STUDY GUIDE

STUDY GUIDE

Richard O. Straub
University of Michigan, Dearborn

with
**Focus on Vocabulary and Language
by *Cornelius Rea***
Douglas College, British Columbia

to accompany

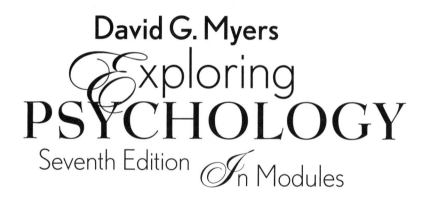

David G. Myers
Exploring
PSYCHOLOGY
Seventh Edition *In* Modules

WORTH PUBLISHERS

Study Guide
by Richard O. Straub
to accompany
Myers: **Exploring Psychology, Seventh Edition in Modules**

Printed in the United States of America

ISBN 13: 978-1-4292-0983-0
ISBN 10: 1-4292-0983-6

First printing

Worth Publishers
41 Madison Avenue
New York, NY 10010
www.worthpublishers.com

Contents

Preface

This Study Guide is designed for use with *Exploring Psychology, Seventh Edition in Modules*, by David G. Myers. It is intended to help you to learn material in the textbook, to evaluate your understanding of that material, and then to review any problem areas. Beginning on page ix, "How to Manage Your Time Efficiently and Study More Effectively" provides detailed instructions on how to use the textbook and this Study Guide for maximum benefit. It also offers additional study suggestions based on principles of time management, effective notetaking, evaluation of exam performance, and an effective program for improving your comprehension while studying from textbooks.

The seventh edition of this Study Guide offers many useful features. Each module includes a review test: In addition to questions asking about facts and definitions, several items evaluate your understanding of the module's broader conceptual material and its application to real-world situations. At the back of the module are the correct answers as well as complete explanations not only of why the answer is correct but also of why the other choices are incorrect.

The Module Review is organized by major text section. For each section the fill-in and essay-type questions are organized under their relevant learning objectives. In addition, each module includes Focus on Vocabulary and Language, written by Cornelius Rea of Douglas College, British Columbia. This section provides brief, clear explanations of some of the idioms and expressions used by David Myers that may be unfamiliar to some students. They are first listed at the beginning of the module, then explained at the back of the module.

Acknowledgments

I would like to thank all the students and instructors who used this Study Guide in its previous editions and provided such insightful and useful suggestions. Special thanks are also due to Betty Shapiro Probert for her extraordinary editorial contributions and to Don Probert for his skill and efficiency in the composition of this guide. I would also like to thank Peter Twickler, Jenny Chiu, and Stacey Alexander of Worth Publishers for their dedication and energy in skillfully coordinating various aspects of production. Most important, I want to thank Jeremy, Rebecca, Melissa, and Pam for their enduring love and patience.

Richard O. Straub
August 2007

How to Manage Your Time Efficiently and Study More Effectively

How effectively do you study? Good study habits make the job of being a college student much easier. Many students, who *could* succeed in college, fail or drop out because they have never learned to manage their time efficiently. Even the best students can usually benefit from an in-depth evaluation of their current study habits.

There are many ways to achieve academic success, of course, but your approach may not be the most effective or efficient. Are you sacrificing your social life or your physical or mental health in order to get A's on your exams? Good study habits result in better grades *and* more time for other activities.

Evaluate Your Current Study Habits

To improve your study habits, you must first have an accurate picture of how you currently spend your time. Begin by putting together a profile of your present living and studying habits. Answer the following questions by writing *yes* or *no* on each line.

_____ 1. Do you usually set up a schedule to budget your time for studying, recreation, and other activities?

_____ 2. Do you often put off studying until time pressures force you to cram?

_____ 3. Do other students seem to study less than you do, but get better grades?

_____ 4. Do you usually spend hours at a time studying one subject, rather than dividing that time between several subjects?

_____ 5. Do you often have trouble remembering what you have just read in a textbook?

_____ 6. Before reading a module in a textbook, do you skim through it and read the section headings?

_____ 7. Do you try to predict exam questions from your lecture notes and reading?

_____ 8. Do you usually attempt to paraphrase or summarize what you have just finished reading?

_____ 9. Do you find it difficult to concentrate very long when you study?

_____ 10. Do you often feel that you studied the wrong material for an exam?

Thousands of college students have participated in similar surveys. Students who are fully realizing their academic potential usually respond as follows: (1) yes, (2) no, (3) no, (4) no, (5) no, (6) yes, (7) yes, (8) yes, (9) no, (10) no.

Compare your responses to those of successful students. The greater the discrepancy, the more you could benefit from a program to improve your study habits. The questions are designed to identify areas of weakness. Once you have identified your weaknesses, you will be able to set specific goals for improvement and implement a program for reaching them.

Manage Your Time

Do you often feel frustrated because there isn't enough time to do all the things you must and want to do? Take heart. Even the most productive and successful people feel this way at times. But they establish priorities for their activities and they learn to budget time for each of them. There's much in the saying "If you want something done, ask a busy person to do it." A busy person knows how to get things done.

If you don't now have a system for budgeting your time, develop one. Not only will your academic accomplishments increase, but you will actually find more time in your schedule for other activities. And you won't have to feel guilty about "taking time off," because all your obligations will be covered.

Establish a Baseline

As a first step in preparing to budget your time, keep a diary for a few days to establish a summary, or baseline, of the time you spend in studying, socializing, working, and so on. If you are like many students, much of your "study" time is nonproductive; you may sit at your desk and leaf through a book, but the time is actually wasted. Or you may procrastinate. You are always getting ready to study, but you rarely do.

Besides revealing where you waste time, your diary will give you a realistic picture of how much time you need to allot for meals, commuting, and other fixed activities. In addition, careful records should indicate the times of the day when you are consistently most productive. A sample time-management diary is shown in Table 1.

Plan the Term

Having established and evaluated your baseline, you are ready to devise a more efficient schedule. Buy a calendar that covers the entire school term and has ample space for each day. Using the course outlines provided by your instructors, enter the dates of all exams, term paper deadlines, and other important academic obligations. If you have any long-range personal plans (concerts, weekend trips, etc.), enter the dates on the calendar as well. Keep your calendar up to date and refer to it often. I recommend carrying it with you at all times.

Develop a Weekly Calendar

Now that you have a general picture of the school term, develop a weekly schedule that includes all of your activities. Aim for a schedule that you can live with for the entire school term. A sample weekly schedule, incorporating the following guidelines, is shown in Table 2.

1. Enter your class times, work hours, and any other fixed obligations first. *Be thorough.* Using information from your time-management diary, allow plenty of time for such things as commuting, meals, laundry, and the like.

Table 1   Sample Time-Management Diary

| Behavior | Monday | |
	Time Completed	Duration Hours: Minutes
Sleep	7:00	7:30
Dressing	7:25	:25
Breakfast	7:45	:20
Commute	8:20	:35
Coffee	9:00	:40
French	10:00	1:00
Socialize	10:15	:15
Video game	10:35	:20
Coffee	11:00	:25
Psychology	12:00	1:00
Lunch	12:25	:25
Study Lab	1:00	:35
Psych. Lab	4:00	3:00
Work	5:30	1:30
Commute	6:10	:40
Dinner	6:45	:35
TV	7:30	:45
Study Psych.	10:00	2:30
Socialize	11:30	1:30
Sleep		

Prepare a similar chart for each day of the week. When you finish an activity, note it on the chart and write down the time it was completed. Then determine its duration by subtracting the time the previous activity was finished from the newly entered time.

2. Set up a study schedule for each of your courses. The study habits survey and your time-management diary will help direct you. The following guidelines should also be useful.

(a) Establish regular study times for each course. The 4 hours needed to study one subject, for example, are most profitable when divided into shorter periods spaced over several days. If you cram your studying into one 4-hour block, what you attempt to learn in the third or fourth hour will interfere with what you studied in the first 2 hours. Newly acquired knowledge is like wet cement. It needs some time to "harden" to become memory.

(b) Alternate subjects. The type of interference just mentioned is greatest between similar topics. Set up a schedule in which you spend time on several *different* courses during each study session. Besides reducing the potential for interference, alternating subjects will help to prevent mental fatigue with one topic.

(c) Set weekly goals to determine the amount of study time you need to do well in each course. This will depend on, among other things, the difficulty of your courses and the effectiveness of your methods. Many

Table 2   Sample Weekly Schedule

Time	Mon.	Tues.	Wed.	Thurs.	Fri.	Sat.
7–8	Dress Eat	Dress Eat	Dress Eat	Dress Eat	Dress Eat	
8–9	Psych.	Study Psych.	Psych.	Study Psych.	Psych.	Dress Eat
9–10	Eng.	Study Eng.	Eng.	Study Eng.	Eng.	Study Eng.
10–11	Study French	Free	Study French	Open Study	Study French	Study Stats.
11–12	French	Study Psych. Lab	French	Open Study	French	Study Stats.
12–1	Lunch	Lunch	Lunch	Lunch	Lunch	Lunch
1–2	Stats.	Psych. Lab	Stats.	Study or Free	Stats.	Free
2–3	Bio.	Psych. Lab	Bio.	Free	Bio.	Free
3–4	Free	Psych.	Free	Free	Free	Free
4–5	Job	Job	Job	Job	Job	Free
5–6	Job	Job	Job	Job	Job	Free
6–7	Dinner	Dinner	Dinner	Dinner	Dinner	Dinner
7–8	Study Bio.	Study Bio.	Study Bio.	Study Bio.	Free	Free
8–9	Study Eng.	Study Stats.	Study Psych.	Open Study	Open Study	Free
9–10	Open Study	Open Study	Open Study	Open Study	Free	Free

This is a sample schedule for a student with a 16-credit load and a 10-hour-per-week part-time job. Using this chart as an illustration, make up a weekly schedule, following the guidelines outlined here.

professors recommend studying at least 1 to 2 hours for each hour in class. If your time-management diary indicates that you presently study less time than that, do not plan to jump immediately to a much higher level. Increase study time from your baseline by setting weekly goals [see (4)] that will gradually bring you up to the desired level. As an initial schedule, for example, you might set aside an amount of study time for each course that matches class time.

(d) Schedule for maximum effectiveness. Tailor your schedule to meet the demands of each course. For the course that emphasizes lecture notes, schedule time for a daily review soon after the class. This will give you a chance to revise your notes and clean up any hard-to-decipher shorthand while the material is still fresh in your mind. If you are evaluated for class participation (for example, in a language course), allow time for a review just *before* the class meets. Schedule study time for your most difficult (or least motivating) courses during hours when you are the most alert and distractions are fewest.

(e) Schedule open study time. Emergencies, additional obligations, and the like could throw off your

schedule. And you may simply need some extra time periodically for a project or for review in one of your courses. Schedule several hours each week for such purposes.

3. After you have budgeted time for studying, fill in slots for recreation, hobbies, relaxation, household errands, and the like.

4. Set specific goals. Before each study session, make a list of specific goals. The simple note "7–8 PM: study psychology" is too broad to ensure the most effective use of the time. Formulate your daily goals according to what you know you must accomplish during the term. If you have course outlines with advance assignments, set systematic daily goals that will allow you, for example, to cover 6 modules before the exam. And be realistic: Can you actually expect to cover a 30-page module in one session? Divide large tasks into smaller units; stop at the most logical resting points. When you complete a specific goal, take a 5- or 10-minute break before tackling the next goal.

5. Evaluate how successful or unsuccessful your studying has been on a daily or weekly basis. Did you

reach most of your goals? If so, reward yourself immediately. You might even make a list of 5 to 10 rewards to choose from. If you have trouble studying regularly, you may be able to motivate yourself by making such rewards contingent on completing specific goals.

6. Finally, until you have lived with your schedule for several weeks, don't hesitate to revise it. You may need to allow more time for chemistry, for example, and less for some other course. If you are trying to study regularly for the first time and are feeling burned out, you probably have set your initial goals too high. Don't let failure cause you to despair and abandon the program. Accept your limitations and revise your schedule so that you are studying only 15 to 20 minutes more each evening than you are used to. The point is to *identify a regular schedule with which you can achieve some success.* Time management, like any skill, must be practiced to become effective.

Techniques for Effective Study

Knowing how to put study time to best use is, of course, as important as finding a place for it in your schedule. Here are some suggestions that should enable you to increase your reading comprehension and improve your notetaking. A few study tips are included as well.

Using SQ3R to Increase Reading Comprehension

How do you study from a textbook? If you are like many students, you simply read and reread in a *passive* manner. Studies have shown, however, that most students who simply read a textbook cannot remember more than half the material 10 minutes after they have finished. Often, what is retained is the unessential material rather than the important points upon which exam questions will be based.

This Study Guide employs a program known as SQ3R (Survey, Question, Read, Rehearse, and Review) to facilitate, and allow you to assess, your comprehension of the important facts and concepts in *Exploring Psychology, Seventh Edition in Modules,* by David G. Myers.

Research has shown that students using SQ3R achieve significantly greater comprehension of texts than students reading in the more traditional passive manner. Once you have learned this program, you can improve your comprehension of any textbook.

Survey Before you read a text module, determine whether the text or the study guide has an outline or list of objectives. Read this material and the summary at the end of the module. Next, read the textbook

module fairly quickly, paying special attention to the major headings and subheadings. This survey will give you an idea of the module's contents and organization. You will then be able to divide the module into logical sections in order to formulate specific goals for a more careful reading of the module.

In this Study Guide, the *Module Overview* summarizes the major topics of the textbook module. This section also provides a few suggestions for approaching topics you may find difficult.

Question You will retain material longer when you have a use for it. If you use a term from a module in order to express an idea, for example, you will remember it longer than if you merely try to memorize the term's definition. Previewing the module will allow you to generate important questions that the module will proceed to answer. These questions correspond to "mental files" into which knowledge will be sorted for easy access.

As you survey, jot down several questions for each module section. One simple technique is to generate questions by rephrasing a section heading. For example, the "Preoperational Thought" head could be turned into "What is preoperational thought?" Good questions will allow you to focus on the important points in the text. Examples of good questions are those that begin as follows: "List two examples of . . . ." "What is the function of . . .?" "What is the significance of . . .?" Such questions give a purpose to your reading. Similarly, you can formulate questions based on the module outline.

Read When you have established "files" for each section of the module, review your first question, begin reading, and continue until you have discovered its answer. If you come to material that seems to answer an important question you don't have a file for, stop and write down the question.

Using this Study Guide, read the module one section at a time. First, preview the section by skimming it, noting headings and boldface items. Next, study the appropriate section objectives in the *Module Review.* Then, as you read the module section, search for the answer to each objective.

Be sure to read everything. Don't skip photo or art captions, graphs, or marginal notes. In some cases, what may seem vague in reading will be made clear by a simple graph. Keep in mind that test questions are sometimes drawn from illustrations and charts.

Rehearse When you have found the answer to a question, close your eyes and mentally recite the question and its answer. Then *write* the answer next to the question. It is important that you recite an answer in your own words rather than the author's. Don't rely on your short-term memory to repeat the author's words verbatim.

In responding to the objectives, pay close attention to what is called for. If you are asked to identify or list, do just that. If asked to compare, contrast, or do both, you should focus on the similarities (compare) and differences (contrast) between the concepts or theories. Answering the objectives carefully not only will help you to focus your attention on the important concepts of the text but also will provide excellent practice for essay exams.

Rehearsal is an extremely effective study technique, recommended by many learning experts. In addition to increasing reading comprehension, it is useful for review. Trying to explain something in your own words clarifies your knowledge, often by revealing aspects of your answer that are vague or incomplete. If you repeatedly rely upon "I know" in recitation, you really *may not know.*

Rehearsal has the additional advantage of simulating an exam, especially an essay exam; the same skills are required in both cases. Too often students study without ever putting the book and notes aside, which makes it easy for them to develop false confidence in their knowledge. When the material is in front of you, you may be able to *recognize* an answer, but will you be able to *recall* it later, when you take an exam that does not provide these retrieval cues?

After you have recited and written your answer, continue with your next question. Read, recite, and so on.

Review When you have answered the last question on the material you have designated as a study goal, go back and review. Read over each question and your written answer to it. Your review might also include a brief written summary that integrates all of your questions and answers. This review need not take longer than a few minutes, but it is important. It will help you retain the material longer and will greatly facilitate a final review of each module before the exam.

In this Study Guide, the *Module Review* contains fill-in and brief essay questions for you to complete after you have finished reading the section and have written answers to the objectives. The correct answers are given at the end of the module. Generally, your answer to a fill-in question should match exactly (as in the case of important terms, theories, or people). In some cases, the answer is not a term or name, so a word close in meaning will suffice. You should answer these questions several times before taking an exam, so it's a good idea to mentally fill in the

answers until you are ready for a final pretest review. Text page references are provided with each section title, in case you need to reread any of the material.

Also provided to facilitate your review is a *Progress Test* that includes multiple-choice questions and, where appropriate, matching or true–false questions. This test is *not* to be taken until you have read the module and completed the *Module Review.* Correct answers, along with explanations of why each alternative is correct or incorrect, are provided at the end of the module. If you miss a question, read these explanations and, if necessary, review the text discussion to further understand why. The *Progress Test* does not test every aspect of a concept, so you should treat an incorrect answer as an indication that you need to review the concept.

The *Progress Test* usually includes questions that test your ability to analyze, integrate, and apply the concepts in the chapter. Some modules also include an essay question dealing with a major concept covered in the module.

The core of each chapter concludes with *Key Terms.* As with the *Module Review* learning objectives, it is important that these answers be written from memory, and in your own words. The *Answers* section at the end of the chapter gives a definition of each term, sometimes along with an example of its usage and/or a tip to help you remember its meaning.

Following the answers is a list of potentially unfamiliar idioms, words, and expressions (*Focus on Vocabulary and Language*), presented in the order in which they occur in the text and accompanied by definitions and examples.

One final suggestion: Incorporate SQ3R into your time-management calendar. Set specific goals for completing SQ3R with each assigned module. Keep a record of modules completed, and reward yourself for being conscientious. Initially, it takes more time and effort to "read" using SQ3R, but with practice, the steps will become automatic. More important, you will comprehend significantly more material and retain what you have learned longer than passive readers do.

Taking Lecture Notes

Are your class notes as useful as they might be? One way to determine their worth is to compare them with those taken by other good students. Are yours as thorough? Do they provide you with a comprehensible outline of each lecture? If not, then the following suggestions might increase the effectiveness of your notetaking.

1. Keep a separate notebook for each course. Use letter-sized pages. Consider using a ring binder, which would allow you to revise and insert notes while still preserving lecture order.

2. Take notes in the format of a lecture outline. Use roman numerals for major points, letters for supporting arguments, and so on. Some instructors will make this easy by delivering organized lectures and, in some cases, by outlining their lectures on the board. If a lecture is disorganized, you will probably want to reorganize your notes soon after the class.

3. As you take notes in class, leave a wide margin on one side of each page. After the lecture, expand or clarify any shorthand notes while the material is fresh in your mind. Use this time to write important questions in the margin next to notes that answer them. This will facilitate later review and will allow you to anticipate similar exam questions.

Evaluate Your Exam Performance

How often have you received a grade on an exam that did not do justice to the effort you spent preparing for the exam? This is a common experience that can leave one feeling bewildered and abused. "What do I have to do to get an A?" "The test was unfair!" "I studied the wrong material!"

The chances of this happening are greatly reduced if you have an effective time-management schedule and use the study techniques described here. But it can happen to the best-prepared student and is most likely to occur on your first exam with a new professor.

Remember that there are two main reasons for studying. One is to learn for your own general academic development. Many people believe that such knowledge is all that really matters. Of course, it is possible, though unlikely, to be an expert on a topic without achieving commensurate grades, just as one can, occasionally, earn an excellent grade without truly mastering the course material. During a job interview or in the workplace, however, your A in Cobol won't mean much if you can't actually program a computer.

In order to keep career options open after you graduate, you must know the material and maintain competitive grades. In the short run, this means performing well on exams, which is the second main objective in studying.

Probably the single best piece of advice to keep in mind when studying for exams is to *try to predict exam questions.* This means ignoring the trivia and focusing on the important questions and their answers (with your instructor's emphasis in mind).

A second point is obvious. How well you do on exams is determined by your mastery of *both* lecture and textbook material. Many students (partly because of poor time management) concentrate too much on one at the expense of the other.

To evaluate how well you are learning lecture and textbook material, analyze the questions you missed on the first exam. If your instructor does not review exams during class, you can easily do it yourself. Divide the questions into two categories: those drawn primarily from lectures and those drawn primarily from the textbook. Determine the percentage of questions you missed in each category. If your errors are evenly distributed and you are satisfied with your grade, you have no problem. If you are weaker in one area, you will need to set future goals for increasing and/or improving your study of that area.

Similarly, note the percentage of test questions drawn from each category. Although exams in most courses cover *both* lecture notes and the textbook, the relative emphasis of each may vary from instructor to instructor. While your instructors may not be entirely consistent in making up future exams, you may be able to tailor your studying for each course by placing *additional* emphasis on the appropriate area.

Exam evaluation will also point out the types of questions your instructor prefers. Does the exam consist primarily of multiple-choice, true–false, or essay questions? You may also discover that an instructor is fond of wording questions in certain ways. For example, an instructor may rely heavily on questions that require you to draw an analogy between a theory or concept and a real-world example. Evaluate both your instructor's style and how well you do with each format. Use this information to guide your future exam preparation.

Important aids, not only in studying for exams but also in determining how well prepared you are, are the *Progress Tests* provided in this Study Guide. If these tests don't include all of the types of questions your instructor typically writes, make up your own practice exam questions. Spend extra time testing yourself with question formats that are most difficult for you. There is no better way to evaluate your preparation for an upcoming exam than by testing yourself under the conditions most likely to be in effect during the actual test.

A Few Practical Tips

Even the best intentions for studying sometimes fail. Some of these failures occur because students attempt to work under conditions that are simply not conducive to concentrated study. To help ensure the success of your time-management program, here are a few suggestions that should assist you in reducing the possibility of procrastination or distraction.

1. If you have set up a schedule for studying, make your roommate, family, and friends aware of this commitment, and ask them to honor your quiet study time. Close your door and post a "Do Not Disturb" sign.

2. Set up a place to study that minimizes potential distractions. Use a desk or table, not your bed or an extremely comfortable chair. Keep your desk and the walls around it free from clutter. If you need a place other than your room, find one that meets as many of these requirements as possible—for example, in the library stacks.

3. Do nothing but study in this place. It should become associated with studying so that it "triggers" this activity, just as a mouth-watering aroma elicits an appetite.

4. Never study with the television on or with other distracting noises present. If you must have music in the background in order to mask outside noise, for example, play soft instrumental music. Don't pick vocal selections; your mind will be drawn to the lyrics.

5. Study by yourself. Other students can be distracting or can break the pace at which *your* learning is most efficient. In addition, there is always the possibility that group studying will become a social gathering. Reserve that for its own place in your schedule.

If you continue to have difficulty concentrating for very long, try the following suggestions.

6. Study your most difficult or most challenging subjects first, when you are most alert.

7. Start with relatively short periods of concentrated study, with breaks in between. If your attention starts to wander, get up immediately and take a break. It is better to study effectively for 15 minutes and then take a break than to fritter away 45 minutes out of an hour. Gradually increase the length of study periods, using your attention span as an indicator of successful pacing.

Some Closing Thoughts

I hope that these suggestions help make you more successful academically, and that they enhance the quality of your college life in general. Having the necessary skills makes any job a lot easier and more pleasant. Let me repeat my warning not to attempt to make too drastic a change in your life-style immediately. Good habits require time and self-discipline to develop. Once established, they can last a lifetime.

STUDY GUIDE

Introduction to the History and Science of Psychology

The History and Scope of Psychology

MODULE OVERVIEW

Psychology's historical development and current activities lead us to define the field as the science of behavior and mental processes. Module 1 discusses the development of psychology from its beginnings until today and the range of behaviors and mental processes being investigated by psychologists in each of the various specialty areas. It also introduces the biopsychosocial approach that integrates the three main levels of analysis followed by psychologists working from the major perspectives. Next is an overview of the diverse subfields in which psychologists conduct research and provide services.

The module concludes with tips for how to get your study of psychology off on the right foot by learning (and pledging to follow!) the SQ3R study method. This study method is also discussed in the essay at the beginning of this Study Guide.

NOTE: Answer guidelines for all Module 1 questions begin on page 10.

MODULE REVIEW

First, skim each section, noting headings and boldface items. After you have read the section, review each objective by answering the fill-in questions that follow it. As you proceed, evaluate your performance by consulting the answers on page 10. Do not continue with the next section until you understand each answer. If you need to, review or reread the section in the textbook before continuing.

> David Myers at times uses idioms that are unfamiliar to some readers. If you do not know the meaning of any of the following words, phrases, or expressions in the context in which they appear in the text, refer to pages 13–14 for an explanation: *remedy their own woes, peekaboo; grist for psychology's mill; "Magellans of the mind"; unpack this definition; mushrooming;*

> *wrestled with some issues; nature-nurture tension dissolves; "Red in the face" and "hot under the collar"; But there is a payoff; psychoceramics; spaced practice . . . . massed practice.*

Psychology's Roots (pp. 3–5)

Objective 1: Describe the evolution of scientific psychology from its early pioneers to contemporary concerns.

1. The Greek philosopher _____ developed early theories about _____ , _____ , _____ , _____ , _____ , and _____ .

2. The first psychological laboratory was founded in 1879 by Wilhelm _____ .

3. The historical roots of psychology include the fields of _____ and _____ .

4. Some early psychologists included Ivan Pavlov, who pioneered the study of _____ ; the personality theorist _____ ; Jean Piaget, who studied _____ ; and _____ , author of an important 1890 psychology textbook.

5. The first female president of the American Psychological Association was _____ . The first woman to receive a Ph.D. in psychology was _____ .

6. In its earliest years, psychology was defined as the science of _____ life. From the 1920s into the 1960s, psychology in America was redefined as the science of _____ behavior. Today, we define psychology as the scientific study of _____ and _____ processes.

7. As a response to Freudian psychology and to _____ , which they considered too mechanistic, pioneers _____ and _____ forged _____ psychology. This new perspective emphasized the _____ potential of _____ people.

8. During the 1960s, psychology underwent a _____ revolution as it began to recapture interest in _____ processes. The study of the interaction of thought processes and _____ function is called _____ _____ .

9. Worldwide, the number of psychologists is _____ (increasing/decreasing). The field is also _____ , which means that we are moving toward a single world of psychological science.

Contemporary Psychology (pp. 5–9)

Objective 2: Summarize the nature-nurture debate in psychology.

1. The nature-nurture issue is the controversy over the relative contributions of _____ and _____ .

2. The Greek philosopher who assumed that character and intelligence are inherited is _____ . The Greek philosopher who argued that all knowledge comes from sensory experience is _____ . Today, we are more likely to find that _____ works on what _____ endows because of our species' ability to learn and to _____ .

Objective 3: Identify the three main levels of analysis in the biopsychosocial approach, and explain psychology's current perspectives.

3. Each person is a complex _____ that is part of a larger _____ _____ and at the same time composed of smaller systems. For this reason, psychologists work from three main _____ of _____ — biological, _____ , and _____ - _____ — which together form an integrated _____ approach to the study of behavior and mental processes.

4. Psychologists who study how the body and brain enable emotions, memories, and sensory experiences are working from the _____ perspective.

5. Psychologists who study how natural selection influences behavior tendencies are working from the _____ perspective, whereas those concerned with the relative influences of genes and environment on individual differences are working from the _____ _____ perspective.

6. Psychologists who believe that behavior springs from unconscious drives and conflicts are working from the _____ perspective.

7. Psychologists who study the mechanisms by which observable responses are acquired and changed are working from the _____ perspective, while psychologists working from the _____ perspective explore how our minds encode, process, store, and retrieve information.

8. Psychologists who study how thinking and behavior vary in different situations are working from the _____ - _____ perspective.

9. The different perspectives _____ (contradict/complement) one another.

Objective 4: Identify some of psychology's subfields, and explain the difference between clinical psychology and psychiatry.

10. Psychologists may be involved in conducting

    _____ ,

    which builds psychology's knowledge base, or

    _____ ,

    which seeks solutions to practical problems.

11. Psychologists who help people cope with problems in living are called _____ psychologists. Psychologists who study, assess, and treat troubled people are called _____ psychologists.

12. Medical doctors who provide psychotherapy and treat physical causes of psychological disorders are called _____ .

Tips for Studying Psychology (pp. 9–11)

Objective 5: Describe several effective study techniques.

1. In order to master any subject, you must _____ process it.

2. The _____ study method incorporates five steps: **a.** _____ ,

    b. _____ , **c.** _____ ,

    d. _____ , and

    e. _____ .

List five additional study tips identified in the text.

   a. _____

   b. _____

   c. _____

   d. _____

   e. _____

PROGRESS TEST

Multiple-Choice Questions

Circle your answers to the following questions and check them with the answers beginning on page 10. If your answer is incorrect, read the explanation for why it is incorrect and then consult the appropriate pages of the text.

1. In its earliest days, *psychology* was defined as the:
   a. science of mental life.
   b. study of conscious and unconscious activity.
   c. scientific study of observable behavior.
   d. scientific study of behavior and mental processes.

2. Who would be most likely to agree with the statement, "Psychology should investigate only behaviors that can be observed"?
   a. Wilhelm Wundt
   b. Sigmund Freud
   c. John B. Watson
   d. William James

3. Today, *psychology* is defined as the:
   a. scientific study of mental phenomena.
   b. scientific study of conscious and unconscious activity.
   c. scientific study of behavior.
   d. scientific study of behavior and mental processes.

4. Who wrote an early psychology textbook?
   a. Wilhelm Wundt   c. Jean Piaget
   b. Ivan Pavlov   d. William James

5. Psychologists who study the degree to which genes influence our personality are working from the _____ perspective.
   a. behavioral   c. behavior genetics
   b. evolutionary   d. neuroscience

6. Which of the following exemplifies the issue of the relative importance of nature and nurture on our behavior?
   a. the issue of the relative influence of biology and experience on behavior
   b. the issue of the relative influence of rewards and punishments on behavior
   c. the debate as to the relative importance of heredity and instinct in determining behavior
   d. the debate as to whether mental processes are a legitimate area of scientific study

7. Which psychological perspective emphasizes the interaction of the brain and body in behavior?
   a. neuroscience
   b. cognitive
   c. behavioral
   d. behavior genetics

8. A psychologist who explores how Asian and North American definitions of attractiveness differ is working from the _____ perspective.
   a. behavioral
   b. evolutionary
   c. cognitive
   d. social-cultural

9. A psychologist who conducts experiments solely intended to build psychology's knowledge base is engaged in:
   a. basic research.
   b. applied research.
   c. industrial/organizational research.
   d. clinical research.

10. Psychologists who study, assess, and treat troubled people are called:
    a. basic researchers.
    b. applied psychologists.
    c. clinical psychologists.
    d. psychiatrists.

11. Today, psychology is a discipline that:
    a. connects with a diversity of other fields.
    b. is largely independent of other disciplines.
    c. is focused primarily on basic research.
    d. is focused primarily on applied research.

12. In order, the sequence of steps in the SQ3R method is:
    a. survey, review, question, read, reflect.
    b. review, question, survey, read, reflect.
    c. question, review, survey, read, reflect.
    d. survey, question, read, review, reflect.

13. The first psychology laboratory was established by _____ in the year _____ .
    a. Wundt; 1879
    b. James; 1890
    c. Freud; 1900
    d. Watson; 1913

14. Who would be most likely to agree with the statement, "Psychology is the science of mental life"?
    a. Wilhelm Wundt
    b. John Watson
    c. Ivan Pavlov
    d. virtually any American psychologist during the 1960s

15. In psychology, *behavior* is best defined as:
    a. anything a person says, does, or feels.
    b. any action we can observe and record.
    c. any action, whether observable or not.
    d. anything we can infer from a person's actions.

16. Carl Rogers and Abraham Maslow are most closely associated with:
    a. cognitive psychology.
    b. behaviorism.
    c. psychodynamic theory.
    d. humanistic psychology.

17. In defining psychology, the text notes that psychology is most accurately described as a:
    a. way of asking and answering questions.
    b. field engaged in solving applied problems.
    c. set of findings related to behavior and mental processes.
    d. nonscientific approach to the study of mental disorders.

18. Two historical roots of psychology are the disciplines of:
    a. philosophy and chemistry.
    b. physiology and chemistry.
    c. philosophy and biology.
    d. philosophy and physics.

19. The Greek philosopher who believed that intelligence was inherited was:
    a. Aristotle.
    b. Plato.
    c. Calkins.
    d. Randi.

20. The way the mind encodes, processes, stores, and retrieves information is the primary concern of the _____ perspective.
    a. neuroscience
    b. evolutionary
    c. social-cultural
    d. cognitive

21. Which of the following individuals is also a physician?
    a. clinical psychologist
    b. experimental psychologist
    c. psychiatrist
    d. biological psychologist

22. Dr. Jones' research centers on the relationship between changes in our thinking over the life span and changes in moral reasoning. Dr. Jones is most likely a:
    a. clinical psychologist.
    b. personality psychologist.
    c. psychiatrist.
    d. developmental psychologist.

23. Which subfield is most directly concerned with studying human behavior in the workplace?
    a. clinical psychology
    b. personality psychology
    c. industrial/organizational psychology
    d. psychiatry

24. Dr. Ernst explains behavior in terms of different situations. Dr. Ernst is working from the _____ perspective.

    a. behavioral   **c.** social-cultural
    b. evolutionary   **d.** cognitive

25. Which perspective emphasizes the learning of observable responses?

    a. behavioral   **c.** neuroscience
    b. social-cultural   **d.** cognitive

26. A psychologist who studies how worker productivity might be increased by changing office layout is engaged in _____ research.

    a. applied   **c.** clinical
    b. basic   **d.** developmental

27. A major principle underlying the SQ3R study method is that:

    a. people learn and remember material best when they actively process it.
    b. many students overestimate their mastery of text and lecture material.
    c. study time should be spaced over time rather than crammed into one session.
    d. "overlearning" disrupts efficient retention.

28. The biopsychosocial approach emphasizes the importance of:

    a. different levels of analysis in exploring behavior and mental processes.
    b. basic research over pure research.
    c. pure research over basic research.
    d. having a single academic perspective to guide research.

29. *Psychology* is defined as the "scientific study of behavior and mental processes." Wilhelm Wundt would have omitted which of the following words from this definition?

    a. scientific study
    b. behavior and
    c. and mental processes
    d. Wundt would have agreed with the definition as stated.

30. Dharma's term paper on the history of American psychology notes that:

    a. psychology began as the science of mental life.
    b. from the 1920s into the 1960s, psychology was defined as the scientific study of observable behavior.
    c. contemporary psychologists study both overt behavior and covert thoughts.
    d. all of these answers are true.

31. Terrence wants to talk to a professional to help him cope with some academic challenges he's facing. You recommend that he contact a(n):

    a. industrial/organizational psychologist.
    b. developmental psychologist.
    c. counseling psychologist.
    d. psychiatrist.

32. Professor Gutierrez, who believes that human emotions are best understood as being jointly determined by heredity, learning, and the individual's social and cultural contexts, is evidently a proponent of the:

    a. psychodynamic perspective.
    b. biopsychosocial approach.
    c. evolutionary perspective.
    d. neuroscience perspective.

33. To say that "psychology is a science" means that:

    a. psychologists study only observable behaviors.
    b. psychologists approach the study of thoughts and actions with careful observation and rigorous analysis.
    c. it has ties only to the biological sciences.
    d. all of these answers are true.

34. In concluding her report on the "nature-nurture debate in contemporary psychology," Karen notes that:

    a. most psychologists believe that nature is a more important influence on the development of most human traits.
    b. most psychologists believe that nurture is more influential.
    c. the issue is more heatedly debated than ever before.
    d. nurture works on what nature endows.

35. Dr. Waung investigates how a person's interpretation of a situation affects his or her reaction. Evidently, Dr. Waung is working from the _____ perspective.
    a. neuroscience   c. cognitive
    b. behavioral   d. social-cultural

36. Dr. Aswad is studying people's enduring inner traits. Dr. Aswad is most likely a(n):
    a. clinical psychologist.
    b. psychiatrist.
    c. personality psychologist.
    d. industrial/organizational psychologist.

37. The psychological perspective that places the *most* emphasis on how observable responses are learned is the _____ perspective.
    a. behavioral   c. behavior genetics
    b. cognitive   d. evolutionary

38. During a dinner conversation, a friend says that the cognitive and behavioral perspectives are quite similar. You disagree and point out that the cognitive perspective emphasizes_____ , whereas the behavioral perspective emphasizes _____ .

    a. conscious processes; observable responses
    b. unconscious processes; conscious processes
    c. overt behaviors; covert behaviors
    d. environmental influences; genetic influences

39. Concerning the major psychological perspectives on behavior, the text author suggests that:
    a. researchers should work within the framework of only one of the perspectives.

    b. only those perspectives that emphasize objective measurement of behavior are useful.
    c. the different perspectives often complement one another; together, they provide a fuller understanding of behavior than provided by any single perspective.
    d. psychologists should avoid all of these traditional perspectives.

40. Your roommate announces that her schedule permits her to devote three hours to studying for an upcoming quiz. You advise her to:
    a. spend most of her time reading and rereading the text material.
    b. focus primarily on her lecture notes.
    c. space study time over several short sessions.
    d. cram for three hours just before the quiz.

41. A fraternity brother rationalizes the fact that he spends very little time studying by saying that he "doesn't want to peak too soon and have the test material become stale." You tell him that:
    a. he is probably overestimating his knowledge of the material.
    b. if he devotes extra time to studying, his retention of the material will be improved.
    c. the more often students review material, the better their exam scores.
    d. all of these answers are true.

Matching Items

Match each psychological perspective, school, and subfield with its definition or description.

Terms

_____ 1. neuroscience perspective
_____ 2. social-cultural perspective
_____ 3. psychiatry
_____ 4. clinical psychology
_____ 5. behavior genetics perspective
_____ 6. behavioral perspective
_____ 7. industrial/organizational psychology
_____ 8. cognitive perspective
_____ 9. basic research
_____ 10. applied research
_____ 11. evolutionary perspective
_____ 12. psychodynamic perspective

Definitions or Descriptions

a. the study of behavior in the workplace
b. how people differ as products of different environments
c. the study of practical problems
d. the mechanisms by which observable responses are acquired and changed
e. how the body and brain create emotions, memories, and sensations
f. how the mind encodes, processes, stores, and retrieves information
g. how natural selection favors traits that promote the perpetuation of one's genes
h. the study, assessment, and treatment of troubled people
i. the medical treatment of psychological disorders
j. the disguised effects of unfulfilled wishes and childhood traumas
k. adds to psychology's knowledge base
l. how much genes and environment contribute to individual differences

Essay Question

Explain how researchers working from each of psychology's major perspectives might investigate an emotion such as love. (Use the space below to list the points you want to make, and organize them. Then write the essay on a separate piece of paper.)

KEY TERMS

Using your own words, on a separate piece of paper write a brief definition or explanation of each of the following.

1. behaviorism
2. humanistic psychology
3. psychology
4. nature-nurture issue
5. levels of analysis
6. biopsychosocial approach
7. basic research
8. applied research
9. counseling psychology
10. clinical psychology
11. psychiatry
12. SQ3R

ANSWERS

Module Review

Psychology's Roots

1. Aristotle; learning; memory; motivation; emotion; perception; personality

2. Wundt

3. biology; philosophy

4. learning; Sigmund Freud; children; William James

5. Mary Calkins; Margaret Washburn

6. mental; observable; behavior; mental

7. behaviorism; Carl Rogers; Abraham Maslow; humanistic; growth; healthy

8. cognitive; mental; brain; cognitive neuroscience

9. increasing; globalizing

Contemporary Psychology

1. biology; experience

2. Plato; Aristotle; nurture; nature; adapt

3. system; social system; levels; analysis; psychological; social-cultural; biopsychosocial

4. neuroscience

5. evolutionary; behavior genetics

6. psychodynamic

7. behavioral; cognitive

8. social-cultural

9. complement

10. basic research; applied research

11. counseling; clinical

12. psychiatrists

Tips for Studying Psychology

1. actively

2. SQ3R; a. survey; b. question; c. read; d. review; e. reflect
   a. Distribute study time.
   b. Listen actively in class.
   c. Overlearn material.
   d. Focus on the big ideas.
   e. Be a smart test-taker.

Progress Test

Multiple-Choice Questions

1. **a.** is the answer.
   b. Psychology has never been defined in terms of conscious and unconscious activity.

c. From the 1920s into the 1960s, psychology was defined as the scientific study of observable behavior.
d. *Psychology* today is defined as the scientific study of behavior and mental processes. In its earliest days, however, psychology focused exclusively on mental phenomena.

2. **c.** is the answer.
   a. Wilhelm Wundt, the founder of the first psychology laboratory, was seeking to measure the simplest mental processes.
   b. Sigmund Freud developed an influential theory of personality that focused on unconscious processes.
   d. William James, author of an important 1890 textbook, was a philosopher and was more interested in mental phenomena than observable behavior.

3. **d.** is the answer.
   a. In its earliest days psychology was defined as the science of mental phenomena.
   b. Psychology has never been defined in terms of conscious and unconscious activity.
   c. From the 1920s into the 1960s, psychology was defined as the scientific study of behavior.

4. **d.** is the answer.
   a. Wilhelm Wundt founded the first psychology laboratory.
   b. Ivan Pavlov pioneered the study of learning.
   c. Jean Piaget was this century's most influential observer of children.

5. **c.** is the answer.

6. **a.** is the answer. Biology and experience are internal and external influences, respectively.
   b. Rewards and punishments are both external influences on behavior.
   c. Heredity and instinct are both internal influences on behavior.
   d. The legitimacy of the study of mental processes does not relate to the internal/external issue.

7. **a.** is the answer.
   b. The cognitive perspective is concerned with how we encode, process, store, and retrieve information.
   c. The behavioral perspective studies the mechanisms by which observable responses are acquired and changed.
   d. The behavior genetics perspective focuses on the relative contributions of genes and environment to individual differences.

8. **d.** is the answer.
   a. Behavioral psychologists investigate how behaviors are learned. They tend not to focus on subjective opinions, such as attractiveness.

b. The evolutionary perspective studies how natural selection favors traits that promote the perpetuation of one's genes.

c. Cognitive psychologists study the mechanisms of thinking and memory, and generally do not investigate attitudes. Also, because the question specifies that the psychologist is interested in comparing two cultures, d. is the best answer.

9. **a.** is the answer.
   b. & c. Applied and industrial/organizational psychologists tackle practical problems.
   d. Clinical psychologists (and researchers) focus on treating troubled people.

10. **c.** is the answer.
    d. Psychiatrists are medical doctors rather than psychologists.

11. **a.** is the answer.
    c. & d. Psychologists are widely involved in *both* basic and applied research.

12. **d.** is the answer.

13. **a.** is the answer.

14. **a.** is the answer.
    b. & d. John Watson, like many American psychologists during this time, believed that psychology should focus on the study of observable behavior.
    c. Because he pioneered the study of learning, Pavlov focused on observable behavior and would certainly have *disagreed* with this statement.

15. **a.** is the answer.

16. **d.** is the answer.

17. **a.** is the answer.
    b. Psychology is equally involved in basic research.
    c. Psychology's knowledge base is constantly expanding.
    d. Psychology is the *scientific study* of behavior and mental processes.

18. **c.** is the answer.

19. **b.** is the answer.
    a. Aristotle believed that all knowledge originates with sensory experience.
    c. Mary Whiton Calkins was the first woman president of APA.
    d. Randi is a magician who has debunked a variety of psychic phenomena.

20. **d.** is the answer.
    a. The neuroscience perspective studies the biological bases for a range of psychological phenomena.

b. The evolutionary perspective studies how natural selection favors traits that promote the perpetuation of one's genes.

c. The social-cultural perspective is concerned with variations in behavior across situations and cultures.

21. **c.** is the answer. After earning their MD degrees, psychiatrists specialize in the diagnosis and treatment of mental health disorders.
    a., b., & d. These psychologists generally earn a Ph.D. rather than an MD.

22. **d.** is the answer. The emphasis on change during the life span indicates that Dr. Jones is most likely a developmental psychologist.
    a. Clinical psychologists study, assess, and treat people who are psychologically troubled.
    b. Personality psychologists study our inner traits.
    c. Psychiatrists are medical doctors.

23. **c.** is the answer.
    a. Clinical psychologists study, assess, and treat people with psychological disorders.
    b. & d. Personality psychologists and psychiatrists do not usually study people in work situations.

24. **c.** is the answer.
    a. Psychologists who follow the behavioral perspective emphasize observable, external influences on behavior.
    b. The evolutionary perspective focuses on how natural selection favors traits that promote the perpetuation of one's genes.
    d. The cognitive perspective places emphasis on conscious, rather than unconscious, processes.

25. **a.** is the answer.

26. **a.** is the answer. The research is addressing a practical issue.
    b. Basic research is aimed at contributing to the base of knowledge in a given field, not at resolving particular practical problems.
    c. & d. Clinical and developmental research would focus on issues relating to psychological disorders and life-span changes, respectively.

27. **a.** is the answer.
    b. & c. Although each of these is true, SQ3R is based on the more *general* principle of active learning.
    d. In fact, just the opposite is true.

28. **a.** is the answer.
    b. & c. The biopsychosocial approach has nothing to do with the relative importance of basic research and applied research and is equally applicable to both.

d. On the contrary, the biopsychosocial approach is based on the idea that single academic perspectives are often limited.

29. **b.** is the answer.

   a. As the founder of the first psychology laboratory, Wundt certainly based his research on the scientific method.

   c. The earliest psychologists, including Wilhelm Wundt, were concerned with the self-examination of covert thoughts, feelings, and other mental processes.

30. **d.** is the answer.

31. **c.** is the answer.

   a. Industrial/organizational psychologists study and advise on behavior in the workplace.

   b. Developmental psychologists investigate behavior and mental processes over the life span.

   d. Psychiatrists are medical doctors who treat medical disorders. There is no indication that Terrence is suffering from a medical disorder.

32. **b.** is the answer.

   a., c., & d. Each of these perspectives is too narrow to apply to Professor Gutierrez's belief. Moreover, the psychodynamic perspective (a.) emphasizes unconscious processes, which Professor Gutierrez has not expressed a belief in.

33. **b.** is the answer.

   a. Psychologists study both overt (observable) behaviors and covert thoughts and feelings.

   c. Psychology has ties to many disciplines, including biological and other social sciences.

34. **d.** is the answer. Because both nature and nurture influence most traits and behaviors, the tension surrounding this issue has dissolved.

35. **c.** is the answer.

   a. This perspective emphasizes the influences of physiology on behavior.

   b. This perspective emphasizes environmental influences on observable behavior.

   d. This perspective emphasizes how behavior and thinking vary across situations and cultures.

36. **c.** is the answer.

   a. Clinical psychology is concerned with the study and treatment of psychological disorders.

   b. Psychiatry is the branch of medicine concerned with the physical diagnosis and treatment of psychological disorders.

   d. Industrial/organizational psychologists study behavior in the workplace.

37. **a.** is the answer.

38. **a.** is the answer.

   b. Neither perspective places any special emphasis on unconscious processes.

c. Neither perspective emphasizes covert behaviors.

d. If anything, the behavioral perspective emphasizes environmental influences.

39. **c.** is the answer.

   a. The text suggests just the opposite: By studying behavior from several perspectives, psychologists gain a fuller understanding.

   b. & d. Each perspective is useful in that it calls researchers' attention to different aspects of behavior. This is equally true of those perspectives that do not emphasize objective measurement.

40. **c.** is the answer.

   a. To be effective, study must be *active* rather than passive in nature.

   b. Most exams are based on lecture *and* text material.

   d. Cramming hinders retention.

41. **d.** is the answer.

Matching Items

1.	e	6.	d	11.	g
2.	b	7.	a	12.	j
3.	i	8.	f		
4.	h	9.	k		
5.	l	10.	c		

Essay Question

A psychologist working from the neuroscience perspective might study the brain circuits and body chemistry that trigger attraction and sexual arousal. A psychologist working from the evolutionary perspective might analyze how love has facilitated the survival of our species. A psychologist working from the behavior genetics perspective might attempt to compare the extent to which the emotion is attributable to our genes and the extent to which it is attributable to our environment. A psychologist working from the psychodynamic perspective might search for evidence that a person's particular emotional feelings are disguised effects of unfulfilled wishes. A psychologist working from the behavioral perspective might study the external stimuli, such as body language, that elicit and reward approach behaviors toward another person. A psychologist working from a cognitive perspective might study how our thought processes, attitudes, and beliefs foster attachment to loved ones, and a psychologist working from a social-cultural perspective might explore situational influences on attraction and how the development and expression of love vary across cultural groups.

Key Terms

1. **Behaviorism** is the view that psychology should focus only on the scientific study of observable behaviors without reference to mental processes.

2. **Humanistic psychology** is the branch of psychology that emphasizes the growth potential of healthy people.

3. **Psychology** is the scientific study of behavior and mental processes.

4. The **nature-nurture issue** is the controversy over the relative contributions that genes (nature) and experience (nurture) make to the development of psychological traits and behaviors.

5. Psychologists analyze behavior and mental processes from differing complementary views, or **levels of analysis.**

6. The **biopsychosocial approach** is an integrated approach that focuses on biological, psychological, and social-cultural levels of analysis for a given behavior or mental process.

7. **Basic research** is pure science that aims to increase psychology's scientific knowledge base rather than to solve practical problems.

8. **Applied research** is scientific study that aims to solve practical problems.

9. **Counseling psychology** is the branch of psychology that helps people cope with challenges in their daily lives.

10. **Clinical psychology** is the branch of psychology concerned with the study, assessment, and treatment of people with psychological disorders.

11. **Psychiatry** is the branch of medicine concerned with the physical diagnosis and treatment of psychological disorders.

12. **SQ3R** is a study method consisting of five steps: *Survey, Question, Read, Rehearse,* and *Review.*

FOCUS ON VOCABULARY AND LANGUAGE

. . . to remedy their own woes, millions turn to "psychology." In order to alleviate or fix (*remedy*) their misery, anxiety, grief, pain, and suffering (*woes*), people seek help from "psychology." (Psychology is in quotes because Myers wants to point out that not everything you think of as "psychology" is part of scientific psychology.)

Have you ever played *peekaboo* with a 6- month-old . . . ? Peekaboo is a game played in most cultures where a person hides or pretends to hide from a child and then reappears saying "PEEKABOO!" The important question for psychologists is, why do infants all over the world react similarly to this game; what are they actually feeling, perceiving, and thinking?

Such questions provide *grist for psychology's mill* . . . . The expression *"provide grist for the mill"* derives from the practice in the past where farmers brought their grain (*grist*) to the *mill* (a building with machinery for grinding grain into flour). Today the expression means that a greater volume of work (*grist*) does not present a problem; in fact, it is welcomed. The amount of grain (*grist*) is analogous to the variety of questions asked, and the research conducted to answer them is like the *mill* producing flour from the grist. Thus, psychology is a science that thrives on attempting to answer a variety of questions about how we think, feel, and act through scientific methodology (research).

Psychology's Roots

This list of pioneering psychologists—"*Magellans of the mind,*" . . . . Ferdinand Magellan (1489–1521) was a famous Portuguese navigator who made many discoveries and explored areas of the world previously unknown to his fellow Europeans. Because early psychologists made exciting discoveries and explored unknown frontiers, they were preparing the way (they were *pioneers*) for future psychologists and can thus be considered "*Magellans of the mind.*"

Let's *unpack* this definition. *Unpack* here means to take apart or disassemble. So psychology, defined as the science of behavior and mental processes, is broken down into overt behavior (i.e., observable events) and covert processes (i.e., events hidden within, such as thoughts, feelings, perceptions, beliefs, and so on) and is studied using the scientific or empirical method.

Contemporary Psychology

. . . mushrooming . . . Membership in psychological societies is growing at a rapid rate (*mushrooming*), and psychology is becoming more and more international (*globalizing*).

. . . psychology has wrestled with some issues . . . . Psychology has struggled (*wrestled*) with a number of debates, the biggest and most enduring of which is the controversy over the relative influence that genes (biology) and environment (experience) have on the development of psychological traits and behaviors (the **nature-nurture issue**).

Yet over and over again we will see that in contemporary science the nature-nurture *tension dissolves:* . . . The main point is that both sides of the debate have something to offer: Each contributes to the search for the truth. Thus, in modern science the strained relations (*tension*) over this issue diminish (*dissolve*). As Myers notes, we are biologically predisposed (*genetic influences*) to adapt and learn from experiences (*environmental influences*); *nurture works on what nature endows.*

"*Red in the face*" and "*hot under the collar*" refer to the physical changes that often accompany emotional arousal (e.g., anger). A person's face may become red due to blood rushing to it (blushing), and he or she may feel hot and perspire (*hot under the collar*). Different perspectives (neuroscience, evolutionary, behavior genetics, psychodynamic, behavioral, cognitive, and social-cultural) examine the same event (emotional change) using different levels of analysis (see Table 1.1). Myers points out that these different levels of analysis are not necessarily in opposition to each other but, rather, are complementary; that is, each level helps to complete the puzzle of why the event occurs by supplying answers from different points of view (*perspectives*).

But there is a *payoff:* Psychology is a *meeting ground* for different disciplines and is thus a *perfect home* for those with *wide-ranging* interests. Myers points out that there is much diversity in the discipline of psychology (i.e., it lacks unity), but this is beneficial (a *payoff*) because it is a nice place (area) to work in (a *perfect home*) for those who have broad or diverse (*wide-ranging*) interests. Thus, psychology is the ideal meeting place or *meeting ground* for different disciplines.

. . . *psychoceramics* (the study of crackpots). This joke derives its humor from the fact that some English words or phrases have more than one meaning, and it is this "play on words" that makes the joke funny. *Ceramics* is concerned with the work (or art) of making pottery, porcelain, and so on. Some of the pots may develop small breaks or splits and consequently would be referred to as "cracked pots." The term *crackpot*, on the other hand, is a colloquial (informal) expression used to describe a useless, impractical, or even crazy person. Although psychologists engage in a variety of interdisciplinary studies, such as psychohistory, psycholinguistics, and so on, there is obviously no such thing as "*psychoceramics*—the study of crackpots." Clinical psychologists, of course, assess and treat mental, emotional, and behavioral disorders (mental illness or psychopathology). (Note that Myers confesses in a footnote that he wrote this sentence on April 1st, April Fools' Day, which traditionally involves people playing practical jokes on other people. Did he fool you?)

Tips for Studying Psychology

One of psychology's oldest findings is that "*spaced practice*" promotes better retention than "*massed practice.*" *Spaced practice* refers to studying over a longer period of time, say 2 hours a day over 5 days rather than 10 hours on 1 day (*massed practice* or cramming). Distributing your study time is much better for learning and retention than one long study period (a *blitz*).

Research Strategies: How Psychologists Ask and Answer Questions

MODULE OVERVIEW

Module 2 begins by explaining the limits of intuition and common sense in reasoning about behavior and mental processes. To counteract our human tendency toward faulty reasoning, psychologists adopt a scientific attitude that is based on curiosity, skepticism, humility, and critical thinking. Module 2 also explains how psychologists, using the scientific method, employ the research strategies of description, correlation, and experimentation in order to objectively describe, predict, and explain behavior.

Next is a discussion of several questions people often ask about psychology, including why animal research is relevant, whether laboratory experiments are artificial, whether behavior varies with culture and gender, and whether psychology's principles have the potential for misuse.

Module 2 introduces a number of concepts and issues that will play an important role in later modules. Pay particular attention to the strengths and weaknesses of descriptive and correlational research. In addition, make sure that you understand the method of experimentation, especially the importance of control conditions and the difference between independent and dependent variables.

NOTE: Answer guidelines for all Module 2 questions begin on page 24.

MODULE REVIEW

First, skim each section, noting headings and boldface items. After you have read the section, review each objective by answering the fill-in questions that follow it. As you proceed, evaluate your performance by consulting the answers on page 24. Do not continue with the next section until you understand each answer. If you need to, review or reread the section in the textbook before continuing.

David Myers at times uses idioms that are unfamiliar to some readers. If you do not know the meaning of any of the following words, phrases, or expressions in the context in which they appear in the text, refer to pages 29–31 for an explanation: *our intuition often goes awry; dresses it in jargon; bull's eye; "Out of sight, out of mind"; "Absence makes the heart grow fonder"; familiarity breeds contempt; drop a course; sift reality from illusions; hard-headed curiosity; leap of faith; the proof is in the pudding; auras; crazy-sounding ideas; arena of competing ideas; so much the worse for our ideas; "The rat is always right"; the spectacles of our preconceived ideas; gut feelings; debunked; "play the tape"; hunches; Numbers can be numbing; a thimbleful; snapshot of the opinions; flipped a coin; "cold hand" . . . "hot hand"; recap; plunge in; To understand how a combustion engine works; screen; color "the facts."*

Thinking Critically With Psychological Science
(pp. 13–17)

Objective 1: Explain how hindsight bias and overconfidence can make research findings seem like mere common sense.

1. Psychologists use the science of _____ and _____ processes to better understand why people _____ , _____ , and _____ as they do.

2. The tendency to perceive an outcome that has occurred as being obvious and predictable is called the _____ _____ . This phenomenon is _____ (rare/common) in _____ (children/adults/both children and adults).

3. Because it is _____ (after the fact/usually wrong), this tendency makes research findings seem like mere common sense.

4. Our everyday thinking is also limited by _____ in what we think we know.

5. Most people are _____ (better/worse/equally wrong) in predicting their social behavior.

Objective 2: Explain how the scientific attitude encourages critical thinking.

6. The scientific approach is characterized by the attitudes of _____ , _____ , and _____ .

7. Scientific inquiry thus encourages reasoning that examines assumptions, discerns hidden values, evaluates evidence, and assesses conclusions, which is called _____ _____ .

The Scientific Method (pp. 17–27)

Objective 3: Describe how psychological theories guide scientific research.

1. Psychologists use the _____ _____ to guide their study of behavior and mental processes. They make self-reports and _____ and form _____ , which are _____ or rejected based on whether or not their predictions are correct.

2. An explanation using an integrated set of principles that organizes observations and predicts behaviors or events is a _____ . Testable predictions that allow a scientist to evaluate a theory are called _____ . These predictions give direction to _____ .

3. In order to prevent theoretical biases from influencing scientific observations, research must be reported precisely—using clear _____ _____ of all concepts—so that others can _____ the findings.

4. The test of a useful theory is the extent to which it effectively _____ observations and implies clear _____ .

5. Psychologists conduct research using _____ , _____ , and _____ methods.

Objective 4: Compare and contrast case studies, surveys, and naturalistic observation, and explain the importance of random sampling.

6. The research strategy in which one or more individuals is studied in depth in order to reveal universal principles of behavior is the _____ _____ .

7. Although case studies can suggest _____ for further study, a potential problem with this method is that any given individual may be _____ .

8. The method in which a group of people is questioned about their attitudes or behavior is the _____ .

9. An important factor in the validity of survey research is the _____ of questions.

10. We are more likely to overgeneralize from select samples that are especially _____ .

11. Surveys try to obtain a _____ sample, one that will be representative of the _____ being studied. In such a sample, every person _____ (does/does not) have a chance of being included.

12. Large, representative samples _____ (are/are not) better than small ones.

13. The research method in which people or animals are directly observed in their natural environments is called _____ _____ .

14. Case studies, surveys, and naturalistic observation do not explain behavior; they simply _____ it.

15. Using naturalistic observation, researchers have found that people are more likely to laugh in _____ situations than in _____ situations. Also, using

observations of walking speed and the accuracy of public clocks, researchers have concluded that the pace of life _____ (varies/does not vary) from one culture to another.

Objective 5: Describe positive and negative correlations, and explain how correlational measures can aid the process of prediction but not provide evidence of cause-effect relationships.

16. When changes in one factor are accompanied by changes in another, the two factors are said to be _____ , and one is thus able to _____ the other. The statistical expression of this relationship is called a _____ _____ .

17. If two factors increase or decrease together, they are _____ _____ . If, however, one decreases as the other increases, they are _____ _____ . Another way to state the latter is that the two variables relate _____ .

18. A negative correlation between two variables does not indicate the _____ or _____ of the relationship. Nor does correlation prove _____ ; rather, it merely indicates the possibility of a _____-_____ relationship.

If your level of test anxiety goes down as your time spent studying for the exam goes up, would you say these events are positively or negatively correlated? Explain your reasoning.

19. A correlation between two events or behaviors means only that one event can be _____ from the other.

20. Because two events may both be caused by some other _____ , a correlation does not mean that one _____ the other. For this reason, correlation thus does not enable _____ .

Objective 6: Describe how people form illusory correlations, and explain the human tendency to perceive order in random sequences.

21. A perceived correlation that does not really exist is an _____ _____ .

22. People are more likely to notice and recall events that _____ their beliefs. This error in thinking helps explain many _____ beliefs.

23. Another common tendency is to perceive order in _____ _____ .

24. Patterns and streaks in random sequences occur _____ (more/less) often than people expect, and they _____ (do/do not) appear random.

Objective 7: Explain how experiments help researchers isolate cause and effect, focusing on the characteristics of experimentation that make this possible.

25. To isolate _____ and _____ , researchers _____ control for other _____ .

26. Research studies have found that breast-fed infants _____ (do/do not) grow up with higher intelligence scores than those of infants who are bottle-fed with cow's milk. To study cause-effect relationships, psychologists conduct _____ . Using this method, a researcher _____ the factor of interest while _____ (controlling) other factors. By _____ assigning participants to

groups, researchers are able to hold
_____ all factors except the one
being investigated.

27. If a _____ changes when an
_____ factor is varied, the
researcher knows the factor is having an
_____ .

28. Researchers sometimes give certain participants a
pseudotreatment, called a _____ ,
and compare their behavior with that of participants who receive the actual treatment. When
merely thinking that one is receiving a treatment
produces results, a _____
_____ is said to occur.

29. When neither the participants nor the person collecting the data knows which condition a participant is in, the researcher is making use of the
_____-_____
procedure.

30. An experiment must involve at least two conditions: the _____ condition, in
which the experimental treatment is present, and
the _____ condition, in which it is
absent.

31. To ensure that the two groups are identical,
experimenters rely on the _____
_____ of individuals to the experimental conditions.

32. The factor that is being manipulated in an experiment is called the _____ variable.
The measurable factor that may change as a result
of these manipulations is called the
_____ variable.

33. The aim of an experiment is to _____
a(n) _____ variable, _____
the _____ variable, and
_____ all other _____ .

Explain at least one advantage of the experiment as a
research method.

Frequently Asked Questions About Psychology (pp. 27–31)

Objective 8: Explain the value of simplified laboratory conditions in discovering general principles of
behavior.

1. In laboratory experiments, psychologists' concern
is not with specific behaviors but with the underlying theoretical _____ .

2. Psychologists conduct experiments on simplified
behaviors in a laboratory environment in order to
gain _____ over the many vari-
ables present in the "real world." In doing so,
they are able to test _____
_____ of behavior that also operate in the real world.

Objective 9: Discuss whether psychological research
can be generalized across cultures and
genders.

3. Culture refers to _____ ,
_____ , _____ , and
_____ shared by a large group of
people that one generation passes on to the next.

4. Although specific attitudes and behaviors vary
across cultures, the underlying _____
are the same. For instance, throughout the world
people diagnosed with _____
exhibit the same _____ malfunc-
tion. Likewise, similarities between the
_____ far outweigh differences.

Objective 10: Explain why psychologists study animals, and discuss the ethics of experimentation with
both animals and humans.

5. Many psychologists study animals because they
are fascinating. More important, they study animals because of the _____ (simi-
larities/differences) between humans and other
animals. These studies have led to treatments for
human _____ and to a better
understanding of human functioning.

6. Some people question whether experiments with animals are _____ . They wonder whether it is right to place the _____ of humans over those of animals.

7. Opposition to animal experimentation also raises the question of what _____ should protect the well-being of animals.

Describe the goals of the ethical guidelines for psychological research.

Objective 11: Describe how personal values can influence psychologists' research and its application, and discuss psychology's potential to manipulate people.

8. Psychologists' values _____ (do/do not) influence their theories, observations, and professional advice.

9. Although psychology _____ (can/cannot) be used to manipulate people, its purpose is to _____ .

PROGRESS TEST

Multiple-Choice Questions

Circle your answers to the following questions and check them with the answers beginning on page 25. If your answer is incorrect, read the explanation for why it is incorrect and then consult the appropriate pages of the text.

1. After detailed study of a gunshot wound victim, a psychologist concludes that the brain region destroyed is likely to be important for memory functions. Which type of research did the psychologist use to deduce this?
  a. the case study
  b. a survey
  c. correlation
  d. experimentation

2. In an experiment to determine the effects of exercise on motivation, exercise is the:
  a. control condition.
  b. intervening variable.
  c. independent variable.
  d. dependent variable.

3. In order to determine the effects of a new drug on memory, one group of people is given a pill that contains the drug. A second group is given a sugar pill that does not contain the drug. This second group constitutes the:
  a. random sample.
  b. experimental group.
  c. control group.
  d. test group.

4. *Theories* are defined as:
  a. testable propositions.
  b. factors that may change in response to manipulation.
  c. statistical indexes.
  d. principles that help to organize, predict, and explain facts.

5. A psychologist studies the play behavior of third-grade children by watching groups during recess at school. Which type of research is she using?
  a. correlation
  b. case study
  c. experimentation
  d. naturalistic observation

6. To ensure that other researchers can repeat their work, psychologists use:
  a. control groups.
  b. random assignment.
  c. double-blind procedures.
  d. operational definitions.

7. The scientific attitude of skepticism is based on the belief that:
  a. people are rarely candid in revealing their thoughts.
  b. mental processes can't be studied objectively.
  c. the scientist's intuition about behavior is usually correct.
  d. ideas need to be tested against observable evidence.

8. Which of the following is *not* a basic research technique used by psychologists?
  a. description
  b. replication
  c. experimentation
  d. correlation

9. Psychologists' personal values:
   a. have little influence on how their experiments are conducted.
   b. do not influence the interpretation of experimental results because of the use of statistical techniques that guard against subjective bias.
   c. can bias both scientific observation and interpretation of data.
   d. have little influence on investigative methods but a significant effect on interpretation.

10. If shoe size and IQ are negatively correlated, which of the following is true?
    a. People with large feet tend to have high IQs.
    b. People with small feet tend to have high IQs.
    c. People with small feet tend to have low IQs.
    d. IQ is unpredictable based on a person's shoe size.

11. Which of the following would be best for determining whether alcohol impairs memory?
    a. case study   c. survey
    b. naturalistic observation d. experiment

12. Well-done surveys measure attitudes in a representative subset, or _____ , of an entire group, or _____ .
    a. population; random sample
    b. control group; experimental group
    c. experimental group; control group
    d. random sample; population

13. Which of the following research methods does *not* belong with the others?
    a. case study   c. naturalistic observation
    b. survey   d. experiment

14. To prevent the possibility that a placebo effect or researchers' expectations will influence a study's results, scientists employ:
    a. control groups.
    b. experimental groups.
    c. random assignment.
    d. the double-blind procedure.

15. Which statement about the ethics of experimentation with people and animals is *false*?
    a. Only a small percentage of animal experiments use shock.
    b. Allegations that psychologists routinely subject animals to pain, starvation, and other inhumane conditions have been proven untrue.
    c. The American Psychological Association and the British Psychological Society have set strict guidelines for the care and treatment of human and animal subjects.

   d. Animals are used in psychological research more often than they are killed by humane animal shelters.

16. In an experiment to determine the effects of attention on memory, memory is the:
    a. control condition.
    b. intervening variable.
    c. independent variable.
    d. dependent variable.

17. Which of the following *best* describes the hindsight bias?
    a. Events seem more predictable before they have occurred.
    b. Events seem more predictable after they have occurred.
    c. A person's intuition is usually correct.
    d. A person's intuition is usually not correct.

18. The procedure designed to ensure that the experimental and control groups do not differ in any way that might affect the experiment's results is called:
    a. variable controlling.
    b. random assignment.
    c. representative sampling.
    d. stratification.

19. Illusory correlation refers to:
    a. the perception that two negatively correlated variables are positively correlated.
    b. the perception of a correlation where there is none.
    c. an insignificant correlation.
    d. a correlation that equals –1.0.

20. The strength of the relationship between two vivid events will most likely be:
    a. significant.
    b. positive.
    c. negative.
    d. overestimated.

21. Which of the following is true, according to the text?
    a. Because laboratory experiments are artificial, any principles discovered cannot be applied to everyday behaviors.
    b. No psychological theory can be considered a good one until it produces testable predictions.
    c. Psychology's theories reflect common sense.
    d. We tend to think we know less than we do.

22. Which type of research would allow you to determine whether students' college grades accurately predict later income?
    a. case study
    b. naturalistic observation
    c. experimentation
    d. correlation

23. In a test of the effects of air pollution, groups of students performed a reaction-time task in a polluted or an unpolluted room. To what condition were students in the unpolluted room exposed?
    a. experimental
    b. control
    c. randomly assigned
    d. dependent

24. In order to study the effects of lighting on mood, Dr. Cooper had students fill out questionnaires in brightly lit or dimly lit rooms. In this study, the independent variable consisted of:
    a. the number of students assigned to each group.
    b. the students' responses to the questionnaire.
    c. the room lighting.
    d. the subject matter of the questions asked.

25. You decide to test your belief that men drink more soft drinks than women by finding out whether more soft drinks are consumed per day in the men's dorm than in the women's dorm. Your belief is a(n) _____ , and your research prediction is a(n) _____ .
    a. hypothesis; theory
    b. theory; hypothesis
    c. independent variable; dependent variable
    d. dependent variable; independent variable

26. Your roommate is conducting a survey to learn how many hours the typical college student studies each day. She plans to pass out her questionnaire to the members of her sorority. You point out that her findings will be flawed because:
    a. she has not specified an independent variable.
    b. she has not specified a dependent variable.
    c. the sample will probably not be representative of the population of interest.
    d. of all of these reasons.

27. The concept of control is important in psychological research because:
    a. without control over independent and dependent variables, researchers cannot describe, predict, or explain behavior.
    b. experimental control allows researchers to study the influence of one or two independent variables on a dependent variable while holding other potential influences constant.

    c. without experimental control, results cannot be generalized from a sample to a population.
    d. of all of these reasons.

28. Martina believes that high doses of caffeine slow a person's reaction time. In order to test this belief, she has five friends each drink three 8-ounce cups of coffee and then measures their reaction time on a learning task. What is wrong with Martina's research strategy?
    a. No independent variable is specified.
    b. No dependent variable is specified.
    c. There is no control condition.
    d. There is no provision for replication of the findings.

29. A researcher was interested in determining whether her students' test performance could be predicted from their proximity to the front of the classroom. So she matched her students' scores on a math test with their seating position. This study is an example of:
    a. experimentation.
    b. correlational research.
    c. a survey.
    d. naturalistic observation.

30. Your best friend criticizes psychological research for being artificial and having no relevance to behavior in real life. In defense of psychology's use of laboratory experiments you point out that:
    a. psychologists make every attempt to avoid artificiality by setting up experiments that closely simulate real-world environments.
    b. psychologists who conduct research are not concerned with the applicability of their findings to the real world.
    c. most psychological research is not conducted in a laboratory environment.
    d. psychologists intentionally study behavior in simplified environments in order to gain greater control over variables and to test general principles that help to explain many behaviors.

31. A professor constructs a questionnaire to determine how students at the university feel about nuclear disarmament. Which of the following techniques should be used in order to survey a random sample of the student body?
    a. Every student should be sent the questionnaire.
    b. Only students majoring in psychology should be asked to complete the questionnaire.
    c. Only students living on campus should be asked to complete the questionnaire.
    d. From an alphabetical listing of all students, every tenth (or fifteenth, for example) student should be asked to complete the questionnaire.

32. If eating saturated fat and the likelihood of contracting cancer are positively correlated, which of the following is true?
    a. Saturated fat causes cancer.
    b. People who are prone to develop cancer prefer foods containing saturated fat.
    c. A separate factor links the consumption of saturated fat to cancer.
    d. None of these answers is necessarily true.

33. Rashad, who is participating in a psychology experiment on the effects of alcohol on perception, is truthfully told by the experimenter that he has been assigned to the "high-dose condition." What is wrong with this experiment?
    a. There is no control condition.
    b. Rashad's expectations concerning the effects of "high doses" of alcohol on perception may influence his performance.
    c. Knowing that Rashad is in the "high-dose" condition may influence the experimenter's interpretations of Rashad's results.
    d. Both b. and c. are correct.

34. A friend majoring in anthropology is critical of psychological research because it often ignores the influence of culture on thoughts and actions. You point out that:
    a. there is very little evidence that cultural diversity has a significant effect on specific behaviors and attitudes.
    b. most researchers assign participants to experimental and control conditions in such a way

as to fairly represent the cultural diversity of the population under study.
    c. it is impossible for psychologists to control for every possible variable that might influence research participants.
    d. even when specific thoughts and actions vary across cultures, as they often do, the underlying processes are much the same.

35. The scientific attitude of humility is based on the idea that:
    a. researchers must evaluate new ideas and theories objectively rather than accept them blindly.
    b. scientific theories must be testable.
    c. simple explanations of behavior make better theories than do complex explanations.
    d. researchers must be prepared to reject their own ideas in the face of conflicting evidence.

36. Which of the following procedures is an example of the use of a placebo?
    a. In a test of the effects of a drug on memory, a participant is led to believe that a harmless pill actually contains an active drug.
    b. A participant in an experiment is led to believe that a pill, which actually contains an active drug, is harmless.
    c. Participants in an experiment are not told which treatment condition is in effect.
    d. Neither the participants nor the experimenter knows which treatment condition is in effect.

37. If height and body weight are positively correlated, which of the following is true?
    a. There is a cause-effect relationship between height and weight.
    b. As height increases, weight decreases.
    c. Knowing a person's height, one can predict his or her weight.
    d. All of these answers are true.

38. Joe believes that his basketball game is always best when he wears his old gray athletic socks. Joe is a victim of the phenomenon called:
    a. the placebo effect.
    b. overconfidence.
    c. illusory correlation.
    d. hindsight bias.

Matching Items

Match each term with its definition or description.

Terms

_____ 1. placebo effect
_____ 2. hindsight bias
_____ 3. critical thinking
_____ 4. illusory correlation
_____ 5. hypothesis
_____ 6. theory
_____ 7. independent variable
_____ 8. dependent variable
_____ 9. experimental condition
_____ 10. control condition
_____ 11. case study
_____ 12. survey
_____ 13. replication
_____ 14. random assignment
_____ 15. experiment
_____ 16. double-blind
_____ 17. culture

Definitions or Descriptions

a. an in-depth observational study of one person
b. false perception of a relationship between two variables
c. the variable being manipulated in an experiment
d. the variable being measured in an experiment
e. experimental results caused by expectations alone
f. the "treatment-absent" condition in an experiment
g. testable proposition
h. "I-knew-it-all-along" phenomenon
i. repeating an experiment to see whether the same results are obtained
j. the process in which research participants are selected by chance for different groups in an experiment
k. reasoning that does not blindly accept arguments
l. an explanation using an integrated set of principles that organizes observations and predicts behavior
m. the research strategy in which the effects of one or more variables on behavior are tested
n. shared ideas and behaviors passed from one generation to the next
o. the "treatment-present" condition in an experiment
p. the research strategy in which a representative sample of individuals is questioned
q. experimental procedure in which neither the research participant nor the experimenter knows which condition the participant is in

Essay Question

Elio has a theory that regular exercise can improve thinking. Help him design an experiment evaluating this theory. (Use the space below to list the points you want to make, and organize them. Then write the essay on a separate piece of paper.)

KEY TERMS

Using your own words, on a separate piece of paper write a brief definition or explanation of each of the following.

1. hindsight bias
2. critical thinking
3. theory
4. hypothesis
5. operational definition
6. replication
7. case study
8. survey
9. population

10. random sample
11. naturalistic observation
12. correlation
13. illusory correlation
14. experiment
15. random assignment
16. double-blind procedure
17. placebo effect
18. experimental condition
19. control condition
20. independent variable
21. dependent variable
22. culture

ANSWERS

Module Review

Thinking Critically With Psychological Science

1. behavior; mental; think; feel; act
2. hindsight bias; common; both children and adults
3. after the fact
4. overconfidence
5. equally wrong
6. curiosity; skepticism; humility
7. critical thinking

The Scientific Method

1. scientific method; observations; theories; revised
2. theory; hypotheses; research
3. operational definitions; replicate
4. organizes; predictions
5. descriptive; correlation; experimental
6. case study
7. hypotheses; atypical
8. survey
9. wording
10. vivid
11. random; population; does
12. are
13. naturalistic observation
14. describe
15. social; solitary; varies
16. correlated; predict; correlation coefficient

17. positively correlated; negatively correlated; inversely
18. strength; weakness; causation; cause-effect

This is an example of a negative correlation. As one factor (time spent studying) increases, the other factor (anxiety level) decreases.

19. predicted
20. event; caused; explanation
21. illusory correlation
22. confirm; superstitious
23. random events
24. more; do not
25. cause; effect; statistically; factors
26. do; experiments; manipulates; holding constant; randomly; constant
27. behavior; experimental; effect
28. placebo; placebo effect
29. double-blind
30. experimental; control
31. random assignment
32. independent; dependent
33. manipulate; independent; measure; dependent; control; variables

Experimentation has the advantage of increasing the investigator's control of both relevant and irrelevant variables that might influence behavior. Experiments also permit the investigator to go beyond observation and description to uncover cause-effect relationships in behavior.

Frequently Asked Questions About Psychology

1. principles
2. control; general principles
3. ideas; behaviors; attitudes; traditions
4. principles or processes; dyslexia; brain; genders
5. similarities; diseases
6. ethical; well-being
7. safeguards

Ethical guidelines require investigators to (1) obtain informed consent of potential participants, (2) protect them from harm and discomfort, (3) treat information about participants confidentially, and (4) fully explain the research afterward.

8. do
9. can; enlighten

Progress Test

Multiple-Choice Questions

1. **a.** is the answer. In a case study, one subject is studied in depth.
   b. In survey research, a group of people is interviewed.
   c. Correlations identify whether two factors are related.
   d. In an experiment, an investigator manipulates one variable to observe its effect on another.

2. **c.** is the answer. Exercise is the variable being manipulated in the experiment.
   a. A control condition for this experiment would be a group of people not permitted to exercise.
   b. An intervening variable is a variable other than those being manipulated that may influence behavior.
   d. The dependent variable is the behavior measured by the experimenter—in this case, the effects of exercise.

3. **c.** is the answer. The control condition is that for which the experimental treatment (the new drug) is absent.
   a. A random sample is a subset of a population in which every person has an equal chance of being selected.
   b. The experimental condition is the group for which the experimental treatment (the new drug) is present.
   d. "Test group" is an ambiguous term; both the experimental and control group are tested.

4. **d.** is the answer.
   a. Hypotheses are testable propositions.
   b. Dependent variables are factors that may change in response to manipulated independent variables.
   c. Statistical indexes may be used to test specific hypotheses (and therefore as indirect tests of theories), but they are merely mathematical tools, not general principles, as are theories.

5. **d.** is the answer. In this case, the children are being observed in their normal environment rather than in a laboratory.
   a. Correlational research measures relationships between two factors. The psychologist may later want to determine whether there are correlations between the variables studied under natural conditions.
   b. In a case study, one subject is studied in depth.
   c. This is not an experiment because the psychologist is not directly controlling the variables being studied.

6. **d.** is the answer.

7. **d.** is the answer.

8. **b.** is the answer. Replication is the repetition of an experiment in order to determine whether its findings are reliable. It is not a research method.

9. **c.** is the answer.
   a., b., & d. Psychologists' personal values can influence all of these.

10. **b.** is the answer.
    a. & c. These answers would have been correct had the question stated that there is a *positive* correlation between shoe size and IQ. Actually, there is probably no correlation at all!

11. **d.** is the answer. In an experiment, it would be possible to manipulate alcohol consumption and observe the effects, if any, on memory.
    a., b., & c. These answers are incorrect because only by directly controlling the variables of interest can a researcher uncover cause-effect relationships.

12. **d.** is the answer.
    a. A sample is a subset of a population.
    b. & c. Control and experimental groups are used in experimentation, not in survey research.

13. **d.** is the answer. Only experiments can reveal cause-effect relationships; the other methods can only *describe* relationships.

14. **d.** is the answer.
    a. & b. The double-blind procedure is one way to create experimental and control groups.
    c. Research participants are randomly assigned to either an experimental or a control group.

15. **d.** is the answer. Animal shelters are forced to kill 50 times as many dogs and cats as are used in research.

16. **d.** is the answer.
    a. The control condition is the comparison group, in which the experimental treatment (the treatment of interest) is absent.
    b. Memory is a directly observed and measured dependent variable in this experiment.
    c. Attention is the independent variable, which is being manipulated.

17. **b.** is the answer.
    a. The phenomenon is related to hindsight rather than foresight.
    c. & d. The phenomenon doesn't involve whether or not the intuitions are correct but rather people's attitude that they had the correct intuition.

18. **b.** is the answer. If enough participants are used in an experiment and they are randomly assigned to the two groups, any differences that emerge between the groups should stem from the experiment itself.
    a., c., & d. None of these terms describes precautions taken in setting up groups for experiments.

19. **b.** is the answer.

20. **d.** is the answer. Because we are sensitive to dramatic or unusual events, we are especially likely to perceive a relationship between them.
a., b., & c. The relationship between vivid events is no more likely to be significant, positive, or negative than that between less dramatic events.

21. **b.** is the answer.
a. In fact, the artificiality of experiments is part of an intentional attempt to create a controlled environment in which to test theoretical principles that are applicable to all behaviors.
c. Some psychological theories go against what we consider common sense; furthermore, on many issues that psychology addresses, it's far from clear what the "common sense" position is.
d. In fact, just the opposite is true.

22. **d.** is the answer. Correlations show how well one factor can be predicted from another.
a. Because a case study focuses in great detail on the behavior of an individual, it's probably not useful in showing whether predictions are possible.
b. Naturalistic observation is a method of describing, rather than predicting, behavior.
c. In experimental research, the effects of manipulated independent variables on dependent variables are measured. It is not clear how an experiment could help determine whether college grades predict later income.

23. **b.** is the answer. The control condition is the one in which the treatment—in this case, pollution—is absent.
a. Students in the polluted room would be in the experimental condition.
c. Presumably, all students in both conditions were randomly assigned to their groups. Random assignment is a method for establishing groups, rather than a condition.
d. The word *dependent* refers to a kind of variable in experiments; conditions are either experimental or control.

24. **c.** is the answer. The lighting is the factor being manipulated.
a. & d. These answers are incorrect because they involve aspects of the experiment other than the variables.
b. This answer is the dependent, not the independent, variable.

25. **b.** is the answer. A general belief such as this one is a theory; it helps organize, explain, and generate testable predictions (called hypotheses) such as "men drink more soft drinks than women."

c. & d. Independent and dependent variables are experimental treatments and behaviors, respectively. Beliefs and predictions may involve such variables, but are not themselves those variables.

26. **c.** is the answer. The members of one sorority are likely to share more interests, traits, and attitudes than will the members of a random sample of college students.
a. & b. Unlike experiments, surveys do not specify or directly manipulate independent and dependent variables. In a sense, survey questions are independent variables, and the answers, dependent variables.

27. **b.** is the answer.
a. Although the descriptive methods of case studies, surveys, naturalistic observation, and correlational research do not involve control of variables, they nevertheless enable researchers to describe and predict behavior.
c. Whether or not a sample is representative of a population, rather than control over variables, determines whether results can be generalized from a sample to a population.

28. **c.** is the answer. In order to determine the effects of caffeine on reaction time, Martina needs to measure reaction time in a control, or comparison, group that does not receive caffeine.
a. Caffeine is the independent variable.
b. Reaction time is the dependent variable.
d. Whether Martina's experiment can be replicated is determined by the precision with which she reports her procedures, which is not an aspect of research strategy.

29. **b.** is the answer.
a. This is not an experiment because the researcher is not manipulating the independent variable (seating position); she is merely measuring whether variation in this factor predicts test performance.
c. If the study were based entirely on students' self-reported responses, this would be a survey.
d. This study goes beyond naturalistic observation, which merely describes behavior as it occurs, to determine if test scores can be predicted from students' seating position.

30. **d.** is the answer.

31. **d.** is the answer. Selecting every tenth person would probably result in a representative sample of the population of students at the university.
a. It would be difficult, if not impossible, to survey every student on campus.
b. Psychology students are not representative of the entire student population.

c. This answer is incorrect for the same reason as b. This would constitute a biased sample.

32. **d.** is the answer.
    a. Correlation does not imply causality.
    b. Again, a positive correlation simply means that two factors tend to increase or decrease together; further relationships are not implied.
    c. A separate factor may or may not be involved. That the two factors are correlated does not imply a separate factor. There may, for example, be a direct causal relationship between the two factors themselves.

33. **d.** is the answer.
    a. The low-dose comparison group is the control group.

34. **d.** is the answer.
    a. In fact, just the opposite is true.
    b. Actually, psychological experiments tend to use the most readily available people, often white North American college students.
    c. Although this may be true, psychological experiments remain important because they help explain underlying processes of human behavior everywhere. Therefore, d. is a much better response than c.

35. **d.** is the answer.
    a. This follows from the attitude of skepticism, rather than humility.
    b. & c. Although both of these are true of the scientific method, neither has anything to do with humility.

36. **a.** is the answer.
    b. Use of a placebo tests whether the behavior of a research participant, who mistakenly believes that a treatment (such as a drug) is in effect, is the same as it would be if the treatment were actually present.
    c. & d. These are examples of *blind* and *double-blind* control procedures.

37. **c.** is the answer. If height and weight are positively correlated, increased height is associated with increased weight. Thus, one can predict a person's weight from his or her height.
    a. Correlation does not imply causality.
    b. This situation depicts a negative correlation between height and weight.

38. **c.** is the answer. A correlation that is perceived but doesn't actually exist, as in the example, is known as an illusory correlation.
    a. The placebo effect occurs when a person's expectations cause a result.
    b. Overconfidence is the tendency to think we are more right than we actually are.

d. Hindsight bias is the tendency to believe, after learning an outcome, that one would have foreseen it.

Essay Question

Elio's hypothesis is that daily aerobic exercise for one month will improve memory. Exercise is the independent variable. The dependent variable is memory. Exercise could be manipulated by having people in an experimental group jog for 30 minutes each day. Memory could be measured by comparing the number of words they recall from a test list studied before the exercise experiment begins, and again afterward. A control group that does not exercise *is* needed so that any improvement in the experimental group's memory can be attributed to exercise, and not to some other factor, such as the passage of one month's time or familiarity with the memory test. The control group should engage in some nonexercise activity for the same amount of time each day that the experimental group exercises. The participants should be randomly selected from the population at large, and then randomly assigned to the experimental and control groups.

Matching Items

1. e	6. l	11. a	16. q
2. h	7. c	12. p	17. n
3. k	8. d	13. i	
4. b	9. o	14. j	
5. g	10. f	15. m	

Key Terms

1. **Hindsight bias** refers to the tendency to believe, after learning an outcome, that one would have foreseen it; also called the *I-knew-it-all-along phenomenon*.

2. **Critical thinking** is careful reasoning that examines assumptions, discerns hidden values, evaluates evidence, and assesses conclusions.

3. A **theory** is an explanation using an integrated set of principles that organizes observations and predicts behaviors or events.

4. A **hypothesis** is a testable prediction, often implied by a theory; testing the hypothesis helps scientists to test the theory.
   Example: In order to test his theory of why people conform, Solomon Asch formulated the testable **hypothesis** that an individual would be more likely to go along with the majority opinion of a large group than with that of a smaller group.

5. An **operational definition** is a precise statement of the procedures (operations) used to define research variables.

6. **Replication** is the process of repeating an experiment, often with different participants and in different situations, to see whether the basic finding generalizes to other people and circumstances.

7. The **case study** is an observation technique in which one person is studied in great depth, often with the intention of revealing universal principles.

8. The **survey** is a technique for ascertaining the self-reported attitudes or behaviors of a representative, random sample of people.

9. A **population** consists of all the members of a group being studied.

10. A **random sample** is one that is representative because every member of the population has an equal chance of being included.

11. **Naturalistic observation** involves observing and recording behavior in naturally occurring situations without trying to manipulate and control the situation.

12. **Correlation** is a measure of the extent to which two factors vary together, and thus of how well either factor predicts the other. The correlation coefficient is a statistical measure of the relationship; it can be positive or negative.

    Example: If there is a **positive correlation** between air temperature and ice cream sales, the warmer (higher) it is, the more ice cream is sold. If there is a **negative correlation** between air temperature and sales of cocoa, the cooler (lower) it is, the more cocoa is sold.

13. **Illusory correlation** is the perception of a relationship where none exists.

14. An **experiment** is a research method in which a researcher manipulates one or more factors (independent variables) in order to observe their effect on some behavior or mental process (the dependent variable); experiments therefore make it possible to establish cause-effect relationships.

15. **Random assignment** is the procedure of assigning participants to the experimental and control conditions by chance in order to minimize preexisting differences between those assigned to the different groups.

16. A **double-blind procedure** is an experimental procedure in which neither the experimenter nor the research participants are aware of which condition is in effect. It is used to prevent experimenters' and participants' expectations from influencing the results of an experiment.

17. The **placebo effect** occurs when the results of an experiment are caused by a participant's expectations about what is really going on.

18. The **experimental condition** of an experiment is one in which participants are exposed to the independent variable being studied.

    Example: In the study of the effects of a new drug on reaction time, participants in the **experimental condition** would actually receive the drug being tested.

19. The **control condition** of an experiment is one in which the treatment of interest, or independent variable, is withheld so that comparison to the experimental condition can be made.

    Example: The **control condition** for an experiment testing the effects of a new drug on reaction time would be a group of participants given a placebo (inactive drug or sugar pill) instead of the drug being tested.

20. The **independent variable** of an experiment is the factor being manipulated and tested by the investigator.

    Example: In the study of the effects of a new drug on reaction time, the drug is the **independent variable**.

21. The **dependent variable** of an experiment is the factor being measured by the investigator.

    Example: In the study of the effects of a new drug on reaction time, the participants' reaction time is the **dependent variable.**

22. **Culture** is the enduring behaviors, ideas, attitudes, and traditions shared by a large group of people and transmitted from one generation to the next.

FOCUS ON VOCABULARY AND LANGUAGE

Introduction

Although in some ways we *outsmart* the smartest computers, our *intuition* often goes *awry*. The main point is that humans are in many ways superior to computers (*we outsmart them*), but our beliefs, feelings, and perceptions (*intuition*) can often lead us astray (*awry*) or away from the truth. To be human means we can, and do, make mistakes (*to err is human*).

Thinking Critically With Psychological Science

Some people think psychology merely *documents* what people already know and *dresses it in jargon*. Some people criticize psychology, saying that it simply reports (*documents*) common sense, or what's obvious to everyone. Instead of stating something plainly, the critics suggest, psychology translates the information into the specialized and obscure vocabulary of the discipline (*dresses it up in jargon*). Myers makes it very clear with some good examples that this criticism is not justified and points out that our intuitions about reality can often be very mistaken (they can *lead us astray*).

How easy it is to seem *astute* when *drawing the bull's eye after the arrow has struck*. In the sport of archery the task is to shoot the arrow at the red circle in the center of the target (the *bull's eye*). If we first shoot an arrow, then draw the target so that the arrow is in the center (in the *bull's eye*), we can appear to be very accurate. Myers uses this analogy to illustrate how the hindsight bias (or the *I-knew-it all-along phenomenon*) can lead us to believe that we are shrewd (*astute*) and would have been able to predict outcomes that we have learned after-the-fact.

"Out of sight, out of mind" . . . *"Absence makes the heart grow fonder."* These two sayings, or expressions, about romantic love have opposite meanings. The first one suggests that when couples are apart (*out of sight*) they are less likely to think about each other (*out of mind*) than when they are together. The second saying makes the point that being separated (*absence*) increases the feelings of love the couple shares (*makes the heart grow fonder*). People who are told that the results of a study support the first expression (*out of sight, out of mind*) see this as mere common sense. People told that the results support the second expression (*absence makes the heart grow fonder*) also say this is obviously true. There is clearly a problem here; relying on common sense can lead to opposite conclusions.

. . . that *familiarity breeds contempt*. . . . This expression and others are based on many casual observations but are often wrong. For example, is it true that the better you know someone (*familiarity*), the more likely it is that you will dislike the person (have *contempt*)? In fact, research shows that the opposite is probably true. (Your text, again and again, will emphasize the fact that our common sense and intuition do not always provide us with reliable evidence.)

. . . *drop a course* . . . This means to stop going to class and to have your name removed from the class list.

But scientific inquiry, fed by curious skepticism and by humility, can help us *sift* reality from illusions. Literally, *sift* means to separate the finer particles from the coarser ones by passing material through a sieve. Myers uses the word sift to explain how a scientific approach can separate (*sift*) what is true and factual (real) from what is not real (illusion). (Be sure you understand the word *sift* because Myers uses it quite often.)

Underlying all science is, first, a *hard-headed curiosity* . . . *Hard-headed* here means to be practical, uncompromising, realistic, or unswayed by sentiment. All science, including psychology, is guided by this realistic desire to know (*curiosity*) about nature and life.

. . . *leap of faith.* This is a belief in something in the absence of demonstrated proof. Some questions—about the existence of God or life after death, for example—cannot be answered by science and cannot be scientifically proved or disproved; if a person believes, then it is on the basis of trust and confidence alone (*leap of faith*).

. . . the *proof is in the pudding*. This comes from the expression *"the proof of the pudding is in the eating."* A *pudding* is a sweet dessert. We can test (or prove) the quality of the dessert (*pudding*) by trying it (*eating*). Likewise, many questions, even if they appear to make little sense (*crazy-sounding ideas*), can be tested using the scientific method.

. . . *auras* . . . An *aura* is a bright glow surrounding a figure or an object. Some believe that humans have auras which only those with extrasensory abilities can see. The magician James Randi proposed a simple test of this claim, but nobody who is alleged to have this magical power (*aura-seer*) has taken the test.

More often, science relegates *crazy-sounding ideas* to the *mountain* of forgotten claims. . . . The use of scientific inquiry can get rid of or dispose of (*relegate*) non-sensible concepts (*crazy-sounding ideas*) to the large stack or pile (*mountain*) of ridiculous claims no longer remembered.

In the *arena* of competing ideas . . . An *arena* is an area where games, sports, and competitions take place. Myers is suggesting that in an area (*arena*) where there is a contest between ideas (*competing ideas*), skeptical testing can help discover the truth.

. . . *then so much the worse for our ideas*. This means that we have to give up, or get rid of, our ideas if they are shown to be wrong (*so much the worse for them*). We have to be humble (i.e., have humility).

"The rat is always right." This early *motto* (a phrase used as a maxim or guiding principle) comes from the fact that for most of the first half of the twentieth century psychology used animals in its research (especially in the study of learning). The *rat* became a symbol of this research, and its behavior or performance in experiments demonstrated the truth. If the truth, as shown by the rat, is contrary to the prediction or hypothesis, then one has to be humble about it and try another way.

We all view nature through the *spectacles* of our *preconceived ideas*. This means that what we already believe (*our preconceived ideas*) influences, and to some extent determines, what we look for and actually see or discover in nature. It's as though the type of eyeglasses (*spectacles*) we wear limits what we can see.

. . . *gut feelings* . . . This refers to basic intuitive reactions or responses. Critical thinking requires determining whether a conclusion is based simply on a subjective opinion (*gut feeling*) or anecdote (a story someone tells) or on reliable scientific evidence.

. . . *debunked* . . . This means to remove glamour or credibility from established ideas, persons, and traditions. Myers points out that scientific evidence and critical inquiry have indeed discredited (*debunked*) many popular presumptions.

. . . one *cannot* simply *"play the tape"* and relive long-buried or *repressed* memories. . . . This is an example of a discredited (*debunked*) idea that hidden (*repressed*) memories can be accurately and reliably retrieved (*brought back*) intact and complete in the same way that *playing a tape* on a VCR allows us to watch exactly the same show over and over again.

The Scientific Method

. . . it [psychological science] welcomes *hunches* and plausible-sounding theories. In popular usage, a *hunch* is an intuitive feeling about a situation or event. Psychology can use subjective ideas to help formulate hypotheses or predictions, which can then be tested empirically or scientifically.

Numbers can be numbing . . . We are often overwhelmed and our senses deadened (*numbed*) by the sometimes inappropriate use of statistics and numbers.

As psychologist Gordon Allport (1954, p. 9) said, "Given a *thimbleful* of [dramatic] facts we rush to make *generalizations as large as a tub*." A *thimble* is a small metal container which fits over the top of the thumb or finger and is used while sewing to push the needle through the material; a *tub* is a very large container (e.g., a *bathtub*). Allport is saying that given a *small* amount of information (a *thimbleful*), we tend to make very *big* assumptions (*generalizations as large as a tub*).

. . . 1500 randomly sampled people, drawn from all areas of a country, provide a remarkably accurate *snapshot* of the opinions of a nation. A *snapshot* is a picture taken with a camera, and it captures what people are doing at a given moment in time. A good survey (*1500 randomly selected representative people*) gives an accurate picture (*snapshot*) of the opinions of the whole population of interest (the *target group*).

If someone *flipped a coin* six times, which of the following sequences of heads (H) and tails (T) would be most likely: HHHTTT or HTTHTH or HHHH-HH? *Flipping a coin* means throwing or tossing the coin into the air and observing which side is facing up when it lands. (The side of the coin that usually has the imprint of the face of a famous person on it—e.g., the president or the queen—is called *heads* (*H*) and the other side is called *tails* (*T*).) By the way, all of the above sequences are equally likely, but most people pick HTTHTH. Likewise, any series of five playing cards (e.g., a bridge or poker hand in a game of cards) is just as likely as any other hand.

"cold hand" . . . *"hot hand"* . . . In this context, "hot" and "cold" do not refer to temperature. Here, being hot (or having a *"hot hand"*) means doing well, and doing well consistently is having a hot streak. Having a run of poor luck is a cold streak. The crucial point, however, is that our intuition about sequences of events (*streaks* or *streaky patterns*) often deceives us. True random sequences often are not what we think they should be, and thus, they don't *appear* to be really random. When we think we're doing well (have a *"hot hand"*), very often we are not; we are merely noting or overinterpreting certain sequences (*streaks*) found in any random data.

Let's *recap.* Recap is an abbreviation of *recapitulate,* which means to repeat or go over briefly, to summarize. Myers summarizes (*recaps*) the important points in each section of the module.

Frequently Asked Questions About Psychology

. . . *plunge in* . . . In this context, *plunge in* means to move ahead quickly with the discussion. (Similarly, when you dive into a swimming pool [*plunge in*], you do so quickly.) Before going on with the discussion of psychology (*plunging in*), Myers addresses some important issues and questions.

To understand how a combustion engine works, you would do better to study *a lawn mower's engine than a Mercedes'.* A *Mercedes* is a very complex luxury car, and a *lawn mower* (a machine for cutting grass in the garden) has a very simple engine. To under-stand the principles underlying both machines, it is easier to study the simpler one. Likewise, when trying to understand the nervous system, it is better to study a simple one (e.g., a sea slug) than a complex one (a human).

. . . most universities today screen research proposals through an *ethics committee.* . . . *Ethics committees* (groups of people concerned with moral behavior and acceptable standards of conduct) subject research proposals to rigorous tests (*screen them*) to ensure that they are fair and reasonable and that they do not harm the participants' well-being.

Values can also *color* "the facts." Our values (what we believe is right and true) can influence (*color*) our observations, interpretations, and conclusions ("the facts").

Biology and Behavior

Neural and Hormonal Systems

3 **M O D U L E**

MODULE OVERVIEW

Module 3 is concerned with the basis of the body's neural systems, which underlie all human behavior. Under the direction of the brain, the nervous and endocrine systems coordinate a variety of voluntary and involuntary behaviors and serve as the body's mechanisms for communication with the external environment.

Many students find the technical material in this and the next module difficult to master. Not only are there many terms for you to remember, but you must also know the organization and function of the various divisions of the nervous system. Learning this material will require a great deal of rehearsal. Working the module review several times and mentally reciting terms are useful techniques for rehearsing this type of material.

NOTE: Answer guidelines for all Module 3 questions begin on page 41.

MODULE REVIEW

First, skim each section, noting headings and boldface items. After you have read the section, review each objective by answering the fill-in and essay-type questions that follow it. As you proceed, evaluate your performance by consulting the answers on page 41. Do not continue with the next section until you understand each answer. If you need to, review or reread the section in the textbook before continuing.

> David Myers at times uses idioms that are unfamiliar to some readers. If you do not know the meaning of any of the following words, phrases, or expressions in the context in which they appear in the text, refer to pages 45–46 for an explanation: *an ill-fated theory; a wrongheaded theory; happy fact of nature; building blocks;*

> *a sluggish 2 miles per hour to . . . a breakneck 200 or more miles; somewhat like pushing a neuron's accelerator . . . more like pushing its brake; How do we distinguish a gentle touch from a big hug; "protoplasmic kisses"; "runner's high"; Agonists excite . . . Antagonists inhibit; some chemicals can slither through this [blood-brain] barrier; Like an automatic pilot, this system may be consciously overridden; yield an ever-changing wiring diagram that dwarfs a powerful computer; work groups; information highway; The knee-jerk response . . . a headless warm body could do it; kindred systems; Conducting and coordinating this whole electrochemical orchestra is that maestro we call the brain.*

Introduction (pp. 36, 37)

Objective 1: Explain why psychologists are concerned with human biology, and describe the ill-fated phrenology theory.

1. In the most basic sense, every idea, mood, memory, and behavior that an individual has ever experienced is a _____ phenomenon.

2. The theory that linked our mental abilities to bumps on the skull was _____ .

3. Researchers who study the links between biology and behavior are called _____

   _____ .

Neural Communication (pp. 37–41)

Objective 2: Describe the parts of a neuron, and explain how its impulses are generated.

1. Our body's neural system is built from billions of nerve cells, or _____ .

2. The extensions of a neuron that receive messages from other neurons are the _____ .

3. The extension of a neuron that transmits information to other neurons is the _____ ; some of these extensions are insulated by a fatty sheath called _____ , which helps speed the neuron's impulses.

4. Identify the major parts of the neuron diagrammed here:

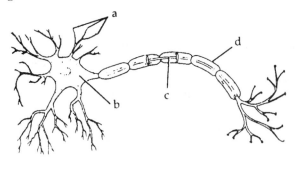

a. _____   c. _____
b. _____   d. _____

5. The neural impulse, or _____ _____ , is a brief electrical charge that travels down a(n) _____ .

6. In order to trigger a neural impulse, _____ signals minus _____ signals must exceed a certain intensity, called the _____ . Increasing a stimulus above this level _____ (will/will not) increase the neural impulse's intensity. This phenomenon is called an _____-_____-_____ response.

7. The strength of a stimulus _____ (does/does not) affect the speed of a neural impulse.

Objective 3: Describe how nerve cells communicate.

8. The junction between two neurons is called a _____ , and the gap is called the _____ _____ . This discovery was made by _____ .

9. The chemical messengers that convey information across the gaps between neurons are called _____ . These chemicals unlock tiny channels on receptor sites, allowing electrically charged _____ to enter the neuron.

10. Neurotransmitters influence neurons either by _____ or _____ their readiness to fire. Excess neurotransmitters are reabsorbed by the sending neuron in a process called _____ .

Outline the sequence of reactions that occur when a neural impulse is generated and transmitted from one neuron to another.

Objective 4: Describe how neurotransmitters influence behavior, and explain how drugs and other chemicals affect neurotransmission.

11. A neurotransmitter that is important in muscle contraction is _____ ; it is also important in learning and _____ .

12. Naturally occurring opiatelike neurotransmitters that are present in the brain are called _____ . When the brain is flooded with drugs such as _____ or _____ , it may stop producing these neurotransmitters.

13. Drugs that produce their effects by mimicking neurotransmitters are called _____ . Drugs that block the effects of neurotransmitters by occupying their _____ are called _____ .

While certain _____ drugs create a temporary "high" by mimicking the endorphins, the poison _____ produces paralysis by blocking the activity of the neurotransmitter ACh.

14. The molecular shape of some drugs prevents them from passing through the

_____-_____

_____ by which the brain fences out unwanted chemicals.

15. The tremors of _____ disease are due to the death of neurons that produce the neurotransmitter _____ . People with this condition can be helped to regain control over their muscles by taking

_____ .

The Nervous System (pp. 41–44)

Objective 5: Identify the two major divisions of the nervous system, and describe their basic functions.

1. Taken altogether, the neurons of the body form the _____ _____ .

2. The brain and spinal cord comprise the _____ nervous system. The neurons that link the brain and spinal cord to the body's sense receptors, muscles, and glands form the _____ nervous system.

3. Sensory and motor axons are bundled into electrical cables called _____ .

4. Information arriving in the central nervous system from the body travels in _____ neurons. The central nervous system sends instructions to the body's tissues by means of _____ neurons.

5. The neurons that enable internal communication within the central nervous system are called

_____ .

6. The division of the peripheral nervous system that enables voluntary control of the skeletal muscles is the _____ nervous system.

7. Involuntary, self-regulating responses—those of the glands and muscles of internal organs—are controlled by the _____ nervous system.

8. The body is made ready for action by the _____ division of the autonomic nervous system.

9. The _____ division of the autonomic nervous system produces relaxation.

Describe and explain the sequence of physical reactions that occur in the body as an emergency is confronted and then passes.

10. Neurons cluster into work groups called

_____ _____ .

11. Automatic responses to stimuli, called _____ , illustrate the work of the _____ _____ . Simple pathways such as these are involved in the _____-_____ response and in the _____ reflex.

Beginning with the sensory receptors in the skin, trace the course of a spinal reflex as a person reflexively jerks his or her hand away from an unexpectedly hot burner on a stove.

The Endocrine System (pp. 44–46)

Objective 6: Describe the nature and functions of the endocrine system and its interaction with the nervous system.

1. The body's chemical communication network is called the _____ _____ .

This system transmits information through chemical messengers called _____
at a much _____ (faster/slower) rate than the nervous system, and its effects last _____ (a longer time/a shorter time).

2. In a moment of danger, the _____ glands release _____ and _____ .

3. The most influential gland is the _____ , which, under the control of an adjacent brain area called the _____ , helps regulate _____ and the release of hormones by other endocrine glands.

Write a paragraph describing the feedback system that links the nervous and endocrine systems.

PROGRESS TEST

Multiple-Choice Questions

Circle your answers to the following questions and check them with the answers beginning on page 42. If your answer is incorrect, read the explanation for why it is incorrect and then consult the appropriate pages of the text.

1. The axons of certain neurons are covered by a layer of fatty tissue that helps speed neural transmission. This tissue is:
   a. dopamine.
   b. the myelin sheath.
   c. acetylcholine.
   d. an endorphin.

2. Heartbeat, digestion, and other self-regulating bodily functions are governed by the:
   a. voluntary nervous system.
   b. autonomic nervous system.
   c. sympathetic division of the autonomic nervous system.
   d. somatic nervous system.

3. A strong stimulus can increase the:
   a. speed of the impulse the neuron fires.
   b. intensity of the impulse the neuron fires.
   c. number of times the neuron fires.
   d. threshold that must be reached before the neuron fires.

4. The pain of heroin withdrawal may be attributable to the fact that:
   a. under the influence of heroin the brain ceases production of endorphins.
   b. under the influence of heroin the brain ceases production of all neurotransmitters.
   c. during heroin withdrawal the brain's production of all neurotransmitters is greatly increased.
   d. heroin destroys endorphin receptors in the brain.

5. The effect of a drug that is an antagonist is to:
   a. cause the brain to stop producing certain neurotransmitters.
   b. mimic a particular neurotransmitter.
   c. block a particular neurotransmitter.
   d. disrupt a neuron's all-or-none firing pattern.

6. Which is the correct sequence in the transmission of a simple reflex?
   a. sensory neuron, interneuron, sensory neuron
   b. interneuron, motor neuron, sensory neuron
   c. sensory neuron, interneuron, motor neuron
   d. interneuron, sensory neuron, motor neuron

7. Dr. Hernandez is studying neurotransmitter abnormalities in depressed patients. She would most likely describe herself as a:
   a. personality psychologist.
   b. phrenologist.
   c. psychoanalyst.
   d. biological psychologist.

8. Voluntary movements, such as writing with a pencil, are directed by the:
   a. sympathetic nervous system.
   b. somatic nervous system.
   c. parasympathetic nervous system.
   d. autonomic nervous system.

9. A neuron will generate action potentials more often when it:
   a. remains below its threshold.
   b. receives an excitatory input.
   c. receives more excitatory than inhibitory inputs.
   d. is stimulated by a neurotransmitter.

10. Which is the correct sequence in the transmission of a neural impulse?
    a. axon, dendrite, cell body, synapse
    b. dendrite, axon, cell body, synapse
    c. synapse, axon, dendrite, cell body
    d. dendrite, cell body, axon, synapse

11. Chemical messengers produced by endocrine glands are called:
    a. agonists.
    b. neurotransmitters.
    c. hormones.
    d. enzymes.

12. When Sandy scalded her toe in a tub of hot water, the pain message was carried to her spinal cord by the _____ nervous system.
    a. somatic
    b. sympathetic
    c. parasympathetic
    d. central

13. Which of the following are governed by the simplest neural pathways?
    a. emotions
    b. physiological drives, such as hunger
    c. reflexes
    d. movements, such as walking

14. Melissa has just completed running a marathon. She is so elated that she feels little fatigue or discomfort. Her lack of pain is probably the result of the release of:
    a. ACh.
    b. endorphins.
    c. dopamine.
    d. norepinephrine.

15. Parkinson's disease involves:
    a. the death of nerve cells that produce a vital neurotransmitter.
    b. impaired function in the right hemisphere only.
    c. impaired function in the left hemisphere only.
    d. excess production of the neurotransmitters dopamine and acetylcholine.

16. Which of the following is true regarding the myelin sheath that is found on some neurons?
    a. It increases the speed of neural transmission.
    b. It covers the dendrites of a neuron.
    c. It regulates the release of neurotransmitters.
    d. It is found in the cell body of a neuron.

17. I am a relatively fast-acting chemical messenger that affects mood, hunger, sleep, and arousal. What am I?
    a. acetylcholine
    b. dopamine
    c. norepinephrine
    d. serotonin

18. The neurotransmitter acetylcholine (ACh) is most likely to be found:
    a. at the junction between sensory neurons and muscle fibers.
    b. at the junction between motor neurons and muscle fibers.
    c. at junctions between interneurons.
    d. in all of these locations.

19. The gland that regulates body growth is the:
    a. adrenal.
    b. thyroid.
    c. hypothalamus.
    d. pituitary.

20. Epinephrine and norepinephrine are _____ that are released by the _____ gland.
    a. neurotransmitters; pituitary
    b. hormones; pituitary
    c. neurotransmitters; thyroid
    d. hormones; adrenal

21. The effect of a drug that is an agonist is to:
    a. cause the brain to stop producing certain neurotransmitters.
    b. mimic a particular neurotransmitter.
    c. block a particular neurotransmitter.
    d. disrupt a neuron's all-or-none firing pattern.

22. A biological psychologist would be *more* likely to study:
    a. how you learn to express emotions.
    b. how to help people overcome emotional disorders.
    c. life-span changes in the expression of emotion.
    d. the chemical changes that accompany emotions.

23. You are able to pull your hand quickly away from hot water before pain is felt because:
    a. movement of the hand is a reflex that involves intervention of the spinal cord only.
    b. movement of the hand does not require intervention by the central nervous system.
    c. the brain reacts quickly to prevent severe injury.
    d. the autonomic division of the peripheral nervous system intervenes to speed contraction of the muscles of the hand.

24. Several shy neurons send an inhibitory message to neighboring neuron Joni. At the same time, a larger group of party-going neurons send Joni excitatory messages. What will Joni do?
    a. fire, assuming that her threshold has been reached
    b. not fire, even if her threshold has been reached
    c. enter a refractory period
    d. become hyperpolarized

25. I am a relatively fast-acting chemical messenger that influences movement, learning, attention, and emotion. What am I?
    a. dopamine
    b. a hormone
    c. acetylcholine
    d. glutamate

26. Since Malcolm has been taking a drug prescribed by his doctor, he no longer enjoys the little pleasures of life, such as eating and drinking. His doctor explains that this is because the drug:
    a. triggers release of dopamine.
    b. inhibits release of dopamine.
    c. triggers release of ACh.
    d. inhibits release of ACh.

27. Which of the following was a major problem with phrenology?
    a. It was "ahead of its time" and no one believed it could be true.
    b. The brain is not neatly organized into structures that correspond to our categories of behavior.
    c. The brains of humans and animals are much less similar than the theory implied.
    d. All of these answers were problems with phrenology.

28. I am a relatively slow-acting (but long-lasting) chemical messenger carried throughout the body by the bloodstream. What am I?
    a. a hormone
    b. a neurotransmitter
    c. acetylcholine
    d. dopamine

29. Your brother has been taking prescription medicine and experiencing a number of unpleasant side effects, including unusually rapid heartbeat and excessive perspiration. It is likely that the medicine is exaggerating activity in the:
    a. central nervous system.
    b. sympathetic nervous system.
    c. parasympathetic nervous system.
    d. somatic nervous system.

Essay Question

Discuss how the endocrine and nervous systems become involved when a student feels stress—such as that associated with an upcoming final exam. (Use the space below to list the points you want to make, and organize them. Then write the essay on a separate sheet of paper.)

KEY TERMS

Using your own words, on a piece of paper write a brief definition or explanation of each of the following terms.

1. biological psychology
2. neuron
3. dendrite
4. axon
5. action potential
6. threshold
7. synapse
8. neurotransmitters
9. endorphins
10. nervous system
11. central nervous system (CNS)
12. peripheral nervous system (PNS)

13. nerves
14. sensory neurons
15. motor neurons
16. interneurons
17. somatic nervous system
18. autonomic nervous system
19. sympathetic nervous system
20. parasympathetic nervous system
21. reflex
22. endocrine system
23. hormones
24. adrenal glands
25. pituitary gland

ANSWERS

Module Review

Introduction
1. biological
2. phrenology
3. biological psychologists

Neural Communication
1. neurons
2. dendrites
3. axon; myelin
4. a. dendrites
   b. cell body
   c. axon
   d. myelin sheath
5. action potential; axon
6. excitatory; inhibitory; threshold; will not; all-or-none
7. does not
8. synapse; synaptic cleft (gap); Sir Charles Sherrington
9. neurotransmitters; atoms
10. exciting; inhibiting; reuptake

A neural impulse is generated by excitatory signals minus inhibitory signals exceeding a certain threshold. The stimuli are received through the dendrites, combined in the cell body, and electrically transmitted in an all-or-none fashion down the length of the axon. When the combined signal reaches the end of the axon, chemical messengers called neurotransmitters are released into the synaptic cleft, or gap, between two neurons. Neurotransmitter molecules bind to receptor sites on the dendrites of neighboring neurons and have either an excitatory or inhibitory influence on that neuron's tendency to generate its own neural impulse.

11. acetylcholine (ACh); memory
12. endorphins; heroin; morphine
13. agonists; receptor sites; antagonists; opiate; curare
14. blood-brain barrier
15. Parkinson's; dopamine; L-dopa

The Nervous System
1. nervous system
2. central; peripheral
3. nerves
4. sensory; interneurons
5. motor
6. somatic
7. autonomic
8. sympathetic
9. parasympathetic

The sympathetic division of the autonomic nervous system becomes aroused in response to an emergency. The physiological changes that occur include accelerated heartbeat, elevated blood sugar, dilation of arteries, slowing of digestion, and increased perspiration to cool the body. When the emergency is over, the parasympathetic nervous system produces the opposite physical reactions.

10. neural networks
11. reflexes; spinal cord; knee-jerk; pain

From sensory receptors in the skin the message travels via sensory neurons to an interneuron in the spinal cord, which in turn activates a motor neuron. This motor neuron causes the muscles in the hand to contract, and the person jerks his or her hand away from the heat.

The Endocrine System
1. endocrine system; hormones; slower; a longer time
2. adrenal; epinephrine; norepinephrine
3. pituitary; hypothalamus; growth

The hypothalamus in the brain influences secretions by the pituitary. The pituitary regulates other endocrine glands, which release hormones that influence behavior.

Progress Test

Multiple-Choice Questions

1. **b.** is the answer.
   a. Dopamine is a neurotransmitter that influences movement, learning, attention, and emotion.
   c. Acetylcholine is a neurotransmitter that triggers muscle contraction.
   d. Endorphins are opiatelike neurotransmitters linked to pain control and to pleasure.

2. **b.** is the answer. The autonomic nervous system controls internal functioning, including heartbeat, digestion, and glandular activity.
   a. The functions mentioned are all automatic, not voluntary, so this answer cannot be correct.
   c. This answer is incorrect because most organs are affected by both divisions of the autonomic nervous system.
   d. The somatic nervous system transmits sensory input to the central nervous system and enables voluntary control of skeletal muscles.

3. **c.** is the answer. Stimulus strength can affect only the number of times a neuron fires or the number of neurons that fire.
   a., b., & d. These answers are incorrect because firing is an all-or-none response, so intensity remains the same regardless of stimulus strength. Nor can stimulus strength change the neuronal threshold or the impulse speed.

4. **a.** is the answer. Endorphins are neurotransmitters that function as natural painkillers. When the body has a supply of artificial painkillers such as heroin, endorphin production stops.
   b. The production of neurotransmitters other than endorphins does not cease.
   c. Neurotransmitter production does not increase during withdrawal.
   d. Heroin makes use of the same receptor sites as endorphins.

5. **c.** is the answer.

6. **c.** is the answer. In a simple reflex, a sensory neuron carries the message that a sensory receptor has been stimulated to an interneuron in the spinal cord. The interneuron responds by activating motor neurons that will enable the appropriate response.

7. **d.** is the answer. Biological psychologists study the links between biology (in this case, neurotransmitters) and psychology (depression, in this example).

8. **b.** is the answer.
   a., c., & d. The autonomic nervous system, which is divided into the sympathetic and parasympathetic divisions, is concerned with regulating basic bodily maintenance functions.

9. **c.** is the answer.
   a. An action potential will occur only when the neuron's threshold is *exceeded*.
   b. An excitatory input that does not reach the neuron's threshold will not trigger an action potential.
   d. This answer is incorrect because some neurotransmitters inhibit a neuron's readiness to fire.

10. **d.** is the answer. A neuron receives incoming stimuli on its dendrites and cell body. These electrochemical signals are combined in the cell body, generating an impulse that travels down the axon, causing the release of neurotransmitter substances into the synaptic cleft or gap.

11. **c.** is the answer.
    a. Agonists are drugs that excite neural firing by mimicking a particular neurotransmitter.
    b. Neurotransmitters are the chemicals involved in synaptic transmission in the nervous system.
    d. Enzymes are chemicals that facilitate various chemical reactions throughout the body but are not involved in communication within the endocrine system.

12. **a.** is the answer. Sensory neurons in the somatic nervous system relay such messages.
    b. & c. These divisions of the autonomic nervous system are concerned with the regulation of bodily maintenance functions such as heartbeat, digestion, and glandular activity.
    d. The spinal cord itself is part of the central nervous system, but the message is carried to the spinal cord by the somatic division of the peripheral nervous system.

13. **c.** is the answer. As automatic responses to stimuli, reflexes are the simplest complete units of behavior and require only simple neural pathways.
    a., b., & d. Emotions, drives, and voluntary movements are all behaviors that are much more complex than reflexes and therefore involve much more complicated neural pathways.

14. **b.** is the answer. Endorphins are neurotransmitters that function as natural painkillers and are evidently involved in the "runner's high" and other situations in which discomfort or fatigue is expected but not experienced.
    a. ACh is a neurotransmitter involved in muscular control.

c. Dopamine is a neurotransmitter involved in, among other things, motor control.

d. Norepinephrine is an adrenal hormone released to help us respond in moments of danger.

15. **a.** is the answer. Parkinson's disease causes the death of brain tissue that produces dopamine.
b. & c. This disease affects both hemispheres of the cortex.
d. This disease causes insufficient production of the neurotransmitters.

16. **a.** is the answer.
b., c., & d. Myelin sheaths cover the axon and are not involved in regulating the release of neurotransmitters.

17. **d.** is the answer.

18. **b.** is the answer. ACh is a neurotransmitter that causes the contraction of muscle fibers when stimulated by motor neurons. This function explains its location.
a. & c. Sensory neurons and interneurons do not directly stimulate muscle fibers.

19. **d.** is the answer. The pituitary regulates body growth, and some of its secretions regulate the release of hormones from other glands.
a. The adrenal glands are stimulated by the autonomic nervous system to release epinephrine and norepinephrine.
b. The thyroid gland affects metabolism, among other things.
c. The hypothalamus regulates the pituitary but does not itself directly regulate growth.

20. **d.** is the answer. Also known as adrenaline and noradrenaline, epinephrine and norepinephrine are hormones released by the adrenal glands.

21. **b.** is the answer.
a. Abuse of certain drugs, such as heroin, may have this effect.
c. This describes the effect of an antagonist.
d. Drugs do not have this effect on neurons.

22. **d.** is the answer. Biological psychologists study the links between biology (chemical changes in this example) and behavior (emotions in this example).
a., b., & c. Experimental, clinical, and developmental psychologists would be more concerned with the learning of emotional expressions, the treatment of emotional disorders, and life-span changes in emotions, respectively.

23. **a.** is the answer. Since this reflex is an automatic response and involves only the spinal cord, the hand is jerked away before the brain has even received the information that causes the sensation of pain.

b. The spinal cord, which organizes simple reflexes such as this one, is part of the central nervous system.
c. The brain is not involved in directing spinal reflexes.
d. The autonomic nervous system controls the glands and the muscles of the internal organs; it does not influence the skeletal muscles controlling the hand.

24. **a.** is the answer.
b. Because she has reached her threshold, she will probably fire.
c. The refractory period is a resting period. Because Joni has received a large number of excitatory messages, she will not be at rest.
d. *Hyperpolarization* is not a term.

25. **c.** is the answer.

26. **b.** is the answer.
a. By triggering release of dopamine, such a drug would probably *enhance* Malcolm's enjoyment of the pleasures of life.
c. & d. ACh is the neurotransmitter at synapses between motor neurons and muscle fibers.

27. **b.** is the answer.
a. "Ahead of its time" implies the theory had merit, which later research clearly showed it did not. Moreover, phrenology *was* accepted as an accurate theory of brain organization by many scientists.
c. Phrenology said nothing about the similarities of human and animal brains.

28. **a.** is the answer.
b., c., & d. Acetylcholine and dopamine are fast-acting neurotransmitters released at synapses, not in the bloodstream.

29. **b.** is the answer. Sympathetic arousal produces several effects, including accelerated heartbeat and excessive perspiration.
a. The central nervous system does not control autonomic functions.
c. Arousal of the parasympathetic nervous system would have effects opposite to those stated.
d. The somatic nervous system enables voluntary control of the skeletal muscles.

Essay Question

The body's response to stress is regulated by the nervous system. As the date of the exam approaches, the stressed student's cerebral cortex activates the hypothalamus, triggering the release of hormones that in turn activate the sympathetic branch of the autonomic nervous system and the endocrine system. The autonomic nervous system controls involuntary bodily responses such as breathing, heartbeat, and digestion. The endocrine system contains glands that secrete hormones into the bloodstream that regulate the functions of body organs.

In response to activation by the hypothalamus, the student's pituitary gland would secrete a hormone which in turn triggers the release of epinephrine, norepinephrine, and other stress hormones from the adrenal glands. These hormones would help the student's body manage stress by making nutrients available to meet the increased demands for energy stores the body often faces in coping with stress. As these hormones activate the sympathetic division of the autonomic system, the body's fight-or-flight response occurs, including increased heart rate, breathing, and blood pressure and the suppression of digestion. After the exam date has passed, the student's body would attempt to restore its normal, pre-stress state. The parasympathetic branch of the autonomic system would slow the student's heartbeat and breathing and digestive processes would no longer be suppressed, perhaps causing the student to feel hungry.

Key Terms

1. **Biological psychology** is the study of the links between biology and behavior.
2. The **neuron**, or nerve cell, is the basic building block of the nervous system.
3. The **dendrites** of a neuron are the bushy, branching extensions that receive messages from other nerve cells and conduct impulses toward the cell body.
4. The **axon** of a neuron is the extension that sends impulses to other nerve cells or to muscles or glands.
5. An **action potential** is a neural impulse generated by the movement of positively charged atoms in and out of channels in the axon's membrane.
6. A neuron's **threshold** is the level of stimulation that must be exceeded in order for the neuron to fire, or generate an electrical impulse.
7. A **synapse** is the junction between the axon tip of the sending neuron and the dendrite or cell body of the receiving neuron. The tiny gap at this junction is called the synaptic gap or cleft.
8. **Neurotransmitters** are chemicals that are released into synaptic gaps and so *transmit neural messages* from neuron to neuron.

9. **Endorphins** are natural, opiatelike neurotransmitters linked to pain control and to pleasure.
   Memory aid: Endorphins *end* pain.
10. The **nervous system** is the speedy, electrochemical communication system, consisting of all the nerve cells in the peripheral and central nervous systems.
11. The **central nervous system (CNS)** consists of the brain and spinal cord; it is located at the *center*, or internal core, of the body.
12. The **peripheral nervous system (PNS)** includes the sensory and motor neurons that connect the central nervous system to the body's sense receptors, muscles, and glands; it is at the *periphery* of the body relative to the brain and spinal cord.
13. **Nerves** are bundles of neural axons, which are part of the PNS, that connect the central nervous system with muscles, glands, and sense organs.
14. **Sensory neurons** carry information from the sense receptors to the central nervous system for processing.
15. **Motor neurons** carry information and instructions for action from the central nervous system to muscles and glands.
16. **Interneurons** are the neurons of the central nervous system that link the sensory and motor neurons in the transmission of sensory inputs and motor outputs.
17. The **somatic nervous system** is the division of the peripheral nervous system that enables voluntary control of the skeletal muscles; also called the skeletal nervous system.
18. The **autonomic nervous system** is the division of the peripheral nervous system that controls the glands and the muscles of internal organs and thereby controls internal functioning; it regulates the *automatic* behaviors necessary for survival.
19. The **sympathetic nervous system** is the division of the autonomic nervous system that arouses the body, mobilizing its energy in stressful situations.
20. The **parasympathetic nervous system** is the division of the autonomic nervous system that calms the body, conserving its energy.
21. A **reflex** is a simple, automatic, inborn response to a sensory stimulus; it is governed by a very simple neural pathway.
22. The **endocrine system**, the body's "slower" chemical communication system, consists of

glands that secrete hormones into the bloodstream.

23. **Hormones** are chemical messengers, mostly those manufactured by the endocrine glands, that are produced in one tissue and circulate through the bloodstream to their target tissues, on which they have specific effects.

24. The **adrenal glands** produce epinephrine and norepinephrine, hormones that prepare the body to deal with emergencies or stress.

25. The **pituitary gland**, under the influence of the hypothalamus, regulates growth and controls other endocrine glands; sometimes called the "master gland."

FOCUS ON VOCABULARY AND LANGUAGE

. . . an ill-fated theory. . . . Myers is referring to the theory that bumps or lumps on the skull could reveal our personality (*phrenology*). It was a theory destined for failure (*ill-fated*), despite its popularity during the early 1800s.

(caption): A *wrongheaded* theory. Even though phrenology was without any scientific merit (*wrongheaded*), it did suggest the idea that different parts of the brain influence a variety of functions and behaviors.

Neural Communication

For scientists, it is a *happy fact of nature* that the information systems of humans and other animals operate similarly. . . . The structure and function of neurons are very similar in humans and other animals (e.g., squids and sea slugs) and this is a good thing (*a happy fact of nature*) for those researching the nervous system. Myers makes the important point about this similarity, noting that it would not be possible to tell the difference between a small piece of your brain tissue and that of a monkey.

Its *building blocks* are **neurons,** or nerve cells. Building blocks are the basic or fundamental parts (e.g., bricks) that make up a structure (e.g., a house). The structure of our nervous system, or neural information system, is made up of neurons (*its building blocks*).

. . . the neural impulse travels at speeds ranging from a *sluggish* 2 miles per hour to a *breakneck* 200 or more miles per hour. The speed of the neural impulse ranges from extremely slow (*sluggish*) to very fast (a *breakneck* speed). Compared to the speed of electricity or sophisticated electronics systems your neural impulses travel at a relatively slow pace.

Most of these signals are *excitatory, somewhat like pushing a neuron's accelerator.* Other signals are *inhibitory, more like pushing its brake.* Myers is making a comparison between the effect of a neuron firing and the effect of speeding up a car when accelerating (*excitatory effect*) or slowing it down by applying the brake (*inhibitory effect*). He also likens excitatory signals to those who love social gatherings (*party animals*) and inhibitory signals to those who do not (*party poopers*); if those who want to have a party outvote those who don't, then the party (*action potential*) will happen (i.e., *the party's on*).

How do we distinguish a gentle touch from a big hug? This question is concerned with how we become aware of the magnitude of a stimulus, from a soft stroke or pat (*gentle touch*) to a strong embrace (*big hug*). The answer is that the intensity of the stimulus is a function of the number and frequency of neurons firing. A strong stimulus (*big hug*) does not initiate (*trigger*) a more powerful or faster impulse than a weak stimulus (*gentle touch*); rather, it triggers more neurons to fire, and to fire more often.

. . . these near-unions of neurons—"protoplasmic kisses". . . were another of nature's marvels. The reference here is to the fact that the axon terminal of one neuron is separated from the receiving neuron by a tiny space called the synaptic gap. Protoplasm is the material that constitutes all living cells, and the communication between cells is likened to a kiss between cells (*protoplasmic kisses*). The transmission between sender and receiver is via chemicals called neurotransmitters. The cells don't actually touch but send messages across the synaptic gap.

. . . "runner's high" . . . This refers to the feeling of emotional well-being or euphoria (*high*) following vigorous exercise such as running or jogging and is the result of the release of opiatelike substances called endorphins.

Agonists excite. . . . *Antagonists* inhibit. An *agonist* drug molecule is enough like the neurotransmitter to imitate (*mimic*) its effects (for example, by producing a temporary euphoric feeling—a "high") or it may prevent (*block*) the *reuptake* of the neurotransmitter (for example, too much ACh flooding the synapses causes muscle contractions, convulsions, or even death). An *antagonist* drug, on the other hand, can stop (*inhibit*) the release of a neurotransmitter (for example, preventing the release of ACh from the sending neuron can cause paralysis), or it may *occupy* the receptor sites on the receiving neuron so the neuron can't fire (for example, toxins such as curare fill the ACh receptor sites, and paralysis will result when the neurons can't fire).

But some chemicals can *slither through* this [blood-brain] barrier. The *blood-brain barrier* is a system that blocks or obstructs unwanted chemicals circulating in the blood from getting into the brain (*the brain fences them out*). Some neurotransmitter substances (chemicals) such as L-dopa can slide or slip smoothly (*slither*) through the blood-brain barrier. The brain then transforms this raw material into dopamine (which cannot cross the blood-brain barrier), allowing many Parkinson's patients to obtain better muscle control.

The Nervous System

Like an *automatic pilot*, this system may be consciously *overridden*. . . . The autonomic nervous system automatically takes care of the operation of our internal organs much as a plane can be flown by the automatic (*or mechanical/computerized*) pilot. The system can, however, be consciously taken over (*overridden*) in the same way that the real pilot can take over flying the plane.

Tens of billions of neurons, each communicating with thousands of other neurons, *yield an ever-changing wiring diagram that dwarfs a powerful computer*. The complexity of the central nervous system, which allows or makes possible (*enables*) our thinking, feeling, and behavior, is similar to the electronic circuitry (*wiring diagrams*) of the best computer, except, by comparison, the computer would appear to be extremely tiny or small (*dwarfed by*) and the brain's wiring would seem to be constantly modifying or altering itself (*ever-changing*).

Neurons cluster into *work groups* called *neural networks*. Myers points out that the brain works much like a computer making many simultaneous computations. This is accomplished by neural networks which are clusters of interconnected neurons (*work groups*). Neurons work with nearby neurons for much the same reason people live in cities—it is easier for brief, quick interactions.

. . . information highway. . . . The spinal cord is similar to the freeway (*highway*), but instead of cars moving up and down, sensory and motor messages (*information*) travel between the peripheral nervous system and the brain. This information moves either up (*ascending*) to the brain or down (*descending*) from the brain.

The knee-jerk response, for example, involves one such simple pathway; *a headless warm body could do it.* When the patellar tendon of a bent knee is struck, the whole leg reflexively straightens out (*the knee-jerk response*). This automatic reaction is a function of a simple spinal reflex pathway so it does not require mediation by the brain (*a headless warm* [live] *body could do it*).

The Endocrine System

The endocrine system and nervous system are therefore *kindred* systems. These two systems are very similar and have a close relationship (*kindred systems*). The hormones of the endocrine system are chemically equivalent to neurotransmitters, but operate at a much slower speed. Messages in the nervous system move very rapidly (they zip along as fast as e-mail) compared to endocrine system messages which move relatively slowly (they trudge along like regular or "snail" mail).

Conducting and coordinating this whole *electrochemical orchestra* is that *maestro* we call the brain. Myers is comparing the functioning of the neurotransmitters and hormones to a large group of musicians (*electrochemical orchestra*) whose movements and actions are directed by the conductor or master (*maestro*), the brain.

The Brain

MODULE OVERVIEW

Module 4 is concerned with the structures and functions of the brain, the large, wrinkled mass that makes us what we are. The brain consists of the brainstem, the thalamus, the cerebellum, the limbic system, and the cerebral cortex. Knowledge of how the brain works has increased with advances in neuroscientific methods. Studies of split-brain patients have also given researchers a great deal of information about the specialized functions of the brain's right and left hemispheres.

Many students find the technical material in this and the previous module difficult to master. Learning this material will require a great deal of rehearsal. Working the module review several times, drawing and labeling brain diagrams, and mentally reciting terms are all useful techniques for rehearsing this type of material.

NOTE: Answer guidelines for all Module 4 questions begin on page 54.

MODULE REVIEW

First, skim each section, noting headings and boldface items. After you have read the section, review each objective by answering the fill-in and essay-type questions that follow it. As you proceed, evaluate your performance by consulting the answers beginning on page 54. Do not continue with the next section until you understand each answer. If you need to, review or reread the section in the textbook before continuing.

> David Myers at times uses idioms that are unfamiliar to some readers. If you do not know the meaning of any of the following words, phrases, or expressions in the context in which they appear in the text, refer to pages 59–60 for an explanation: *we live in our heads; This*

> *peculiar cross-wiring is but one of many surprises the brain has to offer; . . . what London is to England's trains; neural cartographers; snoop on the messages . . . and eavesdrop on the chatter of billions of neurons; Newer windows into the brain . . . Supermanlike; snapshots of the brain's changing activity provide . . . divides its labor; the doughnut-shaped limbic system; magnificent mistake; wrinkled organ, shaped somewhat like the meat of an oversized walnut; Being human takes a lot of nerve; "one of the hardiest weeds in the garden of psychology"; frontal lobes ruptured . . . Gage's moral compass; What you experience as . . . the visible tip of the information-processing iceberg; one even managed to quip that he had a "splitting headache"; When the "two minds" are at odds; so alike to the naked eye . . . harmony of the whole; dwarfs.*

Older Brain Structures (pp. 48–53)

Objective 1: Describe the components of the brainstem, and summarize the functions of the brainstem, thalamus, and cerebellum.

1. The oldest and innermost region of the brain is the _____ .

2. At the base of the brainstem, where the spinal cord enters the skull, lies the
_____ , which controls
_____ and _____ .
Just above this part is the _____ ,
which helps coordinate movements.

3. Nerves from each side of the brain cross over to connect with the body's opposite side in the
_____ .

4. At the top of the brainstem sits the
_____ , which serves as the brain's
sensory switchboard, receiving information from
all the senses except _____ and
routing it to the regions dealing with those
senses. These egg-shaped structures also receive
replies from the higher regions, which they direct
to the _____ and the
_____ .

5. The _____ _____ is a
nerve network inside the brainstem that plays an
important role in controlling _____ .
Electrically stimulating this area will produce
a(n) _____ animal. Lesioning this
area will cause an animal to lapse into a(n)
_____ .

6. At the rear of the brainstem lies the
_____ . It influences one type of
_____ _____ and
memory, but its major function is coordination of
voluntary movement and _____
control.

7. The lower brain functions occur without
_____ effort, indicating that our
brains process most information _____
(inside/outside) of our awareness.

Objective 2: Describe several techniques for studying
the brain.

8. (Close-Up) Researchers sometimes study brain
function by producing _____ or by
selectively destroying brain cells. The oldest technique for studying the brain involves _____
_____ of patients with brain
injuries or diseases.

9. (Close-Up) The _____ is a record-
ing of the electrical activity of the whole brain.

10. (Close-Up) The technique depicting the level of
activity of brain areas by measuring the brain's
consumption of glucose is called the
_____ _____ .

(Close-Up) Briefly explain the purpose of the PET
scan.

11. (Close-Up) A technique that produces clearer
images of the brain (and other body parts) by
using magnetic fields and radio waves is known
as _____ .

12. (Close-Up) By taking pictures less than a second
apart, the _____ _____
detects blood rushing to the part of the cortex
thought to control the bodily activity being
studied. Using this technique, researchers found
that blood flow to the back of the brain
_____ (increases/decreases) when
people view a face because that is where the
_____ cortex is located.

Objective 3: Describe the structures and functions of
the limbic system, and explain how one of these
structures controls the pituitary gland.

13. Between the brainstem and cerebral hemispheres
is the _____ system. One
component of this system that processes memory
is the _____ .

14. Aggression or fear will result from stimulation of
different regions of the _____ .

15. We must remember, however, that the brain
_____ (is/is not) neatly organized
into structures that correspond to our categories
of behavior. For example, aggressive behavior
_____ (does/does not) involve
neural activity in all brain levels.

16. Below the thalamus is the _____ ,
which regulates bodily maintenance behaviors
such as _____ , _____ ,
_____ _____ , and
_____ . This area also regulates
behavior by secreting _____
that enable it to control the _____

gland. Olds and Milner discovered that this region also contains _____ centers, which animals will work hard to have stimulated.

17. Some researchers believe that alcoholism, drug abuse, binge eating, and other _____ disorders may stem from a genetic _____

_____ _____ .

in the natural brain systems for pleasure and well-being.

The Cerebral Cortex (pp. 53–60)

Objective 4: Identify the four lobes of the cerebral cortex, and explain their importance to the human brain.

1. The most complex functions of human behavior are linked to the most developed part of the brain, the _____ _____ .
This thin layer of interconnected neural cells is the body's ultimate control and

_____-_____

center.

2. Compared to the cortexes of lower mammals, the human cortex has a _____ (smoother/more wrinkled) surface. This _____ (increases/decreases) the overall surface area of our brains.

3. List the four lobes of the brain.

a. _____   c. _____

b. _____   d. _____

Objective 5: Summarize some of the findings on the functions of the motor cortex and the sensory cortex, and discuss the importance of the association areas.

4. Electrical stimulation of one side of the _____ cortex, an arch-shaped region at the back of the _____ lobe, will produce movement on the opposite side of the body. The more precise the control needed, the _____ (smaller/ greater) amount of cortical space occupied. Findings from clinical trials involving

_____ _____ , in

which, for example, recording electrodes are implanted in this area of a 25-year-old man's brain, raise hopes that people who are

_____ may one day be able to control machines directly with their

_____ .

5. At the front of the parietal lobes lies the _____ cortex, which, when stimulated, elicits a sensation of _____ .

6. The more sensitive a body region, the greater the area of _____

_____ devoted to it.

7. Visual information is received in the _____ lobes, whereas auditory information is received in the _____ lobes.

8. Areas of the brain that don't receive sensory information or direct movement but, rather, integrate and interpret information received by other regions are known as _____

_____ . Approximately _____ of the human cortex is of this type. Such areas in the _____ lobe are involved in judging, planning, and processing of new memories and in some aspects of personality. In the _____ lobe, these areas enable mathematical and spatial reasoning, and an area of the _____ lobe enables us to recognize faces.

9. Brain injuries may produce an impairment in language use called _____ . Studies of people with such impairments have shown that _____ _____ is involved in producing speech, _____ _____ is involved in understanding speech, and the _____ _____ is involved in recoding printed words into auditory form.

10. Although the mind's subsystems are localized in particular brain regions, the brain _____ (does/does not) act as a unified whole.

Objective 6: Discuss the brain's plasticity following injury or illness.

11. The quality of the brain that makes it possible for undamaged brain areas to take over the functions of damaged regions is known as _____ . This quality is especially apparent in the brains of _____ (young children/adolescents/adults).

12. Although most severed neurons _____ (will/will not) regenerate, neural tissue can _____ in response to damage. New evidence suggests that adult mice and humans _____ (can/cannot) generate new brain cells in two older brain regions; research also reveals the existence of master _____ cells in the human embryo that can develop into any type of brain cell.

Our Divided Brain (pp. 60–63)

Objective 7: Describe split-brain research, and explain how it helps us understand the functions of our left and right hemispheres.

1. The brain's two sides serve differing functions, which is referred to as hemispheric specialization, or _____ . Because damage to it will impair language and understanding, the _____ hemisphere came to be known as the _____ hemisphere.

2. In treating several patients with severe epilepsy, Vogel and Bogen separated the two hemispheres of the brain by cutting the _____ _____ . When this structure is severed, the result is referred to as a _____ _____ .

3. In a split-brain patient, only the _____ hemisphere will be aware of an unseen object held in the left hand. In this

case, the person would not be able to _____ the object. When different words are shown in the left and right visual fields, if the patient fixates on a point on the center line between the fields, the patient will be able to say only the word shown on the _____ .

Explain why a split-brain patient would be able to read aloud the word *pencil* flashed to his or her right visual field, but would be unable to identify a *pencil* by touch using only the left hand.

4. When the "two minds" of a split brain are at odds, the _____ hemisphere tries to rationalize what it doesn't understand. The _____ hemisphere often acts on autopilot. This phenomenon demonstrates that the _____ mind _____ (can/cannot) control our behavior.

5. Deaf people use the _____ hemisphere to process sign language.

6. Although the _____ hemisphere is better at making quick, literal interpretations of language, the _____ hemisphere excels at making inferences and at copying drawings, _____ _____ , perceiving differences, and perceiving _____ .

Reflections on the Biological Revolution in Psychology (p. 63)

1. An overriding principle emphasized in the text is that everything _____ is simultaneously _____ .

PROGRESS TEST

Multiple-Choice Questions

Circle your answers to the following questions and check them with the answers beginning on page 55. If your answer is incorrect, read the explanation for why it is incorrect and then consult the appropriate pages of the text.

1. The brain research technique that involves monitoring the brain's usage of glucose is called (in abbreviated form) the:
   a. PET scan.　　　c. EEG.
   b. fMRI.　　　　 d. MRI.

2. Though there is no single "control center" for emotions, their regulation is primarily attributed to the brain region known as the:
   a. limbic system.　　c. brainstem.
   b. reticular formation.　d. cerebellum.

3. Damage to _____ will usually cause a person to lose the ability to comprehend language.
   a. the angular gyrus
   b. Broca's area
   c. Wernicke's area
   d. frontal lobe association areas

4. Which of the following is typically controlled by the right hemisphere?
   a. language
   b. learned voluntary movements
   c. arithmetic reasoning
   d. perceptual tasks

5. The increasing complexity of animals' behavior is accompanied by an:
   a. increase in the size of the brainstem.
   b. increase in the depth of the corpus callosum
   c. increase in the size of the frontal lobes.
   d. increase in the amount of association area.

6. Following a head injury, a person has ongoing difficulties staying awake. Most likely, the damage occurred to the:
   a. thalamus.　　　c. reticular formation.
   b. corpus callosum.　d. cerebellum.

7. An experimenter flashes the word FLYTRAP onto a screen facing a split-brain patient so that FLY projects to her right hemisphere and TRAP to her left hemisphere. When asked what she saw, the patient will
   a. say she saw FLY.
   b. say she saw TRAP.

   c. point to FLY using her right hand.
   d. point to TRAP using her left hand.

8. Cortical areas that are not primarily concerned with sensory, motor, or language functions are:
   a. called projection areas.
   b. called association areas.
   c. located mostly in the parietal lobe.
   d. located mostly in the temporal lobe.

9. The visual cortex is located in the:
   a. occipital lobe.　　c. frontal lobe.
   b. temporal lobe.　　d. parietal lobe.

10. Which of the following is typically controlled by the left hemisphere?
    a. spatial reasoning
    b. word recognition
    c. the left side of the body
    d. perceptual skills

11. The technique that uses magnetic fields and radio waves to produce computer images of structures within the brain is called:
    a. the EEG.　　　c. a PET scan.
    b. a lesion.　　　d. MRI.

12. Jessica experienced difficulty keeping her balance after receiving a blow to the back of her head. It is likely that she injured her:
    a. medulla.　　　c. hypothalamus.
    b. thalamus.　　　d. cerebellum.

13. Moruzzi and Magoun caused a cat to lapse into a coma by severing neural connections between the cortex and the:
    a. reticular formation.　c. thalamus.
    b. hypothalamus.　　d. cerebellum.

14. Research has found that the amount of representation in the motor cortex reflects the:
    a. size of the body parts.
    b. degree of precise control required by each of the parts.
    c. sensitivity of the body region.
    d. area of the occipital lobe being stimulated by the environment.

15. The nerve fibers that enable communication between the right and left cerebral hemispheres and that have been severed in split-brain patients form a structure called the:
    a. reticular formation.　c. corpus callosum.
    b. association areas.　　d. parietal lobes.

16. Beginning at the front of the brain and moving toward the back of the head, then down the skull and back around to the front, which of the following is the correct order of the cortical regions?
    a. occipital lobe; temporal lobe; parietal lobe; frontal lobe
    b. temporal lobe; frontal lobe; parietal lobe; occipital lobe
    c. frontal lobe; occipital lobe; temporal lobe; parietal lobe
    d. frontal lobe; parietal lobe; occipital lobe; temporal lobe

17. Following a nail gun wound to his head, Jack became more uninhibited, irritable, dishonest, and profane. It is likely that his personality change was the result of injury to his:
    a. parietal lobe.   c. occipital lobe.
    b. temporal lobe.   d. frontal lobe.

18. Three-year-old Marco suffered damage to the speech area of the brain's left hemisphere when he fell from a swing. Research suggests that:
    a. he may never speak again.
    b. his motor abilities may improve so that he can easily use sign language.
    c. his right hemisphere may take over much of the language function.
    d. his earlier experience with speech may enable him to continue speaking.

19. The part of the human brain that is most like that of a fish is the:
    a. cortex.
    b. limbic system.
    c. brainstem.
    d. right hemisphere.

20. In order to pinpoint the location of a tumor, a neurosurgeon electrically stimulated parts of the patient's sensory cortex. If the patient was conscious during the procedure, which of the following was probably experienced?
    a. "hearing" faint sounds
    b. "seeing" random visual patterns
    c. movement of the arms or legs
    d. a sense of having the skin touched

21. If Dr. Rogers wishes to conduct an experiment on the effects of stimulating the reward centers of a rat's brain, he should insert an electrode into the:
    a. thalamus.
    b. sensory cortex.
    c. hypothalamus.
    d. corpus callosum.

22. A split-brain patient has a picture of a knife flashed to her left hemisphere and that of a fork to her right hemisphere. She will be able to:
    a. identify the fork using her left hand.
    b. identify a knife using her left hand.
    c. identify a knife using either hand.
    d. identify a fork using either hand.

23. Following Jayshree's near-fatal car accident, her physician noticed that the pupillary reflex of her eyes was abnormal. This *may* indicate that Jayshree's _____ was damaged in the accident.
    a. occipital cortex
    b. autonomic nervous system
    c. left temporal lobe
    d. cerebellum

24. Anton is applying for a technician's job with a neurosurgeon. In trying to impress his potential employer with his knowledge of the brain, he says, "After my father's stroke I knew immediately that the blood clot had affected his left cerebral hemisphere because he no longer recognized a picture of his friend." Should Anton be hired?
    a. Yes. Anton obviously understands brain structure and function.
    b. No. The right hemisphere, not the left, specializes in picture recognition.
    c. Yes. Although blood clots never form in the left hemisphere, Anton should be rewarded for recognizing the left hemisphere's role in picture recognition.
    d. No. Blood clots never form in the left hemisphere, and the right hemisphere is more involved than the left in recognizing pictures.

25. Dr. Johnson briefly flashed a picture of a key in the right visual field of a split-brain patient. The patient could probably:
    a. verbally report that a key was seen.
    b. write the word *key* using the left hand.
    c. draw a picture of a key using the left hand.
    d. do none of these things.

26. In primitive vertebrate animals, the brain primarily regulates _____ ; in lower mammals, the brain enables _____ .
    a. emotion; memory
    b. memory; emotion
    c. survival functions; emotion
    d. reproduction; emotion

27. A scientist from another planet wishes to study the simplest brain mechanisms underlying emotion and memory. You recommend that the scientist study the:

   a. brainstem of a frog.
   b. limbic system of a dog.
   c. cortex of a monkey.
   d. cortex of a human.

28. Dr. Frankenstein made a mistake during neurosurgery on his monster. After the operation, the monster "saw" with his ears and "heard" with his eyes. It is likely that Dr. Frankenstein "rewired" neural connections in the monster's:

   a. hypothalamus.   c. amygdala.
   b. cerebellum.   d. thalamus.

29. Raccoons have much more precise control of their paws than dogs. You would expect that raccoons have more cortical space dedicated to "paw control" in the _____ of their brains.

   a. frontal lobes   c. temporal lobes
   b. parietal lobes   d. occipital lobes

Matching Items 1

Match each structure or technique with its corresponding function or description.

Structures or Techniques

_____ 1. hypothalamus
_____ 2. lesion
_____ 3. EEG
_____ 4. fMRI
_____ 5. reticular formation
_____ 6. MRI
_____ 7. thalamus
_____ 8. corpus callosum
_____ 9. cerebellum
_____ 10. amygdala
_____ 11. medulla

Functions or Descriptions

a. amplified recording of brain waves
b. technique that uses radio waves and magnetic fields to image brain anatomy
c. serves as sensory switchboard
d. contains reward centers
e. tissue destruction
f. technique that uses radio waves and magnetic fields to show brain function
g. helps control arousal
h. links the cerebral hemispheres
i. influences rage and fear
j. regulates breathing and heartbeat
k. enables coordinated movement

Matching Items 2

Match each structure or term with its corresponding function or description.

Structures or Terms

_____ 1. right hemisphere
_____ 2. brainstem
_____ 3. aphasia
_____ 4. plasticity
_____ 5. Broca's area
_____ 6. Wernicke's area
_____ 7. limbic system
_____ 8. association areas
_____ 9. left hemisphere
_____ 10. angular gyrus

Functions or Descriptions

a. controls speech production
b. specializes in rationalizing reactions
c. translates writing into speech
d. specializes in spatial relations
e. language disorder
f. oldest part of the brain
g. regulates emotion
h. the brain's capacity for modification
i. responsible for language comprehension
j. brain areas involved in higher mental functions

In the diagrams to the right, the numbers refer to brain locations that have been damaged. Match each location with its probable effect on behavior.

Location		Behavioral Effect
_____	1.	a. vision disorder
_____	2.	b. insensitivity to touch
_____	3.	c. motor paralysis
_____	4.	d. hearing problem
_____	5.	e. lack of coordination
_____	6.	f. abnormal hunger
_____	7.	g. split brain
_____	8.	h. sleep/arousal
_____	9.	disorder
		i. altered personality

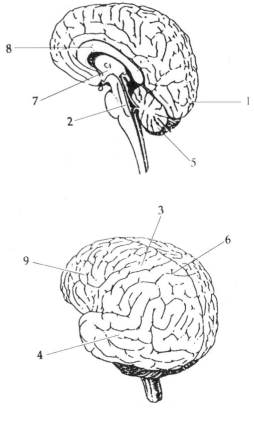

KEY TERMS

Using your own words, on a piece of paper write a brief definition or explanation of each of the following terms.

1. brainstem
2. medulla
3. thalamus
4. reticular formation
5. cerebellum
6. lesion
7. electroencephalogram (EEG)
8. PET (positron emission tomography) scan
9. MRI (magnetic resonance imaging)
10. fMRI (functional magnetic resonance imaging)
11. limbic system
12. amygdala
13. hypothalamus
14. cerebral cortex
15. frontal lobes
16. parietal lobes

17. occipital lobes
18. temporal lobes
19. motor cortex
20. sensory cortex
21. association areas
22. aphasia
23. Broca's area
24. Wernicke's area
25. plasticity
26. corpus callosum
27. split brain

ANSWERS

Module Review

Older Brain Structures

1. brainstem
2. medulla; breathing; heartbeat; pons
3. brainstem

4. thalamus; smell; medulla; cerebellum

5. reticular formation; arousal; alert (awake); coma

6. cerebellum; nonverbal learning; balance

7. conscious; outside

8. lesions; clinical observation

9. electroencephalogram (EEG)

10. PET scan

By depicting the brain's consumption of radioactively labeled glucose, the PET scan allows researchers to see which brain areas are most active as a person performs various tasks. This provides additional information on the specialized functions of various regions of the brain.

11. MRI (magnetic resonance imaging)

12. functional MRI; increases; visual

13. limbic; hippocampus

14. amygdala

15. is not; does

16. hypothalamus; hunger; thirst; body temperature; sex; hormones; pituitary; reward

17. addictive; reward deficiency syndrome

The Cerebral Cortex

1. cerebral cortex; information-processing

2. more wrinkled; increases

3. a. frontal lobe
   b. parietal lobe
   c. occipital lobe
   d. temporal lobe

4. motor; frontal; greater; neural prosthetics; paralyzed; thoughts (or brains)

5. sensory; touch

6. sensory cortex

7. occipital; temporal

8. association areas; three-fourths; frontal; parietal; temporal

9. aphasia; Broca's area; Wernicke's area; angular gyrus

10. does

11. plasticity; young children

12. will not; reorganize; can; stem

Our Divided Brain

1. lateralization; left; dominant (major)

2. corpus callosum; split brain

3. right; name; right

The word *pencil* when flashed to a split-brain patient's right visual field would project only to the opposite, or left, hemisphere of the patient's brain. Because the left hemisphere contains the language control centers of the brain, the patient would be able to read the word aloud. The left hand is controlled by the right hemisphere of the brain. Because the right hemisphere would not be aware of the word, it would not be able to guide the left hand in identifying a pencil by touch.

4. left; right; unconscious; can

5. left

6. left; right; recognizing faces; emotion

Reflections on the Biological Revolution in Psychology

1. psychological; biological

Progress Test

Multiple-Choice Questions

1. **a.** is the answer. The PET scan measures glucose consumption in different areas of the brain to determine their levels of activity.
   b. The fMRI compares MRI scans taken less than a second apart to reveal brain anatomy and function.
   c. The EEG is a measure of electrical activity in the brain.
   d. MRI uses magnetic fields and radio waves to produce computer-generated images of soft tissues of the body.

2. **a.** is the answer.
   b. The reticular formation is linked to arousal.
   c. The brainstem governs the mechanisms of basic survival—heartbeat and breathing, for example—and has many other roles.
   d. The cerebellum coordinates movement output and balance.

3. **c.** is the answer. Wernicke's area is involved in comprehension, and people with aphasia who have damage to Wernicke's area are unable to understand what is said to them.
   a. The angular gyrus translates printed words into speech sounds; damage would result in the inability to read aloud.
   b. Broca's area is involved in the physical production of speech; damage would result in the inability to speak fluently.
   d. The cortex's association areas are involved in, among other things, processing language;

damage to these areas wouldn't specifically affect comprehension.

4. **d.** is the answer.
   a. In most persons, language is primarily a left hemisphere function.
   b. Learned movements are unrelated to hemispheric specialization.
   c. Arithmetic reasoning is generally a left hemisphere function.

5. **d.** is the answer. As animals increase in complexity, there is an increase in the amount of association areas.
   a. The brainstem controls basic survival functions and is not related to the complexity of an animal's behavior.
   b. The corpus callosum connects the brain's two hemispheres; it's not necessarily related to more complex behaviors.
   c. The frontal lobe is concerned with personality, planning, and other mental functions, but its size is unrelated to intelligence or the complexity of behavior.

6. **c.** is the answer. The reticular formation plays an important role in arousal.
   a. The thalamus relays sensory input.
   b. The corpus callosum links the two cerebral hemispheres.
   d. The cerebellum is involved in coordination of movement output and balance.

7. **b.** is the answer.

8. **b.** is the answer. Association areas interpret, integrate, and act on information from other areas of the cortex.

9. **a.** is the answer. The visual cortex is located at the very back of the brain.

10. **b.** is the answer.
    a., c., & d. Spatial reasoning, perceptual skills, and the left side of the body are primarily influenced by the right hemisphere.

11. **d.** is the answer.
    a. The EEG is an amplified recording of the brain's electrical activity.
    b. A lesion is destruction of tissue.
    c. The PET scan is a visual display of brain activity that detects the movement of a radioactive form of glucose as the brain performs a task.

12. **d.** is the answer. The cerebellum is involved in the coordination of voluntary muscular movements.
    a. The medulla regulates breathing and heartbeat.
    b. The thalamus relays sensory inputs to the appropriate higher centers of the brain.

c. The hypothalamus is concerned with the regulation of basic drives and emotions.

13. **a.** is the answer. The reticular formation controls arousal via its connections to the cortex. Thus, separating the two produces a coma.
    b., c., & d. None of these structures controls arousal. The hypothalamus regulates hunger, thirst, sexual behavior, and other basic drives; the thalamus is a sensory relay station; and the cerebellum is involved in the coordination of voluntary movement.

14. **b.** is the answer.
    c. & d. These refer to the sensory cortex.

15. **c.** is the answer. The corpus callosum is a large band of neural fibers linking the right and left cerebral hemispheres. To sever the corpus callosum is in effect to split the brain.

16. **d.** is the answer. The frontal lobe is in the front of the brain. Just behind is the parietal lobe. The occipital lobe is located at the very back of the head and just below the parietal lobe. Next to the occipital lobe and toward the front of the head is the temporal lobe.

17. **d.** is the answer. As demonstrated in the case of Phineas Gage, injury to the frontal lobe may produce such changes in personality.
    a. Damage to the parietal lobe might disrupt functions involving the sensory cortex.
    b. Damage to the temporal lobe might impair hearing.
    c. Occipital damage might impair vision.

18. **c.** is the answer.

19. **c.** is the answer. The brainstem is the oldest and most primitive region of the brain. It is found in lower vertebrates, such as fish, as well as in humans and other mammals. The structures mentioned in the other choices are associated with stages of brain evolution beyond that seen in the fish.

20. **d.** is the answer. Stimulation of the sensory cortex elicits a sense of touch, as the experiments of Penfield demonstrated.
    a., b., & c. Hearing, seeing, or movement might be expected if the temporal, occipital, and motor regions of the cortex, respectively, were stimulated.

21. **c.** is the answer. As Olds and Milner discovered, electrical stimulation of the hypothalamus is a highly reinforcing event because it is the location of the animal's reward centers. The other brain regions mentioned are not associated with reward centers.

22. **a.** is the answer. The left hand, controlled by the right hemisphere, would be able to identify the fork, the picture of which is flashed to the right hemisphere.

23. **b.** is the answer. Simple reflexes, such as this one, are governed by activity in the autonomic nervous system.
   a. The occipital lobes process sensory messages from the eyes; they play no role in the reflexive response of the pupils to light.
   c. The left temporal lobe specializes in processing language.
   d. The cerebellum specializes in coordinating movement.

24. **b.** is the answer.
   a., c., & d. The left hemisphere does not specialize in picture recognition. And blood clots can form anywhere in the brain.

25. **a.** is the answer. The right visual field projects directly to the verbal left hemisphere.
   b. & c. The left hand is controlled by the right hemisphere, which, in this situation, would be unaware of the word since the picture has been flashed to the left hemisphere.

26. **c.** is the answer.
   d. Reproduction is only one of the basic survival functions the brain regulates.

27. **b.** is the answer. The hippocampus of the limbic system is involved in processing memory. The amygdala of the limbic system influences fear and anger.
   a. The brainstem controls vital functions such as breathing and heartbeat; it is not directly involved in either emotion or memory.
   c. & d. These answers are incorrect because the limbic system is an older brain structure than the cortex. Its involvement in emotions and memory is therefore more basic than that of the cortex.

28. **d.** is the answer. The thalamus relays sensory messages from the eyes, ears, and other receptors to the appropriate projection areas of the cortex. "Rewiring" the thalamus, theoretically, could have the effects stated in this question.
   a., b., & c. These brain structures are not directly involved in brain processes related to sensation or perception.

29. **a.** is the answer. The motor cortex, which determines the precision with which various parts of the body can be moved, is located in the frontal lobes.
   b. The parietal lobes contain the sensory cortex, which controls sensitivity to touch.

c. The temporal lobes contain the primary projection areas for hearing and, on the left side, are also involved in language use.
   d. The occipital lobes contain the primary projection areas for vision.

Matching Items 1

1. d	5. g	9. k
2. e	6. b	10. i
3. a	7. c	11. j
4. f	8. h	

Matching Items 2

1. d	5. a	9. b
2. g	6. i	10. c
3. e	7. g	
4. h	8. j	

Brain Damage Diagram

1. a	4. d	7. f
2. h	5. e	8. g
3. c	6. b	9. i

Key Terms

1. The **brainstem**, the oldest and innermost region of the brain, is an extension of the spinal cord and is the central core of the brain; its structures direct automatic survival functions.

2. Located in the brainstem, the **medulla** controls breathing and heartbeat.

3. Located atop the brainstem, the **thalamus** routes incoming messages to the appropriate cortical centers and transmits replies to the medulla and cerebellum.

4. Also part of the brainstem, the **reticular formation** is a nerve network that plays an important role in controlling arousal.

5. The **cerebellum** processes sensory input and coordinates movement output and balance.

6. A **lesion** is destruction of tissue; studying the consequences of lesions in different regions of the brain—both surgically produced in animals and naturally occurring—helps researchers to determine the normal functions of these regions.

7. An **electroencephalogram (EEG)** is an amplified recording of the waves of electrical activity of the brain. *Encephalo* comes from a Greek word meaning "related to the brain."

8. The **PET (positron emission tomography) scan** measures the levels of activity of different areas

of the brain by tracing their consumption of a radioactive form of glucose, the brain's fuel.

9. **MRI (magnetic resonance imaging)** uses magnetic fields and radio waves to produce computer-generated images that show brain structures more clearly.

10. In a **fMRI (functional magnetic resonance imaging)**, MRI scans taken less than a second apart are compared to reveal blood flow and, therefore, brain anatomy and function.

11. A doughnut-shaped neural system, the **limbic system** is associated with emotions such as fear and aggression and basic physiological drives.

   Memory aid: Its name comes from the Latin word *limbus*, meaning "border"; the **limbic system** is at the border of the brainstem and cerebral hemispheres.

12. The **amygdala** is part of the limbic system and influences the emotions of fear and aggression.

13. Also part of the limbic system, the **hypothalamus** regulates hunger, thirst, body temperature, and sex; helps govern the endocrine system via the pituitary gland; and contains the so-called reward centers of the brain.

14. The **cerebral cortex** is a thin intricate covering of interconnected neural cells atop the cerebral hemispheres. The seat of information processing, the cortex is responsible for those complex functions that make us distinctively human.

   Memory aid: Cortex in Latin means "bark." As bark covers a tree, the **cerebral cortex** is the "bark of the brain."

15. Located at the front of the brain, just behind the forehead, the **frontal lobes** are involved in speaking and muscle movements and in making plans and judgments.

16. Situated between the frontal and occipital lobes, the **parietal lobes** contain the sensory cortex.

17. Located at the back and base of the brain, the **occipital lobes** contain the visual cortex, which receives information from the eyes.

18. Located on the sides of the brain, the **temporal lobes** contain the auditory areas, which receive information from the ears.

   Memory aid: The **temporal lobes** are located near the *temples.*

19. Located at the back of the frontal lobe, the **motor cortex** controls voluntary movement.

20. The **sensory cortex** is located at the front of the parietal lobes, just behind the motor cortex. It registers and processes body touch and movement sensations.

21. Located throughout the cortex, **association areas** of the brain are involved in higher mental functions, such as learning, remembering, and abstract thinking.

   Memory aid: Among their other functions, **association areas** of the cortex are involved in integrating, or *associating*, information from different areas of the brain.

22. **Aphasia** is an impairment of language as a result of damage to any of several cortical areas, including Broca's area and Wernicke's area.

23. **Broca's area**, located in the left frontal lobe, is involved in controlling the motor ability to produce speech.

24. **Wernicke's area,** located in the left temporal lobe, is involved in language comprehension and expression.

25. **Plasticity** is the brain's capacity for modification, as evidenced by brain reorganization following damage (especially in children).

26. The **corpus callosum** is the large band of neural fibers that links the right and left cerebral hemispheres. Without this band of nerve fibers, the two hemispheres could not interact.

27. **Split brain** is a condition in which the major connections between the two cerebral hemispheres (the corpus callosum) are severed, literally resulting in a split brain.

FOCUS ON VOCABULARY AND LANGUAGE

Introduction

. . . we live in our heads. What this means is that you subjectively feel that the essence of your being, your mind, resides in your brain, which is inside your head. The brain in our head allows us to function psychologically as well as physically: *the mind is what the brain does.*

Older Brain Structures

This peculiar cross-wiring is but one of many surprises the brain has to offer. In the brainstem most nerves from the left side of the body connect to the right side of the brain and those from the right connect to the left side of the brain. This strange (*peculiar*) traverse of nerves from one side to the other (*cross-wiring*), which occurs in the pons, is one of the many marvels or astonishing findings (*surprises*) about the brain.

Think of the thalamus as being to sensory input what *London is to England's trains.* London is the relay center for trains going to all parts of the country just as Chicago is the hub or relay center for many airlines flying to different parts of the United States. Myers uses this as an analogy for the thalamus, which receives messages from sensory neurons and sends them on, or relays them to higher brain areas (it also receives some of the higher brain's responses and directs them to the medulla and the cerebellum).

The known universe's most amazing organ is being probed and mapped by a new generation of neural cartographers. A cartographer is someone who prepares or makes maps. Myers is suggesting that the brain (*the known universe's most amazing organ*) is going to be graphically depicted (*mapped*) by a new younger group of neuroscientists (a new generation of neural *cartographers*).

Today's scientists can . . . *snoop on* the messages of individual neurons and *eavesdrop on the chatter* of billions of neurons . . . With today's technological tools it is possible to unobtrusively view or spy on (*snoop on*) single nerve cells (neurons) as well as covertly listen to (*eavesdrop on*) the back-and-forth communication (*chatter*) of millions and millions of cells.

Newer windows into the brain give us a *Supermanlike* ability to see inside the living brain. Modern technological means of viewing the brain (*new windows into the brain*), such as the PET scan, MRI, and fMRI, provide us with a greater than normal (*Supermanlike*) ability to look inside the cortex without destroying

tissue. (*Note:* Superman is a comic-book, TV, and movie character with x-ray vision which allows him to see through solid matter.)

Such *snapshots* of the brain's changing *activity* provide new insights into how the brain *divides its labor.* The fMRI technique allows pictures (*snapshots*) to be taken of different brain areas at work (the brain *divides its labor*) while a person is carrying out various mental tasks.

. . . the *doughnut-shaped* **limbic system.** This system is in the shape of a ring (*doughnut-shaped*) and has three components: the **hippocampus,** which is involved in forming (*laying down*) new memories; the **amygdala,** which influences aggression and fear; and the **hypothalamus,** which regulates hunger, thirst, body temperature, and sexuality.

. . . they made *a magnificent mistake.* Olds and Milner accidentally discovered (*stumbled upon*) a brain area that provides a pleasurable reward and then went on to find other similar areas which they called "*pleasure centers.*" Myers calls this a splendid and spectacular error (*a magnificent mistake*). When rats are allowed to stimulate these areas by pressing a bar or lever (*pedal*) they seem to prefer this to any other activity and will continue at a very rapid rate (*feverish pace*) until they are too tired to go on (*until they drop from exhaustion*).

The Cerebral Cortex

If you opened a human skull, exposing the brain, you would see a *wrinkled* organ, shaped somewhat like the *meat of an oversized walnut.* The human brain has a convoluted (*wrinkled*) surface, and the cerebral cortex is divided into two halves or hemispheres just like the two lobes of the edible portion (*the meat or seed*) in the shell of a very large (*oversized*) walnut.

Being human *takes a lot of nerve.* Myers is using humor to make a point here. The expression "it takes a lot of nerve" means to be very brave or courageous (another expression, "it takes a lot of guts," means the same thing!). Thus, when Myers states that being human takes a lot of nerve, the literal meaning in this context is that humans are made up of many, many nerves (the humor is derived from the double meaning).

Their [association areas] silence has led to what Donald McBurney (1966, p. 44) calls "one of the *hardiest weeds in the garden of psychology*": that we ordinarily use only 10 percent of our brains. Just as weeds in a garden are extremely difficult to eradicate despite efforts to get rid of them, the myth that we use only 10 percent of our brain persists. This incorrect notion may have arisen because early researchers were unsure about the function of the association areas. However, more recent research into the brain's association areas showed that while these areas don't have specific functions, they are involved in many different operations such as interpreting, integrating, and acting on information processed by the sensory areas. Remember, we use all of our brain, all the time. Damage to the association areas would result in very serious deficits.

With his frontal lobes *ruptured*, Gage's *moral compass* had disconnected from his behavior. Phineas Gage's frontal lobes were severely damaged (*ruptured*) when the tamping iron shot through his head. As a result, he lost many of his normal inhibitions, which caused him to veer away from his previous honest ways (he lost his moral compass).

What you experience as a continuous, indivisible stream of perception is actually but the visible tip of the information-processing iceberg, most of which lies beneath the surface of your conscious awareness. Myers is making an analogy here. Most of the important functions that allow you to see the world as a whole are not part of conscious experience, but, like most of the mass of an iceberg, are below the surface and out of awareness.

Our Divided Brain

Waking from the surgery, one even managed to *quip* that he had a *"splitting headache"* . . . . People have had their corpus callosum severed or cut in order to control epileptic seizures. Despite such a major operation this patient managed to joke (*quip*) that he had a very bad headache (*a splitting headache*). Personality and intellectual functioning were not affected by this procedure, and you would not be able to detect anything unusual if you were having a casual conversation with a split-brain patient.

When the "two minds" are at odds, the left hemisphere does *mental gymnastics* to *rationalize* reactions it does not understand. In split-brain patients, if information or commands are delivered to the right hemisphere (which does not have language), then the left hemisphere, which can talk, would not be aware of what was requested. So if the patient carried out the command to do something (e.g., "walk" or "clap"), the left hemisphere will go through all kinds of contortions (*mental gymnastics*) to create some plausible story that accounts for the response (it rationalizes and constructs theories to explain our behavior).

Simply looking at the two hemispheres, so *alike* to the *naked eye*, who would suppose that they contribute so uniquely to *the harmony of the whole?* Myers points out that research with split-brain people and normal people shows that we have unified brains with different parts that have specialized functions. Thus, if we observe the two hemispheres without optical aids (*with the naked eye*), they may seem to be the same (*appear alike*); however, their differential functioning combines to produce an integrated unit (*the harmony of the whole*).

Reflections on the Biological Revolution in Psychology

Yet what is unknown still *dwarfs* what is known. This means that all that has been discovered so far is very, very small (*dwarfed*) compared to what yet remains to be discovered.

Behavior Genetics and Evolutionary Psychology

MODULE OVERVIEW

Module 5 is concerned with the ways in which our biological heritage, or nature, interacts with our individual experiences, or nurture, to shape who we are. After a brief explanation of basic terminology, the chapter explores the fields of behavior genetics, which studies twins and adopted children to weigh genetic and environmental influences on behaviors. The next section discusses psychology's use of evolutionary principles to answer universal questions about human behavior.

NOTE: Answer guidelines for all Module 5 questions begin on page 68.

MODULE REVIEW

First, skim each section, noting headings and boldface items. After you have read the section, review each objective by answering the fill-in and essay-type questions that follow it. As you proceed, evaluate your performance by consulting the answers on page 68. Do not continue with the next section until you understand each answer. If you need to, review or reread the section in the textbook before continuing.

> David Myers at times uses idioms that are unfamiliar to some readers. If you do not know the meaning of the following words, phrases, or expressions in the context in which they appear in the text, refer to pages 71–72 for an explanation: *To scientifically tease apart; blue-collar families; Stories of startling twin similarities; "Mom may be holding a full house while Dad has a straight flush"; go barefoot . . . tenderfoot; blueprints; the area of a field is more the result of its length or width; cash-strapped; tight genetic leash; In our ancestral history, females most often sent*

> *their genes into the future by pairing wisely, men by pairing widely; stick-around dads over likely cads; mobile gene machines.*

Introduction (p. 66)

Objective 1: Give examples of differences and of similarities within the human family, and describe the types of questions that interest behavior geneticists.

1. Our differences as humans include our

   _____ , _____ , and

   _____ and _____

   backgrounds.

2. Our similarities as human beings include our

   common _____ _____ ,

   our shared _____ architecture, our

   ability to use _____ , and our

   _____ behaviors.

3. The term *environment* refers to every

   _____ influence.

4. A fundamental question in psychology deals with the extent to which we are shaped by our heredity, called our _____ , and by our life history, called our _____ .

Behavior Genetics: Predicting Individual Differences (pp. 66–73)

1. Researchers who specifically study the effects of genes on behavior are called _____

   _____ .

Objective 2: Define *chromosome, DNA, gene,* and *genome,* and describe their relationships.

2. The master plans for development are stored in the _____ . In number, each person inherits _____ of these structures, _____ from each parent. Each is composed of a coiled chain of the molecule _____ .

3. If chromosomes are the "books" of heredity, the "words" that make each of us a distinctive human being are called _____ .

4. The complete instructions for making an organism are referred to as the human _____ .

Objective 3: Describe how twin and adoption studies help us differentiate hereditary and environmental influences on human behavior.

5. To study the power and limits of genetic influences on behavior, researchers use _____ and _____ studies.

6. Twins who developed from a single egg are genetically _____ . Twins who developed from different fertilized eggs are no more genetically alike than siblings and are called _____ twins.

7. In terms of the personality traits of extraversion and neuroticism, identical twins are _____ (more/no more) alike than are fraternal twins.

Identify other dimensions that show strong genetic influences.

8. Through research on identical twins raised apart, psychologists are able to study the influence of the _____ .

9. Studies tend to show that the personalities of adopted children _____ (do/do not) closely resemble those of their adoptive parents.

10. Adoption studies show that parenting _____ (does/does not) matter. For example, adopted children often score _____ (higher/lower) than their biological parents on intelligence tests.

Objective 4: Discuss how the relative stability of our temperament illustrates the influence of heredity on development, and give examples of the interaction of genes and environment on specific traits.

11. The term that refers to the inborn personality, especially the child's emotional excitability, is _____ , which _____ (does/does not) endure over time.

12. From the first weeks of life, _____ babies are more _____ , _____ , and _____ . In contrast, _____ babies are _____ , _____ , and _____ in feeding and sleeping.

13. Faced with a new or strange situation, high-strung infants become _____ (more/less) physiologically aroused than less excitable infants.

14. Genes are self-_____ ; rather than acting as _____ that always lead to the same result, they _____ to the environmental context.

15. For _____ phenomena, human differences are nearly always the result of both _____ and _____ influences.

16. Throughout life, we are the product of the _____ of our _____ predispositions and our surrounding _____ .

17. Environments trigger activity in _____ , and our genetically influenced traits evoke _____ in other people. This may explain why _____ twins recall

greater variations in their early family life than do _____ twins.

Evolutionary Psychology: Understanding Human Nature (pp. 73–77)

Objective 5: Describe the area of psychology that interests evolutionary psychologists, and point out some possible effects of natural selection in the development of human characteristics.

1. Researchers who study natural selection and the adaptive nature of human behavior are called _____ _____ .

2. Researchers in this field focus mostly on what makes people so _____ (much alike/different from one another).

3. According to the principle of _____ _____ , traits that contribute to reproduction and survival will be most likely to be passed on to succeeding generations.

4. Genetic _____ are random errors in genetic replication that are the source of all genetic _____ .

5. Genetic constraints on human behavior are generally _____ (tighter/looser) than those on animal behavior. The human species' ability to _____ and to _____ in responding to different _____ contributes to our _____ , defined as our ability to _____ and _____ . Because of our genetic legacy, we love the tastes of sweets and _____ , which we tend to _____ , even though famine is unlikely in industrialized societies.

Objective 6: Identify some gender differences in sexuality, and describe evolutionary explanations for those differences.

6. The characteristics by which people define *male* and *female* constitute _____ . These characteristics are subject to _____ and _____ influences.

7. Compared to females, males are _____ (equally/more/less) likely to engage in casual, impulsive sex, and they are _____ (equally/more/less) likely to initiate sexual activity. This is an example of a _____ difference.

8. The _____ explanation of gender differences in attitudes toward sex is based on differences in the optimal strategy by which women and men pass on their _____ . According to this view, males and females _____ (are/are not) selected for different patterns of sexuality.

9. Cross-cultural research reveals that men judge women as more attractive if they have a _____ appearance, whereas women judge men who appear _____ , _____ , _____ , and _____ as more attractive.

Objective 7: Summarize the criticisms of evolutionary explanations of human behaviors, and describe the evolutionary psychologists' responses to these criticisms.

10. Critics of the evolutionary explanation of the gender sexuality difference argue that it often works _____ (forward/backward) to propose a _____ explanation.

11. Another critique is that gender differences in sexuality vary with _____ expectations and social and family structures.

12. Gender differences in mate preferences are largest in cultures characterized by greater gender _____ (equality/inequality).

13. Evolutionary psychologists counter the criticisms by noting that the sexes, having faced similar adaptive problems, are more _____ (alike/different) than they are _____ (alike/different). They also note that evolutionary principles offer testable _____ .

PROGRESS TEST

Multiple-Choice Questions

Circle your answers to the following questions and check them with the answers beginning on page 68. If your answer is incorrect, read the explanation for why it is incorrect and then consult the appropriate pages of the text.

1. Dr. Ross believes that principles of natural selection help explain why infants come to fear strangers about the time they become mobile. Dr. Ross is most likely a(n):
   a. behavior geneticist.
   b. molecular geneticist.
   c. evolutionary psychologist.
   d. molecular biologist.

2. A pair of adopted children or identical twins reared in the same home are most likely to have similar:
   a. temperaments.
   b. personalities.
   c. religious beliefs.
   d. emotional reactivity.

3. If a fraternal twin develops schizophrenia, the likelihood of the other twin developing serious mental illness is much lower than with identical twins. This suggests that:
   a. schizophrenia is caused by genes.
   b. schizophrenia is influenced by genes.
   c. environment is unimportant in the development of schizophrenia.
   d. identical twins are especially vulnerable to mental disorders.

4. Of the following, the best way to separate the effects of genes and environment in research is to study:
   a. fraternal twins.
   b. identical twins.
   c. adopted children and their adoptive parents.
   d. identical twins raised in different environments.

5. Through natural selection, the traits that are most likely to be passed on to succeeding generations are those that contribute to survival and:
   a. happiness.   c. aggressiveness.
   b. reproduction.   d. temperament.

6. Which of the following is *not* true regarding gender and sexuality?
   a. Men more often than women attribute a woman's friendliness to sexual interest.
   b. Women are more likely than men to cite affection as a reason for first intercourse.
   c. Men are more likely than females to initiate sexual activity.
   d. Gender differences in sexuality are noticeably absent among gay men and lesbian women.

7. Evolutionary psychologists attribute gender differences in sexuality to the fact that women have:
   a. greater reproductive potential than do men.
   b. lower reproductive potential than do men.
   c. weaker sex drives than men.
   d. stronger sex drives than men.

8. According to evolutionary psychology, men are drawn sexually to women who seem _____, while women are attracted to men who seem _____.
   a. nurturing; youthful
   b. youthful and fertile; mature and affluent
   c. slender; muscular
   d. exciting; dominant

9. Unlike _____ twins, who develop from a single fertilized egg, _____ twins develop from separate fertilized eggs.
   a. fraternal; identical
   b. identical; fraternal
   c. placental; nonplacental
   d. nonplacental; placental

10. Temperament refers to a person's characteristic:
    a. emotional reactivity and intensity.
    b. attitudes.
    c. behaviors.
    d. role-related traits.

11. When evolutionary psychologists use the word "fitness," they are specifically referring to:
    a. an animal's ability to adapt to changing environments.
    b. the diversity of a species' gene pool.
    c. the total number of members of the species currently alive.
    d. our ability to survive and reproduce.

12. Physiological tests reveal that anxious, inhibited infants:
    a. become less physiologically aroused when facing new situations.
    b. have slow, steady heart rates.
    c. have high and variable heart rates.
    d. have underreactive nervous systems.

13. Each cell of the human body has a total of:
    a. 23 chromosomes.
    b. 23 genes.
    c. 46 chromosomes.
    d. 46 genes.

14. Genes direct our physical development by synthesizing:
    a. hormones.
    b. proteins.
    c. DNA.
    d. chromosomes.

15. The human genome is best defined as:
    a. a complex molecule containing genetic information that makes up the chromosomes.
    b. a segment of DNA.
    c. the complete instructions for making an organism.
    d. the code for synthesizing protein.

16. Most human traits are:
    a. learned.
    b. determined by a single gene.
    c. influenced by many genes acting together.
    d. unpredictable.

17. Mutations are random errors in _____ replication.
    a. gene
    b. chromosome
    c. DNA
    d. protein

18. Casual, impulsive sex is most frequent among:
    a. males with high circulating levels of testosterone.
    b. males with traditional masculine attitudes.
    c. females and males who are weakly gender-typed.
    d. females and males who are strongly gender-typed.

19. Evolutionary explanations of gender differences in sexuality have been criticized because:
    a. they offer "after-the-fact" explanations.
    b. standards of attractiveness vary with time and place.
    c. they underestimate cultural influences on sexuality.
    d. of all of these reasons.

20. Several studies of long-separated identical twins have found that these twins:
    a. have little in common, due to the different environments in which they were raised.
    b. have many similarities, in everything from medical histories to personalities.
    c. have similar personalities, but very different likes, dislikes, and life-styles.
    d. are no more similar than are fraternal twins reared apart.

21. Adoption studies show that the personalities of adopted children:
    a. closely match those of their adoptive parents.
    b. bear more similarities to their biological parents than to their adoptive parents.
    c. closely match those of the biological children of their adoptive parents.
    d. closely match those of other children reared in the same home, whether or not they are biologically related.

22. Chromosomes are composed of small segments of
    a. DNA called genes.
    b. DNA called neurotransmitters.
    c. genes called DNA.
    d. DNA called enzymes.

23. When the effect of one factor (such as environment) depends on another (such as heredity), we say there is a(n) _____ between the two factors.
    a. norm
    b. positive correlation
    c. negative correlation
    d. interaction

24. An evolutionary psychologist would be most interested in studying:
    a. why most parents are so passionately devoted to their children.
    b. hereditary influences on skin color.
    c. why certain diseases are more common among certain age groups.
    d. genetic differences in personality.

25. If chromosomes are the "books" of heredity, the "words" are the _____ .

    a. genes   c. genomes
    b. molecules   d. DNA

26. After comparing divorce rates among identical and fraternal twins, Dr. Alexander has concluded that genes do play a role. Dr. Alexander is most likely a(n):

    a. evolutionary psychologist.
    b. behavior geneticist.
    c. molecular geneticist.
    d. divorcee.

27. One of the best ways to distinguish how much genetic and environmental factors affect behavior is to compare children who have:

    a. the same genes and environments.
    b. different genes and environments.
    c. similar genes and environments.
    d. the same genes but different environments.

28. My sibling and I developed from a single fertilized egg. Who are we?

    a. opposite-sex identical twins.
    b. same-sex identical twins.
    c. opposite-sex fraternal twins.
    d. same-sex fraternal twins.

29. A psychologist working from the evolutionary perspective is likely to suggest that people are biologically predisposed to:

    a. protect their offspring.
    b. like sweets.
    c. be attracted to fertile-appearing members of the opposite sex.
    d. do all of these answers.

30. Of the relatively few genetic differences among humans _____ are differences among population groups.

    a. less than 1 percent
    b. less than 10 percent
    c. approximately 25 percent
    d. approximately 40 to 50 percent

31. Responding to the argument that gender differences are often by-products of a culture's social and family structures, an evolutionary psychologist is most likely to point to:

    a. our great human capacity for learning.
    b. the tendency of cultural arguments to reinforce traditional gender inequalities.
    c. the infallibility of hindsight explanations.
    d. all of these answers.

32. A person whose twin has Alzheimer's disease has _____ risk of sharing the disease if they are identical twins than if they are fraternal twins.

    a. less
    b. about the same
    c. a much greater
    d. It is unpredictable.

33. Which of the following is an example of an interaction?

    a. Swimmers swim fastest during competition against other swimmers.
    b. Swimmers with certain personality traits swim fastest during competition, while those with other personality traits swim fastest during solo time trials.
    c. As the average daily temperature increases, sales of ice cream decrease.
    d. As the average daily temperature increases, sales of lemonade increase.

34. Which of the following most accurately summarizes the findings of the 40-year fox-breeding study described in the text?

    a. Wild wolves cannot be domesticated.
    b. "Survival of the fittest" seems to operate only when animals live in their natural habitats.
    c. By mating aggressive and unaggressive foxes, the researchers created a mutant species.
    d. By selecting and mating the tamest males and females, the researchers have produced affectionate, unaggressive offspring.

35. Compared to men, women are more likely to:

    a. be concerned with their partner's physical attractiveness.
    b. initiate sexual activity.
    c. cite "liking one another" as a justification for having sex in a new relationship.
    d. be less accepting of casual sex.

Matching Items

Match each term with its corresponding definition or description.

Terms

_____ 1. fraternal
_____ 2. genes
_____ 3. DNA
_____ 4. identical
_____ 5. environment

Functions or Descriptions

a. the biochemical units of heredity
b. twins that develop from a single egg
c. twins that develop from separate eggs
d. nongenetic influences
e. a complex molecule containing the genetic information that makes up the chromosomes

True–False Items

Indicate whether each statement is true or false by placing *T* or *F* in the blank next to the item.

_____ 1. Gender differences in mate preferences vary widely from one culture to another.

_____ 2. The most emotionally reactive newborns tend to be the most restrained 9-month-olds.

_____ 3. Research on twins shows a substantial genetic influence on attitudes toward organized religion and many other issues.

_____ 4. Genes act as blueprints that lead to the same result no matter the context.

_____ 5. Compared to identical twins reared in different families, fraternal twins recall their early family life more differently.

_____ 6. Nature selects behavioral tendencies that increase the likelihood of sending one's genes into the future.

Essay Question

Lakia's new boyfriend has been pressuring her to become more sexually intimate than she wants to at this early stage in their relationship. Strongly gender-typed and "macho" in attitude, Jerome is becoming increasingly frustrated with Lakia's hesitation, while Lakia is starting to wonder if a long-term relationship with this type of man is what she really wants. In light of your understanding of the evolutionary explanation of gender differences in sexuality, explain why the tension between Lakia and Jerome would be considered understandable.

KEY TERMS

Using your own words, on a piece of paper write a brief definition or explanation of each of the following terms.

1. environment
2. behavior genetics
3. chromosomes
4. DNA
5. genes
6. genome
7. identical twins
8. fraternal twins
9. temperament
10. interaction
11. evolutionary psychology
12. natural selection
13. mutation
14. gender

ANSWERS
Module Review

Introduction
1. personalities; interests; cultural; family
2. biological heritage; brain; language; social
3. nongenetic
4. nature; nurture

Behavior Genetics: Predicting Individual Differences
1. behavior geneticists
2. chromosomes; 46; 23; DNA
3. genes
4. genome
5. twin; adoption
6. identical; fraternal
7. more

Other dimensions that reflect genetic influences are abilities, personal traits, and interests.

8. environment
9. do not

10. does; higher
11. temperament; does
12. difficult; irritable; intense; unpredictable; easy; cheerful; relaxed; predictable
13. more
14. regulating; blueprints; react
15. psychological; genetic; environmental
16. interaction; genetic; environment
17. genes; responses; fraternal; identical

Evolutionary Psychology: Understanding Human Nature
1. evolutionary psychologists
2. much alike
3. natural selection
4. mutations; diversity
5. looser; learn; adapt; environments; fitness; survive; reproduce; fats; store
6. gender; biological; social
7. more; more; gender
8. evolutionary; genes; are
9. youthful; mature; dominant; bold; affluent
10. backward; hindsight
11. cultural
12. inequality
13. alike; different; predictions

Progress Test

Multiple-Choice Questions

1. **c.** is the answer.
   a., b., & d. Whereas evolutionary psychologists attempt to explain universal human tendencies, these researchers investigate genetic differences among individuals.

2. **c.** is the answer. Research has not shown a strong parental influence on personality, temperament, or emotional reactivity.

3. **b.** is the answer.
   a. & c. Although an identical twin is at increased risk, the relationship is far from perfect. Mental disorders, like all psychological traits, are influenced by *both* nature and nurture.
   d. This is not at all implied by the evidence from twin studies.

4. **d.** is the answer.

a., b., & c. In order to pinpoint the influence of one of the two factors (genes and environment), it is necessary to hold one of the factors constant.

5. **b.** is the answer.
a., c., & d. Natural selection favors traits that send one's genes into the future; thus, people with those traits survive longer and reproduce more often. Aggression, happiness, and temperament have nothing to do with either survival or reproduction.

6. **d.** is the answer. Such gender differences characterize both heterosexual and homosexual people.

7. **b.** is the answer. Women can incubate only one infant at a time.
c. & d. The text does not suggest that there is a gender difference in the strength of the sex drive.

8. **b.** is the answer.
a. According to this perspective, women prefer mates with the potential for long-term nurturing investment in their joint offspring.
c. While men are drawn to women whose waists are roughly a third narrower than their hips, the text does not suggest that women equate muscularity with fertility.
d. Excitement was not mentioned as a criterion for mating.

9. **b.** is the answer.
c. & d. There are no such things as "placental" or "nonplacental" twins. All twins have a placenta during prenatal development.

10. **a.** is the answer.

11. **d.** is the answer.
a. Survival ability is only one aspect of fitness.
b. & c. Neither of these is related to fitness.

12. **c.** is the answer.
a., b., & d. The reactions of these infants are the opposite of what these choices describe.

13. **c.** is the answer.
b. & d. Each cell of the human body contains hundreds of genes.

14. **b.** is the answer.
a. Hormones are chemical messengers produced by the endocrine glands.
c. & d. Genes are segments of DNA, which are the make-up of chromosomes.

15. **c.** is the answer.
a. This defines DNA.
b. This defines a gene.
d. The genes provide the code for synthesizing proteins.

16. **c.** is the answer.

17. **a.** is the answer.

18. **b.** is the answer.
a. Testosterone levels have not been linked to the frequency of casual sex.
c. & d. Males are far more accepting of casual sex than are females.

19. **d.** is the answer.

20. **b.** is the answer.
a., c., & d. Despite being raised in different environments, long-separated identical twins often have much in common, including likes, dislikes, and life-styles. This indicates the significant heritability of many traits.

21. **b.** is the answer.
a., c., & d. The personalities of adopted children do not much resemble those of their adoptive parents (therefore, not a.) or other children reared in the same home (therefore, not c. or d.).

22. **a.** is the answer.
b. Neurotransmitters are the chemicals involved in synaptic transmission in the nervous system.
d. Enzymes are chemicals that facilitate various chemical reactions throughout the body but are not involved in heredity.

23. **d.** is the answer.
a. A norm is a culturally determined set of expected behaviors for a particular role, such as a gender role.
b. & c. When two factors are correlated, it means either that increases in one factor are accompanied by increases in the other (positive correlation) or that increases in one factor are accompanied by decreases in the other (negative correlation).

24. **a.** is the answer. This is an example of a trait that contributes to survival of the human species and the perpetuation of one's genes.
b., c., & d. These traits and issues would likely be of greater interest to a behavior geneticist, since they concern the influence of specific genes on behavior.

25. **a.** is the answer.
b. DNA is a molecule.
c. & d. Genes are segments of DNA.

26. **b.** is the answer.
a. Evolutionary psychologists study the evolution of behavior using the principles of natural selection.
c. Molecular geneticists search for the specific genes that influence behaviors. In his example, the researcher is merely comparing twins.
d. Who knows?

27. **d.** is the answer. To separate the influences of heredity and experience on behavior, one of the two must be held constant.

    a., b., & c. These situations would not allow one to separate the contributions of heredity and environment.

28. **b.** is the answer

    a. Because they are genetically the same, identical twins are always of the same sex.

    c. & d. Fraternal twins develop from two fertilized eggs.

29. **d.** is the answer.

30. **b.** is the answer. Actually, only 5 percent are differences among population groups.

31. **a.** is the answer.

    b. & c. In fact, these are typical criticisms of evolutionary psychology.

32. **c.** is the answer.

33. **b.** is the answer.

    a. An interaction requires at least two variables; in this example there is only one (competition).

    c. This is an example of a negative correlation.

    d. This is an example of a positive correlation.

34. **d.** is the answer.

35. **d.** is the answer.

    a., b., & c. These are typical male attitudes and behaviors.

Matching Items

1.	c	4.	b
2.	a	5.	d
3.	e		

True–False Items

1.	F	4.	F
2.	F	5.	T
3.	F	6.	T

Essay Question

Evolutionary psychologists would not be surprised by the tension between Lakia and Jerome and would see it as a reflection of women's more relational and men's more recreational approach to sex. Since eggs are expensive, compared with sperm, women prefer mates with the potential for long-term investment in their joint offspring. According to this perspective, this may be why Lakia is not in a hurry to become sexually intimate with Jerome. Men, on the other hand, are selected for "pairing widely" but not necessarily wisely in order to maximize the spreading of their genes. This is especially true of men like Jerome, who have traditional masculine attitudes.

Key Terms

1. In behavior genetics, **environment** refers to every nongenetic, or external, influence on our traits and behaviors.

2. **Behavior genetics** is the study of the relative power and limits of genetic and environmental influences on behavior.

3. **Chromosomes** are threadlike structures made of DNA molecules, which contain the genes. In conception, the 23 chromosomes in the egg are paired with the 23 chromosomes in the sperm.

4. **DNA** (deoxyribonucleic acid) is a complex molecule containing the genetic information that makes up the chromosomes.

5. **Genes** are the biochemical units of heredity that make up the chromosomes; they are segments of the DNA molecules capable of synthesizing a protein.

6. A **genome** is the complete genetic instructions for making an organism.

7. **Identical twins** develop from a single fertilized egg that splits in two and therefore are genetically identical.

8. **Fraternal twins** develop from two separate eggs fertilized by different sperm and therefore are no more genetically similar than ordinary siblings.

9. **Temperament** refers to a person's characteristic emotional reactivity and intensity.

10. An **interaction** occurs when the effects of one factor (such as environment) depend on another factor (such as heredity).

    Example: Because the way people react to us (an environmental factor) depends on our genetically influenced temperament (a genetic factor), there is an **interaction** between environment and heredity.

11. **Evolutionary psychology** is the study of the evolution of behavior and the mind, using the principles of natural selection.

12. **Natural selection** is the evolutionary principle that traits that contribute to reproduction and survival are the most likely to be passed on to succeeding generations.

13. **Mutations** are random errors in gene replication that are the source of genetic diversity within a species.

14. **Gender** refers to the biological and social characteristics by which people define *male* and *female*.

FOCUS ON VOCABULARY AND LANGUAGE

Behavior Genetics: Predicting Individual Differences

To scientifically *tease apart* heredity and environment . . . . Myers is using an analogy here: in an attempt to discover and separate out (*tease apart*) the differential effects of the environment and genes, behavior geneticists use two approaches: twin studies and adoption studies.

blue-collar families . . . This phrase refers to a social category based on the type of work people do. Traditionally, manual workers wore blue (denim) work shirts (*blue-collar workers*) in contrast to office workers, managers, etc., who wore white shirts (*white-collar workers*). The identical twins (both named Jim) were adopted by similar working-class (*blue-collar*) families.

Stories of *startling twin similarities* do not impress Bouchard's critics, who remind us that "the plural of anecdote is not data." Bouchard's investigation into the similarities between separated twins suggests that genes influence many behaviors, such as career choices, TV-watching habits, and food likes and dislikes (*startling stories*). The critics point out that any two strangers of the same sex and age would probably have many coincidental things in common if they were to spend hours comparing their behaviors and life histories. Furthermore, stories by, or about, individuals (*single anecdotes*) do not constitute scientific data, even if there are many of them (*the plural of anecdote is not data*).

(margin): "Mom may be *holding a full house while Dad has a straight flush,* yet when Junior gets a random half of each of their cards his *poker-hand may be a loser*" (David Lykken, 2001). To make sense of this quote you need to be familiar with card games such as poker. In this game, a "full house" and a "straight flush" are sequences of cards (*hands*) that usually are winners. Even if Mom and Dad have "winner" sets of genes, similar to the winning cards in poker, the random genes they pass on to their offspring (*Junior*) will not necessarily be a "winning" set of genes too (*his poker-hand may be a loser*).

Go barefoot for a summer and you will develop toughened callused feet—a biological adaptation to friction. Meanwhile, your *shod neighbor will remain a tenderfoot.* The enormous adaptive capacity is a common, but extremely valuable, characteristic of human beings (*the behavioral hallmark of our species*). If someone doesn't wear shoes (*he goes barefoot*), his feet will become tough, which is a biological adapta-

tion. If a person wears shoes (*your shod neighbor*), his feet will be tender or soft (he will be a *tenderfoot*); this is also the product of a biological mechanism. However, it is the environment that causes the difference between the two people. (Note: the word *tenderfoot* traditionally referred to someone who was new to ranching in the western United States and is now used to describe any newcomer or novice.)

. . . blueprints . . . A *blueprint* is an architectural term for a copy of an original diagram or plan used as a working drawing for creating a building or structure. Myers notes that genes and environment interact. Genes, rather than acting as master plans (*blueprints*) that always lead to the same result, instead react and respond to their environments. Thus, people with identical genes (identical twins) but with different experiences end up with similar but not identical minds.

Thus, asking whether your personality is more a product of your genes or environment is like asking . . . whether *the area of a field is more the result of its length or width.* The area of a space, such as a soccer field or a football field, is determined by multiplying the length by the width. Obviously, you cannot find the area of the field without both length and width. Likewise, we do not become who we are without both nature and nurture. As Myers notes, genes and experience are both important, and neither operates apart from the other; rather, they interact.

Evolutionary Psychology: Understanding Human Nature

cash-strapped . . . This means to be in desperate need of money (*strapped for cash*). Russian researchers selectively bred only the tamest and friendliest foxes from each of 30 generations over a 40-year period. The present breed of foxes is affectionate, docile, and eager to please; in order to raise funds for the financially destitute (*cash-strapped*) institute, they are being marketed as house pets.

But the tight genetic *leash* . . . is looser on humans. Just as a dog is restrained or held in check by a strap or cord (*leash*), genes generally determine the fairly rigid or fixed patterns of behaviors of many animals. In humans, however, genes are less influential; thus, the usually strong genetic constraints (*tight genetic leash*) operate in a less determined way (*are looser*).

In our *ancestral history*, women most often sent their genes into the future by *pairing wisely*, men by *pairing widely.* Evolutionary psychologists note that our normal desires (*natural yearnings*) help perpetuate our genes. In our evolutionary past (*ancestral history*) females accomplished this best by being selective in their choice of mate (*pairing wisely*) and men by more promiscuous behavior (*pairing widely*). Myers points out, however, that environmental factors, such as cultural expectations, can alter or shape how sexual behavior is expressed by both males and females (*culture can bend the genders*).

They (women) prefer *stick-around dads over likely cads*. Women tend to prefer males who are more likely to be supportive of their children (their *joint offspring*) and who are also more willing to make a lasting contribution to their protection (*stick-around dads*) rather than males who indicate little or no will-

ingness to make such a co-parenting commitment (*likely cads*).

As *mobile gene machines*, we are designed to prefer whatever worked for our ancestors in their environments. Evolutionary psychologists believe that behavioral tendencies that increase the probability of getting one's genes into the future have been selected for over the course of evolution. Humans who actively seek out mates and successfully procreate (*mobile gene machines*) are passing on inherited tendencies to behave in certain ways (*our natural yearnings*) because these behaviors were adaptive for our ancestors.

Environmental Influences on Behavior

MODULE OVERVIEW

Module 6 focuses on environmental influences on behavior. The impact of the prenatal environment, parents, early experience, peers, and culture on the development of the brain and behavior are each discussed. The final section of the module explores how genes and environment interact to shape both the biological and social aspects of our gender. In the end, the message is clear: our genes and our experience together form who we are.

NOTE: Answer guidelines for all Module 6 questions begin on page 79.

MODULE REVIEW

First, skim each section, noting headings and boldface items. After you have read the section, review each objective by answering the fill-in and essay-type questions that follow it. As you proceed, evaluate your performance by consulting the answers beginning on page 79. Do not continue with the next section until you understand each answer. If you need to, review or reread the section in the textbook before continuing.

David Myers at times uses idioms that are unfamiliar to some readers. If you do not know the meaning of the following words, phrases, or expressions in the context in which they appear in the text, refer to pages 82–83 for an explanation: *pathways through a forest; while the excess connections are still on call; shuffle their gene decks; as a potter molds clay; vapors of a toxic climate are seeping into a child's life; cerebral hard drive . . . cultural software; norms grease the social machinery; cultures collide; standoffish; surface early; throws a master switch; initiate dates . . . pick up the check; with the flick of an apron; won the day; boggles the mind.*

Parents and Peers (pp. 79–81)

Objective 1: Describe how experience can modify the brain.

1. Environmental influences begin during the period of _____ development.

2. Rosenzweig and Krech discovered that rats raised from a young age in enriched environments had _____ (thicker/thinner) cortexes than animals raised in isolation.

Describe the effects of sensory stimulation on neural development.

3. Experience shapes the brain by preserving activated _____ connections and allowing unused connections to _____ . This process, called _____ , results in a massive loss of unused connections by _____ .

Objective 2: Explain why we should be careful about attributing children's successes and failures to their parents' influence, and evaluate the importance of peer influence on development.

4. The idea that parents shape their children's futures came from _____ _____ and _____ .

5. Parents do influence some areas of their children's lives, such as their _____ _____ , _____ _____ , and _____ _____ .

6. In areas such as _____ , the environment siblings share at home accounts for less than _____ percent of their differences.

7. Experiences with _____ have a powerful effect on how children develop, partly as a result of a _____ effect by which kids seek out others with similar attitudes and interests.

Cultural Influences (pp. 82–87)

Objective 3: Describe how behavior is influenced by cultural norms.

1. The enduring behaviors, ideas, attitudes, and traditions of a group of people and transmitted from one generation to the next defines the group's _____ .

2. One landmark of human culture is the preservation of _____ , which is derived from our mastery of _____ , so that we can pass it on to future generations. Culture also enables an efficient division of _____ .

3. All cultural groups evolve their own rules for expected behavior, called _____ .

4. One such rule involves the buffer zone that people maintain around their bodies, called _____ _____ .

Identify several cultural differences in personal space, expressiveness, and pace of life.

5. Cultures change _____ (slowly/ rapidly).

6. Many changes in Western culture have been driven by the discovery of new forms of _____ .

7. The speed at which culture changes is much _____ (faster/slower) than the pace of evolutionary changes in the human _____ _____ .

Objective 4: Identify some ways a primarily individualist culture differs from a primarily collectivist culture, and compare their effects on personal identity and child-rearing.

8. Cultures based on _____ value personal _____ and individual _____ . Examples of such cultures occur in the _____ _____ , _____ , and _____ .

9. In contrast, cultures based on _____ value _____ , _____ , and _____ . Examples of such cultures occur in parts of _____ and _____ .

10. Whereas people in _____ cultures value freedom, they suffer more _____ , divorce, _____ , and _____ -related disease.

11. Whereas most Western parents place more emphasis on _____ (emotional closeness/independence) in their children, many Asian and African parents focus on cultivating _____ (emotional closeness/independence).

12. Children in collectivist cultures grow up with a strong sense of _____ _____ , a sense that what shames or honors the person also shames or honors the family.

13. In general, differences between groups are _____ (smaller/larger) than person-to-person differences within groups.

Gender Development (pp. 87–93)

Objective 5: Discuss gender similarities and differences in psychological traits such as aggression, social power, and social connectedness.

1. Among your _____ (how many?) chromosomes, _____ (how many?) are unisex.

2. Compared to the average man, an average woman has more _____ , less _____ , and is a few inches _____ . Women are more likely than men to suffer from _____ , _____ , and _____ .

3. Compared to women, men are more likely to commit _____ and to suffer _____ . They are also more likely to be diagnosed with _____ , _____-_____ , _____ , and _____ _____ .

4. *Aggression* is defined as _____ or _____ behavior that is _____ to hurt someone.

5. Throughout the world, men are more likely than women to engage in _____ , _____ , and _____ .

6. The aggression gender gap pertains to _____ rather than _____ aggression.

7. Compared to women, men are perceived as being more _____ , _____ , and _____ . As leaders, they tend to be more _____ , while women are more _____ .

8. Compared to men, women are perceived as being more _____ , _____ , and _____ .

9. These perceived differences occur _____ (throughout the world/only in certain cultures).

10. According to Carol Gilligan, women are more concerned than men in making _____ with others.

11. This difference is noticeable in how children _____ , and it continues throughout the teen and adult years. Girls play in groups that are _____ and less _____ than boys' groups.

12. Because they are more _____ , women are likely to use conversation to _____ , while men are likely to use conversation to _____ _____ .

13. Women tend and befriend—for example, they turn to others for _____ , especially when coping with _____ .

Objective 6: Explain how biological sex is determined, and describe the role of sex hormones in biological development and gender differences.

14. The twenty-third pair of chromosomes determines the developing person's _____ . The mother always contributes a(n) _____ chromosome. When the father contributes a(n) _____ chromosome, the testes begin producing the hormone _____ . In about the _____ (what week?), this hormone initiates the development of external male sex organs.

15. Sex chromosomes control _____ that influence the brain's wiring. In adulthood, part of the _____ lobe, an area involved in _____ fluency, is thicker in women. Part of the brain's _____ lobe, a key area for _____ perception, is thicker in men.

Objective 7: Discuss the importance of gender roles in development, and describe two theories of gender-typing.

16. Our expectations about the way men and women behave define our culture's _____ .

17. Gender roles _____ (are/are not) rigidly fixed by evolution, as evidenced by the fact that they vary across _____ and over _____ . For instance, in _____ societies there tends to be minimal division of labor by sex; by contrast, in _____ societies, women remain close to home while men roam freely, herding cattle or sheep.

18. Our individual sense of being male or female is called our _____ _____ . The degree to which we exhibit traditionally male or female traits and interests is called _____- _____ .

19. According to _____ _____ theory, children learn gender-linked behaviors by observing others and being rewarded or punished. When their families discourage traditional gender-typing, children _____ (do/do not) organize them- selves into "boy worlds" and "girl worlds."

20. Another theory, called _____ _____ theory, combines _____ _____ theory with _____ . According to this theory, children learn from their _____ what it means to be male or female and adjust their behavior accordingly.

Reflections on Nature and Nurture
(pp. 93–95)

Objective 8: Describe the biopsychosocial approach to development.

1. As _____ _____ becomes more and more irrelevant to power and status, gender roles are _____ (converging/diverging).

2. We are the product of both _____ and _____ , but we are also a sys- tem that is _____ .

3. The principle that we should prefer the simplest of competing explanations for a phenomenon is called _____ _____ .

PROGRESS TEST

Multiple-Choice Questions

Circle your answers to the following questions and check them with the answers beginning on page 80. If your answer is incorrect, read the explanation for why it is incorrect and then consult the appropriate pages of the text.

1. Collectivist cultures:
   a. give priority to the goals of their groups.
   b. value the maintenance of social harmony.
   c. foster social interdependence.
   d. are characterized by all of these.

2. The traditions of a culture are passed from one generation to the next by means of:
   a. norms.
   b. temperaments.
   c. genes.
   d. chromosomes.

3. Which of the following most accurately expresses the extent of parental influence on personality?
   a. It is more extensive than most people believe.
   b. It is weaker today than in the past.
   c. It is more limited than popular psychology supposes.
   d. It is almost completely unpredictable.

4. Gender refers to:
   a. the biological and social definition of male and female.
   b. the biological definition of male and female.
   c. one's sense of being male or female.
   d. the extent to which one exhibits traditionally male or female traits.

5. The fertilized egg will develop into a boy if, at conception:
   a. the sperm contributes an X chromosome.
   b. the sperm contributes a Y chromosome.
   c. the egg contributes an X chromosome.
   d. the egg contributes a Y chromosome.

6. Which theory states that gender becomes a lens through which children view their experiences?
   a. social learning theory
   b. sociocultural theory
   c. cognitive theory
   d. gender schema theory

7. The hormone testosterone:
   a. is found only in females.
   b. determines the sex of the developing person.
   c. stimulates growth of the female sex organs.
   d. stimulates growth of the male sex organs.

8. Research studies have found that when infant rats and premature human babies are regularly touched or massaged, they:
   a. gain less weight.
   b. develop faster neurologically.
   c. have more agreeable temperaments.
   d. develop a more complete sense of self.

9. Of the following, parents are most likely to influence their children's:
   a. temperament.
   b. personality.
   c. faith.
   d. emotional reactivity.

10. Compared to children raised in Western societies, those raised in communal societies, such as Japan or China:
    a. grow up with a stronger integration of the sense of family into their self-concepts.
    b. exhibit greater shyness toward strangers.
    c. exhibit greater concern for loyalty and social harmony.
    d. have all of these characteristics.

11. The *selection effect* in peer influence refers to the tendency of children and youth to:
    a. naturally separate into same-sex playgroups.
    b. establish large, fluid circles of friends.
    c. seek out friends with similar interests and attitudes.
    d. choose friends their parents like.

12. Which of the following is *not* true regarding cultural diversity?
    a. Culture influences emotional expressiveness.
    b. Culture influences personal space.
    c. Culture does not have a strong influence on how strictly social roles are defined.
    d. All cultures evolve their own norms.

13. Women and men are most likely to be attracted to strongly gender-typed mates in cultures characterized by:
    a. gender inequality.
    b. gender equality.
    c. flexible gender roles.
    d. few norms.

14. Children who are raised by parents who discourage traditional gender-typing:
    a. are less likely to display gender-typed behaviors themselves.
    b. often become confused and develop an ambiguous gender identity.
    c. nevertheless organize themselves into "girl worlds" and "boy worlds."
    d. display excessively masculine and feminine traits as adults.

15. Genetically male children who underwent sex-reassignment surgery and were raised as girls later:
    a. all described themselves as female.
    b. all described themselves as male.
    c. all had an unclear sexual identity.
    d. described themselves either as female or male, or had an unclear sexual identity.

16. Providing a child with a stimulating educational environment during early childhood is likely to:
    a. ensure the formation of a strong attachment with parents.
    b. foster the development of a calm, easygoing temperament.
    c. prevent neural connections from degenerating.
    d. accomplish all of these.

17. Although the fitness center has many unused lockers, Rabab picks a locker right next to Chalina's, who feels uncomfortable because Rabab has intruded into her:
    a. gender norm.
    b. personal space.
    c. gender role.
    d. cultural schema.

18. Despite growing up in the same home environment, Karen and her brother John have personalities as different from each other as two people selected randomly from the population. Why is this so?
    a. Personality is inherited. Because Karen and John are not identical twins, it is not surprising they have very different personalities.
    b. Gender is the most important factor in personality. If Karen had a sister, the two of them would probably be much more alike.
    c. The interaction of their individual genes and nonshared experiences accounts for the common finding that children in the same family are usually very different.
    d. Their case is unusual; children in the same family usually have similar personalities.

19. I am a rat whose cortex is lighter and thinner than my litter mates. What happened to me?
    a. You were born prematurely.
    b. You suffer from fetal alcohol syndrome.
    c. You were raised in an enriched environment.
    d. You were raised in a deprived environment.

20. Chad, who grew up in the United States, is more likely to encourage _____ in his future children than Asian-born Hidiyaki, who is more likely to encourage _____ in his future children.
    a. obedience; independence
    b. independence; emotional closeness
    c. emotional closeness; obedience
    d. loyalty; emotional closeness

21. Rod has always felt pressure to be the driver when traveling in a car with Sue because he learned that this was expected of men. Rod's feelings illustrate the influence of:
    a. testosterone.
    b. gender roles.
    c. the selection effect.
    d. collectivism.

22. Compared with men, women:
    a. use conversation to communicate solutions.
    b. emphasize freedom and self-reliance.
    c. talk more openly.
    d. do all of these.

23. When his son cries because another child has taken his favorite toy, Brandon admonishes him by saying, "Big boys don't cry." Evidently, Brandon is an advocate of _____ in accounting for the development of gender-linked behaviors.
    a. gender schema theory
    b. gender identity theory
    c. gender-typing theory
    d. social learning theory

24. The fact that language forces children age 2 and older to begin organizing their worlds on the basis of gender is most consistent with which theory of how gender-linked behaviors develop?
    a. gender schema theory
    b. gender identity theory
    c. gender-typing theory
    d. social learning theory

25. Three-year-old Jack is inhibited and shy. As an adult, Jack is likely to be:
    a. cautious and unassertive.
    b. spontaneous and fearless.
    c. socially assertive.
    d. Who knows? This aspect of personality is not very stable over the life span.

Matching Items

Match each term with its corresponding definition or description.

Terms

_____ 1. X chromosome
_____ 2. norm
_____ 3. Y chromosome
_____ 4. gender role
_____ 5. gender identity
_____ 6. gender-typing

Functions or Descriptions

a. one's personal sense of being female or male
b. a set of expected behaviors for males and females
c. an understood rule for accepted and expected behavior
d. the sex chromosome found in both women and men
e. the acquisition of a traditional gender role
f. the sex chromosome found only in men

True–False Items

Indicate whether each statement is true or false by placing *T* or *F* in the blank next to the item.

_____ 1. Parents have a stronger influence than do peers on whether a youth starts smoking.
_____ 2. People from individualist cultures say what they feel and what they presume others feel.
_____ 3. Parental influence on personality is more limited than popular psychology supposes.
_____ 4. North Americans prefer more personal space than do Latin Americans.
_____ 5. Lacking any exposure to language before adolescence, a person will never master any language.

9. testosterone
10. role
11. gender role
12. gender identity
13. gender-typing
14. social learning theory
15. gender schema theory

KEY TERMS

Using your own words, on a piece of paper write a brief definition or explanation of each of the following terms.

1. culture
2. norm
3. personal space
4. individualism
5. collectivism
6. aggression
7. X chromosome
8. Y chromosome

ANSWERS

Module Review

Parents and Peers

1. prenatal
2. thicker

Research has shown that human and animal infants given extra sensory stimulation develop faster neurologically. Throughout life, sensory stimulation activates and strengthens particular neural connections, while other connections weaken with disuse. In this way, our experiences shape the very structure of the neural pathways that process those experiences.

3. neural; degenerate; pruning; puberty
4. Freudian psychiatry; psychology
5. political attitudes; personal manners; religious beliefs
6. personality; 10
7. peers; selection

Cultural Influences

1. culture
2. innovation; language; labor

3. norms

4. personal space

Most North Americans, the British, and Scandinavians prefer more personal space than do Latin Americans, Arabs, and the French. Cultural differences in expressiveness and the pace of life often create misunderstandings. For example, people with northern European roots may perceive people from Mediterranean cultures as warm and charming but inefficient, while Mediterraneans may see the northern Europeans as efficient but emotionally cold.

5. rapidly

6. technology

7. faster; gene pool

8. individualism; independence (or control); achievement; United States; Canada; Western Europe

9. collectivism; interdependence; tradition; harmony; Africa; Asia

10. individualist; loneliness; homicide; stress

11. independence; emotional closeness

12. family self

13. smaller

Gender Development

1. 46; 45

2. fat; muscle; shorter; depression; anxiety; eating disorders

3. suicide; alcoholism; autism, color-blindness, hyperactivity, antisocial personality disorder

4. physical; verbal; intended

5. hunting; fighting; warring

6. physical; verbal

7. dominant; forceful; independent; directive (or autocratic); democratic

8. deferential; nurturant; affiliative

9. throughout the world

10. connections

11. play; smaller; competitive

12. interdependent; explore relationships; communicate solutions

13. support; stress

14. sex; X; Y; testosterone; seventh

15. hormones; frontal; verbal; parietal; space

16. gender roles

17. are not; cultures; time; nomadic; agricultural

18. gender identity; gender-typing

19. social learning; do

20. gender schema; social learning; cognition; schemas

Reflections on Nature and Nurture

1. brute strength; converging

2. nature; nurture; open

3. Occam's razor

Progress Test

Multiple-Choice Questions

1. **d.** is the answer.

2. **a.** is the answer.

3. **c.** is the answer.

4. **a.** is the answer.
   b. This definition is incomplete.
   c. This defines gender identity.
   d. This defines gender-typing.

5. **b.** is the answer.
   a. In this case, a female would develop.
   c. & d. The egg can contribute only an X chromosome. Thus, the sex of the child is determined by which chromosome the sperm contributes.

6. **d.** is the answer.
   a. According to social learning theory, gender-typing evolves through imitation and reinforcement.
   b. & c. Neither theory focuses on gender-typing.

7. **d.** is the answer.
   a. Although testosterone is the principal male hormone, it is present in both females and males.
   b. This is determined by the sex chromosomes.
   c. In the absence of testosterone, female sex organs will develop.

8. **b.** is the answer.

9. **c.** is the answer.
   a. & d. Temperament, which refers to a person's emotional reactivity, is determined primarily by genes.
   b. Genes limit parents' influence on their children's personalities.

10. **d.** is the answer.

11. **c.** is the answer.

12. **c.** is the answer.

13. **a.** is the answer.
    b. In such cultures gender differences in mate preferences tend to be much smaller.

c. Although flexibility in gender roles was not discussed per se, it is likely that greater flexibility would equate with greater equality in gender roles.

d. All cultures develop norms.

14. **c.** is the answer.

b. & d. There is no evidence that being raised in a "gender neutral" home confuses children or fosters a backlash of excessive gender-typing.

15. **d.** is the answer. Some later described themselves as female, and some as male.

16. **c.** is the answer.

a. Although early experiences are a factor in the development of attachment (discussed in Module 8), educational stimulation is probably less important than warmth and nurturance.

b. Because temperament appears to be a strongly genetic trait, it is unlikely that early educational experiences would affect its nature.

17. **b.** is the answer.

18. **c.** is the answer.

a. Although heredity does influence certain traits, such as outgoingness and emotional instability, it is the interaction of heredity and experience that ultimately molds personality.

b. There is no single "most important factor" in personality. Moreover, for the same reason two sisters or brothers often have dissimilar personalities, a sister and brother may be very much alike.

d. Karen and John's case is not at all unusual.

19. **d.** is the answer.

a. & b. Premature birth and fetal alcohol syndrome (discussed in Module 7) usually do not have this effect on the developing brain.

c. If the question had stated "I have a heavier and thicker cortex," this answer would be correct.

20. **b.** is the answer. Although parental values differ from one time and place to another, studies reveal that Western parents today want their children to think for themselves, while Asian and African parents place greater value on emotional closeness.

d. Both of these values are more typical of Asian than Western cultures.

21. **b.** is the answer.

22. **c.** is the answer.

23. **d.** is the answer. Following social learning theory, Brandon is using verbal punishment to discourage what he believes to be an inappropriate gender-linked behavior in his son.

a. Gender schema theory maintains that children adjust their behaviors to match their cultural con-

cept of gender. In this example, we have only the father's behavior on which to base our answer.

b. & c. No such theories were discussed.

24. **a.** is the answer. Many aspects of language, including masculine and feminine pronouns, provide children with schemas through which they begin organizing their worlds on the basis of gender.

25. **a.** is the answer.

b., c., & d. Temperament is one of the most stable personality traits.

Matching Items

1. d   4. b
2. c   5. a
3. f   6. e

True–False Items

1. F   4. T
2. F   5. T
3. T

Key Terms

1. A **culture** is the enduring behaviors, ideas, attitudes, and traditions shared by a large group of people and transmitted from one generation to the next.

2. **Norms** are understood rules for accepted and expected behavior.

3. **Personal space** refers to the buffer zone that people like to maintain around their bodies.

4. **Individualism** is giving priority to personal goals over group goals and defining one's identity in terms of personal attributes rather than group identification.

5. **Collectivism** is giving priority to the goals of one's group, and defining one's identity accordingly.

6. **Aggression** is physical or verbal behavior intended to hurt someone.

7. The **X chromosome** is the sex chromosome found in both men and women. Females inherit an X chromosome from each parent.

8. The **Y chromosome** is the sex chromosome found only in men. Males inherit an X chromosome from their mothers and a Y chromosome from their fathers.

9. **Testosterone** is the principal male sex hormone. During prenatal development, testosterone stimulates the development of the external male sex organs.

10. A **role** is a cluster of prescribed behaviors expected of those who occupy a particular social position.

11. A **gender role** is a set of expected behaviors for males and females.

12. **Gender identity** is one's sense of being male or female.

13. **Gender-typing** is the acquisition of a traditional feminine or masculine role.

14. According to **social learning theory**, people learn social behavior (such as gender roles) by observing and imitating and by being rewarded or punished.

15. According to **gender schema theory**, children acquire a cultural concept of what it means to be female or male and adjust their behavior accordingly.

FOCUS ON VOCABULARY AND LANGUAGE

Parents and Peers

Similar to *pathways* through a forest, less traveled paths gradually disappear, and *popular paths* are broadened. This analogy suggests that brain development goes on throughout life. Neural connections (*pathways*) that are frequently used (*popular paths*) are widened and more clearly defined, while those connections that are seldom used (*in disuse*) become weakened and may eventually disappear.

During early childhood—while excess connections are *still on call*— . . . . To *be on call* means to be ready and available for use. Thus, during the early childhood years while there are many neural connections ready for use (*still on call*), an enriched and stimulating environment is extremely important for intellectual, perceptual, and social development. As Myers puts it, "... use it or lose it."

In procreation, a woman and a man *shuffle their gene decks and deal a life-forming hand* to their child-to-be . . . The idea here is that just as cards are randomly interspersed (*shuffled*) and then passed on (*dealt*) to the players, a man and a woman intermingle their genes (*shuffle their gene decks*) and conceive offspring (*deal a life-forming hand to their child-to-be*). The child is then exposed to numerous environmental factors beyond parental control that limit how much the parents influence the child's development (*children are not formless blobs sculpted by parental nurture*).

Society reinforces such parent-blaming: Believing that parents shape their children as a *potter molds clay*, people readily praise parents for their children's virtues and blame them for their children's vices. Myers suggests that, because some factors that affect development are under the parent's control and others are not, it is not appropriate to be judgmental. We should be slower to praise parents for their children's achievements (children's virtues) and slower yet to be critical when the children do not perform up to our expectations (children's

vices). Children are not simply formed by their parents' child-rearing abilities (*as a potter molds clay*) but rather are influenced by many factors beyond their control.

If the vapors of a toxic climate are seeping into a child's life, that climate—not just the child—needs *reforming*. Myers is suggesting that when problem behaviors arise it is important to look at the whole context that is influencing the child rather than just focusing on the youngster. If the environment (*neighborhood and schools*) is unhealthy and dangerous (*a toxic climate*) and is slowly leaking (*seeping*) into a child's life, then it is important to change (*reform*) these environmental influences instead of simply trying to change the child.

Cultural Influences

We come equipped with a huge *cerebral hard drive ready to receive many gigabytes of cultural software.* Myers is comparing our capacity to learn and adapt through cultural transmission to that of a computer's operating system (*cerebral hard drive*) which, like a human, is capable of receiving very large amounts of information through programming (*gigabytes of cultural software*).

Yet, norms *grease the social machinery* . . . Every society has its own rules and regulations about accepted and appropriate modes of conduct (social norms), and these standards differ from culture to culture. These proscriptions may sometimes seem unjust or senseless, but because they are known and practiced by most people, they serve the function of helping society run smoothly (*they grease the social machinery*).

When cultures collide, their differing norms often *befuddle*. When people from different cultures meet, the interaction can be confusing (*befuddling*). Personal space (the distance we like to have between us and others) varies; someone who prefers more space may end up constantly retreating (*back-*

pedaling) from someone who needs to be close in order to have a comfortable conversation.

. . . *standoffish* . . . This means to be distant or unfriendly in social interactions. North Americans have a need for a bigger personal space than do people from some other cultures. So, when that space is infringed upon (*invaded*), the natural reaction is to back away, which may give the impression of being aloof and unfriendly (*standoffish*).

Gender Development

These gender differences in connectedness *surface early,* in children's play. Males and females differ in their feelings of belonging (*connectedness*), a disparity that is noticeable from a young age (*surfaces early*). When playing, boys tend to engage in competitive group activity without much close, confidential, or affectionate dialogue. Girls typically are more intimate with each other and play in smaller groups, frequently with one friend, and they are less competitive and more supportive and empathic.

The Y chromosome includes a single gene that *throws a master switch* triggering the testes to develop and produce the principal male hormone, **testosterone** . . . We all get an X chromosome from our mothers and either an X (you'll be a girl) or a Y (you'll be a boy) from our fathers. Thus, the Y chromosome is crucial to making males, and a single gene is responsible for initiating the process (*it throws the switch*) that activates (*triggers*) the production of testosterone by the testes.

Thirty years ago, it was standard for men to *initiate dates*, drive the car, and *pick up the check*, and for women to decorate the home, buy and care for the children's clothes, and select the wedding gifts. Gender roles are a culture's expectations for male and female behaviors, but these behaviors change over time and across cultures, and vary from generation to generation. Traditionally (*as was common practice 30 years ago*), males asked females to go out (*initiated dates*) and paid for the meal and entertainment (*picked up the check*), and women looked after domestic concerns, including purchasing and looking after the children's clothes and choosing presents for those who were getting married (*wedding gifts*).

In that same century [the twentieth century], with the *flick of an apron*, the number of U.S. college women hoping to be full-time homemakers *plunged* during the late 1960s and early 1970s (Figure 6.3). Over time, gender roles have changed. Within a relatively brief period of time (*with the flick of an apron*), the number of women engaged in the traditional female role (full-time homemaker) declined rapidly (*plunged*) and the number of women in the work force increased substantially, especially in traditional male fields such as medicine, law, and engineering.

Reflections on Nature and Nurture

won the day . . . Galileo's theory that the Earth revolved around the Sun, and not the other way around (vice-versa), was eventually accepted (*it won the day*). His explanation was a coherent account (*it hung together*) of the way the solar system actually works.

It *boggles* the mind—the entire universe *popping out of a single point* some 14 billion years ago. . . . When something is startling, unexpected, or hard to comprehend, we say that "it *boggles* the mind." The idea that the entire universe arose from a singularity (*popped out of a single point*) approximately 14 billion years ago is one such "mind-boggling" idea that leaves even scientists full of reverence and wonder (*they are awestruck*).

Developing Through the Life Span

Developmental Issues, Prenatal Development, and the Newborn

7
MODULE

MODULE OVERVIEW

Developmental psychologists study the life cycle, from conception to death, examining how we develop physically, mentally, and socially. Modules 5 and 6 discuss the relative impact of genes and experience on behavior. Module 7 introduces two other major issues in developmental psychology: (1) whether development is best described as gradual and continuous or as a discontinuous sequence of stages and (2) whether the individual's personality remains stable or changes over the life span.

Module 7 begins the discussion of lifelong development with the events of prenatal development, then continues with a description of the newborn's surprising competencies.

NOTE: Answer guidelines for all Module 7 questions begin on page 89.

MODULE REVIEW

First, skim this section, noting headings and boldface items. After you have read the section, review each objective by completing the sentences and answering the questions that follow it. As you proceed, evaluate your performance by consulting the answers on page 89. Do not continue with the next section until you understand each answer. If you need to, review or reread the section in the textbook before continuing.

> David Myers at times uses idioms that are unfamiliar to some readers. If you do not know the meaning of the following expressions in the context in which they appear in the text, refer to page 90 for an explanation: *journey through life—from womb to tomb; as a giant redwood differs from its seedling; goof-off.*

Introduction and Two Major Developmental Issues (pp. 98, 99–100)

Objective 1: State three areas of change that developmental psychologists study, and summarize current views regarding continuity versus stages and stability versus change in lifelong development.

1. Scientists who study physical, cognitive, and social changes throughout the life cycle are called

   _____ _____ .

2. One of the major issues in developmental psychology concerns the relative importance of genes and experience in determining behavior; this is called the _____ /

   _____ issue.

3. A second developmental issue concerns whether developmental changes are gradual or abrupt: this is called the _____ /

   _____ issue.

4. Those who emphasize _____ and

   _____ see development as a slow, continuous process.

5. Those who emphasize _____

   _____ see development as a series of stages. The stage theory that all children pass through four discrete, age-linked stages of cognitive development was proposed by

   _____ .

87

6. Although research casts doubt on the idea that life proceeds through age-linked _____ , there are spurts of _____ growth during childhood and puberty that correspond roughly to the stages proposed by _____ .

7. A third controversial issue concerns the consistency of personality and whether development is characterized more by _____ over time or by change.

8. The first two years of life _____ (do/do not) provide a good basis for predicting a person's eventual traits.

9. Research on the consistency of personality shows that some traits, such as those related to _____ , are more stable than others, such as social attitudes.

Conception and Prenatal Development
(pp. 100–102)

Objective 2: Discuss the course of prenatal development and the destructive impact of teratogens.

1. Conception begins when a woman's _____ releases a mature _____ .

2. The few _____ from the man that reach the egg release digestive _____ that eat away the egg's protective covering. As soon as one sperm penetrates the egg, the egg's surface _____ all other sperm.

3. The egg and sperm _____ fuse and become one.

4. Fertilized human eggs are called _____ . During the first week, the cells in this cluster begin to specialize in structure and function, that is, they begin to _____ . The outer part of the fertilized egg attaches to the _____ wall, forming the _____ .

5. From about 2 until 8 weeks of age the developing human, formed from the inner cells of the fertilized egg, is called a(n) _____ . During the final stage of prenatal development,

the developing human is called a(n) _____ .

6. Along with nutrients, a range of harmful substances known as _____ can pass through the placenta.

7. Moderate consumption of alcohol during pregnancy _____ (usually does not affect/can affect) the fetal brain. If a mother drinks heavily, her baby is at risk for the birth defects and mental retardation that accompany _____ _____ .

The Competent Newborn (pp. 102–103)

Objective 3: Describe some abilities of the newborn.

1. Newborns come equipped with _____ responses suited to their survival. When an infant's cheek is touched, for example, it will vigorously _____ for a nipple.

Give some evidence supporting the claim that a newborn's sensory equipment is biologically prewired to facilitate social responsiveness.

PROGRESS TEST

Circle your answers to the following questions and check them with the answers on page 90. If your answer is incorrect, read the explanation for why it is incorrect and then consult the appropriate pages of the text.

Multiple-Choice Questions

1. Dr. Joan Goodman is studying how memory changes as people get older. She is most likely a(n) _____ psychologist.
   a. social
   b. cognitive
   c. developmental
   d. experimental

2. Babies will vigorously *root* when:
   a. their foot is tickled.
   b. their cheek is touched.
   c. they hear a loud noise.
   d. they make eye contact with their caregiver.

3. A child can be born a drug addict because:
   a. drugs used by the mother will pass into the child's bloodstream.
   b. addiction is an inherited personality trait.
   c. drugs used by the mother create genetic defects in her chromosomes.
   d. the fetus' blood has not yet developed a resistance to drugs.

4. A child whose mother drank heavily when she was pregnant is at heightened risk of:
   a. being emotionally excitable during childhood.
   b. becoming insecurely attached.
   c. being born with the physical and cognitive abnormalities of fetal alcohol syndrome.
   d. addiction to a range of drugs throughout life.

5. Which is the correct order of stages of prenatal development?
   a. zygote, fetus, embryo
   b. zygote, embryo, fetus
   c. embryo, zygote, fetus
   d. embryo, fetus, zygote

6. Which of the following statements is consistent with the current thinking of developmental psychologists?
   a. Development occurs in a series of sharply defined stages.
   b. The first two years are the most crucial in determining the individual's personality.
   c. The consistency of personality in most people tends to increase over the life span.
   d. Social and emotional style are among the characteristics that show the least stability over the life span.

7. Most contemporary developmental psychologists believe that:
   a. personality is essentially formed by the end of infancy.
   b. personality continues to be formed until adolescence.
   c. the shaping of personality continues during adolescence and well beyond.
   d. adolescent development has very little impact on adult personality.

KEY TERMS

Using your own words, on a piece of paper write a brief definition or explanation of each of the following terms.

1. developmental psychology
2. zygote
3. embryo
4. fetus
5. teratogens
6. fetal alcohol syndrome (FAS)

ANSWERS

Module Review

Introduction and *Two Major Developmental Issues*
1. developmental psychologists
2. nature/nurture
3. continuity/stages
4. experience; learning
5. biological maturation; Piaget
6. stages; brain; Piaget
7. stability
8. do not
9. temperament

Conception and Prenatal Development
1. ovary; egg
2. sperm; enzymes; blocks
3. nuclei
4. zygotes; differentiate; uterine; placenta
5. embryo; fetus
6. teratogens
7. can affect; fetal alcohol syndrome

The Competent Newborn
1. automatic; root

Newborns reflexively turn their heads in the direction of human voices. They gaze longer at a drawing of a facelike image than at a bull's-eye pattern. They focus best on objects about 8 to 12 inches away, which is about the distance between a nursing infant's eyes and the mother's. Within days, they recognize their mother's smell and voice.

Progress Test

Multiple-Choice Questions

1. **c.** is the answer. Developmental psychologists study physical, cognitive (memory, in this example), and social change throughout the life span.
   a. Social psychologists study how people influence and are influenced by others.
   b. Cognitive psychologists *do* study memory; because Dr. Goodman is interested in life-span *changes* in memory, she is more likely a developmental psychologist.
   d. Experimental psychologists study physiology, sensation, perception, learning, and other aspects of behavior. Only developmental psychologists focus on developmental changes in behavior and mental processes.

2. **b.** is the answer. The infant turns its head and begins sucking when its cheek is stroked.
   a., c., & d. These stimuli produce other reflexes in the newborn.

3. **a.** is the answer. Any drug taken by the mother passes through the placenta and enters the child's bloodstream.
   b. Addiction cannot be inherited; it requires exposure to an addictive drug.
   c. Drugs may disrupt the mechanisms of heredity, but there is no evidence that such changes promote addiction.
   d. This answer is incorrect because at no age does the blood "resist" drugs.

4. **c.** is the answer.
   a., b., & d. A child's emotional temperament, attachment, and addiction have not been linked to the mother's drinking while pregnant.

5. **b.** is the answer.

6. **c.** is the answer. Although some researchers emphasize consistency and others emphasize potential for change, they all agree that consistency increases over the life span.
   a. One criticism of stage theories is that development does not occur in sharply defined stages.
   b. Research has shown that individuals' adult personalities cannot be predicted from their first two years.
   d. Social and emotional style are two of the most stable traits.

7. **c.** is the answer.

Key Terms

1. **Developmental psychology** is the branch of psychology concerned with physical, cognitive, and social change throughout the life span.

2. The **zygote** (a term derived from the Greek word for "joint") is the fertilized egg, that is, the cluster of cells formed during conception by the union of sperm and egg.

3. The **embryo** is the developing prenatal organism from about 2 weeks through 2 months after conception.

4. The **fetus** is the developing prenatal human from 9 weeks after conception to birth.

5. **Teratogens** (literally, poisons) are any chemicals and viruses that cross the mother's placenta and can harm the developing embryo or fetus.

6. **Fetal alcohol syndrome (FAS)** refers to the physical and cognitive abnormalities that heavy drinking by a pregnant woman may cause in the developing child.

FOCUS ON VOCABULARY AND LANGUAGE

As we *journey* through life—from *womb to tomb*—when, how, and why do we develop? In the process of becoming who we are, and as we travel (*journey*) through life, from conception to death (*womb to tomb*) we change and mature physically, psychologically, and socially. (Another humorous expression describing the life span or life cycle is from "sperm to worm.")

Two Major Developmental Issues

But do they differ as a giant redwood differs from its seedling? Or do they differ as a butterfly differs from a caterpillar . . . ? The giant redwood is a large coniferous tree that grows in a continuous, cumulative way from seedling to mature tree. On the other hand, the butterfly emerges as a different creature after passing through a stage as a caterpillar. The question developmental psychologists ask is: Are changes throughout the life span (from infant to adult) due to a slow, continuous shaping process (like the tree), or do we go through a series of genetically preprogrammed stages (like the butterfly)?

Many a 20-year-old *goof-off* has matured into a 40-year-old business or cultural leader. To *goof off* means to avoid work and act in a lazy manner; a person who behaves this way is called a *goof-off*. Some traits, such as temperament, are relatively stable over time, but everyone changes in some way with age. Thus, a lazy youth (*20-year-old goof-off*) may develop (*mature*) into a more productive adult (*40-year-old leader*).

Infancy and Childhood

MODULE OVERVIEW

Development continues at a fairly rapid pace in infancy and childhood, although physical growth begins to slow a bit in the middle years of childhood. Module 8 describes physical, cognitive, and social development through age 11, focusing on the stage theory of Piaget and the effects of attachment or lack of attachment on development. Although today's theorists see development as more continuous than Piaget did, his theory continues to provide a broad framework for studying development.

NOTE: Answer guidelines for all Module 8 questions begin on page 97.

MODULE REVIEW

First, skim this section, noting headings and boldface items. After you have read the section, review each objective by completing the sentences and answering the questions that follow it. As you proceed, evaluate your performance by consulting the answers on page 97. Do not continue with the next section until you understand each answer. If you need to, review or reread the section in the textbook before continuing.

> David Myers at times uses idioms that are unfamiliar to some readers. If you do not know the meaning of the following words, phrases, or expressions in the context in which they appear in the text, refer to pages 100–101 for an explanation: *toddler; wild growth spurt; smothering crib death; flop his beret; double take; realizes her "grandmother" is really a wolf; cognitive milestones; concrete demonstrations . . . think for themselves; pit the drawing power; gosling; Mere exposure; mobile sperm banks; footprints on the brain; Parenting styles . . . lax.*

Physical Development (pp. 105–106)

Objective 1: Describe some developmental changes in brain and motor abilities during infancy and childhood, and explain why our earliest memories rarely predate our third birthdays.

1. The developing brain _____ (over/under)produces neurons. At birth, the human nervous system _____ (is/is not) fully mature.

2. Between 3 and 6 years of age, the brain is developing most rapidly in the _____ lobes, which enable _____ _____ . The last cortical areas to develop are the _____ _____ .

3. After puberty, a process of _____ shuts down some neural connections and strengthens others.

4. Biological growth processes that enable orderly changes in behavior are called _____ .

5. Infants pass the milestones of _____ development at different rates, but the basic _____ of stages is fixed. They sit before they _____ and walk before they _____ .

6. Genes play a _____ (major/minor) role in motor development.

7. Until the necessary muscular and neural maturation is complete, including the rapid development of the brain's _____ , experience has a _____ (large/small) effect on behavior.

8. Our earliest memories generally do not occur before age _____ .

9. This phenomenon has been called

   _____ _____ .

Cognitive Development (pp. 107–112)

Objective 2: State Piaget's understanding of how the mind develops, and outline Piaget's four stages of cognitive development, noting current thinking regarding cognitive stages.

1. The first researcher to show that the thought processes of adults and children are very different was _____ .

2. The term for all the mental activities associated with thinking, remembering, communicating, and knowing is _____ .

3. To organize and interpret his or her experiences, the developing child constructs cognitive concepts called _____ .

4. The interpretation of new experiences in terms of existing ideas is called _____ . The adaptation of existing ideas to fit new experiences is called _____ .

5. In Piaget's first stage of development, the _____ stage, children experience the world through their motor and sensory interactions with objects. This stage occurs between infancy and nearly age _____ .

6. The awareness that things continue to exist even when they are removed from view is called

   _____ _____ . This awareness begins to develop at about _____ months of age.

7. Developmental researchers have found that Piaget and his followers _____ (overestimated/underestimated) young children's competence. For instance, babies have

an understanding of _____ , as Karen Wynn demonstrated.

8. According to Piaget, during the preschool years and up to age _____ , children are in the _____ stage.

9. The principle that the quantity of a substance remains the same even when the shape of its container changes is called _____ . Piaget believed that preschoolers _____ (have/have not) developed this concept.

10. Preschoolers have difficulty perceiving things from another person's point of view. This inability is called _____ .

11. The child's growing ability to take another's perspective is evidence that the child is acquiring a

    _____ _____ . Between about 3½ and 4½, children come to realize that others may hold

    _____ _____ .

12. (Close-Up) The disorder characterized by deficient _____ and _____ interaction and an impaired _____ _____ is _____ . This disorder is related to malfunctions of brain areas that enable _____ to others. The "high functioning" form of this disorder is called

    _____ _____ .

13. (Close-Up) A new theory proposes that autism represents an "extreme _____ brain." According to this theory, girls tend to be _____ , who are better than boys at reading facial expressions and gestures. Boys tend to be _____ , who understand things in terms of rules or laws.

14. Piaget believed that children acquire the mental abilities needed to comprehend mathematical transformations and conservation by about _____ years of age. At this time, they enter the _____ _____ stage.

15. Russian psychologist _____ noted that by age _____ children stop

thinking aloud and instead rely on

_____ _____ . When

parents give children words, they provide, according to this theorist, a _____ upon which the child can build higher-level thinking.

16. In Piaget's final stage, the _____

_____ stage, reasoning expands from the purely concrete to encompass

_____ thinking. Piaget believed most children begin to enter this stage by age

_____ .

17. In contrast to Piaget's findings, researchers have discovered that the ability to perform mental

_____ , to think

_____ , and to take another's

_____ develops

_____ (abruptly/gradually) during the preschool years.

Explain briefly how contemporary researchers view Piaget's theory.

Social Development (pp. 113–118)

Objective 3: Discuss the effects of nourishment, body contact, and familiarity on infant social attachment.

1. Soon after _____

_____ emerges and children become mobile, a new fear, called

_____ _____ ,

emerges.

2. This fear emerges at about age _____ .

3. The development of a strong emotional bond between infant and parent is called

_____ .

4. The Harlows' studies of monkeys have shown that mother-infant attachment does not depend on the mother providing nourishment as much as it does on her providing the comfort of

_____ _____ . Another

key to attachment is _____ .

5. Human attachment involves one person providing another with a _____

_____ when distressed and a

_____ _____ from

which to explore.

6. In some animals, attachment will occur only during a restricted time called a

_____ _____ .

Konrad Lorenz discovered that young birds would follow almost any object if it were the first moving thing they observed. This phenomenon is called _____ .

7. Human infants _____ (do/do not) have a precise critical period for becoming attached. However, because of _____

_____ , they attach to what they

know.

Objective 4: Contrast secure and insecure attachment, and discuss the roles of parents and infants in the development of attachment and an infant's feelings of basic trust.

8. Placed in a research setting called the

_____ _____ , children

show one of two patterns of attachment:

_____ attachment or

_____ attachment.

Contrast the responses of securely and insecurely attached infants to strange situations.

Discuss the impact of responsive parenting on infant attachment.

9. A father's love and acceptance for his children are _____ (comparable to/less important than) a mother's love in predicting their children's health and well-being.

10. Separation anxiety peaks in infants around _____ months, then _____ (gradually declines/remains constant for about a year). This is true of children _____ (in North America/throughout the world).

11. According to Erikson, securely attached infants approach life with a sense of _____ _____ .

Objective 5: Assess the impact of parental neglect and different parenting styles on attachment patterns and development.

12. The Harlows found that when monkeys reared in social isolation were placed with other monkeys, they reacted with either fear or _____ .

13. Most abused children _____ (do/do not) later become abusive parents.

14. Although most children who grow up under adversity are _____ and become normal adults, early abuse may alter the development of the brain chemical _____ .

15. Parents who impose rules and expect obedience are exhibiting a(n) _____ style of parenting.

16. Parents who make few demands of their children and tend to submit to their children's desires are identified as _____ parents.

17. Setting and enforcing standards after discussion with their children is the approach taken by _____ parents.

18. Studies have shown that children with high self-esteem, self-restraint, and social competence tend to have _____ parents. Remember, though, that these correlational studies _____ (do/do not) prove causation.

PROGRESS TEST

Circle your answers to the following questions and check them with the answers beginning on page 97. If your answer is incorrect, read the explanation for why it is incorrect and then consult the appropriate pages of the text.

Multiple-Choice Questions

1. In Piaget's stage of concrete operational intelligence, the child acquires an understanding of the principle of:
   a. conservation.   c. attachment.
   b. deduction.   d. object permanence.

2. Piaget held that egocentrism is characteristic of the:
   a. sensorimotor stage.
   b. preoperational stage.
   c. concrete operational stage.
   d. formal operational stage.

3. During which stage of cognitive development do children acquire object permanence?
   a. sensorimotor   c. concrete operational
   b. preoperational   d. formal operational

4. The Harlows' studies of attachment in monkeys showed that:
   a. provision of nourishment was the single most important factor motivating attachment.
   b. a cloth mother produced the greatest attachment response.

c. whether a cloth or wire mother was present mattered less than the presence or absence of other infants.

d. attachment in monkeys is based on imprinting.

5. When psychologists discuss maturation, they are referring to stages of growth that are *not* influenced by:

a. conservation.   c. nurture.
b. nature.   d. continuity.

6. The developmental theorist who suggested that securely attached children develop an attitude of basic trust is:

a. Piaget.   c. Vygotsky.
b. Harlow.   d. Erikson.

7. Research findings on infant motor development are consistent with the idea that:

a. cognitive development lags significantly behind motor skills development.

b. maturation of physical skills is relatively unaffected by experience.

c. in the absence of relevant earlier learning experiences, the emergence of motor skills will be slowed.

d. in humans, the process of maturation may be significantly altered by cultural factors.

8. According to Piaget, the ability to think logically about abstract propositions is indicative of the stage of:

a. preoperational thought.
b. concrete operations.
c. formal operations.
d. sensorimotor thought.

9. Stranger anxiety develops soon after:

a. the concept of conservation.
b. egocentrism.
c. a theory of mind.
d. the concept of object permanence.

10. Before Piaget, people were more likely to believe that:

a. the child's mind is a miniature model of the adult's.

b. children think about the world in radically different ways from adults.

c. the child's mind develops through a series of stages.

d. children interpret their experiences in terms of their current understandings.

11. Which is the correct sequence of stages in Piaget's theory of cognitive development?

a. sensorimotor, preoperational, concrete operational, formal operational

b. sensorimotor, preoperational, formal operational, concrete operational

c. preoperational, sensorimotor, concrete operational, formal operational

d. preoperational, sensorimotor, formal operational, concrete operational

12. The term *critical period* refers to:

a. prenatal development.
b. the initial 2 hours after a child's birth.
c. the preoperational stage.
d. a restricted time for learning.

13. Which of the following was *not* found by the Harlows in socially deprived monkeys?

a. They had difficulty mating.

b. They showed extreme fear or aggression when first seeing other monkeys.

c. They showed abnormal physical development.

d. The females were abusive mothers.

14. Most people's earliest memories do not predate _____ of age.

a. 6 months   c. 2 years
b. 1 year   d. 3 years

15. Insecurely attached infants who are left by their mothers in an unfamiliar setting often will:

a. hold fast to their mothers on their return.

b. explore the new surroundings confidently.

c. be indifferent toward their mothers on their return.

d. display little emotion at any time.

16. Compared to when he was younger, 4-year-old Antonio is better able to empathize with his friend's feelings. This growing ability to take another's perspective indicates that Antonio is acquiring a:

a. self-concept.   c. temperament.
b. schema.   d. theory of mind.

17. Calvin, who is trying to impress his psychology professor with his knowledge of infant motor development, asks why some infants learn to roll over before they lift their heads from a prone position, while others develop these skills in the opposite order. What should Calvin's professor conclude from this question?

    a. Calvin clearly understands that the sequence of motor development is not the same for all infants.
    b. Calvin doesn't know what he's talking about. Although some infants reach these developmental milestones ahead of others, the order is the same for all infants.
    c. Calvin needs to be reminded that rolling over is an inherited reflex, not a learned skill.
    d. Calvin understands an important principle: motor development is unpredictable.

18. As a child observes, liquid is transferred from a tall, thin tube into a short, wide jar. The child is asked if there is now less liquid in order to determine if she has mastered:

    a. the schema for liquids.
    b. the concept of object permanence.
    c. the concept of conservation.
    d. the ability to reason abstractly.

19. I am 14 months old and fearful of strangers. I am in Piaget's _____ stage of cognitive development.

    a. sensorimotor   c. concrete operational
    b. preoperational   d. formal operational

20. I am 3 years old, can use language, and have trouble taking another person's perspective. I am in Piaget's ____ stage of cognitive development.

    a. sensorimotor   c. concrete operational
    b. preoperational   d. formal operational

21. In Piaget's theory, conservation is to egocentrism as the _____ stage is to the _____ stage.

    a. sensorimotor; formal operational
    b. formal operational; sensorimotor
    c. preoperational; sensorimotor
    d. concrete operational; preoperational

22. Four-year-old Jamail has a younger sister. When asked if he has a sister, he is likely to answer _____ ; when asked if his sister has a brother, Jamail is likely to answer _____ .

    a. yes; yes   c. yes; no
    b. no; no   d. no; yes

23. In a 1998 movie, a young girl finds that a gaggle of geese follow her wherever she goes because she was the first "object" they saw after they were born. This is an example of:

    a. conservation.   c. egocentrism.
    b. imprinting.   d. basic trust.

24. Joshua and Ann Bishop have a 13-month-old boy. According to Erikson, the Bishops' sensitive, loving care of their child contributes to their child's:

    a. sense of basic trust.
    b. secure attachment.
    c. sense of control.
    d. moral development.

True–False Items

Indicate whether each statement is true or false by placing *T* or *F* in the blank next to the item.

_____ 1. Most abused children later become abusive parents.
_____ 2. At birth, the brain and nervous system of a healthy child are fully developed.
_____ 3. The sequence in which children develop motor skills varies from one culture to another.
_____ 4. Research shows that young children are more capable and development is more continuous than Piaget believed.

KEY TERMS

Using your own words, on a piece of paper write a brief definition or explanation of each of the following terms.

1. maturation
2. cognition
3. schema
4. assimilation
5. accommodation
6. sensorimotor stage
7. object permanence
8. preoperational stage
9. conservation
10. egocentrism
11. theory of mind
12. concrete operational stage
13. formal operational stage
14. autism

15. stranger anxiety
16. attachment
17. critical period
18. imprinting
19. basic trust

ANSWERS

Module Review

Physical Development

1. over; is not
2. frontal; rational planning; association areas
3. pruning
4. maturation
5. motor; sequence; crawl; run
6. major
7. cerebellum; small
8. 3
9. infantile amnesia

Cognitive Development

1. Piaget
2. cognition
3. schemas
4. assimilation; accommodation
5. sensorimotor; 2
6. object permanence; 8
7. underestimated; numbers
8. 6 or 7; preoperational
9. conservation; have not
10. egocentrism
11. theory of mind; false beliefs
12. communication; social; theory of mind; autism; attending; Asperger syndrome
13. male; empathizers; systemizers
14. 6 or 7; concrete operational
15. Lev Vygotsky; 7; inner speech; scaffold
16. formal operational; abstract; 12
17. operations; symbolically; perspective; gradually

Contemporary researchers see development as more continuous than did Piaget. By detecting the beginnings of each type of thinking at earlier ages, they have revealed conceptual abilities that Piaget missed. They also see formal logic as a smaller part of cognition than Piaget did. Despite these revisions to Piaget's theory, studies support the basic idea that cognitive development unfolds as a sequence of distinct stages.

Social Development

1. object permanence; stranger anxiety
2. 8 months
3. attachment
4. body contact; familiarity
5. safe haven; secure base
6. critical period; imprinting
7. do not; mere exposure
8. strange situation; secure; insecure

Placed in a strange situation, securely attached infants play comfortably, happily exploring their new environment. In contrast, insecurely attached infants are less likely to explore their surroundings and may even cling to their mothers. When separated from their mothers, insecurely attached infants are much more distressed than securely attached infants. When reunited with their mothers, insecurely attached infants may be indifferent.

Research studies conducted by Mary Ainsworth have revealed that sensitive, responsive mothers tend to have securely attached infants, whereas insensitive, unresponsive mothers often have insecurely attached infants. Other studies have found that temperamentally difficult infants whose mothers receive training in responsive parenting are more likely to become securely attached than are control infants. This points to the importance of considering the infant's temperament in studying attachment.

9. comparable to
10. 13; gradually declines; throughout the world
11. basic trust
12. aggression
13. do not
14. resilient; serotonin
15. authoritarian
16. permissive
17. authoritative
18. authoritative; do not

Progress Test

Multiple-Choice Questions

1. **a.** is the answer.
   b. Deduction, or deductive reasoning, is a formal operational ability.
   c. Piaget's theory is not concerned with attachment.

d. Attaining object permanence is the hallmark of sensorimotor thought.

2. b. is the answer. The preoperational child sees the world from his or her own vantage point.
a. As immature as egocentrism is, it represents a significant cognitive advance over the sensorimotor child, who knows the world only through senses and actions. Even simple self-awareness takes a while to develop.
c. & d. As children attain the operational stages, they become more able to see the world through the eyes of others.

3. a. is the answer. Before object permanence is attained, "out of sight" is truly "out of mind."
b., c., & d. Developments during the preoperational, concrete operational, and formal operational stages include the use of language, conservation, and abstract reasoning, respectively.

4. b. is the answer.
a. When given the choice between a wire mother with a bottle and a cloth mother without, the monkeys preferred the cloth mother.
c. The presence of other infants made no difference.
d. Imprinting plays no role in the attachment of higher primates.

5. c. is the answer. Through maturation—an orderly sequence of biological growth processes that are relatively unaffected by experience—all humans develop.
a. Conservation is the cognitive awareness that objects do not change with changes in shape.
b. The forces of nature *are* those that direct maturation.
d. The continuity/stages debate has to do with whether development is a gradual and continuous process or a discontinuous, stagelike process. Those who emphasize maturation see development as occurring in stages, not continuously.

6. d. is the answer. Erikson proposed that development occurs in a series of stages, in the first of which the child develops an attitude of either basic trust or mistrust.
a. Piaget's theory is concerned with cognitive development.
b. Harlow conducted research on attachment and deprivation.
c. Vygotsky focused on the influence of social factors on cognitive development.

7. b. is the answer.

8. c. is the answer. Once formal operational thought has been attained, thinking is no longer limited to concrete propositions.

a. & b. Preoperational thought and concrete operational thought emerge before, and do not include, the ability to think logically about abstract propositions.
d. Sensorimotor thought is the first of Piaget's stages, in which the infant experiences his or her world through senses and action.

9. d. is the answer. With object permanence, a child develops schemas for familiar objects, including faces, and may become upset by a stranger who does not fit any of these schemas.
a. The concept of conservation develops during the concrete operational stage, whereas stranger anxiety develops during the sensorimotor stage.
b. & c. Egocentrism and a theory of mind both develop during the preoperational stage. This follows the sensorimotor stage, during which stranger anxiety develops.

10. a. is the answer.
b., c., & d. Each of these is an understanding developed by Piaget.

11. a. is the answer.

12. d. is the answer. A critical period is a restricted time during which an organism must be exposed to certain influences or experiences for a particular kind of learning to occur.
a. Critical periods refer to developmental periods after birth.
b. Critical periods vary from behavior to behavior, but they are not confined to the hours following birth.
c. Critical periods are not specifically associated with the preoperational period.

13. c. is the answer. Deprived monkeys were impaired in their social behaviors but not in their physical development.
a., b., & d. Each of these was found in socially deprived monkeys.

14. d. is the answer.

15. c. is the answer.
a. Insecurely attached infants often cling to their mothers when placed in a new situation; yet, when the mother returns after an absence, the infant's reaction tends to be one of indifference.
b. These behaviors are characteristic of securely attached infants.
d. Insecurely attached infants in unfamiliar surroundings will often exhibit a range of emotional behaviors.

16. d. is the answer.

17. b. is the answer.

a. & d. Although the rate of motor development varies from child to child, the basic sequence is universal and, therefore, predictable.

c. Rolling over and head lifting are both learned.

18. **c.** is the answer. This test is designed to determine if the child understands that the quantity of liquid is conserved, despite the shift to a container that is different in shape.

   a. These are general processes related to concept building.

   b. Object permanence is the concept that an object continues to exist even when not perceived; in this case, the water is perceived throughout the experiment.

   d. This experiment does not require abstract reasoning, only the ability to reason logically about the concrete.

19. **a.** is the answer. This child's age and stranger anxiety clearly place him within Piaget's sensorimotor stage.

20. **b.** is the answer. This child's age, ability to use language, and egocentrism clearly place her within Piaget's preoperational stage.

21. **d.** is the answer. Conservation is a hallmark of the concrete operational stage; egocentrism is a hallmark of the preoperational stage.

22. **c.** is the answer. Being 4 years old, Jamail would be in Piaget's preoperational stage. Preoperational thinking is egocentric, which means Jamail would find it difficult to "put himself in his sister's shoes" and perceive that she has a brother.

23. **b.** is the answer.

   a. Conservation is the ability to realize that the amount of an object does not change even if its shape changes.

   c. Egocentrism is having difficulty perceiving things from another's perspective.

   d. According to Erikson, basic trust is feeling that the world is safe as a result of sensitive, loving caregivers.

24. **a.** is the answer. Although loving parents will also produce securely attached children, Erikson's theory deals with trust or mistrust.

   c. Control is not a factor in this stage of Erikson's theory.

   d. Moral development is not part of Erikson's theory.

True–False Items

1. F		**3.** F	
2. F		**4.** T	

Key Terms

1. **Maturation** refers to the biological growth processes that enable orderly changes in behavior, relatively uninfluenced by experience or other environmental factors.

   Example: The ability to walk depends on a certain level of neural and muscular **maturation**. For this reason, until the toddler's body is physically ready to walk, practice "walking" has little effect.

2. **Cognition** refers to all the mental processes associated with thinking, knowing, remembering, and communicating.

3. In Piaget's theory of cognitive development, **schemas** are mental concepts or frameworks that organize and interpret information.

4. In Piaget's theory, **assimilation** refers to interpreting a new experience in terms of an existing schema.

5. In Piaget's theory, **accommodation** refers to changing an existing schema to incorporate new information that cannot be assimilated.

6. In Piaget's theory of cognitive stages, the **sensorimotor stage** lasts from birth to about age 2. During this stage, infants gain knowledge of the world through their senses and their motor activities.

7. **Object permanence,** which develops during the sensorimotor stage, is the awareness that things do not cease to exist when not perceived.

8. In Piaget's theory, the **preoperational stage** lasts from about 2 to 6 or 7 years of age. During this stage, language development is rapid, but the child is unable to understand the mental operations of concrete logic.

9. **Conservation** is the principle that properties such as number, volume, and mass remain constant despite changes in the forms of objects; it is acquired during the concrete operational stage.

10. In Piaget's theory, **egocentrism** refers to the difficulty that preoperational children have in considering another's viewpoint. *Ego* means "self," and *centrism* indicates "in the center"; the preoperational child is "self-centered."

11. Our ideas about our own and others' thoughts, feelings, and perceptions and the behaviors these might predict constitute our **theory of mind**.

12. During the **concrete operational stage,** lasting from about ages 6 or 7 to 11, children can think logically about concrete events and objects.

13. In Piaget's theory, the **formal operational stage** normally begins about age 12. During this stage people begin to think logically about abstract concepts.

    Memory aid: To help differentiate Piaget's stages remember that "operations" are mental transformations. *Pre*operational children, who lack the ability to perform transformations, are "before" this developmental milestone. Concrete operational children can operate on real, or concrete, objects. Formal operational children can perform logical transformations on abstract concepts.

14. **Autism** is a disorder that appears in childhood and is marked by deficient communication, social interaction, and understanding of others' states of mind.

15. **Stranger anxiety** is the fear of strangers that infants begin to display by about 8 months of age.

16. **Attachment** is an emotional tie with another person, shown in young children by their seeking closeness to a caregiver and showing distress on separation.

17. A **critical period** is a limited time shortly after birth during which an organism must be exposed to certain stimuli or experiences if it is to develop properly.

18. **Imprinting** is the process by which certain animals form attachments during a limited critical period early in life.

19. According to Erikson, **basic trust** is a sense that the world is predictable and trustworthy—a concept that infants form if their needs are met by responsive caregiving.

FOCUS ON VOCABULARY AND LANGUAGE

Introduction

. . . *toddler* . . . This describes a child who is beginning to learn to walk and who walks with short, uneven steps.

Physical Development

After birth, the neural networks that eventually enabled you to walk, talk, and remember had a *wild growth spurt*. Myers points out that when you were born, you had all the brain cells that you will ever have. But after birth there is a very rapid development (*a wild growth spurt*) in the number of connections between neurons.

. . . *smothering crib death* . . . When it's time for sleep, parents usually put their babies in small beds with high sides (*cribs*). If babies sleep face down, they may not be able to breathe properly and could suffocate (a *smothering crib death*). However, the recommendation that babies sleep face up on their backs (*back-to-sleep position*) has been associated with somewhat later crawling (moving on hands and knees) but not with later walking.

Cognitive Development

In one test, Piaget showed an infant an appealing toy and then *flopped his beret over it* to see whether the infant would search for it. When Piaget tested object permanence, he showed the child an attractive toy and then covered it with his soft round hat (*he flopped his beret over it*). Very young babies do not

search for the hidden toy—when they can't see it, they don't appear to think about it (*what is out of sight is out of mind*).

When she lifted the screen, the infants sometimes *did a double take*, staring longer when shown a wrong number of objects. In this experiment with 5-month-old infants, Karen Wynn showed that these very young children were capable of conceptual thinking. She did this by measuring their reaction time to expected and unexpected outcomes. Shown an impossible outcome, infants stared longer (*they did a double take*) and they also demonstrated a mental capacity for detecting changes or differences in the frequency of events (*they have a head for numbers*).

When Little Red Riding Hood realizes her "*grandmother*" *is really a wolf,* she swiftly revises her ideas about the creature's intentions and races away. Preschoolers gradually begin to understand that other people have mental capacities, intentions, motivations, feelings, etc. (*children form a theory of mind*). This is illustrated when the young girl in the children's story called *Little Red Riding Hood* recognizes that the big bad wolf (disguised as her grandmother) has very bad intentions toward her, and she quickly escapes (*races away*).

. . . *cognitive milestones* . . . A milestone is an event of significance or importance. (Originally, a milestone was a large stone by the roadside inscribed with the distance in miles to nearby towns.) Myers notes that the age at which children usually succeed at important mental tasks (*cognitive milestones*) is of less relevance than the developmental order or sequence in which these abilities appear.

Better to *build on* what they [children] already know, engaging them in *concrete demonstrations* and stimulating them to *think for themselves*. Preschool and elementary school children think differently from adults. In order for them to become independent thinkers (*think for themselves*), Piaget recommends that they be given specific, tangible examples (*concrete demonstrations*) that utilize (*build on*) their existing knowledge.

Social Development

To pit the drawing power of a food source against the contact comfort of the blanket, they created two artificial mothers. The Harlows' experiment was designed to test whether food or nourishment was more rewarding than the comfort of a soft terry cloth. Thus, when they tested the attraction (*pitted the drawing power*) of the artificial mother who supplied food against the soft comfort of the terry cloth mother (*contact comfort*), they were surprised that the monkeys preferred the cloth mother. They used "her" as a *secure base* from which to explore and a safe place (*safe haven*) to return to when frightened or anxious.

For *goslings, ducklings, or chicks,* that period falls in the hours shortly after *hatching* when the first moving object they see is normally their mother. A *gosling* is a young goose, a *duckling* a young duck, and a *chick* a young chicken. What all these young fowl have in common is a tendency to follow, or trail after, the first larger moving object they see shortly after they emerge (*hatch*) from the eggshell. This attachment process is called **imprinting**.

Mere exposure to people and things fosters *fondness*. Children do not imprint in the same way that duck-

lings and other animals do; nevertheless, repeated encounters with (or *exposure to*) other humans and objects encourage or promote liking and attachment (*fosters fondness*). As Myers puts it, "familiarity breeds content." This is a twist on the old saying "familiarity breeds contempt" and suggests that intimacy creates (*breeds*) satisfaction (*contentment*) rather than scorn (*contempt*).

But fathers are more than just *mobile sperm banks.* A *sperm bank* is where donated sperm is stored until it is used for artificial insemination. More and more research shows that fathers are not simply sperm producers who can move around (*mobile sperm banks*) and get mothers pregnant. Rather, evidence suggests they are capable caregivers who may interact with their babies much as mothers do.

. . . can leave *footprints* on the brain. Traumatic experiences that occur early in development can have an effect on brain functioning; metaphorically, they can leave impressions (*footprints*) on the brain. The production of neurotransmitters such as serotonin, which calms aggressive impulses, is slower (*sluggish*) in abused children who become aggressive teens and adults.

Parenting styles vary. Some parents *spank*, some *reason.* Some are *strict*, some are *lax.* When it comes to child-rearing practices (*parenting styles*), there is much variability: (a) some parents use strict controls and physical punishment (*spanking*); (b) others talk and discuss problems and issues with their children (*reason with them*); and (c) still others allow the children to do what they want and make few demands of them (*they are lax*). Myers identifies these parenting styles as (a) *authoritarian*, (b) *authoritative*, and (c) *permissive.*

Adolescence

MODULE OVERVIEW

Adolescence begins with the sexual maturity of puberty and ends with the social independence of emerging adulthood. Module 9 details the physical, cognitive, and social development of this period that has variously been referred to as a time of "storm and stress" and as a time of exciting discoveries and new possibilities. In discussing cognitive development, the module focuses on Kohlberg's theory of moral reasoning, pointing out both its strengths and its weaknesses, and on Erikson's psychosocial stages of development.

NOTE: Answer guidelines for all Module 9 questions begin on page 108.

MODULE REVIEW

First, skim this section, noting headings and boldface items. After you have read the section, review each objective by completing the sentences and answering the questions that follow it. As you proceed, evaluate your performance by consulting the answers on page 108. Do not continue with the next section until you understand each answer. If you need to, review or reread the section in the textbook before continuing.

> David Myers at times uses idioms that are unfamiliar to some readers. If you do not know the meaning of the following words, phrases, or expressions in the context in which they appear in the text, refer to pages 110–111 for an explanation: *morphing; pays dividends; out of sync; intellectual summit; character—the psychological muscles for controlling impulses; moral ladder; throw a switch; psychosocial task; forge their identity; emotional ties with parents loosen.*

Introduction and Physical Development
(pp. 120–122)

Objective 1: Define *adolescence,* and identify the major physical changes that occur during this period.

1. Adolescence is defined as the transition period between _____ and

   _____ .

2. The "storm and stress" view of adolescence is credited to _____ , one of the first American psychologists to describe adolescence.

3. Adolescence begins with the time of developing sexual maturity known as _____ . A two-year period of rapid physical development begins in girls at about the age of _____ and in boys at about the age of _____ . This growth spurt is marked by the development of the reproductive organs and external genitalia, or _____ _____ characteristics, as well as by the development of traits such as pubic hair and enlarged breasts in females and facial hair in males. These nonreproductive traits are known as _____ _____ characteristics.

4. The first menstrual period is called _____ . In boys, the first ejaculation is called _____ .

5. The _____ (timing/sequence) of pubertal changes is more predictable than their _____ (timing/sequence).

6. Boys who mature _____ (early/late) tend to be more popular, self-assured, and independent; they also are at increased risk for _____

   _____ .

   For girls, _____ (early/late) maturation can be stressful, especially when their bodies are out of sync with their _____

   _____ . This reminds us that

   _____ and _____

   interact.

7. Within the adolescent brain, the continuing growth of the fatty issue _____ around _____ helps speed neurotransmission. Also, teens' occasional impulsiveness and risky behaviors may be due, in part, to the fact that development in the brain's

   _____ _____ lags

   behind that of the _____

   _____ .

Cognitive Development (pp. 122–124)

Objective 2: Describe adolescents' reasoning abilities and moral development, according to Piaget and Kohlberg.

1. Adolescents' developing ability to reason gives them a new ability to think about what is _____ possible.

2. During the early teen years, reasoning is often _____ , as adolescents often feel their experiences are unique.

3. Piaget's final stage of cognitive development is the stage of _____

   _____ . The adolescent in this stage is capable of thinking logically about

   _____ as well as concrete propositions. This enables them to detect

   _____ in others' reasoning and to spot hypocrisy.

4. The theorist who proposed that moral thought progresses through stages is _____ . These stages are divided into three basic levels:

   _____ , _____ , and

   _____ .

5. In the preconventional stages of morality, characteristic of children, the emphasis is on obeying rules in order to avoid _____ or gain

   _____ .

6. Conventional morality usually emerges by early _____ . The emphasis is on gaining social _____ or upholding the social

   _____ .

7. Individuals who base moral judgments on their own perceptions of basic ethical principles are said by Kohlberg to employ _____ morality.

Summarize the criticisms of Kohlberg's theory of moral development.

8. Morality involves doing the right thing, and what we do depends on _____ influences. Today's _____

   _____ _____ focus on moral issues and doing the right thing.

9. Children who learn to delay _____ become more socially responsible, often engaging in responsible action through _____ learning. They also become more _____ successful and productive.

Social Development (pp. 124–127)

Objective 3: Identify Erikson's eight stages of psychosocial development and their accompanying issues.

Complete the missing information in the following table of Erikson's stages of psychosocial development.

Group Age	Psychosocial Stage
Infancy	_____
_____	Autonomy vs. shame and doubt
Preschooler	_____
_____	Competence vs. inferiority
Adolescence	_____
_____	Intimacy vs. isolation
Middle adulthood	_____
_____	Integrity vs. despair

1. To refine their sense of identity, adolescents in Western cultures experiment with different _____ in different situations. The result may be role _____ , which is resolved by forming a self-definition, or _____ .

2. Cultures that place less value on _____ inform adolescents about who they are, rather than letting them decide on their own. Some adolescents may form an identity defined in _____ to parents.

3. During the early to mid-teen years, self-esteem generally _____ (rises/falls/remains stable). During the late teens and twenties, self-esteem generally _____ (rises/falls/remains stable).

4. Erikson saw the formation of identity as a prerequisite for the development of _____ in young adulthood.

Objective 4: Contrast parental and peer influences during adolescence.

5. Adolescence is typically a time of increasing influence from one's _____ and decreasing influence from _____ .

6. Most adolescents report that they _____ (do/do not) get along with their parents. They see their parents as having the most influence in shaping their _____ _____ , for example.

7. When rejected adolescents withdraw, they are vulnerable to _____ , low _____ , and _____ .

Objective 5: Discuss the characteristics of emerging adulthood.

8. In earlier times, society marked the transition to adulthood with an elaborate initiation called a public _____ _____ _____ . As a result of increased _____ _____ and weakened _____-_____ bonds, sexual maturity is beginning _____ (earlier/later) than in the past.

9. Because the time from 18 to the mid-twenties is increasingly a not-yet-settled phase of life, some psychologists refer to this period as a time of _____ _____ .

PROGRESS TEST

Circle your answers to the following questions and check them with the answers beginning on page 108. If your answer is incorrect, read the explanation for why it is incorrect and then consult the appropriate pages of the text.

Multiple-Choice Questions

1. According to Erikson, the central psychological challenges pertaining to adolescence, young adulthood, and middle age, respectively, are:
   a. identity formation; intimacy; generativity.
   b. intimacy; identity formation; generativity.
   c. generativity; intimacy; identity formation.
   d. intimacy; generativity; identity formation.

2. In preconventional morality, the person:
   a. obeys out of a sense of social duty.
   b. conforms to gain social approval.
   c. obeys to avoid punishment or to gain concrete rewards.
   d. follows the dictates of his or her conscience.

3. Which of the following is correct?
   a. Early maturation places both boys and girls at a distinct social advantage.
   b. Early maturing girls are more popular and self-assured than girls who mature late.
   c. Early maturation places both boys and girls at a distinct social disadvantage.
   d. Early maturing boys are more popular and self-assured than boys who mature late.

4. Among the hallmarks of growing up are a boy's first ejaculation and a girl's first menstrual period, which also is called:
   a. puberty.   c. menarche.
   b. spermarche.   d. generativity.

5. The average age at which puberty begins is _____ in boys; in girls, it is _____ .
   a. 14; 13   c. 11; 10
   b. 13; 11   d. 10; 9

6. After puberty, the self-concept usually becomes:
   a. more positive in boys.
   b. more positive in girls.
   c. more positive in both boys and girls.
   d. more negative in both boys and girls.

7. Adolescence is marked by the onset of:
   a. an identity crisis.
   b. parent-child conflict.
   c. the concrete operational stage.
   d. puberty.

8. Whose stage theory of moral development was based on how people reasoned about ethical dilemmas?
   a. Erikson   c. Hall
   b. Piaget   d. Kohlberg

9. To which of Kohlberg's levels would moral reasoning based on the existence of fundamental human rights pertain?
   a. preconventional morality
   b. conventional morality
   c. postconventional morality
   d. generative morality

10. In Erikson's theory, individuals generally focus on developing _____ during adolescence and then _____ during young adulthood.
    a. identity; intimacy
    b. intimacy; identity
    c. basic trust; identity
    d. identity; basic trust

11. Based on the text discussion of maturation and popularity, who among the following is probably the most popular sixth grader?
    a. Jessica, the most physically mature girl in the class
    b. Roger, the most intellectually mature boy in the class
    c. Rob, the tallest, most physically mature boy in the class
    d. Cindy, who is average in physical development and is on the school debating team

12. Fourteen-year-old Cassandra feels freer and more open with her friends than with her family. Knowing this is the case, Cassandra's parents should:
    a. be concerned, because deteriorating parent-teen relationships, such as this one, are often followed by a range of problem behaviors.
    b. encourage Cassandra to find new friends.
    c. seek family counseling.
    d. not worry, since adolescence is typically a time of growing peer influence and diminishing parental influence.

13. Thirteen-year-old Irene has no trouble defeating her 11-year-old brother at a detective game that requires following clues in order to deduce the perpetrator of a crime. How might Piaget explain Irene's superiority at the game?

   a. Being older, Irene has had more years of schooling.

   b. Girls develop intellectually at a faster rate than boys.

   c. Being an adolescent, Irene is beginning to develop abstract reasoning skills.

   d. Girls typically have more experience than boys at playing games.

14. Which of the following was *not* mentioned in the text as a criticism of Kohlberg's theory of moral development?

   a. It does not account for the fact that the development of moral reasoning is culture-specific.

   b. Postconventional morality appears mostly in educated, middle-class persons.

   c. The theory is biased against the moral reasoning of people in communal societies such as China.

   d. The theory is biased in favor of moral reasoning in men.

15. Sam, a junior in high school, regularly attends church because his family and friends think he should. Which stage of moral reasoning is Sam in?

   a. preconventional

   b. conventional

   c. postconventional

   d. too little information to tell

16. Research on social relationships between parents and their adolescent children shows that:

   a. parental influence on children increases during adolescence.

   b. high school girls who have the most affectionate relationships with their mothers tend to enjoy the most intimate friendships with girlfriends.

   c. high school boys who have the most affectionate relationships with their fathers tend to enjoy the most intimate friendships with friends.

   d. most teens are strongly influenced by parents in matters of personal taste.

17. After a series of unfulfilling relationships, 30-year-old Carlos tells a friend that he doesn't want to marry because he is afraid of losing his freedom and independence. Erikson would say that Carlos is having difficulty with the psychosocial task of:

   a. trust versus mistrust.

   b. autonomy versus doubt.

   c. intimacy versus isolation.

   d. identity versus role confusion.

Essay Question

Sheryl is 12 years old and in the sixth grade. Describe the developmental changes she is likely to be experiencing according to Piaget, Kohlberg, and Erikson. (Use the space below to list the points you want to make, and organize them. Then write the essay on a separate sheet of paper.)

KEY TERMS

Using your own words, on a piece of paper write a brief definition or explanation of each of the following terms.

1. adolescence

2. puberty

3. primary sex characteristics

4. secondary sex characteristics

5. menarche

6. identity

7. intimacy

ANSWERS

Module Review

Introduction and Physical Development

1. childhood; adulthood
2. G. Stanley Hall
3. puberty; 11; 13; primary sex; secondary sex
4. menarche; spermarche
5. sequence; timing
6. early; alcohol use and premature sexual activity; early; emotional maturity; heredity; environment
7. myelin; axons; frontal lobe; limbic system

Cognitive Development

1. ideally
2. self-focused
3. formal operations; abstract; inconsistencies
4. Kohlberg; preconventional; conventional; postconventional
5. punishment; rewards
6. adolescence; approval; order
7. postconventional

Critics of Kohlberg's theory argue that the perception of postconventional moral reasoning as the highest level of moral development reflects a Western middle-class bias. Others have argued that for women, morality is less a matter of abstract, impersonal justice and more an ethic of caring relationships.

8. social; character education programs
9. gratification; service; academically

Social Development

Erikson's stages of psychosocial development

Group Age	Psychosocial Stage
Infancy	Trust vs. mistrust
Toddlerhood	Autonomy vs. shame and doubt
Preschooler	Initiative vs. guilt
Elementary school	Competence vs. inferiority
Adolescence	Identity vs. role confusion
Young adulthood	Intimacy vs. isolation
Middle adulthood	Generativity vs. stagnation
Late adulthood	Integrity vs. despair

1. selves; confusion; identity
2. individualism; opposition
3. falls; rises
4. intimacy
5. peers; parents
6. do; religious faith
7. loneliness; self-esteem; depression
8. rite of passage; body fat; parent-child; earlier
9. emerging adulthood

Progress Test

Multiple-Choice Questions

1. **a.** is the answer.
2. **c.** is the answer. At the preconventional level, moral reasoning centers on self-interest, whether this means obtaining rewards or avoiding punishment.
   a. & b. Moral reasoning based on a sense of social duty or a desire to gain social approval is associated with the conventional level of moral development.
   d. Reasoning based on ethical principles is characteristic of the postconventional level of moral development.
3. **d.** is the answer. Boys who show early physical maturation are generally stronger and more athletic than boys who mature late; these qualities may lead to greater popularity and self-assurance.
   a. & c. Early maturation tends to be socially advantageous for boys but not for girls.
   b. Early maturing girls often suffer embarrassment and are objects of teasing.
4. **c.** is the answer.
   a. Puberty refers to the early adolescent period during which accelerated growth and sexual maturation occur, not to the first menstrual period.
   b. Spermarche is the boy's first ejaculation.
   d. In Erikson's theory, generativity, or the sense of contributing and being productive, is the task of middle adulthood.
5. **b.** is the answer.
6. **c.** is the answer. Because the late teen years provide many new opportunities for trying out possible roles, adolescents' identities typically incorporate an increasingly positive self-concept.
7. **d.** is the answer. The physical changes of puberty mark the onset of adolescence.

a. & b. An identity crisis or parent-child conflict may or may not occur during adolescence; neither of these formally marks its onset.

c. Formal operational thought, rather than concrete reasoning, typically develops in adolescence.

8. **d.** is the answer.

a. Erikson is known for his theory of psychosocial development.

b. Piaget is known for his theory of cognitive development.

c. Hall categorized adolescence as a period of "storm and stress."

9. **c.** is the answer.

a. Preconventional morality is based on avoiding punishment and obtaining rewards.

b. Conventional morality is based on gaining the approval of others and/or on following the law and social convention.

d. There is no such thing as generative morality.

10. **a.** is the answer.

b. According to Erikson, identity develops before intimacy.

c. & d. The formation of basic trust is the task of infancy.

11. **c.** is the answer. Early maturing boys tend to be more popular.

a. Early maturing girls may temporarily suffer embarrassment and be the objects of teasing.

b. & d. The social benefits of early or late maturation are based on physical development, not on cognitive skills.

12. **d.** is the answer.

a. This description of Cassandra's feelings does not suggest that her relationship with her parents is deteriorating. Cassandra's social development, like that of most adolescents, is coming under increasing peer influence and diminishing parental influence.

b. & c. Because Cassandra's feelings are normal, there is no reason for her to change her circle of friends or for her parents to seek counseling.

13. **c.** is the answer.

a., b., & d. Piaget did not link cognitive ability to amount of schooling, gender, or differences in how boys and girls are socialized.

14. **a.** is the answer. Children in various cultures do seem to progress through Kohlberg's preconventional and conventional levels, which indicates that some aspects of the development of moral reasoning are universal.

15. **b.** is the answer. Conventional morality is based in part on a desire to gain others' approval.

a. Preconventional reasoning is based on external incentives such as gaining a reward or avoiding punishment.

c. Postconventional morality reflects an affirmation of agreed-upon rights or universal ethical principles.

d. Fear of others' disapproval is one of the bases of conventional moral reasoning.

16. **b.** is the answer.

a. In fact, just the opposite is true: parental influence on children *decreases* during adolescence.

d. Teens reflect their parents' social, political, and religious views, but rely on peers for matters of personal taste.

17. **c.** is the answer. Carlos' age and struggle to form a close relationship place him squarely in this stage.

a. Trust versus mistrust is the psychosocial task of infancy.

b. Autonomy versus doubt is the psychosocial task of toddlerhood.

d. Identity versus role confusion is the psychosocial task of adolescence.

Essay Question

Sheryl's age would place her at the threshold of Piaget's stage of formal operations. Although her thinking is probably still somewhat self-focused, Sheryl is becoming capable of abstract, logical thought. This will increasingly allow her to reason hypothetically and deductively. Because her logical thinking also enables her to detect inconsistencies in others' reasoning and between their ideals and actions, Sheryl and her parents may be having some heated debates about now.

According to Kohlberg, Sheryl is probably at the threshold of postconventional morality. When she was younger, Sheryl probably abided by rules in order to gain social approval, or simply because "rules are rules" (conventional morality). Now that she is older, Sheryl's moral reasoning will increasingly be based on her own personal code of ethics and an affirmation of people's agreed-upon rights. Because she is a woman, her morality may be more concerned with caring about relationships.

According to Erikson, psychosocial development occurs in eight stages, each of which focuses on a particular task. As an adolescent, Sheryl's psychosocial task is to develop a sense of self by testing roles, then integrating them to form a single identity. Erikson called this stage "identity versus role confusion."

Key Terms

1. **Adolescence** refers to the life stage from puberty to independent adulthood, denoted physically by a growth spurt and maturation of primary and secondary sex characteristics, cognitively by the onset of formal operational thought, and socially by the formation of identity.

2. **Puberty** is the early adolescent period of sexual maturation, during which a person becomes capable of reproduction.

3. The **primary sex characteristics** are the body structures (ovaries, testes, and external genitalia) that enable reproduction.

4. The **secondary sex characteristics** are the nonreproductive sexual characteristics, for example, female breasts, male voice quality, and body hair.

5. **Menarche** is the first menstrual period.

6. In Erikson's theory, establishing an **identity**, or one's sense of self, is the primary task of adolescence.

7. In Erikson's theory, **intimacy**, or the ability to establish close, loving relationships, is the primary task of late adolescence and early adulthood.

FOCUS ON VOCABULARY AND LANGUAGE

Adolescence—the years spent *morphing* from child to adult—. . . The time period between the end of childhood and the beginning of adulthood involves many social and biological changes; the person is transformed (*morphed*) from one type of entity (a child) to something quite different (an adult).

Physical Development

For boys, early maturation *pays dividends*. If onset of puberty occurs before the expected or usual time (*early maturation*), it will be much less stressful for boys than for girls. In general, for boys in their early teen years, being stronger and more athletic leads to more self-assurance, greater popularity, and greater independence (*it pays dividends*).

If a young girl's body is *out of sync* with her own emotional maturity and her friends' physical development and experiences, she may begin associating with older adolescents or may suffer teasing or sexual harassment. *Sync* is an abbreviation of *synchronize*, which means to occur at the same time. So, if a girl's biological development is not proceeding at the same rate (*out of sync*) with her emotional and social development, she may start fraternizing (*associating*) with and imitating the behavior of older girls. Thus, early maturation can be a problem for girls, especially if the people around them react in an inappropriate or suggestive manner to their physical development (*sexual harassment*) or make fun of them (*tease them*).

Cognitive Development

Gradually, though, most achieve the *intellectual summit* that Piaget called *formal operations*. The *formal operational* stage is the highest level in Piaget's theory of cognitive development (*intellectual summit*). Most adolescents reach this stage and are capable of logical and abstract reasoning. For example, many think about (*ponder*) and discuss (*debate*) such issues as good and evil, truth and justice, and other abstract topics about human nature.

A crucial task of childhood and adolescence is discerning right from wrong and developing *character—the psychological muscles for controlling impulses*. *Character* refers to the total qualities a person possesses, including attitudes, beliefs, interests, actions, and a philosophy of life. By developing *character*, adolescents learn to have the intellectual strength (*psychological muscles*) to refrain from acting immorally (*controlling impulses*). Kohlberg proposed a controversial stage theory of moral development which has three levels: preconventional, conventional, and postconventional.

Kohlberg claimed these levels form a *moral ladder*. In Kohlberg's view children have to go through each of the three stages (preconventional, conventional, and postconventional) in succession much as a person climbs a ladder, one rung at a time, from bottom to top. The lowest rung on this *moral ladder* involves self-interest and avoidance of punishment; the highest rung, which often develops during and after adolescence, is concerned with personal ethical principles and universal justice. Critics contend that the theory has cultural and gender biases.

Social Development

. . . *psychosocial task* . . . According to Erikson, each stage of life involves a dilemma (*crisis*) that has to be resolved before we can move on to the next stage.

These tasks involve interactions between ourselves, our surroundings, and other people; thus, they are *social* in nature. The psychosocial assignment (*psychosocial task*) of adolescence involves *role confusion vs. forming an identity*. (This is sometimes called an **identity crisis.**)

Erikson noticed that some adolescents *forge* their identity early, simply by taking on their parents' values and expectations. *Forge* literally means to form or shape by heating and hammering metal. Erikson observed that some young people form (*forge*) their identities early, while others never quite appear to acquire a strong feeling of who they are (i.e., they don't *find themselves*).

In young adulthood, *emotional ties with parents loosen*. During their early twenties, many people still *lean heavily on their parents*. The time period between 18 and the mid-twenties is sometimes called the emerging adulthood stage. During this period, young adults have less need for close emotional contact with parents (*emotional ties with parents loosen*); nevertheless, many still rely on their parents for financial and social support (*they still lean heavily on their parents*).

Adulthood

MODULE OVERVIEW

Module 10 takes us from middle adulthood through old age and dying and death. It describes the physical, cognitive, and social developments that occur in each age group. At one time, psychologists believed that adolescence marked the end of developmental growth; today, they know that development occurs throughout the life span and that how we age depends on how we live. Of particular interest is the relationship between intelligence and aging. This module discusses research findings in this area.

NOTE: Answer guidelines for all Module 10 questions begin on page 117.

MODULE REVIEW

First, skim this section, noting headings and boldface items. After you have read the section, review each objective by completing the sentences and answering the questions that follow it. As you proceed, evaluate your performance by consulting the answers on page 117. Do not continue with the next section until you understand each answer. If you need to, review or reread the section in the textbook before continuing.

> David Myers at times uses idioms that are unfamiliar to some readers. If you do not know the meaning of the following words, phrases, or expressions in the context in which they appear in the text, refer to pages 118–119 for an explanation: *stairs get steeper, the print gets smaller, and people seem to mumble more; levies a tax; "Use it or lose it"; "Pair-bonding is a trademark of the human animal"; test-driving life together; Highs become less high.*

Physical Development (pp. 129–132)

Objective 1: Identify the major changes in physical and sensory abilities that occur in middle adulthood and later life.

1. During adulthood, age _____ (is/is not) a very good predictor of people's traits.

2. The mid-twenties are the peak years for

   _____ _____ ,

   _____ _____ ,

   _____ _____ , and

   _____ _____ . Because

   they mature earlier, _____
   (women/men) also peak earlier.

3. During early and middle adulthood, physical vigor has less to do with _____ than with a person's _____ and _____ habits.

4. The cessation of the menstrual cycle, known as _____ , occurs within a few years of _____ . This biological change results from lowered levels of the hormone _____ . A woman's experience during this time depends largely on her _____ and _____ .

5. Although men experience no equivalent to menopause, they do experience a more gradual decline in _____ count, level of the hormone _____ , and speed of erection and ejaculation during later life.

6. With age, the eye's pupil _____ (shrinks/enlarges) and its lens becomes _____ (more/less) transparent. As a result, the amount of light that reaches the retina is _____ (increased/reduced).

7. Although older adults are _____ (more/less) susceptible to life-threatening ailments, they suffer from short-term ailments such as flu _____ (more/less) often than younger adults.

8. Aging _____ (slows/speeds/has no effect on) neural processing and causes a gradual loss of _____ _____ .

9. Physical exercise stimulates _____ _____ development and _____ connections, thanks to increased _____ and nutrient flow.

Cognitive Development (pp. 132–134)

Objective 2: Assess the impact of aging on memory and intelligence.

1. Studies of developmental changes in learning and memory show that during adulthood there is a decline in the ability to _____ (recall/recognize) new information but not in the ability to _____ (recall/recognize) such information. One factor that influences memory in the elderly is the _____ of material.

2. The accumulation of stored information that comes with education and experience is called _____ intelligence, which tends to _____ with age.

3. The ability to reason abstractly is referred to as _____ intelligence, which tends to _____ with age.

Social Development (pp. 134–139)

Objective 3: Explain why the path of adult development need not be tightly linked to one's chronological age.

1. Contrary to popular opinion, job and marital dissatisfaction do not surge during the forties, thus suggesting that a midlife _____ need not occur.

2. The term used to refer to the culturally preferred timing for leaving home, getting a job, marrying, and so on is the _____ _____ .

3. Today, the timing of such life events is becoming _____ (more/less) predictable. More important than age are _____ _____ and chance encounters.

Objective 4: Discuss the importance of love, marriage, children, and work in adulthood.

4. According to Erikson, the two basic tasks of adulthood are achieving _____ and _____ . According to Freud, the healthy adult is one who can _____ and _____ .

5. Human societies have nearly always included a relatively _____ bond. Marriage bonds are usually lasting when couples marry after age _____ and are _____ _____ .

6. Marriages today are _____ (half/twice) as likely to end in divorce as they were in the 1960s. Couples who live together before marrying have a _____ (higher/ lower) divorce rate than those who do not.

7. Marriage is a predictor of _____ , _____ _____ , _____ , and _____ . Lesbian couples report _____ (greater/less) well-being than those who are alone.

8. As children begin to absorb time and energy, satisfaction with the marriage itself _____ (increases/decreases). This is particularly true among _____ women, who shoulder most of the burden.

9. For most couples, the children's leaving home produces a(n) _____ (increase/decrease) in marital satisfaction.

10. For men and women, happiness is having work that fits their interests and provides them with a sense of _____ and _____ .

Objective 5: Describe trends in people's life satisfaction across the life span.

11. From early adulthood to midlife, people typically experience a strengthening sense of _____ , _____ , and _____ .

12. According to studies, older people _____ (do/do not) report as much happiness and satisfaction with life as younger people do. In addition, their feelings _____ (do/do not) mellow.

13. As we age, the brain area called the _____ shows _____ (increased/decreased) activity in response to negative events.

Objective 6: Describe the range of reactions to the death of a loved one.

14. Grief over a loved one's death is especially severe when it comes _____ .

15. Reactions to a loved one's death _____ (do/do not) vary according to cultural norms. Those who express the strongest grief immediately _____ (do/do not) purge their grief more quickly.

16. Terminally ill and bereaved people _____ (do/do not) go through predictable stages.

17. According to Erikson, the final task of adulthood is to achieve a sense of _____ .

PROGRESS TEST

Circle your answers to the following questions and check them with the answers beginning on page 117. If your answer is incorrect, read the explanation for why it is incorrect and then consult the appropriate pages of the text.

Multiple-Choice Questions

1. A person's general ability to think abstractly is called _____ intelligence. This ability generally _____ with age.
   a. fluid; increases
   b. fluid; decreases
   c. crystallized; decreases
   d. crystallized; increases

2. An elderly person who can look back on life with satisfaction and reminisce with a sense of completion has attained Erikson's stage of:
   a. generativity.   c. isolation.
   b. intimacy.   d. integrity.

3. The cognitive ability that has been shown to decline during adulthood is the ability to:
   a. recall new information.
   b. recognize new information.
   c. learn meaningful new material.
   d. use judgment in dealing with daily life problems.

4. Which of the following statements concerning the effects of aging is true?
   a. Aging almost inevitably leads to total memory failure if the individual lives long enough.
   b. Aging increases susceptibility to short-term ailments such as the flu.
   c. Significant increases in life satisfaction are associated with aging.
   d. The aging process can be significantly affected by the individual's activity patterns.

5. The end of menstruation is called:
   a. crystallization.
   b. menopause.
   c. the midlife crisis.
   d. generativity.

6. The popular idea that terminally ill and bereaved people go through predictable stages, such as denial, anger, and so forth:
   a. is widely supported by research.
   b. more accurately describes grieving in some cultures than others.
   c. is true of women but not men.
   d. is not supported by research studies.

7. The social clock refers to:
   a. an individual or society's distribution of work and leisure time.
   b. adulthood responsibilities.
   c. typical ages for starting a career, marrying, and so on.
   d. age-related changes in one's circle of friends.

8. The emotional impact of menopause on a woman depends on:
   a. whether she is still married.
   b. the amount of estrogen secreted.
   c. how supportive her children are.
   d. her expectations and attitudes.

9. Notable achievements in fields such as _____ are often made by younger adults in their late twenties or early thirties, when _____ intelligence is at its peak.
   a. mathematics; fluid
   b. philosophy; fluid
   c. science; crystallized
   d. literature; crystallized

10. After their grown children have left home, most couples experience:
    a. the distress of the "empty nest syndrome."
    b. increased strain in their marital relationship.
    c. the loss of the child's financial help.
    d. greater happiness and enjoyment in their relationship.

11. A person's accumulation of stored information, called ____ intelligence, generally ____ with age.
    a. fluid; decreases
    b. fluid; increases
    c. crystallized; decreases
    d. crystallized; increases

12. In terms of incidence, susceptibility to short-term illnesses _____ with age and susceptibility to long-term ailments _____ with age.
    a. decreases; increases
    b. increases; decreases
    c. increases; increases
    d. decreases; decreases

13. Deborah is a mathematician and Willie is a philosopher. Considering their professions:
    a. Deborah will make her most significant career accomplishments at an earlier age than Willie will.
    b. Deborah will make her most significant career accomplishments at a later age than Willie will.
    c. Deborah will make her most significant career accomplishments at about the same time as Willie.
    d. there is still not enough information for predicting such accomplishments.

14. Sixty-five-year-old Calvin cannot reason as well as he could when he was younger. More than likely, Calvin's _____ intelligence has declined.
    a. analytic   c. fluid
    b. crystallized   d. recognition.

15. Which statement illustrates cognitive development during the course of adult life?
    a. Adults in their forties have better recognition memory than do adults in their seventies.
    b. Recall and recognition memory both remain strong throughout life.
    c. Recognition memory decreases sharply at midlife.
    d. Adults in their forties have better recall memory than adults in their seventies.

16. Given the text discussion of life satisfaction patterns, which of the following people is likely to report the greatest life satisfaction?
    a. Billy, a 7-year-old second-grader
    b. Kathy, a 17-year-old high-school senior
    c. Mildred, a 70-year-old retired teacher
    d. too little information to tell

True–False Items

Indicate whether each statement is true or false by placing *T* or *F* in the blank next to the item.

_____ 1. The process of grieving is much the same throughout the world.
_____ 2. During adulthood, age only moderately correlates with people's traits.
_____ 3. Intelligence declines throughout adulthood.
_____ 4. By the age of 50, most adults have experienced a "midlife crisis."
_____ 5. Compared to those who are younger, elderly people are more susceptible to short-term ailments such as flu and cold viruses.

KEY TERMS

Using your own words, on a piece of paper write a brief definition or explanation of each of the following terms.

1. menopause
2. crystallized intelligence
3. fluid intelligence
4. social clock

ANSWERS
Module Review

Physical Development

1. is not
2. muscular strength, reaction time, sensory keenness, cardiac output; women
3. age; health; exercise
4. menopause; 50; estrogen; expectations; attitude
5. sperm; testosterone
6. shrinks; less; reduced
7. more; less
8. slows; brain cells
9. brain cell; neural; oxygen

Cognitive Development

1. recall; recognize; meaningfulness
2. crystallized; increase
3. fluid; decrease

Social Development

1. transition (crisis)
2. social clock
3. less; life events
4. intimacy; generativity; love; work
5. monogamous; 20; well educated
6. twice; higher
7. happiness; sexual satisfaction; health; income; greater
8. decreases; employed
9. increase
10. competence; accomplishment
11. identity; confidence; self-esteem
12. do; do
13. amygdala; decreased

14. suddenly and before its expected time on the social clock
15. do; do not
16. do not
17. integrity

Progress Test

Multiple-Choice Questions

1. **b.** is the answer.
   a. Fluid intelligence tends to decrease with age.
   c. & d. Crystallized intelligence refers to the accumulation of facts and general knowledge that takes place during a person's life. Crystallized intelligence generally *increases* with age.

2. **d.** is the answer.
   a. Generativity is associated with middle adulthood.
   b. & c. Intimacy and isolation are associated with young adulthood.

3. **a.** is the answer.
   b., c., & d. These cognitive abilities remain essentially unchanged as the person ages.

4. **d.** is the answer. "Use it or lose it" seems to be the rule: often, changes in activity patterns contribute significantly to problems regarded as being part of usual aging.
   a. Most elderly people suffer some memory loss but remember some events very well.
   b. Although the elderly are more subject to long-term ailments than younger adults, they actually suffer fewer short-term ailments.
   c. People of all ages report equal happiness or satisfaction with life.

5. **b.** is the answer.
   a. There is no such term as crystallization. Crystallized intelligence is the type of intelligence that increases with age.
   c. When it does occur, the midlife crisis is a psychological, rather than biological, phenomenon.
   d. Generativity is Erikson's term for productivity during middle adulthood.

6. **d.** is the answer.

7. **c.** is the answer. Different societies and eras have somewhat different ideas about the age at which major life events should ideally occur.

8. **d.** is the answer.

9. **a.** is the answer. A mathematician's skills are likely to reflect abstract reasoning, or fluid intelligence, which declines with age.
   b. & d. Philosophy and literature are fields in which individuals often do their most notable

work later in life, after more experiential knowledge (crystallized intelligence) has accumulated.
c. Scientific achievements generally reflect fluid, rather than crystallized, intelligence.

10. **d.** is the answer.
a., b., & c. Most couples do not feel a loss of purpose or marital strain following the departure of grown children. And it's unlikely that their children had been supporting them financially.

11. **d.** is the answer.
a. & b. Fluid intelligence, which decreases with age, refers to the ability to reason abstractly.
c. Crystallized intelligence increases with age.

12. **a.** is the answer.

13. **a.** is the answer. Mathematical and philosophical reasoning involve fluid and crystallized intelligence, respectively. Because fluid intelligence generally declines with age while crystallized intelligence increases, it is likely that significant mathematical accomplishments will occur at an earlier age than philosophical accomplishments.

14. **c.** is the answer. Reasoning is based on fluid intelligence.
a. There is no "analytic" intelligence.
b. Crystallized intelligence increases up to old age.
d. There is no term "recognition intelligence." However, older people's recognition memory is still quite good.

15. **d.** is the answer.
a. & c. In tests of recognition memory, the performance of older persons shows little decline.

b. The ability to recall material, especially meaningless material, declines with age.

16. **d.** is the answer. Research has not uncovered a tendency for people of any particular age group to report greater feelings of satisfaction or well-being.

True–False Items

1. F
2. T
3. F
4. F
5. F

Key Terms

1. **Menopause** is the cessation of menstruation and typically occurs in the early fifties. It also refers to the biological and psychological changes experienced during a woman's years of declining ability to reproduce.

2. **Crystallized intelligence** refers to those aspects of intellectual ability, such as vocabulary and general knowledge, that reflect accumulated learning. Crystallized intelligence tends to increase with age.

3. **Fluid intelligence** refers to a person's ability to reason speedily and abstractly. Fluid intelligence tends to decline with age.

4. The **social clock** refers to the culturally preferred timing of social events, such as leaving home, marrying, having children, and retiring.

FOCUS ON VOCABULARY AND LANGUAGE

Physical Development

In later life, the stairs get steeper, the print gets smaller, and people seem to *mumble* more. This is not meant to be taken literally. Myers is pointing out that as we become older, our sensory and perceptual abilities change so that our reaction time and our ability to see and hear decline. Thus, the stairs *appear* steeper, the print *seems* smaller, and people do not appear to be speaking clearly (*they mumble*).

Aging *levies a tax* on the brain by slowing our neural processing. Myers is pointing out that aging is accompanied by a decrease in some perceptual and cognitive abilities. Just as you have less money after taxes have been assessed (*levied*) on your income, there are some losses in the brain's ability to function optimally due to the aging process.

We are more likely to *rust from disuse than to wear out from overuse*. "Use it or lose it" is sound advice. When adults remain active physically, sexually, and mentally (they *"use it"*), they are less likely to become inactive later in life (*"lose it"*). If we follow sedentary life-styles, we will be like unused pieces of metal machinery that suffer from rust; on the other hand, keeping active will not do us any harm (*we won't wear out from overuse*); instead, we may benefit both mentally and physically.

Social Development

"Pair-bonding is a trademark of the human animal," observed anthropologist Helen Fisher (1993). *Pair-bonding* refers to the monogamous attachment formed between one person and another, such as with a marriage partner, and this affiliation is characteristic (*a trademark*) of human beings.

Might *test-driving life together* in a "trial marriage" minimize divorce risk? Does premarital cohabitation or a "trial marriage" (*test-driving life together*) increase the probability of a successful later marriage and reduce the likelihood of divorce (*minimize divorce risk*)? The research suggests it does not. Those who live together before marriage are more likely to get divorced than those who don't. (These findings are correlational and can't be used to make causal inferences.)

As the years go by, *feelings mellow. . . . Highs become less high, lows less low.* Our feelings become less extreme (*they mellow*) as we age: the excitement and elation (*highs*) and the depression and gloom (*lows*) do not encompass such a broad range of feelings as they once did. Myers states it nicely when he says, "As we age, life becomes less an emotional roller coaster, more like paddling a canoe."

Sensation and Perception

Introduction to Sensation and Perception: Vision

11 MODULE

MODULE OVERVIEW

Sensation refers to the process by which we detect physical energy from the environment and encode it as neural signals. Perception refers to the processes by which we select, organize, and interpret that energy. This module describes the basic principles underlying sensation and perception. For example, sensory adaptation enables us to ignore many of the stimuli constantly bombarding us while focusing on important stimuli.

The module then describes the sense of vision, including the structure of the eye and the process through which the stimulus energy is transmitted through the eye and interpreted in the brain. It also covers problems in acuity. The module concludes with a discussion of the major theories proposed to explain color vision.

In this module there are many terms to learn. Many of the terms are related to the structure of the eye. Doing the module review several times, labeling the diagram of the eye, and rehearsing the material frequently will help you to memorize the parts of the eye and their functions. As you study the Young-Helmholtz three-color and opponent-process theories of color vision, concentrate on understanding the strengths and weaknesses of each.

NOTE: Answer guidelines for all Module 11 questions begin on page 130.

MODULE REVIEW

First, skim each section, noting headings and boldface items. After you have read the section, review each objective by answering the fill-in and essay-type questions that follow it. As you proceed, evaluate your performance by consulting the answers on page 130. Do not continue with the next section until you understand each answer. If you need to, review or reread the section in the textbook before continuing.

David Myers at times uses idioms that are unfamiliar to some readers. If you do not know the meaning of the following words, phrases, or expressions in the context in which they appear in the text, refer to pages 134–135 for an explanation: *in a mirror she is again stumped; A frog could starve to death knee-deep in motionless flies; The shades on our senses are open just a crack; price hike . . . to raise the eyebrows; So everywhere that Mary looks, the scene is sure to go; blind spot; Rods have no such hotline; Holy Grail; blindsight; Color, like all aspects of vision, . . . the theater of our brains.*

Introduction (p. 143)

Objective 1: Contrast sensation and perception, and explain the difference between bottom-up and top-down processing.

1. The process by which we detect physical energy from the environment and encode it as neural signals is _____ . The process by which sensations are selected, organized, and interpreted is _____ .

2. Sensory analysis, which starts at the entry level and works up, is called _____-_____ _____ .

   Perceptual analysis, which works from our experience and expectations, is called

   _____-_____

   _____ .

3. The perceptual disorder in which a person has lost the ability to recognize familiar faces is

   _____ .

Sensing the World: Some Basic Principles
(pp. 143–147)

Objective 2: Distinguish between absolute and difference thresholds, and discuss research findings on subliminal stimulation.

1. The study of relationships between the physical characteristics of stimuli and our psychological experience of them is _____ .

2. The _____ _____ refers to the minimum stimulation necessary for a stimulus to be detected _____ percent of the time.

3. Some entrepreneurs claim that exposure to "below threshold," or _____ , stimuli can be persuasive, but their claims are probably unwarranted.

4. Some weak stimuli may trigger in our sensory receptors a response that is processed by the brain, even though the response doesn't cross the threshold into _____ awareness.

5. Under certain conditions, an invisible image or word can _____ a person's response to a later question. The _____ _____ illustrates that much of our information processing occurs _____ .

6. The minimum difference required to distinguish two stimuli 50 percent of the time is called the _____ _____ .

   Another term for this value is the _____ _____ _____ .

7. The principle that the difference threshold is not a constant amount, but a constant proportion, is known as _____ _____ . The proportion depends on the _____ .

Objective 3: Describe the phenomenon of sensory adaptation, and explain its functional value.

8. After constant exposure to an unchanging stimulus, the receptor cells of our senses begin to fire less vigorously; this phenomenon is called _____ _____ .

9. This phenomenon illustrates that sensation is designed to focus on _____ changes in the environment.

Vision (pp. 147–155)

Objective 4: Describe the characteristics of visible light, and explain the process by which the eye converts light energy into neural messages.

1. Stimulus energy is _____ (converted) into _____ messages by our eyes.

2. The visible spectrum of light is a small portion of the larger spectrum of _____ radiation.

3. The distance from one light wave peak to the next is called _____ . This value determines the wave's color, or _____ .

4. The amount of energy in light waves, or _____ , determined by a wave's _____ , or height, influences the _____ of a light.

5. Light enters the eye through the _____ , then passes through a small opening called the _____ ; the size of this opening is controlled by the colored _____ .

6. By changing its curvature, the _____ can focus the image of an object onto the _____ , the light-sensitive inner surface of the eye.

7. The process by which the lens changes shape to focus images is called _____ .

8. The retina's receptor cells are the _____ and _____ .

9. The neural signals produced in the rods and cones activate the neighboring _____ cells, which then activate a network of _____ cells. The axons of ganglion cells converge to form the _____ _____ , which carries the visual information to the _____ .

10. Where this nerve leaves the eye, there are no receptors; thus, the area is called the _____ _____ .

11. Most cones are clustered around the retina's point of central focus, called the

_____, whereas the rods are con-centrated in more _____ regions of the retina. Many cones have their own _____ cells to communicate with the visual cortex.

12. It is the _____ (rods/cones) of the eye that permit the perception of color, whereas _____ (rods/cones) enable black-and-white vision.

13. Unlike cones, in dim light the rods are _____ (sensitive/insensitive). Adapting to a darkened room will take the retina approximately _____ minutes.

Objective 5: Discuss the different levels of processing that occur as information travels from the retina to the brain's cortex.

14. Visual information percolates through progres-sively more _____ levels. In the brain, it is routed by the _____ to higher-level brain areas. Hubel and Wiesel dis-covered that certain neurons in the _____ of the brain respond only to specific features of what is viewed. They called these neurons _____ _____.

15. Feature detectors pass their information to higher-level cells in the brain, which respond to specific visual scenes. Research has shown that in monkey brains such cells specialize in responding to a specific _____, _____ _____, _____, or _____ _____. In many cortical areas, teams of cells (_____ _____) respond to complex patterns.

16. The brain achieves its remarkable speed in visual perception by processing several subdivisions of a stimulus _____ (simultaneous-ly/sequentially). This procedure, called _____ _____, may

explain why people who have suffered a stroke may lose just one aspect of vision. Other brain-damaged people may demonstrate _____ by responding to a stimulus that is not consciously perceived.

Objective 6: Explain how the Young-Helmholtz and opponent-process theories help us understand color vision.

17. An object appears to be red in color because it _____ the long wavelengths of red and because of our mental _____ of the color.

18. One out of every 50 people is color deficient; this is usually a male because the defect is genetically _____-_____.

19. According to the _____-_____ _____ theory, the eyes have three types of color receptors: one reacts most strongly to _____, one to _____, and one to _____.

20. After staring at a green square for a while, you will see the color red, its _____ color, as an _____.

21. Hering's theory of color vision is called the _____-_____ theory. According to this theory, after visual information leaves the receptors it is analyzed in terms of pairs of opposing colors: _____ versus _____, _____ versus _____, and _____ versus _____.

Summarize the two stages of color processing.

PROGRESS TEST

Multiple-Choice Questions

Circle your answers to the following questions and check them with the answers beginning on page 131. If your answer is incorrect, read the explanation for why it is correct and then consult the appropriate pages of the text.

1. Which of the following is true?
   a. The absolute threshold for any stimulus is a constant.
   b. The absolute threshold for any stimulus varies somewhat.
   c. The absolute threshold is defined as the minimum amount of stimulation necessary for a stimulus to be detected 75 percent of the time.
   d. The absolute threshold is defined as the minimum amount of stimulation necessary for a stimulus to be detected 60 percent of the time.

2. If you can just notice the difference between 10- and 11-pound weights, which of the following weights could you differentiate from a 100-pound weight?
   a. 101-pound weight
   b. 105-pound weight
   c. 110-pound weight
   d. There is no basis for prediction.

3. A decrease in sensory responsiveness accompanying an unchanging stimulus is called:
   a. sensory fatigue.
   b. accommodation.
   c. sensory adaptation.
   d. sensory interaction.

4. The size of the pupil is controlled by the:
   a. lens.   c. cornea.
   b. retina.   d. iris.

5. The process by which the lens changes its curvature is:
   a. accommodation.   c. feature detection.
   b. sensory adaptation. d. transduction.

6. The receptor of the eye that functions best in dim light is the:
   a. fovea.   c. bipolar cell.
   b. cone   d. rod.

7. The Young-Helmholtz theory proposes that:
   a. there are three different types of color-sensitive cones.

   b. retinal cells are excited by one color and inhibited by its complementary color.
   c. there are four different types of cones.
   d. rod, not cone, vision accounts for our ability to detect fine visual detail.

8. The transduction of light energy into nerve impulses takes place in the:
   a. iris.   c. lens.
   b. retina.   d. optic nerve.

9. The brain breaks vision into separate dimensions such as color, depth, movement, and form, and works on each aspect simultaneously. This is called:
   a. feature detection.
   b. parallel processing.
   c. accommodation.
   d. opponent processing.

10. One light may appear reddish and another greenish if they differ in:
    a. wavelength.   c. opponent processes.
    b. amplitude.   d. brightness.

11. Which of the following explains why a rose appears equally red in bright and dim light?
    a. the Young-Helmholtz theory
    b. the opponent-process theory
    c. feature detection
    d. color constancy

12. Which of the following is an example of sensory adaptation?
    a. finding the cold water of a swimming pool warmer after you have been in it for a while
    b. developing an increased sensitivity to salt the more you use it in foods
    c. becoming very irritated at the continuing sound of a dripping faucet
    d. All of these answers are examples.

13. Most color-deficient people will probably:
    a. lack functioning red- or green-sensitive cones.
    b. see the world in only black and white.
    c. also suffer from poor vision.
    d. have above-average vision to compensate for the deficit.

14. _____ processing refers to how the physical characteristics of stimuli influence their interpretation.
    a. Top-down   c. Sensory
    b. Bottom-up   d. Psychophysical

15. The study of perception is primarily concerned with how we:
    a. detect sights, sounds, and other stimuli.
    b. sense environmental stimuli.
    c. develop sensitivity to illusions.
    d. interpret sensory stimuli.

16. According to the opponent-process theory:
    a. there are three types of color-sensitive cones.
    b. the process of color vision begins in the cortex.
    c. neurons involved in color vision are stimulated by one color's wavelength and inhibited by another's.
    d. all of the above are true.

17. Hubel and Wiesel discovered feature detectors in the visual:
    a. fovea.   c. iris.
    b. optic nerve.   d. cortex.

18. Weber's law states that:
    a. the absolute threshold for any stimulus is a constant.
    b. the jnd for any stimulus is a constant.
    c. the absolute threshold for any stimulus is a constant proportion.
    d. the jnd for any stimulus is a constant proportion.

19. Which of the following is the correct order of the structures through which light passes after entering the eye?
    a. lens, pupil, cornea, retina
    b. pupil, cornea, lens, retina
    c. pupil, lens, cornea, retina
    d. cornea, pupil, lens, retina

20. In the opponent-process theory, the three pairs of processes are:
    a. red-green, blue-yellow, black-white.
    b. red-blue, green-yellow, black-white.
    c. red-yellow, blue-green, black-white.
    d. dependent upon the individual's experience.

21. Wavelength is to _____ as _____ is to brightness.
    a. hue; intensity
    b. intensity; hue
    c. frequency; amplitude
    d. brightness; hue

22. Concerning the evidence for subliminal stimulation, which of the following is the best answer?
    a. The brain processes some information without our awareness.
    b. Stimuli too weak to cross our thresholds for awareness may trigger a response in our sense receptors.
    c. Because the "absolute" threshold is a statistical average, we are able to detect weaker stimuli some of the time.
    d. All of these answers are true.

23. Which of the following is the most accurate description of how we process color?
    a. Throughout the visual system, color processing is divided into separate red, green, and blue systems.
    b. Red-green, blue-yellow, and black-white opponent processes operate throughout the visual system.
    c. Color processing occurs in two stages: (1) a three-color system in the retina and (2) opponent-process cells en route to the visual cortex.
    d. Color processing occurs in two stages: (1) an opponent-process system in the retina and (2) a three-color system en route to the visual cortex.

24. One reason that your ability to detect fine visual details is greatest when scenes are focused on the fovea of your retina is that:
    a. there are more feature detectors in the fovea than in the peripheral regions of the retina.
    b. cones in the fovea are nearer to the optic nerve than those in peripheral regions of the retina.
    c. many rods, which are clustered in the fovea, have individual bipolar cells to relay their information to the cortex.
    d. many cones, which are clustered in the fovea, have individual bipolar cells to relay their information to the cortex.

25. Given normal sensory ability, a person standing atop a mountain on a dark, clear night can see a candle flame atop a mountain 30 miles away. This is a description of vision's:
    a. difference threshold.   c. absolute threshold.
    b. jnd.   d. feature detection.

26. _____ processing refers to how our knowledge and expectations influence perception.
    a. Top-down   c. Sensory
    b. Bottom-up   d. Psychophysical

27. In shopping for a new stereo, you discover that you cannot differentiate between the sounds of models X and Y. The difference between X and Y is below your:
    a. absolute threshold.   c. receptor threshold.
    b. subliminal threshold. d. difference threshold.

28. In order to maximize your sensitivity to fine visual detail you should:
    a. stare off to one side of the object you are attempting to see.
    b. close one eye.
    c. decrease the intensity of the light falling upon the object.
    d. stare directly at the object.

29. In comparing the human eye to a camera, the film would be located in the eye's:
    a. pupil.   c. cornea.
    b. lens.   d. retina.

30. Sensation is to _____ as perception is to _____ .
    a. recognizing a stimulus; interpreting a stimulus
    b. detecting a stimulus; recognizing a stimulus
    c. interpreting a stimulus; detecting a stimulus
    d. seeing; hearing

31. I am a cell in the thalamus that is excited by red and inhibited by green. I am a(n):
    a. feature detector.   c. bipolar cell.
    b. cone.   d. opponent-process cell.

32. Which of the following is true of cones?
    a. Cones enable color vision.
    b. Cones are highly concentrated in the foveal region of the retina.
    c. Cones have a higher absolute threshold for brightness than rods.
    d. All of these answers are true.

33. Assuming that the visual systems of humans and other mammals function similarly, you would expect that the retina of a nocturnal mammal (one active only at night) would contain:
    a. mostly cones.
    b. mostly rods.
    c. an equal number of rods and cones.
    d. more bipolar cells than an animal active only during the day.

34. As the football game continued into the night, LeVar noticed that he was having difficulty distinguishing the colors of the players' uniforms. This is because the _____ , which enable color vision, have a _____ absolute threshold for brightness than the available light intensity.
    a. rods; higher   c. rods; lower
    b. cones; higher   d. cones; lower

35. After staring at a very intense red stimulus for a few minutes, Carrie shifted her gaze to a beige wall and "saw" the color _____ . Carrie's experience provides support for the _____ theory.
    a. green; trichromatic
    b. blue; opponent-process
    c. green; opponent-process
    d. blue; trichromatic

36. Superman's eyes used _____ , while his brain used _____ .
    a. perception; sensation
    b. top-down processing; bottom-up processing
    c. bottom-up processing; top-down processing
    d. sensory adaptation; subliminal perception

Matching Items

Match each of the structures with its function or description.

Structures or Conditions
_____ 1. lens
_____ 2. iris
_____ 3. pupil
_____ 4. rods
_____ 5. cones

Functions or Descriptions
a. controls pupil
b. accommodation
c. admits light
d. vision in dim light
e. color vision

Summing Up

Use the diagram to identify the parts of the eye, then describe how each contributes to vision. Also, briefly explain the role of each structure.

The Eye

1. _____
   _____

2. _____
   _____

3. _____
   _____

4. _____
   _____

5. _____
   _____

6. _____
   _____

7. _____

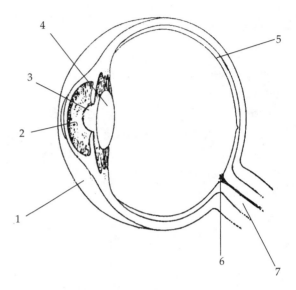

KEY TERMS

Using your own words, on a piece of paper write a brief definition or explanation of each of the following terms.

1. sensation
2. bottom-up processing
3. perception
4. top-down processing
5. psychophysics
6. absolute threshold
7. subliminal
8. priming
9. difference threshold
10. Weber's law
11. sensory adaptation
12. wavelength and hue

13. intensity
14. retina
15. accommodation
16. rods and cones
17. optic nerve
18. blind spot
19. fovea
20. feature detectors
21. parallel processing
22. Young-Helmholtz trichromatic (three-color) theory
23. opponent-process theory

ANSWERS

Module Review

Introduction

1. sensation; perception
2. bottom-up processing; top-down processing
3. prosopagnosia

Sensing the World: Some Basic Principles

1. psychophysics
2. absolute threshold; 50
3. subliminal
4. conscious
5. prime; priming effect; automatically
6. difference threshold; just noticeable difference
7. Weber's law; stimulus
8. sensory adaptation
9. informative

Vision

1. transduced; neural
2. electromagnetic
3. wavelength; hue
4. intensity; amplitude; brightness
5. cornea; pupil; iris
6. lens; retina
7. accommodation
8. rods; cones
9. bipolar; ganglion; optic nerve; brain
10. blind spot
11. fovea; peripheral; bipolar
12. cones; rods
13. sensitive; 20
14. abstract; thalamus; visual cortex; feature detectors
15. gaze; head angle; posture; body movement; supercell clusters
16. simultaneously; parallel processing; blindsight
17. reflects (rejects); construction
18. sex-linked
19. Young-Helmholtz trichromatic; red; green; blue
20. opponent; afterimage
21. opponent-process; red; green; yellow; blue; black; white

In the first stage of color processing, the retina's red, green, and blue cones respond in varying degrees to different color stimuli, as suggested by the three-color theory. The resulting signals are then processed in the thalamus by red-green, blue-yellow, and black-white opponent-process cells, which are stimulated by one wavelength and inhibited by its opponent.

Progress Test

Multiple-Choice Questions

1. **b.** is the answer. Psychological factors can affect the absolute threshold for a stimulus.
   a. The absolute threshold for detecting a stimulus depends not only on the strength of the stimulus but also on psychological factors such as experience, expectations, motivation, and fatigue. Thus, the threshold cannot be a constant.
   c. & d. The absolute threshold is defined as the minimum stimulus that is detected 50 percent of the time.

2. **c.** is the answer. According to Weber's law, the difference threshold is a constant proportion of the stimulus. There is a 10 percent difference between 10 and 11 pounds; since the difference threshold is a constant proportion, the weight closest to 100 pounds that can nonetheless be differentiated from it is 110 pounds (or 100 pounds plus 10 percent).

3. **c.** is the answer.
   a. "Sensory fatigue" is not a term in psychology.
   b. Accommodation refers to an adaptive change in shape by the lens of the eye.
   d. Sensory interaction is the principle that one sense may influence another.

4. **d.** is the answer.
   a. The lens lies behind the pupil and focuses light on the retina.
   b. The retina is the inner surface of the eyeball and contains the rods and cones.
   c. The cornea lies in front of the pupil and is the first structure that light passes through as it enters the eye.

5. **a.** is the answer.
   b. Sensory adaptation is our diminishing sensitivity to an unchanging stimulus.
   c. Feature detection is the process by which neural cells in the brain respond to specific visual features.
   d. Transduction refers to the conversion of an environmental stimulus, such as light, into a neural impulse by a receptor—a rod or a cone.

6. **d.** is the answer.
   a. The fovea is not a receptor; it is a region of the retina that contains only cones.

b. Cones have a higher threshold for brightness than rods and therefore do not function as well in dim light.

c. Bipolar cells are not receptors; they are neurons in the retina that link rods and cones with ganglion cells, which make up the optic nerve.

7. **a.** is the answer. The Young-Helmholtz theory proposes that there are red-, green-, and blue-sensitive cones.

b. This answer describes Hering's opponent-process theory.

c. The Young-Helmholtz theory proposes that there are three types of cones, not four.

d. The Young-Helmholtz theory concerns only color vision, not the detection of visual detail.

8. **b.** is the answer.

a. The iris controls the diameter of the pupil.

c. The lens accommodates its shape to focus images on the retina.

d. The optic nerve carries nerve impulses from the retina to the visual cortex.

9. **b.** is the answer.

a. Feature detection is the process by which nerve cells in the brain respond to specific visual features of a stimulus, such as movement or shape.

c. Accommodation is the process by which the lens changes its curvature to focus images on the retina.

d. The opponent-process theory suggests that color vision depends on the response of brain cells to red-green, yellow-blue, and black-white opposing colors.

10. **a.** is the answer. Wavelength determines hue, or color.

b. & d. The amplitude of light determines its brightness.

c. Opponent processes are neural systems involved in color vision, not properties of light.

11. **d.** is the answer. Color constancy is the perception that a familiar object has consistent color, even if changing illumination alters the wavelengths reflected by that object.

a. & b. These theories explain how the visual system detects color; they do not explain why colors do not seem to change when lighting does.

c. Feature detection explains how the brain recognizes visual images by analyzing their distinctive features of shape, movement, and angle.

12. **a.** is the answer. Sensory adaptation means a diminishing sensitivity to an unchanging stimulus. Only the adjustment to cold water involves a decrease in sensitivity; the other examples involve an increase.

13. **a.** is the answer. Thus, they have difficulty discriminating these two colors.

b. Those who are color deficient are usually not "color blind" in a literal sense. Instead, they are unable to distinguish certain hues, such as red from green.

c. Failure to distinguish red and green is separate from, and does not usually affect, general visual ability.

d. Color deficiency does not enhance vision. A deficit in one sense often is compensated for by overdevelopment of another sense—for example, hearing in blind people.

14. **b.** is the answer.

a. Top-down processing refers to how our knowledge and expectations influence perception.

c. Sensory processing refers to how stimuli enter our awareness.

d. Psychophysics is the study of the relationship between the physical characteristics of objects and our psychological experience of them.

15. **d.** is the answer.

a. & b. The study of sensation is concerned with these processes.

c. Although studying illusions has helped psychologists understand ordinary perceptual mechanisms, it is not the primary focus of the field of perception.

16. **c.** is the answer. After leaving the receptor cells, visual information is analyzed in terms of pairs of opponent colors; neurons stimulated by one member of a pair are inhibited by the other.

a. The idea that there are three types of color-sensitive cones is the basis of the Young-Helmholtz three-color theory.

b. According to the opponent-process theory, and all other theories of color vision, the process of color vision begins in the retina.

17. **d.** is the answer. Feature detectors are cortical neurons and hence are located in the visual cortex.

a. The fovea contains cones.

b. The optic nerve contains neurons that relay nerve impulses from the retina to higher centers in the visual system.

c. The iris is simply a ring of muscle tissue, which controls the diameter of the pupil.

18. **d.** is the answer. Weber's law concerns difference thresholds (jnd's), not absolute thresholds, and states that these are constant proportions of the stimuli, not that they remain constant.

19. **d.** is the answer.

20. **a.** is the answer.

21. **a.** is the answer. Wavelength determines hue, and intensity determines brightness.

22. **d.** is the answer.

23. **c.** is the answer.

    a. This answer is incorrect because separate red, green, and blue systems operate only in the retina.

    b. This answer is incorrect because opponent-process systems operate en route to the brain, after visual processing in the receptors is completed.

    d. This answer is incorrect because it reverses the correct order of the two stages of processing.

24. **d.** is the answer.

    a. Feature detectors are nerve cells located in the visual cortex, not in the fovea of the retina.

    b. The proximity of rods and cones to the optic nerve does not influence their ability to resolve fine details.

    c. Rods are concentrated in the peripheral regions of the retina, not in the fovea; moreover, several rods share a single bipolar cell.

25. **c.** is the answer. The absolute threshold is the minimum stimulation needed to detect a stimulus.

    a. & b. The difference threshold, which is also known as the jnd, is the minimum difference between two stimuli that a person can detect. In this example, there is only one stimulus—the sight of the flame.

    d. Feature detection refers to nerve cells in the brain responding to specific features of a stimulus.

26. **a.** is the answer.

    b. Bottom-up processing refers to the physical characteristics of stimuli rather than their perceptual interpretation.

    c. Sensory processing refers to how stimuli enter our awareness.

    d. Psychophysics is the study of the relationship between the physical characteristics of objects and our psychological experience of them.

27. **d.** is the answer.

    a. The absolute threshold refers to whether a single stimulus can be detected, not to whether two stimuli can be differentiated.

    b. Subliminal refers to stimuli below the absolute threshold.

    c. A receptor threshold is a minimum amount of energy that will elicit a neural impulse in a receptor cell.

28. **d.** is the answer. Greater sensitivity to fine visual detail is associated with the cones, which have their own bipolar cells to relay information to the cortex. The cones are concentrated in the fovea, the retina's point of central focus. For this reason, staring directly at an object maximizes sensitivity to fine detail.

    a. If you stare off to one side, the image falls onto peripheral regions of the retina, where rods are concentrated and sensitivity to fine visual detail is poor.

    b. Sensitivity to detail is not directly influenced by whether one or both eyes are stimulated.

    c. Decreasing the intensity of light would only impair the functioning of the cones, which are sensitive to visual detail but have a high threshold for light intensity.

29. **d.** is the answer. Just as light strikes the film of a camera, visual images entering the eye are projected onto the retina.

    a. The pupil would be analogous to the aperture of a camera, since both control the amount of light permitted to enter.

    b. The lens of the eye performs a focusing function similar to the lens of the camera.

    c. The cornea would be analogous to a camera's lens cap in that both protect delicate inner structures.

30. **b.** is the answer.

    a. Both recognition and interpretation are examples of perception.

    c. This answer would have been correct if the question had read, "Perception is to sensation as _____ is to _____ ."

    d. Sensation and perception are important processes in both hearing and seeing.

31. **d.** is the answer.

    a. Feature detectors are located in the visual cortex and respond to features such as movement, shape, and angle.

    b. & c. Cones and bipolar cells are located in the retina. Moreover, neither are excited by some colors and inhibited by others.

32. **d.** is the answer.

33. **b.** is the answer. Rods and cones enable vision in dim and bright light, respectively. If an animal is active only at night, it is likely to have more rods than cones in its retinas.

    d. Bipolar cells link both cones and rods to ganglion cells. There is no reason to expect that a nocturnal mammal would have more bipolar cells than a mammal active both during the day and at night. If anything, because several rods share a single bipolar cell, whereas many cones have their own, a nocturnal animal (with a visual system consisting mostly of rods) might be expected to have fewer bipolar cells than an animal active during the day (with a visual system consisting mostly of cones).

34. **b.** is the answer.

    a. & c. It is the cones, rather than the rods, that enable color vision.

    d. If the cones' threshold were lower than the available light intensity, they would be able to function and therefore detect the colors of the players' uniforms.

35. **c.** is the answer.

    a. The trichromatic theory cannot account for the experience of afterimages.

    b. & d. Afterimages are experienced as the complementary color of a stimulus. Green, not blue, is red's complement.

36. **c.** is the answer.

Matching Items

1. b   4. d
2. a   5. e
3. c

Summing Up

1. Cornea. Light enters the eye through this transparent membrane, which protects the inner structures from the environment.
2. Iris. The colored part of the eye, the iris functions like the aperture of a camera, controlling the size of the pupil to optimize the amount of light that enters the eye.
3. Pupil. The adjustable opening in the iris, the pupil allows light to enter.
4. Lens. This transparent structure behind the pupil changes shape to focus images on the retina.
5. Retina. The light-sensitive inner surface of the eye, the retina contains the rods and cones, which transduce light energy into neural impulses.
6. Blind spot. The region of the retina where the optic nerve leaves the eye, the blind spot contains no rods or cones and so there is no vision here.
7. Optic nerve. This bundle of nerve fibers carries neural impulses from the retina to the brain.

Key Terms

1. **Sensation** is the process by which we detect physical energy from the environment and encode it as neural signals.

2. **Bottom-up processing** is analysis that begins with the sensory receptors and works up to the brain's integration of sensory information.
3. **Perception** is the process by which we select, organize, and interpret sensory information.
4. **Top-down processing** is information processing guided by higher-level mental processes.
5. **Psychophysics** is the study of relationships between the physical characteristics of stimuli and our psychological experience of them.
6. The **absolute threshold** is the minimum stimulation needed to detect a stimulus 50 percent of the time.
7. A stimulus that is **subliminal** is one that is below the absolute threshold for conscious awareness.

    Memory aid: Limen is the Latin word for "threshold." A stimulus that is **subliminal** is one that is *sub-* ("below") the *limen*, or threshold.
8. **Priming** is the activation, often unconsciously, of an association by an imperceptible stimulus, the effect of which is to predispose a perception, memory, or response.
9. The **difference threshold** (also called the *just noticeable difference,* or *jnd*), is the minimum difference between two stimuli required for detection 50 percent of the time.
10. **Weber's law** states that the just noticeable difference between two stimuli is a constant minimum proportion of the stimulus.

    Example: If a difference of 10 percent in weight is noticeable, **Weber's law** predicts that a person could discriminate 10- and 11-pound weights or 50- and 55-pound weights.
11. **Sensory adaptation** refers to the decreased sensitivity that occurs with continued exposure to an unchanging stimulus.
12. **Wavelength**, which refers to the distance from the peak of one light (or sound) wave to the next, gives rise to the perceptual experiences of **hue**, or color, in vision (and **pitch** in sound).
13. The **intensity** of light and sound is determined by the amplitude of the waves and is experienced as brightness and loudness, respectively.

    Example: Sounds that exceed 85 decibels in amplitude, or **intensity**, will damage the auditory system.
14. The **retina** is the light-sensitive, multilayered inner surface of the eye that contains the rods and cones as well as neurons that form the beginning of the optic nerve.
15. **Accommodation** is the process by which the lens of the eye changes shape to focus near objects on the retina.

16. The **rods** and **cones** are visual receptors that convert light energy into neural impulses. The rods are concentrated in the periphery of the retina, the cones in the fovea. The rods have poor sensitivity; detect black, white, and gray; function well in dim light; and are needed for peripheral vision. The cones have excellent sensitivity, enable color vision, and function best in daylight or bright light.

17. Comprised of the axons of retinal ganglion cells, the **optic nerve** carries neural impulses from the eye to the brain.

18. The **blind spot** is the region of the retina where the optic nerve leaves the eye. Because there are no rods or cones in this area, there is no vision here.

19. The **fovea** is the retina's point of central focus. It contains only cones; therefore, images focused on the fovea are the clearest.

20. **Feature detectors**, located in the visual cortex of the brain, are nerve cells that selectively respond to specific visual features, such as movement, shape, or angle. Feature detectors are evidently the basis of visual information processing.

21. **Parallel processing** is information processing in which several aspects of a stimulus, such as light or sound, are processed simultaneously.

22. The **Young-Helmholtz trichromatic (three-color) theory** maintains that the retina contains red-, green-, and blue-sensitive color receptors that in combination can produce the perception of any color. This theory explains the first stage of color processing.

23. The **opponent-process theory** maintains that color vision depends on pairs of opposing retinal processes (red-green, yellow-blue, and white-black). This theory explains the second stage of color processing.

FOCUS ON VOCABULARY AND LANGUAGE

Shown her own face in a mirror, she is again *stumped*. This person (E. H.) is suffering from *prosopagnosia* and cannot recognize faces and even fails (*she is stumped*) to recognize her own face in the mirror. What is interesting in this case is that she can process incoming sensory information (*bottom up*) but is unable to make any sense of it (*top down*). As Myers notes earlier, she has sensation (*bottom-up processing*), but her perception (*top-down processing*) is not working properly.

Sensing the World: Some Basic Principles

A frog could starve to death *knee-deep* in motionless flies. But let one *zoom by* and the frog's *"bug detector"* cells *snap awake*. The frog's eyes and brain are organized in such a way that only fast moving (*zooming*), small, dark objects will cause these specialized feature detector nerve cells (*"bug detectors"*) to become active (*snap awake*). If the frog is surrounded by flies that don't move (*knee-deep in motionless flies*), it will die of hunger, completely unaware of the food at its feet.

The *shades* on our senses are open just a *crack*, allowing us only a restricted awareness of this *vast sea* of energy. Just as sunblinds or curtains (*shades*) let only a little light in through any small opening (*a crack*), our sensory system is only able to detect a very small part of the large amount (*vast sea*) of the physical energy that exists in the world.

. . . it might take a 30 cent *price hike* in a $3 gallon of gasoline to similarly *raise the eyebrows. Raised eyebrows* express surprise. So a 30 cent increase (*price hike*) in the cost of gasoline would be noticed by consumers (*would raise their eyebrows*). **Weber's law** states that a constant proportion of the original stimulus is needed in order for the difference to be detected, and the precise proportion will change depending on the stimulus. Thus, a $5 increase in the price of the car would not be a **just noticeable difference**, or **jnd**, but a $5 dollar increase (*price hike*) in the cost of a hamburger and fries would exceed a **jnd**.

So everywhere that Mary looks, the scene is sure to go. In order to understand this sentence you need to be familiar with the old nursery rhyme: Mary had a little lamb, its fleece was white as snow, and *everywhere that Mary went the lamb was sure to go.* When a volunteer (*Mary*) is fitted with a special contact lens and miniature projector she sees the same image no matter where her eyes "look" (*everywhere that Mary looks the scene is sure to go*). When an image is projected onto the retina in this manner the scene disappears bit by bit and then reappears and disappears again (in meaningful units). This happens because the image, which normally would be moving back and forth rapidly (*quivering*) as a result of tiny eye movements, is now stationary with respect to the retina and its receptors. As the receptors fatigue the image disappears.

Vision

. . . blind spot . . . You can use the suggestion in Figure 11.8 of the text to demonstrate that there are two small parts of your visual field (one in the left and one in the right) where you have no sight. These tiny areas (*blind spots*) are where the optic nerve exits the eye.

Rods have no such *hotline* [to the brain]. . . . Cones, which are mostly clustered in the **fovea** and detect color and fine detail, have many more individual connections to the brain than the rods. Rods, which give us our black-and-white vision, have to share bipolar cells and so do not have as many individual connections (*hotlines*) to the brain (in dim light, however, this can be an advantage as several rods can focus or funnel their individual faint energy output onto a single bipolar cell).

(caption): The answer to this question is the *Holy Grail* of vision research. The reference here is to the medieval legend that the cup (*grail*) Jesus Christ drank from at the Last Supper, and which was later used to catch his blood when he was crucified, survived and may have been brought to England. The quest, or search, for this sacred cup (*Holy Grail*) symbolized spiritual regeneration and enlightenment.

Similarly, attempting to answer the question about how the brain deals with multiple aspects of a visual scene at the same time, automatically, and without our awareness (*parallel processing*), is an important undertaking that, if successful, will enlighten us about brain functioning (*the Holy Grail of vision research*).

. . . blindsight . . . *Blindsight* refers to the fact that some people with neurological damage have the ability to see, to some degree, without any conscious awareness of the visual experience. They are blind, yet they can see (*blindsight*). This suggests that there are two parallel processing systems operating, one that unconsciously guides our actions (the zombie within), and one that gives us our conscious perceptions.

Color, like all aspects of vision, resides not in the object but in the *theater of our brains* . . . . Myers notes that when we view a colored object (for example, a blue balloon), it absorbs all the wavelengths except its own (blue) and reflects the wavelengths of blue back to us. The color we perceive is a product of our brain and exists only in the perceiver's mind (*theater of the brain*).

The Other Senses

12

MODULE OVERVIEW

This module describes the senses of hearing, touch, pain, taste, smell, and kinesthesis and the vestibular sense. It begins with the sense of hearing, including the structure of the ear and the process through which the stimulus energy is transmitted through the ear and interpreted in the brain.

Although vision and hearing are the most important human senses, the other senses are also vital to our ability to function. Without pain, for example, we might not realize when we cut ourselves or when some internal organ is not functioning properly.

In this module there are many terms to learn. Many of the terms are related to the structures of the relevant organs. Doing the module review several times, labeling the diagram of the ear, and rehearsing the material frequently will help you to memorize the parts of the various structures and their functions.

NOTE: Answer guidelines for all Module 12 questions begin on page 142.

MODULE REVIEW

First, skim each section, noting headings and boldface items. After you have read the section, review each objective by answering the fill-in and essay-type questions that follow it. As you proceed, evaluate your performance by consulting the answers on page 142. Do not continue with the next section until you understand each answer. If you need to, review or reread the section in the textbook before continuing.

> David Myers at times uses idioms that are unfamiliar to some readers. If you do not know the meaning of the following words, phrases, or expressions in the context in which they appear in the text, refer to pages 145–146 for

> an explanation: *sensitive to faint sounds, an obvious boon; A piccolo produces much shorter, faster sound waves than does a bass guitar; If a car to the right honks; cock your head; we yearn to touch—to kiss, to stroke, to snuggle; Rubbing the area around your stubbed toe; A well-trained nurse may distract needle-shy patients by chatting with them; there's more to taste than meets the tongue; bathing your nostrils in a stream of scent-laden molecules; biological gyroscopes.*

Hearing (pp. 157–160)

Objective 1: Describe the auditory process, including the stimulus input and the structure and function of the ear.

1. The stimulus for hearing, or _____ , is sound waves, created by the compression and expansion of _____

   _____ .

2. The amplitude of a sound wave determines the sound's _____ .

3. The frequency of a sound wave determines the _____ we perceive.

4. Sound energy is measured in units called _____ . The absolute threshold for hearing is arbitrarily defined as _____ such units.

5. The ear is divided into three main parts: the _____ ear, the _____ ear, and the _____ ear.

6. The outer ear channels sound waves toward the _____ , a tight membrane that then vibrates.

7. The middle ear transmits the vibrations through a piston made of three small bones: the
_____ , _____ , and
_____ .

8. In the inner ear, a coiled, bony, fluid-filled tube called the _____ contains the receptor cells for hearing. The incoming vibrations cause the _____
_____ to vibrate the fluid that fills the tube, which causes ripples in the
_____ _____ ,
which is lined with _____
_____ . This movement triggers impulses in adjacent nerve fibers that converge to form the auditory nerve, which carries the neural messages (via the _____) to the
_____ lobe's auditory cortex.

Objective 2: Describe how sounds are located.

9. We locate a sound by sensing differences in the
_____ and _____
with which it reaches our ears.

10. A sound that comes from directly ahead will be
_____ (easier/harder) to locate than a sound that comes from off to one side.

Touch (p. 161)

Objective 3: Describe the sense of touch.

1. The sense of touch is a mixture of at least four senses: _____ ,
_____ , _____ , and
_____ . Other skin sensations, such as tickle, itch, hot, and wetness, are
_____ of the basic ones.

2. The _____-_____
influence on touch is illustrated by the fact that a self-produced tickle produces less activation in the _____ _____
than someone else's tickle.

Pain (pp. 162–164)

Objective 4: Describe the basis of pain.

1. People born without the ability to feel pain may be unaware of experiencing severe

_____ . People with illness-related
_____ experience extreme sensitivity to things others find only mildly painful.

2. Pain is a property of the _____
as well as of the _____ and our
_____ .

3. A sensation of pain in an amputated leg is referred to as a _____
_____ sensation. Another example is _____ , experienced by people who have a ringing-in-the-ears sensation.

4. Pain-producing brain activity may be triggered with or without _____
_____ .

5. The pain system _____ (is/is not) triggered by one specific type of physical energy. The body _____ (does/does not) have specialized receptor cells for pain.

6. Melzack and Wall have proposed a theory of pain called the _____-
_____ theory, which proposes that there is a neurological _____ in the _____ _____
that blocks pain signals or lets them through. It may be opened by activation of
_____ (small/large) nerve fibers and closed by activation of _____
(small/large) fibers or by information from the
_____ .

List some pain control techniques used in health care situations.

Taste and Smell (pp. 164–167)

Objective 5: Describe the senses of taste and smell, and comment on the nature of sensory interaction.

1. The basic taste sensations are _____ ,
_____ , _____ ,
_____ , and a meaty taste called
_____ .

2. Taste, which is a _____ sense, is enabled by the 200 or more _____ _____ on the top and sides of the tongue. Each contains a _____ that catches food chemicals.

3. Taste receptors reproduce themselves every _____ . As we age, the number of taste buds _____ (increases/decreases/remains unchanged) and our taste sensitivity _____ (increases/decreases/remains unchanged). Taste is also affected by _____ and by _____ use.

4. When the sense of smell is blocked, as when we have a cold, foods do not taste the same; this illustrates the principle of _____ _____ . The _____ effect occurs when we _____ a speaker saying one syllable while _____ another.

5. Like taste, smell, or _____ , is a _____ sense.

6. Odors are able to evoke memories and feelings because there is a direct link between the brain area that gets information from the nose and the ancient _____ centers associated with memory and emotion.

Body Position and Movement (pp. 167–168)

Objective 6: Distinguish between kinesthesis and the vestibular sense.

1. The system for sensing the position and movement of body parts is called _____ . The receptors for this sense are located in the _____ , _____ , and _____ of the body.

2. The sense that monitors the position and movement of the head (and thus the body) is the _____ _____ . The receptors for this sense are located in the _____ _____ and _____ _____ of the inner ear.

PROGRESS TEST

Multiple-Choice Questions

Circle your answers to the following questions and check them with the answers beginning on page 142. If your answer is incorrect, read the explanation for why it is correct and then consult the appropriate pages of the text.

1. Frequency is to pitch as _____ is to _____ .
   a. wavelength; loudness
   b. amplitude; loudness
   c. wavelength; intensity
   d. amplitude; intensity

2. Our experience of pain when we are injured depends on:
   a. our biological make-up and the type of injury we have sustained.
   b. how well medical personnel deal with our injury.
   c. our physiology, experiences and attention, and surrounding culture.
   b. what our culture allows us to express in terms of feelings of pain.

3. According to the gate-control theory, a way to alleviate chronic pain would be to stimulate the _____ nerve fibers that _____ the spinal gate.
   a. small; open   c. large; open
   b. small; close   d. large; close

4. Kinesthesis involves:
   a. the bones of the middle ear.
   b. information from the muscles, tendons, and joints.
   c. membranes within the cochlea.
   d. the body's sense of balance.

5. Which of the following is *not* one of the basic tastes?
   a. sweet   c. umami
   b. salty   d. bland

6. Of the four distinct skin senses, the only one that has definable receptors is:
   a. warmth.   c. pressure.
   b. cold.   d. pain.

7. The receptors for taste are located in the:
   a. taste buds.   c. fovea.
   b. cochlea.   d. cortex.

8. The inner ear contains receptors for:
   a. audition and kinesthesis.
   b. kinesthesis and the vestibular sense.
   c. audition and the vestibular sense.
   d. audition, kinesthesis, and the vestibular sense.

9. What enables you to feel yourself wiggling your toes even with your eyes closed?
   a. vestibular sense
   b. sense of kinesthesis
   c. the skin senses
   d. sensory interaction

10. The principle that one sense may influence another is:
    a. transduction.
    b. the gate-control theory.
    c. audition.
    d. sensory interaction.

11. The phantom limb sensation indicates that:
    a. pain is a purely sensory phenomenon.
    b. the central nervous system plays only a minor role in the experience of pain.
    c. pain involves the brain's interpretation of neural activity.
    d. all of these answers are true.

12. While competing in the Olympic trials, marathoner Kirsten O'Brien suffered a stress fracture in her left leg. That she did not experience significant pain until the race was over is probably attributable to the fact that during the race:
    a. the pain gate in her spinal cord was closed by information coming from her brain.
    b. her body's production of endorphins decreased.
    c. an increase in the activity of small pain fibers closed the pain gate.
    d. a decrease in the activity of large pain fibers closed the pain gate.

13. Which of the following is an example of sensory interaction?
    a. finding that despite its delicious aroma, a weird-looking meal tastes awful
    b. finding that food tastes bland when you have a bad cold
    c. finding it difficult to maintain your balance when you have an ear infection
    d. All of these answers are examples.

14. Which of the following correctly lists the order of structures through which sound travels after entering the ear?
    a. auditory canal, eardrum, middle ear, cochlea
    b. eardrum, auditory canal, middle ear, cochlea
    c. eardrum, middle ear, cochlea, auditory canal
    d. cochlea, eardrum, middle ear, auditory canal

15. Dr. Frankenstein has forgotten to give his monster an important part; as a result, the monster cannot transduce sound. Dr. Frankenstein omitted the:
    a. eardrum.   c. semicircular canals.
    b. middle ear.   d. basilar membrane.

16. Elderly Mrs. Martinez finds that she must spice her food heavily or she cannot taste it. Unfortunately, her son often finds her cooking inedible because it is so spicy. What is the likely explanation for their taste differences?
    a. Women have higher taste thresholds than men.
    b. Men have higher taste thresholds than women.
    c. Being elderly, Mrs. Martinez probably has fewer taste buds than her son.
    d. All of these answers are likely explanations.

17. When admiring the texture of a piece of fabric, Calvin usually runs his fingertips over the cloth's surface. He does this because:
    a. if the cloth were held motionless, sensory adaptation to its feel would quickly occur.
    b. the sense of touch does not adapt.
    c. a relatively small amount of brain tissue is devoted to processing touch from the fingertips.
    d. of all of these reasons.

18. How does pain differ from other senses?
    a. It has no special receptors.
    b. It has no single stimulus.
    c. It is influenced by both physical and psychological phenomena.
    d. All of these answers are true.

19. Tamiko hates the bitter taste of her cough syrup. Which of the following would she find most helpful in minimizing the syrup's bad taste?
    a. tasting something very sweet before taking the cough syrup
    b. keeping the syrup in her mouth for several seconds before swallowing it
    c. holding her nose while taking the cough syrup
    d. gulping the cough syrup so that it misses her tongue

Matching Items

Match each of the structures with its function or description.

Structures or Conditions

_____   **1.** middle ear
_____   **2.** inner ear
_____   **3.** large nerve fiber
_____   **4.** small nerve fiber
_____   **5.** semicircular canals
_____   **6.** sensors in joints

Functions or Descriptions

a. amplifies sounds
b. closes pain gate
c. vestibular sense
d. opens pain gate
e. transduction of sound
f. kinesthesis

Essay Question

A dancer in a chorus line uses many sensory cues when performing. Discuss three senses that dancers rely on and explain why each is important. (Use the space below to list the points you want to make, and organize them. Then write the essay on a separate sheet of paper.)

Summing Up

Use the diagram to identify the parts of the ear, then describe how each contributes to hearing. Also, briefly explain the role of each structure.

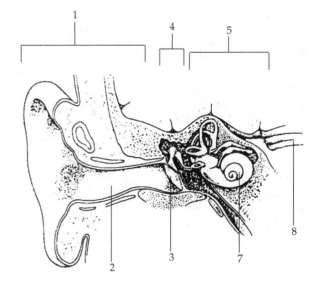

The Ear

1. _____

_____

2. _____

_____

3. _____

_____

4. _____

_____

5. _____

_____

6. _____

_____

7. _____

_____

8. _____

_____

KEY TERMS

Using your own words, on a piece of paper write a brief definition or explanation of each of the following terms.

1. audition

2. frequency and pitch

3. middle ear

4. cochlea

5. inner ear

6. gate-control theory

7. sensory interaction

8. kinesthesis

9. vestibular sense

ANSWERS

Module Review

Hearing

1. audition; air molecules

2. loudness

3. pitch

4. decibels; zero

5. outer; middle; inner

6. eardrum

7. hammer; anvil; stirrup

8. cochlea; oval window; basilar membrane; hair cells; thalamus; temporal

9. speed (timing); intensity

10. harder

Touch

1. pressure; warmth; cold; pain; variations

2. top-down; somatosensory cortex

Pain

1. injury; hyperalgesia

2. senses; brain; expectations

3. phantom limb; tinnitus

4. sensory input

5. is not; does not

6. gate-control; gate; spinal cord; small; large; brain

Pain control techniques include drugs, surgery, acupuncture, thought distraction, exercise, hypnosis, relaxation training, electrical stimulation, and massage. Similarly, for burn victims, distraction during painful wound care can be created by immersion in a computer generated 3-D world.

Taste and *Smell*

1. sweet; sour; salty; bitter; umami

2. chemical; taste buds; pore

3. week or two; decreases; decreases; smoking; alcohol

4. sensory interaction; McGurk; see; hearing

5. olfaction; chemical

6. limbic

Body Position and Movement

1. kinesthesis; muscles; tendons; joints

2. vestibular sense; semicircular canals; vestibular sacs

Progress Test

Multiple-Choice Questions

1. **b.** is the answer. Just as wave frequency determines pitch, so wave amplitude determines loudness.

   a. Amplitude is the physical basis of loudness; wavelength determines frequency and thereby pitch.

   c. & d. Wavelength, amplitude, and intensity are physical aspects of light and sound. Because the question is based on a relationship between a physical property (frequency) of a stimulus and its psychological attribute (pitch), these answers are incorrect.

2. **c.** is the answer. The biopsychosocial approach tells us that our experience of pain depends on biological, psychological, and social-cultural factors.

3. **d.** is the answer. The small fibers conduct most pain signals; the large fibers conduct most other sensory signals from the skin. The gate either allows pain signals to pass on to the brain or blocks them from passing. When the large fibers are stimulated, the pain gate is closed and other sensations are felt in place of pain.

4. **b.** is the answer. Kinesthesis, or the sense of the position and movement of body parts, is based on information from the muscles, tendons, and joints.
a. & c. The ear plays no role in kinesthesis.
d. Equilibrium, or the vestibular sense, is not involved in kinesthesis but is, rather, a companion sense.

5. **d.** is the answer.

6. **c.** is the answer. Researchers have identified receptors for pressure but have been unable to do so for the other skin senses.

7. **a.** is the answer.
b. The cochlea contains receptors for hearing.
c. The fovea contains receptors for vision (the cones).
d. The cortex is the outer layer of the brain, where information detected by the receptors is processed.

8. **c.** is the answer. The inner ear contains the receptors for audition (hearing) and the vestibular sense; those for kinesthesis are located in the muscles, tendons, and joints.

9. **b.** is the answer. Kinesthesis, the sense of movement of body parts, would enable you to feel your toes wiggling.
a. The vestibular sense is concerned with movement and position, or balance, of the whole body, not of its parts.
c. The skin, or tactile, senses are pressure, pain, warmth, and cold; they have nothing to do with movement of body parts.
d. Sensory interaction, the principle that the senses influence each other, does not play a role in this example, which involves only the sense of kinesthesis.

10. **d.** is the answer.
a. Transduction is the process by which stimulus energy is converted into nerve impulses.
b. The gate-control theory is the concept that a "gate" in our spinal cord determines whether pain reaches our brain.
c. Audition is the sense of hearing.

11. **c.** is the answer. Since pain is felt in the limb that does not exist, the pain is simply the brain's (mis)interpretation of neural activity.

a. If pain were a purely sensory phenomenon, phantom limb pain would not occur, since the receptors are no longer present.
b. That pain is experienced when a limb is missing indicates that the central nervous system, especially the brain, is where pain is sensed.

12. **a.** is the answer.
b. Since endorphins relieve pain, a decrease in their production would have made Kirsten more likely to experience pain. Moreover, because endorphins are released in response to pain, their production probably would have increased.
c. Neural activity in small fibers tends to open the pain gate.
d. An *increase* in large-fiber activity would tend to *close* the pain gate.

13. **d.** is the answer. Each of these is an example of the interaction of two senses—vision and taste in the case of (a.), taste and smell in the case of (b.), and hearing and the vestibular sense in the case of (c.).

14. **a.** is the answer.

15. **d.** is the answer. The hair cells, which transduce sound energy, are located on the basilar membrane.
a. & b. The eardrum and bones of the middle ear merely conduct sound waves to the inner ear, where they are transduced.
c. The semicircular canals are involved in the vestibular sense, not hearing.

16. **c.** is the answer. As people age they lose taste buds and their taste thresholds increase. For this reason, Mrs. Martinez needs more concentrated tastes than her son to find food palatable.
a. & b. There is no evidence that women and men differ in their absolute thresholds for taste.

17. **a.** is the answer.
b. The sense of touch (pressure) adapts very quickly.
c. On the contrary, the extreme sensitivity of the fingertips is due to the relatively large amount of cortical tissue that processes neural impulses from the fingertips.

18. **d.** is the answer.

19. **c.** is the answer. Because of the powerful sensory interaction between taste and smell, eliminating the odor of the cough syrup should make its taste more pleasant.
a. If anything, the contrasting tastes might make the bitter syrup even less palatable.
b. If Tamiko keeps the syrup in her mouth for several seconds, it will ensure that her taste pores fully "catch" the stimulus, thus intensifying the bitter taste.

d. It's probably impossible to miss the tongue completely.

Matching Items

1. a   4. d
2. e   5. c
3. b   6. f

Essay Question

The senses that are most important to dancers are vision (see Module 11), hearing, kinesthesis, and the vestibular sense. Your answer should refer to any three of these senses and include, at minimum, the following information.

Dancers rely on vision to gauge their body position relative to other dancers as they perform specific choreographed movements. Vision also helps dancers assess the audience's reaction to their performance. Whenever dance is set to music, hearing is necessary so that the dancers can detect musical cues for certain parts of their routines. Hearing also helps the dancers keep their movements in time with the music. Kinesthetic receptors in dancers' muscles, tendons, and joints provide their brains with information about the position and movement of body parts to determine if their hands, arms, legs, and heads are in the proper positions. Receptors for the vestibular sense located in the dancers' inner ears send messages to their brains that help them maintain their balance and determine the correctness of the position and movement of their bodies.

Summing Up

The Ear

1. Outer ear. Hearing begins as sound waves enter the auditory canal of the outer ear.
2. Auditory canal. Sound waves passing through the auditory canal are brought to a point of focus at the eardrum.
3. Eardrum. Lying between the outer and middle ear, this membrane vibrates in response to sound waves.
4. Middle ear. Lying between the outer and inner ear, this air-filled chamber contains the hammer, anvil, and stirrup.
5. Hammer, anvil, and stirrup. These tiny bones of the middle ear concentrate the eardrum's vibrations on the cochlea's oval window.

6. Inner ear. This region of the ear contains the cochlea and the semicircular canals, which play an important role in balance.
7. Cochlea. This fluid-filled multichambered structure contains the hair cell receptors that transduce sound waves into neural impulses.
8. Auditory nerve. This bundle of fibers carries nerve impulses from the inner ear to the brain.

Key Terms

1. **Audition** refers to the sense of hearing.
2. **Frequency** is directly related to wavelength: longer waves produce lower pitch; shorter waves produce higher pitch. The **pitch** of a sound is determined by its frequency, that is, the number of complete wavelengths that can pass a point in a given time.
3. The **middle ear** is the chamber between the eardrum and cochlea containing the three bones (hammer, anvil, and stirrup) that concentrate the eardrum's vibrations on the cochlea's oval window.
4. The **cochlea** is the coiled, bony, fluid-filled tube of the inner ear through which sound waves trigger neural impulses.
5. The **inner ear** contains the semicircular canals and the cochlea, which includes the receptors that sound energy into neural impulses. Because it also contains the vestibular sac, the inner ear plays an important role in balance, as well as in audition.
6. Melzack and Wall's **gate-control theory** maintains that a "gate" in the spinal cord determines whether pain signals are permitted to reach the brain. Neural activity in small nerve fibers opens the gates; activity in large fibers or information from the brain closes the gate.

   Example: The **gate-control theory** gained support with the discovery of endorphins. Production of these opiatelike chemicals may be the brain's mechanism for closing the spinal gate.
7. **Sensory interaction** is the principle that one sense may influence another.
8. **Kinesthesis** is the sense of the position and movement of the parts of the body.
9. The sense of body movement and position, including the sense of balance, is called the **vestibular sense.**

FOCUS ON VOCABULARY AND LANGUAGE

Hearing

We also are remarkably sensitive to *faint sounds*, an obvious *boon* for our ancestors' survival when *hunting* or being *hunted*, or for detecting a *child's whimper*. Humans are very good at detecting very quiet noises (*faint sounds*), which was clearly beneficial (*a boon*) to our predecessors' ability to survive when they were both predator (*hunter*) and prey (*being hunted*). Likewise, the ability to notice and respond to a youngster's quiet cry of distress (*a child's whimper*) would have had adaptive value. We are also very sensitive to changes in sounds and we have the ability to differentiate among thousands of human voices.

A *piccolo* produces much shorter, faster sound waves than does a *bass guitar*. Musical instruments produce stimulus energy called sound waves—molecules of air that bump and push each other along—and these may be long (low frequency) or short (high frequency). A *bass guitar* produces low-frequency sound waves and thus has a lower pitch than a *piccolo* (a small flute), which produces high-frequency waves and has a higher pitch.

If a car to the right *honks*, your right ear receives a more *intense* sound, and it receives sound slightly *sooner* than your left ear (Figure 12.4). We locate sounds because our ears are about 6 inches apart and there is a time, as well as a loudness difference, between auditory reception in each ear. If we hear the sound of a car horn (*it honks*) to our right, the left ear receives a less intense sound somewhat later than the right ear, and thus we locate the direction of the sound to the right.

That is why, when trying to *pinpoint* a sound, you *cock your head*, so that your two ears will receive slightly different messages. When a sound is equidistant from our two ears (directly ahead, behind, or above), and there is no visual clue, we have trouble locating (*pinpointing*) the source. In this situation it helps to tilt (*cock*) our heads so that each ear receives a slightly different message (the sound will be a little louder and sensed a little sooner by one ear, and the brain uses this information to detect where the sound is coming from).

Touch

As lovers, we *yearn* to touch—to kiss, to stroke, *to snuggle*. Our sense of touch involves a mixture of at least four distinct senses: pressure, warmth, cold, and pain. Intimate relations often involve a desire or longing (*we yearn*) to caress, kiss, and closely embrace each other (*snuggle*).

Pain

Rubbing the area around your *stubbed toe* will create competing stimulation that will *block* some of the pain messages. If you hit your toe against a solid object (*stub your toe*), it really hurts. If, however, you massage (*rub*) the part around the sore spot, it makes you feel better because stimulation interferes with (*blocks*) some of the pain messages. This supports the **gate-control** model, which suggests that this stimulation (*rubbing*) will activate "gate-closing" in large neural fibers and, thus, will reduce pain.

A well-trained nurse may distract *needle-shy* patients by chatting with them and asking them to look away when inserting the needle. One method of pain control is through distraction. If you are nervous or anxious about being injected with a hypodermic needle (*a needle-shy patient*), the nurse may talk to you about unimportant matters (*she chats with you*) and request that you do not watch the procedure. This type of distraction can reduce the intensity of the pain.

Taste

Essential as taste buds are, *there's more to taste than meets the tongue*. The common expression "*there is more to this than meets the eye*" suggests that there is something extra going on over and above the obvious or apparent. Myers creates a variation of this expression using a different sense (taste). The flavors we experience are a function of more than just the taste buds in the tongue; they involve **sensory interaction** with the sense of smell (**olfaction**). Thus, the sense of taste involves more than simply responding to the chemicals that stimulate taste receptors in the tongue (there is more to taste than meets the tongue).

Smell

Between those two moments, you will daily inhale and exhale nearly 20,000 breaths of life-sustaining air, *bathing* your nostrils in a *stream of scent-laden molecules*. Smell (**olfaction**) is a chemical sense and as substances (flowers, feet, fish, fertilizer, etc.) release molecules, they are carried by the air we breathe (*a stream of scent-laden molecules*) and wash over (*bathe*) receptors in our nasal cavities (nostrils).

Body Position and Movement

The biological *gyroscopes* for this sense of *equilibrium* are in the inner ear. A *gyroscope* is a mechanical device used as a stabilizer in navigation and scientific instruments. Likewise, we have biological stabilizers that monitor the movement and position of our bodies and provide us with a sense of balance (*equilibrium*). They are called the *semicircular canals* and the *vestibular sacs* and are located in the inner ear.

Perceptual Organization

MODULE OVERVIEW

Module 13 explores how we select and organize our sensations into meaningful perceptions. The module introduces a wide range of terminology, especially in the sections on form perception and depth perception. Doing the module review several times and rehearsing the material frequently will help you to memorize the processes by which we perceive objects in our environment. Also, trying some of the illusions presented in the text will help you to understand how the brain interprets what the senses take in.

NOTE: Answer guidelines for all Module 13 questions begin on page 151.

MODULE REVIEW

First, skim each section, noting headings and boldface items. After you have read the section, review each objective by answering the fill-in and essay-type questions that follow it. As you proceed, evaluate your performance by consulting the answers on page 151. Do not continue with the next section until you understand each answer. If you need to, review or reread the section in the textbook before continuing.

> David Myers at times uses idioms that are unfamiliar to some readers. If you do not know the meaning of the following words, phrases, or expressions in the context in which they appear in the text, refer to page 154 for an explanation: *Sometimes, however, they lead us astray; mothers then coaxed them to crawl out onto the glass; The floating finger sausage; through a paper tube.*

Introducing Perceptual Organization (p. 171)

Objective 1: Describe Gestalt psychology's contribution to our understanding of perception.

1. According to the _____ school of psychology, we tend to organize a cluster of sensations into a _____ , or form.

Form Perception (pp. 171–173)

Objective 2: Explain the figure-ground relationship, and identify principles of perceptual grouping in form perception.

1. When we view a scene, we see the central object, or _____ , as distinct from surrounding stimuli, or the _____ .

2. Proximity, similarity, closure, continuity, and connectedness are examples of Gestalt rules of

   _____ .

3. The principle that we organize stimuli into smooth, continuous patterns is called

   _____ . The principle that we fill in gaps to create a complete, whole object is

   _____ . The grouping of items that are close to each other is the principle of

   _____ ; the grouping of items that look alike is the principle of

   _____ . The tendency to perceive uniform or attached items as a single unit is the

   principle of _____ .

Depth Perception (pp. 173–175)

Objective 3: Discuss research on depth perception involving the use of the visual cliff, and describe the binocular and monocular cues we use to perceive depth.

1. The ability to see objects in three dimensions despite their two-dimensional representations on our retinas is called _____ _____ . It enables us to estimate _____ .

2. Gibson and Walk developed the _____ _____ to test depth perception in infants. They found that each species, by the time it is _____ , has the perceptual abilities it needs.

Summarize the results of Gibson and Walk's studies of depth perception.

For questions 3–11, identify the depth perception cue that is defined.

3. Any cue that requires both eyes: _____ .

4. The greater the difference between the images received by the two eyes, the nearer the object: _____ _____ . 3-D movies simulate this cue by photographing each scene with two cameras.

5. Any cue that requires either eye alone: _____ .

6. If two objects are presumed to be the same size, the one that casts a smaller retinal image is perceived as farther away: _____ _____ .

7. An object partially covered by another is seen as farther away: _____ .

8. Objects lower in the visual field are seen as nearer: _____ _____ .

9. As we move, objects at different distances appear to move at different rates: _____ _____ .

10. Parallel lines appear to converge in the distance: _____ _____ .

11. The dimmer of two objects seems farther away: _____ _____ _____ .

Perceptual Constancy (pp. 176–179)

Objective 4: Describe the perceptual constancies, and show how the perceived size-distance relationship operates in visual illusions.

1. Our tendency to see objects as unchanging while the stimuli from them change in size, shape, and lightness is called _____ _____ .

2. The experience of color depends on the surrounding _____ in which an object is seen. In an unvarying context, a familiar object will be perceived as having consistent color, even as the light changes. This phenomenon is called _____ _____ .

3. We see color as a result of our brains' computations of the light _____ by any object relative to its _____ _____ .

4. Due to shape and size constancy, familiar objects _____ (do/do not) appear to change shape or size despite changes in our _____ images of them.

5. Several illusions, including the _____ and _____ illusions, are explained by the interplay between perceived _____ and perceived _____ . When distance cues are removed, these illusions are _____ (diminished/strengthened).

6. The brain computes an object's brightness _____ (relative to/independent of) surrounding objects.

7. The amount of light an object reflects relative to its surroundings is called

_____ _____ .

PROGRESS TEST

Multiple-Choice Questions

Circle your answers to the following questions and check them with the answers beginning on page 151. If your answer is incorrect, read the explanation for why it is correct and then consult the appropriate pages of the text.

1. The historical movement associated with the idea that the perceived whole differs from the sum of its parts is:
   a. cognitive psychology.
   b. behavioral psychology.
   c. functional psychology.
   d. Gestalt psychology.

2. Figures tend to be perceived as whole, complete objects, even if spaces or gaps exist in the representation, thus demonstrating the principle of:
   a. connectedness.   c. continuity.
   b. similarity.   d. closure.

3. The figure-ground relationship has demonstrated that:
   a. perception is largely innate.
   b. perception is simply a point-for-point representation of sensation.
   c. the same stimulus can trigger more than one perception.
   d. different people see different things when viewing a scene.

4. When we stare at an object, each eye receives a slightly different image, providing a depth cue known as:
   a. interposition.   c. relative motion.
   b. linear perspective. d. retinal disparity.

5. As we move, viewed objects cast changing shapes on our retinas, although we do not perceive the objects as changing. This is part of the phenomenon of:
   a. perceptual constancy.
   b. relative motion.
   c. linear perspective.
   d. continuity.

6. Which of the following is *not* a monocular depth cue?
   a. light and shadow   c. retinal disparity
   b. relative height   d. interposition

7. The Moon illusion occurs in part because distance cues at the horizon make the Moon seem:
   a. farther away and therefore larger.
   b. closer and therefore larger.
   c. farther away and therefore smaller.
   d. closer and therefore smaller.

8. Figure is to ground as _____ is to _____ .
   a. night; day
   b. top; bottom
   c. cloud; sky
   d. sensation; perception

9. The tendency to organize stimuli into smooth, uninterrupted patterns is called:
   a. closure.   c. similarity.
   b. continuity.   d. proximity.

10. Which of the following statements is consistent with the Gestalt theory of perception?
    a. Perception develops largely through learning.
    b. Perception is the product of heredity.
    c. The mind organizes sensations into meaningful perceptions.
    d. Perception results directly from sensation.

11. The phenomenon of size constancy is based on the close connection between an object's perceived _____ and its perceived _____ .
    a. size; shape   c. size; brightness
    b. size; distance   d. shape; distance

12. The depth cue that occurs when we watch stable objects at different distances as we are moving is:
    a. linear perspective. c. relative clarity.
    b. interposition.   d. relative motion.

13. Each time you see your car, it projects a different image on the retinas of your eyes, yet you do not perceive it as changing. This is because of:
    a. interposition.
    b. retinal disparity.
    c. perceptual constancy.
    d. figure-ground.

14. The term *gestalt* means:
    a. grouping.   c. perception.
    b. sensation.   d. whole.

15. Studies of the visual cliff have provided evidence that much of depth perception is:
    a. innate.
    b. learned.
    c. innate in lower animals, learned in humans.
    d. innate in humans, learned in lower animals.

16. All of the following are laws of perceptual organization *except*:
    a. proximity.   c. continuity.
    b. closure.   d. retinal disparity.

● ● ● ● ● ●

17. You probably perceive the diagram above as three separate objects due to the principle of:
    a. proximity.   c. closure.
    b. continuity.   d. connectedness.

18. The fact that a white object under dim illumination appears lighter than a gray object under bright illumination is called:
    a. relative luminance.
    b. retinal disparity.
    c. color contrast.
    d. lightness constancy.

19. When two familiar objects of equal size cast unequal retinal images, the object that casts the smaller retinal image will be perceived as being:
    a. closer than the other object.
    b. more distant than the other object.
    c. larger than the other object.
    d. smaller than the other object.

20. As her friend Milo walks toward her, Noriko perceives his size as remaining constant because his perceived distance _____ at the same time that her retinal image of him _____ .
    a. increases; decreases
    b. increases; increases
    c. decreases; decreases
    d. decreases; increases

21. In the *absence* of perceptual constancy:
    a. objects would appear to change size as their distance from us changed.
    b. depth perception would be based exclusively on monocular cues.
    c. depth perception would be based exclusively on binocular cues.
    d. depth perception would be impossible.

22. How do we perceive a pole that partially covers a wall?
    a. as farther away
    b. as nearer
    c. as larger
    d. There is not enough information to determine the object's size or distance.

23. An artist paints a tree orchard so that the parallel rows of trees converge at the top of the canvas. Which cue has the artist used to convey distance?
    a. interposition   c. linear perspective
    b. retinal disparity d. figure-ground

24. Objects higher in our field of vision are perceived as _____ due to the principle of _____ .
    a. nearer; relative height
    b. nearer; linear perspective
    c. farther away; relative height
    d. farther away; linear perspective

25. Your friend tosses you a frisbee. You know that it is getting closer instead of larger because of:
    a. shape constancy.   c. size constancy.
    b. relative motion.   d. all of these answers.

26. Studying the road map before her trip, Colleen had no trouble following the route of the highway she planned to travel. Colleen's ability illustrates the principle of:
    a. closure.   c. continuity.
    b. similarity.   d. proximity.

True–False Items

Indicate whether each statement is true or false by placing *T* or *F* in the blank next to the item.

_____ 1. Once we perceive an item as a figure, it is impossible to see it as ground.

_____ 2. Six-month-old infants will cross a visual cliff if their mother calls.

_____ 3. It is just as easy to touch two pencil tips together with only one eye open as it is with both eyes open.

_____ 4. As our distance from an object changes, the object's size seems to change.

Essay Question

In many movies from the 1930s, dancers performed seemingly meaningless movements which, when viewed from above, were transformed into intricate patterns and designs. Similarly, the formations of marching bands often create pictures and spell words. Identify and describe at least four Gestalt principles of grouping that explain the audience's perception of the images created by these types of formations. (Use the space below to list the points you want to make, and organize them. Then write the essay on a separate piece of paper.)

KEY TERMS

Using your own words, on a piece of paper write a brief definition or explanation of each of the following terms.

1. gestalt

2. figure-ground

3. grouping

4. depth perception

5. visual cliff

6. binocular cue

7. retinal disparity

8. monocular cue

9. perceptual constancy

10. color constancy

ANSWERS
Module Review

Introducing Perceptual Organization

1. Gestalt; whole

Form Perception

1. figure; ground

2. grouping

3. continuity; closure; proximity; similarity; connectedness

Depth Perception

1. depth perception; distance

2. visual cliff; mobile

Research on the visual cliff suggests that in many species the ability to perceive depth is present at, or very shortly after, birth.

3. binocular

4. retinal disparity

5. monocular

6. relative size

7. interposition

8. relative height

9. relative motion

10. linear perspective

11. light and shadow

Perceptual Constancy

1. perceptual constancy

2. context; color constancy

3. reflected; surrounding objects

4. do not; retinal

5. Moon; Ponzo; size; distance; diminished

6. relative to

7. relative luminance

Progress Test

Multiple-Choice Questions

1. **d.** is the answer. Gestalt psychology, which developed in Germany early in the twentieth century, was interested in how clusters of sensations are organized into "whole" perceptions.

a. Cognitive psychology is the study of how we perceive, think, and solve problems.

b. & c. Behavioral and functional psychology developed later in the United States.

2. **d.** is the answer.

   a. Connectedness refers to the tendency to see uniform and linked items as a unit.

   b. Similarity refers to the tendency to group similar items.

   c. Continuity refers to the tendency to group stimuli into smooth, continuous patterns.

3. **c.** is the answer. Although we always differentiate a stimulus into figure and ground, those elements of the stimulus we perceive as figure and those as ground may change. In this way, the same stimulus can trigger more than one perception.

   a. The idea of a figure-ground relationship has no bearing on the issue of whether perception is innate.

   b. Perception cannot be simply a point-for-point representation of sensation, since in figure-ground relationships a single stimulus can trigger more than one perception.

   d. Figure-ground relationships demonstrate the existence of general, rather than individual, principles of perceptual organization. Significantly, even the same person can see different figure-ground relationships when viewing a scene.

4. **d.** is the answer. The greater the retinal disparity, or difference between the images, the less the distance.

   a. Interposition is the monocular distance cue in which an object that partially blocks another object is seen as closer.

   b. Linear perspective is the monocular distance cue in which parallel lines appear to converge in the distance.

   c. Relative motion is the monocular distance cue in which objects at different distances change their relative positions in our visual image, with those closest moving most.

5. **a.** is the answer. Perception of constant shape, like perception of constant size, is part of the phenomenon of perceptual constancy.

   b. Relative motion is a monocular distance cue in which objects at different distances appear to move at different rates.

   c. Linear perspective is a monocular distance cue in which lines we know to be parallel converge in the distance, thus indicating depth.

   d. Continuity is the perceptual tendency to group items into continuous patterns.

6. **c.** is the answer. Retinal disparity is a *binocular* cue; all the other cues mentioned are monocular.

7. **a.** is the answer. The Moon appears larger at the horizon than overhead in the sky because objects at the horizon provide distance cues that make the Moon seem farther away and therefore larger. In the open sky, of course, there are no such cues.

8. **c.** is the answer. We see a cloud as a figure against the background of sky.

   a., b., & d. The figure-ground relationship refers to the organization of the visual field into objects (figures) that stand out from their surroundings (ground).

9. **b.** is the answer.

   a. Closure refers to the tendency to perceptually fill in gaps in recognizable objects in the visual field.

   c. Similarity refers to the tendency to group items that are similar.

   d. Proximity refers to the tendency to group items that are near one another.

10. **c.** is the answer.

    a. & b. The Gestalt psychologists did not deal with the origins of perception; they were more concerned with its form.

    d. In fact, they argued just the opposite: Perception is more than mere sensory experience.

11. **b.** is the answer.

12. **d.** is the answer. When we move, stable objects we see also appear to move, and the distance and speed of the apparent motion cue us to the objects' relative distances.

    a., b., & c. These depth cues are unrelated to movement and thus work even when we are stationary.

13. **c.** is the answer. Because of perceptual constancy, we see the car's shape and size as always the same.

    a. Interposition is the monocular cue that objects that block our view of other objects are perceived as closer.

    b. Retinal disparity means that our right and left eyes each receive slightly different images.

    d. Figure-ground refers to the organization of the visual field into two parts.

14. **d.** is the answer. Gestalt means a "form" or "organized whole."

15. **a.** is the answer. Most infants refused to crawl out over the "cliff" even when coaxed, suggesting that much of depth perception is innate. Studies with the young of "lower" animals show the same thing.

16. **d.** is the answer.

17. **d.** is the answer.
   a. Proximity is the tendency to group objects near to one another. The diagram is perceived as three distinct units, even though the points are evenly spaced.
   b. Continuity is the tendency to group stimuli into smooth, uninterrupted patterns. There is no such continuity in the diagram.
   c. Closure is the perceptual tendency to fill in gaps in a form. In the diagram, three disconnected units are perceived rather than a single whole.

18. **d.** is the answer. Although the amount of light reflected from a white object is less in dim light than in bright light—and may be less than the amount of light reflected from a brightly lit gray object—the brightness of the white object is perceived as remaining constant. Because a white object reflects a higher percentage of the light falling on it than does a gray object, and the brightness of objects is perceived as constant despite variations in illumination, white is perceived as brighter than gray even under dim illumination.
   a. Relative luminance refers to the relative intensity of light falling on surfaces that are in proximity. Lightness constancy is perceived despite variations in illumination.
   b. Retinal disparity refers to the differences between the images received by the left eye and the right eye.
   c. Color contrast is not discussed in this text.

19. **b.** is the answer. The phenomenon described is the basis for the monocular cue of relative size.
   a. The object casting the *larger* retinal image would be perceived as closer.
   c. & d. Because of size constancy, the perceived size of familiar objects remains constant, despite changes in their retinal image size.

20. **d.** is the answer.

21. **a.** is the answer. Because we perceive the size of a familiar object as constant even as its retinal image grows smaller, we perceive the object as being farther away.
   b. & c. Perceptual constancy is a cognitive, rather than sensory, phenomenon. Therefore, the absence of perceptual constancy would not alter sensitivity to monocular or binocular cues.
   d. Although the absence of perceptual constancy would impair depth perception based on the size-distance relationship, other cues to depth could still be used.

22. **b.** is the answer. This is an example of the principle of interposition in depth perception.
   a. The partially *obscured* object is perceived as farther away.

c. The perceived size of an object is not altered when that object overlaps another.

23. **c.** is the answer.
   a. Interposition is a monocular depth cue in which an object that partially covers another is perceived as closer.
   b. Retinal disparity refers to the difference between the two images received by our eyes that allows us to perceive depth. It has nothing to do with the way the artist placed the trees.
   d. Figure-ground refers to the organization of the field into objects that stand out from their surroundings.

24. **c.** is the answer.
   b. & d. Linear perspective is the apparent convergence of parallel lines as a cue to distance.

25. **a.** is the answer.

26. **c.** is the answer. She perceives the line for the road as continuous, even though it is interrupted by lines indicating other roads.
   a. Closure refers to the perceptual filling in of gaps in a stimulus to create a complete, whole object.
   b. Similarity is the tendency to perceive similar objects as belonging together. On a road map, all the lines representing roads appear similar. Thus, this cue could not be the basis for Colleen's ability to trace the route of a particular road.
   d. Proximity is the tendency to group objects near to one another as a single unit.

True–False Items

   1. F   3. F
   2. F   4. F

Essay Question

   1. *Proximity.* We tend to perceive items that are near each other as belonging together. Thus, a small section of dancers or members of a marching band may separate themselves from the larger group in order to form part of a particular image.

   2. *Similarity.* Because we perceive similar figures as belonging together, choreographers and band directors often create distinct visual groupings within the larger band or dance troupe by having the members of each group wear a distinctive costume or uniform.

   3. *Continuity.* Because we perceive smooth, continuous patterns rather than discontinuous ones, dancers or marching musicians moving together (as in a column, for example) are perceived as a separate unit.

   4. *Closure.* If a figure has gaps, we complete it, filling in the gaps to create a whole image. Thus, we

perceptually fill in the relatively wide spacing between dancers or marching musicians in order to perceive the complete words or forms they are creating.

Key Terms

1. **Gestalt** means "organized whole." The Gestalt psychologists emphasized our tendency to integrate pieces of information into meaningful wholes.

2. **Figure-ground** refers to the organization of the visual field into two parts: the figure, which stands out from its surroundings, and the surroundings, or background.

3. **Grouping** is the perceptual tendency to organize stimuli into coherent groups. Gestalt psychologists identified various principles of grouping.

4. **Depth perception** is the ability to see objects in three dimensions although the images that strike the retina are two-dimensional; it allows us to judge distance.

5. The **visual cliff** is a laboratory device for testing depth perception, especially in infants and young animals. In their experiments with the visual cliff,

Gibson and Walk found strong evidence that depth perception is at least in part innate. (p. 165)

6. **Binocular cues** are depth cues that depend on information from both eyes.

   Memory aid: *Bi-* indicates "two"; *ocular* means something pertaining to the eye. **Binocular cues** are cues for the "two eyes."

7. **Retinal disparity** refers to the differences between the images received by the left eye and the right eye as a result of viewing the world from slightly different angles. It is a binocular depth cue, since the greater the difference between the two images, the nearer the object.

8. **Monocular cues** are depth cues that depend on information from either eye alone.

   Memory aid: *Mono-* means one; a monocle is an eyeglass for one eye. A **monocular cue** is one that is available to either the left or the right eye.

9. **Perceptual constancy** is the perception that objects have consistent lightness, color, shape, and size, even as illumination and retinal images change.

10. **Color constancy** is the perception that familiar objects have consistent color despite changes in illumination that shift the wavelengths they reflect.

FOCUS ON VOCABULARY AND LANGUAGE

Form Perception

Usually, these and other grouping principles help us construct reality. Sometimes, however, they *lead us astray*. Although we put together elements of sensation through active organization (the Gestalt grouping principles) and end up with a unitary experience, we sometimes make mistakes in the process (*we are led astray*).

Depth Perception

Their mothers then *coaxed* them to *crawl* out onto the glass. In the experiment with the **visual cliff**, 6- to 14-month-old children were gently encouraged (*coaxed*) by their mothers to move, on their hands and knees (*crawl*), onto the invisible glass top on the "deep" side of the apparatus. Most could not be persuaded to do so, leading to the conclusion that depth perception may be innate (inborn). The idea for this famous experiment came to Gibson when she was at the Grand Canyon and wondered if a young child (toddler) looking (*peering*) over the edge of the canyon would recognize the steep, unsafe, incline (*dangerous drop-off*) and retreat (*draw back*).

The floating *finger sausage* (Figure 13.6). Try the demonstration and you will experience the effect of **retinal disparity** and see a tubular shape (*finger sausage*) made by your brain from the two different images of your fingers.

Take away these distance cues—by looking at the horizon Moon (or each monster or each bar) through a *paper tube*—and the object immediately shrinks. Observers have argued for centuries about why the Moon near the horizon seems so much larger than the Moon overhead in the sky. One explanation involves the interaction of perceived size and perceived distance. Distance cues at the horizon make the Moon appear farther away than when it is overhead (where there are no distance cues). The Moon casts the *same retinal image* in both situations, so the image that appears to be more distant (i.e., near the horizon) will therefore seem larger. We can eliminate the distance cues by looking at the Moon through a rolled-up piece of paper (*paper tube*); the Moon will appear much smaller (*it shrinks*).

Perceptual Interpretation

MODULE OVERVIEW

Module 14 explores how we interpret our sensations into meaningful perceptions. It deals with two important issues. The first issue is the role of experience, as opposed to heredity, in perception. Make sure you understand the results of studies of recovery from blindness, early sensory restriction, adaptation to distorted environments, and perceptual set. The second is the possible existence of ESP, or perception without sensation. You should be able to discuss both the claims made for ESP and the criticisms of these claims.

Human factors psychologists study the interaction of people and machines and try to find ways to increase safety and productivity.

NOTE: Answer guidelines for all Module 14 questions begin on page 158.

MODULE REVIEW

First, skim each section, noting headings and boldface items. After you have read the section, review each objective by answering the fill-in and essay-type questions that follow it. As you proceed, evaluate your performance by consulting the answers on page 158. Do not continue with the next section until you understand each answer. If you need to, review or reread the section in the textbook before continuing.

> David Myers at times uses idioms that are unfamiliar to some readers. If you do not know the meaning of the following words, phrases, or expressions in the context in which they appear in the text, refer to page 160 for an explanation: *Ping-Pong ball; we may feel slightly disoriented, even dizzy; to see is to believe . . . to*

> *believe is to see; a "monster" in Scotland's Loch Ness; from what's behind our eyes and between our ears; in the eyes of their beholders; uncanny; mind-blowing performances; uncanny; mind-blowing performances.*

Introduction and Sensory Deprivation and Restored Vision (pp. 181–182)

Objective 1: Describe the debate over the role of nature and nurture in perception, and discuss what research findings on sensory deprivation and restored vision have contributed to this debate.

1. The idea that knowledge comes from inborn ways of organizing sensory experiences was proposed by the philosopher _____ .

2. On the other side were philosophers who maintained that we learn to perceive the world by experiencing it. One philosopher of this school was _____ .

3. Studies of cases in which vision has been restored to a person who was blind from birth show that, upon *seeing* tactilely familiar objects for the first time, the person _____ (can/cannot) recognize them.

4. Studies of sensory restriction demonstrate that visual experiences during _____ are crucial for perceptual development. Such experiences suggest that there is a

   _____ _____ for normal sensory and perceptual development. For this reason, human infants born with an opaque lens, called a _____ , typically have corrective surgery within a few months.

Perceptual Adaptation (pp. 182–183)

Objective 2: Explain what the use of distorting goggles indicates regarding the adaptability of perception.

1. Humans given glasses that shift or invert the visual field _____ (will/will not) adapt to the distorted perception. This is called _____ _____ .

2. Animals such as chicks _____ (adapt/do not adapt) to distorting lenses.

Perceptual Set (pp. 183–185)

Objective 3: Discuss the effects of assumptions, expectations, and context on our perceptions.

1. A mental predisposition that influences perception is called a _____

    _____ .

2. How a stimulus is perceived depends on our perceptual schemas and the _____ in which it is experienced.

3. The context of a stimulus creates a _____ (top-down/bottom-up) expectation that influences our perception as we match our _____ (top-down/bottom-up) signal against it.

4. Our perception is also influenced by _____ about gender and the _____ context of our experiences.

(Thinking Critically) Is There Extrasensory Perception? (pp. 186–187)

Objective 4: Identify the three most testable forms of ESP, and explain why most research psychologists remain skeptical of ESP claims.

1. Perception outside the range of normal sensation is called _____

    _____ .

2. Psychologists who study ESP are called

    _____ .

3. The form of ESP in which people claim to be capable of reading others' minds is called _____ . A person who "senses" that a friend is in danger might claim to have the

ESP ability of _____ . An ability to "see" into the future is called _____ . A person who claims to be able to levitate and move objects is claiming the power of

_____ .

4. Analyses of psychic visions and premonitions reveal _____ (high/chance-level) accuracy. Nevertheless, some people continue to believe in their accuracy because vague predictions often are later_____ to match events that have already occurred. In addition, people are more likely to recall or _____ dreams that seem to have come true.

5. Critics point out that a major difficulty for parapsychology is that ESP phenomena are not consistently _____ .

6. Researchers who tried to reduce external distractions between a "sender" and a "receiver" in an ESP experiment reported performance levels that _____ (beat/did not beat) chance levels. More recent studies _____ (failed to replicate the results/found equally high levels of performance).

Perception and the Human Factor (pp. 185, 188–189)

Objective 5: Explain how psychologists contribute to the development of user-friendly machines and work settings.

1. Psychologists who study the importance of considering perceptual principles in the design of machines, appliances, and work settings are called _____

    _____ _____ .

2. Victims of the *curse of knowledge*, technology developers who assume that others share their _____ , may create designs that are unclear to others. Another example of failure to consider the human factor in design is the

    _____ _____ technology that provides embarrassing headsets that amplify sound for people with hearing loss.

PROGRESS TEST

Multiple-Choice Questions

Circle your answers to the following questions and check them with the answers beginning on page 158. If your answer is incorrect, read the explanation for why it is correct and then consult the appropriate pages of the text.

1. A person claiming to be able to read another's mind is claiming to have the ESP ability of:

   a. psychokinesis.   c. clairvoyance.
   b. precognition.   d. telepathy.

2. Which philosopher maintained that knowledge comes from inborn ways of organizing our sensory experiences?

   a. Locke   c. May
   b. Kant   d. Warren

3. Kittens and monkeys reared seeing only diffuse, unpatterned light:

   a. later had difficulty distinguishing color and brightness.
   b. later had difficulty perceiving color and brightness, but eventually regained normal sensitivity.
   c. later had difficulty perceiving the shape of objects.
   d. showed no impairment in perception, indicating that neural feature detectors develop even in the absence of normal sensory experiences.

4. Adults who are born blind but later have their vision restored:

   a. are almost immediately able to recognize familiar objects.
   b. typically fail to recognize familiar objects.
   c. are unable to follow moving objects with their eyes.
   d. have excellent eye-hand coordination.

5. Which of the following influences perception?

   a. biological maturation
   b. the context in which stimuli are perceived
   c. expectations
   d. all of these answers

6. Jack claims that he often has dreams that predict future events. He claims to have the power of:

   a. telepathy.   c. precognition.
   b. clairvoyance.   d. psychokinesis.

7. Researchers who investigated telepathy found that:

   a. when external distractions are reduced, both the "sender" and the "receiver" become much more accurate in demonstrating ESP.
   b. only "senders" become much more accurate.
   c. only "receivers" become much more accurate.
   d. over many studies, none of these events occur.

8. Experiments with distorted visual environments demonstrate that:

   a. adaptation rarely takes place.
   b. animals adapt readily, but humans do not.
   c. humans adapt readily, while lower animals typically do not.
   d. adaptation is possible during a critical period in infancy but not thereafter.

9. The phenomenon that refers to the ways in which an individual's expectations influence perception is called:

   a. perceptual set.
   b. parapsychology.
   c. perceptual adaptation.
   d. psychokinesis.

10. According to the philosopher _____ , we learn to perceive the world.

    a. Locke   c. May
    b. Kant   d. Warren

11. Which of the following statements best describes the effects of sensory restriction?

    a. It produces functional blindness when experienced for any length of time at any age.
    b. It has greater effects on humans than on animals.
    c. It has more damaging effects when experienced during infancy.
    d. It has greater effects on adults than on children.

12. Psychologists who study ESP are called:

    a. clairvoyants.   c. parapsychologists.
    b. telepaths.   d. levitators.

13. Which of the following statements concerning ESP is true?

    a. Most ESP researchers are quacks.
    b. There have been a large number of reliable demonstrations of ESP.
    c. Most research psychologists are skeptical of the claims of defenders of ESP.
    d. There have been reliable laboratory demonstrations of ESP, but the results are no different from those that would occur by chance.

14. Regina claims that she can bend spoons, levitate furniture, and perform many other "mind over matter" feats. Regina apparently believes she has the power of:

   a. telepathy.   **c.** precognition.

   b. clairvoyance.   **d.** psychokinesis.

15. The predictions of leading psychics are:

   a. often ambiguous prophecies later interpreted to match actual events.

   b. no more accurate than guesses made by others.

   c. nearly always inaccurate.

   d. all of these answers.

16. Thanks to _____ , TiVo has solved the TV recording problem caused by the complexity of VCRs.

   a. Gestalt psychologists

   b. human factors psychologists

   c. cognitive psychologists

   d. social psychologists

True–False Items

Indicate whether each statement is true or false by placing *T* or *F* in the blank next to the item.

_____ **1.** Laboratory experiments have laid to rest all criticisms of ESP.

_____ **2.** Unlike other animals, humans have no critical period for visual stimulation.

_____ **3.** Immanuel Kant argued that experience determined how we perceive the world.

_____ **4.** After a period of time, humans are able to adjust to living in a world made upside down by distorting goggles.

_____ **5.** Perception is influenced by psychological factors such as set and expectation as well as by physiological events.

_____ **6.** John Locke argued that perception is inborn.

KEY TERMS

Using your own words, on a piece of paper write a brief definition or explanation of each of the following terms.

1. perceptual adaptation

2. perceptual set

3. extrasensory perception (ESP)

4. parapsychology

ANSWERS
Module Review

Introduction and *Sensory Deprivation and Restored Vision*

1. Kant
2. Locke
3. cannot
4. infancy; critical period; cataract

Perceptual Adaptation

1. will; perceptual adaptation
2. do not adapt

Perceptual Set

1. perceptual set
2. context
3. top-down; bottom-up
4. stereotypes; emotional

(Thinking Critically) Is There Extrasensory Perception?

1. extrasensory perception
2. parapsychologists
3. telepathy; clairvoyance; precognition; psychokinesis
4. chance-level; interpreted (retrofitted); reconstruct
5. reproducible
6. beat; failed to replicate the results

Perception and the Human Factor

1. human factors psychologists
2. expertise; assistive listening

Progress Test

Multiple-Choice Questions

1. **d.** is the answer.
   a. Psychokinesis refers to the claimed ability to perform acts of "mind over matter."
   b. Precognition refers to the claimed ability to perceive future events.
   c. Clairvoyance refers to the claimed ability to perceive remote events.

2. **b.** is the answer.
   a. Locke argued that knowledge is not inborn but comes through learning.

c. & d. Michael May, born blind, was given sight as an adult. His case demonstrated the importance of experience for vision. Richard Warren investigated context effects.

3. c. is the answer.

a. & b. The kittens had difficulty only with lines they had never experienced, and never regained normal sensitivity.

d. Both perceptual and feature-detector impairment resulted from visual restriction.

4. b. is the answer. Because they have not had early visual experiences, these adults typically have difficulty learning to perceive objects.

a. Such patients typically could not visually recognize objects with which they were familiar by touch, and in some cases this inability persisted.

c. Being able to perceive figure-ground relationships, patients *are* able to follow moving objects with their eyes.

d. This answer is incorrect because eye-hand coordination is an acquired skill and requires much practice.

5. d. is the answer.

6. c. is the answer.

a. This answer would be correct had Jack claimed to be able to read someone else's mind.

b. This answer would be correct had Jack claimed to be able to sense remote events, such as a friend in distress.

d. This answer would be correct had Jack claimed to be able to levitate objects or bend spoons without applying any physical force.

7. d. is the answer.

8. c. is the answer. Humans and certain animals, such as monkeys, are able to adjust to upside-down worlds and other visual distortions, figuring out the relationship between the perceived and the actual reality; lower animals, such as chickens and fish, are typically unable to adapt.

a. Humans and certain animals are able to adapt quite well to distorted visual environments (and then to readapt).

b. This answer is incorrect because humans are the most adaptable of creatures.

d. Humans are able to adapt at any age to distorted visual environments.

9. a. is the answer.

b. Parapsychology is the study of paranormal phenomena.

c. Perceptual adaptation is the ability to adjust to an artificially displaced or even inverted visual field.

d. Psychokinesis is the ability to levitate objects.

10. a. is the answer.

b. Kant claimed that knowledge is inborn.

c. & d. Michael May, born blind, was given sight as an adult. Richard Warren investigated context effects.

11. c. is the answer. There appears to be a critical period for perceptual development, in that sensory restriction has severe, even permanent, disruptive effects when it occurs in infancy but not when it occurs later in life.

a. & d. Sensory restriction does not have the same effects at all ages, and it is more damaging to children than to adults. This is because there is a critical period for perceptual development; whether functional blindness will result depends in part on the nature of the sensory restriction.

b. Research studies have not indicated that sensory restriction is more damaging to humans than to animals.

12. c. is the answer.

a., b., & d. These psychics claim to exhibit the phenomena studied by parapsychologists.

13. c. is the answer.

a. Many ESP researchers are sincere, reputable researchers.

b. & d. There have been no reliable demonstrations of ESP.

14. d. is the answer.

a. Telepathy is the claimed ability to "read" minds.

b. Clairvoyance refers to the claimed ability to perceive remote events.

c. Precognition refers to the claimed ability to perceive future events.

15. d. is the answer.

16. b. is the answer.

True–False Items

1.	F	4.	T
2.	F	5.	T
3.	F	6.	F

Key Terms

1. **Perceptual adaptation** refers to our ability to adjust to an artificially displaced or even inverted visual field. Given distorting lenses, we perceive things accordingly but soon adjust by learning the relationship between our distorted perceptions and the reality.

2. **Perceptual set** is a mental predisposition to perceive one thing and not another.

3. **Extrasensory perception (ESP)** refers to the controversial claim that perception can occur without sensory input. Supposed ESP powers include telepathy, clairvoyance, and precognition.

   Memory aid: *Extra-* means "beyond" or "in addition to"; **extrasensory perception** is perception outside or beyond the normal senses.

4. **Parapsychology** is the study of ESP, psychokinesis, and other paranormal forms of interaction between the individual and the environment.

   Memory aid: *Para-*, like *extra-*, indicates "beyond"; thus, paranormal is beyond the normal and **parapsychology** is the study of phenomena beyond the realm of psychology and known natural laws.

FOCUS ON VOCABULARY AND LANGUAGE

Sensory Deprivation and Restored Vision

Most had been born with cataracts—clouded lenses that allowed them to see only diffused light, rather as you or I might see a diffuse fog through a *Ping-Pong* ball sliced in half. People born with cataracts cannot see clearly because the normally transparent lenses in their eyes are opaque. To understand what their vision is like, imagine what you would see if you had your eyes covered with half of a small, white, plastic ball that is used in table tennis (*Ping-Pong*). When cataract patients have their vision restored, after being blind since birth, they can sense colors and distinguish figure from ground (innate capacities), but they cannot visually recognize things that were familiar by touch.

Perceptual Adaptation

Given a new pair of glasses, we may feel slightly disoriented, even dizzy. When we start wearing ordinary eyeglasses or when we are fitted with a new pair, our initial reaction is a little confusion and vertigo (*dizziness*). However, we quickly adapt within a few days. We can also adapt to lenses that distort what we are looking at by 40° to one side, and even to distortion lenses that invert reality (turn the visual image upside down—a topsy-turvy world). Fish, frogs, salamanders, and young chickens cannot adapt in this way.

Perceptual Set

As everyone knows, *to see is to believe.* As we also know, but less fully appreciate, *to believe is to see.* The expression *"seeing is believing"* means that we put much reliance on visual information when deciding (believing) what is true. Myers shows us that, on the contrary, what we believe may actually affect what we see. Our assumptions, expectations, and mental predispositions (**perceptual sets**) determine, to a large extent, our perceptions.

In 1972, a British newspaper published genuine, unretouched photographs of *a "monster"* in Scotland's Loch Ness. . . . People who had heard about, or believed in, the Loch Ness Monster before seeing a very ambiguous picture of a log were more inclined to see what they expected to see (i.e., a monster) because of their **perceptual set**.

Clearly, much of what we perceive comes not just from the world "out there" but also *from what's behind our eyes and between our ears*. Myers is reiterating the point that our mental predispositions, expectations, beliefs, etc. (*what's behind our eyes and between our ears*) influence much more of what we perceive than the sensory stimulation received from the outside world.

Some differences, it seems, exist merely in the eyes of their beholders. The familiar saying *"beauty is in the eye of the beholder"* means that what is perceived as beautiful has more to do with what the perceiver subjectively believes than with the absolute qualities of the person or object being judged. Likewise, our stereotypes (rigid, conventional ideas or beliefs) about gender or culture can greatly influence (*color*) what is perceived.

(Thinking Critically) Is There Extrasensory Perception?

. . . uncanny . . . People who have dreams that coincide, by pure chance, with later events often have an eerie or strange (*uncanny*) feeling about the accuracy of their *apparent* precognitions.

. . . mind-blowing performances. Some alleged (*so-called*) psychics, using magic tricks and not extrasensory ability, unethically manipulate and deceive (*exploit*) gullible (*unquestioning*) audiences with impressive and wondrous demonstrations (*mind-blowing performances*). As Myers points out, after many, many years of investigation and thousands of experiments there is no scientific evidence that extrasensory abilities exist (believers in the paranormal need only produce one person who can demonstrate a single, reproducible ESP phenomenon to refute the claim that there is no ESP—this has not happened).

States of Consciousness

Waking and Sleeping Rhythms

15 MODULE

MODULE OVERVIEW

Consciousness—our awareness of ourselves and our environment—can be experienced in various states. Module 15 examines not only waking consciousness but also sleep and dreaming. Most of the terminology in this module is introduced in the section on Sleep and Dreams. Doing the module review several times and rehearsing the material frequently will help you to memorize all the terms associated with the stages of sleep.

NOTE: Answer guidelines for all Module 15 questions begin on page 170.

MODULE REVIEW

First, skim each section, noting headings and boldface items. After you have read the section, review each objective by answering the fill-in and essay-type questions that follow it. As you proceed, evaluate your performance by consulting the answers on page 170. Do not continue with the next section until you understand each answer. If you need to, review or reread the section in the textbook before continuing.

> David Myers at times uses idioms that are unfamiliar to some readers. If you do not know the meaning of any of the following words, phrases, or expressions in the context in which they appear in the text, refer to pages 173–175 for an explanation (note that one item appears in the module introduction): *a fundamental yet slippery concept; psychology had nearly lost consciousness; your attentional spotlight shifts; saunter; pop-out; it is but the tip of the information-processing iceberg; Running on automatic pilot; move in concert; Pulling an all-nighter; the machine go wild . . . deep zigzags; in deep slumber, you ascend from your initial sleep dive; As the*

> *night wears on; drowsy; suffer from patterns that . . . thwart; Many fill this need by using their first class for an early siesta and after-lunch study hall for a slumber party; "spring forward" . . . "fall backward"; riddle of sleep; next-day blahs; "snoozing is second only to boozing"; Dreams provide a psychic safety valve; it is time to wake up; buzz.*

Waking Consciousness (pp. 193–195)

Objective 1: Discuss the significance of consciousness in the history of psychology.

1. The study of _____ was central in the early years of psychology and in recent decades, but for quite some time it was displaced by the study of observable

   _____ .

2. Advances in neuroscience made it possible to relate _____ _____ to various mental states; as a result,

   _____ _____ began

   to reenter psychology.

Define consciousness in a sentence.

Objective 2: Discuss how our perceptions are directed and limited by selective attention.

3. When we focus our conscious awareness on a particular stimulus we are using _____

   _____ . Normally, our attention

   _____ (is/is not) divided.

163

4. When researchers distracted participants with a counting task, the participants displayed _____ _____ and failed to notice a gorilla-suited assistant who passed through. Two specific forms of this phenomenon are _____ and _____ _____ .

5. Some stimuli are so powerful they demand our attention, causing us to experience _____-_____ .

Objective 3: Contrast conscious and unconscious information processing.

6. In comparison with unconscious processing, conscious processing has a(n) _____ (limited/unlimited) capacity, is relatively _____ (fast/slow), and processes pieces of information _____ (simultaneously/serially).

7. Novel tasks _____ (require/do not require) conscious attention.

Sleep and Dreams (pp. 195–208)

Objective 4: Describe the cycle of our circadian rhythm, and identify some events that can disrupt this biological clock.

1. Our bodies' internal "clocks" control several _____ _____ .

2. The sleep-waking cycle follows a 24-hour clock called the _____ _____ .

3. Body temperature _____ (rises/falls) as morning approaches and begins to _____ (rise/fall) again before we go to sleep.

4. When people are at their daily peak in circadian arousal, _____ is sharpest and _____ is most accurate.

5. Our biological clock is reset each day by exposure to _____ _____ , which triggers proteins in the _____ of the eyes to signal the

brain's _____ gland to increase or decrease its production of _____ .

6. In the brain, the cluster of cells called the _____ _____ controls the circadian clock.

Objective 5: List the stages of the sleep cycle, and explain how they differ.

7. The sleep cycle consists of _____ distinct stages.

8. The rhythm of sleep cycles was discovered when Aserinsky noticed that, at periodic intervals during the night, the _____ of a sleeping child moved rapidly. This stage of sleep, during which _____ occur, is called _____ _____ .

9. The relatively slow brain waves of the awake but relaxed state are known as _____ waves.

10. During Stage 1 sleep, people often experience _____ sensations similar to _____ . These sensations may later be incorporated into _____ .

11. The bursts of brain-wave activity that occur during Stage 2 sleep are called _____ _____ .

12. Large, slow brain waves are called _____ waves. They occur first in Stage _____ , and increasingly during Stage _____ sleep, which are therefore called _____-_____ sleep. A person in the latter stage of sleep generally will be _____ (easy/difficult) to awaken. It is during this stage that people may engage in sleep _____ .

Describe the bodily changes that accompany REM sleep.

13. During REM sleep, the motor cortex is _____ (active/relaxed), while the muscles are _____ (active/relaxed). For this reason, REM is often referred to as _____ sleep.

14. The rapid eye movements generally signal the beginning of a _____ , which during REM sleep is often storylike, _____ , and more richly hallucinatory.

15. The sleep cycle repeats itself about every _____ minutes. As the night progresses, Stage 4 sleep becomes _____ (longer/briefer) and REM periods become _____ (longer/briefer). Approximately _____ percent of a night's sleep is spent in REM sleep.

Objective 6: Describe individual differences in sleep duration and the effects of sleep loss, noting four reasons that we need sleep.

16. Newborns spend nearly _____ (how much?) of their day asleep, while adults spend no more than _____ .

17. Sleep patterns are influenced by _____ , as indicated by the fact that sleep patterns among _____ (identical/fraternal) twins are very similar. Sleep is also influenced by _____ , as indicated by the fact that people now sleep _____ (more/less) than they did a century ago.

18. Allowed to sleep unhindered, most people will sleep _____ (how many?) hours a night.

19. Teenagers typically need _____ hours of sleep but now average nearly _____ hours less sleep than teenagers of 80 years ago. To psychologist William _____ , this indicates that the vast majority of students are dangerously sleep-deprived. One indication of the hazards of this state is that the rate of _____ tends to increase immediately after the spring time change in Canada and the United States. Another is that sleep deprivation may suppress the functioning of the body's _____ system and alter metabolic and hormonal functioning in ways that mimic _____ and are conducive to _____ , _____ , and _____ .

Describe the effects of sleep loss.

20. Two possible reasons for sleep are to _____ us and to help restore body tissues, especially those of the _____ . Animals with high waking _____ produce an abundance of chemical _____ _____ that are toxic to _____ . Sleep also facilitates our _____ of the day's experiences and stimulates _____ thinking.

21. During sleep a growth hormone is released by the _____ gland. Adults spend _____ (more/less) time in deep sleep than children and so release _____ (more/less) growth hormone.

Objective 7: Identify the major sleep disorders.

22. A persistent difficulty in falling or staying asleep is characteristic of _____ . Sleeping pills and alcohol may make the problem worse since they tend to _____ (increase/reduce) REM sleep.

23. The sleep disorder in which a person experiences uncontrollable sleep attacks is _____ . People with severe cases of this disorder may collapse directly into _____ sleep and experience a loss of _____

_____ .

24. Individuals suffering from _____ _____ stop breathing while sleeping. This disorder is especially prevalent among _____ _____ .

25. The sleep disorder characterized by extreme fright and rapid heartbeat and breathing is called _____ _____ . Unlike nightmares, these episodes usually happen early in the night, during Stage _____ sleep. The same is true of episodes of _____ and _____ , problems that _____ (run/do not run) in families. These sleep episodes are most likely to be experienced by _____ (young children/adolescents/older adults), in whom this stage tends to be the _____ and _____ .

Objective 8: Describe the most common content of dreams, and compare the five major perspectives on why we dream.

26. Dreams experienced during _____ sleep are vivid, emotional, and bizarre.

27. For both men and women, 8 in 10 dreams are marked by _____ (positive/negative) emotions, such as fears of being _____ .

28. Freud referred to the actual content of a dream as its _____ content. Freud believed that this is a censored, symbolic version of the true meaning, or _____ _____ , of the dream.

29. According to Freud, most of the dreams of adults reflect _____ wishes and are the key to understanding inner _____ . To Freud, dreams serve as a psychic

_____ _____ that discharges otherwise unacceptable feelings.

30. Researchers who believe that dreams serve an _____-processing function receive support from the fact that REM sleep facilitates _____ .

31. Brain scans confirm the link between _____ sleep and _____ .

32. Other theories propose that dreaming serves some _____ function, for example, that REM sleep provides the brain with needed _____ . Such an explanation is supported by the fact that _____ (infants/adults) spend the most time in REM sleep.

33. Still other theories propose that dreams are elicited by random bursts of _____ activity originating in lower regions of the brain, such as the _____ . According to the _____-_____ theory, dreams are the brain's attempt to make sense of this activity. The bursts are believed to be given their emotional tone by the brain's _____ system. PET scans of sleeping people reveal increased activity in the brain's _____ system, especially the _____ . Other theorists see dreams as a natural part of brain _____ and _____ development.

34. Researchers agree that we _____ (need/do not need) REM sleep. After being deprived of REM sleep, a person spends more time in REM sleep; this is the _____ _____ effect.

35. REM sleep _____ (does/does not) occur in other mammals. Animals such as fish, whose behavior is less influenced by learning, _____ (do/do not) dream. This finding supports the _____-_____ theory of dreaming.

PROGRESS TEST

Multiple-Choice Questions

Circle your answers to the following questions and check them with the answers beginning on page 171. If your answer is incorrect, read the explanation for why it is incorrect and then consult the appropriate pages of the text.

1. As defined by the text, consciousness includes which of the following?
   a. focused attention
   b. sleeping
   c. hypnosis
   d. all of these answers

2. The cluster of brain cells that control the circadian rhythm is the:
   a. amygdala.
   b. suprachiasmatic nucleus.
   c. NPY.
   d. pineal.

3. Compared to their counterparts of 80 years ago, teenagers today average _____ sleep each night.
   a. 2 hours less
   b. 4 hours less
   c. 1 hour more
   d. about the same amount of

4. Sleep spindles predominate during which stage of sleep?
   a. Stage 2
   b. Stage 3
   c. Stage 4
   d. REM sleep

5. During which stage of sleep does the body experience increased heart rate, rapid breathing, and genital arousal?
   a. Stage 2
   b. Stage 3
   c. Stage 4
   d. REM sleep

6. The sleep cycle is approximately _____ minutes.
   a. 30
   b. 50
   c. 75
   d. 90

7. The effects of chronic sleep deprivation include:
   a. suppression of the immune system.
   b. altered metabolic and hormonal functioning.
   c. impaired creativity.
   d. all of these answers.

8. One effect of sleeping pills is to:
   a. decrease REM sleep.
   b. increase REM sleep.
   c. decrease Stage 2 sleep.
   d. increase Stage 2 sleep.

9. People who heard unusual phrases prior to sleep were awakened each time they began REM sleep. The fact that they remembered less the next morning provides support for the _____ theory of dreaming.
   a. manifest content
   b. physiological
   c. information-processing
   d. activation-synthesis

10. According to Freud, dreams are:
    a. a symbolic fulfillment of erotic wishes.
    b. the result of random neural activity in the brainstem.
    c. the brain's mechanism for self-stimulation.
    d. the disguised expressions of inner conflicts.

11. At its beginning, psychology focused on the study of:
    a. observable behavior.
    b. consciousness.
    c. abnormal behavior.
    d. all of these answers.

12. Which of the following is *not* a theory of dreaming mentioned in the text?
    a. Dreams facilitate information processing.
    b. Dreaming stimulates the developing brain.
    c. Dreams result from random neural activity originating in the brainstem.
    d. Dreaming is an attempt to escape from social stimulation.

13. The sleep-waking cycles of young people who stay up too late typically are _____ hours in duration.
    a. 23
    b. 24
    c. 25
    d. 26

14. Which of the following statements regarding REM sleep is true?
    a. Adults spend more time than infants in REM sleep.
    b. REM sleep deprivation results in a REM rebound.
    c. People deprived of REM sleep adapt easily.
    d. Sleeping medications tend to increase REM sleep.

15. The perceptual error in which we fail to see an object when our attention is directed elsewhere is
    a. a hallucination.
    b. inattentional blindness.
    c. perceptual adaptation.
    d. narcolepsy.

16. A person whose EEG shows a high proportion of alpha waves is most likely:
    a. dreaming.
    b. in Stage 2 sleep.
    c. in Stage 3 or 4 sleep.
    d. awake and relaxed.

17. Circadian rhythms are the:
    a. brain waves that occur during Stage 4 sleep.
    b. muscular tremors that occur during opiate withdrawal.
    c. regular body cycles that occur on a 24-hour schedule.
    d. brain waves that are indicative of Stage 2 sleep.

18. Which of the following is *not* an example of a biological rhythm?
    a. the circadian rhythm
    b. the 90-minute sleep cycle
    c. the five sleep stages
    d. sudden sleep attacks during the day

19. Which of the following is characteristic of REM sleep?
    a. genital arousal
    b. increased muscular tension
    c. night terrors
    d. alpha waves

20. *Consciousness* is defined in the text as:
    a. mental life.
    b. selective attention to ongoing perceptions, thoughts, and feelings.
    c. information processing.
    d. our awareness of ourselves and our environment.

21. According to the activation-synthesis theory, dreaming represents:
    a. the brain's efforts to integrate unrelated bursts of activity in visual brain areas with the emotional tone provided by limbic system activity.
    b. a mechanism for coping with the stresses of daily life.
    c. a symbolic depiction of a person's unfulfilled wishes.
    d. an information-processing mechanism for converting the day's experiences into long-term memory.

22. A person who falls asleep in the midst of a heated argument probably suffers from:
    a. sleep apnea.
    b. narcolepsy.
    c. night terrors.
    d. insomnia.

23. REM sleep is referred to as *paradoxical sleep* because:
    a. studies of people deprived of REM sleep indicate that REM sleep is unnecessary.
    b. the body's muscles remain relaxed while the brain and eyes are active.
    c. it is very easy to awaken a person from REM sleep.
    d. the body's muscles are very tense while the brain is in a nearly meditative state.

24. Although her eyes are closed, Adele's brain is generating bursts of electrical activity. It is likely that Adele is:
    a. experiencing sleep spindles.
    b. under the influence of melatonin.
    c. in REM sleep.
    d. having a night terror.

25. Concluding his presentation on levels of information processing, Miguel states that:
    a. humans process both conscious and unconscious information in parallel.
    b. conscious processing occurs in parallel, while unconscious processing is serial.
    c. conscious processing is serial, while unconscious processing is parallel.
    d. all information processing is serial in nature.

26. Jill dreams that she trips and falls as she walks up the steps to the stage to receive her college diploma. Her psychoanalyst suggests that the dream might symbolize her fear of moving on to the next stage of her life—a career. The analyst is evidently attempting to interpret the _____ content of Jill's dream.

    a. manifest   c. REM
    b. latent   d. overt

27. Barry has participated in a sleep study for the last four nights. He was awakened each time he entered REM sleep. Now that the experiment is over, which of the following can be expected to occur?

    a. Barry will be too tired to sleep, so he'll continue to stay awake.
    b. Barry will sleep so deeply for several nights that dreaming will be minimal.
    c. There will be an increase in sleep Stages 1–4.
    d. There will be an increase in Barry's REM sleep.

28. A PET scan of a sleeping person's brain reveals increased activity in the amygdala of the limbic system. This most likely indicates that the sleeper:

    a. has a neurological disorder.
    b. is not truly asleep.
    c. is in REM sleep.
    d. suffers from narcolepsy.

29. *Selective attention* is most accurately defined as:

    a. the focusing of conscious awareness on a particular stimulus.
    b. our awareness of ourselves and our environment.
    c. failing to see visible objects when our attention is directed elsewhere.
    d. separating our conscious awareness to focus on two tasks at the same time.

30. Concluding her presentation on contemporary theories of why sleep is necessary, Marilynn makes all of the following points *except*:

    a. Sleep may have evolved because it kept our ancestors safe during potentially dangerous periods.
    b. Sleep gives the brain time to heal, as it restores and repairs damaged neurons.
    c. Sleep encourages growth through a hormone secreted during Stage 4.
    d. Slow-wave sleep provides a "psychic safety valve" for stressful waking experiences.

Matching Items

Match each term with its appropriate definition or description.

Definitions or Descriptions

_____ 1. surface meaning of dreams
_____ 2. deeper meaning of dreams
_____ 3. stage(s) of sleep associated with delta waves
_____ 4. stage(s) of sleep associated with muscular relaxation and dreaming
_____ 5. sleep disorder in which breathing stops
_____ 6. sleep disorder occurring in Stage 4 sleep
_____ 7. twilight stage of sleep associated with imagery resembling hallucinations
_____ 8. disorder in which sleep attacks occur
_____ 9. brain wave of awake, relaxed person
_____ 10. brain-wave activity during Stage 2 sleep
_____ 11. our awareness of ourselves and our environment
_____ 12. theory that dreaming reflects our erotic drives

Terms

a. Stage 1 sleep
b. night terrors
c. manifest content
d. narcolepsy
e. sleep apnea
f. Stages 3 and 4 sleep
g. REM sleep
h. latent content
i. Freud's theory
j. alpha
k. consciousness
l. sleep spindle

KEY TERMS

Using your own words, on a separate piece of paper write a brief definition or explanation of each of the following terms.

1. consciousness

2. selective attention

3. inattentional blindness

4. circadian rhythm

5. REM sleep

6. alpha waves

7. sleep

8. hallucinations

9. delta waves

10. insomnia

11. narcolepsy

12. sleep apnea

13. night terrors

14. dream

15. manifest content

16. latent content

17. REM rebound

ANSWERS

Module Review

Waking Consciousness

1. consciousness; behavior

2. brain activity; mental concepts

Consciousness is our awareness of ourselves and our environment.

3. selective attention; is

4. inattentional blindness; change blindness; choice blindness

5. pop-out

6. limited; slow; serially

7. require

Sleep and Dreams

1. biological rhythms

2. circadian rhythm

3. falls; rise

4. thinking; memory

5. bright light; retinas; pineal; melatonin

6. suprachiasmatic nucleus

7. 5

8. eyes; dreams; REM sleep

9. alpha

10. hypnagogic; hallucinations; memories

11. sleep spindles

12. delta; 3; 4; slow-wave; difficult; walking

During REM sleep, brain waves become as rapid as those of Stage 1 sleep, heart rate and breathing become more rapid and irregular, and genital arousal and rapid eye movements occur.

13. active; relaxed; paradoxical

14. dream; emotional

15. 90; briefer; longer; 20 to 25

16. two-thirds; one-third

17. genes; identical; culture; less

18. 9

19. 8 or 9; 2; Dement; accidents; immune; aging; obesity; hypertension; memory impairment

The major effect of sleep deprivation is sleepiness. Other effects include impaired creativity, concentration, and communication; slowed performance; and irritability.

20. protect; brain; metabolism; free radicals; neurons; memory; creative

21. pituitary; less; less

22. insomnia; reduce

23. narcolepsy; REM; muscular tension

24. sleep apnea; overweight men

25. night terrors; 4; sleepwalking; sleeptalking; run; young children; lengthiest; deepest

26. REM

27. negative; attacked, pursued, or rejected, or of experiencing misfortune

28. manifest; latent content

29. erotic; conflicts; safety valve

30. information; memory

31. REM; memory

32. physiological; stimulation; infants

33. neural; brainstem; activation-synthesis; limbic; limbic; amygdala; maturation; cognitive

34. need; REM rebound

35. does; do not; information-processing

Progress Test

Multiple-Choice Questions

1. **d.** is the answer.

2. **b.** is the answer.
   a. The amygdala is an emotion center in the limbic system.
   c. NPY is a brain chemical that has been found to be reduced in rats who prefer alcohol to water.
   d. The pineal is a gland that produces the sleep-inducing hormone melatonin.

3. **a.** is the answer.

4. **a.** is the answer.
   b. & c. Delta waves predominate during Stages 3 and 4. Stage 3 is the transition between Stages 2 and 4 and is associated with a pattern that has elements of both stages.
   d. Faster, nearly waking brain waves occur during REM sleep.

5. **d.** is the answer.
   a., b., & c. During non-REM Stages 1–4 heart rate and breathing are slow and regular and the genitals are not aroused.

6. **d.** is the answer.

7. **d.** is the answer.

8. **a.** is the answer. Like alcohol, sleeping pills carry the undesirable consequence of reducing REM sleep and may make insomnia worse in the long run.
   b., c., & d. Sleeping pills do not produce these effects.

9. **c.** is the answer. They remembered less than if they were awakened during other stages.

10. **a.** is the answer. Freud saw dreams as psychic safety valves that discharge unacceptable feelings that are often related to erotic wishes.
    b. & c. These physiological theories of dreaming are not associated with Freud.
    d. According to Freud, dreams represent the individual's conflicts and wishes but in disguised, rather than transparent, form.

11. **b.** is the answer.
    a. The behaviorists' emphasis on observable behavior occurred much later in the history of psychology.
    c. Psychology has never been primarily concerned with abnormal behavior.

12. **d.** is the answer.
    a., b., & c. Each of these describes a valid theory of dreaming that was mentioned in the text.

13. **c.** is the answer. We can reset our biological clocks by adjusting our sleep schedules. Thus, young adults adopt something closer to a 25-hour day by staying up too late to get 8 hours of sleep.

14. **b.** is the answer. Following REM deprivation, people temporarily increase their amount of REM sleep, in a phenomenon known as REM rebound.
    a. Just the opposite is true: the amount of REM sleep is greatest in infancy.
    c. Deprived of REM sleep by repeated awakenings, people return more and more quickly to the REM stages after falling back to sleep. They by no means adapt easily to the deprivations.
    d. Just the opposite occurs: they tend to suppress REM sleep.

15. **b.** is the answer.

16. **d.** is the answer.
    a. The brain waves of REM sleep (dream sleep) are more like those of Stage 1 sleepers.
    b. Stage 2 is characterized by sleep spindles.
    c. Stages 3 and 4 are characterized by slow, rolling delta waves.

17. **c.** is the answer.

18. **d.** is the answer.

19. **a.** is the answer.
    b. During REM sleep, muscular tension is low.
    c. Night terrors are associated with Stage 4 sleep.
    d. Alpha waves are characteristic of the relaxed, awake state.

20. **d.** is the answer.

21. **a.** is the answer.
    b. & c. These essentially Freudian explanations of the purpose of dreaming are based on the idea that a dream is a psychic safety valve that harmlessly discharges otherwise inexpressible feelings.
    d. This explanation of the function of dreaming is associated with the information-processing viewpoint.

22. **b.** is the answer. Narcolepsy is characterized by uncontrollable sleep attacks.
    a. Sleep apnea is characterized by the temporary cessation of breathing while asleep.
    c. Night terrors are characterized by high arousal and terrified behavior, occurring during Stage 4 sleep.
    d. Insomnia refers to chronic difficulty in falling or staying asleep.

23. **b.** is the answer. Although the body is aroused internally, the messages of the activated motor cortex do not reach the muscles.
    a. Studies of REM-deprived people indicate just the opposite.

c. It is difficult to awaken a person from REM sleep.

d. Just the opposite occurs in REM sleep: the muscles are relaxed, yet the brain is aroused.

24. **c.** is the answer. The rapid eye movements of REM sleep coincide with bursts of activity in the visual cortex.

25. **c.** is the answer.

26. **b.** is the answer. The analyst is evidently trying to go beyond the events in the dream and understand the dream's hidden meaning, or the dream's latent content.

    a. The manifest content of a dream is its actual story line.

    c. REM refers to the rapid eye movements that occur during dreaming.

    d. There is no such term. In any case, "overt" would be the same as "manifest" content.

27. **d.** is the answer. Because of the phenomenon known as REM rebound, Barry, having been deprived of REM sleep, will now increase his REM sleep.

    a. Increased irritability is an effect of sleep deprivation in general, not of REM deprivation specifically.

    b. REM rebound will cause Barry to dream more than normal.

    c. The increase in REM sleep is necessarily accompanied by decreases in Stages 1–4 sleep.

28. **c.** is the answer.

    a. & d. Increased activity in the visual and auditory areas of the sleeping brain is perfectly normal during REM sleep.

    b. In fact, people cannot easily be awakened from REM sleep.

29. **a.** is the answer.

    b. This is the definition of consciousness.

    c. This defines inattentional blindness.

    d. In selective attention, awareness is focused on one stimulus.

30. **d.** is the answer. Freud's theory proposed that dreams, which occur during fast-wave, REM sleep, serve as a psychic safety valve.

Matching Items

1. c	**6.** b	**11.** k
2. h	**7.** a	**12.** i
3. f	**8.** d	
4. g	**9.** j	
5. e	**10.** l	

Key Terms

1. For most psychologists, **consciousness** is our awareness of ourselves and our environment.

2. **Selective attention** is the focusing of our awareness on a particular stimulus.

3. **Inattentional blindness** is a perceptual error in which we fail to see a visible object when our attention is directed elsewhere.

4. A **circadian rhythm** is any regular bodily rhythm, such as body temperature and sleep-wakefulness, that follows a 24-hour cycle.

   Memory aid: In Latin, *circa* means "about" and *dies* means "day." A **circadian rhythm** is one that is about a day, or 24 hours, in duration.

5. **REM sleep** is the sleep stage in which the brain and eyes are active, the muscles are relaxed, and vivid dreaming occurs; also known as *paradoxical sleep*.

   Memory aid: **REM** is an acronym for rapid eye movement, the distinguishing feature of this sleep stage that led to its discovery.

6. **Alpha waves** are the relatively slow brain waves characteristic of an awake, relaxed state.

7. **Sleep** is the natural, periodic, reversible loss of consciousness, on which the body and mind depend for healthy functioning.

8. **Hallucinations** are false sensory experiences that occur without any sensory stimulus.

9. **Delta waves** are the large, slow brain waves associated with deep sleep.

10. **Insomnia** is a sleep disorder in which the person regularly has difficulty in falling or staying asleep.

11. **Narcolepsy** is a sleep disorder in which the victim suffers sudden, uncontrollable sleep attacks, often characterized by entry directly into REM.

12. **Sleep apnea** is a sleep disorder in which the person ceases breathing while asleep, briefly arouses to gasp for air, falls back asleep, and repeats this cycle throughout the night.

    Example: One theory of the sudden infant death syndrome is that it is caused by **sleep apnea**.

13. A person suffering from **night terrors** experiences episodes of high arousal with apparent terror. Night terrors usually occur during Stage 4 sleep.

14. **Dreams** are vivid sequences of images, emotions, and thoughts, the most vivid of which occur during REM sleep.

15. In Freud's theory of dreaming, the **manifest content** is the remembered story line.

16. In Freud's theory of dreaming, the **latent content** is the underlying but censored meaning of a dream.

    Memory aids for 15 and 16: *Manifest* means "clearly apparent, obvious"; *latent* means "hidden, concealed." A dream's **manifest content** is that which is obvious; its **latent content** remains hidden until its symbolism is interpreted.

17. **REM rebound** is the tendency for REM sleep to increase following REM sleep deprivation.

FOCUS ON VOCABULARY AND LANGUAGE

To psychologists, consciousness is similarly a *fundamental* yet *slippery* concept. In science many fundamental concepts are difficult to define (e.g., life, matter, energy). Consciousness is one of the most basic (*fundamental*) ideas in psychology, yet it is an elusive and difficult concept to grasp (*a slippery concept*).

Waking Consciousness

... psychology had nearly *lost consciousness* ... Myers is using a little humor here in order to illustrate the fact that changes (*swings*) have taken place during psychology's history. To *"lose consciousness"* can have two meanings in the above sentence: (1) to fall unconscious or pass out and (2) to fail to keep (lose) "consciousness" as the subject matter of psychology. Psychology started out as the study of conscious experience; then, because of problems in scientifically investigating the mind, overt behavior replaced consciousness in the 1920s. Finally, in the 1960s, psychology regained consciousness as a legitimate subject for psychologists to study.

Now, suddenly, *your attentional spotlight shifts.* Your *feet feel encased, your nose stubbornly intrudes on the page* before you. **Selective attention** refers to our tendency to focus on only a small part of what is possible for us to experience. If you do attend to more aspects of your experience (*your attentional spotlight shifts*), you will be surprised at the amount of stimulation you process without awareness, such as the feel of the shoes on your feet (*your feet feel encased*) and the fact that your nose actually blocks your line of vision (*your nose stubbornly intrudes on the page*).

... they failed to notice a young woman carrying an umbrella *saunter* across the screen midway through the tape. In this experiment, viewers had to watch a video of basketball players and signal when the ball was passed. Because of their intense selective attention, they generally failed to notice a female walking slowly (*sauntering*) through the players.

... *pop-out* ... A very unique object or event (a *strikingly distinct stimulus*) will automatically attract our attention (*it draws our eye*). This experience is called the *pop-out phenomenon*.

... yet it [consciousness] is but *the tip of the information-processing iceberg*. Just as most of the mass or volume of an iceberg is below the surface of the ocean and out of sight, most mental functioning goes on without conscious awareness. Consciousness is a small part (*the tip of the iceberg*) of total information processing.

Running on automatic pilot allows consciousness—the mind's *CEO*—to monitor the whole system and deal with new challenges ... Myers is pointing out that much of our information processing occurs outside of conscious awareness (*we run on automatic pilot*) and that conscious awareness is similar to the top manager of an organization (*CEO or chief executive officer*) whose many assistants take care of all the routine tasks, allowing him or her to pay attention to (*monitor*) the total system and tackle (*deal with*) new challenges.

Sleep and Dreams

... limbs often *move in concert.* ... To *"move in concert"* is to move simultaneously or in synchrony. When we dream of doing something, our arms and legs do *not* move in synchrony (*do not move in concert*) with the activity in the dream.

Pulling an all-nighter, we feel *groggiest* about 4:00 A.M., and then *we get a second wind* after our normal wake-up time arrives. If we decide to stay up all night (*pull an all-nighter*), say, to finish a term paper by the deadline, we feel most mentally confused and uncoordinated (*groggiest*) around the middle of the night, but as our usual time for getting up approaches, we begin to feel renewed energy (*we get a second wind*).

Aserinsky watched the machine *go wild*, tracing *deep zigzags* on the graph paper. The discovery of REM (Rapid Eye Movement) occurred accidentally. To see if an EEG (electroencephalograph) was working properly Aserinsky placed the electrodes near his 8-year-old son's eyes. Periodically during the night the machine responded vigorously (*went wild*), producing a pattern of high-frequency waves (*deep zigzags*) on the printout. These patterns were produced by rapid, spasmodic (*jerky*) eye movements and accompanied by very frantic brain activity, and when awakened during one of these periods the boy said he was dreaming.

Rather than continuing in deep *slumber*, you *ascend* from your initial *sleep dive*. During a typical night's sleep (*slumber*) you go through a number of distinct stages. If you are awake and relaxed, perhaps with your eyes closed, an EEG would show alpha waves. As you fall deeper and deeper into sleep (*sleep dive*), your brain waves continue to slow down. By Stage 4 your brain waves are long and slow (*delta waves*), but you don't stay here all night; instead, you go back up (*ascend*) through the stages into the most unique and interesting stage of all, REM (Rapid Eye Movement) sleep, where most dreams occur. Here, the brain waves resemble the fast, uneven Stage 1 waves (*saw-toothed*), but there is much more internal physiological arousal now, and, paradoxically, your muscles are almost paralyzed.

As the night *wears on*, deep Stage 4 sleep gets progressively briefer and then disappears. As the night progresses (*wears on*), the time spent in Stage 4 deep sleep gets shorter (and eventually ceases altogether) and time spent in REM sleep gets longer.

. . . *drowsy* . . . If you were deprived of sleep for a few nights, you would feel very tired and sleepy (*drowsy*) and also unsteady and dazed (*groggy*).

People today more than ever suffer from patterns that not only leave them sleepy but also *thwart* their having an energized feeling of well-being. Because of the pressures of work, school, social obligations, and so on, we often have sleep schedules that prevent (*thwart*) us from getting the amount of sleep we need. The consequence of this "sleep debt" (*accumulated insufficient sleep*) is a general lack of energy and discomfort (*malaise*) and a frequent feeling of sleepiness.

Many fill this need [for sleep] by using their first class for an *early siesta* and after-lunch *study hall for a slumber party*. Today's young students often get much less sleep than they need and consequently many end up using the first class of the day for a short sleep or nap (*siesta*), and the quiet school period meant for study (*study hall*) may be occupied by whole groups of sleeping students (*slumber party*). Even so, 80 percent of students are still seriously sleep deprived (*they have a large sleep debt*), which results in diminished cognitive and intellectual functioning ("*a large sleep debt makes you stupid*") and a tendency to fall asleep during routine lectures (*when the going gets boring, the students start snoring*).

. . . "*spring forward*" to "daylight savings" time and "*fall backward*" to "standard" time. Many countries adopt daylight savings time, which means that in the spring people move their clocks ahead one hour (*spring forward*) and back one hour in the fall (*fall backward*). Consequently, people lose one hour of sleep in the spring, which results in more traffic accidents on the Monday following the Sunday time change; with the extra hour of sleep in the fall, traffic accidents decline on the Monday following the time change.

Such discoveries are beginning to solve the ongoing *riddle* of sleep. Recent research has shown that sleep helps us repair and restore body tissue (*recuperate*), promotes physical growth, increases memory and learning capacity, provides a protective mechanism (this was especially true in our evolutionary past), and enhances (*feeds*) creative thinking. These findings are starting to clear up the continuing puzzle (*riddle*) of why we need to sleep.

The most common quick fixes for true insomnia—sleeping pills and alcohol—can aggravate the problem, reducing REM sleep and leaving the person with *next-day blahs*. The most popular fast remedies (*quick fixes*) for insomnia are sleeping pills and alcohol. Unfortunately, they can make the problem worse (*aggravate it*) by suppressing REM sleep; the next day the person may have less energy and feel very tired (*next-day blahs*). When these "remedies" are discontinued, the insomnia may get worse.

As a traffic menace, "*snoozing is second only to boozing*," says the American Sleep Disorders Association, and those with narcolepsy are especially at risk (Aldrich, 1989). Falling asleep (*snoozing*) while driving is almost as serious a problem as drinking (*boozing*) and driving. People with **narcolepsy** suffer from occasional periods of uncontrollable sleepiness often associated with emotional arousal, and are thus in danger, and dangerous, while driving.

. . . Dreams provide a *psychic safety valve* that discharges otherwise unacceptable feelings. The story line of the dream (**manifest content**) is a disguised version of the real, but hidden, meaning of the dream (**latent content**). According to Freud, by symbolically expressing our hidden desires and erotic wishes, dreams allow us to ventilate unconscious drives that might otherwise be harmful (*acts as a psychic safety valve*). (A *safety valve* allows a system to dissipate built-up pressure and thus may prevent an explosion.)

However, his critics say *it is time to wake up* from Freud's dream theory, which is a scientific *nightmare*. Myers is having some fun with a play on words here. The expression "it is time to wake up from something" means one should start paying attention to reality and facts, rather than fantasy, and to say something is "a nightmare" means that it is unruly, difficult, or even frightening. Most contemporary psychologists believe that REM sleep and dreams are important aspects of our life but that Freud's theory of dream interpretation is erroneous, unscientific, and misguided (*a nightmare*); thus, we should not place much reliance on its explanations (*it is time to wake up from it*).

The brain regions that *buzz* as rats learn to navigate a maze, or as people learn to perform a visual-discrimination task, *buzz again* later during REM sleep . . . Studies demonstrate that sleeping helps memory and learning. The areas of the brain that are active (*that buzz*) when learning is taking place are also active once more (*they buzz again*) during REM sleep. This is important news for sleep-deprived students who tend to learn and remember less than their non-sleep-derived counterparts. Attempting to make up for the loss of sleep by sleeping longer and later on weekends (*a kind of sleep bulimia . . . binge sleeping*) will not compensate for the lower levels of learning and recall.

Hypnosis

16 **MODULE**

MODULE OVERVIEW

Module 16 explores whether hypnosis is a unique state of consciousness. Since it was first introduced, hypnosis has been surrounded by many unproven myths, such as the idea that a person under hypnosis will act in ways that he or she would not in the waking stage.

NOTE: Answer guidelines for all Module 16 questions begin on page 179.

MODULE REVIEW

First, skim each section, noting headings and boldface items. After you have read the section, review each objective by answering the fill-in and essay-type questions that follow it. As you proceed, evaluate your performance by consulting the answers on page 179. Do not continue with the next section until you understand each answer. If you need to, review or reread the section in the textbook before continuing.

> David Myers at times uses idioms that are unfamiliar to some readers. If you do not know the meaning of either of the following phrases in the context in which they appear in the text, refer to page 180 for an explanation: "*psychological truth serum . . . considerable mischief*"; *might the two views . . . be bridged?*

Facts and Falsehoods (pp. 211–213)

Objective 1: Discuss the characteristics of people who are susceptible to hypnosis.

1. Hypnosis is a _____
_____ in which a hypnotist suggests that a subject will experience certain feelings or thoughts, for example.

2. The weight of research evidence suggests that hypnosis _____ (does/does not) allow a person to perform feats that are impossible in the normal waking state. The strength, stamina, learning, and perceptual abilities of hypnotized people _____ (are/are not) like those of motivated unhypnotized people.

3. Most people are _____ (somewhat/not at all) hypnotically suggestible.

Describe people who are the most susceptible to hypnosis.

Objective 2: Evaluate claims that hypnosis can influence people's memory, will, health, and perception of pain.

4. Research studies show that "hypnotically refreshed" memories combine _____ with _____ .

5. An _____ person in a legitimate _____ can induce people—hypnotized or not—to perform some unlikely acts.

6. Hypnotherapists have helped some people alleviate headaches, asthma, and stress-related skin disorders through the use of _____ suggestions.

7. Hypnosis _____ (is/is not) especially helpful for the treatment of obesity.

8. Hypnosis _____ (can/cannot) relieve pain. One theory of hypnotic pain relief is that hypnosis separates, or _____ , the sensory and emotional aspects of pain. Another is that hypnotic pain relief is due to selective _____ , that is, to the person's focusing on stimuli other than pain.

9. PET scans show that hypnosis reduces brain activity in a region involved in _____ to painful stimuli, but not in the _____ cortex that receives the raw _____ input.

Explaining the Hypnotized State (pp. 213–214)

Objective 3: Give arguments for and against hypnosis as an altered state of consciousness.

1. Skeptics believe that hypnosis may reflect the workings of _____

_____ . These findings provide support for the _____ _____ theory of hypnosis.

Summarize the argument that hypnosis is not an altered state of consciousness.

2. Hilgard has advanced the idea that during hypnosis there is a _____ , or split, between different levels of consciousness.

Discuss the current view of hypnosis as a blend of the two views.

PROGRESS TEST

Multiple-Choice Questions

Circle your answers to the following questions and check them with the answers beginning on page 179. If your answer is incorrect, read the explanation for why it is incorrect and then consult the appropriate pages of the text.

1. Which of the following statements concerning hypnosis is true?
   a. People will do anything under hypnosis.
   b. Hypnosis is the same as sleeping.
   c. Hypnosis is in part an extension of the division between conscious awareness and automatic behavior.
   d. Hypnosis improves memory recall.

2. Hypnotic responsiveness is:
   a. the same in all people.
   b. generally greater in women than men.
   c. generally greater in men than women.
   d. greater when people are led to *expect* it.

3. According to Hilgard, hypnosis is:
   a. no different from a state of heightened motivation.
   b. the same as dreaming.
   c. a dissociation between different levels of consciousness.
   d. a type of "animal magnetism."

4. As a form of therapy for relieving problems such as warts, hypnosis is:
   a. ineffective.
   b. no more effective than positive suggestions given without hypnosis.
   c. highly effective.
   d. more effective with adults than children.

5. Those who believe that hypnosis is a social phenomenon argue that "hypnotized" individuals are:
   a. consciously faking their behavior.
   b. merely acting out a role.
   c. underachievers striving to please the hypnotist.
   d. all of these answers.

6. An attorney wants to know if the details and accuracy of an eyewitness's memory for a crime would be improved under hypnosis. Given the results of relevant research, what should you tell the attorney?
   a. Most hypnotically retrieved memories are either false or contaminated.
   b. Hypnotically retrieved memories are usually more accurate than conscious memories.
   c. Hypnotically retrieved memories are purely the product of the subject's imagination.
   d. Hypnosis only improves memory of anxiety-provoking childhood events.

7. Of the following individuals, who is likely to be the most hypnotically suggestible?
   a. Bill, a reality-oriented stockbroker
   b. Janice, an actress with a rich imagination
   c. Megan, a sixth-grader who has trouble focusing her attention on a task
   d. Darren, who has never been able to really "get involved" in movies or novels

8. Research studies of the effectiveness of hypnosis as a form of therapy have demonstrated that:
   a. for problems of self-control, such as smoking, hypnosis is equally effective with people who can be deeply hypnotized and those who cannot.
   b. posthypnotic suggestions have helped alleviate headaches, asthma, and stress-related skin disorders.
   c. as a form of therapy, hypnosis is no more effective than positive suggestions given without hypnosis.
   d. all of these answers are true.

9. Those who consider hypnosis a social phenomenon contend that:
   a. hypnosis is an altered state of consciousness.
   b. hypnotic phenomena are unique to hypnosis.
   c. hypnotized subjects become unresponsive when they are no longer motivated to act as instructed.
   d. all of the above are true.

KEY TERMS

Using your own words, on a separate piece of paper write a brief definition or explanation of each of the following terms.

1. hypnosis
2. posthypnotic suggestion
3. dissociation

ANSWERS
Module Review

Facts and Falsehoods

1. social interaction
2. does not; are
3. somewhat

Those who are most susceptible frequently become deeply absorbed in imaginative activities. They also tend to have rich fantasy lives.

4. fact; fiction
5. authoritative; context
6. posthypnotic
7. is
8. can; dissociates; attention
9. attending; sensory; sensory

Explaining the Hypnotized State

1. normal consciousness; social influence

The behavior of hypnotized subjects is not fundamentally different from that of other people. Therefore, hypnosis may be mainly a social phenomenon, with hypnotized subjects acting out the role of a "good hypnotic subject."

2. dissociation

The social influence and divided consciousness views work together to explain hypnosis as an extension both of normal principles of social influence and of everyday dissociations between our conscious awareness and our automatic behaviors.

Progress Test

Multiple-Choice Questions

1. **c.** is the answer.
   a. Hypnotized subjects usually perform only acts they might perform normally.
   b. The text does not suggest that sleeping and hypnosis are the same states. In fact, the brain waves of hypnotized subjects are not like those associated with sleeping.
   d. Hypnosis typically *disrupts*, or contaminates, memory.

2. **d.** is the answer.
   a. Hypnotic responsiveness varies greatly from person to person.
   b. & c. There is no evidence of a gender difference in hypnotic responsiveness.

3. **c.** is the answer. Hilgard believes that hypnosis reflects a dissociation, or split, in consciousness, as occurs normally, only to a much greater extent.

4. **b.** is the answer.

   a. & c. Hypnosis *can* be helpful in treating these problems, but it is no more effective than other forms of therapy.

   d. Adults are not more responsive than children to hypnosis.

5. **b.** is the answer.

   a. & c. There is no evidence that hypnotically responsive individuals fake their behaviors or that they are underachievers.

6. **a.** is the answer. Although people recall more under hypnosis, they "recall" a lot of fiction along with fact and appear unable to distinguish between the two.

   b. Hypnotically refreshed memories are usually no more accurate than conscious memories.

   c. Although the hypnotized subject's imagination may influence the memories retrieved, some actual memory retrieval also occurs.

   d. Hypnotically retrieved memories don't normally focus on anxiety-provoking events.

7. **b.** is the answer. People with rich fantasy lives and the ability to become imaginatively absorbed have essentially the characteristics associated with hypnotic suggestibility. The fact that Janice is an actress also suggests she possesses such traits.

   a. Bill's reality orientation makes him an unlikely candidate for hypnosis.

   c. The hypnotically suggestible are generally able to focus on tasks or on imaginative activities.

   d. People who are hypnotically suggestible tend to become deeply engrossed in novels and movies.

8. **d.** is the answer.

9. **c.** is the answer.

Key Terms

1. **Hypnosis** is a social interaction in which one person (the hypnotist) suggests to another (the subject) that certain perceptions, feelings, thoughts, or behaviors will spontaneously occur.

2. A **posthypnotic suggestion** is a suggestion made during a hypnosis session that is to be carried out when the subject is no longer hypnotized.

3. **Dissociation** is a split between different levels of consciousness, allowing a person to divide attention between two or more thoughts.

FOCUS ON VOCABULARY AND LANGUAGE

Facts and Falsehoods

(margin): "Hypnosis is not a psychological *truth serum*, and to regard it as such has been a source of considerable *mischief*." Research shows that hypnotists can subtly influence what people recall and they may inadvertently create false memories by making suggestions and asking leading questions. Thus, hypnosis is not like a so-called *truth serum* (a drug alleged to make people tell the truth) but rather has caused a great deal of annoying—and possibly harmful—effects (*considerable mischief*).

Explaining the Hypnotized State

So, might the two views—social influence and divided consciousness—*be bridged?* Although there are a number of different explanations about what hypnosis really is, Myers suggests that it may be possible to bring together some of these theories (*bridge the differences*). Thus, hypnosis may be both a part of normal aspects of social influence and our ability to have a divided (*or split*) consciousness.

Drugs and Consciousness

17

M O D U L E

MODULE OVERVIEW

Module 17 examines drug-altered states and near-death experiences. Although drug use and near-death experiences are very different, they often produce similar altered perceptions. Most of the terminology in this module is introduced in the section on Psychoactive Drugs. Doing the module review several times and rehearsing the material frequently will help you to memorize the names of the drugs and their effects on the nervous system. Also, pay particular attention to the section on the possible psychological and social roots of drug use.

NOTE: Answer guidelines for all Module 17 questions begin on page 187.

MODULE REVIEW

First, skim each section, noting headings and boldface items. After you have read the section, review each objective by answering the fill-in and essay-type questions that follow it. As you proceed, evaluate your performance by consulting the answers on page 187. Do not continue with the next section until you understand each answer. If you need to, review or reread the section in the textbook before continuing.

> David Myers at times uses idioms that are unfamiliar to some readers. If you do not know the meaning of any of the following words, phrases, or expressions in the context in which they appear in the text, refer to pages 189–190 for an explanation: *tipsy on one can of beer; kicked the habit; tipsy restaurant patrons leave extravagant tips; a staggering problem; quicker pick-her-upper; one may pay a long-term price: a gnawing craving for another fix; crack.*

Dependence and Addiction (pp. 216–217)

Objective 1: Discuss the nature of drug dependence and addiction, and identify three common misconceptions about addiction.

1. Drugs that alter moods and perceptions are called _____ drugs.

2. Drug users who require increasing doses to experience a drug's effects have developed _____ for the drug. The user's brain counteracts the disruption to its normal functioning; thus, the user experiences _____ .

3. After ceasing to use a drug, a person who experiences _____ symptoms has developed a physical _____ . Regular use of a drug to relieve stress is an example of a _____ dependence. A person who has a compulsive craving for a substance despite adverse consequences is _____ to that substance.

Briefly state three common misconceptions about addiction.

4. The three broad categories of drugs discussed in the text include _____ , which tend to slow body functions; _____ , which speed body functions; and _____ , which alter perception.

These drugs all work by mimicking, stimulating, or inhibiting the activity of the brain's _____ . Psychologically, our _____ also play a role.

Psychoactive Drugs (pp. 217–225)

Objective 2: Explain how depressants affect nervous system activity and behavior, and summarize the findings on alcohol use and abuse.

1. Depressants _____ nervous system activity and _____ body function. Low doses of alcohol, which is classified as a _____ , slow the activity of the _____ nervous system.

2. Alcohol may make a person more _____ , more _____ , or more _____ daring. Alcohol affects memory by interfering with the process of trans-ferring experiences into _____-_____ memory. Also, blackouts after drinking result from alcohol's suppression of _____ _____ .

3. Excessive use of alcohol can also affect cognition by _____ the brain, especially in _____ (men/women). Alcohol also reduces _____ and focuses one's attention on the _____ _____ and away from _____ _____ , thus lessening _____ _____ .

Describe how a person's expectations can influence the behavioral effects of alcohol.

4. Tranquilizers, which are also known as _____ , have effects similar to those of alcohol.

5. Opium, morphine, and heroin all _____ (excite/depress) neural functioning. Together, these drugs are called the _____ . When they are present, the brain eventually stops producing _____ .

Objective 3: Identify the major stimulants, and explain how they affect neural activity and behavior.

6. The most widely used stimulants are _____ , _____ , the _____ , _____ , _____ , and _____ . Stimulants _____ (are/are not) addictive.

7. Methamphetamine triggers the release of the neurotransmitter _____ , which stimulates brain cells that enhance _____ and _____ .

8. Eliminating _____ would increase life expectancy more than any other preventive measure. Smoking usually begins during _____ _____ . Smokers _____ (do/do not) become depen-dent on _____ , and they _____ (do/do not) develop toler-ance to the drug. Quitting causes _____-_____ symp-toms that include _____ _____ .

9. Nicotine quickly triggers the release of _____ and _____ , two neurotransmitters that diminish _____ and boost _____ and _____ _____ . Nicotine also stimulates the _____ _____ system to release _____ and _____ , neu-rotransmitters that calm _____ and reduce sensitivity to _____ .

10. Cocaine and crack deplete the brain's supply of the neurotransmitters _____ , _____ , and _____ and result in depression as the drugs' effects wear off. They do this by blocking the _____ of the neurotransmitters, which remain in the nerve cells' _____ .

11. Cocaine's psychological effects depend not only on dosage and form but also on _____ , _____ , and the _____ .

12. The drug _____ , or MDMA, is both a _____ and a _____ _____ . This drug triggers the release of the neurotransmitters _____ and _____ and blocks the reabsorption of _____ . Among the adverse effects of this drug are disruption of the body's _____ clock, suppression of the _____ _____ , and impaired _____ and other _____ functions.

Objective 4: Describe the physiological and psychological effects of hallucinogens, and summarize the effects of LSD and marijuana.

13. Hallucinogens are also referred to as _____ . Two common synthetic hallucinogens are _____ and LSD, which is chemically similar to a subtype of the neurotransmitter _____ . LSD works by _____ the actions of this neurotransmitter.

14. The reports of LSD users are very similar to the _____-_____ experiences reported by some people who survive a brush with death. These experiences may be the result of a deficient supply of _____ or other insults to the brain.

15. The active ingredient in marijuana is abbreviated _____ .

Describe some of the physical and psychological effects of marijuana.

16. All psychoactive drugs trigger _____ _____ , which helps explain both _____ and _____ .

Influences on Drug Use (pp. 225–228)

Objective 5: Discuss the biological, psychological, and social-cultural factors that contribute to drug use.

1. Drug use by North American youth _____ (increased/declined) during the 1970s, then declined until the early 1990s due to increased _____ _____ and efforts by the media to deglamorize drug use.

2. Adopted individuals are more susceptible to alcoholism if they had a(n) _____ (adoptive/biological) parent with a history of alcoholism. Boys who at age 6 are _____ (more/less) excitable are more likely as teens to smoke, drink, and use other drugs. Genes that are more common among people predisposed to alcoholism may cause deficiencies in the brain's _____ _____ system.

Identify some of the psychological and social-cultural roots of drug use.

3. Among teenagers, drug use _____ (varies/is about the same) across

_____ and _____

groups.

4. African-American high school seniors report the

_____ (highest/lowest) rates of

drug use. A major social influence on drug use is

the _____ culture.

5. State three possible channels of influence for drug prevention and treatment programs.

a. _____

b. _____

c. _____

PROGRESS TEST

Multiple-Choice Questions

Circle your answers to the following questions and check them with the answers beginning on page 187. If your answer is incorrect, read the explanation for why it is incorrect and then consult the appropriate pages of the text.

1. Cocaine and crack produce a euphoric rush by:
   a. blocking the actions of serotonin.
   b. depressing neural activity in the brain.
   c. blocking the reuptake of dopamine in brain cells.
   d. stimulating the brain's production of endorphins.

2. Which of the following is classified as a depressant?
   a. methamphetamine   c. marijuana
   b. LSD   d. alcohol

3. Which of the following preventive measures would have the greatest impact on average life expectancy?
   a. eliminating obesity
   b. eliminating smoking
   c. eliminating sleep deprivation
   d. eliminating binge drinking

4. Psychoactive drugs affect behavior and perception through:
   a. the power of suggestion.
   b. the placebo effect.
   c. alteration of neural activity in the brain.
   d. psychological, not physiological, influences.

5. All of the following are common misconceptions about addiction, *except* the statement that
   a. to overcome an addiction a person almost always needs professional therapy.
   b. psychoactive and medicinal drugs very quickly lead to addiction.
   c. biological factors place some individuals at increased risk for addiction.
   d. many other repetitive, pleasure-seeking behaviors fit the drug-addiction-as-disease-needing-treatment model.

6. The lowest rates of drug use among high school seniors is reported by:
   a. Asian-Americans.
   b. Hispanic-Americans.
   c. African-Americans.
   d. Native Americans.

7. Alcohol has the most profound effect on:
   a. the transfer of experiences to long-term memory.
   b. immediate memory.
   c. previously established long-term memories.
   d. all of these answers.

8. A person who requires increasing amounts of a drug in order to feel its effect is said to have developed:
   a. tolerance.
   b. physical dependency.
   c. psychological dependency.
   d. resistance.

9. Which of the following is *not* a stimulant?
   a. amphetamines   c. nicotine
   b. caffeine   d. alcohol

10. Which of the following was *not* cited in the text as evidence that heredity influences alcohol use?
    a. Children whose parents abuse alcohol have a lower tolerance for multiple alcoholic drinks taken over a short period of time.
    b. Boys who are impulsive and fearless at age 6 are more likely to drink as teenagers.
    c. Laboratory mice have been selectively bred to prefer alcohol to water.
    d. Adopted children are more susceptible if one or both of their biological parents has a history of alcoholism.

11. Which of the following is usually the most powerful determinant of whether teenagers begin using drugs?
    a. family strength   c. school adjustment
    b. religiosity   d. peer influence

12. THC is the major active ingredient in:
    a. nicotine.   c. marijuana.
    b. MDMA.   d. cocaine.

13. I am a synthetic stimulant and mild hallucinogen that produces euphoria and social intimacy by triggering the release of dopamine and serotonin. What am I?
    a. LSD   c. THC
    b. MDMA   d. cocaine

14. How a particular psychoactive drug affects a person depends on:
    a. the dosage and form in which the drug is taken.
    b. the user's expectations and personality.
    c. the situation in which the drug is taken.
    d. all of these answers.

15. Which of the following was *not* suggested by the text as an important aspect of drug prevention and treatment programs?
    a. education about the long-term costs of a drug's temporary pleasures
    b. efforts to boost people's self-esteem and purpose in life
    c. attempts to modify peer associations
    d. "scare tactics" that frighten prepubescent children into avoiding drug experimentation

16. Dan has recently begun using an addictive, euphoria-producing drug. Which of the following will probably occur if he repeatedly uses this drug?
    a. As tolerance to the drug develops, Dan will experience increasingly pleasurable "highs."
    b. The dosage needed to produce the desired effect will increase.
    c. After each use, he will become more and more elated.
    d. Dependence will become less of a problem.

17. Roberto is moderately intoxicated by alcohol. Which of the following changes in his behavior is likely to occur?
    a. If angered, he is more likely to become aggressive than when he is sober.
    b. He will be less self-conscious about his behavior.
    c. If sexually aroused, he will be less inhibited about engaging in sexual activity.
    d. All of these answers are likely.

18. Which of the following statements concerning alcoholism is *not* true?
    a. Adopted individuals are more susceptible to alcoholism if they had an adoptive parent with alcoholism.
    b. Having an identical twin with alcoholism puts a person at increased risk for alcohol problems.
    c. Geneticists have identified genes that are more common among people predisposed to alcoholism.
    d. Researchers have bred rats that prefer alcohol to water.

19. Which of the following statements concerning marijuana is true?
    a. The by-products of marijuana are cleared from the body more slowly than are the by-products of alcohol.
    b. Regular users may need a larger dose of the drug to achieve a high than occasional users would need to get the same effect.
    c. Marijuana is as addictive as nicotine or cocaine.
    d. Even small doses of marijuana hasten the loss of brain cells.

20. Which of the following statements concerning near-death experiences is true?
    a. Fewer than 1 percent of patients who come close to dying report having them.
    b. They typically consist of fantastic, mystical imagery.
    c. They are more commonly experienced by females than by males.
    d. They are more commonly experienced by males than by females.

21. Which of the following statements concerning the roots of drug use is true?
    a. Heavy users of alcohol, marijuana, and cocaine often are always on a high.
    b. If an adolescent's friends use drugs, odds are that he or she will, too.
    c. Teenagers who are academically average students seldom use drugs.
    d. It is nearly impossible to predict whether or not a particular adolescent will experiment with drugs.

Matching Items

Match each term with its appropriate definition or description.

Definitions or Descriptions

_____ 1. drug that depresses central nervous system activity
_____ 2. a hallucinogen that distorts perception
_____ 3. drug that temporarily excites neural activity and arouses body functions
_____ 4. drug that is both a stimulant and mild hallucinogen
_____ 5. drugs that increase energy and stimulate neural activity
_____ 6. drugs that reduce anxiety and depress central nervous system activity
_____ 7. natural painkillers produced by the brain
_____ 8. neurotransmitter that LSD resembles

Terms

a. marijuana
b. alcohol
c. cocaine
d. serotonin
e. Ecstasy
f. amphetamines
g. endorphins
h. barbiturates

Essay Question

You have just been assigned the task of writing an article tentatively titled "Alcohol and Alcoholism: Roots, Effects, and Prevention." What information should you include in your article? (Use the space below to list the points you want to make, and organize them. Then write the essay on a separate piece of paper.)

KEY TERMS

Using your own words, on a separate piece of paper write a brief definition or explanation of each of the following terms.

1. psychoactive drugs
2. tolerance
3. withdrawal
4. physical dependence
5. psychological dependence
6. addiction
7. depressants
8. barbiturates
9. opiates
10. stimulants
11. amphetamines

12. methamphetamines

13. Ecstasy (MDMA)

14. hallucinogens

15. LSD

16. near-death experience

17. THC

ANSWERS

Module Review

Dependence and Addiction

1. psychoactive

2. tolerance; neuroadaptation

3. withdrawal; dependence; psychological; addicted

The following myths about addiction are false:

a. Taking a psychoactive drug automatically leads to addiction.

b. One cannot overcome an addiction without professional help.

c. The addiction-as-disease-needing-treatment model is applicable to a broad spectrum of pleasure-seeking behaviors.

4. depressants; stimulants; hallucinogens; neuro-transmitters; expectations

Psychoactive Drugs

1. calm; slow; depressant; sympathetic

2. aggressive; helpful; sexually; long-term; REM sleep

3. shrinking; women; self-awareness; immediate situation; future consequences; impulse control

Studies have found that if people believe that alcohol affects social behavior in certain ways, then, when they drink alcohol (or even mistakenly think that they have been drinking alcohol), they will behave according to their expectations, which vary by culture. For example, if people believe alcohol promotes sexual feeling, on drinking they are likely to behave in a sexually aroused way.

4. barbiturates

5. depress; opiates; endorphins

6. caffeine; nicotine; amphetamines; cocaine; Ecstasy; methamphetamine; are

7. dopamine; energy; mood

8. smoking; early adolescence; do; nicotine; do; nicotine-withdrawal; craving, insomnia, anxiety, and irritability

9. epinephrine; norepinephrine; appetite; alertness; mental efficiency; central nervous; dopamine; opioids; anxiety; pain

10. dopamine; serotonin; norepinephrine; reuptake (reabsorption); synapse

11. expectations; personality; situation

12. Ecstasy; stimulant; mild hallucinogen; dopamine; serotonin; serotonin; circadian; immune system; memory; cognitive

13. psychedelics; MDMA; serotonin; blocking

14. near-death; oxygen

15. THC

Like alcohol, marijuana relaxes, disinhibits, and may produce a euphoric feeling. Also like alcohol, marijuana impairs perceptual and motor skills. Marijuana is a mild hallucinogen; it can amplify sensitivity to colors, sounds, tastes, and smells. Marijuana also interrupts memory formation.

16. negative aftereffects; tolerance; withdrawal

Influences on Drug Use

1. increased; drug education

2. biological; more; dopamine reward

A psychological factor in drug use is the feeling that one's life is meaningless and lacks direction. Regular users of psychoactive drugs often have experienced stress or failure and are somewhat depressed. Drug use often begins as a temporary way to relieve depression, anger, anxiety, or insomnia. A powerful social factor in drug use, especially among adolescents, is peer influence. Peers shape attitudes about drugs, provide drugs, and establish the social context for their use.

3. varies; cultural; ethnic

4. lowest; peer

5. **a.** education about the long-term costs of a drug's temporary pleasures

b. efforts to boost people's self-esteem and purpose in life

c. attempts to "inoculate" youth against peer pressures

Progress Test

Multiple-Choice Questions

1. **c.** is the answer. They also block the reuptake of serotonin and norepinephrine.
a. This answer describes the effect of LSD.

b. Depressants such as alcohol have this effect. Cocaine and crack are classified as stimulants.
d. None of the psychoactive drugs has this effect. Opiates, however, *suppress* the brain's production of endorphins.

2. **d.** is the answer. Alcohol, which slows body functions and neural activity, is a depressant.
   a. Methamphetamine is a stimulant.
   b. & c. LSD and marijuana are hallucinogens.

3. **b.** is the answer.

4. **c.** is the answer. Such drugs work primarily at synapses, altering neural transmission.
   a. What people believe will happen after taking a drug will likely have some effect on their individual reactions, but psychoactive drugs actually work by altering neural transmission.
   b. Since a placebo is a substance without active properties, this answer is incorrect.
   d. This answer is incorrect because the effects of psychoactive drugs on behavior, perception, and so forth have a physiological basis.

5. **c.** is the answer. This is true. Heredity, for example, influences tendencies toward alcoholism.

6. **c.** is the answer.

7. **a.** is the answer. Alcohol disrupts the processing of experiences into long-term memory but has little effect on either immediate or previously established memories.

8. **a.** is the answer.
   b. Physical dependence may occur in the absence of tolerance. The hallmark of physical dependence is the presence of withdrawal symptoms when the person is off the drug.
   c. Psychological dependence refers to a felt, or psychological, need to use a drug, for example, a drug that relieves stress.
   d. There is no such thing as drug "resistance."

9. **d.** is the answer. Alcohol is a depressant.

10. **a.** is the answer. Compared with other children, children whose parents abuse alcohol have a *higher* tolerance for multiple drinks, making it more likely that they will, in fact, consume more alcohol.

11. **d.** is the answer. If adolescents' friends use drugs, the odds are that they will, too.
    a., b., & c. These are also predictors of drug use but seem to operate mainly through their effects on peer association.

12. **c.** is the answer.

13. **b.** is the answer.
    a. & c. Unlike stimulants, LSD and THC do not speed up body functions.

d. Unlike hallucinogens, cocaine is a stimulant and does not generally distort perceptions.

14. **d.** is the answer.

15. **d.** is the answer.

16. **b.** is the answer. Continued use of a drug produces a tolerance; to experience the same "high," Dan will have to use larger and larger doses.

17. **d.** is the answer. Alcohol loosens inhibitions and reduces self-consciousness, making people more likely to act on their feelings of anger or sexual arousal. It also disrupts the processing of experience into long-term memory.

18. **a.** is the answer. Adopted individuals are more susceptible to alcoholism if they had a *biological* parent with alcoholism.
    b., c., & d. Each of these is true, which indicates that susceptibility to alcoholism is at least partially determined by heredity.

19. **a.** is the answer. THC, the active ingredient in marijuana, and its by-products linger in the body for a month or more.

20. **b.** is the answer.
    a. Approximately 12 to 40 percent of people who have come close to death report some sort of near-death experience.
    c. & d. There is no gender difference in the prevalence of near-death experiences.

21. **b.** is the answer.

Matching Items

1. b		**5.** f	
2. a		**6.** h	
3. c		**7.** g	
4. e		**8.** d	

Essay Question

As a depressant, alcohol slows neural activity and body functions. Although low doses of alcohol may produce relaxation, with larger doses reactions slow, speech slurs, skilled performance deteriorates, and the processing of recent experiences into long-term memories is disrupted. Alcohol also reduces self-awareness and may facilitate sexual and aggressive urges the individual might otherwise resist.

Some people may be biologically vulnerable to alcoholism. This is indicated by the fact that individuals who have a biological parent with alcoholism, or people who have an identical twin with alcoholism, are more susceptible to alcoholism.

Stress, depression, and the feeling that life is meaningless and without direction are common feelings among heavy users of alcohol and may create a psychological vulnerability to alcoholism.

Especially for teenagers, peer group influence is strong. If an adolescent's friends use alcohol, odds are that he or she will too.

Research suggests three important channels of influence for drug prevention and treatment programs: (1) education about the long-term consequences of alcohol use; (2) efforts to boost people's self-esteem and purpose in life; and (3) attempts to counteract peer pressure that leads to experimentation with drugs.

Key Terms

1. **Psychoactive drugs**—which include stimulants, depressants, and hallucinogens—are chemical substances that alter mood and perceptions. They work by affecting or mimicking the activity of neurotransmitters.

2. **Tolerance** is the diminishing of a psychoactive drug's effect that occurs with repeated use, requiring progressively larger doses in order to produce the same effect.

3. **Withdrawal** refers to the discomfort and distress that follow the discontinued use of addictive drugs.

4. **Physical dependence** is a physiological need for a drug that is indicated by the presence of withdrawal symptoms when the drug is not taken.

5. The psychological need to use a drug is referred to as **psychological dependence**.

6. An **addiction** is a compulsive craving for a drug despite adverse consequences and withdrawal symptoms.

7. **Depressants** are psychoactive drugs, such as alcohol, opiates, and barbiturates, that reduce neural activity and slow body functions.

8. **Barbiturates** are depressants, sometimes used to induce sleep or reduce anxiety.

9. **Opiates** are depressants derived from the opium poppy, such as opium, morphine, and heroin; they reduce neural activity and temporarily lessen pain and anxiety.

10. **Stimulants** are psychoactive drugs, such as caffeine, nicotine, amphetamines, and cocaine, that excite neural activity and speed up body functions.

11. **Amphetamines** are a type of stimulant and, as such, speed up body functions and neural activity.

12. **Methamphetamine** is a powerfully addictive stimulant that speeds up body functions and is associated with energy and mood changes.

13. Classified as both a (synthetic) stimulant and a mild hallucinogen, **Ecstasy (MDMA)** produces short-term euphoria by increasing serotonin levels in the brain. Repeated use may permanently damage serotonin neurons, suppress immunity, and disrupt cognition.

14. **Hallucinogens** are psychoactive drugs, such as LSD and marijuana, that distort perception and evoke sensory images in the absence of sensory input.

15. **LSD** (lysergic acid diethylamide) is a powerful hallucinogen capable of producing vivid false perceptions and disorganization of thought processes. LSD produces its unpredictable effects partially because it blocks the action of the neurotransmitter serotonin.

16. The **near-death experience** is an altered state of consciousness that has been reported by some people who have had a close brush with death.

17. The major active ingredient in marijuana, **THC** is classified as a mild hallucinogen.

FOCUS ON VOCABULARY AND LANGUAGE

Dependence and Addiction

Why might a person who rarely drinks alcohol get *tipsy* on one can of beer, but an experienced drinker may show few effects until the *second six-pack*? Prolonged use of a psychoactive drug produces the ability, through neuroadaptation, to take more and more of the substance (*tolerance*). Thus, an infrequent user of alcohol may get somewhat intoxicated (*tipsy*) from one beer, but for a regular drinker there might be little effect until six or more beers have been consumed (*until the second six-pack [of beer]*).

. . . kicked the habit . . . This means that the person who has been using the substance on a regular basis

(*habitual* or *addictive behavior*) has now stopped doing so (*has kicked the habit*). Myers notes that addiction is not a disease (such as diabetes) and many people voluntary stop using addictive drugs without treatment or therapy.

Psychoactive Drugs

. . . as when *tipsy* restaurant patrons leave extravagant tips. Alcohol can increase both harmful and helpful inclinations. Thus, it often happens that restaurant clientele give a larger gratuity (extravagant *tips*) when they are more intoxicated (*tipsy*). Whatever tendencies you have when sober will be more obvious when you are drunk.

In larger doses, alcohol can become a *staggering problem*. Myers is using humor here to make an important point. To describe a problem as *staggering* means that the problem is enormous and has serious consequences (for example, a *staggering debt* is one that is overwhelming). One of the consequences of ingesting large amounts of alcohol is slowed reaction time, memory loss (*blackouts*), language disruptions (*slurred speech*), and uncoordinated physical movement (the person *staggers*). Thus, drinking too much alcohol has serious implications (it is a *staggering problem*).

If, as commonly believed, liquor is the *quicker pick-her-upper*, the effect lies partly in that powerful sex organ, the mind. Alcohol (liquor) is thought by many to speed up the process of meeting members of the opposite sex and to lower sexual inhibitions. Thus, a male may believe that use of alcohol will facilitate his ability to initiate contact and get to know a female (a *quicker pick-her-upper*). Myers points out that not only alcohol is involved, but also our beliefs about its effects on sexual behavior (the effect lies partly in that *powerful sex organ, the mind*).

But for this short-term pleasure *one may pay a long-term price: a gnawing craving* for another *fix* . . . . There is a cost (*one pays a long-term price*) for enjoying drug-induced pleasures, and for an addict this may be a persistent inner torment (*gnawing*) and an urgent, persistent desire (*craving*) for another dose of the drug (a *fix*).

. . . *crack* . . . *Crack* is a very potent, synthetic form of cocaine which produces a feeling of euphoria (*a rush*) followed by deep depression, tiredness, and irritability (*a "crash"*).

Learning

Classical Conditioning

18 MODULE

MODULE OVERVIEW

"No topic is closer to the heart of psychology than learning, a relatively permanent change in an organism's behavior due to experience." Module 18 covers the basic principles of classical, or respondent, conditioning, in which we learn associations between events. The module also covers several important issues, including the generality of principles of learning, the role of cognitive processes in learning, and the ways in which learning is constrained by the biological predispositions of different species.

NOTE: Answer guidelines for all Module 18 questions begin on page 198.

MODULE REVIEW

First, skim each section, noting headings and boldface items. After you have read the section, review each objective by answering the fill-in and essay-type questions that follow it. As you proceed, evaluate your performance by consulting the answers on page 198. Do not continue with the next section until you understand each answer. If you need to, review or reread the section in the textbook before continuing.

> David Myers at times uses idioms that are unfamiliar to some readers. If you do not know the meaning of any of the following words, phrases, or expressions in the context in which they appear in the introduction to Learning and in this module, refer to pages 201–202 for an explanation: *Learning breeds hope; mugged; the clever rancher has outfitted his herd with electronic pagers; For many people, the name Ivan Pavlov . . . rings a bell; drooled; sets your mouth to watering; red-light district; breaking up . . .*

> *fire-breathing heartthrob; your heart may race; the thought that counts; we stand on his shoulders; crack cocaine users often feel a craving; legendary significance.*

Introducing Learning (pp. 232–234)

Objective 1: Define *learning,* and identify three different forms of learning.

1. A relatively permanent change in an organism's behavior due to experience is called

   _____ .

2. More than 200 years ago, philosophers such as John Locke and David Hume argued that an important factor in learning is our tendency to _____ events that occur in sequence. Even simple animals, such as the sea slug *Aplysia*, can learn simple _____ between stimuli. This type of learning is called _____

   _____ .

3. The type of learning in which the organism learns to associate two stimuli is _____ conditioning.

4. The tendency of organisms to associate a response and its consequence forms the basis of _____ conditioning.

5. Complex animals often learn behaviors merely by _____ others perform them.

Introduction and Pavlov's Experiments
(pp. 235–239)

Objective 2: Discuss early attempts at studying learning experimentally, and describe the basic components of classical conditioning.

1. Classical conditioning was first explored by the Russian physiologist _____ . Early in the twentieth century, psychologist _____ urged psychologists to discard references to inner thoughts, feelings, and motives in favor of studying observable behavior. This view, called _____ , influenced American psychology during the first half of that century.

2. In Pavlov's classic experiment, a tone, or _____ _____ , is sounded just before food, the _____ _____ , is placed in the animal's mouth.

3. An animal will salivate when food is placed in its mouth. This salivation is called the _____ _____ .

4. Eventually, the dogs in Pavlov's experiment would salivate on hearing the tone. This salivation is called the _____ _____ .

Objective 3: Summarize the processes and survival value of acquisition, extinction, spontaneous recovery, generalization, and discrimination.

5. The initial learning of a conditioned response is called _____ . For many conditioning situations, the optimal interval between a neutral stimulus and the US is _____ _____ .

6. When the US is presented prior to a neutral stimulus, conditioning _____ (does/does not) occur.

Explain why learning theorists consider classically conditioned behaviors to be biologically adaptive.

7. Michael Domjan's sexual conditioning studies with quail demonstrate that classical conditioning is highly adaptive because it helps animals _____ and _____ .

8. If a CS is repeatedly presented without the US, _____ soon occurs; that is, the CR diminishes.

9. Following a pause, however, the CR reappears in response to the CS; this phenomenon is called _____ _____ .

10. Subjects often respond to a similar stimulus as they would to the original CS. This phenomenon is called _____ .

11. Subjects can also be trained not to respond to _____ stimuli. This learned ability is called _____ .

12. Being able to recognize differences among stimuli has _____ value because it lets us limit our learned responses to appropriate stimuli.

Extending Pavlov's Understanding
(pp. 239–242)

Objective 4: Discuss the importance of cognitive processes and biological predispositions in classical conditioning.

1. The early behaviorists believed that to understand behavior in various organisms, any presumption of _____ was unnecessary.

2. Experiments by Rescorla and Wagner demonstrate that a CS must reliably _____ the US for an association to develop and, more generally, that _____ processes play a role in conditioning. It is as if the animal learns to _____ that the US will occur.

3. The importance of cognitive processes in human conditioning is demonstrated by the failure of classical conditioning as a treatment for _____ .

4. Some psychologists once believed that any natural _____ could be conditioned to any neutral _____ .

5. Garcia discovered that rats would associate _____ with taste but not with other stimuli. Garcia found that taste-aversion conditioning _____ (would/would not) occur when the delay between the CS and the US was more than an hour.

6. Results such as these demonstrate that the principles of learning are constrained by the _____ predispositions of each animal species and that they help each species _____ to its environment. They also demonstrate the importance of different _____ _____ _____ in understanding complex phenomena.

Pavlov's Legacy (pp. 242–243)

Objective 5: Summarize Pavlov's contribution to our understanding of learning and to improvements in human health and well-being.

1. Classical conditioning is one way that virtually all organisms learn to _____ to their environment.

2. Another aspect of Pavlov's legacy is that he showed how a process such as learning could be studied _____ .

Explain why the study of classical conditioning is important.

3. Through classical conditioning, drug users often develop a _____ when they encounter _____ associated with previous highs.

4. Research studies demonstrate that the body's immune system _____ (can/cannot) be classically conditioned.

Describe the Watson and Rayner experiment.

PROGRESS TEST

Multiple-Choice Questions

Circle your answers to the following questions and check them with the answers beginning on page 198. If your answer is incorrect, read the explanation for why it is incorrect and then consult the appropriate pages of the text.

1. *Learning* is best defined as:
   a. any behavior produced by an organism without being provoked.
   b. a change in the behavior of an organism.
   c. a relatively permanent change in the behavior of an organism due to experience.
   d. behavior based on operant rather than respondent conditioning.

2. In Pavlov's original experiment with dogs, the meat served as a(n):
   a. CS.   c. US.
   b. CR.   d. UR.

3. In Pavlov's original experiment with dogs, the tone was initially a(n) _____ stimulus; after it was paired with meat, it became a(n) _____ stimulus.
   a. conditioned; neutral
   b. neutral; conditioned
   c. conditioned; unconditioned
   d. unconditioned; conditioned

4. When a conditioned stimulus is presented without an accompanying unconditioned stimulus, _____ will soon take place.
   a. generalization   c. extinction
   b. discrimination   d. aversion

5. In Garcia and Koelling's studies of taste-aversion learning, rats learned to associate:
   a. taste with electric shock.
   b. sights and sounds with sickness.
   c. taste with sickness.
   d. taste and sounds with electric shock.

6. In Pavlov's original experiment with dogs, salivation to meat was the:
   a. CS.   c. US.
   b. CR.   d. UR.

7. Classical conditioning experiments by Rescorla and Wagner demonstrate that an important factor in conditioning is the:
   a. subject's age.
   b. strength of the stimuli.
   c. predictability of an association.
   d. similarity of stimuli.

8. Which of the following is a form of associative learning?
   a. classical conditioning
   b. operant conditioning
   c. observational learning
   d. All of these are examples.

9. For the most rapid conditioning, a CS should be presented:
   a. about 1 second after the US.
   b. about one-half second before the US.
   c. about 15 seconds before the US.
   d. at the same time as the US.

10. During extinction, the _____ is omitted; as a result, the _____ seems to disappear.
    a. US; UR   c. US; CR
    b. CS; CR   d. CS; UR

11. In Watson and Rayner's experiment, the loud noise was the _____ and the white rat was the _____.
    a. CS; CR   c. CS; US
    b. US; CS   d. US; CR

12. In which of the following may classical conditioning play a role?
    a. emotional problems
    b. the body's immune response
    c. helping drug addicts
    d. all of these situations

13. In Pavlov's studies of classical conditioning of a dog's salivary responses, spontaneous recovery occurred:
    a. during acquisition, when the CS was first paired with the US.
    b. during extinction, when the CS was first presented by itself.
    c. when the CS was reintroduced following extinction of the CR and a rest period.
    d. during discrimination training, when several conditioned stimuli were introduced.

14. Experiments on taste-aversion learning demonstrate that:
    a. for the conditioning of certain stimuli, the US need not immediately follow the CS.
    b. any perceivable stimulus can become a CS.
    c. all animals are biologically primed to associate illness with the taste of a tainted food.
    d. all of these statements are true.

15. You always rattle the box of dog biscuits before giving your dog a treat. As you do so, your dog salivates. Rattling the box is a(n) _____ ; your dog's salivation is a(n) _____ .
    a. CS; CR   c. US; CR
    b. CS; UR   d. US; UR

16. A pigeon can easily be taught to flap its wings in order to avoid shock but not for food reinforcement. According to the text, this is most likely so because:
    a. pigeons are biologically predisposed to flap their wings in order to escape aversive events and to use their beaks to obtain food.
    b. shock is a more motivating stimulus for birds than food is.
    c. hungry animals have difficulty delaying their eating long enough to learn *any* new skill.
    d. of all of these reasons.

For questions 17–20, use the following information.
As a child, you were playing in the yard one day when a neighbor's cat wandered over. Your mother (who has a terrible fear of animals) screamed and snatched you into her arms. Her behavior caused you to cry. You now have a fear of cats.

17. Identify the CS.
    a. your mother's behavior   c. the cat
    b. your crying   d. your fear today

18. Identify the US.
    a. your mother's behavior   c. the cat
    b. your crying   d. your fear today

19. Identify the CR.
    a. your mother's behavior   c. the cat
    b. your crying   d. your fear today

20. Identify the UR.
    a. your mother's behavior   c. the cat
    b. your crying   d. your fear today

21. Bill once had a blue car that was in the shop more than it was out. Since then he will not even consider owning blue- or green-colored cars. Bill's aversion to green cars is an example of:
    a. discrimination.
    b. generalization.
    c. spontaneous recovery.
    d. extinction.

22. Two groups of rats receive classical conditioning trials in which a tone and electric shock are presented. For Group 1, the electric shock always follows the tone. For Group 2, the tone and shock occur randomly. Which of the following is likely to result?
    a. The tone will become a CS for Group 1 but not for Group 2.
    b. The tone will become a CS for Group 2 but not for Group 1.
    c. The tone will become a CS for both groups.
    d. The tone will not become a CS for either group.

23. Last evening May-ling ate her first cheeseburger and french fries at an American fast-food restaurant. A few hours later she became ill. It can be expected that:
    a. May-ling will develop an aversion to the sight of a cheeseburger and french fries.
    b. May-ling will develop an aversion to the taste of a cheeseburger and french fries.
    c. May-ling will not associate her illness with the food she ate.
    d. May-ling will associate her sickness with something she experienced immediately before she became ill.

Matching Items

Match each definition or description with the appropriate term.

Definitions or Descriptions

_____ 1. tendency for similar stimuli to evoke a CR
_____ 2. the reappearance of a weakened CR
_____ 3. the ability to differentiate between similar stimuli
_____ 4. the weakening of the CR when the CS is no longer followed by the US
_____ 5. the initial stage of conditioning

Terms

a. spontaneous recovery
b. generalization
c. extinction
d. discrimination
e. acquisition

True–False Items

Indicate whether each statement is true or false by placing *T* or *F* in the blank next to the item.

_____ 1. The optimal interval between CS and US is about 15 seconds.
_____ 2. Cognitive processes are of relatively little importance in learning.
_____ 3. All animals, including rats and birds, are biologically predisposed to associate taste cues with sickness.
_____ 4. Whether the CS or US is presented first seems not to matter in terms of the ease of classical conditioning.
_____ 5. Spontaneous recovery refers to the tendency of extinguished behaviors to reappear suddenly.

KEY TERMS

Using your own words, on a piece of paper write a brief definition or explanation of each of the following terms.

1. associative learning
2. classical conditioning
3. learning
4. behaviorism
5. unconditioned response (UR)
6. unconditioned stimulus (US)
7. conditioned response (CR)
8. conditioned stimulus (CS)
9. acquisition
10. extinction
11. spontaneous recovery
12. generalization
13. discrimination

ANSWERS

Module Review

Introducing Learning

1. learning
2. associate; associations; associative learning
3. classical
4. operant
5. observing

Introduction and Pavlov's Experiments

1. Ivan Pavlov; John Watson; behaviorism
2. conditioned stimulus; unconditioned stimulus
3. unconditioned response
4. conditioned response
5. acquisition; one-half second
6. (usually) does not

Learning theorists consider classical conditioning to be adaptive because conditioned responses help organisms to prepare for good or bad events (unconditioned stimuli) that are about to occur.

7. survive; reproduce
8. extinction
9. spontaneous recovery
10. generalization

11. similar; discrimination
12. survival

Extending Pavlov's Understanding

1. cognition
2. predict; cognitive; expect
3. alcoholism
4. response; stimulus
5. sickness; would
6. biological; adapt; levels of analysis

Pavlov's Legacy

1. adapt
2. objectively

Classical conditioning led to the discovery of general principles of learning that are the same for all species tested, including humans. Classical conditioning also provided an example to the young field of psychology of how complex, internal processes could be studied objectively. In addition, classical conditioning has proven to have many helpful applications to human health and well-being.

3. craving; cues
4. can

In Watson and Rayner's experiment, classical conditioning was used to condition fear of a rat in Albert, an 11-month-old infant. When Albert touched the white rat (neutral stimulus), a loud noise (unconditioned stimulus) was sounded. After several pairings of the rat with the noise, Albert began crying at the mere sight of the rat. The rat had become a conditioned stimulus, triggering a conditioned response of fear.

Progress Test

Multiple-Choice Questions

1. c. is the answer.
   a. This answer is incorrect because it simply describes any behavior that is automatic rather than being triggered by a specific stimulus.
   b. This answer is too general, since behaviors can change for reasons other than learning.
   d. Respondently conditioned behavior also satisfies the criteria of our definition of learning.

2. c. is the answer. Meat automatically triggers the response of salivation and is therefore an unconditioned stimulus.

a. A conditioned stimulus acquires its response-triggering powers through learning. A dog does not learn to salivate to meat.

b. & d. Responses are behaviors triggered in the organism, in this case the dog's salivation. The meat is a stimulus.

3. **b.** is the answer. Prior to its pairing with meat (the US), the tone did not trigger salivation and was therefore a neutral stimulus. Afterward, the tone triggered salivation (the CR) and was therefore a conditioned stimulus (CS).

c. & d. Unconditioned stimuli, such as meat, innately trigger responding. Pavlov's dogs had to learn to associate the tone with the food.

4. **c.** is the answer. In this situation, the CR will decline, a phenomenon known as extinction.

a. Generalization occurs when the subject makes a CR to stimuli similar to the original CS.

b. Discrimination is when the subject does not make a CR to stimuli other than the original CS.

d. An aversion is a CR to a CS that has been associated with an unpleasant US, such as shock or a nausea-producing drug.

5. **c.** is the answer.

a. & d. These studies also indicated that rats are biologically predisposed to associate visual and auditory stimuli, but not taste, with shock.

b. Rats are biologically predisposed to associate taste with sickness.

6. **d.** is the answer. A dog does not have to learn to salivate to food; therefore, this response is unconditioned.

a. & c. Salivation is a response, not a stimulus.

7. **c.** is the answer.

a., b., & d. Rescorla and Wagner's research did not address the importance of these factors in classical conditioning.

8. **d.** is the answer.

9. **b.** is the answer.

a. Backward conditioning, in which the US precedes the CS, is ineffective.

c. This interval is longer than is optimum for the most rapid acquisition of a CS-US association.

d. Simultaneous presentation of CS and US is ineffective because it does not permit the subject to anticipate the US.

10. **c.** is the answer.

11. **b.** is the answer. The loud noise automatically triggered Albert's fear and therefore functioned as a US. After being associated with the US, the white rat acquired the power to trigger fear and thus became a CS.

12. **d.** is the answer.

13. **c.** is the answer.

a., b., & d. Spontaneous recovery occurs after a CR has been extinguished, and in the absence of the US. The situations described here all involve the continued presentation of the US and, therefore, the further strengthening of the CR.

14. **a.** is the answer. Taste-aversion experiments demonstrate conditioning even with CS-US intervals as long as several hours.

b. Despite being perceivable, a visual or auditory stimulus cannot become a CS for illness in some animals, such as rats.

c. Some animals, such as birds, are biologically primed to associate the *appearance* of food with illness.

15. **a.** is the answer. Your dog had to learn to associate the rattling sound with the food. Rattling is therefore a conditioned, or learned, stimulus, and salivation in response to this rattling is a learned, or conditioned, response.

16. **a.** is the answer. As in this example, conditioning must be consistent with the particular organism's biological predispositions.

b. Some behaviors, but certainly not all, are acquired more rapidly than others when shock is used as negative reinforcement.

c. Pigeons are able to acquire many new behaviors when food is used as reinforcement.

17. **c.** is the answer. Because the cat was associated with your mother's scream, it triggered a fear response, and is thus the CS.

18. **a.** is the answer. Your mother's scream and evident fear, which naturally caused you to cry, was the US.

19. **d.** is the answer. Your fear of cats is the CR. An acquired fear is always a conditioned response.

20. **b.** is the answer. Your crying, automatically triggered by your mother's scream and fear, was the UR.

21. **b.** is the answer. Not only is Bill extending a learned aversion to a specific blue car to all blue cars but also to cars that are green.

a. Whereas discrimination involves responding only to a particular stimulus, Bill is extending his aversive response to other stimuli (green cars) as well.

c. Spontaneous recovery is the reappearance of an extinguished CR after a pause.

d. Extinction is the weakening of the CR when the CS is no longer followed by the US.

22. **a.** is the answer. Classical conditioning proceeds most effectively when the CS and US are reliably

paired and therefore appear predictably associated. Only for Group 1 is this likely to be true.

23. **b.** is the answer.
a., c., & d. Taste-aversion research demonstrates that humans and some other animals, such as rats, are biologically primed to associate illness with the taste of tainted food, rather than with other cues, such as the food's appearance. Moreover, taste aversions can be acquired even when the interval between the CS and the illness is several hours.

Matching Items

1. b   4. c
2. a   5. e
3. d

True–False Items

1. F   4. F
2. F   5. T
3. F

Key Terms

1. In **associative learning**, organisms learn that certain events occur together. Two variations of associative learning are classical conditioning and operant conditioning.

2. Also known as Pavlovian conditioning, **classical conditioning** is a type of learning in which an organism learns to associate stimuli; a neutral stimulus becomes capable of triggering a conditioned response after having become associated with an unconditioned stimulus.

3. **Learning** is any relatively permanent change in an organism's behavior due to experience.

4. **Behaviorism** is the view that psychology should be an objective science that studies only observable behaviors without reference to mental processes.

Example: Because he was an early advocate of the study of observable behavior, John Watson is often called the father of behaviorism.

5. In classical conditioning, the **unconditioned response (UR)** is the unlearned, involuntary response to the unconditioned stimulus.

6. In classical conditioning, the **unconditioned stimulus (US)** is the stimulus that naturally and automatically triggers the reflexive unconditioned response.

7. In classical conditioning, the **conditioned response (CR)** is the learned response to a previously neutral conditioned stimulus, which results from the acquired association between the CS and US.

8. In classical conditioning, the **conditioned stimulus (CS)** is an originally neutral stimulus that comes to trigger a CR after association with an unconditioned stimulus.

9. In a learning experiment, **acquisition** refers to the initial stage of conditioning in which the new response is established and gradually strengthened. In operant conditioning, it is the strengthening of a reinforced response.

10. **Extinction** refers to the weakening of a CR when the CS is no longer followed by the US; in operant conditioning extinction occurs when a response is no longer reinforced.

11. **Spontaneous recovery** is the reappearance of an extinguished CR after a pause.

12. **Generalization** refers to the tendency, once a response has been conditioned, for stimuli similar to the original CS to evoke a CR.

13. **Discrimination** in classical conditioning refers to the ability to distinguish the CS from similar stimuli that do not signal a US. In operant conditioning, it refers to responding differently to stimuli that signal a behavior will be reinforced or will not be reinforced.

FOCUS ON VOCABULARY AND LANGUAGE

Introducing Learning

Learning breeds hope. The fact that we can change and adapt as a result of experience (*learn*) in so many different areas gives rise to optimism (*breeds hope*) about our future prospects.

. . . watching a TV character get mugged . . . To be mugged means to be attacked, (sometimes) beaten, and robbed. This example shows how associations are formed between events, such as between the sounds that precede an attack and the *mugging* itself. In movies and on TV, a certain type of music is often played before a frightening event or scene. After a few such associations, the music itself can elicit fear before you actually see the frightening or scary event. This is an example of classical conditioning.

. . . the clever [Japanese] rancher has outfitted his *herd* with electronic *pagers*, which he calls from his cellphone. In this example of conditioning, the cattle farmer (*rancher*) has trained his animals (steers or cattle) to gather together and move (*he herds them*) to the feeding station (*food trough*). They have learned to associate the sound of the tone (*the beep*) made by the signaling device (*electronic pager*) with the delivery of food (classical conditioning), and they have also learned that moving fast (*hustling*) to the food container (*trough*) is followed by the good feeling of satiating their hunger (operant conditioning).

Introduction

For many people, the name Ivan Pavlov (1849–1936) *rings a bell.* Myers is making a little joke here. A common expression when hearing something familiar but vague is to say, *"That rings a bell."* Pavlov's name is familiar to many people, who may also be vaguely aware that his research involved dogs and ringing bells (classical conditioning).

Pavlov's Experiments

. . . what the dog was thinking and feeling as it drooled. . . . To *drool* means to salivate or produce spit. When food (US) is placed in a dog's mouth, the dog will automatically salivate or *drool* (UR). If a tone (CS) is sounded before (or precedes) the US over a number of trials, then the CS alone (the tone) will be able to elicit salivation (CR). Pavlov decided that the dog's internal mental state (thinking and feeling) was not important in reaching an understanding of fundamental learning principles, and that focusing attention on cognitive processes only led to futile arguments (*fruitless debates*).

(margin note): If the *aroma* of cake baking *sets your mouth to watering*, what is the US? The CS? The CR? When you bake a cake in the oven, there is a lovely smell (*aroma*) which makes you salivate or drool (*sets your mouth to watering*). This is an example of classical conditioning: the taste of the cake in your mouth is the US (this automatically produces saliva, the UR), the aroma is the CS, and, because of its past associations with the US, it can now, by itself, elicit saliva (the CR).

They [male quail] developed a preference for their cage's *red-light district* . . . Traditionally, a red lamp hung in the window identified the house as a brothel, and the area of town populated by many brothels became known as the *red-light district*. In Domjan's experiments with male quail a red light (CS) was used to signal the arrival of a receptive female quail (US), which elicited sexual arousal (UR). Eventually, the red light (CS) alone elicited sexual arousal (CR), and the male quail appeared to develop a general liking (*preference*) for the cage with the red light (*the red-light district*).

After *breaking up* with his *fire-breathing heartthrob*, Tirrell also experienced extinction and spontaneous recovery. He recalls that "the smell of onion breath (CS), no longer paired with the kissing (US), lost its ability to *shiver my timbers*." This paragraph describes the end of the relationship (*breaking up*) with his girlfriend (*heartthrob*) who loved to eat onions and thus had hot, smelly breath (*fire-breathing*). The repeated smell of onions or onion breath (CS) without the US (kissing) resulted in extinction of his conditioned aroused state (CR), and, consequently, the CS lost its ability to get him excited (*shiver his timbers*). He later experienced spontaneous recovery (the extinguished CR returned briefly) when he smelled onion breath once more. [The idiom "shiver my timbers" has no simple explanation; it may be an old expression dating back to the days of wooden (*timbered*) sailing ships that would tremble or shiver in a storm, or alternatively, it may have been used in the game of cricket to describe what happens when the cricket ball shakes and scatters (*shivers*) the wooden wicket and stumps (*timbers*).]

Confronted by a pit bull, *your heart may race*; confronted by a golden retriever, it probably will not. Pit bulls are dogs (*not cattle*) that are generally perceived as aggressive and potentially dangerous; golden retrievers are dogs that are usually gentle and friendly. Thus, when you encounter a pit bull, you may experience physiological arousal (*your heart may race*) and you may experience fear, but the sight of a golden retriever will not likely cause the same reaction. To be able to tell the difference (*discriminate*) between two stimuli (in this case, two types of dogs) is an adaptive ability that has obvious survival value.

Extending Pavlov's Understanding

So, even in classical conditioning, it is (especially with humans) not only the simple CS–US association but also *the thought that counts*. The expression "it's the thought that counts" recognizes that a person's intentions and motivations (*thoughts*) are just as important as the actual behavior. Myers is making the point that cognitions (*thoughts, perceptions, expectation*) are now viewed as being critically important in the process of learning through classical conditioning.

Pavlov's Legacy

But if we *see further* than Pavlov did, it is because we *stand on his shoulders*. This phrase is not to be taken literally; it simply means that we now know more than Pavlov did (*we see further*) because we can build and expand on his great work (*stand on his shoulders*).

Former *crack* cocaine users often feel a *craving* when they again encounter cues (people, places) associated with previous *highs*. Crack cocaine users are drug addicts who use a drug that is a synthetic, but very potent, form of cocaine (*crack*). For those who are attempting abstinence, the strong desire (*craving*) for the drug may be a classically conditioned response (CR) to the sight or presence of people or places (CSs). These people or places (CSs) were associated with taking the drug (US) which produced the UR (euphoric feelings or *highs*). Drug addicts are therefore advised to avoid (steer clear of) settings, equipment (*paraphernalia*), or people related to previous drug-taking activity.

. . . legendary significance . . . Watson and Rayner's work with Little Albert was the first investigation of how phobias or irrational fears might develop through the process of classical conditioning. Thus, the story was passed on to future generations of psychologists (it became a legend) and influenced their research.

Operant Conditioning

MODULE OVERVIEW

Module 19 covers the basic principles of operant conditioning, in which we learn to engage in behaviors that are rewarded and to avoid behaviors that are punished. The module also covers the role of cognitive processes in operant conditioning and the ways in which learning is constrained by the biological predispositions of different species. It includes a discussion of how operant conditioning principles are applied in everyday life. The module concludes by contrasting classical and operant conditioning techniques.

NOTE: Answer guidelines for all Module 19 questions begin on page 210.

MODULE REVIEW

First, skim each section, noting headings and boldface items. After you have read the section, review each objective by answering the fill-in and essay-type questions that follow it. As you proceed, evaluate your performance by consulting the answers beginning on page 210. Do not continue with the next section until you understand each answer. If you need to, review or reread the section in the textbook before continuing.

> David Myers at times uses idioms that are unfamiliar to some readers. If you do not know the meaning of any of the following words, phrases, or expressions in the context in which they appear in the text, refer to pages 214–216 for an explanation: *to pull habits out of a rat; . . . between Bach's music and Stravinsky's; pastes gold stars; snooze button; goofing off; a sale with every pitch; fly fishing; a choppy stop-start pattern; "You've got mail"; loses a treat; drawbacks; spanking is a hit; backfire; piggy bank; stirred a hornet's nest.*

Introduction (p. 246)

Objective 1: Identify the two major characteristics that distinguish classical conditioning from operant conditioning.

1. Learning that certain events occur together is referred to as _____

   _____ .

2. Classical conditioning associates _____ stimuli with stimuli that trigger responses that are _____ . Thus, in this form of conditioning, the organism _____ (does/does not) control the responses.

3. The reflexive responses of classical conditioning involve _____ behavior.

4. In contrast, behavior that is more spontaneous and that is influenced by its consequences is called _____ behavior.

Skinner's Experiments (pp. 246–252)

Objective 2: Describe the process of operant conditioning, including the shaping procedure.

1. B. F. Skinner used Thorndike's _____

   _____ _____

   as a starting point in developing a *behavioral technology*. This principle states that _____ behavior is likely to

   _____ .

2. Skinner designed an apparatus, called the

   _____ _____ , to

   investigate _____ in animals, that is, those changes in behavior that are due to experience.

3. The procedure in which a person teaches an animal to perform an intricate behavior by building up to it in small steps is called _____ . This method involves reinforcing successive _____ of the desired behavior.

4. In experiments to determine what an animal can perceive, researchers have found that animals are capable of forming _____ and _____ between stimuli. Similar experiments have been conducted with babies, who also can't verbalize their responses.

5. A situation, event, or signal that a certain response will be reinforced is a _____ _____ .

Objective 3: Identify the different types of reinforcers, and describe the major schedules of partial reinforcement.

6. An event that increases the frequency of a preceding response is a _____ .

7. A stimulus that strengthens a response by presenting a typically pleasurable stimulus after a response is a _____ _____ .

8. A stimulus that strengthens a response by reducing or removing an aversive (unpleasant) stimulus is a _____ _____ .

9. Reinforcers, such as food and shock, that are related to basic needs and therefore do not rely on learning are called _____ _____ . Reinforcers that must be conditioned and therefore derive their power through association are called _____ _____ .

10. Children who are able to delay gratification tend to become _____ (more/less) socially competent and high achieving as they mature.

11. Immediate reinforcement _____ (is/is not) more effective than its alternative, _____ reinforcement. This explains in part the tendency of some teens to engage in risky _____ use and _____ _____ .

12. The procedure involving reinforcement of each and every response is called _____ _____ . Under these conditions, learning is _____ (rapid/slow). When this type of reinforcement is discontinued, extinction is _____ (rapid/slow).

13. The procedure in which responses are reinforced only part of the time is called _____ reinforcement. Under these conditions, learning is generally _____ (faster/slower) than it is with continuous reinforcement. Behavior reinforced in this manner is _____ (very/not very) resistant to extinction.

14. When behavior is reinforced after a set number of responses, a _____-_____ schedule is in effect.

15. Three-year-old Yusef knows that if he cries when he wants a treat, his mother will sometimes give in. When, as in this case, reinforcement occurs after an unpredictable number of responses, a _____-_____ schedule is being used.

16. Reinforcement of the first response after a set interval of time defines the _____-_____ schedule. An example of this schedule is _____ .

17. When the first response after varying amounts of time is reinforced, a _____-_____ schedule is in effect.

Describe the typical patterns of response under fixed-interval, fixed-ratio, variable-interval, and variable-ratio schedules of reinforcement.

Objective 4: Discuss how punishment and negative reinforcement differ, and list some drawbacks of punishment as a behavior-control technique.

18. Unlike _____ _____ , which increases the behavior that preceded it, _____ is an aversive consequence that decreases the likelihood of the behavior that preceded it. Thus, taking aspirin to relieve a headache is an example of _____ _____ , and a child being sent to his room after spilling his milk is an example of _____ .

19. Because punished behavior is merely _____ , it may reappear.

20. Punishment can also lead to _____ and a sense of helplessness, as well as to the association of the aversive event with _____ .

21. Punishment also often increases _____ and does not guide the individual toward more desirable behavior.

Extending Skinner's Understanding
(pp. 253–255)

Objective 5: Explain the importance of cognitive processes and biological predispositions in operant conditioning.

1. Skinner and other behaviorists resisted the growing belief that expectations, perceptions, and other _____ processes have a valid place in the science of psychology.

2. When a well-learned route in a maze is blocked, rats sometimes choose an alternative route, acting as if they were consulting a _____ _____ .

3. Animals may learn from experience even when reinforcement is not available. When learning is not apparent until reinforcement has been provided, _____ _____ is said to have occurred.

4. Excessive rewards may undermine _____ _____ , which is the desire to perform a behavior for its own sake. The motivation to seek external rewards and avoid

punishment is called _____ _____ .

5. Operant conditioning _____ (is/is not) constrained by an animal's biological predispositions.

6. For instance, with animals it is difficult to use food as a _____ to _____ behaviors that are not naturally associated with _____ .

7. Biological constraints predispose organisms to learn associations that are naturally _____ . When animals revert to their biologically predisposed patterns, they are exhibiting what is called "_____ _____ ."

Skinner's Legacy (pp. 255–257)

Objective 6: Describe the controversy over Skinner's views of human behavior, and identify some ways to apply operant conditioning principles at school, at work, and at home.

1. Skinner's views were controversial because he insisted that _____ influences, rather than _____ _____ and _____ , shape behavior.

2. Skinner also advocated the use of _____ principles to influence people in ways that promote more desirable _____ .

3. Skinner's critics argued that he _____ people by neglecting their personal _____ and by seeking to _____ their actions.

4. The use of teaching machines and programmed textbooks was an early application of the operant conditioning procedure of _____ to education. On-line _____ systems, software that is _____ , and _____-based learning are newer examples of this application of operant principles.

5. In boosting productivity in the workplace, positive reinforcement is _____ (more/less) effective when applied to specific

behaviors than when given to reward general merit and when the desired performance is well defined and _____ . For such behaviors, immediate reinforcement is _____ (more/no more) effective than delayed reinforcement.

6. In using operant conditioning to change your own behavior, you would follow these four steps:

    a. _____

    b. _____

    c. _____

    d. _____

Contrasting Classical and Operant Conditioning (pp. 257–258)

Objective 7: Identify the major similarities and differences between classical and operant conditioning.

1. Classical conditioning and operant conditioning are both forms of _____ _____ .

2. Both types of conditioning involve similar processes of _____ , _____ , _____ , _____ , _____ , and _____ .

3. Classical and operant conditioning are both subject to the influences of _____ processes and _____ predispositions.

4. Through classical conditioning, an organism associates different _____ that it does not _____ and responds _____ .

5. Through operant conditioning, an organism associates its _____ _____ with their _____ .

PROGRESS TEST

Multiple-Choice Questions

Circle your answers to the following questions and check them with the answers beginning on page 211. If your answer is incorrect, read the explanation for why it is incorrect and then consult the appropriate pages of the text.

1. The type of learning associated with Skinner is:
    a. classical conditioning.
    b. operant conditioning.
    c. respondent conditioning.
    d. observational learning.

2. In order to obtain a reward a monkey learns to press a lever when a 1000-Hz tone is on but not when a 1200-Hz tone is on. What kind of training is this?
    a. extinction
    b. generalization
    c. classical conditioning
    d. discrimination

3. Which of the following statements concerning reinforcement is correct?
    a. Learning is most rapid with intermittent reinforcement, but continuous reinforcement produces the greatest resistance to extinction.
    b. Learning is most rapid with continuous reinforcement, but intermittent reinforcement produces the greatest resistance to extinction.
    c. Learning is fastest and resistance to extinction is greatest after continuous reinforcement.
    d. Learning is fastest and resistance to extinction is greatest following intermittent reinforcement.

4. The highest and most consistent rate of response is produced by a _____ schedule.
    a. fixed-ratio   c. fixed-interval
    b. variable-ratio   d. variable-interval

5. A response that leads to the removal of an unpleasant stimulus is one being:
    a. positively reinforced.
    b. negatively reinforced.
    c. punished.
    d. extinguished.

6. One difference between classical and operant conditioning is that:
    a. in classical conditioning the responses operate on the environment to produce rewarding or punishing stimuli.
    b. in operant conditioning the responses are triggered by preceding stimuli.
    c. in classical conditioning the responses are automatically triggered by stimuli.
    d. in operant conditioning the responses are reflexive.

7. Punishment is a controversial way of controlling behavior because:
   a. behavior is not forgotten and may return.
   b. punishing stimuli often create fear.
   c. punishment often increases aggressiveness.
   d. of all of these reasons.

8. Which of the following is an example of reinforcement?
   a. presenting a positive stimulus after a response
   b. removing an unpleasant stimulus after a response
   c. being told that you have done a good job
   d. All of these are examples.

9. Shaping is a(n) _____ technique for _____ a behavior.
   a. operant; establishing
   b. operant; suppressing
   c. respondent; establishing
   d. respondent; suppressing

10. For operant conditioning to be most effective, when should the reinforcers be presented in relation to the desired response?
    a. immediately before
    b. immediately after
    c. at the same time as
    d. at least a half hour before

11. In distinguishing between negative reinforcers and punishment, we note that:
    a. punishment, but not negative reinforcement, involves use of an aversive stimulus.
    b. in contrast to punishment, negative reinforcement decreases the likelihood of a response by the presentation of an aversive stimulus.
    c. in contrast to punishment, negative reinforcement increases the likelihood of a response by the presentation of an aversive stimulus.
    d. in contrast to punishment, negative reinforcement increases the likelihood of a response by the termination of an aversive stimulus.

12. The commission method of payment is an example of which reinforcement schedule?
    a. fixed-interval   c. fixed-ratio
    b. variable-interval   d. variable-ratio

13. Putting on your coat when it is cold outside is a behavior that is maintained by:
    a. discrimination learning.
    b. punishment.
    c. negative reinforcement.
    d. classical conditioning.

14. On an intermittent reinforcement schedule, reinforcement is given:
    a. in very small amounts.
    b. randomly.
    c. for successive approximations of a desired behavior.
    d. only some of the time.

15. You teach your dog to fetch the paper by giving him a cookie each time he does so. This is an example of:
    a. operant conditioning.
    b. classical conditioning.
    c. conditioned reinforcement.
    d. partial reinforcement.

16. A cognitive map is a:
    a. mental representation of one's environment.
    b. sequence of thought processes leading from one idea to another.
    c. set of instructions detailing the most effective means of teaching a particular concept.
    d. biological predisposition to learn a particular skill.

17. After exploring a complicated maze for several days, a rat subsequently ran the maze with very few errors when food was placed in the goal box for the first time. This performance illustrates:
    a. classical conditioning.
    b. discrimination learning.
    c. observational learning.
    d. latent learning.

18. Leon's psychology instructor has scheduled an exam every third week of the term. Leon will probably study the most just before an exam and the least just after an exam. This is because the schedule of exams is reinforcing studying according to which schedule?
    a. fixed-ratio   c. fixed-interval
    b. variable-ratio   d. variable-interval

19. On-line testing systems and interactive software are applications of the operant conditioning principles of:
    a. shaping and immediate reinforcement.
    b. immediate reinforcement and punishment.
    c. shaping and primary reinforcement.
    d. continuous reinforcement and punishment.

20. Which of the following is the best example of a conditioned reinforcer?
    a. putting on a coat on a cold day
    b. relief from pain after the dentist stops drilling your teeth
    c. receiving a cool drink after washing your mother's car on a hot day
    d. receiving an approving nod from the boss for a job well done

21. You are expecting an important letter in the mail. As the regular delivery time approaches you glance more and more frequently out the window, searching for the letter carrier. Your behavior in this situation typifies that associated with which schedule of reinforcement?
    a. fixed-ratio
    b. variable-ratio
    c. fixed-interval
    d. variable-interval

22. Jack finally takes out the garbage in order to get his father to stop pestering him. Jack's behavior is being influenced by:
    a. positive reinforcement.
    b. negative reinforcement.
    c. a primary reinforcer.
    d. punishment.

23. From a casino owner's viewpoint, which of the following jackpot-payout schedules would be the most desirable for reinforcing customer use of a slot machine?
    a. variable-ratio
    b. fixed-ratio
    c. variable-interval
    d. fixed-interval

24. After discovering that her usual route home was closed due to road repairs, Sharetta used her knowledge of the city and sense of direction to find an alternate route. This is an example of:
    a. latent learning.
    b. observational learning.
    c. shaping.
    d. using a cognitive map.

25. The manager of a manufacturing plant wishes to use positive reinforcement to increase the productivity of workers. Which of the following procedures would probably be the most effective?
    a. Deserving employees are given a general merit bonus at the end of each fiscal year.
    b. A productivity goal that seems attainable, yet is unrealistic, is set for each employee.

    c. Employees are given immediate bonuses for specific behaviors related to productivity.
    d. Employees who fail to meet standards of productivity receive pay cuts.

26. Reggie's mother tells him that he can watch TV after he cleans his room. Evidently, Reggie's mother is attempting to use _____ to increase room cleaning.
    a. operant conditioning
    b. conditioned reinforcement
    c. positive reinforcement
    d. all of these techniques

27. Which of the following is an example of shaping?
    a. A dog learns to salivate at the sight of a box of dog biscuits.
    b. A new driver learns to stop at an intersection when the light changes to red.
    c. A parrot is rewarded first for making any sound, then for making a sound similar to "Laura," and then for "speaking" its owner's name.
    d. A psychology student reinforces a laboratory rat only occasionally, to make its behavior more resistant to extinction.

28. Lars, a shoe salesman, is paid every two weeks, whereas Tom receives a commission for each pair of shoes he sells. Evidently, Lars is paid on a _____ schedule of reinforcement, and Tom on a _____ schedule of reinforcement.
    a. fixed-ratio; fixed-interval
    b. continuous; intermittent
    c. fixed-interval; fixed-ratio
    d. variable-interval; variable-ratio

29. Nancy decided to take introductory psychology because she has always been interested in human behavior. Jack enrolled in the same course because he thought it would be easy. Nancy's behavior was motivated by _____, Jack's by _____.
    a. extrinsic motivation; intrinsic motivation
    b. intrinsic motivation; extrinsic motivation
    c. drives; incentives
    d. incentives; drives

Matching Items

Match each definition or description with the appropriate term.

Definitions or Descriptions

_____ 1. presentation of a desired stimulus
_____ 2. removal of an aversive stimulus
_____ 3. an innately reinforcing stimulus
_____ 4. an acquired reinforcer
_____ 5. responses are reinforced after an unpredictable amount of time
_____ 6. the motivation to perform a behavior for its own sake
_____ 7. reinforcing closer and closer approximations of a behavior
_____ 8. presentation of an aversive stimulus
_____ 9. learning that becomes apparent only after reinforcement is provided
_____ 10. each and every response is reinforced
_____ 11. a desire to perform a behavior due to promised rewards

Terms

a. shaping
b. punishment
c. latent learning
d. positive reinforcement
e. negative reinforcement
f. primary reinforcer
g. conditioned reinforcer
h. continuous reinforcement
i. variable-interval schedule
j. extrinsic motivation
k. intrinsic motivation

True–False Items

Indicate whether each statement is true or false by placing *T* or *F* in the blank next to the item.

_____ 1. Operant conditioning involves behavior that is primarily reflexive.
_____ 2. Negative reinforcement decreases the likelihood that a response will recur.
_____ 3. The learning of a new behavior proceeds most rapidly with continuous reinforcement.
_____ 4. As a rule, variable schedules of reinforcement produce more consistent rates of responding than fixed schedules.
_____ 5. Although punishment may be effective in suppressing behavior, it can have several undesirable side effects.

Essay Question

Describe the best way for a pet owner to condition her dog to roll over. (Use the space below to list the points you want to make, and organize them. Then write the essay on a separate piece of paper.)

KEY TERMS

Using your own words, on a piece of paper write a brief definition or explanation of each of the following terms.

1. associative learning
2. respondent behavior
3. operant conditioning
4. operant behavior
5. operant chamber (Skinner box)
6. learning
7. shaping
8. reinforcer
9. positive reinforcement
10. negative reinforcement
11. primary reinforcers
12. conditioned reinforcers
13. continuous reinforcement
14. partial (intermittent) reinforcement
15. fixed-ratio schedule
16. variable-ratio schedule
17. fixed-interval schedule
18. variable-interval schedule
19. punishment
20. cognitive map
21. latent learning
22. intrinsic motivation
23. extrinsic motivation

ANSWERS

Module Review

Introduction

1. associative learning
2. neutral; automatic; does not
3. respondent
4. operant

Skinner's Experiments

1. law of effect; rewarded; recur
2. operant chamber (Skinner box); learning
3. shaping; approximations
4. concepts; discriminating
5. discriminative stimulus

6. reinforcer
7. positive reinforcer
8. negative reinforcer
9. primary reinforcers; conditioned reinforcers
10. more
11. is; delayed; drug; unprotected sex
12. continuous reinforcement; rapid; rapid
13. partial (intermittent); slower; very
14. fixed-ratio
15. variable-ratio
16. fixed-interval; checking the mail as delivery time approaches
17. variable-interval

Following reinforcement on a fixed-interval schedule, there is a pause in responding and then an increasing rate of response as time for the next reinforcement draws near. On a fixed-ratio schedule there also is a post-reinforcement pause, followed, however, by a return to a consistent, high rate of response. Both kinds of variable schedules produce steadier rates of response, without the pauses associated with fixed schedules. In general, schedules linked to responses produce higher response rates and variable schedules produce more consistent responding than the related fixed schedules.

18. negative reinforcement; punishment; negative reinforcement; punishment
19. suppressed
20. fear; the person who administered it
21. aggressiveness

Extending Skinner's Understanding

1. cognitive
2. cognitive map
3. latent learning
4. intrinsic motivation; extrinsic motivation
5. is
6. reinforcer; shape; food
7. adaptive; instinctive drift

Skinner's Legacy

1. external; internal thoughts; feelings
2. operant; behavior
3. dehumanized; freedom; control
4. shaping; testing; interactive; Web
5. more; achievable; more

6. a. State your goal.

b. Monitor the behavior (when and where it occurs).

c. Reinforce the desired behavior.

d. Reduce the incentives to perform the undesirable behavior.

Contrasting Classical and Operant Conditioning

1. associative learning

2. acquisition; extinction; spontaneous recovery; generalization; discrimination

3. cognitive; biological

4. stimuli; control; automatically

5. operant behaviors; consequences

Progress Test

Multiple-Choice Questions

1. b. is the answer.
a. & c. Classical conditioning is associated with Pavlov; respondent conditioning is another name for classical conditioning.
d. Observational learning is most closely associated with Bandura.

2. d. is the answer. In learning to distinguish between the conditioned stimulus and another, similar stimulus, the monkey has received training in discrimination.
a. In extinction training, a stimulus and/or response is allowed to go unreinforced.
b. Generalization training involves responding to stimuli similar to the conditioned stimulus; here the monkey is being trained not to respond to a similar stimulus.
c. This cannot be classical conditioning since the monkey is acting in order to obtain a reward. Thus, this is an example of operant conditioning.

3. b. is the answer. A continuous association will naturally be easier to learn than one that occurs on only some occasions, so learning is most rapid with continuous reinforcement. Yet, once the continuous association is no longer there, as in extinction training, extinction will occur more rapidly than it would have had the organism not always experienced reinforcement.

4. b. is the answer.
a. With fixed-ratio schedules, there is a pause following each reinforcement.
c. & d. Because reinforcement is not contingent on the rate of response, interval schedules, especially fixed-interval schedules, produce lower response rates than ratio schedules.

5. b. is the answer.
a. Positive reinforcement involves presenting a favorable stimulus following a response.
c. Punishment involves presenting an unpleasant stimulus following a response.
d. In extinction, a previously reinforced response is no longer followed by reinforcement. In this situation, a response causes a stimulus to be terminated or removed.

6. c. is the answer.
a. In *operant* conditioning the responses operate on the environment.
b. In *classical* conditioning responses are triggered by preceding stimuli.
d. In *classical* conditioning responses are reflexive.

7. d. is the answer.

8. d. is the answer. a. is an example of positive reinforcement, b. is an example of negative reinforcement, and c. is an example of conditioned reinforcement.

9. a. is the answer. Shaping works on operant behaviors by reinforcing successive approximations to a desired goal.

10. b. is the answer.
a., c., & d. Reinforcement that is delayed, presented before a response, or presented at the same time as a response does not always increase the response's frequency of occurrence.

11. d. is the answer.
a. Both involve an aversive stimulus.
b. All reinforcers, including negative reinforcers, increase the likelihood of a response.
c. In negative reinforcement, an aversive stimulus is withdrawn following a desirable response.

12. c. is the answer. Payment is given after a fixed number of pieces have been completed.
a. & b. Interval schedules reinforce according to the passage of time, not the amount of work accomplished.
d. Fortunately for those working on commission, the work ratio is fixed and therefore predictable.

13. c. is the answer. By learning to put on your coat before going outside, you have learned to reduce the aversive stimulus of the cold.
a. Discrimination learning involves learning to make a response in the presence of the appropriate stimulus and not other stimuli.
b. Punishment is the suppression of an undesirable response by the presentation of an aversive stimulus.

d. Putting on a coat is a response that operates on the environment. Therefore, this is an example of operant, not classical, conditioning.

14. **d.** is the answer.
    a. Intermittent reinforcement refers to the ratio of responses to reinforcers, not the overall quantity of reinforcement delivered.
    b. Unlike intermittent reinforcement, in which the delivery of reinforcement is contingent on responding, random reinforcement is delivered independently of the subject's behavior.
    c. This defines the technique of shaping, not intermittent reinforcement.

15. **a.** is the answer. You are teaching your dog by rewarding him when he produces the desired behavior.
    b. This is not classical conditioning because the cookie is a primary reinforcer presented after the operant behavior of the dog fetching the paper.
    c. Food is a primary reinforcer; it satisfies an innate need.
    d. Rewarding your dog each time he fetches the paper is continuous reinforcement.

16. **a.** is the answer.

17. **d.** is the answer. The rat had learned the maze but did not display this learning until reinforcement became available.
    a. Negotiating a maze is clearly operant behavior.
    b. This example does not involve learning to distinguish between stimuli.
    c. This is not observational learning because the rat has no one to observe!

18. **c.** is the answer. Because reinforcement (earning a good grade on the exam) is available according to the passage of time, studying is reinforced on an interval schedule. Because the interval between exams is constant, this is an example of a fixed-interval schedule.

19. **a.** is the answer. On-line testing systems apply operant principles such as reinforcement, immediate feedback, and shaping to the teaching of new skills.
    b. & d. On-line testing systems provide immediate, and continuous, reinforcement for correct responses, but do not use aversive control procedures such as punishment.
    c. On-line testing systems are based on feedback for correct responses; this feedback constitutes conditioned, rather than primary, reinforcement.

20. **d.** is the answer. An approving nod from the boss is a conditioned reinforcer in that it doesn't satisfy an innate need but has become linked with

desirable consequences. Cessation of cold, cessation of pain, and a drink are all primary reinforcers, which meet innate needs.

21. **c.** is the answer. Reinforcement (the letter) comes after a fixed interval, and as the likely end of the interval approaches, your behavior (glancing out the window) becomes more frequent.
    a. & b. These answers are incorrect because with ratio schedules, reinforcement is contingent upon the number of responses rather than on the passage of time.
    d. Assuming that the mail is delivered at about the same time each day, the interval is fixed rather than variable. Your behavior reflects this, since you glance out the window more often as the delivery time approaches.

22. **b.** is the answer. By taking out the garbage, Jack terminates an aversive stimulus—his father's nagging.
    a. Positive reinforcement would involve a desirable stimulus that increases the likelihood of the response that preceded it.
    c. This answer would have been correct if Jack's father had rewarded Jack for taking out the garbage by providing his favorite food.
    d. Punishment suppresses behavior; Jack is behaving in order to obtain reinforcement.

23. **a.** is the answer. Ratio schedules maintain higher rates of responding—gambling in this example—than do interval schedules. Furthermore, variable schedules are not associated with the pause in responding following reinforcement that is typical of fixed schedules. The slot machine would therefore be used more often, and more consistently, if jackpots were scheduled according to a variable-ratio schedule.

24. **d.** is the answer. Sharetta is guided by her mental representation of the city, or cognitive map.
    a. Latent learning, or learning in the absence of reinforcement that is demonstrated when reinforcement becomes available, has no direct relevance to the example.
    b. Observational learning refers to learning from watching others.
    c. Shaping is the technique of reinforcing successive approximations of a desired behavior.

25. **c.** is the answer.
    a. Positive reinforcement is most effective in boosting productivity in the workplace when specific behavior, rather than vaguely defined general merit, is rewarded. Also, immediate reinforcement is much more effective than the delayed reinforcement described in a.

b. Positive reinforcement is most effective in boosting productivity when performance goals are achievable, rather than unrealistic.

d. The text does not specifically discuss the use of punishment in the workplace. However, it makes the general point that although punishment may temporarily suppress unwanted behavior, it does not guide one toward more desirable behavior. Therefore, workers who receive pay cuts for poor performance may learn nothing about how to improve their productivity.

26. **d.** is the answer. By making a more preferred activity (watching TV) contingent on a less preferred activity (room cleaning), Reggie's mother is employing the operant conditioning technique of positive reinforcement.

27. **c.** is the answer. The parrot is reinforced for making successive approximations of a goal behavior. This defines shaping.

   a. Shaping is an operant conditioning procedure; salivation at the sight of dog biscuits is a classically conditioned response.

   b. Shaping involves the systematic reinforcement of successive approximations of a more complex behavior. In this example there is no indication that the response of stopping at the intersection involved the gradual acquisition of simpler behaviors.

   d. This is an example of the partial reinforcement of an established response, rather than the shaping of a new response.

28. **c.** is the answer. Whereas Lars is paid (reinforced) after a fixed period of time (fixed-interval), Tom is reinforced for each sale (fixed-ratio) he makes.

29. **b.** is the answer. Wanting to do something for its own sake is intrinsic motivation; wanting to do something for a reward (in this case, presumably, a high grade) is extrinsic motivation.

   a. The opposite is true. Nancy was motivated to take the course for its own sake, whereas Jack was evidently motivated by the likelihood of a reward in the form of a good grade.

   c. & d. A good grade, such as the one Jack is expecting, is an incentive. Drives, however, are aroused states that result from physical deprivation; they are not involved in this example.

Matching Items

1. d	**5.** i	**9.** c
2. e	**6.** k	**10.** h
3. f	**7.** a	**11.** j
4. g	**8.** b	

True–False Items

1. F		**4.** T
2. F		**5.** T
3. T		

Essay Question

The first step in shaping an operant response, such as rolling over, is to find an effective reinforcer. Some sort of biscuit or dog treat is favored by animal trainers. This primary reinforcement should be accompanied by effusive praise (secondary reinforcement) whenever the dog makes a successful response.

Rolling over (the goal response) should be divided into a series of simple approximations, the first of which is a response, such as lying down on command, that is already in the dog's repertoire. This response should be reinforced several times. The next step is to issue a command, such as "Roll over," and withhold reinforcement until the dog (usually out of frustration) makes a closer approximation (such as rotating slightly in one direction). Following this example, the trainer should gradually require closer and closer approximations until the goal response is attained. When the new response has been established, the trainer should switch from continuous to partial reinforcement, in order to strengthen the skill.

Key Terms

1. In **associative learning**, organisms learn that certain events occur together. Two variations of associative learning are classical conditioning and operant conditioning.

2. **Respondent behavior** is that which occurs as an automatic response to some stimulus.

   Example: In classical conditioning, conditioned and unconditioned responses are examples of **respondent behavior** in that they are automatic responses triggered by specific stimuli.

3. **Operant conditioning** is a type of learning in which behavior is strengthened if followed by a reinforcer or diminished if followed by a punisher.

   Example: Unlike classical conditioning, which works on automatic behaviors, **operant conditioning** works on behaviors that operate on the environment.

4. **Operant behavior** is behavior that operates on the environment, producing consequences.

5. An **operant chamber** (*Skinner box*) is an experimental chamber for the operant conditioning of an animal such as a pigeon or rat. The controlled environment enables the investigator to present visual or auditory stimuli, deliver reinforcement or punishment, and precisely measure simple responses such as bar presses or key pecking.

6. **Learning** is any relatively permanent change in an organism's behavior due to experience.

7. **Shaping** is the operant conditioning procedure for establishing a new response by reinforcing successive approximations of the desired behavior.

8. In operant conditioning, a **reinforcer** is any event that strengthens the behavior it follows.

9. In operant conditioning, **positive reinforcement** strengthens a response by *presenting* a typically pleasurable stimulus after that response.

10. In operant conditioning, **negative reinforcement** strengthens a response by *removing* an aversive stimulus after that response.

11. The powers of **primary reinforcers** are inborn and do not depend on learning.

12. **Conditioned reinforcers** are stimuli that acquire their reinforcing power through their association with primary reinforcers.

13. **Continuous reinforcement** is the operant procedure of reinforcing the desired response every time it occurs. In promoting the acquisition of a new response it is best to use continuous reinforcement.

14. **Partial (intermittent) reinforcement** is the operant procedure of reinforcing a response intermittently. A response that has been partially reinforced is much more resistant to extinction than one that has been continuously reinforced.

15. In operant conditioning, a **fixed-ratio schedule** is one in which reinforcement is presented after a set number of responses.

Example: Continuous reinforcement is a special kind of **fixed-ratio schedule**: Reinforcement is presented after *each* response, so the ratio of reinforcements to responses is one to one.

16. In operant conditioning, a **variable-ratio schedule** is one in which reinforcement is presented after a varying number of responses.

17. In operant conditioning, a **fixed-interval schedule** is one in which a response is reinforced after a specified time has elapsed.

18. In operant conditioning, a **variable-interval schedule** is one in which responses are reinforced after varying intervals of time.

19. In operant conditioning, **punishment** is the presentation of an aversive stimulus, such as shock, which decreases the behavior it follows.

Memory aid: People often confuse negative reinforcement and **punishment**. The former strengthens behavior, while the latter weakens it.

20. A **cognitive map** is a mental picture of one's environment.

21. **Latent learning** is learning that occurs in the absence of reinforcement but only becomes apparent when there is an incentive to demonstrate it.

22. **Intrinsic motivation** is the desire to perform a behavior for its own sake, rather than for some external reason, and to be effective.

Memory aid: Intrinsic means "internal": A person who is **intrinsically motivated** is motivated from within.

23. **Extrinsic motivation** is the desire to perform a behavior in order to obtain a reward or avoid a punishment.

Memory aid: Extrinsic means "external": A person who is extrinsically motivated is motivated by some outside factor.

FOCUS ON VOCABULARY AND LANGUAGE

Skinner's Experiments

. . . to pull habits out of a rat. David Myers is having fun playing with the English language here. The expression "to pull rabbits out of a hat" refers to stage magicians who are able to extract rabbits from a seemingly empty hat. Can you see the way Myers has twisted this expression? Both classical and operant conditioning involve teaching new habits to various organisms, including rats. Following classical conditioning the CS triggers a new response from the animal (i.e., the CS "*pulls a habit out of the rat*"), or the sight of the lever may elicit the habit of lever pressing (operant conditioning).

They [pigeons] have even been trained to discriminate between *Bach's music and Stravinsky's*. Bach and Stravinsky were composers whose styles of musical composition were quite different. Through shaping (rewarding behaviors that are closer and closer to the target or desired response), psychologists have been able to train pigeons to discriminate (or choose) between the two musical sounds. For example, pigeons may be rewarded for pecking a disk when Bach is playing and for refraining from pecking when Stravinsky is playing. They can be trained to discriminate, or tell the difference, between the two.

Or consider a teacher who pastes *gold stars on a wall chart* after the names of children scoring 100 percent on spelling tests. Teachers often use extrinsic rewards such as small, bright stickers (*gold stars*) and typically display them on a classroom bulletin board (*pastes them on a wall chart*) for, say, the very best spellers in the class. Unfortunately, if only the top few students (*academic all-stars*) are recognized in this way, the rest of the students may lose motivation because, even if they improve their spelling and work very hard (but still don't get 100%), they don't get any reinforcers. Myers recommends a shaping procedure that rewards even small improvements and recognizes the child for making the effort to do better and better.

Pushing the *snooze button* silences your annoying alarm. When your radio alarm goes off in the morning, you may press the switch (*snooze button*) which turns off the irritating tone for a brief period of time. The ensuing quiet period, which may allow you to go back to sleep for a while (*snooze*), and the absence of the buzzer are negative reinforcers for pushing the snooze button. (Your button-pushing behavior has been strengthened because it removed an aversive event, the alarm.) Likewise, a regular drug user (*drug addict*) may be negatively reinforced for continuing or resuming drug taking because doing so diminishes the pain associated with going without the drug (*withdrawal pangs*).

. . . goofing off and getting a bad exam grade . . . Students may score poorly on an exam because they were doing something unproductive, such as watching TV, instead of studying (they were *goofing off*). As a consequence, they may decide to change their behavior and work hard to avoid further exam anxiety and the unpleasant possibility of getting a low grade. The new behavior may be strengthened if it avoids the aversive consequences of anxiety (negative reinforcement); in addition, getting a good score on the exam can positively reinforce good study habits. Remember, reinforcers of either kind (positive or negative) always strengthen behavior.

Salespeople do not make a sale with every *pitch,* nor do *anglers* get a bite with every *cast*. The *pitch* referred to here is the sales talk (*pitch*) that the salesperson uses to promote the product or service. The

bite the angler (fisherman) does not get refers to the fact that throwing out the line (*casting*) does not always result in fish biting the bait. The idea is that much of our behavior is not continuously reinforced but persists, nevertheless, by being partially reinforced (you make a sale or catch a fish only once in a while despite many responses). Thus, intermittent rewards encourage the expectation of future reinforcement (*hope springs eternal*) and create greater resistance to extinction of the behavior compared to a continuous schedule.

. . . fly fishing . . . This refers to a style of fishing in which artificial insects, such as flies, are used as bait to catch the fish. People who fly fish are reinforced only once in a while despite making many responses. This variable-ratio schedule of reinforcement makes the target behavior very persistent and hard to suppress (the behavior is very resistant to extinction) because ultimately the more responding, the more reinforcement.

. . . a choppy stop-start pattern . . . When reinforcement is for the first response after a set time period (a **fixed-interval schedule**), responding is typically more frequent as the expected time for the reinforcer gets closer (*draws near*) and is much less frequent after the reward has been received. The pattern of responding is consequently uneven (*choppy*) because cycles of post-reinforcement pauses followed by higher levels of responding (a *stop-start pattern*) are characteristic of the fixed-interval schedule.

. . . "You've got mail" . . . E-mails can arrive at unpredictable times, so it is best to check on-line every once in a while if you are expecting an e-mail from someone. Slow, steady responding like this, typical of a **variable-interval schedule,** may be reinforced with the *"You've got mail"* announcement.

. . . the child who loses a treat after running into the street . . . Here the phrase *"loses a treat"* refers to the withholding of some pleasant consequence such as a candy bar or piece of cake (appetitive stimulus) following some unwanted behavior. This is one type of punishment; it decreases the probability of the behavior being repeated. Another example is *time out*, in which the child is put in a situation (such as in the corner) in which no reinforcement is available.

. . . drawbacks . . . This means problems or bad consequences. One problem (*drawback*) with using punishment is that the behavior may be temporarily suppressed in the presence of the punisher but may reappear in other, safer settings. In addition, punishment may elicit aggression, create fear and appre-

hension, and generate avoidance behavior in those being punished. As Myers notes, punishment teaches what not to do, whereas reinforcement teaches what to do.

No wonder *spanking is a hit* with so many U.S. parents of 3- and 4-year-olds. . . . *Hit* has a number of meanings; it can mean to physically strike someone or something (*hit the ball*), but it can also mean to be popular (*to be a hit*). Parents who physically punish (*hit or swat*) their young children are negatively reinforced for doing so if the bad behavior is suppressed or eliminated. It is not surprising then that spanking (*hitting or swatting*) is popular (*it is a hit*) with so many parents.

Promising people a reward for a task they already enjoy can *backfire*. If children enjoy doing something because it is fun (intrinsic motivation), they may lose interest in the task if they are promised a reward for it (extrinsic motivation). Thus, in some circumstances offering material gains (a *payoff*) may have an effect opposite to the one expected (it can *backfire*). Applied properly, however, rewards can motivate high performance levels (*they fuel your efforts*), increase creativity, enhance enjoyment of tasks, and raise (*boost*) feelings of competence, especially if they suggest (*signal*) that a job was well done.

Extending Skinner's Understanding

. . . *piggy bank* . . . This is a small container for saving money (usually coins) that is often in the shape of a pig. Children can learn to save their money by putting it in their *piggy bank*. However, as Myers points out, pigs who were trained to put big wooden coins in a large *piggy bank* soon reverted to their natural behavior of pushing the coins with their snouts (noses) despite the fact that they received no reward for doing this. This is an example of the biological constraints on learning. This example of *instinctive drift* illustrates the biological constraints on learning.

Skinner's Legacy

. . . *stirred a hornet's nest.* . . . A hornet is a large yellow and black stinging insect belonging to the wasp family. Up to 200 hornets live together in a sheltered home (*nest*); if disturbed or agitated (*stirred*), they will attack in an angry and aggressive manner. B. F. Skinner aroused a great deal of anger and hostility and was vehemently attacked by many people (*he stirred a hornet's nest*) for insisting that mental events and free will (internal events) were of little relevance as determinants of behavior compared to environmental factors such as rewards and punishments (external influences).

Learning by Observation

MODULE OVERVIEW

Module 20 covers observational learning, in which we learn by observing and imitating others. Although the basic forms of learning—classical and operant conditioning—account for much of human behavior, we also learn indirectly, by observing other people.

NOTE: Answer guidelines for all Module 20 questions appear on page 219.

MODULE REVIEW

First, skim each section, noting headings and boldface items. After you have read the section, review each objective by answering the fill-in and essay-type questions that follow it. As you proceed, evaluate your performance by consulting the answers on page 219. Do not continue with the next section until you understand each answer. If you need to, review or reread the section in the textbook before continuing.

> David Myers at times uses idioms that are unfamiliar to some readers. If you do not know the meaning of following expression in the context in which it appears in the text, refer to page 220 for an explanation: *those who observed the model's actions were much more likely to lash out at the doll.*

Introduction (pp. 261–262)

Objective 1: Explain the process of observational learning.

1. A relatively permanent change in behavior due to experience defines _____ .

2. Learning by observing and imitating others is called _____ _____ , or _____ when it involves a specific _____ .

3. Neuroscientists have found _____ neurons in the brain's _____ lobe that provide a neural basis for _____ learning. These neurons have been observed to fire when monkeys perform a simple task and when they _____ . This type of neuron _____ (has/has not) been found in human brains and may help give rise to _____ and to a child's ability to infer another's mental state, called _____ _____ _____ .

4. By age _____ , infants will imitate novel play behaviors. By age _____ , they will imitate acts modeled on television.

Bandura's Experiments (pp. 262–263)

Objective 2: Describe Bandura's findings on what determines whether we will imitate a model.

1. The psychologist best known for research on observational learning is _____ .

2. In one experiment, the child who viewed an adult punch an inflatable doll played _____ (more/less) aggressively than the child who had not observed the adult.

3. Bandura believes people imitate a model because of _____ and _____, those received by the model as well as by imitators.

4. Models are most effective when they are perceived as _____, _____, or _____.

Applications of Observational Learning
(pp. 263–265)

Objective 3: Discuss the impact of prosocial modeling and the relationship between watching violent TV and antisocial behavior.

1. Children will model positive, or _____, behaviors. Models are also most effective when their words and actions are _____.

2. Observational learning may also have _____ effects. These results may help explain why _____ parents might have _____ children. However, _____ factors may also be involved.

3. Children in developed countries spend more time _____ _____ than they spend in school.

4. Compared to real-world crimes, television depicts a much higher percentage of crimes as being _____ in nature.

5. Correlational studies _____ (link/do not link) watching television violence with violent behavior.

6. The more hours children spend watching violent programs, the more at risk they are for _____ and _____ as teens and adults.

7. Correlation does not prove _____. Most researchers believe that watching violence on television _____ (does/does not) lead to aggressive behavior.

8. The violence effect stems from several factors, including _____ of observed aggression and the tendency of prolonged exposure to violence to _____ viewers.

PROGRESS TEST

Multiple-Choice Questions

Circle your answers to the following questions and check them with the answers on page 219. If your answer is incorrect, read the explanation for why it is incorrect and then consult the appropriate pages of the text.

1. Learning by imitating others' behaviors is called _____ learning. The researcher best known for studying this type of learning is _____.
   a. secondary; Skinner
   b. observational; Bandura
   c. secondary; Pavlov
   d. observational; Watson

2. Mirror neurons are found in the brain's _____ and are believed to be the neural basis for _____.
   a. frontal lobe; observational learning
   b. frontal lobe; classical conditioning
   c. temporal lobe; operant conditioning
   d. temporal lobe; observational learning

3. In promoting observational learning, the most effective models are those we perceive as:
   a. similar to ourselves.
   b. respected and admired.
   c. successful.
   d. having any of these characteristics.

4. Regarding the impact of watching television violence on children, most researchers believe that:
   a. aggressive children simply prefer violent programs.
   b. television simply reflects, rather than contributes to, violent social trends.
   c. watching violence on television leads to aggressive behavior.
   d. there is only a weak correlation between exposure to violence and aggressive behavior.

5. Mrs. Ramirez often tells her children that it is important to buckle their seat belts while riding in the car, but she rarely does so herself. Her children will probably learn to:
   a. use their seat belts and tell others it is important to do so.
   b. use their seat belts but not tell others it is important to do so.
   c. tell others it is important to use seat belts but rarely use them themselves.
   d. neither tell others that seat belts are important nor use them.

6. After watching coverage of the Olympics on television recently, Lynn and Susan have been staging their own "summer games." Which of the following best accounts for their behavior?

   a. classical conditioning   c. latent learning
   b. observational learning   d. shaping

KEY TERMS

Using your own words, on a piece of paper write a brief definition or explanation of each of the following terms.

1. learning
2. observational learning
3. modeling
4. mirror neurons
5. prosocial behavior

ANSWERS
Module Review

Introduction

1. learning
2. observational learning; modeling; behavior
3. mirror; frontal; observational; observe other monkeys performing the same task; has; empathy; theory of mind
4. 9 months; 14 months

Bandura's Experiments

1. Albert Bandura
2. more
3. rewards; punishments
4. similar; successful; admirable

Applications of Observational Learning

1. prosocial; consistent
2. antisocial; abusive; aggressive; genetic
3. watching television
4. violent
5. link
6. aggression; crime
7. causation; does
8. imitation; desensitize

Progress Test

Multiple-Choice Questions

1. **b.** is the answer.
   a. Skinner is best known for studies of *operant* learning. Moreover, there is no such thing as secondary learning.
   c. Pavlov is best known for classical conditioning.
   d. Watson is best known as an early proponent of behaviorism.
2. **a.** is the answer.
3. **d.** is the answer.
4. **c.** is the answer.
5. **c.** is the answer. Studies indicate that when a model says one thing but does another, subjects do the same and learn not to practice what they preach.
6. **b.** is the answer. The girls are imitating behavior they have observed and admired.
   a. Because these behaviors are clearly willful rather than involuntary, classical conditioning plays no role.
   c. Latent learning plays no role in this example.
   d. Shaping is a procedure for teaching the acquisition of a new response by reinforcing successive approximations of the behavior.

Key Terms

1. **Learning** is any relatively permanent change in an organism's behavior due to experience.
2. **Observational learning** is learning by watching and imitating the behavior of others.
3. **Modeling** is the process of watching and then imitating a specific behavior and is thus an important means through which observational learning occurs.
4. Found in the brain's frontal lobe, **mirror neurons** may be the neural basis for observational learning. These neurons generate impulses when certain actions are performed or when another individual who performs those actions is observed.
5. The opposite of antisocial behavior, **prosocial behavior** is positive, helpful, and constructive and is subject to the same principles of observational learning as is undesirable behavior, such as aggression.

FOCUS ON VOCABULARY AND LANGUAGE

Bandura's Experiments

Compared with children not exposed to the adult model, those who observed the model's actions were much more likely to *lash out* at the doll. Bandura's experiments on observational learning demonstrated that children who saw an adult engage in (*model*) violent behavior (an *aggressive outburst*) were more inclined to attack and beat up (*lash out at*) a Bobo doll and copy (*imitate*) the words and gestures used by the role model.

Memory

Information Processing

MODULE OVERVIEW

Module 21 explores human memory as a system that processes information in three steps. Encoding refers to the process of putting information into the memory system. Storage is the purely passive mechanism by which information is maintained in memory. Retrieval is the process by which information is accessed from memory through recall or recognition.

Module 21 also discusses the important role of meaning, imagery, and organization in encoding new memories, as well as how memory is represented physically in the brain.

NOTE: Answer guidelines for all Module 21 questions begin on page 232.

MODULE REVIEW

First, skim this section, noting headings and boldface items. After you have read the section, review each objective by completing the sentences and answering the questions that follow it. As you proceed, evaluate your performance by consulting the answers on page 232. Do not continue with the next section until you understand each answer. If you need to, review or reread the section in the textbook before continuing.

> David Myers at times uses idioms that are unfamiliar to some readers. If you do not know the meaning of any of the following words, phrases, or expressions in the context in which they appear in the text, refer to pages 237–238 for an explanation: *medal winners in a memory Olympics; shine the flashlight beam of our attention on; boost; nonsense syllables; a raw script . . . finished stage production; "peg-word"; lightning flash; Sherlock Holmes; champion memorist; Arousal can sear certain events into the brain;*

> *mirror-image writing . . . jigsaw puzzle; London cabbie; buoyant mood . . . rose-colored glasses; morph from devils into angels.*

The Phenomenon of Memory and Studying Memory: Information-Processing Models
(pp. 269–271)

Objective 1: Describe Atkinson-Shiffrin's classic three-stage processing model of memory, and explain how the contemporary model of working memory differs.

1. Learning that persists over time indicates the existence of _____ for that learning.

2. Both human memory and computer memory can be viewed as _____-_____ systems that perform three tasks: _____ , _____ , and _____ .

3. The classic model of memory has been Atkinson and Shiffrin's _____-_____ _____ model. According to this model, we first record information as a fleeting _____ . _____ , from which it is processed into _____-_____ memory, where the information is _____ through rehearsal into _____-_____ memory for later retrieval.

4. The phenomenon of short-term memory has been clarified by the concept of _____ memory, which focuses more on the _____ processing of briefly stored

information. This form of memory processes incoming _____ and _____-_____ information retrieved from _____-_____ memory.

Encoding: Getting Information In (pp. 271–276)

Objective 2: Describe the types of information we encode automatically, and contrast effortful processing with automatic processing, giving examples of each.

1. Encoding that does not require conscious attention or effort is called _____ _____ . Some processing requires effort at first but with _____ and _____ it becomes effortless.

Give examples of material that is typically encoded with little or no effort.

2. Encoding that requires attention and effort is called _____ _____ .

3. With novel information, conscious repetition, or _____ , boosts memory.

4. A pioneering researcher in verbal memory was _____ . In one experiment, he found that the longer he studied a list of nonsense syllables, the _____ (fewer/greater) the number of repetitions he required to relearn it later. Additional rehearsal (or _____) increases retention.

5. Memory studies also reveal that distributed rehearsal is more effective for retention; this is called the _____ _____ .

6. The tendency to remember the first and last items in a list best is called the _____ _____ _____ .

7. People briefly recall the last items in a list quickly and well, called the _____ effect. Following a delay, first items are remembered _____ (better/less well) than last items, called the _____ effect.

Objective 3: Compare the benefits of visual, acoustic, and semantic encoding in remembering verbal information, and describe some memory-enhancing encoding strategies.

8. Encoding the meaning of words is referred to as _____ encoding; encoding by sound is called _____ encoding; encoding the image of words is _____ encoding.

9. Research has shown that comparing visual, acoustic, and semantic encoding showed that memory was best with _____ encoding.

10. Memory that consists of mental pictures is based on the use of _____ .

11. Concrete, high-imagery words tend to be remembered _____ (better/less well) than abstract, low-imagery words.

12. Memory for concrete nouns is facilitated when we encode them _____ and _____ .

13. Our tendency to recall the high points of pleasurable events such as family vacations illustrates the phenomenon of _____ _____ .

14. Memory aids are known as _____ devices.

15. Using a jingle, such as the one that begins "one is a bun," is an example of the "_____-_____" system.

16. Memory may be aided by grouping information into meaningful units called _____ . An example of this technique involves forming words from the first letters of to-be-remembered words; the resulting word is called an _____ .

17. In addition, material may be processed into _____ , which are composed of a few broad concepts divided into lesser concepts, categories, and facts.

Storage: Retaining Information (pp. 277–283)

Objective 4: Contrast two types of sensory memory, and describe the duration and working capacity of short-term memory.

1. Stimuli from the environment are first recorded in _____ memory.

2. George Sperling found that when people were briefly shown three rows of letters, they could recall _____ (virtually all/about half) of them. When Sperling sounded a tone immediately after a row of letters was flashed to indicate which letters were to be recalled, the subjects were much _____ (more/less) accurate. This suggests that people have a brief photographic, or _____ , memory lasting about a few tenths of a second.

3. Sensory memory for sounds is called _____ memory. This memory fades _____ (more/less) rapidly than photographic memory, lasting for as long as _____ .

4. Peterson and Peterson found that when _____ was prevented by asking subjects to count backward, memory for letters was gone after 12 seconds. Without _____ processing, short-term memories have a limited life.

5. Our short-term memory capacity is about _____ chunks of information. This capacity was discovered by _____ .

6. Short-term memory for random _____ (digits/letters) is slightly better than for random _____ (digits/letters), and memory for information we hear is somewhat _____ (better/worse) than that for information we see.

7. Both children and adults have short-term recall for roughly as many words as they can speak in _____ (how many?) seconds.

Objective 5: Describe the capacity and duration of long-term memory, and discuss the biological changes that may underlie memory formation and storage.

8. In contrast to short-term memory—and contrary to popular belief—the capacity of permanent memory is essentially _____ .

9. Psychologist _____ attempted to locate memory by cutting out pieces of rats' _____ after they had learned a maze. He found that no matter where he cut, the rats _____ (remembered/forgot) the maze.

10. Researchers believe that the physical basis of memory, or the _____ _____ , involves a strengthening of certain neural connections, which occurs at the _____ between neurons.

11. Kandel and Schwartz have found that when learning occurs in the sea slug *Aplysia*, the neurotransmitter _____ is released in greater amounts, making synapses more efficient.

12. After learning has occurred, a sending neuron needs _____ (more/less) prompting to fire, and the number of _____ _____ it stimulates may increase. This phenomenon, called _____ - _____ _____ , may be the neural basis for learning and memory. Blocking this process with a specific _____ , or by genetic engineering that causes the absence of an _____ , interferes with learning. Rats given a drug that enhances _____ will learn a maze _____ (faster/more slowly).

13. After LTP has occurred, an electric current passed through the brain _____ (will/will not) disrupt old memories and _____ (will/will not) wipe out recent experiences.

14. Hormones released when we are excited or under stress often _____ (facilitate/impair) learning and memory.

15. Two emotion-processing clusters, the
_____ , in the brain's
_____ system increase activity in
the brain's memory-forming areas.

16. Drugs that block the effects of stress hormones
_____ (facilitate/disrupt) memo-
ries of emotional events.

17. Memories for surprising, significant moments
that are especially clear are called
_____ memories. Like other memories, these memories _____ (can/
cannot) err.

Objective 6: Distinguish between implicit and explicit memory, and identify the main brain structure
associated with each.

18. The loss of memory is called _____ .
Studies of people who have lost their memory
suggest that there _____ (is/is not)
a single unified system of memory.

19. Although amnesia victims typically _____
(have/have not) lost their capacity for learning,
which is called _____ memory,
they _____ (are/are not) able to
declare their memory, suggesting a deficit in their
_____ memory systems.

20. Amnesia patients typically have suffered damage
to the _____ of their limbic system.
This brain structure is important in the processing and storage of _____
memories. Damage on the left side of this structure impairs _____ memory;
damage on the right side impairs memory for
_____ designs and locations. The
rear part of this structure processes
_____ memory.

21. The hippocampus seems to function as a zone
where the brain _____ (temporari-
ly/permanently) stores the elements of a memory. However, memories _____ (do/
do not) migrate for storage elsewhere. The hippocampus is active during _____-
_____ sleep, as memories are

processed for later retrieval. Recalling past experiences activates various parts of the
_____ and _____
lobes.

22. The cerebellum is important in the processing of
_____ memories. Humans and lab-
oratory animals with a damaged cerebellum are
incapable of simple _____-
_____ conditioning.

23. The dual explicit-implicit memory system helps
explain _____ amnesia. We do not
have explicit memories of our first three years
because the _____ is one of the last
brain structures to mature.

Retrieval: Getting Information Out (pp. 283–287)

Objective 7: Contrast the recall, recognition, and
relearning measures of memory, and explain how
retrieval cues can help us access stored memories.

1. The ability to retrieve information not in conscious awareness is called _____ .

2. Bahrick found that 25 years after graduation, people were not able to _____
(recall/recognize) the names of their classmates
but were able to _____
(recall/recognize) 90 percent of their names and
their yearbook pictures.

3. If you have learned something and then forgotten
it, you will probably be able to _____
it _____ (more/less) quickly than
you did originally.

4. The best retrieval cues come from the associations
formed at the time we _____ a
memory.

5. The process by which associations can lead to
retrieval is called _____ .

Objective 8: Describe the impact of environmental
contexts and internal emotional states on retrieval.

6. Studies have shown that retention is best when
learning and testing are done in
_____ (the same/different)
contexts.

Summarize the text explanation of the déjà vu experience.

7. The type of memory in which emotions serve as retrieval cues is referred to as

_____-_____

memory.

8. Our tendency to recall experiences that are consistent with our current emotional state is called

_____-_____

memory.

Describe the effects of mood on memory.

9. People who are currently depressed may recall their parents as _____

_____ . People who have recovered from depression typically recall their parents about the same as do people who _____

_____ .

PROGRESS TEST

Multiple-Choice Questions

Circle your answers to the following questions and check them with the answers beginning on page 233. If your answer is incorrect, read the explanation for why it is incorrect and then consult the appropriate pages of the text.

1. The three steps in memory information processing are:
   a. input, processing, output.
   b. input, storage, output.
   c. input, storage, retrieval.
   d. encoding, storage, retrieval.

2. Visual sensory memory is referred to as:
   a. iconic memory.   c. photomemory.
   b. echoic memory.   d. semantic memory.

3. Echoic memories fade after approximately:
   a. 1 hour.   c. 1 second.
   b. 1 minute.   d. 3 to 4 seconds.

4. Which of the following is *not* a measure of retention?
   a. recall   c. relearning
   b. recognition   d. retrieval

5. Our short-term memory span is approximately _____ items.
   a. 2   c. 7
   b. 5   d. 10

6. Memory techniques such as acronyms and the peg-word system are called:
   a. consolidation devices.
   b. imagery techniques.
   c. encoding strategies.
   d. mnemonic devices.

7. One way to increase the amount of information in memory is to group it into larger, familiar units. This process is referred to as:
   a. consolidating.   c. encoding.
   b. organization.   d. chunking.

8. Kandel and Schwartz have found that when learning occurs, more of the neurotransmitter _____ is released into synapses.
   a. ACh   c. serotonin
   b. dopamine   d. noradrenaline

9. In a study on context cues, people learned words while on land or when they were underwater. In a later test of recall, those with the best retention had:
   a. learned the words on land, that is, in the more familiar context.
   b. learned the words underwater, that is, in the more exotic context.
   c. learned the words and been tested on them in different contexts.
   d. learned the words and been tested on them in the same context.

10. The spacing effect means that:
    a. distributed study yields better retention than cramming.
    b. retention is improved when encoding and retrieval are separated by no more than 1 hour.
    c. learning causes a reduction in the size of the synaptic gap between certain neurons.
    d. delaying retrieval until memory has consolidated improves recall.

11. Studies demonstrate that learning causes permanent neural changes in which part of animals' neurons?
    a. myelin   c. synapses
    b. cell bodies   d. all of these parts

12. In Sperling's memory experiment, research participants were shown three rows of three letters, followed immediately by a low, medium, or high tone. The participants were able to report:
    a. all three rows with perfect accuracy.
    b. only the top row of letters.
    c. only the middle row of letters.
    d. any one of the three rows of letters.

13. Studies of amnesia victims suggest that:
    a. memory is a single, unified system.
    b. there are two distinct types of memory.
    c. there are three distinct types of memory.
    d. memory losses following brain trauma are unpredictable.

14. Memory for skills is called:
    a. explicit memory.   c. prime memory.
    b. declarative memory.   d. implicit memory.

15. The eerie feeling of having been somewhere before is an example of:
    a. state dependency.   c. priming.
    b. encoding failure.   d. déjà vu.

16. When Gordon Bower presented words grouped by category or in random order, recall was:
    a. the same for all words.
    b. better for the categorized words.
    c. better for the random words.
    d. improved when participants developed their own mnemonic devices.

17. The three-stage processing model of memory was proposed by:
    a. Atkinson and Shiffrin.
    b. Herman Ebbinghaus.
    c. Eric Kandel.
    d. George Sperling.

18. Which area of the brain is most important in the processing of implicit memories?
    a. hippocampus   c. hypothalamus
    b. cerebellum   d. amygdala

19. Which of the following measures of retention is the least sensitive in triggering retrieval?
    a. recall   c. relearning
    b. recognition   d. They are equally sensitive.

20. Amnesia victims typically have experienced damage to the _____ of the brain.
    a. frontal lobes   c. thalamus
    b. cerebellum   d. hippocampus

21. According to the serial position effect, when recalling a list of words you should have the greatest difficulty with those:
    a. at the beginning of the list.
    b. at the end of the list.
    c. at the end and in the middle of the list.
    d. in the middle of the list.

22. Experimenters gave people a list of words to be recalled. When the participants were tested after a delay, the items that were best recalled were those:
    a. at the beginning of the list.
    b. in the middle of the list.
    c. at the end of the list.
    d. at the beginning and the end of the list.

23. Which type of word processing—visual, acoustic, or semantic—results in the greatest retention?
    a. visual
    b. acoustic
    c. semantic
    d. Acoustic and semantic processing were equally beneficial.

24. Lashley's studies, in which rats learned a maze and then had various parts of their brains surgically removed, showed that the memory:
    a. was lost when surgery took place within 1 hour of learning.
    b. was lost when surgery took place within 24 hours of learning.
    c. was lost when any region of the brain was removed.
    d. remained no matter which area of the brain was tampered with.

25. The disruption of memory that occurs when football players have been knocked out provides evidence for the importance of:

a. consolidation in the formation of new memories.

b. consolidation in the retrieval of long-term memories.

c. nutrition in normal neural functioning.

d. all of these answers.

26. *Long-term potentiation* refers to:

a. the disruptive influence of old memories on the formation of new memories.

b. the disruptive influence of recent memories on the retrieval of old memories.

c. our tendency to recall experiences that are consistent with our current mood.

d. the increased efficiency of synaptic transmission between certain neurons following learning.

27. The process of getting information out of memory storage is called:

a. encoding.   c. rehearsal.

b. retrieval.   d. storage.

28. Amnesia patients typically experience disruption of:

a. implicit memories.   c. iconic memories.

b. explicit memories.   d. echoic memories.

29. Information is maintained in short-term memory only briefly unless it is:

a. encoded.   c. iconic or echoic.

b. rehearsed.   d. retrieved.

30. Textbook chapters are often organized into _____ in order to facilitate information processing.

a. mnemonic devices   c. hierarchies

b. chunks   d. recognizable units

31. It is easier to recall information that has just been presented when the information:

a. consists of random letters rather than words.

b. is seen rather than heard.

c. is heard rather than seen.

d. is experienced in an unusual context.

32. Complete this analogy: Fill-in-the-blank test questions are to multiple-choice questions as:

a. encoding is to storage.

b. storage is to encoding.

c. recognition is to recall.

d. recall is to recognition.

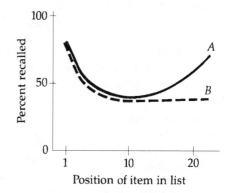

33. The above figure depicts the recall of a list of words under two conditions. Which of the following best describes the difference between the conditions?

a. In *A*, the words were studied and retrieved in the same context; in *B*, the contexts were different.

b. In *B*, the words were studied and retrieved in the same context; in *A*, the contexts were different.

c. The delay between presentation of the last word and the test of recall was longer for *A* than for *B*.

d. The delay between presentation of the last word and the test of recall was longer for *B* than for *A*.

34. Darren was asked to memorize a list of letters that included *v, q, y,* and *j*. He later recalled these letters as *e, u, i,* and *k*, suggesting that the original letters had been encoded:

a. automatically.   c. semantically.

b. visually.   d. acoustically.

35. Being in a bad mood after a hard day of work, Susan could think of nothing positive in her life. This is best explained as an example of:

a. priming.

b. memory consolidation.

c. mood-congruent memory.

d. retrieval failure.

36. In an effort to remember the name of the class-mate who sat behind her in fifth grade, Martina mentally recited the names of other classmates who sat near her. Martina's effort to refresh her memory by activating related associations is an example of:
    a. priming.
    b. déjà vu.
    c. encoding.
    d. relearning.

37. Walking through the halls of his high school 10 years after graduation, Tom experienced a flood of old memories. Tom's experience showed the role of:
    a. state-dependent memory.
    b. context effects.
    c. the serial position effect.
    d. echoic memory.

38. The first thing Karen did when she discovered that she had misplaced her keys was to re-create in her mind the day's events. That she had little difficulty in doing so illustrates:
    a. automatic processing.
    b. effortful processing.
    c. state-dependent memory.
    d. priming.

39. Which of the following is the best example of a flashbulb memory?
    a. suddenly remembering to buy bread while standing in the checkout line at the grocery store
    b. recalling the name of someone from high school while looking at his or her yearbook snapshot
    c. remembering to make an important phone call
    d. remembering what you were doing on September 11, 2001, when terrorists crashed planes into the World Trade Center towers.

40. Elderly Mr. Flanagan, a retired electrician, can easily remember how to wire a light switch, but he cannot remember the name of the president of the United States. Evidently, Mr. Flanagan's _____ memory is better than his _____ memory.
    a. implicit; explicit
    b. explicit; implicit
    c. declarative; nondeclarative
    d. explicit; declarative

41. Although you can't recall the answer to a question on your psychology midterm, you have a clear mental image of the textbook page on which it appears. Evidently, your _____ encoding of the answer was _____ .
    a. semantic; automatic
    b. visual; automatic
    c. semantic; effortful
    d. visual; effortful

42. Brenda has trouble remembering her new five-digit ZIP plus four-digit address code. What is the most likely explanation for the difficulty Brenda is having?
    a. Nine digits are at or above the upper limit of most people's short-term memory capacity.
    b. Nine digits are at or above the upper limit of most people's iconic memory capacity.
    c. The extra four digits cannot be organized into easily remembered chunks.
    d. Brenda evidently has an impaired implicit memory.

43. Brad, who suffered accidental damage to the left side of his hippocampus, has trouble remembering:
    a. visual designs.
    b. locations.
    c. all nonverbal information.
    d. verbal information.

44. During basketball practice Jan's head was painfully elbowed. If the trauma to her brain disrupts her memory, we would expect that Jan would be most likely to forget:
    a. the name of her teammates.
    b. her telephone number.
    c. the name of the play during which she was elbowed.
    d. the details of events that happened shortly after the incident.

45. After suffering damage to the hippocampus, a person would probably:
    a. lose memory for skills such as bicycle riding.
    b. be incapable of being classically conditioned.
    c. lose the ability to store new facts.
    d. experience all of these changes.

Matching Items

Match each definition or description with the appropriate term.

Definitions or Descriptions

_____ 1. sensory memory that decays more slowly than visual sensory memory

_____ 2. the process by which information gets into the memory system

_____ 3. mental pictures that aid memory

_____ 4. the phenomenon in which one's mood can influence retrieval

_____ 5. memory for a list of words is affected by word order

_____ 6. "one is a bun, two is a shoe" mnemonic device

_____ 7. word that chunks to-be-remembered information into a more familiar form

_____ 8. a measure of memory

Terms

a. relearning
b. serial position effect
c. peg-word system
d. acronym
e. imagery
f. mood-congruent memory
g. echoic memory
h. encoding

True–False Items

Indicate whether each statement is true or false by placing *T* or *F* in the blank next to the item.

_____ 1. Generally speaking, memory for random digits is better than memory for random letters.

_____ 2. Most people do not have memories of events that occurred before the age of 3.

_____ 3. Time spent in developing imagery, chunking, and associating material with what you already know is more effective than time spent repeating information again and again.

_____ 4. After long-term potentiation has occurred, passing an electric current through the brain will disrupt old memories.

_____ 5. Memory is a single, unified conscious system.

KEY TERMS

Using your own words, on a separate piece of paper write a brief definition or explanation of each of the following terms.

1. memory

2. encoding

3. storage

4. retrieval

5. sensory memory

6. short-term memory

7. long-term memory

8. working memory

9. automatic processing

10. effortful processing

11. rehearsal

12. spacing effect

13. serial position effect

14. imagery

15. mnemonics

16. chunking

17. iconic memory

18. echoic memory

19. long-term potentiation (LTP)

20. flashbulb memory

21. amnesia

22. implicit memory

23. explicit memory

24. hippocampus

25. recall

26. recognition

27. relearning

28. priming

29. déjà vu

30. mood-congruent memory

ANSWERS

Module Review

The Phenomenon of Memory and *Studying Memory: Information-Processing Models*

1. memory

2. information-processing; encoding; storage; retrieval

3. three-stage processing; sensory memory; short-term; encoded; long-term

4. working; active; auditory; visual-spatial; long-term

Encoding: Getting Information In

1. automatic processing; practice; experience

Automatic processing includes the encoding of information about space, time, and frequency. It also includes the encoding of word meaning, a type of encoding that appears to be learned.

2. effortful processing

3. rehearsal

4. Hermann Ebbinghaus; fewer; overlearning

5. spacing effect

6. serial position effect

7. recency; better; primacy

8. semantic; acoustic; visual

9. semantic

10. imagery

11. better

12. semantically; visually

13. rosy retrospection

14. mnemonic

15. peg-word

16. chunks; acronym

17. hierarchies

Storage: Retaining Information

1. sensory

2. about half; more; iconic

3. echoic; less; 3 or 4 seconds

4. rehearsal; active

5. 7; George Miller

6. digits; letters; better

7. 2

8. unlimited (limitless)

9. Karl Lashley; cortexes; remembered

10. memory trace; synapses

11. serotonin

12. less; receptor sites; long-term potentiation; drug; enzyme; LTP; faster

13. will not; will

14. facilitate

15. amygdala; limbic

16. disrupt

17. flashbulb; can

18. amnesia; is not

19. have not; implicit; are not; explicit

20. hippocampus; explicit; verbal; visual; spatial

21. temporarily; do; slow-wave; frontal; temporal

22. implicit; eye-blink

23. infantile; hippocampus

Retrieval: Getting Information Out

1. recall

2. recall; recognize

3. relearn; more

4. encode

5. priming

6. the same

The déjà vu experience is most likely the result of being in a context similar to one that we have actually been in before. If we have previously been in a similar situation, though we cannot recall what it was, the current situation may present cues that subconsciously help us to retrieve the earlier experience.

7. state-dependent

8. mood-congruent

When happy, for example, we perceive things in a positive light and recall happy events; these perceptions and memories, in turn, prolong our good mood.

9. rejecting, punitive, and guilt-promoting; have never suffered depression

Progress Test

Multiple-Choice Questions

1. **d.** is the answer. Information must be encoded, or put into appropriate form; stored, or retained over time; and retrieved, or located and gotten out when needed.

2. **a.** is the answer. Iconic memory is our fleeting memory of visual stimuli.
   b. Echoic memory is auditory sensory memory.
   c. There is no such thing as photomemory.
   d. Semantic memory is memory for meaning, not a form of sensory memory.

3. **d.** is the answer. Echoic memories last 3 to 4 seconds.

4. **d.** is the answer. Retrieval refers to the *process* of remembering.

5. **c.** is the answer.

6. **d.** is the answer.
   a. There is no such term as "consolidation techniques."
   b. & c. Imagery and encoding strategies are important in storing new memories, but mnemonic device is the general designation of techniques that facilitate memory, such as acronyms and the peg-word system.

7. **d.** is the answer.
   a. There is no such process of "consolidating."
   b. Organization *does* enhance memory, but it does so through hierarchies, not grouping.
   c. Encoding refers to the processing of information into the memory system.

8. **c.** is the answer. Kandel and Schwartz found that when learning occurred in the sea slug *Aplysia*, serotonin was released at certain synapses, which then became more efficient at signal transmission.

9. **d.** is the answer. In general, being in a context similar to that in which you experienced something will tend to help you recall the experience.
   a. & b. The learning environment per se—and its familiarity or exoticness—did not affect retention.

10. **a.** is the answer.
    b. & d. The text does not suggest that there is an optimal interval between encoding and retrieval.
    c. Learning increases the efficiency of synaptic transmission in certain neurons, but not by altering the size of the synapse.

11. **c.** is the answer.

12. **d.** is the answer. When asked to recall all the letters, participants could recall only about half; however, if immediately after the presentation they were signaled to recall a particular row, their recall was near perfect. This showed that they had a brief photographic memory—so brief that it faded in less time than it would have taken to say all nine letters.

13. **b.** is the answer. Because amnesia victims lose their fact (explicit) memories but not their skill (implicit) memories or their capacity to learn, it appears that human memory can be divided into two distinct types.
    d. As studies of amnesia victims show, memory losses following damage to the hippocampus are quite predictable.

14. **d.** is the answer.
    a. & b. Explicit memory (also called declarative memory) is memory of facts and experiences that one can consciously know and declare.
    c. There is no such thing as prime memory.

15. **d.** is the answer.
    a. State-dependent memory is the phenomenon in which information is best retrieved when the person is in the same emotional or physiological state he or she was in when the material was learned.
    b. Encoding failure occurs when a person has not processed information sufficiently for it to enter the memory system.
    c. Priming is the process by which a memory is activated through retrieval of an associated memory.

16. **b.** is the answer. When the words were organized into categories, recall was two to three times better, indicating the benefits of hierarchical organization in memory.
    d. This study did not examine the use of mnemonic devices.

17. **a.** is the answer.
    b. Herman Ebbinghaus conducted pioneering studies of verbal learning and memory.
    c. With James Schwartz, Eric Kandel studied synaptic changes during learning in the sea slug.
    d. George Sperling is known for his research studies of iconic memory.

18. **b.** is the answer.
    a. The hippocampus is a temporary processing site for *explicit memories*.
    c. & d. These areas of the brain are not directly involved in the memory system.

19. **a.** is the answer. A test of recall presents the fewest retrieval cues and usually produces the most limited retrieval.

20. **d.** is the answer.

21. **d.** is the answer. According to the serial position effect, items at the beginning and end of a list tend to be remembered best.

22. **a.** is the answer.
b. In the serial position effect, the items in the middle of the list always show the *poorest* retention.
c. & d. Delayed recall erases the memory facilitation for items at the end of the list.

23. **c.** is the answer. Processing a word in terms of its meaning (semantic encoding) produces much better retention than does visual or acoustic encoding.

24. **d.** is the answer. Surprisingly, Lashley found that no matter where he cut, the rats had at least a partial memory of how to solve the maze.
a. & b. Lashley's studies did not investigate the significance of the interval between learning and cortical lesioning.

25. **a.** is the answer. A blow to the head wipes out recent experiences because information in STM did not have time to consolidate into LTM.
b. Such injuries disrupt the formation, rather than the retrieval, of memories.
c. Although nutrition plays an important role in neural functioning, the effects of such injuries are independent of nutrition.

26. **d.** is the answer.

27. **b.** is the answer.
a. Encoding is the process of getting information *into* memory.
c. Rehearsal is the conscious repetition of information in order to maintain it in memory.
d. Storage is the maintenance of encoded material over time.

28. **b.** is the answer. Amnesia patients typically have suffered damage to the hippocampus, a brain structure involved in processing explicit memories for facts.
a. Amnesia patients do retain implicit memories for how to do things; these are processed in the cerebellum.
c. & d. Amnesia patients generally do not experience impairment in their iconic and echoic sensory memories.

29. **b.** is the answer.
a. Information in short-term memory has *already* been encoded.
c. Iconic and echoic are types of *sensory* memory.
d. Retrieval is the process of getting material out of storage and into conscious, short-term memory. Thus, all material in short-term memory has either already been retrieved or is about to be placed in storage.

30. **c.** is the answer. By breaking concepts down into subconcepts and yet smaller divisions and showing the relationships among these, hierarchies facilitate information processing. Use of main heads and subheads is an example of the organization of textbook chapters into hierarchies.
a. Mnemonic devices are the method of loci, acronyms, and other memory *techniques* that facilitate retention.
b. Chunks are organizations of knowledge into familiar, manageable units.
d. Recognition is a measure of retention.

31. **c.** is the answer. Short-term recall is slightly better for information we hear rather than see, because echoic memory momentarily outlasts iconic memory.
a. Meaningful stimuli, such as words, are usually remembered more easily than meaningless stimuli, such as random letters.
b. Iconic memory does not last as long as echoic memory in short-term recall.
d. Although context is a powerful retrieval cue, there is no general facilitation of memory in an unusual context.

32. **d.** is the answer.
a. & b. In order to correctly answer either type of question, the knowledge must have been encoded and stored.
c. With fill-in-the-blank questions, the answer must be recalled with no retrieval cues other than the question. With multiple-choice questions, the correct answer merely has to be recognized from among several alternatives.

33. **d.** is the answer.
a. & b. A serial position effect would presumably occur whether the study and retrieval contexts were the same or different.
c. As researchers found, when recall is delayed, only the first items in a list are recalled more accurately than the others. With immediate recall, both the first and last items are recalled more accurately.

34. **d.** is the answer. That all four mistakes are based on a sound confusion suggests that the letters were encoded acoustically.
a. Memorizing a list of letters would involve effortful, rather than automatic, processing.
b. The mistakes do not involve letters that are similar in appearance.
c. Semantic encoding would have been suggested by errors based on similarities in meaning.

35. **c.** is the answer. Susan's memories are affected by her bad mood.

a. Priming refers to the conscious or unconscious activation of particular associations in memory.

b. Memory consolidation refers to the idea that information from STM is combined as it enters LTM.

d. Although Susan's difficulty in recalling the good could be considered retrieval failure, it is caused by the mood-congruent effect, which is therefore the best explanation.

36. **a.** is the answer. Priming is the conscious or unconscious activation of particular associations in memory.

    b. Déjà vu is the false impression of having previously experienced a current situation.

    c. That Martina is able to retrieve her former classmates' names implies that they already have been encoded.

    d. Relearning is a measure of retention based on how long it takes to relearn something already mastered. Martina is recalling her former classmates' names, not relearning them.

37. **b.** is the answer. Being back in the context in which the original experiences occurred triggered memories of these experiences.

    a. The memories were triggered by similarity of place, not mood.

    c. The serial position effect refers to our tendency to remember best items at the beginning and end of a list.

    d. Echoic memory refers to momentary memory of auditory stimuli.

38. **a.** is the answer. Time and space—and therefore sequences of events—are often automatically processed.

    b. That she had *little difficulty* indicates that the processing was automatic, rather than effortful.

    c. & d. State-dependent memory and priming have nothing to do with the automatic processing of space and time.

39. **d.** is the answer. Flashbulb memories are unusually clear memories of emotionally significant moments in life.

40. **a.** is the answer.

    b., c., & d. Explicit memory, also called declarative memory, is the memory of facts that one can consciously "declare." Nondeclarative memory is what Mr. Flanagan has retained.

41. **b.** is the answer.

    a. & c. Your failure to recall the answer indicates that it was never encoded semantically.

    d. Spatial information, such as the location of an answer (but not the actual answer) on a textbook page, is often encoded automatically.

42. **a.** is the answer. Short-term memory capacity is approximately seven digits.

    b. Because iconic memory lasts no more than a tenth of a second, regardless of how much material is experienced, this cannot be the explanation for Brenda's difficulty.

    c. The final four digits should be no more difficult to organize into chunks than the first five digits of the address code.

    d. Memory for digits is an example of explicit, rather than implicit, memory.

43. **d.** is the answer.

    a., b., & c. Damage to the right side, not the left side, of the hippocampus would cause these types of memory deficits.

44. **c.** is the answer. Blows to the head usually disrupt the most recent experiences, such as this one, rather than long-term memories like those in choices a. and b., or new learning such as that in choice d.

45. **c.** is the answer. The hippocampus is involved in processing new facts for storage.

    a., b., & d. Studies of amnesia victims with hippocampal damage show that neither classical conditioning nor skill memory are impaired, indicating that these aspects of memory are controlled by other regions of the brain.

Matching Items

1. g   5. b
2. h   6. c
3. e   7. d
4. f   8. a

True–False Items

1. T   4. F
2. T   5. F
3. T

Key Terms

1. **Memory** is the persistence of learning over time through the storage and retrieval of information.

2. **Encoding** is the first step in memory; information is translated into some form that enables it to enter our memory system.

3. **Storage** is the process by which encoded information is maintained over time.

4. **Retrieval** is the process of bringing to consciousness information from memory storage.

5. **Sensory memory** is the immediate, very brief recording of sensory information in the memory system.

6. **Short-term memory** is activated memory, which can hold about seven items for a short time.

7. **Long-term memory** is the relatively permanent and unlimited capacity memory system into which information from short-term memory may pass. It includes knowledge, skills, and experiences.

8. **Working memory** is the newer way of conceptualizing short-term memory as a work site for the active processing of incoming auditory and visual-spatial information, and of information retrieved from long-term memory.

9. **Automatic processing** refers to our unconscious encoding of incidental information such as space, time, and frequency and of well-learned information.

10. **Effortful processing** is encoding that requires attention and conscious effort.

11. **Rehearsal** is the conscious, effortful repetition of information that you are trying either to maintain in consciousness or to encode for storage.

12. The **spacing effect** is the tendency for distributed study or practice to yield better long-term retention than massed study or practice.

13. The **serial position effect** is the tendency for items at the beginning and end of a list to be more easily retained than those in the middle.

14. **Imagery** refers to mental pictures and can be an important aid to effortful processing.

15. **Mnemonics** are memory aids (acronyms, pegwords, etc.), which often use vivid imagery and organizational devices.

16. **Chunking** is the memory technique of organizing material into familiar, meaningful units.

17. **Iconic memory** is the visual sensory memory consisting of a perfect photographic memory, which lasts no more than a few tenths of a second.

    Memory aid: *Icon* means "image" or "representation." **Iconic memory** consists of brief visual images.

18. **Echoic memory** is the momentary sensory memory of auditory stimuli, lasting about 3 or 4 seconds.

19. **Long-term potentiation (LTP)** is an increase in a synapse's firing potential following brief, rapid stimulation. LTP is believed to be the neural basis for learning and memory.

20. A **flashbulb memory** is an unusually vivid memory of an emotionally important moment or event.

21. **Amnesia** is the loss of memory.

22. **Implicit memories** are memories of skills, preferences, and dispositions. These memories are evidently processed, not by the hippocampus, but by a more primitive part of the brain, the cerebellum. They are also called *procedural* or *nondeclarative memories*.

23. **Explicit memories** are memories of facts, including names, images, and events. They are also called declarative memories.

24. The **hippocampus** is a neural center located in the limbic system that is important in the processing of explicit memories for storage.

25. **Recall** is a measure of memory in which the person must remember, with few retrieval cues, information learned earlier.

26. **Recognition** is a measure of memory in which one need only identify, rather than recall, previously learned information.

27. **Relearning** is also a measure of memory in that the less time it takes to relearn information, the more that information has been retained.

28. **Priming** is the activation, often unconscious, of a web of associations in memory in order to retrieve a specific memory.

29. **Déjà vu** is the false sense that you have already experienced a current situation.

30. **Mood-congruent memory** is the tendency to recall experiences that are consistent with our current mood.

FOCUS ON VOCABULARY AND LANGUAGE

The Phenomenon of Memory and Studying Memory: Information-Processing Models

. . . *medal winners in a memory Olympics.* . . . People with exceptional memories are being likened or compared to the top athletes in the Olympic Games. S, for example, would clearly receive the top prize (*medal winner*) in any competition in which remembering vast amounts of information was being tested (*memory Olympics*).

. . . we *shine the flashlight beam of our attention on* certain incoming stimuli—often those that are novel or important. One model of memory suggests that we only focus on (*shine the flashlight beam of our attention on*) and process one part or aspect of the total sensory input, particularly new (*novel*) or important stimuli. We can also locate and bring back stored information from **long-term memory** (**LTM**) into a temporary work site (**working memory**), where it is combined with incoming stimuli and actively processed.

Encoding: Getting Information In

. . . *boost* . . . One way to improve and increase the power of our memory is to use **rehearsal**. Thus, actively repeating some new information (such as a stranger's name or new terminology) will help strengthen (*boost*) our ability to remember this material. As Myers notes it is important for effective retention to space out or distribute rehearsals over time (*the spacing effect*) rather than doing the repetitions all at once (massed practice or cramming).

To create novel verbal material for learning, Ebbinghaus formed a list of all possible *nonsense syllables* by *sandwiching* one vowel between two consonants. In order to avoid using meaningful words with prior associations, Hermann Ebbinghaus invented three-letter words that made no sense and had no meaning (*nonsense syllables*). He did this by putting a vowel (*sandwiching it*) between two consonants. His nonsense (*meaningless*) syllables were consonant (C), vowel (V), consonant (C), or CVCs.

. . . Gordon Bower and Daniel Morrow (1990) liken our minds to theater directors who, *given a raw script,* imagine a *finished stage production.* This suggests that what we remember is not an exact replica of reality. We construct some mental representation or model (*finished stage production*) from the basic sensory information (*raw script*) available to us, and so, when we recall something, it is our own version (*mental model*) that comes to mind and not the real thing.

For example, the *"peg-word"* system requires you to memorize a *jingle*. A *jingle* is an easily remembered succession of words that ring or resound against each other due to alliteration or rhyme and are often used in radio or TV commercials. The mnemonic (memory aid) called the *"peg-word"* method is based on memorizing a short 10-item poem (*jingle*) that can be associated with a new list of 10 items through visual imagery. The new items are hung on, or pegged to, the familiar items.

Storage: Retaining Information

How much of this page could you sense and recall in less time than a *lightning flash*? In his investigation of sensory storage, George Sperling showed his subjects an array of nine letters for a very brief period (for about the length of a *flash of lightning*). He demonstrated that this was sufficient time for them to briefly view (*glimpse*) all nine letters and that an image remained for less than half a second before fading away; he called this brief (*fleeting*) memory of visual stimuli **iconic memory.**

. . . *Sherlock Holmes* . . . Mystery writer Sir Arthur Conan Doyle's most popular character was a very intelligent and logical private detective named Sherlock Holmes. Holmes believed, as did many others, that our memory capacity was limited, much as a small empty room or attic can hold only so much furniture before it overflows. Contemporary psychologists now believe that our ability to store long-term memories is basically without any limit.

(caption): Among animals, one contender for *champion memorist* would be a mere *birdbrain*—the Clark's nutcracker. . . . Clark's nutcracker is a small bird with a small brain (*birdbrain*) but a phenomenal memory (it is a *champion memorist*) of where it buries its food. It can recall, after a period of more than 6 months, 6000 different locations of hidden food (*caches*).

Arousal *can sear* certain events into the brain . . . When arousal level rises because of stress, so too do the levels of certain hormones. These in turn signal the brain that something important has happened and the events that triggered the arousal make an indelible impression on the brain much as a hot grill burns (*sears*) its shape on the surface of the meat placed on it.

They [people with amnesia] can learn to read *mirror-image writing* or do a *jigsaw puzzle.* . . . They can be classically conditioned. People who have lost the ability to remember new information (*amnesics*) may nevertheless be capable of learning through association (classical conditioning) and of learning to solve problems (e.g., *jigsaw puzzles*) even if they are not aware of having done so. Myers notes that these findings suggest that memory is not a single, unified system. Amnesics can learn how to *do* something (**implicit memory**) without any knowledge of this learning (**explicit**, or **declarative**, **memory**).

London cabbie . . . Taxi-cab drivers are often called *cabbies* and those who work in London, England (*London cabbies*), face an enormous challenge trying to memorize the complicated layout (*maze*) of city streets; the longer they work there the larger the rear area of the hippocampus (which specializes in spatial memory) becomes.

Retrieval: Getting Information Out

If put in a *buoyant mood . . .* people recall the world through *rose-colored glasses. . . .* Our memories are affected by our emotional states (*moods*). Thus, if we are in a good or happy (*buoyant*) mood, we are more likely to view the total situation in a more optimistic and hopeful way (*through rose-colored glasses*). And if we are sad and unhappy, our memories are affected, or tainted, by our negative mood (*being depressed sours memories*). Memory of events and people is influenced by the particular mood we are in, whether it is good or bad, and we tend to remember the events accordingly.

When teens are *down*, their parents seem inhuman; as their mood *brightens*, their parents *morph from devils into angels*. Because our memories tend to be **mood-congruent**, we are likely to explain our present emotional state by remembering events and people as being consistent (*congruent*) with how we now feel. In one study when young adolescents were in a bad mood (*down*), they viewed their parents as cruel and uncaring (inhuman), but later when they were in a much better (*brighter*) mood their parents were described in much nicer terms. It seemed as though their parents had undergone an amazing change in character (*morphing from devils to angels*), but the change was simply in the teenagers' mood. As Myers notes, *"passions [or emotions] exaggerate."*

Forgetting, Memory Construction, and Improving Memory

22

MODULE OVERVIEW

Module 22 first explores how forgetting may result from failure to encode or store information or to find appropriate retrieval cues.

The next section of the module discusses the issue of memory construction. How "true" are our memories of events? A particularly controversial issue in this area involves suspicious claims of long-repressed memories of sexual abuse and other traumas that are "recovered" with the aid of hypnosis and other techniques. As you study this module, try applying some of the memory and studying tips discussed in the text.

NOTE: Answer guidelines for all Module 22 questions begin on page 244.

MODULE REVIEW

First, skim this section, noting headings and boldface items. After you have read the section, review each objective by completing the sentences and answering the questions that follow it. As you proceed, evaluate your performance by consulting the answers on page 244. Do not continue with the next section until you understand each answer. If you need to, review or reread the section in the textbook before continuing.

> David Myers at times uses idioms that are un-familiar to some readers. If you do not know the meaning of any of the following words, phrases, or expressions in the context in which they appear in the text, refer to pages 246–247 for an explanation: *applause for memory; lies poised on the tip of our tongue; mental attic; sheepishly; Like relighting a blown-out candle; "hypnotically refreshed"; reconstruction as well as reproduction; sincerely wrong; Sprinkled.*

Forgetting (pp. 290–294)

Objective 1: Explain why we should value our ability to forget, and discuss the roles of encoding failure and storage decay in the process of forgetting.

1. Without the ability to _____ , we would constantly be overwhelmed by information.

2. Memory researcher Daniel Schacter has identified the seven sins of memory, divided into three categories that identify the ways in which our memory can fail: the three sins of _____ , the three sins of _____ , and the one sin of _____ .

3. The first type of forgetting is caused by _____ failure.

4. This type of forgetting occurs because some of the information that we sense never actually _____ .

5. One reason for age-related memory decline is that the brain areas responsible for _____ new information are _____ (more/less) responsive in older adults.

6. Studies by Ebbinghaus and by Bahrick indicate that most forgetting occurs _____ (soon/a long time) after the material is learned.

7. This type of forgetting is known as _____ _____ , which may be caused by a gradual fading of the physical _____ _____ .

8. When information that is stored in memory temporarily cannot be found, _____ failure has occurred.

Objective 2: Contrast proactive and retroactive interference, and discuss whether Freud's concept of repression is supported by current research.

9. Research suggests that memories are also lost as a result of _____ , which is especially possible if we simultaneously learn similar, new material.

10. The disruptive effect of previous learning on current learning is called _____ _____ . The disruptive effect of learning new material on efforts to recall material previously learned is called _____ _____ .

11. Jenkins and Dallenbach found that if subjects went to sleep after learning, their memory for a list of nonsense syllables was _____ (better/worse) than it was if they stayed awake.

12. In some cases, old information facilitates our learning of new information. This is called _____ _____ .

13. Freud proposed that motivated forgetting, or _____ , may protect a person from painful memories.

14. Increasing numbers of memory researchers think that motivated forgetting is _____ (less/more) common than Freud believed.

Memory Construction (pp. 295–301)

Objective 3: Explain how misinformation, imagination, and source amnesia can distort our memory of an event.

1. Research has shown that recall of an event is often influenced by our experiences and assumptions. The workings of these influences illustrate the process of memory _____ .

2. When witnesses to an event receive misleading information about it, they may experience a _____ _____ and

misremember the event. A number of experiments have demonstrated that false memories _____ (can/cannot) be created when people are induced to imagine nonexistent events; that is, these people later experience "_____ _____ ." People who believe they have recovered memories of alien abduction and child sex abuse tend to have _____ _____ .

Describe what Loftus' studies have shown about the effects of misleading postevent information on eyewitness reports.

3. At the heart of many false memories is _____ _____ , which occurs when we _____ an event to the wrong source.

Objective 4: Discuss whether young children's eyewitness reports are reliable and the controversy over reports of repressed and recovered memories.

4. Because memory is reconstruction as well as reproduction, we _____ (can/cannot) be sure whether a memory is real by how real it feels.

5. Research studies of children's eyewitness recall reveal that preschoolers _____ (are/are not) more suggestible than older children or adults. For this reason, whether a child produces an accurate eyewitness memory depends heavily on how he or she is _____ .

6. Children are most accurate when it is a first interview with a _____ person who asks _____ questions.

7. Researchers increasingly agree that memories obtained under the influence of hypnosis or drugs _____ (are/are not) reliable.

8. Memories of events that happened before age _____ are unreliable. This phenomenon is called _____

_____ .

9. Memory construction makes it clear that memory is best understood not only as a _____ and biological event, but also as a

_____-_____

phenomenon.

Improving Memory (pp. 301–302)

Objective 5: Explain how an understanding of memory can contribute to effective study techniques.

1. The SQ3R study technique identifies five strategies for boosting memory: _____ ,

_____ , _____ ,

_____ , and _____ .

Discuss several specific strategies for improving memory.

PROGRESS TEST

Multiple-Choice Questions

Circle your answers to the following questions and check them with the answers beginning on page 244. If your answer is incorrect, read the explanation for why it is incorrect and then consult the appropriate pages of the text.

1. Research on memory construction reveals that memories:
   a. are stored as exact copies of experience.
   b. reflect a person's biases and assumptions.
   c. may be chemically transferred from one organism to another.
   d. even if long term, usually decay within about five years.

2. Hypnotically "refreshed" memories may prove inaccurate—especially if the hypnotist asks leading questions—because of:
   a. encoding failure.
   b. repression.
   c. proactive interference.
   d. memory construction.

3. Which of the following terms does *not* belong with the others?
   a. misattribution   c. suggestibility
   b. blocking   d. bias

4. Which of the following best describes the typical forgetting curve?
   a. a steady, slow decline in retention over time
   b. a steady, rapid decline in retention over time
   c. a rapid initial decline in retention becoming stable thereafter
   d. a slow initial decline in retention becoming rapid thereafter

5. Jenkins and Dallenbach found that memory was better in subjects who were:
   a. awake during the retention interval, presumably because decay was reduced.
   b. asleep during the retention interval, presumably because decay was reduced.
   c. awake during the retention interval, presumably because interference was reduced.
   d. asleep during the retention interval, presumably because interference was reduced.

6. Repression is an example of:
   a. encoding failure.   c. motivated forgetting.
   b. memory decay.   d. all of these answers.

7. Studies by Loftus and Palmer, in which people were quizzed about a film of an accident, indicate that:
   a. when quizzed immediately, people can recall very little, due to the stress of witnessing an accident.
   b. when questioned as little as one day later, their memory was very inaccurate.
   c. most people had very accurate memories as much as 6 months later.
   d. people's recall may easily be affected by misleading information.

8. Which of the following was *not* recommended as a strategy for improving memory?
   a. active rehearsal
   b. distributed study
   c. speed reading
   d. encoding meaningful associations

9. Memory researchers are suspicious of long-repressed memories of traumatic events that are "recovered" with the aid of drugs or hypnosis because:
   a. such experiences usually are vividly remembered.
   b. such memories are unreliable and easily influenced by misinformation.
   c. memories of events happening before about age 3 are especially unreliable.
   d. of all of these reasons.

10. The misinformation effect provides evidence that memory:
    a. is constructed during encoding.
    b. is unchanging once established.
    c. may be reconstructed during recall according to how questions are framed.
    d. is highly resistant to misleading information.

11. According to memory researcher Daniel Schacter, blocking occurs when:
    a. our inattention to details produces encoding failure.
    b. we confuse the source of information.
    c. our beliefs influence our recollections.
    d. information is on the tip of our tongue, but we can't get it out.

12. After finding her old combination lock, Janice can't remember its combination because she keeps confusing it with the combination of her new lock. She is experiencing:
    a. proactive interference.
    b. retroactive interference.
    c. encoding failure.
    d. storage failure.

13. Which of the following sequences would be best to follow if you wanted to minimize interference-induced forgetting in order to improve your recall on the psychology midterm?
    a. study, eat, test
    b. study, sleep, test
    c. study, listen to music, test
    d. study, exercise, test

14. When Carlos was promoted, he moved into a new office with a new phone extension. Every time he is asked for his phone number, Carlos first thinks of his old extension, illustrating the effects of:
    a. proactive interference.
    b. retroactive interference.
    c. encoding failure.
    d. storage failure.

15. At your high school reunion you cannot remember the last name of your homeroom teacher. Your failure to remember is most likely the result of:
    a. encoding failure.
    b. storage failure.
    c. retrieval failure.
    d. state-dependent memory.

16. Lewis cannot remember the details of the torture he experienced as a prisoner of war. According to Freud, Lewis' failure to remember these painful memories is an example of:
    a. repression.
    b. retrieval failure.
    c. encoding failure.
    d. proactive interference.

17. Which of the following illustrates the constructive nature of memory?
    a. Janice keeps calling her new boyfriend by her old boyfriend's name.
    b. After studying all afternoon and then getting drunk in the evening, Don can't remember the material he studied.
    c. After getting some good news, elated Kareem has a flood of good memories from his younger years.
    d. Although elderly Mrs. Harvey, who has Alzheimer's disease, has many gaps in her memory, she invents sensible accounts of her activities so that her family will not worry.

18. When he was 8 years old, Frank was questioned by the police about a summer camp counselor suspected of molesting children. Even though he was not, in fact, molested by the counselor, today 19-year-old Frank "remembers" the counselor touching him inappropriately. Frank's false memory is an example of which "sin" of memory?
    a. blocking
    b. transience
    c. misattribution
    d. suggestibility

Matching Items

Match each definition or description with the appropriate term.

Definitions or Descriptions

_____ 1. the blocking of painful memories
_____ 2. new learning interferes with previous knowledge
_____ 3. old knowledge interferes with new learning
_____ 4. misattributing the origin of an event
_____ 5. the fading of unused information over time
_____ 6. the lingering effects of misinformation
_____ 7. a memory sin of intrusion

Terms

a. repression
b. persistence
c. proactive interference
d. transience
e. retroactive interference
f. source amnesia
g. suggestibility

True–False Items

Indicate whether each statement is true or false by placing *T* or *F* in the blank next to the item.

_____ 1. Studying that is distributed over time produces better retention than cramming.
_____ 2. Preschool children can be induced to report false events through the use of suggestive interview techniques.
_____ 3. Studies by Ebbinghaus show that most forgetting takes place soon after learning.
_____ 4. The persistence of a memory is a good clue as to whether or not it derives from an actual experience.
_____ 5. Recall of newly acquired knowledge is no better after sleeping than after being awake for the same period of time.
_____ 6. Although repression has not been confirmed experimentally, most psychologists believe it happens.
_____ 7. Overlearning material by continuing to restudy it beyond mastery often disrupts recall.

Essay Question

Discuss the points of agreement among experts regarding the validity of recovered memories of child abuse. (Use the space below to list the points you want to make, and organize them. Then write the essay on a separate piece of paper.)

KEY TERMS

Using your own words, on a separate piece of paper write a brief definition or explanation of each of the following terms.

1. proactive interference

2. retroactive interference

3. repression

4. misinformation effect

5. source amnesia

ANSWERS

Module Review

Forgetting

1. forget

2. forgetting; distortion; intrusion

3. encoding

4. enters the memory system

5. encoding; less

6. soon

7. storage decay; memory trace

8. retrieval

9. interference

10. proactive interference; retroactive interference

11. better

12. positive transfer

13. repression

14. less

Memory Construction

1. construction

2. misinformation effect; can; imagination inflation; vivid imaginations

When people viewed a film of a traffic accident and were quizzed a week later, phrasing of questions affected answers; the word "smashed," for instance, made viewers mistakenly think they had seen broken glass.

3. source amnesia; misattribute

4. cannot

5. are; questioned

6. neutral; nonleading

7. are not

8. 3; infantile amnesia

9. cognitive; social-cultural

Improving Memory

1. Survey; Question; Read; Rehearse; Review

Suggestions for improving memory include rehearsing material over many separate and distributed study sessions with the objective of overlearning material. Studying should also involve active rehearsal, rather than mindless repetition of information. Organizing information, relating material to what is already known, developing numerous retrieval cues, and using mnemonic devices that incorporate vivid imagery are helpful, too. Frequent activation of retrieval cues, such as the context and mood in which the original learning occurred, can also help strengthen memory, as can recalling events while they are fresh, before possible misinformation is encountered. Studying should also be arranged to minimize potential sources of interference. Finally, self-tests in the same format (recall or recognition) that will later be used on the actual test are useful.

Progress Test

Multiple-Choice Questions

1. **b.** is the answer. In essence, we construct our memories, bringing them into line with our biases and assumptions, as well as with our subsequent experiences.
   a. If this were true, it would mean that memory construction does not occur. Through memory construction, memories may deviate significantly from the original experiences.
   c. There is no evidence that such chemical transfers occur.
   d. Many long-term memories are apparently unlimited in duration.

2. **d.** is the answer. It is in both encoding and retrieval that we construct our memories, and as Loftus' studies showed, leading questions affect people's memory construction.
   a. The memory encoding occurred at the time of the event in question, not during questioning by the hypnotist.
   b. Repression refers to the prevention of painful and unacceptable memories from entering consciousness.

c. Proactive interference is the interfering effect of prior learning on the recall of new information.

3. **b.** is the answer. Blocking is an example of retrieval failure. Each of the others is an example of a "sin of distortion," in which memories, although inaccurate, are retrieved.

4. **c.** is the answer. As Ebbinghaus and Bahrick both showed, most of the forgetting that is going to occur happens soon after learning.

5. **d.** is the answer.
a. & b. This study did not find evidence that memories fade (decay) with time.
c. When one is awake, there are many *more* potential sources of memory interference than when one is asleep.

6. **c.** is the answer. According to Freud, we repress painful memories to preserve our self-concepts.
a. & b. The fact that repressed memories can sometimes be retrieved suggests that they were encoded and have not decayed with time.

7. **d.** is the answer. When misled by the phrasings of questions, subjects incorrectly recalled details of the film and even "remembered" objects that weren't there.

8. **c.** is the answer. Speed reading, which entails little active rehearsal, yields poor retention.

9. **d.** is the answer.

10. **c.** is the answer. Loftus and Palmer found that eyewitness testimony could easily be altered when questions were phrased to imply misleading information.
a. Although memories *are* constructed during encoding, the misinformation effect is a retrieval, rather than an encoding, phenomenon.
b. & d. In fact, just the opposite is true.

11. **d.** is the answer.
a. This defines absent-mindedness.
b. This is misattribution.
c. This is bias.

12. **b.** is the answer. Retroactive interference is the disruption of something you once learned by new information.
a. Proactive interference occurs when old information makes it difficult to correctly remember new information.
c. & d. Interference produces forgetting even when the forgotten material was effectively encoded and stored. Janice's problem is at the level of retrieval.

13. **b.** is the answer.
a., c., & d. Involvement in other activities, even just eating or listening to music, is more disruptive than sleeping.

14. **a.** is the answer. Proactive interference occurs when old information makes it difficult to recall new information.
b. If Carlos were having trouble remembering the old extension, this answer would be correct.
c. & d. Carlos has successfully encoded and stored the extension; he's just having problems retrieving it.

15. **c.** is the answer.
a. & b. The name of your homeroom teacher, which you probably heard at least once each day of school, was surely processed into memory (encoded) and maintained there for some time (stored).
d. State-dependent memory is the tendency to recall information best in the same emotional or physiological state as when it was learned. It is unlikely that a single state was associated with learning your homeroom teacher's name.

16. **a.** is the answer.
b. Although Lewis' difficulty in recalling these memories could be considered retrieval failure, it is caused by repression, which is therefore the *best* explanation.
c. This answer is incorrect because it is clear that Lewis did encode these events at some time in the past.
d. Proactive interference is the disruptive effect of previously learned material on learning new information, which is not the situation here.

17. **d.** is the answer.
a. This is an example of proactive interference.
b. This is an example of the disruptive effects of depressant drugs, such as alcohol, on the formation of new memories.
c. This is mood-congruent memory.

18. **d.** is the answer. In this example, the questions Frank was asked to answer created misinformation that later became part of his memory.
a. This answer would have been correct if Frank had been molested by the counselor but had failed to encode it in his memory.
b. This answer would have been correct if Frank had been molested but the memory trace had faded with time.
c. Misattribution might have occurred if Frank had witnessed another camper being molested and later recalled himself as the actual victim.

Matching Items

1.	a	**5.**	d
2.	e	**6.**	g
3.	c	**7.**	b
4.	f		

True–False Items

1. T
2. T
3. T
4. F
5. F
6. F
7. F

Essay Question

Experts agree that child abuse is a real problem that can have long-term adverse effects on individuals. They also acknowledge that forgetting of isolated events, both good and bad, is an ordinary part of life. Although experts all accept the fact that recovered memories are commonplace, they warn that memories "recovered" under hypnosis or with the use of drugs are unreliable, as are memories of events before age 3. Finally, they agree that memories can be traumatic, whether real or false.

Key Terms

1. **Proactive interference** is the disruptive effect of something you already have learned on your efforts to learn or recall new information.

2. **Retroactive interference** is the disruptive effect of something recently learned on old knowledge.

   Memory aid: *Retro* means "backward." **Retroactive interference** is "backward-acting" interference.

3. **Repression** is an example of motivated forgetting in that painful and unacceptable memories are prevented from entering consciousness. In psychoanalytic theory, it is the basic defense mechanism.

4. The **misinformation effect** is the tendency of eyewitnesses to an event to incorporate misleading information about the event into their memories.

5. At the heart of many false memories, **source amnesia** refers to attributing an event to the wrong source.

FOCUS ON VOCABULARY AND LANGUAGE

Forgetting

Amid all the *applause for memory* . . . have any voices been heard in praise of forgetting? We tend to focus on the importance of remembering and recalling information (*there is much applause for memory*). However, if we could not forget, we would be like the Russian memory expert (*memory whiz*) S who was overwhelmed by the amount of useless information he had stored (*haunted by his junk heap of memories*). Thus, many people, from William James to contemporary cognitive psychologists, acknowledge the importance of forgetting.

. . . a name *lies poised on the tip of our tongue*, waiting to be retrieved. The expression *"it's on the tip of my tongue"* refers to the feeling you get when you are trying to remember something (a name, place, etc.) but can't, even though you feel you know it and can *almost* say it (*it's on the tip of your tongue*). Given an appropriate retrieval cue (such as the first letter of the name or something it rhymes with, etc.) we can often remember the item.

As you collect more and more information, your *mental attic* never fills, but it certainly gets *cluttered*. We may have an unlimited amount of space in our memory system or *mental attic* (a room at the top of a house), but with a constant flow of new information coming in, the storage can become disorganized (*cluttered*). The new information may get in the way of recalling old material (**retroactive interference**),

or old material may block or disrupt recall of new information (**proactive interference**).

We *sheepishly* accepted responsibility for 89 cookies. Still, we had not come close; there had been 160. The Myers family obviously loves chocolate chip cookies, and the story of how all 160 were devoured (*scarfed, wolfed down, ate, consumed*) within 24 hours (*not a crumb was left*) is quite funny but makes an important point. Embarrassed, guilty, and feeling a little foolish (*sheepish*), they could only account for and remember eating 89. This illustrates the self-serving nature of memory and how, unknowingly, we change and revise our own histories.

Like *relighting a blown-out candle*, these words cued the woman's memory . . . Just as an extinguished (*blown-out*) candle can be reignited (*relit*) with a match, the presentation of a retrieval cue may help someone recall or retrieve a long forgotten memory. Although Freud proposed that we repress memories of painful experiences in the unconscious mind in order to protect our self-concepts and minimize anxiety, Myers notes that most contemporary memory researchers believe repression rarely, if ever, happens.

Memory Construction

Memory construction helps explain why *"hypnotically refreshed"* memories of crimes so easily incorporate errors, some of which originate with the hypnotist's leading questions . . . Because of the tendency to manufacture events without being consciously aware of doing so (*memory construction*), people are likely to be influenced by suggestions and biased questions while under hypnosis. Their subsequent recollections (*"hypnotically refreshed"*) may therefore be a mixture of fact and fiction.

Because memory is *reconstruction* as well as *reproduction*, we can't be sure whether a memory is real by how real it feels. It is difficult to determine if a memory is real simply by noting how real it feels or how confident we are about its accuracy. We not only recall and retrieve real memories (*reproduction*) but we also manufacture false memories (*reconstruction*).

If memories can be *sincere*, yet *sincerely wrong*, might children's recollections of sexual abuse be prone to error? The evidence suggests that under appropriate conditions children's memories can be reliable and accurate (*sincere*), but that they are also prone to the misinformation effect and can be misled by biased questions and suggestions; later, the children are not able to reliably separate real from false (*sincerely wrong*) memories.

Improving Memory

Sprinkled throughout this module and Module 21 and summarized here for easy reference are *concrete* suggestions for improving memory. These modules on memory have many good ideas for memory improvement scattered or interspersed (*sprinkled*) throughout it, and Myers has pulled them together in an easy to understand format—the SQ3R (Survey, Question, Read, Rehearse, Review) method. These are real and tangible (*concrete*) ways that will help you improve your memory. Use them!!!

Thinking, Language, and Intelligence

Thinking

23

M O D U L E

MODULE OVERVIEW

Module 23 deals with thinking, with emphasis on how people logically—or at times illogically—use tools such as algorithms and heuristics when making decisions and solving problems. Also discussed are several common obstacles to problem solving, including fixations that prevent us from taking a fresh perspective on a problem and our bias to search for information that confirms rather than challenges existing hypotheses. The module concludes with a discussion of the power and perils of intuition.

NOTE: Answer guidelines for all Module 23 questions begin on page 256.

MODULE REVIEW

First, skim each section, noting headings and boldface items. After you have read the section, review each objective by answering the fill-in and essay-type questions that follow it. As you proceed, evaluate your performance by consulting the answers on page 256. Do not continue with the next section until you understand each answer. If you need to, review or reread the section in the textbook before continuing.

> David Myers at times uses idioms that are unfamiliar to some readers. If you do not know the meaning of any of the following words, phrases, or expressions in the context in which they appear in the introduction and this module, refer to pages 259–260 for an explanation: *kin to; birdier bird; stumbling upon one that worked; shoot the basketball; seat of their pants; snap judgment; "a broken promise"; plagues; road tested in the Stone Age; flip-flop; fuels social conflict; filled with straw; off-screen . . . displayed on-screen.*

Introduction and Concepts (pp. 307–308)

Objective 1: Define *cognition*, and describe the roles of categories, hierarchies, and prototypes in concept formation.

1. Cognition, or _____ , can be defined as _____

   _____ .

2. Scientists who study these mental activities are called _____ _____ .

3. People tend to organize specific items into mental groupings called_____ , and many such groupings often are further organized into

   _____ .

4. Concepts are typically formed through the development of a best example, or

   _____ , of a category. People more easily detect _____ (male/female) prejudice against _____ (males/females) than vice versa.

Solving Problems (pp. 308–310)

Objective 2: Compare algorithms, heuristics, and insight as problem-solving strategies.

1. Humans are especially capable of using their reasoning powers for coping with new situations, and thus for _____

   _____ .

2. When we try each possible solution to a problem, we are using _____

   _____ _____ .

3. Logical, methodical, step-by-step procedures for solving problems are called _____ .

4. Simple thinking strategies that provide us with problem-solving shortcuts are referred to as

   _____ .

5. When you suddenly realize a problem's solution, _____ has occurred. Research studies show that at such moments the brain displays a burst of activity in the _____

   _____ _____ .

Objective 3: Explain how confirmation bias and fixation can interfere with problem solving.

6. The tendency of people to look for information that verifies their preconceptions is called

   _____ _____ .

7. It is human nature to seek evidence that _____ our ideas more eagerly than to seek evidence that might _____ them.

8. Not being able to take a new perspective when attempting to solve a problem is referred to as

   _____ .

9. When a person is unable to envision using an object in an atypical way, _____ _____ is operating.

Making Decisions and Forming Judgments
(pp. 310–316)

Objective 4: Explain how the representativeness and availability heuristics can cause us to underestimate or ignore important information, and describe the drawbacks and advantages of overconfidence in decision making.

1. People judge how well something matches a particular prototype; this is the _____

   _____ .

2. When we judge the likelihood of something occurring in terms of how readily it comes to mind, we are using the _____

   _____ .

Explain how these two heuristics may lead us to make judgmental errors.

3. (Thinking Critically) Many people fear _____ more than _____ , and _____ more than _____ , despite the fact that these fears are not supported by death and injury statistics. This type of faulty thinking occurs because we fear:

   a. _____
   b. _____
   c. _____
   d. _____

4. The tendency of people to overestimate the accuracy of their knowledge results in

   _____ .

5. Overconfidence has _____ value because self-confident people tend to live _____ (more/less) happily and find it _____ (easier/harder) to make tough decisions.

6. When research participants are given feedback on the accuracy of their judgments, such feedback generally _____ (does/does not) help them become more realistic about how much they know.

Objective 5: Describe the effects that framing, belief perseverance, and intuition can have on our judgments and decision making.

7. The way an issue is posed is called _____ . This effect influences economic and business decisions, suggesting that our judgments _____ (may/may not) always be well reasoned.

8. Research has shown that once we form a belief or a concept, it may take more convincing evidence for us to change the concept than it did to create it; this is because of _____

   _____ .

9. A cure for this is to _____

   _____ _____ .

10. Intuitive reactions allow us to react _____ and in ways that are usually _____ .

PROGRESS TEST

Multiple-Choice Questions

Circle your answers to the following questions and check them with the answers beginning on page 256. If your answer is incorrect, read the explanation for why it is incorrect and then consult the appropriate pages of the text.

1. The text defines *cognition* as:
   a. silent speech.
   b. all mental activity.
   c. mental activity associated with processing, understanding, remembering, and communicating information.
   d. logical reasoning.

2. A mental grouping of similar things, events, or people is called a(n):
   a. prototype.   c. algorithm.
   b. concept.   d. heuristic.

3. When forming a concept, people often develop a best example, or _____ , of a category.
   a. denoter   c. prototype
   b. heuristic   d. algorithm

4. Confirmation bias refers to the tendency to:
   a. overestimate the accuracy of one's beliefs and judgments.
   b. cling to one's initial conceptions after the basis on which they were formed has been discredited.
   c. search randomly through alternative solutions when problem solving.
   d. look for information that is consistent with one's beliefs.

5. Functional fixedness is a type of:
   a. algorithms.   c. fixation.
   b. heuristics.   d. insight.

6. Failing to solve a problem that requires using an object in an unusual way illustrates the phenomenon of:
   a. the representativeness heuristic.
   b. functional fixedness.
   c. framing.
   d. belief perseverance.

7. Which of the following is an example of the use of heuristics?
   a. trying every possible letter ordering when unscrambling a word
   b. considering each possible move when playing chess
   c. using the formula "area = length x width" to find the area of a rectangle
   d. playing chess using a defensive strategy that has often been successful for you

8. The chimpanzee Sultan used a short stick to pull a longer stick that was out of reach into his cage. He then used the longer stick to reach a piece of fruit. Researchers hypothesized that Sultan's discovery of the solution to his problem was the result of:
   a. trial and error.
   b. heuristics.
   c. functional fixedness.
   d. insight.

9. You hear that one of the Smith children is an outstanding Little League player and immediately conclude it's their one son rather than any of their four daughters. You reached your quite possibly erroneous conclusion as the result of:
   a. the confirmation bias.
   b. the availability heuristic.
   c. the representativeness heuristic.
   d. belief perseverance.

10. A common problem in everyday reasoning is our tendency to:
    a. cling to our beliefs in the face of contrary evidence.
    b. accept as logical those conclusions that disagree with our own opinions.
    c. underestimate the accuracy of our knowledge.
    d. accept as logical conclusions that involve unfamiliar concepts.

11. Representativeness and availability are examples of:
    a. fixations.   c. algorithms.
    b. framing.   d. heuristics.

12. Assume that Congress is considering revising its approach to welfare and to this end is hearing a range of testimony. A member of Congress who uses the availability heuristic would be most likely to:

    a. want to experiment with numerous possible approaches to see which of these seems to work best.
    b. want to find the best solution by systematically examining every possibility.
    c. refuse to be budged from his or her beliefs despite persuasive testimony to the contrary.
    d. base his or her ideas on the most vivid, memorable testimony given, even though many of the statistics presented run counter to this testimony.

13. If you want to be absolutely certain that you will find the solution to a problem you know *is* solvable, you should use:

    a. a heuristic.   c. insight.
    b. an algorithm.   d. trial and error.

14. Which of the following illustrates belief perseverance?

    a. Your belief remains intact even in the face of evidence to the contrary.
    b. You refuse to listen to arguments counter to your beliefs.
    c. You tend to become flustered and angered when your beliefs are refuted.
    d. You tend to search for information that supports your beliefs.

15. Complete the following analogy: Rose is to flower as:

    a. concept is to prototype.
    b. prototype is to concept.
    c. concept is to hierarchy.
    d. hierarchy is to concept.

16. Your stand on an issue such as the use of nuclear power for electricity involves personal judgment. In such a case, one memorable occurrence can weigh more heavily than a book full of data, thus illustrating:

    a. belief perseverance.
    b. confirmation bias.
    c. the representativeness heuristic.
    d. the availability heuristic.

17. A dessert recipe that gives you the ingredients, their amounts, and the steps to follow is an example of a(n):

    a. prototype.   c. heuristic.
    b. algorithm.   d. fixation.

18. Dr. Mendoza is studying the mental strategies people use when solving problems. Dr. Mendoza is clearly a(n):

    a. cognitive psychologist.
    b. experimental psychologist.
    c. organizational psychologist.
    d. developmental psychologist.

19. Boris the chess master selects his next move by considering moves that would threaten his opponent's queen. His opponent, a chess-playing computer, selects its next move by considering *all* possible moves. Boris is using a(n) _____ and the computer is using a(n) _____ .

    a. algorithm; heuristic
    b. prototype; algorithm
    c. heuristic; prototype
    d. heuristic; algorithm

20. During a televised political debate, the Republican and Democratic candidates each argued that the results of a recent public opinion poll supported their party's platform regarding sexual harassment. Because both candidates saw the information as supporting their belief, it is clear that both were victims of:

    a. functional fixedness.   c. belief perseverance.
    b. overconfidence.   d. confirmation bias.

21. Experts in a field prefer heuristics to algorithms because heuristics:

    a. guarantee solutions to problems.
    b. often save time.
    c. prevent fixation
    d. do all of these things.

22. Rudy is 6 feet 6 inches tall, weighs 210 pounds, and is very muscular. If you think that Rudy is more likely to be a basketball player than a computer programmer, you are a victim of:

    a. belief perseverance.
    b. the availability heuristic.
    c. functional fixedness.
    d. the representativeness heuristic.

23. Failing to see that an article of clothing can be inflated as a life preserver is an example of:
a. belief perseverance.
b. the availability heuristic.
c. the representativeness heuristic.
d. functional fixedness.

24. Airline reservations typically decline after a highly publicized airplane crash because people overestimate the incidence of such disasters. In such instances, their decisions are being influenced by:
a. belief bias.
b. the availability heuristic.
c. the representativeness heuristic.
d. functional fixedness.

25. Most people tend to:
a. accurately estimate the accuracy of their knowledge and judgments.
b. underestimate the accuracy of their knowledge and judgments.
c. overestimate the accuracy of their knowledge and judgments.
d. lack confidence in their decision-making strategies.

26. In relation to ground beef, consumers respond more positively to an ad describing it as "75 percent lean" than to one referring to its "25 percent fat" content. This is an example of:
a. the framing effect.   c. a prototype.
b. confirmation bias.   d. overconfidence.

Matching Items

Match each definition or description with the appropriate term.

Definitions or Descriptions

_____ **1.** the way an issue or question is posed
_____ **2.** presuming that something is likely if it comes readily to mind
_____ **3.** the tendency to overestimate the accuracy of one's judgments
_____ **4.** being unable to see a problem from a different angle
_____ **5.** haphazard problem solving by trying one solution after another
_____ **6.** the sudden realization of the solution to a problem

Terms

a. trial and error
b. availability heuristic
c. insight
d. framing
e. overconfidence
f. fixation

True–False Items

Indicate whether each statement is true or false by placing *T* or *F* in the blank next to the item.

_____ **1.** According to the confirmation bias, people often interpret ambiguous evidence as support for their beliefs.
_____ **2.** Most human problem solving involves the use of heuristics rather than reasoning that systematically considers every possible solution.
_____ **3.** When asked, most people underestimate the accuracy of their judgments.
_____ **4.** When shown evidence that contradicts our initial beliefs about an issue, we are most likely to change our opinion.
_____ **5.** More often than not, our thinking is without conscious awareness.

KEY TERMS

Using your own words, on a piece of paper write a brief definition or explanation of each of the following terms.

1. cognition
2. concept
3. prototype
4. algorithm
5. heuristic
6. insight
7. confirmation bias
8. fixation
9. functional fixedness
10. representativeness heuristic
11. availability heuristic
12. overconfidence
13. framing
14. belief perseverance

ANSWERS

Module Review

Introduction and *Concepts*

1. thinking; the mental activity associated with processing, knowing, remembering, and communicating
2. cognitive psychologists
3. concepts; hierarchies
4. prototype; male; females

Solving Problems

1. problem solving
2. trial and error
3. algorithms
4. heuristics
5. insight; right temporal lobe
6. confirmation bias
7. verifies; refute
8. fixation
9. functional fixedness

Making Decisions and Forming Judgments

1. representativeness heuristic

2. availability heuristic

Using these heuristics often prevents us from processing other relevant information; because we overlook this information, we make judgmental errors. Thus, in the text example, the representativeness heuristic leads people to overlook the fact that there are many more truck drivers than Ivy League classics professors and, as a result, to wrongly conclude that the poetry reader is more likely to be an Ivy League classics professor. Also as noted in the text, the availability heuristic leads us to incorrectly think that words beginning with *k* are more common than words having *k* as their third letter.

3. flying; driving; terrorism; accidents
   a. what our ancestral history has prepared us to fear.
   b. what we cannot control.
   c. what is immediate.
   b. what is most readily available in memory.
4. overconfidence
5. adaptive; more; easier
6. does
7. framing; may not
8. belief perseverance
9. consider the opposite
10. quickly; adaptive

Progress Test

Multiple-Choice Questions

1. c. is the answer.
2. b. is the answer.
   a. A prototype is the best example of a particular category, or concept.
   c. & d. Algorithms and heuristics are problem-solving strategies.
3. c. is the answer.
   a. There is no such thing as a "denoter."
   b. & d. Heuristics and algorithms are problem-solving strategies.
4. d. is the answer. It is a major obstacle to problem solving.
   a. & b. These refer to overconfidence and belief perseverance, respectively.
   c. This is trial-and-error problem solving.
5. c. is the answer. Both involve failing to see a problem from a new perspective.
   a. & b. Algorithms and heuristics are problem-solving strategies.
   d. Insight is the sudden realization of a problem's solution.

6. **b.** is the answer. Functional fixedness is the tendency to think of things only in terms of their usual functions.

   a. The representativeness heuristic is the tendency to judge the likelihood of things in terms of how well they conform to our prototypes.

   c. Framing refers to the way an issue is posed; this often influences our judgment.

   d. Belief perseverance is the tendency to cling to one's beliefs even after they have been refuted.

7. **d.** is the answer. Heuristics are simple thinking strategies—such as playing chess defensively—that are based on past successes in similar situations.

   a., b., & c. These are all algorithms.

8. **d.** is the answer. Sultan suddenly arrived at a novel solution to his problem, thus displaying apparent insight.

   a. Sultan did not randomly try various strategies of reaching the fruit; he demonstrated the "light bulb" reaction that is the hallmark of insight.

   b. Heuristics are simple thinking strategies.

   c. Functional fixedness is an impediment to problem solving. Sultan obviously solved his problem.

9. **c.** is the answer. Your conclusion is based on sex stereotypes, that is, athletic ability and participation are for you more *representative* of boys. Your conclusion is by no means necessarily right, however, especially since the Smiths have four daughters and only one son.

   a. The confirmation bias is the tendency to look for information that confirms one's preconceptions.

   b. The availability heuristic involves judging the probability of an event in terms of how readily it comes to mind.

   d. Belief perseverance is the tendency to cling to beliefs, even when the evidence has shown that they are wrong.

10. **a.** is the answer. Reasoning in daily life is often distorted by our beliefs, which may lead us, for example, to accept conclusions that haven't been arrived at logically.

    b., c., & d. These are just the opposite of what we tend to do.

11. **d.** is the answer. Both are simple thinking strategies that allow us to make quick judgments.

    a. Fixations are obstacles to problem solving, in which the person is unable to approach a problem in a new way.

    b. Framing refers to the way an issue is posed.

    c. Algorithms are methodical strategies that guarantee a solution to a particular problem.

12. **d.** is the answer. If we use the availability heuristic, we base judgments on the availability of information in our memories, and more vivid information is often the most readily available.

    a. This would exemplify use of the trial-and-error approach to problem solving.

    b. This would exemplify an algorithm.

    c. This would exemplify belief perseverance.

13. **b.** is the answer. Because they involve the systematic examination of all possible solutions to a problem, algorithms guarantee that a solution will be found.

    a., c., & d. None of these methods guarantees that a problem's solution will be found.

14. **a.** is the answer.

    b. & c. These may very well occur, but they do not define belief perseverance.

    d. This is the confirmation bias.

15. **b.** is the answer. A rose is a prototypical example of the concept *flower*.

    c. & d. Hierarchies are organized clusters of concepts. In this example, there is only the single concept *flower*.

16. **d.** is the answer. The availability heuristic is the judgmental strategy that estimates the likelihood of events in terms of how readily they come to mind, and the most vivid information is often the most readily available.

17. **b.** is the answer. Follow the directions precisely and you can't miss!

    a. A prototype is the best example of a concept.

    c. Heuristics are simple thinking strategies that help solve problems but, in contrast to a recipe that is followed precisely, do not guarantee success.

    d. A fixation is an inability to approach a problem in a new way.

18. **a.** is the answer. Cognitive psychologists study how we process, understand, and communicate knowledge. Problem solving involves processing information and is therefore a topic explored by cognitive psychologists.

    b. Cognitive psychologists often use experimentation to study phenomena but, because not all experimental psychologists study cognition, a. is the best answer.

    c. Organizational psychologists study behavior in the workplace.

    d. Developmental psychologists study the ways in which behavior changes over the life span.

19. **d.** is the answer.

    b. & c. Prototypes have nothing to do with chess playing.

20. **d.** is the answer. The confirmation bias is the tendency to search for information that confirms one's preconceptions. In this example, the politicians' preconceptions are biasing their interpretation of the survey results.
   a. Functional fixedness is the inability to perceive an unusual use for a familiar object.
   b. Overconfidence is the tendency to overestimate the accuracy of one's beliefs and judgments.
   c. Belief perseverance is the tendency to cling to one's beliefs despite evidence to the contrary.

21. **b.** is the answer.
   a. & c. Heuristics do not guarantee solutions or prevent fixation.

22. **d.** is the answer. Your conclusion is based on the stereotype that muscular build is more *representative* of athletes than computer programmers.
   a. Belief perseverance is the tendency to cling to one's beliefs even after they have been refuted.
   b. The availability heuristic involves judging the probability of an event in terms of how readily it comes to mind.
   c. Functional fixedness is the tendency to think of things only in terms of their usual functions.

23. **d.** is the answer.

24. **b.** is the answer. The publicity surrounding disasters makes such events vivid and seemingly more probable than they actually are.
   a. Belief perseverance is the tendency to cling to one's beliefs even after they have been refuted.
   c. The representativeness heuristic operates when we judge the likelihood of things in terms of how well they represent particular prototypes. This example does not involve such a situation.
   d. Functional fixedness operates in situations in which effective problem solving requires using an object in an unfamiliar manner.

25. **c.** is the answer. This is referred to as overconfidence.

26. **a.** is the answer. In this example, the way the issue is posed, or framed, has evidently influenced consumers' judgments.
   b. Confirmation bias is the tendency to search for information that confirms one's preconceptions.
   c. A prototype is a best example of a concept.
   d. Overconfidence is the tendency to be more confident than correct.

Matching Items

1.	d	**4.**	f
2.	b	**5.**	a
3.	e	**6.**	c

True–False Items

1.	T	**4.**	F
2.	T	**5.**	T
3.	F		

Key Terms

1. **Cognition** refers to the mental activity associated with thinking, knowing, remembering, and communicating information.

2. A **concept** is a mental grouping of similar objects, events, or people.

3. A **prototype** is a mental image or best example of a category.

4. An **algorithm** is a methodical, logical procedure that, while sometimes slow, guarantees success.

5. A **heuristic** is a simple thinking strategy that often allows us to make judgments and solve problems efficiently. Although they are more efficient than algorithms, heuristics do not guarantee success and sometimes impede problem solving.

6. **Insight** is a sudden and often novel realization of the solution to a problem.

7. The **confirmation bias** is an obstacle to problem solving in which people tend to search for information that validates their preconceptions.

8. **Fixation** is an inability to approach a problem in a new way.

9. **Functional fixedness** is a type of fixation in which a person can think of things only in terms of their usual functions.

10. The **representativeness heuristic** is the tendency to judge the likelihood of things in terms of how well they conform to one's prototypes.

11. The **availability heuristic** is based on estimating the probability of certain events in terms of how readily they come to mind.

12. Another obstacle to problem solving, **overconfidence** refers to the tendency to overestimate the accuracy of one's beliefs and judgments.

13. **Framing** refers to the way an issue or question is posed. It can affect people's perception of the issue or answer to the question.

14. **Belief perseverance** is the tendency for people to cling to a particular belief even after the information that led to the formation of the belief is discredited.

FOCUS ON VOCABULARY AND LANGUAGE

... our species is *kin to* ... Myers notes that we are biological creatures related to (*kin to*) other species of animals. We have exceptional abilities for innovation, learning, memory, and rational thinking; yet, at the same time we are prone to making mistakes and thinking and acting irrationally.

Concepts

For most of us, the robin is the *birdier bird* ... We develop our ideas of how things go together (*concepts*) from definitions or by using **prototypes**. The best example (*prototype*) of a bird is a robin (*the birdier bird*) rather than a penguin, a kiwi, or an ostrich.

Solving Problems

Thomas Edison tried thousands of light bulb filaments before *stumbling upon one that worked*. Edison was a famous inventor and he used a trial-and-error method in developing the metal filament that makes the light bulb glow brightly. Using trial and error, he came upon the solution by chance (*stumbled upon one that worked*). Myers contrasts this method with following an **algorithm** (a step-by-step method that always ends with the answer and is typical of computer programs).

Making Decisions and Forming Judgments

Should I *shoot* the basketball or pass to the player who's *hot*?—we seldom take the time and effort to reason systematically. (Don't take this sentence literally.) For example, in a game of basketball, the player holding the ball has to decide to throw it through the hoop (*shoot the basketball*) or pass it to a player who has scored frequently (*who's hot*). We usually follow our subjective feelings (*intuitions*) rather than taking the time to use logic and reason.

... they do it [make decisions] by *the seat of their pants*. When we make decisions based on subjective or intuitive reasons, rather than using logical, reflective problem-solving strategies, we are using *seat-of-the-pants* judgments. Thus, when we employ **heuristics** (simple thinking strategies), we may make decisions that are incorrect and not very smart (*dumb decisions*).

The **representativeness heuristic** enabled you to make a *snap* judgment. We can make quick (*snap*) judgments using a strategy that allows us to determine the probability of things by how well they appear to be typical of some prototype (*representativeness heuristic*). For example, is person A, who is intelligent, unimaginative, compulsive, and general-ly lifeless, more likely to (a) play jazz for a hobby or (b) play jazz for a hobby and work as an accountant? The representativeness heuristic leads most people to incorrectly pick (b) as the answer.

The faster people can remember an instance of some event (*"a broken promise"*), the more they expect it to recur. We tend to use whatever information is accessible in our memories when making decisions and judgments; similarly, events or mistakes that are easiest to access (i.e., those that most readily come to mind) will most likely be used. This is called the **availability heuristic.** So, if on one occasion, someone did not keep his or her word (*broke a promise*) about doing something, we tend to remember that event and use it in predicting future behavior. Sometimes the availability heuristic can cause errors in judgment.

Overconfidence *plagues* decisions outside the laboratory, too. Many factors combine to produce the tendency to overestimate the accuracy of our decisions, judgments, and knowledge (**overconfidence**). In everyday life, as well as in lab experiments, our judgments are greatly afflicted (*plagued*) by overconfidence.

(Box): Human emotions were *road tested in the Stone Age.* During our evolutionary past, certain traits or characteristics were selected for because they helped our ancestors survive, and those that survived because of these attributes passed them on to their descendants. Fearful reactions to snakes, lizards, spiders, confinement, and heights were selected for (*they were road tested*) during earlier times (*in the Stone Age*) and are part of human nature today.

That our judgments *flip-flop* dramatically is startling. Presenting the same information in two different ways can cause people to react more negatively or positively depending on how the (logically equivalent) information was **framed**. The framing effect can cause alarming and dramatic reversals (*flip-flops*) in people's decisions and judgments. For example, a very fatty food product made by grinding meat (*ground beef*) will be seen more positively if described as "75% lean" as opposed to "25% fat," despite the fact that exactly the same information is conveyed in each case.

Belief perseverance often *fuels social conflict.* ... Our irrationality also shows when we persist (*persevere*) in our views despite evidence to the contrary (**belief perseverance**). This can lead to an increase in strong feelings or passions over controversial issues (*fuels social conflict*). Myers suggests one solution for those who wish to restrain (*rein in*) the effect of belief perseverance, and that is to give serious consideration to beliefs *opposite* to your own.

From this we might conclude that our heads are indeed *filled with straw.* The discussion about human irrationality might lead to the conclusion that we have ineffective and inefficient cognitions (*heads filled with straw*). Myers, however, is optimistic and suggests that we can learn about our irrational propensities (tendencies) and be alert to the dangers that can result in poor or foolish (*dumb*) decisions.

More than we realize, *thinking occurs off-screen,* with the results occasionally *displayed on-screen.* Humans process a great deal of information without any conscious awareness of doing so. This is similar to a computer's hidden processing, which is not displayed on the monitor (*it occurs off-screen*). Once in a while the results of our unconscious processing enter consciousness (the results are occasionally *displayed on-screen*).

Language and Thought

$$24$$

M O D U L E

MODULE OVERVIEW

Module 24 is concerned with language, including its structure, development in children, relationship to thinking, and use by animals. Two theories of language acquisition are evaluated: Skinner's theory that language acquisition is based entirely on learning and Chomsky's theory that humans have a biological predisposition to acquire language.

NOTE: Answer guidelines for all Module 24 questions begin on page 265.

MODULE REVIEW

First, skim each section, noting headings and boldface items. After you have read the section, review each objective by answering the fill-in and essay-type questions that follow it. As you proceed, evaluate your performance by consulting the answers beginning on page 265. Do not continue with the next section until you understand each answer. If you need to, review or reread the section in the textbook before continuing.

> David Myers at times uses idioms that are unfamiliar to some readers. If you do not know the meaning of any of the following words, phrases, or expressions in the context in which they appear in the text, refer to pages 267–268 for an explanation: *catapulting our species forward; combine them on the fly; read lips; switches need to be turned "on" or "off"; chicken-and-egg questions; rhapsodized; Spying the short stick; Were the chimps language champs or were the researchers chumps?*

Language Development (pp. 319–323)

Objective 1: Trace the course of language acquisition from the babbling stage through the two-word stage.

1. The system of rules we use to combine words into grammatically sensible sentences is called
   _____ .

2. By _____ months of age, babies can read lips and discriminate speech sounds. This marks the beginning of their _____ _____ , their ability to comprehend speech. This ability begins to mature before their _____ _____ , or ability to produce words.

3. The first stage of language development, in which children spontaneously utter different sounds, is the _____ stage. This stage typically begins at about _____ months of age. The sounds children make during this stage _____ (do/do not) include only the sounds of the language they hear.

4. Deaf infants _____ (do/do not) babble. Many natural babbling sounds are _____-_____ pairs formed by _____ _____ .

5. By about _____ months of age, infant babbling begins to resemble the household language. At about the same time, the ability to perceive speech sounds outside their native language is _____ (lost/acquired).

261

6. During the second stage, called the
_____-_____ stage,
children convey complete thoughts using single
words. This stage begins at about
_____ year(s) of age.

7. During the _____-_____
stage, children speak in sentences containing
mostly nouns and verbs. This type of speech is
called _____ speech.

8. After this stage, children quickly begin to utter
longer phrases that _____ (do/do
not) follow the rules of syntax.

Objective 2: Discuss Skinner's and Chomsky's contributions to the nature-nurture debate over how children acquire language, and explain why critical periods is an important concept in children's language
learning.

9. Skinner believed that language development follows the general principles of learning, including
_____ , _____ , and
_____ .

10. Other theorists believe that humans are biologically predisposed to learn language. One such
theorist is _____ , who believes that
we all are born with a _____
_____ _____ in
which _____ switches are thrown
as children experience their language. This theorist contends that all human languages have the
same grammatical building blocks, which suggests that there is a _____
_____ .

11. Research studies of infants' knack for soaking up
language suggest that babies come with a built-in
readiness to learn _____
_____ .

12. Childhood seems to represent a _____
_____ for mastering certain aspects
of language. Those who learn a second language
as adults usually speak it with the
_____ of their first language.
Moreover, they typically show
_____ (poorer/better)

mastery of the _____ of the second
language.

13. The window for learning language gradually
begins to close after age _____ .
When a young brain doesn't learn any language,
its language-learning capacity _____
(never/may still) fully develop(s).

Thinking and Language (pp. 323–326)

Objective 3: Discuss Whorf's linguistic determinism
hypothesis in relation to current views regarding
thinking and languages, and describe the value of
thinking in images.

1. According to the _____
_____ hypothesis, language shapes
our thinking. The linguist who proposed this
hypothesis is _____ .

2. Many people who are bilingual report feeling a
different sense of _____ , depend-
ing on which language they are using.

3. In several studies, researchers have found that
using the pronoun "he" (instead of "he or she")
_____ (does/does not) influence
people's thoughts concerning gender.

4. Bilingual children, who learn to inhibit one language while using their other language, are better
able to inhibit their _____ to irrelevant information. This has been called the
_____ _____ .

5. One study of Canadian children found that
English-speaking children who were
_____ in French had higher
_____ scores and math scores than
control children.

6. It appears that thinking _____
(can/cannot) occur without the use of language.
Thinking in terms of mental pictures is called
_____ _____ .
Athletes often supplement physical with
_____ practice.

7. In one study of psychology students preparing
for a midterm exam, the greatest benefits were
achieved by those who visualized themselves
_____ (receiving a high
grade/studying effectively).

Summarize the probable relationship between thinking and language.

Animal Thinking and Language (pp. 326–329)

Objective 4: List four cognitive skills shared by the great apes and humans, and outline the arguments for and against the idea that animals and humans share the capacity for language.

1. Animals are capable of forming
   _____ . Wolfgang Köhler demonstrated that chimpanzees also exhibit the "Aha!" reaction that characterizes reasoning by

   _____ .

2. Forest-dwelling chimpanzees learn to use branches, stones, and other objects as _____ . These behaviors, along with behaviors related to grooming and courtship, _____ (vary/ do not vary) from one group to another, suggesting the transmission of _____ customs.

3. Animals definitely _____ . For example, honeybees do so by means of a

   _____ .

4. The Gardners attempted to communicate with the chimpanzee Washoe by teaching her

   _____ _____ .

5. Skeptics believe that some chimpanzee trainers may be overgenerous in interpreting ambiguous animal signing thanks to the formation of

   _____ _____ .

6. Most now agree that humans _____ (alone/along with primates) possess language that involves complex grammar.

7. The philosopher _____ believed that animals were living robots that could not think.

Summarize some of the arguments of skeptics of the "talking apes" research and some responses of believers.

PROGRESS TEST

Multiple-Choice Questions

Circle your answers to the following questions and check them with the answers on page 266. If your answer is incorrect, read the explanation for why it is incorrect and then consult the appropriate pages of the text.

1. Which of the following is *not* true of babbling?
   a. It is imitation of adult speech.
   b. It is the same in all cultures.
   c. It typically occurs from about age 4 months to 1 year.
   d. Babbling increasingly comes to resemble a particular language.

2. Which of the following has been argued by critics of ape language research?
   a. Ape language is merely imitation of the trainer's behavior.
   b. There is little evidence that apes can equal even a 3-year-old's ability to order words with proper syntax.
   c. By seeing what they wish to see, trainers attribute greater linguistic ability to apes than actually exists.
   d. All of these have been argued.

3. Whorf's linguistic determinism hypothesis states that:
   a. language is primarily a learned ability.
   b. language is partially an innate ability.
   c. the size of a person's vocabulary reflects his or her intelligence.
   d. our language shapes our thinking.

4. Which of the following *best* describes Chomsky's view of language development?
   a. Language is an entirely learned ability.
   b. Language is an innate ability.
   c. Humans have a biological predisposition to acquire language.
   d. There are no cultural influences on the development of language.

5. Researchers who are convinced that animals can think point to evidence that:
   a. monkeys can learn to classify dogs and cats.
   b. chimpanzees regularly use branches, stones, and other objects as tools in their natural habitats.
   c. chimps invent grooming and courtship customs and pass them on to their peers.
   d. animals can do all of these things.

6. Deaf children who are *not* exposed to sign language until they are teenagers:
   a. are unable to master the basic words of sign language.
   b. learn the basic words but not how to order them.
   c. are unable to master either the basic words or syntax of sign language.
   d. never become as fluent as those who learned to sign at a younger age.

7. Several studies have indicated that the generic pronoun "he":
   a. tends for children and adults alike to trigger images of both males and females.
   b. tends for adults to trigger images of both males and females, but for children to trigger images of males.
   c. tends for both children and adults to trigger images of males but not females.
   d. for both children and adults triggers images of females about one-fourth of the time it is used.

8. Skinner and other behaviorists have argued that language development is the result of:
   a. imitation.   c. association.
   b. reinforcement.   d. all of these factors.

9. Many psychologists are skeptical of claims that chimpanzees can acquire language because the chimps have not shown the ability to:
   a. use symbols meaningfully.
   b. acquire speech.
   c. acquire even a limited vocabulary.
   d. use syntax in communicating.

10. Telegraphic speech is typical of the _____ stage.
    a. babbling   c. two-word
    b. one-word   d. three-word

11. Children first demonstrate a rudimentary understanding of syntax during the _____ stage.
    a. babbling   c. two-word
    b. one-word   d. three-word

12. The study in which people who immigrated to the United States at various ages were compared in terms of their ability to understand English grammar found that:
    a. age of arrival had no effect on mastery of grammar.
    b. those who immigrated as children understood grammar as well as native speakers.

c. those who immigrated as adults understood grammar as well as native speakers.
d. whether or not English was spoken in the home was the most important factor in mastering the rules of grammar.

13. Researchers taught the chimpanzee Washoe and the gorilla Koko to communicate by using:
    a. various sounds.
    b. plastic symbols of various shapes and colors.
    c. sign language.
    d. all of these things.

14. Regarding the relationship between thinking and language, which of the following most accurately reflects the position taken in the text?
    a. Language determines everything about our thinking.
    b. Language determines the way we think.
    c. Thinking without language is not possible.
    d. Thinking affects our language, which then affects our thought.

15. Which of the following is true regarding the relationship between thinking and language?
    a. "Real" thinking requires the use of language.
    b. People sometimes think in images rather than in words.
    c. A thought that cannot be expressed in a particular language cannot occur to speakers of that language.
    d. All of these statements are true.

16. A listener hearing a recording of Japanese, Spanish, and North American children babbling would:
    a. not be able to tell them apart.
    b. be able to tell them apart if they were older than 6 months.
    c. be able to tell them apart if they were older than 8 to 10 months.
    d. be able to tell them apart at any age.

17. The child who says "Milk gone" is engaging in _____ . This type of utterance demonstrates that children are actively experimenting with the rules of _____ .
    a. babbling; syntax
    b. telegraphic speech; syntax
    c. babbling; association
    d. telegraphic speech; association

True–False Items

Indicate whether each statement is true or false by placing *T* or *F* in the blank next to the item.

_____ 1. Studies have shown that even animals may sometimes have insight reactions.

_____ 2. Children of all cultures babble using the same speech sounds.

_____ 3. Thinking without using language is not possible.

_____ 4. Language determines the way we think.

_____ 5. If we define language as the ability to communicate through a meaningful sequence of symbols, then apes are not capable of language.

Essay Question

The lectures of your linguistics professor, who happens to be a staunch behaviorist, clearly imply that she believes language development can be explained according to principles of conditioning. What evidence should you present to convince her that she is wrong? (Use the space below to list the points you want to make, and organize them. Then write the essay on a separate piece of paper.)

KEY TERMS

Using your own words, on a piece of paper write a brief definition or explanation of each of the following terms.

1. language

2. babbling stage

3. one-word stage

4. two-word stage

5. telegraphic speech

6. linguistic determinism

ANSWERS
Module Review
Language Development

1. syntax

2. 4; receptive language; productive language

3. babbling; 4; do not

4. do; consonant-vowel; bunching the tongue in front of the mouth

5. 10; lost

6. one-word; 1

7. two-word; telegraphic

8. do

9. association; imitation; reinforcement

10. Noam Chomsky; language acquisition device; grammar; universal grammar

11. grammatical rules

12. critical period; accent; poorer; grammar

13. 7; never

Thinking and Language

1. linguistic determinism; Benjamin Whorf

2. self

3. does

4. attention; bilingual advantage

5. immersed; aptitude

6. can; procedural memory; mental

7. studying effectively

The relationship is probably a two-way one: the linguistic determinism hypothesis suggests that language helps shape thought; that words come into the language to express new ideas indicates that thought also shapes language.

Animal Thinking and Language

1. concepts; insight

2. tools; vary; cultural

3. communicate; dance

4. sign language

5. perceptual set

6. alone

7. Descartes

Chimps have acquired only limited vocabularies and—in contrast to children—have acquired these vocabularies only with great difficulty. Also in contrast to children, it's unclear that chimps can use syntax to express meaning. The signing of chimps is often nothing more than imitation of the trainer's actions. People tend to interpret such ambiguous behavior in terms of what they want to see. Believers contend that although animals do not have our facility for language, they have the abilities to communicate. For example, Washoe signs spontaneously. Also, pygmy chimps can learn to comprehend the spoken nuances of spoken English.

Progress Test

Multiple-Choice Questions

1. **a.** is the answer. Babbling is not the imitation of adult speech since babbling infants produce sounds from languages they have not heard and could not be imitating.

2. **d.** is the answer.

3. **d.** is the answer.
   a. This is Skinner's position regarding language development.
   b. This is Chomsky's position regarding language development.
   c. The linguistic determinism hypothesis is concerned with the content of thought, not intelligence.

4. **c.** is the answer.
   a. This is Skinner's position.
   b. According to Chomsky, although the *ability* to acquire language is innate, the child can only acquire language in association with others.
   d. Cultural influences are an important example of the influence of learning on language development, an influence Chomsky fully accepts.

5. **d.** is the answer.

6. **d.** is the answer. Compared with deaf children exposed to sign language from birth, those who learn to sign as teens have the same grammatical difficulties as do hearing adults trying to learn a second spoken language.

7. **c.** is the answer. The generic pronoun *he* evidently tends, for both adults and children, to conjure up images of males.

8. **d.** is the answer. These are all basic principles of learning and, according to Skinner, explain language development.

9. **d.** is the answer. Syntax is one of the fundamental aspects of language, and chimps seem unable, for example, to use word order to convey differences in meaning.
   a. & c. Chimps' use of sign language demonstrates both the use of symbols and the acquisition of fairly sizable vocabularies.

b. No psychologist would require the use of speech as evidence of language; significantly, all the research and arguments focus on what chimps are and are not able to do in acquiring other facets of language.

10. **c.** is the answer.

11. **c.** is the answer. Although the child's utterances are only two words long, the words are placed in a sensible order. In English, for example, adjectives are placed before nouns.
    a. & b. Syntax specifies rules for *combining* two or more units in speech.
    d. There is no three-word stage.

12. **b.** is the answer.

13. **c.** is the answer.

14. **d.** is the answer.

15. **b.** is the answer.
    a. Researchers do not make a distinction between "real" and other thinking, nor do they consider nonlinguistic thinking less valid than linguistic thinking.
    c. As suggested in the text, this is not true.

16. **a.** is the answer.

17. **b.** is the answer. Such utterances, characteristic of a child of about 2 years, are like telegrams, in that they consist mainly of nouns and verbs and show use of syntax.
    a. & c. Babbling consists of sounds, not words.
    d. Association is one of the ways in which children learn language, according to behaviorists.

True–False Items

1. T	**4.** F
2. T	**5.** F
3. F	

Essay Question

You should point out that the rate at which children acquire words and grammar is too extraordinary to be explained solely according to principles of learning. Children also utter all sorts of word forms they have never heard and could not, therefore, be imitating. Furthermore, children begin using words in a predictable order, which learning theorists would not expect since each child experiences a unique linguistic environment. It therefore seems clear that children are biologically prepared to acquire language and that the behaviorist position is incorrect.

Key Terms

1. **Language** refers to spoken, written, or signed words and how we combine them to communicate meaning.

2. The **babbling stage** of speech development, which begins around 4 months, is characterized by the spontaneous utterance of speech sounds. During the babbling stage, children the world over sound alike.

3. Between 1 and 2 years of age children speak mostly in single words; they are therefore in the **one-word stage** of linguistic development.

4. Beginning about age 2, children are in the **two-word stage** and speak mostly in two-word sentences.

5. **Telegraphic speech** is the economical, telegram-like speech of children in the two-word stage. Utterances consist mostly of nouns and verbs; however, words occur in the correct order, showing that the child has learned some of the language's syntactic rules.

6. **Linguistic determinism** is Benjamin Whorf's hypothesis that language determines the way we think.

FOCUS ON VOCABULARY AND LANGUAGE

Language Development

When the human vocal tract evolved the ability to utter vowels, *our capacity for language exploded, catapulting our species forward* (Diamond, 1989). When the physiological ability for complex vocalization evolved, the ability to communicate orally expanded exponentially (*exploded*). This new linguistic capacity propelled (*catapulted*) our species to new levels of accomplishments, enabling us to communicate from person to person and to transmit civilization's accumulated knowledge from generation to generation.

With remarkably efficiency, we selectively sample tens of thousands of words in memory, effortlessly *combine them on the fly* with near-perfect syntax, and *spew them out three words a second* (Vigliocco & Hartsuiker, 2002). Humans have an amazing facility for language. With little or no effort, we can select the appropriate words from the tens of thousands in memory, put them together hurriedly (*combine them on the fly*), and verbally produce them in rapid succession (*spew them out three words a second*).

Yet by 4 months of age, babies can *read lips* and *discriminate* speech sounds. When people speak, their lips move in ways that correspond to the sounds they utter. Many deaf people can understand what is being said by watching how the lips move (*lip reading*). Very young children can not only tell the difference (*discriminate*) between sounds, but can also recognize lip movements that correspond with certain sounds (*read lips*).

It is as if the *switches need to be turned "on" or "off"* for us to understand and produce language. Myers likens learning a particular grammar during early childhood to turning on switches that influence language acquisition. When the switches have been turned on for one grammar, it becomes much harder to master a second grammar. During the early years of language development, we easily and accurately acquire (*master*) grammar and accent; after that critical period, the language acquisition system tends to work less hard, and mastering another grammar becomes more difficult (*the window for learning language gradually closes*).

Thinking and Language

Thinking and language intricately intertwine. Asking which comes first is one of psychology's *chicken-and-egg* questions. "Which came first: the chicken or the egg?" Clearly, you need an egg to produce a chicken, but you also need a chicken to lay the egg. So, like this age-old conundrum (*riddle*), psychologists have argued over which comes first, our ideas and thoughts or the words we use to name and verbalize them. Myers concludes that language influences (but does not determine) thought, and our thinking affects our language, which in turn affects thought.

If in our use of language we humans are, as the psalmist long ago *rhapsodized*, "little lower than God," where do other animals fit in the scheme of things? The psalmist (an author of religious or sacred songs) spoke in an extravagantly enthusiastic manner (*rhapsodized*) about human nature, and Myers notes that it is our use of human language that elevates us above nonhumans. Nevertheless, we do share a capacity for language with other animals.

Spying the short stick, Sultan (the chimp) grabbed it and tried to reach the fruit. Kohler's experiment with the chimpanzee Sultan showed that our closest relatives are capable of cognition. When the fruit was out of reach, Sultan noticed (*spied*) the short stick and used it to pull a longer stick into the cage, which he then used to get the fruit.

Were the chimps *language champs* or were the researchers *chumps*? Critics of "ape language" argue that for animals, language acquisition is painfully slow, resembles conditioned responses, does not follow syntax, and is little more than imitation. In addition, demonstrations of animal language are always subjectively interpreted by their trainers. Myers asks: Were the chimps exceptionally talented (*language champs*) or were the researchers just easily fooled or duped (*were they chumps*) and were they acting foolishly (*making monkeys out of themselves*)? The answer is that the controversy has led to further research and progress, and a renewed appreciation of our own, as well as our closest relatives', capacity for communication and language.

Intelligence

25 MODULE

MODULE OVERVIEW

Module 25 first discusses whether intelligence is a single general ability or several specific ones as well as research that attempts to assess the neurological basis of intelligence. It also describes the historical origins of intelligence tests and discusses several important issues concerning their use. These include the methods by which intelligence tests are constructed and whether such tests are valid, reliable, and free of bias. The module also explores the stability of intelligence and the extent of genetic and environmental influences on intelligence.

NOTE: Answer guidelines for all Module 25 questions begin on page 279.

MODULE REVIEW

First, skim each section, noting headings and boldface items. After you have read the section, review each objective by answering the fill-in and essay-type questions that follow it. As you proceed, evaluate your performance by consulting the answers beginning on page 279. Do not continue with the next section until you understand each answer. If you need to, review or reread the section in the textbook before continuing.

> David Myers at times uses idioms that are unfamiliar to some readers. If you do not know the meaning of any of the following words, phrases, or expressions in the context in which they appear in the text, refer to pages 284–285 for an explanation: *dumbfounded; island of brilliance; street-smart adolescent; reading people; add spice to life; out of the blue; on the shoulders of others; "dull" child; a bell-shaped pattern; tape measure; bludgeoning native intelligence; more newsworthy; sharpest at the extremes.*

Introduction and **What Is Intelligence?**
(pp. 331–336)

Objective 1: Discuss the difficulty of defining *intelligence*, and present arguments as to whether intelligence should be considered one general ability or many specific abilities.

1. Intelligence is a _____ constructed concept.

2. Whatever attributes enable success is defined by a _____ as intelligence.

3. In any context, intelligence can be defined as

   _____

   _____ .

4. One controversy regarding the nature of intelligence centers on whether intelligence is one _____ ability or several _____ abilities.

5. The statistical procedure used to identify groups of items that appear to measure a common ability is called _____

   _____ .

6. Charles Spearman, one of the developers of this technique, believed that a factor called g, or

   _____ _____ , runs

   through the more specific aspects of intelligence.

7. People with _____ _____ score at the low end of intelligence tests but possess extraordinary specific skills. Many such people also have the developmental disorder

   _____ .

8. Howard Gardner proposes that there are

   _____ _____ , each

   independent of the others. However, critics point

269

out that the world is not so just: People with mental disadvantages often have lesser _____ abilities as well. General intelligence scores _____ (do/do not) predict performance on complex tasks and in various jobs.

9. Sternberg's _____ theory distinguishes three types of intelligence: _____ intelligence, _____ intelligence, and _____ intelligence.

Objective 2: Identify the factors associated with creativity, and explain what psychologists mean by emotional intelligence.

10. The ability to produce ideas that are both novel and valuable is called _____ . The relationship between intelligence and creativity holds only up to a certain point—an intelligence score of about _____ .

11. Standard intelligence tests, which demand single correct answers to questions, measure _____ thinking. Tests that allow multiple possible answers to problems measure _____ thinking. Injury to certain areas of the brain's _____ _____ can destroy imagination.

Describe five components of creativity other than intelligence.

12. Cantor and Kihlstrom distinguish between _____ intelligence and _____ intelligence.

13. A critical part of social intelligence is _____ _____—the ability to _____ , _____ , _____ , and _____ emotions.

14. A test that measures overall emotional intelligence also measures its components: the ability to _____ emotions in faces, the ability to _____ them and how they change and blend, the ability to _____ them correctly in varied situations, and the ability to use them to enable _____ or creative thinking.

Briefly describe emotionally intelligent people.

15. Across 69 studies in many countries, those scoring high in emotional intelligence also exhibit job performance that is _____ (greatly/modestly) better than that of people without emotional intelligence.

16. Some scholars believe that the concept of _____ intelligence stretches the idea of multiple intelligences too far.

Assessing Intelligence (pp. 336–340)

Objective 3: Discuss the history of intelligence testing, and describe modern tests of mental abilities such as the WAIS.

1. Tests that assess a person's mental capacities and compare them to those of others, using numerical scores, are called _____ tests.

2. The French psychologist who devised a test to predict the success of children in school was _____ . Predictions were made by comparing children's chronological ages with their _____ ages, which were determined by the test. This test _____ (was/was not) designed to measure inborn intelligence.

3. Lewis Terman's revision of Binet's test is referred to as the _____-_____ . This test enables one to derive a(n) _____ _____ for an individual.

Give the original formula for computing IQ, and explain any items used in the formula.

4. Today's tests _____ (do/do not) compute an IQ score. They represent the test-taker's performance relative to the average performance of people of _____ (the same/different) age(s). These tests are designed so that a score of _____ is considered average.

5. The most widely used intelligence test is the _____ _____ _____ _____ . Consisting of 11 subtests, it provides not only a general intelligence score but also separate scores for _____ _____ , _____ _____ , _____ _____ , and _____ _____ .

Objective 4: Discuss the criteria for judging intelligence tests, including standardization, reliability, and validity.

6. Tests designed to predict your ability to learn something new are called _____ tests. Tests designed to measure what you have already learned are called _____ tests.

7. One requirement of a good test is the process of defining meaningful scores relative to a pretested comparison group, which is called _____ .

8. When scores on a test are compiled, they generally result in a bell-shaped pattern, or _____ distribution.

Describe the normal curve, and explain its significance in the standardization process.

9. If a test yields consistent results, it is said to be _____ .

10. When a test is administered more than once to the same people, the psychologist is determining its _____-_____ reliability.

11. When a person's scores for the odd- and even-numbered questions on a test are compared, _____-_____ reliability is being assessed.

12. The Stanford-Binet, WAIS, and WISC have reliabilities of about _____ .

13. The degree to which a test measures or predicts what it is supposed to is referred to as the test's _____ .

14. The degree to which a test measures the behavior it was designed to measure is referred to as the test's _____ _____ .

15. The degree to which a test predicts future performance of a particular behavior is referred to as the test's _____ _____ .

16. Generally speaking, the predictive validity of general aptitude tests _____ (is/is not) as high as their reliability. The predictive validity of these tests _____ (increases/diminishes) as individuals move up the educational ladder.

Objective 5: Describe the two extremes of the normal distribution of intelligence.

17. (Close-Up) Individuals whose intelligence scores fall below 70 and who have difficulty adapting to life may be labeled _____ _____ . This label applies to approximately _____ percent of the population.

18. (Close-Up) Mental retardation sometimes has a physical basis, such as _____ _____ , a genetic disorder caused by an extra chromosome.

19. (Close-Up) The current view is that children with mild retardation should be integrated, or _____ , into regular classrooms.

20. (Close-Up) Intelligence test performance has _____ (improved/decreased) over the past decade. This phenomenon is called the _____ _____ .

21. (Close-Up) Although the actual cause of this effect is unknown, one explanation is that it is due to improved _____ . The recent performance gains on the WAIS are greatest among people at the lowest _____ levels.

Genetic and Environmental Influences on Intelligence (pp. 341–345)

Objective 6: Discuss the evidence for the genetic contribution to individual intelligence, and explain what psychologists mean by the heritability of intelligence.

1. The intelligence scores of identical twins reared together are _____ (more/no more) similar than those of fraternal twins. Brain scans also reveal that identical twins have similar volume to their brain's _____ , and those areas associated with _____ and _____ intelligence.

2. By inserting an extra gene that engineers a neural receptor involved in _____ into fertilized mouse eggs, researchers have created smarter mice.

3. The intelligence test scores of fraternal twins are _____ (more alike/no more alike) than the intelligence test scores of other siblings. This provides evidence of a(n) _____ (genetic/environmental) effect because fraternal twins, being the same _____ , are treated more alike.

4. Studies of adopted children and their adoptive and biological families demonstrate that with age, genetic influences on intelligence become _____ (more/less) apparent. Thus, children's intelligence scores are more like those of their _____ (biological/adoptive) parents than those of their _____ (biological/adoptive) parents.

5. The amount of variation in a trait within a group that is attributed to genetic factors is called its _____ . For intelligence, this has been estimated at _____ percent.

6. If we know a trait has perfect heritability, this knowledge _____ (does/does not) enable us to rule out environmental factors in explaining differences between groups.

Objective 7: Discuss the evidence for environmental influences on individual intelligence.

7. Studies indicate that neglected children _____ (do/do not) show signs of recovery in intelligence and behavior when placed in more nurturing environments. Although normal brain development can be retarded by _____ , _____ deprivation, and _____ _____ , there is no sure environment that will produce a "superbaby."

8. High-quality programs for disadvantaged children, such as the government-funded _____ _____ program, increase children's school readiness; that is, they increase their _____ _____ , creating better attitudes toward learning.

Group Differences in Intelligence Test Scores
(pp. 345–352)

Objective 8: Describe ethnic similarities and differences in intelligence test scores, and discuss some genetic and environmental factors that might explain them.

1. Research evidence suggests that group differences in intelligence may be entirely _____ (genetic/environmental).

Explain why heredity may contribute to individual differences in intelligence but not necessarily contribute to group differences.

2. Group differences in intelligence scores _____ (do/do not) provide an accurate basis for judging individuals. Individual differences within a race are _____ (greater than/less than) between-race differences. Furthermore, race _____ (is/is not) a neatly defined biological category.

3. Although Asian students on the average score _____ (higher/lower) than North American students on math tests, this difference may be due to the fact that _____ _____ .

4. On an infant intelligence measure (preference for looking at novel stimuli), black infants score _____ (lower than/higher than/as well as) white infants.

Objective 9: Describe gender differences in abilities.

5. Girls tend to outscore boys on _____ tests and are more _____ fluent.

6. Although girls have an edge in math _____ , boys score higher in math _____ _____ .

Boys tend to outscore girls on tests of _____ _____ .

7. Working from an _____ perspective, some theorists speculate that these gender differences in spatial manipulation helped our ancestors survive.

8. There is evidence that math reasoning and spatial abilities are influenced by _____ _____ during prenatal development.

9. According to many, boys' and girls' interests and abilities are shaped in large part by _____ _____ and divergent opportunities.

Objective 10: Discuss whether intelligence tests are biased, and describe the stereotype threat phenomenon.

10. In the sense that they detect differences caused by cultural experiences, intelligence tests probably _____ (are/are not) biased.

11. Most psychologists agree that, in terms of predictive validity, the major aptitude tests _____ (are/are not) racially biased.

12. When women and members of ethnic minorities are led to expect that they won't do well on a test, a _____ may result, and their scores may actually be lower.

PROGRESS TEST

Multiple-Choice Questions

Circle your answers to the following questions and check them with the answers beginning on page 280. If your answer is incorrect, read the explanation for why it is incorrect and then consult the appropriate pages of the text.

1. A 6-year-old child has a mental age of 9. The child's IQ is:
   - **a.** 96.
   - **b.** 100.
   - **c.** 125.
   - **d.** 150.

2. Which of the following is *not* true?
   a. In math grades, the average girl typically equals or surpasses the average boy.
   b. The gender gap in math and science scores is increasing.
   c. Women are better than men at detecting emotions.
   d. Males score higher than females on tests of spatial abilities.

3. Most psychologists believe that racial gaps in test scores:
   a. have been exaggerated when they are, in fact, insignificant.
   b. indicate that intelligence is in large measure inherited.
   c. are in large measure caused by environmental factors.
   d. are increasing.

4. Standardization refers to the process of:
   a. determining the accuracy with which a test measures what it is supposed to.
   b. defining meaningful scores relative to a representative pretested group.
   c. determining the consistency of test scores obtained by retesting people.
   d. measuring the success with which a test predicts the behavior it is designed to predict.

5. Down syndrome is normally caused by:
   a. an extra chromosome in the person's genetic makeup.
   b. a missing chromosome in the person's genetic makeup.
   c. malnutrition during the first few months of life.
   d. prenatal exposure to an addictive drug.

6. Which of the following is *not* a requirement of a good test?
   a. reliability   c. reification
   b. standardization   d. validity

7. First-time parents Geena and Brad want to give their baby's intellectual abilities a jump-start by providing a super enriched learning environment. Experts would suggest that the new parents should:
   a. pipe stimulating classical music into the baby's room.
   b. hang colorful mobiles and artwork over the baby's crib.

   c. take the child to one of the new "superbaby" preschools that specialize in infant enrichment.
   d. relax, since there is no surefire environmental recipe for giving a child a superior intellect.

8. Which of the following statements is true?
   a. The predictive validity of intelligence tests is not as high as their reliability.
   b. The reliability of intelligence tests is not as high as their predictive validity.
   c. Modern intelligence tests have extremely high predictive validity and reliability.
   d. The predictive validity and reliability of most intelligence tests are very low.

9. Which of the following best describes the relationship between creativity and intelligence?
   a. Creativity appears to depend on the ability to think imaginatively and has little if any relationship to intelligence.
   b. Creativity is best understood as a certain kind of intelligence.
   c. The more intelligent a person is, the greater his or her creativity.
   d. A certain level of intelligence is necessary but not sufficient for creativity.

10. The existence of _____ reinforces the generally accepted notion that intelligence is a multidimensional quality.
    a. adaptive skills   c. general intelligence
    b. mental retardation   d. savant syndrome

11. Current estimates are that _____ percent of the total variation among intelligence scores can be attributed to genetic factors.
    a. less than 10   c. about 50
    b. approximately 25   d. over 75

12. Reported racial gaps in average intelligence scores are most likely attributable to:
    a. the use of biased tests of intelligence.
    b. the use of unreliable tests of intelligence.
    c. genetic factors.
    d. environmental factors.

13. The bell-shaped distribution of intelligence scores in the general population is called a:
    a. *g* distribution.
    b. standardization curve.
    c. bimodal distribution.
    d. normal distribution.

14. Research on the effectiveness of Head Start suggests that enrichment programs:
    a. produce permanent gains in intelligence scores.
    b. improve school readiness and may provide a small boost to emotional intelligence.
    c. improve intelligence scores but not school readiness.
    d. produce temporary gains in intelligence scores.

15. The test created by Alfred Binet was designed specifically to:
    a. measure inborn intelligence in adults.
    b. measure inborn intelligence in children.
    c. predict school performance in children.
    d. identify mentally retarded children so that they could be institutionalized.

16. Which of the following provides the strongest evidence of environment's role in intelligence?
    a. Adopted children's intelligence scores are more like their adoptive parents' scores than their biological parents'.
    b. Children's intelligence scores are more strongly related to their mothers' scores than to their fathers'.
    c. Children moved from a deprived environment into an intellectually enriched one show gains in intellectual development.
    d. The intelligence scores of identical twins raised separately are no more alike than those of siblings.

17. If a test designed to indicate which applicants are likely to perform the best on the job fails to do so, the test has:
    a. low reliability.
    b. low content validity.
    c. low predictive validity.
    d. not been standardized.

18. The formula for the intelligence quotient was devised by:
    a. Sternberg.   c. Terman.
    b. Binet.   d. Stern.

19. Current intelligence tests compute an individual's intelligence score as:
    a. the ratio of mental age to chronological age multiplied by 100.
    b. the ratio of chronological age to mental age multiplied by 100.
    c. the amount by which the test-taker's performance deviates from the average performance of others the same age.

    d. the ratio of the test-taker's verbal intelligence score to his or her nonverbal intelligence score.

20. J. McVicker Hunt found that institutionalized children given "tutored human enrichment":
    a. showed no change in intelligence test performance compared with institutionalized children who did not receive such enrichment.
    b. responded so negatively as a result of their impoverished early experiences that he felt it necessary to disband the program.
    c. thrived intellectually and socially on the benefits of positive caregiving.
    d. actually developed greater intelligence than control subjects who had lived in foster homes since birth.

21. The concept of a *g* factor implies that intelligence:
    a. is a single overall ability.
    b. is several specific abilities.
    c. cannot be defined or measured.
    d. is both a. and c.

22. Gerardeen has superb social skills, manages conflicts well, and has great empathy for her friends and co-workers. Peter Salovey and John Mayer would probably say that Gerardeen possesses a high degree of:
    a. *g*.
    b. social intelligence.
    c. practical intelligence.
    d. emotional intelligence.

23. The Flynn effect refers to the fact that:
    a. white and black infants score equally well on measures of infant intelligence.
    b. Asian students outperform North American students on math achievement tests.
    c. The IQ scores of today's better-fed and educated population exceed that of the 1930s population.
    d. Individual differences within a race are much greater than between-race differences.

24. Most experts view intelligence as a person's:
    a. ability to perform well on intelligence tests.
    b. innate mental capacity.
    c. ability to learn from experience, solve problems, and adapt to new situations.
    d. diverse skills acquired throughout life.

25. Which of the following statements is true?
    a. About 1 percent of the population is mentally retarded.
    b. More males than females are mentally retarded.
    c. A majority of the mentally retarded can learn academic skills.
    d. All of these statements are true.

26. Originally, IQ was defined as:
    a. mental age divided by chronological age and multiplied by 100.
    b. chronological age divided by mental age and multiplied by 100.
    c. mental age subtracted from chronological age and multiplied by 100.
    d. chronological age subtracted from mental age and multiplied by 100.

27. Which of the following statements most accurately reflects the text's position regarding the relative contribution of genes and environment in determining intelligence?
    a. Except in cases of a neglectful early environment, each individual's basic intelligence is largely the product of heredity.
    b. With the exception of those with genetic disorders such as Down syndrome, intelligence is primarily the product of environmental experiences.
    c. Both genes and life experiences significantly influence performance on intelligence tests.
    d. Because intelligence tests have such low predictive validity, the question cannot be addressed until psychologists agree on a more valid test of intelligence.

28. Tests of _____ measure what an individual can do now, whereas tests of _____ predict what an individual will be able to do later.
    a. aptitude; achievement
    b. achievement; aptitude
    c. reliability; validity
    d. validity; reliability

29. To say that the heritability of a trait is approximately 50 percent means that:
    a. genes are responsible for 50 percent of the trait in an individual, and the environment is responsible for the rest.
    b. the trait's appearance in a person will reflect approximately equal genetic contributions from both parents.

    c. of the variation in the trait within a group of people, 50 percent can be attributed to heredity.
    d. all of these answers are true.

30. (Close-Up) Twenty-two-year-old Dan has an intelligence score of 63 and the academic skills of a fourth-grader, and is unable to live independently. Dan *probably*:
    a. has Down syndrome.
    b. has savant syndrome.
    c. is mentally retarded.
    d. will eventually achieve self-supporting social and vocational skills.

31. A school psychologist found that 85 percent of those who scored above 115 on an aptitude test were "A" students and 75 percent of those who scored below 85 on the test were "D" students. The psychologist concluded that the test had high:
    a. content validity because scores on it correlated highly with the criterion behavior.
    b. predictive validity because scores on it correlated highly with the criterion behavior.
    c. content validity because scores on it correlated highly with the target behavior.
    d. predictive validity because scores on it correlated highly with the target behavior.

32. Benito was born in 1937. In 1947, he scored 130 on an intelligence test. What was Benito's mental age when he took the test?
    a. 9   c. 11
    b. 10   d. 13

33. Melvin has been diagnosed as having savant syndrome, which means that he:
    a. has an IQ of 120 or higher.
    b. would score high on a test of analytical intelligence.
    c. is limited in mental ability but has one exceptional ability.
    d. was exposed to high levels of testosterone during prenatal development.

34. The contribution of environmental factors to racial gaps in intelligence scores is indicated by:
    a. evidence that individual differences within a race are much greater than differences between races.
    b. evidence that white and black infants score equally well on certain measures of infant intelligence.

c. the fact that Asian students outperform North American students on math achievement and aptitude tests.

d. all of these answers.

35. Jack takes the same test of mechanical reasoning on several different days and gets virtually identical scores. This suggests that the test has:

a. high content validity.
b. high reliability.
c. high predictive validity.
d. been standardized.

36. You would not use a test of hearing acuity as an intelligence test because it would lack:

a. content reliability.
b. predictive reliability.
c. predictive validity.
d. content validity.

37. If you compare the same trait in people of similar heredity who live in very different environments, heritability for that trait will be _____ ; heritability for the trait is most likely to be _____ among people of very different heredities who live in similar environments.

a. low; high
b. high; low
c. environmental; genetic
d. genetic; environmental

38. If you wanted to develop a test of musical aptitude in North American children, which would be the appropriate standardization group?

a. children all over the world
b. North American children
c. children of musical parents
d. children with known musical ability

39. Don's intelligence scores were only average, but he has been enormously successful as a corporate manager. Psychologists Sternberg and Wagner would probably suggest that:

a. Don's verbal intelligence exceeds his performance intelligence.
b. Don's performance intelligence exceeds his verbal intelligence.
c. Don's academic intelligence exceeds his practical intelligence.
d. Don's practical intelligence exceeds his academic intelligence.

40. If asked to guess the intelligence score of a stranger, your best guess would be:

a. 75.
b. 100.
c. 125.
d. "I don't know, intelligence scores vary too widely."

41. Before becoming attorneys, law students must pass a special licensing exam, which is an _____ test. Before entering college, high school students must take the SAT, which is an _____ test.

a. achievement; aptitude
b. aptitude; achievement
c. achievement; achievement
d. aptitude; aptitude

42. Vanessa is a very creative sculptress. We would expect that Vanessa also:

a. has an exceptionally high intelligence score.
b. is quite introverted.
c. has a venturesome personality and is intrinsically motivated.
d. lacks expertise in most other skills.

Matching Items

Match each definition or description with the appropriate term.

Definitions or Descriptions

_____ 1. the consistency with which a test measures performance

_____ 2. the process of defining meaningful scores relative to a pretested group

_____ 3. the degree to which a test measures what it is designed to measure

_____ 4. Terman's revision of Binet's original intelligence test

_____ 5. an underlying, general intelligence factor

_____ 6. the proportion of variation among individuals that we can attribute to genes

_____ 7. a very low intelligence score accompanied by one extraordinary skill

_____ 8. a statistical technique that identifies related items on a test

Terms

a. standardization
b. heritability
c. *g*
d. savant syndrome
e. factor analysis
f. Stanford-Binet
g. content validity
h. reliability

True–False Items

Indicate whether each statement is true or false by placing *T* or *F* in the blank next to the item.

_____ 1. In the current version of the Stanford-Binet intelligence test, one's performance is compared only with the performance of others the same age.

_____ 2. Intelligence scores in the United States have been dropping over the past 50 years.

_____ 3. The gap in intelligence scores between black and white children is increasing.

_____ 4. The intelligence scores of adopted children are more similar to those of their adoptive parents than their biological parents.

_____ 5. The consensus among psychologists is that most intelligence tests are extremely biased.

_____ 6. Most psychologists agree that intelligence is mainly determined by heredity.

_____ 7. The variation in intelligence scores within a racial group is much larger than that between racial groups.

_____ 8. Telling students they are unlikely to succeed often erodes their performance on aptitude tests.

Essay Question

You have been asked to devise a Psychology Achievement Test (PAT) that will be administered to freshmen who declare psychology as their major. What steps will you take to ensure that the PAT is a good intelligence test? (Use the space below to list the points you want to make, and organize them. Then write the essay on a separate sheet of paper.)

KEY TERMS

Using your own words, on a piece of paper write a brief definition or explanation of each of the following terms.

1. intelligence
2. general intelligence (g)
3. savant syndrome
4. creativity
5. emotional intelligence
6. intelligence test
7. mental age
8. Stanford-Binet
9. intelligence quotient (IQ)
10. Wechsler Adult Intelligence Scale (WAIS)
11. aptitude test
12. achievement test
13. standardization
14. normal curve (normal distribution)
15. reliability
16. validity
17. content validity
18. predictive validity
19. mental retardation
20. Down syndrome
21. heritability
22. stereotype threat

ANSWERS
Module Review

Introduction and What Is Intelligence?

1. socially
2. culture
3. the ability to learn from experience, solve problems, and use knowledge to adapt to new situations
4. overall (general); specific
5. factor analysis
6. general intelligence
7. savant syndrome; autism
8. multiple intelligences; physical; do
9. triarchic; analytical; practical; creative
10. creativity; 120
11. convergent; divergent; frontal lobes

Creative people tend to have expertise, or a solid base of knowledge; imaginative thinking skills, which allow them to see things in new ways, to recognize patterns, and to make connections; intrinsic motivation, or the tendency to focus on the pleasure and challenge of their work; and a venturesome personality that tolerates ambiguity and risk and seeks new experiences. Creative people also have generally benefited from living in creative environments.

12. academic; social
13. emotional intelligence; perceive; understand; manage; use
14. recognize; predict; express; adaptive

Emotionally intelligent people are self-aware. They can manage their emotions and they can delay gratification. They handle others' emotions skillfully.

15. modestly
16. emotional

Assessing Intelligence

1. intelligence
2. Alfred Binet; mental; was not
3. Stanford-Binet; intelligence quotient

In the original formula for IQ, measured mental age is divided by chronological age and multiplied by 100. "Mental age" refers to the chronological age that most typically corresponds to a given level of performance.

4. do not; the same; 100
5. Wechsler Adult Intelligence Scale; verbal comprehension; perceptual organization; working memory; processing speed
6. aptitude; achievement
7. standardization
8. normal

The normal curve describes the distribution of many physical phenomena and psychological attributes (including mental aptitudes), with most scores falling near the average and fewer near the extremes. When a test is standardized on a normal curve, individual scores are assigned according to how much they deviate above or below the distribution's average.

9. reliable
10. test-retest
11. split-half

12. +.9

13. validity

14. content validity

15. predictive validity

16. is not; diminishes

17. mentally retarded; 1

18. Down syndrome

19. mainstreamed

20. improved; Flynn effect

21. nutrition; economic

Genetic and Environmental Influences on Intelligence

1. more; gray matter; verbal; spatial

2. memory

3. more alike; environmental; age

4. more; biological; adoptive

5. heritability; 50

6. does not

7. do; malnutrition; sensory; social isolation

8. Head Start; emotional intelligence

Group Differences in Intelligence Test Scores

1. environmental

Because of the impact of environmental factors such as education and nutrition on intelligence test performance, even if the heritability of intelligence is high within a particular group, differences in intelligence among groups may be environmentally caused. One group may, for example, thrive in an enriched environment while another of the same genetic predisposition may falter in an impoverished one.

2. do not; greater than; is not

3. higher; Asian students have a longer school year and spend more time studying math

4. as well as

5. spelling; verbally

6. computation; problem solving; mental rotation

7. evolutionary

8. male sex hormones

9. social expectations

10. are

11. are not

12. stereotype threat

Progress Test

Multiple-Choice Questions

1. **d.** is the answer. If we divide 9, the measured mental age, by 6, the chronological age, and multiply the result by 100, we obtain 150.

2. **b.** is the answer. As social expectations have changed, the gender gap in math and science scores is narrowing.

3. **c.** is the answer.
   a. On the contrary, many *group* differences are highly significant, even though they tell us nothing about specific *individuals*.
   b. Although heredity contributes to individual differences in intelligence, it does not necessarily contribute to group differences.
   d. In fact, the difference has diminished somewhat in recent years.

4. **b.** is the answer.
   a. This answer refers to a test's content validity.
   c. This answer refers to test-retest reliability.
   d. This answer refers to predictive validity.

5. **a.** is the answer.
   b. Down syndrome is normally caused by an extra, rather than a missing, chromosome.
   c. & d. Down syndrome is a genetic disorder that is manifest during the earliest stages of prenatal development, well before malnutrition and exposure to drugs would produce their harmful effects on the developing fetus.

6. **c.** is the answer. Reification is a reasoning error, in which an abstract concept such as IQ is regarded as though it were real.

7. **d.** is the answer.

8. **a.** is the answer.
   c. & d. Most modern tests have high reliabilities of about +.9; their validity scores are much lower.

9. **d.** is the answer. Up to an intelligence score of about 120, there is a positive correlation between intelligence and creativity. But beyond this point the correlation disappears, indicating that factors other than intelligence are also involved.
   a. The ability to think imaginatively and intelligence are *both* components of creativity.
   b. Creativity, the capacity to produce ideas that are novel and valuable, is related to and depends in part on intelligence but cannot be considered simply a kind of intelligence.
   c. Beyond an intelligence score of about 120 there is no correlation between intelligence scores and creativity.

10. **d.** is the answer. That people with savant syndrome excel in one area but are intellectually retarded in others suggests that there are multiple intelligences.

a. The ability to adapt defines the capacity we call intelligence.

b. Mental retardation is at the lower end of the range of human intelligence.

c. A general intelligence factor was hypothesized by Spearman to underlie each specific factor of intelligent behavior, but its existence is controversial and remains to be proved.

11. **c.** is the answer. Recent estimates are generally about 50 percent.

12. **d.** is the answer. Findings from a range of studies—including studies related to the Flynn effect and adoption studies—have led experts to focus on the influence of environmental factors.

a. Most experts believe that in terms of predictive validity, the major tests are not racially biased.

b. The reliability of the major tests is actually very high.

c. The bulk of the evidence on which experts base their findings points to the influence of environmental factors.

13. **d.** is the answer.

a. *g* is Spearman's term for "general intelligence"; there is no such thing as a "*g* distribution."

b. There is no such thing.

c. A bimodal distribution is one having two (bi-) modes, or averages. The normal distribution has only one mode.

14. **b.** is the answer. Enrichment programs do improve school readiness, create better attitudes toward learning, and reduce school dropouts and criminality.

15. **c.** is the answer. French compulsory education laws brought more children into the school system, and the government didn't want to rely on teachers' subjective judgments to determine which children would require special help.

a. & b. Binet's test was intended for children, and Binet specifically rejected the idea that his test measured inborn intelligence, which is an abstract capacity that cannot be quantified.

d. This was not a purpose of the test, which dealt with children in the school system.

16. **c.** is the answer.

a., b., & d. None of these is true.

17. **c.** is the answer. Predictive validity is the extent to which tests predict what they are intended to predict.

a. Reliability is the consistency with which a test samples the particular behavior of interest.

b. Content validity is the degree to which a test measures what it is designed to measure.

d. Standardization is the process of defining meaningful test scores based on the performance of a representative group.

18. **d.** is the answer.

19. **c.** is the answer.

a. This is William Stern's original formula for the intelligence quotient.

b. & d. Neither of these formulas is used to compute the score on current intelligence tests.

20. **c.** is the answer. Enrichment led to dramatic results and thereby testified to the importance of environmental factors.

a. & d. The study involved neither intelligence tests nor comparisons with control groups.

b. The children showed a dramatic positive response.

21. **a.** is the answer.

22. **d.** is the answer.

a. The concept of general intelligence pertains more to academic skills.

b. Although emotional intelligence *is* a key component of social intelligence, Salovey and Mayer coined the newer term "emotional intelligence" to refer to skills such as Gerardeen's.

c. Practical intelligence is that which is required for everyday tasks, not all of which involve emotions.

23. **c.** is the answer.

24. **c.** is the answer.

a. Performance ability and intellectual ability are separate traits.

b. This has been argued by some, but certainly not most, experts.

d. Although many experts believe that there are multiple intelligences, this would not be the same thing as diverse acquired skills.

25. **d.** is the answer.

26. **a.** is the answer.

27. **c.** is the answer.

a. & b. Studies of twins, family members, and adopted children point to a significant hereditary contribution to intelligence scores. These same studies, plus others comparing children reared in neglectful or enriched environments, indicate that life experiences also significantly influence test performance.

d. Although the issue of how intelligence should be defined is controversial, intelligence tests generally have predictive validity, especially in the early years.

28. **b.** is the answer.
c. & d. Reliability and validity are characteristics of good tests.

29. **c.** is the answer. Heritability is a measure of the extent to which a trait's variation within a group of people can be attributed to heredity.
a. & b. Heritability is *not* a measure of how much of an *individual's* behavior is inherited, nor of the relative contribution of genes from that person's mother and father. Further, the heritability of any trait depends on the context, or environment, in which that trait is being studied.

30. **c.** is the answer. To be labeled mentally retarded a person must have a test score below 70 and experience difficulty adapting to the normal demands of living independently.
a. Down syndrome is a common cause of *severe* mental retardation; Dan's test score places him in the range of mild retardation.
b. There is no indication that Dan possesses one extraordinary skill, as do people with savant syndrome.
d. The text does not suggest that mentally retarded people eventually become self-supporting.

31. **b.** is the answer.
a., c., & d. Content validity is the degree to which a test measures what it claims to measure. Furthermore, "target behavior" is not a term used by intelligence researchers.

32. **d.** is the answer. At the time he took the test, Benito's chronological age (CA) was 10. Knowing that IQ = 130 and CA = 10, solving the equation for mental age yields a value of 13.

33. **c.** is the answer. People with savant syndrome tend to score low on intelligence tests but have one exceptional ability.

34. **d.** is the answer. These reasons, along with other historical and cross-cultural reasons, all argue for the role of environment in creating and perpetuating the gap.

35. **b.** is the answer.

36. **d.** is the answer. Because the hearing acuity test would in no way sample behaviors relevant to intelligence, it would not have content validity as a test of intelligence.
a. & b. There is no such thing as content reliability or predictive reliability.
c. There is nothing to indicate that, used to test hearing, this test would lack predictive validity.

37. **a.** is the answer. If everyone has nearly the same heredity, then heritability—the variation in a trait attributed to heredity—must be low. If individuals within a group come from very similar environments, environmental differences cannot account for variation in a trait; heritability, therefore, must be high.

38. **b.** is the answer. A standardization group provides a representative comparison for the trait being measured by a test. Because this test will measure musical aptitude in North American children, the standardization group should be limited to North American children but should include children of all degrees of musical aptitude.

39. **d.** is the answer. Sternberg and Wagner distinguish among *academic* intelligence, as measured by intelligence tests; *practical* intelligence, which is involved in everyday life and tasks, such as managerial work; and *creative* intelligence.
a. & b. Verbal and performance intelligence are both measured by standard intelligence tests such as the WAIS and would be included in Sternberg and Wagner's academic intelligence.
c. Academic intelligence refers to skills assessed by intelligence tests; practical intelligence applies to skills required for everyday tasks and, often, for occupational success.

40. **b.** is the answer. Modern intelligence tests are periodically restandardized so that the average remains near 100.

41. **a.** is the answer. An exam for a professional license is intended to measure whether you have gained the overall knowledge and skill to practice the profession. The SAT is designed to predict ability, or aptitude, for learning a new skill.

42. **c.** is the answer.
a. Beyond an intelligence score of about 120, creativity and intelligence scores are not correlated.
b. & d. There is no evidence that creative people are more likely to be introverted.

Matching Items

1.	h	5.	c
2.	a	6.	b
3.	g	7.	d
4.	f	8.	e

True–False Items

1.	T	5.	F
2.	F	6.	F
3.	F	7.	T
4.	F	8.	T

Essay Question

The first step in constructing the test is to create a valid set of questions that measure psychological knowledge and therefore give the test content validity. If your objective is to predict students' future achievement in psychology courses, the test questions should be selected to measure a criterion, such as information faculty members expect all psychology majors to master before they graduate.

To enable meaningful comparisons, the test must be standardized. That is, the test should be administered to a representative sample of incoming freshmen at the time they declare psychology to be their major. From the scores of your pretested sample you will then be able to assign an average score and evaluate any individual score according to how much it deviates above or below the average.

To check your test's reliability you might retest a sample of people using the same test or another version of it. If the two scores are correlated, your test is reliable. Alternatively, you might split the test in half and determine whether scores on the two halves are correlated.

Key Terms

1. Most experts define **intelligence** as the ability to learn from experience, solve problems, and use knowledge to adapt to new situations.

2. **General intelligence (g)**, according to Spearman and others, is a general factor that underlies each of the more specific mental abilities identified through factor analysis.

3. A person with **savant syndrome** has a very low intelligence score, yet possesses one exceptional ability, for example, in music or drawing.

4. Most experts agree that **creativity** refers to an ability to produce novel and valuable ideas. People with high IQs may or may not be creative, which indicates that intelligence is only one component of creativity.

5. **Emotional intelligence** is the ability to perceive, manage, understand, and use emotions.

6. **Intelligence tests** measure people's mental aptitudes and compare them to others' through numerical scores.

7. A concept introduced by Binet, **mental age** is the chronological age that most typically corresponds to a given level of performance.

8. The **Stanford-Binet** is Lewis Terman's widely used revision of Binet's original intelligence test.

9. The **intelligence quotient (IQ)** was defined originally as the ratio of mental age to chronological age multiplied by 100. Contemporary tests of intelligence assign a score of 100 to the average performance for a given age and define other scores as deviations from this average.

10. The **Wechsler Adult Intelligence Scale (WAIS)** is the most widely used intelligence test. It is individually administered and contains 11 subtests broken into verbal and performance areas.

11. **Aptitude tests** are designed to predict future performance. They measure your capacity to learn new information, rather than measuring what you already know.

12. **Achievement tests** measure a person's current knowledge.

13. **Standardization** is the process of defining meaningful scores by comparison with a pretested standardization group.

14. The **normal curve** is a bell-shaped curve that represents the distribution (frequency of occurrence) of many physical and psychological attributes. The curve is symmetrical, with most scores near the average and fewer near the extremes.

15. **Reliability** is the extent to which a test produces consistent results.

16. **Validity** is the degree to which a test measures or predicts what it is supposed to.

17. The **content validity** of a test is the extent to which it samples the behavior that is of interest.

18. **Predictive validity** is the extent to which a test predicts the behavior it is designed to predict; also called *criterion-related validity*.

19. The two criteria that designate **mental retardation** are an IQ below 70 and difficulty adapting to the normal demands of independent living.

20. A common cause of severe retardation and associated physical disorders, **Down syndrome** is usually the result of an extra chromosome in the person's genetic makeup.

21. **Heritability** is the proportion of variation in a trait among individuals that can be attributed to genetic factors.

22. **Stereotype threat** is the phenomenon in which a person's concern that he or she will be evaluated based on a negative stereotype (as on an aptitude test, for example) is actually followed by lower performance.

FOCUS ON VOCABULARY AND LANGUAGE

What Is Intelligence?

You may also know a talented artist who is *dumb-founded by* the simplest mathematical problems . . . . Researchers have used a statistical approach (factor analysis) to identify groups of test items that measure a common ability. So, someone who has a group, or cluster, of abilities in one area may be very puzzled by and completely unable to solve (*dumb-founded by*) a relatively simple problem in a different area. Spearman argued that there was a common factor (*general intelligence,* or *g*) underlying particular abilities.

And consider people with **savant syndrome,** who often score low on intelligence tests but have an *island of brilliance* (Treffert & Wallace, 2002). Some people are functionally retarded in almost every aspect except for one very specific ability (*island of brilliance*) in which they are exceptionally gifted **(savant syndrome)**. Despite having very poor language skills and other cognitive dysfunctions, they may be capable of outstanding performance in computation, memory for music heard only once, drawing, etc. Some psychologists argue that this is evidence for the notion of multiple intelligences.

. . . *the street-smart* adolescent who becomes a *crafty* executive . . . Myers is attempting to simplify Howard Gardner's eight intelligences. As an example of one of these intelligences, he uses the adolescent who has the ability to survive in urban environments (he is *street smart*) becoming a clever (*crafty*) executive.

. . . *reading people* . . . People who have good practical managerial intelligence may not score high on academic ability but will be good at motivating people; assigning work to others appropriately; and knowing and understanding peoples' needs, desires, and ambitions (*knowing how to read people*). Other people may demonstrate different types of intelligences (for example, academic, creative, or emotional intelligence).

They also agree that the differing *varieties of giftedness add spice to life* and challenges for education. The expression "variety adds spice to life" suggests that having many different experiences tends to make life more interesting (*adds spice to life*). The fact that people differ in their talents and gifts not only makes life more interesting but also poses opportunities for teachers to capitalize on the variety of abilities that students possess and to apply multiple intelligence in the classroom.

. . . *out of the blue* . . . The solution to a very complex problem can occur unexpectedly and suddenly (*out of the blue*). This happened to Andrew Wiles when he eventually solved Fermat's last theorem after thinking hard and long (*pondering*) about the problem for over 30 years. This example illustrates the creative process, the ability to produce novel and valuable ideas.

Even Wiles *stood on the shoulders of others* and *wrestled* his problem with the collaboration of a former student. Don't take this literally. Wiles made use of the knowledge and wisdom of colleagues and a former student (*he stood on the shoulders of others*) when he was working hard and struggling to find the solution to Fermat's theorem (*he wrestled with the problem*).

Assessing Intelligence

On tests, therefore, a "*dull*" child should perform as does a typical younger child, and a "*bright*" child as does a typical older child. Children develop intellectually at different rates and so Binet and Simon developed the concept of **mental age**. Children who performed below the average level of other children the same age (e.g., a 10-year-old who performed as the average 8-year-old did) would be considered retarded or slow in development ("*dull*"). Those who performed above the average (e.g., a 10-year-old who scored as the average 12-year-old did) would be considered developmentally advanced or precocious ("*bright*").

. . . scores typically form a *normal distribution*, a *bell-shaped* pattern that forms the normal curve. Many variables that we measure (weight, height, mental aptitude, etc.) follow a symmetrical inverted U shape (a *bell-shaped* curve) when plotted on a frequency distribution. On intelligence tests, the average is 100; most scores (68%) are between 85 and 115, so they are gathered close together (*clustered*) near the mean (*average*).

If you use an inaccurate *tape measure* to measure people's heights, your height report would have high *reliability* (consistency) but low *validity*. In order for a test to be *reliable*, the instrument should have consistent results over numerous tests. So, if you use a ruler (*tape measure*) that is not precise (*inaccurate*), it will meet the *reliability* criterion because it will always give you the same result; it will not, however, be valid. To be valid it should *accurately* measure what it is supposed to measure.

Genetic and Environmental Influences on Intelligence

Extreme deprivation was *bludgeoning native intelligence*. In this investigation of a destitute orphanage, Hunt (1982) found that the effect of extreme neglect was severe depression and a general mental and physical passivity (the children became *"glum lumps"*). Their inborn (*native*) intellectual capacity was taking a severe beating (*bludgeoning*) due to the *physical and emotional neglect*. As Myers notes, severe life experiences do leave footprints on the brain; that is, they can affect brain development and subsequent cognitive ability. Hunt's intervention program had dramatic results. This points to the strong influence of environment.

Group Differences in Intelligence Test Scores

Similarly, in the psychological domain, gender similarities vastly outnumber gender differences, but most people find differences *more newsworthy*. Males and females are alike in many more ways than they are different. Although the similarities overwhelm (*vastly outnumber*) the dissimilarities, we are more intrigued by the dissimilarities, and gender differences are more likely to be reported by the media (*we find them more newsworthy*).

The score differences are *sharpest* at the *extremes*. Although the variability in ability is greater within the two groups, people tend to focus on the between-group male-female differences. The differences in scores between males and females on the SAT test are more noticeable (*sharpest*) at the high and low ends of the distribution (*extremes*) than in the middle. Thus, among the very highest scorers in math, the majority are likely to be male.

Motivation

Introduction to Motivation: Hunger

26 MODULE

MODULE OVERVIEW

Motivation is the study of forces that energize and direct our behavior. Module 26 examines the three perspectives that have been most influential in the study of motivation: instinct theory, drive-reduction theory, and arousal theory. Abraham Maslow's hierarchy of needs provides a fourth perspective, addressing the issue of why some motives are more compelling than others at certain times.

This module also discusses the hunger motive. Research on hunger points to the interplay between physiological and psychological (internal and external) factors in motivation.

NOTE: Answer guidelines for all Module 26 questions begin on page 297.

MODULE REVIEW

First, skim each section, noting headings and boldface items. After you have read the section, review each objective by answering the fill-in and essay-type questions that follow it. As you proceed, evaluate your performance by consulting the answers beginning on page 297. Do not continue with the next section until you understand each answer. If you need to, review or reread the section in the textbook before continuing.

> David Myers at times uses idioms that are unfamiliar to some readers. If you do not know the meaning of any of the following words, phrases, or expressions in the context in which they appear in the Introduction to Motivation and this module, refer to pages 301–302 for an explanation: *Having bagged nearly all of Colorado's tallest peaks; this fad for naming instincts collapsed under its own weight; feedback loops; monkey around; feasted their eyes on*

> *delectable forbidden foods; keeping tabs; miser; binge-purge; win the battle of the bulge; apple-shaped; the specifics of our genes predispose the size of our jeans; the long-term result . . . is a thinner wallet; Couch potatoes.*

Introduction and Motivational Concepts
(pp. 357–360)

Objective 1: Define *motivation* as psychologists use the term today, and describe four perspectives useful for studying motivated behavior.

1. Motivation is defined as _____ _____ _____ .

2. Four perspectives on motivation are _____ theory (which was influenced by _____ theory), _____-_____ theory, _____ theory, and the _____ of needs proposed by _____ .

3. As a result of Darwin's influence, many complex behaviors were classified as rigid, unlearned behavior patterns that are characteristic of a species, called _____ .

Discuss why early instinct theory failed as an explanation of human behavior.

4. The idea underlying the theory that _____ predispose species-typical behavior remains popular.

5. According to another view of motivation, organisms may experience a physiological _____ , which creates a state of arousal that _____ the organism to reduce the need.

6. The aim of drive reduction is to maintain a constant internal state, called _____ .

7. Behavior is often not so much pushed by our drives as it is pulled by _____ in the environment.

8. Rather than reduce a physiological need, some motivated behaviors actually _____ arousal. This demonstrates that human motives _____ (do/do not) always satisfy some biological need.

9. Human motivation aims not to eliminate _____ but to seek _____ _____ of arousal.

Objective 2: Describe Maslow's hierarchy of needs.

10. Starting from the idea that some needs take precedence over others, Maslow constructed a _____ of needs.

11. According to Maslow, the _____ needs are the most pressing, whereas the highest-order needs relate to _____ .

12. A criticism of Maslow's theory is that the sequence is _____ and not _____ experienced.

13. Surveys of life satisfaction reveal that _____ satisfaction is strongly predictive of subjective well-being in poorer nations, whereas _____-_____ satisfaction matters more in wealthy nations and _____ in individualist nations.

The Physiology of Hunger (pp. 360–362)

Objective 3: Describe the physiological determinants of hunger.

1. Ancel Keys observed that men became preoccupied with thoughts of food when they underwent _____ .

2. Cannon and Washburn's experiment using a balloon indicated that there is an association between hunger and _____ _____ .

3. When an animal has had its stomach removed, hunger _____ (does/does not) continue.

4. Increases in the hormone _____ diminish blood _____ , partly by converting it to stored fat, which causes hunger to _____ .

5. The brain area that plays a role in hunger and other bodily maintenance functions is the _____ . Animals will begin eating when the _____ _____ is electrically stimulated. When this region is destroyed, hunger _____ (increases/decreases). Animals will stop eating when the _____ _____ is stimulated. When this area is destroyed, animals _____ (overeat/undereat).

6. The hunger-arousing hormone secreted by an empty stomach is _____

7. When a portion of an obese person's stomach is surgically sealed off, the remaining stomach produces _____ (more/less) of this hormone.

For questions 8–12, identify the appetite hormone that is described.

8. Hunger-triggering hormone: _____ .

9. Hormone secreted by empty stomach: _____ .

10. Hormone secreted by pancreas: _____ .

11. Chemical secreted by bloated fat cells: _____ .

12. Digestive tract hormone that signals fullness:

_____ .

13. The weight level at which an individual's body is programmed to stay is referred to as the body's

_____ _____ .

A person whose weight goes beyond this level will tend to feel _____ (more/less) hungry than usual and expend _____ (more/less) energy.

14. The rate of energy expenditure in maintaining basic functions when the body is at rest is the

_____ _____ rate. When food intake is reduced, the body compensates by _____ (raising/ lowering) this rate.

15. The concept of a precise body set point that drives hunger _____ (is accepted/is not accepted) by all researchers. Some researchers believe that set point can be altered by _____

_____ .

In support of this idea is evidence that when people and other animals are given unlimited access to tasty foods, they tend to_____ and _____ _____ .

For these reasons, some researchers prefer to use the term _____ _____ as an alternative to the idea that there is a fixed set point.

The Psychology of Hunger (pp. 363–366)

Objective 4: Discuss psychological and cultural influences on hunger, and explain how anorexia nervosa and bulimia nervosa demonstrate the influence of psychological forces on physiologically motivated behavior.

1. Research with amnesia patients indicates that part of knowing when to eat is our

_____ of our last meal.

2. (Close-Up) The disorder in which a person becomes significantly underweight and yet feels fat is known as _____

_____ .

3. (Close-Up) A more common disorder is

_____ _____ ,

which is characterized by repeated

_____-_____

episodes and by feelings of depression or anxiety.

4. (Close-Up) The families of bulimia patients have a high incidence of _____ and _____ self-evaluation. The families of anorexia patients tend to be

_____ , _____-

_____ , and _____ .

Eating disorders _____ (provide/do not provide) a telltale sign of childhood sexual abuse.

5. (Close-Up) Genetic factors _____ (may/do not) influence susceptibility to eating disorders. The genes for these disorders may be predisposed by _____ .

6. (Close-Up) Vulnerability to eating disorders _____ (increases/does not increase) with greater body dissatisfaction.

7. (Close-Up) Women students in _____ rate their actual shape as closer to the cultural ideal. In _____ cultures, however, the rise in eating disorders has coincided with an increasing number of women having a poor _____ _____ .

8. (Close-Up) Researchers found that when young women were shown pictures of unnaturally thin models, they felt more _____ , _____ , and _____ with their own bodies.

9. Carbohydrates boost levels of the neurotransmitter _____ , which _____ (calms/arouses) the body.

10. Taste preferences for sweet and salty are _____ (genetic/learned). Other influences on taste include _____ and _____ . We have a natural dislike of many foods that are _____ ; this _____ was probably adaptive for our ancestors, and protected them from toxic substances.

Obesity and Weight Control (pp. 366–372)

Objective 5: Describe research findings on obesity and weight control.

1. Being slightly overweight _____ (poses/does not pose) serious health risks. In the United States, over _____ (how many?) percent of adults are obese. Significant obesity increases the risk of _____ _____ _____ .

2. In developing societies where people face _____ , obesity is considered a sign of _____ and _____ _____ .

3. The risks of obesity are greater for people who carry their weight at their _____ . It also has been linked in women to their risk of late-life _____ disease and brain tissue loss.

4. People who are overweight at age 40 die _____ years (how many?) earlier than those who are not.

5. Obese people are often stereotyped as _____ , _____ , and _____ .

6. One study found that obese women earned _____ than a control group of nonobese women and were less likely to be _____ .

7. In one experiment, job applicants were rated as less worthy of hiring when they were made to appear _____ .

8. The energy equivalent of a pound of fat is approximately _____ calories.

9. The immediate determinant of body fat is the size and number of _____ _____ one has. This number is, in turn, determined by several factors, including _____ _____ .

10. The size of fat cells _____ (can/cannot) be decreased by dieting; the number of fat cells _____ (can/cannot) be decreased by dieting.

11. Fat tissue has a _____ (higher/lower) metabolic rate than lean tissue. The result is that fat tissue requires _____ (more/less) food energy to be maintained.

12. The body weight "thermostat" of obese people _____ (is/is not) set to maintain a higher-than-average weight. When weight drops below this setting, _____ increases and _____ decreases.

Explain why, metabolically, many obese people find it so difficult to become and stay thin.

13. Studies of adoptees and twins _____ (do/do not) provide evidence of a genetic influence on obesity.

14. Obesity is _____ (more/less) common among those who watch more daily TV and _____ (more/less) common among people living in communities where walking is common.

15. Most obese persons who lose weight _____ (gain/do not gain) it back.

(Close-Up) State several pieces of advice for those who want to lose weight.

PROGRESS TEST

Multiple-Choice Questions

Circle your answers to the following questions and check them with the answers beginning on page 298. If your answer is incorrect, read the explanation for why it is incorrect and then consult the appropriate pages of the text.

1. Motivation is best understood as a state that:
    a. reduces a drive.
    b. aims at satisfying a biological need.
    c. energizes an organism to act.
    d. energizes and directs behavior.

2. Which of the following is a difference between a drive and a need?
    a. Needs are learned; drives are inherited.
    b. Needs are physiological states; drives are psychological states.
    c. Drives are generally stronger than needs.
    d. Needs are generally stronger than drives.

3. One problem with the idea of motivation as drive reduction is that:
    a. because some motivated behaviors do not seem to be based on physiological needs, they cannot be explained in terms of drive reduction.
    b. it fails to explain any human motivation.
    c. it cannot account for homeostasis.
    d. it does not explain the hunger drive.

4. Increases in insulin will:
    a. lower blood sugar and trigger hunger.
    b. raise blood sugar and trigger hunger.
    c. lower blood sugar and trigger satiety.
    d. raise blood sugar and trigger satiety.

5. Electrical stimulation of the lateral hypothalamus will cause an animal to:
    a. begin eating.
    b. stop eating.
    c. become obese.
    d. begin copulating.

6. The text suggests that a *neophobia* for unfamiliar tastes:
    a. is more common in children than in adults.
    b. protected our ancestors from potentially toxic substances.
    c. may be an early warning sign of an eating disorder.
    d. only grows stronger with repeated exposure to those tastes.

7. I am a protein produced by fat cells and monitored by the hypothalamus. When in abundance, I cause the brain to increase metabolism. What am I?
    a. PYY
    b. ghrelin
    c. orexin
    d. leptin

8. Instinct theory and drive-reduction theory both emphasize _____ factors in motivation.
    a. environmental
    b. cognitive
    c. psychological
    d. biological

9. Few human behaviors are rigidly patterned enough to qualify as:
    a. needs.
    b. drives.
    c. instincts.
    d. incentives.

10. In his study of men on a semistarvation diet, Keys found that:
    a. the metabolic rate of the men increased.
    b. the men eventually lost interest in food.
    c. the men became obsessed with food.
    d. the men's behavior directly contradicted predictions made by Maslow's hierarchy of needs.

11. (Close-Up) Bulimia nervosa involves:
    a. bingeing and purging.
    b. a low basal metabolic rate.
    c. dramatic weight loss.
    d. a damaged ventromedial hypothalamus.

12. Research on genetic influences on obesity reveals that:
    a. the body weights of adoptees correlate with that of their biological parents.
    b. the body weights of adoptees correlate with that of their adoptive parents.
    c. identical twins usually have very different body weights.
    d. the body weights of identical twin women are more similar than those of identical twin men.

13. Research on obesity indicates that:
    a. pound for pound, fat tissue requires more calories to maintain than lean tissue.
    b. once fat cells are acquired they are never lost, no matter how rigorously one diets.
    c. one pound of weight is lost for every 3500-calorie reduction in diet.
    d. when weight drops below the set point, hunger and metabolism also decrease.

14. The number of fat cells a person has is influenced by:
    a. genetic predisposition.
    b. childhood eating patterns.
    c. adulthood eating patterns.
    d. all of these answers.

15. Which of the following influences on hunger motivation does *not* belong with the others?
    a. set/settling point
    b. attraction to sweet and salty tastes
    c. reduced production of ghrelin after stomach bypass surgery
    d. memory of time elapsed since your last meal

16. Homeostasis refers to:
    a. the tendency to maintain a steady internal state.
    b. the tendency to seek external incentives for behavior.
    c. the setting of the body's "weight thermostat."
    d. a theory of the development of sexual orientation.

17. The tendency to overeat when food is plentiful:
    a. is a recent phenomenon that is associated with the luxury of having ample food.
    b. emerged in our prehistoric ancestors as an adaptive response to alternating periods of feast and famine.
    c. is greater in developed, than in developing, societies.
    d. is stronger in women than in men.

18. (Close-Up) Although the cause of eating disorders is still unknown, proposed explanations focus on all the following *except*:
    a. metabolic factors.
    b. genetic factors.
    c. family background factors.
    d. cultural factors.

19. The brain area that when stimulated suppresses eating is the:
    a. lateral hypothalamus.
    b. ventromedial hypothalamus.
    c. lateral thalamus.
    d. ventromedial thalamus.

20. (Close-Up) Women in _____ rate their body ideals closest to their actual shape.
    a. Western cultures
    b. countries such as Africa, where thinness can signal poverty,

    c. countries such as India, where thinness is not idealized,
    d. Australia, New Zealand, and England

21. According to Maslow's theory:
    a. the most basic motives are based on physiological needs.
    b. needs are satisfied in a specified order.
    c. the highest motives relate to self-actualization.
    d. all of these statements are true.

22. Which of the following is *inconsistent* with the drive-reduction theory of motivation?
    a. When body temperature drops below 98.6° Fahrenheit, blood vessels constrict to conserve warmth.
    b. A person is driven to seek a drink when his or her cellular water level drops below its optimum point.
    c. Monkeys will work puzzles even if not given a food reward.
    d. A person becomes hungry when body weight falls below its biological set point.

23. (Close-Up) Which of the following is true concerning eating disorders?
    a. Genetic factors may influence susceptibility.
    b. Cultural pressures for thinness strongly influence teenage girls.
    c. Family background is a significant factor.
    d. All of these statements are true.

24. In animals, destruction of the lateral hypothalamus results in _____ , whereas destruction of the ventromedial hypothalamus results in _____ .
    a. overeating; loss of hunger
    b. loss of hunger; overeating
    c. an elevated set point; a lowered set point
    d. increased thirst; loss of thirst

25. Which of the following is *not* necessarily a reason that obese people have trouble losing weight?
    a. Fat tissue has a lower metabolic rate than lean tissue.
    b. Once a person has lost weight, it takes fewer calories to maintain his or her current weight.
    c. The tendency toward obesity may be genetically based.
    d. Obese people tend to lack willpower.

26. Beginning with the most basic needs, which of the following represents the correct sequence of needs in the hierarchy described by Maslow?
    a. safety; physiological; esteem; belongingness and love; self-fulfillment
    b. safety; physiological; belongingness and love; esteem; self-fulfillment
    c. physiological; safety; esteem; belongingness and love; self-fulfillment
    d. physiological; safety; belongingness and love; esteem; self-fulfillment

27. After an initial rapid weight loss, a person on a diet loses weight much more slowly. This slow-down occurs because:
    a. most of the initial weight loss is simply water.
    b. when a person diets, metabolism decreases.
    c. people begin to "cheat" on their diets.
    d. insulin levels tend to increase with reduced food intake.

28. (Close-Up) Which of the following would be the worst piece of advice to offer to someone trying to lose weight?
    a. "In order to treat yourself to one 'normal' meal each day, eat very little until the evening meal."
    b. "Reduce your consumption of saturated fats."
    c. "Boost your metabolism by exercising regularly."
    d. "Without increasing total caloric intake, increase the relative proportion of carbohydrates in your diet."

29. Mary loves hang-gliding. It would be most difficult to explain Mary's behavior according to:
    a. incentives.
    b. self-actualization.
    c. drive-reduction theory.
    d. Maslow's hierarchy of needs.

30. For two weeks, Orlando has been on a hunger strike in order to protest his country's involvement in what he perceives as an immoral war. Orlando's willingness to starve himself in order to make a political statement conflicts with the theory of motivation advanced by:
    a. Darwin.   c. Keys.
    b. Mandel.   d. Maslow.

31. (Close-Up) Kathy has been undergoing treatment for bulimia. There is an above-average probability that one or more members of Kathy's family have a problem with:
    a. high achievement.   c. obesity.
    b. overprotection.   d. all of these things.

32. One shortcoming of the instinct theory of motivation is that it:
    a. places too much emphasis on environmental factors.
    b. focuses on cognitive aspects of motivation.
    c. applies only to animal behavior.
    d. does not explain human behaviors; it simply names them.

33. (Close-Up) Which of the following is *not* typical of both anorexia and bulimia?
    a. far more frequent occurrence in women than in men
    b. preoccupation with food and fear of being overweight
    c. weight significantly and noticeably outside normal ranges
    d. low self-esteem and feelings of depression

34. Which of the following is *not* an example of homeostasis?
    a. perspiring in order to restore normal body temperature
    b. feeling hungry and eating to restore the level of blood glucose to normal
    c. feeling hungry at the sight of an appetizing food
    d. All of these are examples of homeostasis.

35. Two rats have escaped from their cages in the neurophysiology lab. The technician needs your help in returning them to their proper cages. One rat is grossly overweight; the other is severely underweight. You confidently state that the overweight rat goes in the "_____-destruction" cage, while the underweight rat goes in the "_____-destruction" cage.
    a. hippocampus; amygdala
    b. amygdala; hippocampus
    c. lateral hypothalamus; ventromedial hypothalamus
    d. ventromedial hypothalamus; lateral hypothalamus

36. Ali's parents have tried hard to minimize their son's exposure to sweet, fattening foods. If Ali has the occasion to taste sweet foods in the future, which of the following is likely?
    a. He will have a strong aversion to such foods.
    b. He will have a neutral reaction to sweet foods.
    c. He will display a preference for sweet tastes.
    d. It is impossible to predict Ali's reaction.

37. (Close-Up) Of the following individuals, who might be most prone to developing an eating disorder?
    a. Jason, an adolescent boy who is somewhat overweight and is unpopular with his peers
    b. Jennifer, a teenage girl who has a poor self-image and a fear of not being able to live up to her parents' high standards
    c. Susan, a 35-year-old woman who is a "workaholic" and devotes most of her energies to her high-pressured career
    d. Bill, a 40-year-old man who has had problems with alcoholism and is seriously depressed after losing his job of 20 years

38. Lucille has been sticking to a strict diet but can't seem to lose weight. What is the most likely explanation for her difficulty?
    a. Her body has a very low set point.
    b. Her prediet weight was near her body's set point.
    c. Her weight problem is actually caused by an underlying eating disorder.
    d. Lucille is influenced primarily by external factors.

39. Randy, who has been under a lot of stress lately, has intense cravings for sugary junk foods, which tend to make him feel more relaxed. Which of the following is the most likely explanation for his craving?
    a. Randy feels that he deserves to pamper himself with sweets because of the stress he is under.
    b. The extra sugar gives Randy the energy he needs to cope with the demands of daily life.
    c. Carbohydrates boost levels of serotonin, which has a calming effect.
    d. The extra sugar tends to lower blood insulin level, which promotes relaxation.

Matching Items

Match each term with its definition or description.

Terms

_____ 1. anorexia nervosa
_____ 2. set point
_____ 3. drive
_____ 4. orexin
_____ 5. homeostasis
_____ 6. need
_____ 7. incentive
_____ 8. bulimia nervosa
_____ 9. ghrelin

Definitions or Descriptions

a. the body's tendency to maintain a balanced internal state
b. environmental stimulus that motivates behavior
c. an eating disorder characterized by significantly below normal weight
d. an eating disorder characterized by repeated episodes of overeating following by vomiting, fasting, or laxative use
e. an aroused state arising from some physiological need
f. a state of deprivation
g. the body's weight-maintenance setting
h. hormone secreted by an empty stomach
i. hunger-triggering hormone secreted by the hypothalamus

True–False Items

Indicate whether each statement is true or false by placing *T* or *F* in the blank next to the item.

_____ 1. When body weight rises above set point, hunger increases.

_____ 2. All taste preferences are conditioned.

_____ 3. An increase in insulin increases blood glucose levels and triggers hunger.

_____ 4. Most obese people who lose weight eventually gain it back.

_____ 5. Obesity is often a sign of social status and affluence in developing countries.

Essay Question

Differentiate the three major theories of motivation, discuss their origins, and explain why they cannot fully account for human behavior. (Use the space below to list the points you want to make, and organize them. Then write the essay on a separate sheet of paper.)

KEY TERMS

Using your own words, write on a separate piece of paper a brief definition or explanation of each of the following terms.

1. motivation

2. instinct

3. drive-reduction theory

4. homeostasis

5. incentives

6. hierarchy of needs

7. glucose

8. set point

9. basal metabolic rate

10. anorexia nervosa

11. bulimia nervosa

ANSWERS

Module Review

Introduction and Motivational Concepts

1. a need or desire that energizes behavior and directs it toward a goal

2. instinct; evolutionary; drive-reduction; arousal; hierarchy; Abraham Maslow

3. instincts

According to instinct theory, any human behavior could be regarded as an instinct. The only evidence for each such "instinct" was the behavior used to identify it. Thus, instinct theory offered only circular explanations; it labeled behaviors but did not explain them.

4. genes

5. need; drives

6. homeostasis

7. incentives

8. increase; do not

9. arousal; optimum levels

10. hierarchy

11. physiological; self-actualization

12. arbitrary; universally

13. financial; home-life; self-esteem

The Physiology of Hunger

1. semistarvation

2. stomach contractions

3. does

4. insulin; glucose; increase

5. hypothalamus; lateral hypothalamus; decreases; ventromedial hypothalamus; overeat

6. ghrelin

7. less

8. orexin

9. ghrelin

10. insulin

11. leptin

12. PYY

13. set point; less; more

14. basal metabolic; lowering

15. is not accepted; slow, sustained changes in body weight; overeat; gain weight; settling point

The Psychology of Hunger

1. memory
2. anorexia nervosa
3. bulimia nervosa; binge-purge
4. obesity; negative; competitive; high-achieving; protective; do not provide
5. may; evolution
6. increases
7. India; Western; body image
8. ashamed; depressed; dissatisfied
9. serotonin; calms
10. genetic; conditioning; culture; unfamiliar; neophobia

Obesity and Weight Control

1. does not pose; 30; diabetes, high blood pressure, heart disease, gallstones, arthritis, and certain types of cancer
2. famine; affluence; social status
3. abdomens (stomachs); Alzheimer's
4. 3
5. slow; lazy; sloppy
6. less; married
7. obese
8. 3500
9. fat cells; genetic predisposition, early childhood eating patterns, adult overeating
10. can; cannot
11. lower; less
12. is; hunger; metabolism

Obese persons have higher set-point weights than nonobese persons. During a diet, metabolic rate drops to defend the set-point weight. The dieter therefore finds it hard to progress beyond an initial weight loss. When the diet is concluded, the lowered metabolic rate continues, so that relatively small amounts of food may prove fattening. Also, some people have lower metabolic rates than others.

13. do
14. more; less
15. gain

Begin only if you are motivated and self-disciplined. Minimize exposure to tempting food cues. Eat healthy foods. Don't starve all day and eat one big meal at night. Beware of binge eating. Be realistic and moderate. Boost your metabolism through exercise.

Progress Test

Multiple-Choice Questions

1. **d.** is the answer.
   a. & b. Although motivation is often aimed at reducing drives and satisfying biological needs, this is by no means always the case, as achievement motivation illustrates.
   c. Motivated behavior not only is energized but also is directed at a goal.

2. **b.** is the answer. A drive is the psychological consequence of a physiological need.
   a. Needs are unlearned states of deprivation.
   c. & d. Since needs are physical and drives psychological, their strengths cannot be compared directly.

3. **a.** is the answer. The curiosity of a child or a scientist is an example of behavior apparently motivated by something other than a physiological need.
   b. & d. Some behaviors, such as thirst and hunger, are partially explained by drive reduction.
   c. Drive reduction is directly based on the principle of homeostasis.

4. **a.** is the answer. Increases in insulin increase hunger indirectly by lowering blood sugar, or glucose.

5. **a.** is the answer. This area of the hypothalamus seems to elevate hunger.
   b. Stimulating the ventromedial hypothalamus has this effect.
   c. Lesioning the ventromedial hypothalamus has this effect.
   d. The hypothalamus is involved in sexual motivation, but not in this way.

6. **b.** is the answer.
   a. Neophobia for taste is typical of all age groups.
   c. Neophobia for taste is *not* an indicator of an eating disorder.
   d. With repeated exposure, our appreciation for a new taste typically *increases*.

7. **d.** is the answer.
   a. PYY signals fullness, which is associated with decreased metabolism.
   b. Ghrelin is a hormone secreted by the empty stomach that sends hunger signals.
   c. Orexin is a hormone secreted by the hypothalamus.

8. **d.** is the answer.

9. **c.** is the answer.
   a. & b. Needs and drives are biologically based states that stimulate behaviors but are not themselves behaviors.
   d. Incentives are the external stimuli that motivate behavior.

10. **c.** is the answer. The deprived men focused on food almost to the exclusion of anything else.
    a. In order to conserve energy, the men's metabolic rate actually *decreased*.
    b. & d. Far from losing interest in food, the men came to care only about food—a finding consistent with Maslow's hierarchy, in which physiological needs are at the base.

11. **a.** is the answer.
    b. metabolic rate is not a factor in bulimia.
    c. anorexia patients show dramatic weight loss. Bulimia patients may maintain normal weight.
    d. Bulimia is primarily a result of psychological factors. Although the hypothalamus may be damaged, that would not be why the person binges and purges.

12. **a.** is the answer.

13. **b.** is the answer.

14. **d.** is the answer.
    a. & b. The most effective management style will depend on the situation.
    c. This might be an effective strategy with some, but not all, employees.

15. **d.** is the answer. Memory of the time of the last meal is an example of a psychological influence on hunger motivation.
    a., b., & c. Each of these is a biological influence on hunger motivation.

16. **a.** is the answer.
    b. This describes extrinsic motivation.
    c. This describes set point.
    d. Homeostasis has nothing to do with sexual orientation.

17. **b.** is the answer.
    c. If anything, just the opposite is true.
    d. Men and women do not differ in the tendency to overeat.

18. **a.** is the answer. The text does not indicate whether their metabolism is higher or lower than most.
    b., c., & d. Genes, family background, and cultural influence have all been proposed as factors in eating disorders.

19. **b.** is the answer.
    a. Stimulation of the lateral hypothalamus triggers eating.

   c. & d. The thalamus is a sensory relay station; stimulation of it has no effect on eating.

20. **c.** is the answer.

21. **d.** is the answer.

22. **c.** is the answer. Such behavior, presumably motivated by curiosity rather than any biological need, is inconsistent with a drive-reduction theory of motivation.
    a., b., & d. Each of these examples is consistent with a drive-reduction theory of motivation.

23. **d.** is the answer.

24. **b.** is the answer.
    a. These effects are the reverse of what takes place.
    c. If anything, set point is lowered by destruction of the lateral hypothalamus and elevated by destruction of the ventromedial hypothalamus.
    d. These effects do not occur.

25. **d.** is the answer. Most researchers today discount the idea that people are obese because they lack willpower.

26. **d.** is the answer.

27. **b.** is the answer. Following the initial weight loss, metabolism drops as the body attempts to defend its set-point weight. This drop in metabolism means that eating an amount that once produced a loss in weight may now actually result in weight gain.

28. **a.** is the answer. Dieting, including fasting, lowers the body's metabolic rate and reduces the amount of food energy needed to maintain body weight.
    b., c., & d. Each of these strategies would be a good piece of advice to a dieter.

29. **c.** is the answer. Drive-reduction theory maintains that behavior is motivated when a biological need creates an aroused state, driving the individual to satisfy the need. It is difficult to believe that Mary's hang-gliding is satisfying a biological need.
    a., b., & d. Mary may enjoy hang-gliding because it is a challenge that "is there" (incentive), because it satisfies a high-level need for fulfillment (self-actualization), or because it increases her self-esteem and sense of fulfillment in life (Maslow's hierarchy of needs).

30. **d.** is the answer. According to Maslow's theory, physiological needs, such as the need to satisfy hunger, must be satisfied before a person pursues loftier needs, such as making political statements.
    a. Darwin was concerned with evolution and survival of the fittest.

b. Mandel described the effects of starvation in Nazi concentration camps.

c. Keys described the psychological effects of semi-starvation.

31. **c.** is the answer.
    a. & b. These are more typical of the families of anorexia patients.

32. **d.** is the answer.
    a. & b. Instinct theory emphasizes biological factors rather than environmental or cognitive factors.
    c. Instinct theory applies to both humans and other animals.

33. **c.** is the answer. Although people with anorexia are significantly underweight, those with bulimia often are not unusually thin or overweight.
    a., b., & d. Both anorexia and bulimia victims are more likely to be women than men, preoccupied with food, fearful of becoming overweight, and suffer from depression or low self-esteem.

34. **c.** is the answer. This is an example of salivating in response to an incentive rather than to maintain a balanced internal state.
    a. & b. Both of these are examples of behavior that maintains a balanced internal state (homeostasis).

35. **d.** is the answer. Destruction of the ventromedial hypothalamus produces overeating and rapid weight gains. Destruction of the lateral hypothalamus suppresses hunger and produces weight loss.
    a. & b. The hippocampus and amygdala are not involved in regulating eating behavior.

36. **c.** is the answer. Our preferences for sweet and salty tastes are genetic and universal.

37. **b.** is the answer. Adolescent females with low self-esteem and high-achieving families seem especially prone to eating disorders such as anorexia nervosa.
    a. & d. Eating disorders occur much more frequently in women than in men.
    c. Eating disorders usually develop during adolescence, rather than during adulthood.

38. **b.** is the answer. The body acts to defend its set point, or the weight to which it is predisposed. If Lucille was already near her set point, weight loss would prove difficult.
    a. If the weight level to which her body is predisposed is low, weight loss upon dieting should not be difficult.
    c. The eating disorders relate to eating behaviors and psychological factors and would not explain a difficulty with weight loss.

d. Externals might have greater problems losing weight, since they tend to respond to food stimuli, but this can't be the explanation in Lucille's case, since she has been sticking to her diet.

39. **c.** is the answer. Serotonin is a neurotransmitter that is elevated by the consumption of carbohydrates and has a calming effect.
    a. & b. These answers do not explain the feelings of relaxation that Randy associates with eating junk food.
    d. The consumption of sugar tends to elevate insulin level rather than lower it.

Matching Items

1.	c	6.	f
2.	g	7.	b
3.	e	8.	d
4.	i	9.	h
5.	a		

True–False Items

1.	F	4.	T
2.	F	5.	T
3.	F		

Essay Question

Under the influence of Darwin's evolutionary theory, it became fashionable to classify all sorts of behaviors as instincts. Instinct theory fell into disfavor for several reasons. First, instincts do not explain behaviors, they merely name them. Second, to qualify as an instinct, a behavior must have a fixed and automatic pattern and occur in all people, regardless of differing cultures and experiences. Apart from a few simple reflexes, however, human behavior is not sufficiently automatic and universal to meet these criteria. Although instinct theory failed to explain human motives, the underlying assumption that genes predispose many behaviors is as strongly believed as ever.

Instinct theory was replaced by drive-reduction theory and the idea that biological needs create aroused drive states that motivate the individual to satisfy these needs and preserve homeostasis. Drive-reduction theory failed as a complete account of human motivation because many human motives do not satisfy any obvious biological need. Instead, such behaviors are motivated by environmental incentives.

Arousal theory emerged in response to evidence that some motivated behaviors *increase*, rather than decrease, arousal.

Key Terms

1. **Motivation** is a need or desire that energizes and directs behavior.

2. An **instinct** is a complex behavior that is rigidly patterned throughout a species and is unlearned.

3. **Drive-reduction theory** attempts to explain behavior as arising from a physiological need that creates an aroused tension state (drive) that motivates an organism to satisfy the need.

4. **Homeostasis** refers to the body's tendency to maintain a balanced or constant internal state.

5. **Incentives** are positive or negative environmental stimuli that motivate behavior.

6. Maslow's **hierarchy of needs** proposes that human motives may be ranked from the basic, physiological level through higher-level needs for safety, love, esteem, and self-actualization; until they are satisfied, the more basic needs are more compelling than the higher-level ones.

7. **Glucose**, or blood sugar, is the major source of energy for the body's tissues. Elevating the level of glucose in the body will reduce hunger.

8. **Set point** is an individual's regulated weight level, which is maintained by adjusting food intake and energy output.

9. **Basal metabolic rate** is the body's base rate of energy expenditure when resting.

10. **Anorexia nervosa** is an eating disorder, most common in adolescent females, in which a person restricts food intake to become significantly underweight and yet still feels fat.

11. **Bulimia nervosa** is an eating disorder characterized by episodes of overeating followed by vomiting, laxative use, fasting, or excessive exercise.

FOCUS ON VOCABULARY AND LANGUAGE

Having *bagged* nearly all of Colorado's *tallest peaks*, many of them *solo* and in winter . . . Aron Ralston was an expert mountaineer who had successfully climbed (*bagged*) nearly all of Colorado's highest mountains (*tallest peaks*), many of them as a lone climber (*solo*) and in winter, too. The remarkable story of how he cut off his own arm when it was trapped (pinned) under a large rock illustrates how motivation can energize and direct behavior.

Motivational Concepts

Before long, *this fad for naming instincts collapsed under its own weight*. A good example of the misuse of a theory was when it became very popular (fashionable) to categorize a very broad range of behaviors as innately determined (a fad for naming instincts). In Darwinian theory, an instinct is an unlearned behavior that follows a fixed pattern in all members of the species. This fashion (fad) of naming thousands of behaviors as instincts, rather than explaining them, grew so large and cumbersome that it was finally abandoned as a useful explanatory system (it collapsed under its own weight).

Both systems operate through *feedback loops*. . . . A thermostat in a house and the body's temperature-regulation system are both examples of **homeostasis**. If temperature drops, the change is detected and the information is directed (*fed*) to the system so that necessary steps are taken to bring the temperature back up to its original position. This information is then transmitted back to the system, so that there is a continuous cycle of cooling down and heating up (*feedback loop*) in an attempt to maintain a steady state. This is the basis of **drive-reduction theory**.

Curiosity drives monkeys to *monkey around* trying to figure out how to unlock a latch that opens nothing or how to open a window (Figure 26.1) that allows them to see outside their room (Butler, 1954). The expression *"monkey around"* means to play or fool around (meddle) with something. Monkeys and young children have a very great need to explore and find out about their surroundings. Arousal theory suggests that we are driven to seek stimulation and increase our level of arousal to some comfortable state which is neither too high nor too low (*optimum level*).

The Physiology of Hunger

They talked food. They daydreamed food. They collected recipes, read cookbooks, and *feasted their eyes on delectable forbidden foods*. In this experiment, subjects were given only half their normal intake of food, and the men became lethargic (*listless*), focused all their thoughts on the topic of food, and looked longingly at (*feasted their eyes on*) pictures of delicious, but unobtainable, foods (*delectable forbidden foods*). This behavior is consistent with Maslow's theory that there is a hierarchy of needs.

. . . suggesting that somehow, somewhere, the body is *keeping tabs on* its available resources. People and other animals naturally and automatically tend to control food intake in order to keep a relatively constant body weight. This indicates that there is a mechanism, or mechanisms, which monitor (*keep tabs on*) energy fluctuations. Levels of the blood sugar glucose and certain brain chemicals may play a role in this process.

. . . rather like a *miser* who runs every bit of extra money to the bank and resists taking any out. One theory suggests that two parts of the hypothalamus, the lateral hypothalamus (LH) and ventromedial hypothalamus (VMH), regulate hunger. Stimulation of the LH increases hunger, while activity in the VMH depresses hunger. If the VMH is destroyed (*lesioned*), rats tend to create and store more fat, just as a person who loves money more than anything else (*a miser*) will keep banking money and use as little of it as possible.

The Psychology of Hunger

(*Close-Up*): . . . *binge-purge* . . . People who have an eating disorder called **bulimia nervosa** may have episodes of overeating (*bingeing*) similar to those who engage in drinking bouts (*spurts of drinking*). The bulimic person (typically females in their teens or twenties) usually follows the overeating episode (*gorging*) with self-induced vomiting and excessive laxative use (*purging*).

Obesity and Weight Control

And why do so few overweight people *win the battle of the bulge*? Most overweight people who diet do not manage to permanently lose the many pounds of fat they want to (*they do not win the battle of the bulge*). Myers discusses a number of factors: (a) the number of fat cells in the body does not decrease when you diet; (b) the tissue in fat is easier to maintain and uses less energy than other tissue;

and (c) when body weight drops below the set point, your overall metabolic rate slows down. For those wanting to diet, Myers lists some useful tips (see page 372).

The risks are greater for *apple-shaped* people who carry their weight *in pot bellies* than for *pear-shaped* people with ample hips and thighs. Significant obesity increases the risk of many diseases and thus shortens life expectancy. People who have a more regularly proportioned physical build (*apple-shaped*) but whose excess weight tends to accumulate and protrude around the abdomen (*they carry their weight in pot bellies*) are more at risk than those people with a body shape that has proportionally more mass in the thighs and hips and less in the upper body (*they are pear-shaped*).

So, the specifics of our genes predispose the size of our jeans. Myers is using a play on words here, suggesting that the complex interaction involved in our genetic make-up (*the specifics of our genes*) may influence the amount of excess weight we gain and correspondingly the size of the denim pants we wear (*the size of our jeans*).

(*margin note*): For most people, the only long-term result of participating in a commercial weight-loss program is a *thinner wallet*. Most commercial weight-loss programs cost a great deal of money but, at best, only help people lose weight temporarily. For those who lose and then regain weight over and over again, the end result is usually a greater weight gain each time and ultimately having less money (*thinner wallets*).

(*Close-Up*): *Couch potatoes beware* . . . Myers admonishes those of us who sit around, watch TV, and eat junk food (*couch potatoes*) to get active.

Sexual Motivation

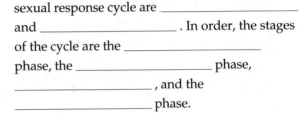

MODULE OVERVIEW

Module 27 discusses sexual motivation, including what factors affect our sexual behavior and the controversy over what determines sexual orientation. Sexual motivation in men and women is triggered less by physiological factors and more by external incentives. Even so, research studies demonstrate that sexual orientation is neither willfully chosen nor easily changed.

NOTE: Answer guidelines for all Module 27 questions begin on page 309.

MODULE REVIEW

First, skim each section, noting headings and boldface items. After you have read the section, review each objective by answering the fill-in and essay-type questions that follow it. As you proceed, evaluate your performance by consulting the answers on page 309. Do not continue with the next section until you understand each answer. If you need to, review or reread the section in the textbook before continuing.

> David Myers at times uses idioms that are unfamiliar to some readers. If you do not know the meaning of any of the following words, phrases, or expressions in the context in which they appear in the text, refer to pages 310–311 for an explanation: *shift it into high gear; X-rated; the pendulum of sexual values has swung; fired; neither willfully chosen nor willfully changed; swung the pendulum toward; double-edged sword; colors our thoughts and emotions; Even to be shunned—given the cold shoulder.*

The Physiology of Sex (pp. 375–377)

Objective 1: Describe the human sexual response cycle, and discuss some causes of sexual disorders.

1. The two researchers who identified a four-stage sexual response cycle are _____ and _____ . In order, the stages of the cycle are the _____ phase, the _____ phase, _____ , and the _____ phase.

2. During resolution, males experience a _____ _____ , during which they are incapable of another orgasm.

3. Problems that consistently impair sexual functioning are called _____ _____ . Examples of such problems include _____ _____ , _____ _____ , and _____ _____ .

Objective 2: Discuss the impact of hormones on sexual motivation and behavior.

4. In most mammals, females are sexually receptive only during ovulation, when the hormone _____ has peaked.

5. The importance of the hormone _____ to male sexual arousal is confirmed by the fact that sexual interest declines in animals if their _____ are removed. In women, low levels of the hormone

303

_____ may cause a waning of sexual interest.

6. Normal hormonal fluctuations in humans have _____ (little/significant) effect on sexual motivation. In later life, frequency of intercourse _____ (increases/decreases) as sex hormone levels _____ (increase/decline).

The Psychology of Sex (pp. 377–378)

Objective 3: Discuss the impact of external stimuli and fantasies on sexual motivation and behavior.

1. Research has shown that erotic stimuli _____ (are/are not) nearly as arousing for women as for men.

2. Brain scans reveal more activity in the _____ among _____ (women/men) who are viewing erotica.

3. With repeated exposure, the emotional response to an erotic stimulus often _____ .

Explain some of the possible harmful consequences of sexually explicit material.

4. Most women and men _____ (have/do not have) sexual fantasies. Compared to women's fantasies, men's sexual fantasies are more _____

_____ .

Sexual fantasies _____ (do/do not) indicate sexual problems or dissatisfaction.

Adolescent Sexuality (pp. 378–380)

Objective 4: Discuss some of the factors that influence adolescent sexual behavior, and describe trends in the spread of sexually transmitted infections.

1. Attitudes toward premarital sex vary widely from one _____ to another and with the passage of _____ . Rates of teen intercourse in the United States and

_____ _____ are much higher than those in _____ and _____ countries.

2. Because teenage sex is often _____ , there is increased risk of _____

_____ _____ .

Compared with European teens, American teens have _____ (higher/lower) rates of intercourse, _____ (higher/lower) rates of contraceptive use, and thus _____ (higher/lower) rates of teen pregnancy and abortion.

State five factors that contribute to the high rate of unprotected sex among teenagers.

3. Unprotected sex has led to an increase in adolescent rates of _____

_____ _____ .

Teenage girls, because of their lower levels of protective _____ , may be especially vulnerable to STIs.

State several predictors of sexual restraint (reduced teen sexuality and pregnancy).

Sexual Orientation (pp. 380–386)

Objective 5: Summarize current views on the number of people whose sexual orientation is homosexual, and discuss the research on environmental and biological influences on sexual orientation.

1. A person's sexual attraction toward members of a particular gender is referred to as

   _____ _____ .

2. Historically, _____ (all/a slight majority) of the world's cultures have been predominantly heterosexual. Most homosexuals begin thinking of themselves as gay or lesbian around age _____ .

3. Studies in Europe and the United States indicate that approximately _____ percent of men and _____ percent of women are exclusively homosexual. This finding suggests that popular estimates of the rate of homosexuality are _____ (high/low/accurate).

4. A person's sexual orientation _____ (does/does not) appear to be voluntarily chosen. Several research studies reveal that sexual orientation among _____ (women/men) tends to be less strongly felt and potentially more changeable than among the other gender. This phenomenon has been called the gender difference in _____

   _____ .

5. Gays and lesbians suffer elevated rates of _____ and risk of _____ attempts.

6. Most gays and lesbians _____ (accept/do not accept) their orientation.

7. Childhood events and family relationships _____ (are/are not) important factors in determining a person's sexual orientation.

8. Homosexuality _____ (does/does not) involve a fear of the other gender that leads people to direct their sexual desires toward members of their own gender.

9. Sex hormone levels _____ (do/do not) predict sexual orientation.

10. As children, most homosexuals _____ (were/were not) sexually victimized.

11. Homosexual and bisexual people appear more often in certain populations, including

    _____ , _____

    _____ , _____ ,

    and _____ .

12. Men who have older brothers are somewhat _____ (more/less) likely to be gay. This phenomenon, which has been called the

    _____ _____-

    _____ _____ ,

    may represent a defensive maternal

    _____ response to substances

    produced by _____ (male/female) fetuses.

13. One theory proposes that people develop a homosexual orientation if they are segregated with _____ (their own/the other) gender at the time their sex drive matures. The fact that early homosexual behavior _____ (does/does not) make people homosexual _____ (supports/conflicts with) this theory.

14. Same-sex attraction _____ (does/does not) occur among animals.

15. Researcher Simon LeVay discovered a cluster of cells in the _____ that is larger in _____ men than in all others. Gays and lesbians differ from their straight counterparts in their preference for sex-related _____ . Other studies have found a section of the brain's

    _____ _____

    that is one-third larger in homosexual men than in heterosexual men.

16. Studies of twins suggest that genes probably _____ (do/do not) play a role in homosexuality. Research has confirmed that homosexual men have more homosexual

relatives on their _____ (mother's/father's) side than on their _____ (mother's/father's) side.

17. In animals and some rare human cases, sexual orientation has been altered by abnormal _____ conditions during prenatal development. In humans, prenatal exposure to hormone levels typical of _____ , particularly between _____ and _____ months after conception, may predispose an attraction to males.

18. Gay males and lesbians may have certain physical traits more typical of those of the other gender, including _____ patterns, greater odds of being _____ (right/left)-handed, and anatomical traits of the _____ within the hearing system.

19. Most psychiatrists now believe that _____ (nature/nurture) plays the larger role in predisposing sexual orientation. Those who believe that sexual orientation is determined by _____ express more accepting attitudes toward homosexual persons.

20. Public opinion surveys reveal a _____ (more/less) accepting attitude toward homosexuality among Americans _____ (and/but not) a liberalization of all sex-related attitudes.

Sex and Human Values (pp. 386–387)

Objective 6: Discuss the place of values in sex research.

1. The study of sexual behavior and what motivates it _____ (can/cannot) be free of values.

2. Researchers' values _____ (should/should not) be openly stated.

The Need to Belong (pp. 387–389)

Objective 7: Describe the adaptive value of social attachments, and discuss the consequences of our need to belong.

1. The philosopher _____ referred to humans as the _____ animal. From an evolutionary standpoint, social bonds in humans boosted our ancestors' _____ rates. If those who felt this need to _____ survived and reproduced more successfully, their _____ would in time predominate.

2. When asked what makes life meaningful, most people mention _____ _____ .

3. Feeling accepted and loved by others boosts our _____ .

4. Much of our _____ behavior aims to increase our belonging. For most people, familiarity leads to _____ (liking/disliking).

5. After years of placing individual refugee and immigrant families in _____ communities, U.S. policies today encourage _____ _____ .

6. _____ (Throughout the world/Only in certain cultures do) people use social exclusion, or _____ , to control social behavior.

7. Researchers have found that people who are rejected are more likely to engage in _____ behaviors and may exhibit more _____ behavior, such as _____ .

PROGRESS TEST

Multiple-Choice Questions

Circle your answers to the following questions and check them with the answers beginning on page 309. If your answer is incorrect, read the explanation for why it is incorrect and then consult the appropriate pages of the text.

1. Some scientific evidence makes a preliminary link between homosexuality and:
   a. late sexual maturation.
   b. the age of an individual's first erotic experience.
   c. atypical prenatal hormones.
   d. early problems in relationships with parents.

2. The correct order of the stages of Masters and Johnson's sexual response cycle is:
   a. plateau; excitement; orgasm; resolution.
   b. excitement; plateau; orgasm; resolution.
   c. excitement; orgasm; resolution; refractory.
   d. plateau; excitement; orgasm; refractory.

3. Which of the following is *not* true regarding sexual orientation?
   a. Sexual orientation is neither willfully chosen nor willfully changed.
   b. Most people accept their orientation.
   c. Men's sexual orientation is potentially more fluid and changeable than women's.
   d. Women, regardless of sexual orientation, respond to both female and male erotic stimuli.

4. When asked what makes life meaningful, most people first mention:
   a. good health.
   b. challenging work.
   c. satisfying relationships.
   d. serving others.

5. Castration of male rats results in:
   a. reduced testosterone and sexual interest.
   b. reduced testosterone, but no change in sexual interest.
   c. reduced estrogen and sexual interest.
   d. reduced estrogen, but no change in sexual interest.

6. It has been said that the body's major sex organ is the brain. With regard to sex education:
   a. transmission of value-free information about the wide range of sexual behaviors should be the primary focus of the educator.
   b. transmission of technical knowledge about the biological act should be the classroom focus, free from the personal values and attitudes of researchers, teachers, and students.
   c. the home, not the school, should be the focus of all instruction about reproductive behavior.
   d. people's attitudes, values, and morals cannot be separated from the biological aspects of sexuality.

7. Of the following parts of the world, teen intercourse rates are highest in:
   a. Western Europe.   c. The United States.
   b. Canada.   d. Asia.

8. Exposure of a fetus to the hormones typical of females between _____ and _____ months after conception may predispose the developing human to become attracted to males.
   a. 1; 3   c. 4; 7
   b. 2; 5   d. 6; 9

9. Which of the following statements concerning homosexuality is true?
   a. Homosexuals have abnormal hormone levels.
   b. As children, most homosexuals were molested by an adult homosexual.
   c. Homosexuals had a domineering opposite-sex parent.
   d. Research indicates that sexual orientation may be at least partly physiological.

10. Sexual orientation refers to:
    a. a person's tendency to display behaviors typical of males or females.
    b. a person's sense of identity as a male or female.
    c. a person's enduring sexual attraction toward members of a particular gender.
    d. all of these answers.

11. According to Masters and Johnson, the sexual response of males is most likely to differ from that of females during:
    a. the excitement phase.
    b. the plateau phase.
    c. orgasm.
    d. the resolution phase.

12. While viewing erotica, men and women differ in the activity levels of which brain area?
    a. anterior cingulate cortex
    b. amygdala
    c. occipital lobe
    d. temporal lobe

13. Which of the following was *not* identified as a contributing factor in the high rate of unprotected sex among adolescents?
    a. alcohol use
    b. thrill-seeking
    c. mass media sexual norms
    d. ignorance

14. Summarizing his presentation on the origins of homosexuality, Dennis explains that the *fraternal birth-order effect* refers to the fact that:
    a. men who have younger brothers are somewhat more likely to be gay.
    b. men who have older brothers are somewhat more likely to be gay.
    c. women with older sisters are somewhat more likely to be gay.
    d. women with younger sisters are somewhat more likely to be gay.

15. Summarizing her report on the need to belong, Rolanda states that:
    a. "Cooperation amongst our ancestors was uncommon."
    b. "Social bonding is not in our nature; it is a learned human trait."
    c. "Because bonding with others increased our ancestors' success at reproduction and survival, it became part of our biological nature."
    d. both a. and b. are true.

16. Which of the following teens is most likely to delay the initiation of sex?
    a. Jack, who has below-average intelligence
    b. Jason, who is not religiously active
    c. Ron, who regularly volunteers his time in community service
    d. It is impossible to predict

True–False Items

Indicate whether each statement is true or false by placing *T* or *F* in the blank next to the item.

_____ 1. According to Masters and Johnson, only males experience a plateau period in the cycle of sexual arousal.
_____ 2. Testosterone affects the sexual arousal of the male only.

_____ 3. Unlike men, women tend not to be aroused by sexually explicit material.
_____ 4. Separated or divorced people are half as likely as married people to say they are happy.
_____ 5. One's sexual orientation is not voluntarily chosen.
_____ 6. Public opinion surveys reveal that Americans today have more liberal attitudes related to homosexuality and all sex-related issues.

KEY TERMS

Using your own words, write on a separate piece of paper a brief definition or explanation of each of the following terms.

1. sexual response cycle

2. refractory period

3. sexual disorder

4. estrogen

5. testosterone

6. sexual orientation

ANSWERS

Module Review

The Physiology of Sex

1. Masters; Johnson; excitement; plateau; orgasm; resolution

2. refractory period

3. sexual disorders; premature ejaculation; erectile dysfunction; orgasmic disorder

4. estrogen

5. testosterone; testes; testosterone

6. little; decreases; decline

The Psychology of Sex

1. are

2. amygdala; men

3. habituates

Erotic material may increase the viewer's acceptance of the false idea that women enjoy rape, may increase men's willingness to hurt women, may lead people to devalue their partners and relationships, and may diminish people's satisfaction with their own sexual partners.

4. have; frequent, physical, and less romantic; do not

Adolescent Sexuality

1. culture; time; Western Europe; Asian; Arab

2. unprotected; sexually transmitted infections (STIs); lower; lower; higher

Among the factors that contribute to unprotected sex among adolescents are (1) ignorance about the safe and risky times of the menstrual cycle, (2) guilt related to sexual activity, (3) minimal communication about birth control, (4) alcohol use that influences judgment, and (5) mass media norms of unprotected promiscuity.

3. sexually transmitted infection (STI); antibodies

Teens with high intelligence test scores, those who are actively religious, those whose father is present, and those who participate in service learning programs more often delay sex. Trends toward commitment show declining teen birth rates and sexual activity.

Sexual Orientation

1. sexual orientation

2. all; 20

3. 3 or 4; 1 or 2; high

4. does not; women; erotic plasticity

5. depression; suicide

6. accept

7. are not

8. does not

9. do not

10. were not

11. poets; fiction writers; artists; musicians

12. more; fraternal birth-order effect; immune; male

13. their own; does not; conflicts with

14. does

15. hypothalamus; heterosexual; odors; anterior commissure

16. do; mother's; father's

17. hormone; females; 2; 5

18. fingerprint; left; cochlea

19. nature; nature

20. more; but not

Sex and Human Values

1. cannot

2. should

The Need to Belong

1. Aristotle; social; survival; belong; genes

2. close, satisfying relationships with family, friends, or romantic partners

3. self-esteem

4. social; liking

5. isolated; chain migration

6. Throughout the world; ostracism

7. self-defeating; antisocial; aggression

Progress Test

Multiple-Choice Questions

1. **c.** is the answer.
a., b., & **d.** None of these is linked to homosexuality.

2. **b.** is the answer.

3. **c.** is the answer. Research studies suggest that women's sexual orientation is potentially more fluid and changeable than men's.

4. **c.** is the answer.

5. **a.** is the answer.
c. & **d.** Castration of the testes, which produce testosterone, does not alter estrogen levels.

6. **d.** is the answer. Sex is much more than just a biological act, and its study therefore inherently involves values, attitudes, and morals, which should thus be discussed openly.

7. **a.** is the answer.

8. **b.** is the answer. The time between the middle of the second and fifth months after conception may be a critical period for the brain's neurohormonal control system. Exposure to abnormal hormonal conditions at other times has no effect on sexual orientation.

9. **d.** is the answer. Researchers have not been able to find any clear differences, psychological or otherwise, between homosexuals and heterosexuals. Thus, the basis for sexual orientation remains unknown, although recent evidence points more to a physiological basis.

10. **c.** is the answer.

11. **d.** is the answer. During the resolution phase males experience a refractory period.
a., b., & c. The male and female responses are very similar in each of these phases.

12. **b.** is the answer.
a. The anterior cingulate cortex has been found to be implicated in feelings of ostracism.
c. & d. The occipital and temporal lobes do not play a major role in motivation.

13. **b.** is the answer.

14. **b.** is the answer.

15. **c.** is the answer.

16. **c.** is the answer.
a., b., & d. Teens with high rather than average intelligence (therefore, not a.), and those who are religiously active (therefore, not b.) are most likely to delay sex.

True–False Items

1. F
2. F
3. F
4. T
5. T
6. F

Key Terms

1. The **sexual response cycle** described by Masters and Johnson consists of four stages of bodily reaction: excitement, plateau, orgasm, and resolution.

2. The **refractory period** is a resting period after orgasm, during which a male cannot be aroused to another orgasm.

3. A **sexual disorder** is a problem—such as erectile disorder, premature ejaculation, and orgasmic dysfunction—that consistently impairs sexual arousal or functioning.

4. **Estrogen** is a sex hormone secreted in greater amounts by females than by males. In mammals other than humans, estrogen levels peak during ovulation and trigger sexual receptivity.

5. **Testosterone** is a sex hormone secreted in greater amounts by males than by females. In males, higher testosterone levels stimulate the prenatal growth of the male sex organs and the development of the male sex characteristics during puberty.

6. **Sexual orientation** refers to a person's enduring attraction to members of either the same or the opposite gender.

FOCUS ON VOCABULARY AND LANGUAGE

The Physiology of Sex

The hormonal fuel is essential, but so are the psychological stimuli that *turn on the engine*, keep it running, and *shift it into high gear*. Myers makes an analogy between sex hormones and the fuel that propels a car. We need the hormones to be sexually motivated just as a car needs fuel to operate. In humans, however, there is a two-way interaction between the chemicals and sexuality. In addition to hormones, psychological factors are needed to initiate sexual desire (*turn on the engine*) and produce the associated behaviors (*shift it into high gear*).

The Psychology of Sex

Viewing *X-rated sex films* similarly tends to diminish people's satisfaction with their own sexual partners (Zillmann, 1989). All films are rated by a censor, and those with an *X-rating* because of their sexually explicit content are restricted to adults only. There is much debate over the influence of such films on people, and some research suggests that there may be adverse effects. For example, they may create the false impression that females enjoy rape; they may increase men's willingness to hurt women; they tend to lead both males and females to devalue their partners and their relationships; and they may reduce people's feeling of fulfillment with their lovers.

Adolescent Sexuality

In recent history, the *pendulum* of sexual values has swung from the European eroticism of the early 1800s to the *conservative Victorian era* of the late 1800s, from the *libertine flapper era* of the 1920s to the family values period of the 1950s. The *pendulum* of a mechanical clock swings back and forth from one side, or extreme, to the other. Myers is pointing out that our views of sexuality tend to move from restrictive (*conservative Victorian*) at one extreme to those with fewer restraints (*libertine flapper*) at the other, during different periods of time (*eras*).

Today's generation may be moving toward an era in which commitment and restraint are more important than sexual expression. (Note: A *flapper* was an emancipated young woman in the 1920s.)

Sexual Orientation

. . . fired . . . To be *fired* means to lose your job (*to be laid off, let go, or sacked*). Myers suggests that one way for heterosexual people to understand how a homosexual feels in a predominantly heterosexual society is to imagine what it would be like if the situation were reversed and homosexuality was the norm. How would it feel as a heterosexual to be ostracized (*ignored*), to lose one's job (*be fired*), or to be confronted by media that showed or indicated homosexuality as the societal norm?

Most of today's psychologists therefore view sexual orientation as neither *willfully chosen* nor *willfully changed*. Myers compares sexual orientation to handedness. You don't deliberately decide (*willfully choose*) to be right-handed or left-handed and you can't intentionally alter (*willfully change*) your inherent inclination to use one hand over the other. Like handedness, sexual orientation is not linked to criminality nor is it associated with personality or psychological disorder.

Regardless of the process, the consistency of the genetic, prenatal, and brain findings has *swung the pendulum toward* a biological explanation of sexual orientation (Rahman & Wilson, 2003). The debate over what causes different sexual orientations has continued for many years. Recent evidence from the research seems to favor (*has swung the pendulum toward*) a biologically based account.

To gay and lesbian activists, the new biological research is a *double-edged sword* (Diamond, 1993). The research supporting a physiological explanation of sexual orientation has both positive and negative aspects (*a double-edged sword*). On the one hand, if sexual orientation is genetically influenced, there is a basis for claiming equal civil rights and there is no need to attribute blame. On the other hand, these findings create a nagging anxiety (*troubling possibility*) that sexual orientation may be controlled through genetic engineering or fetal abortions.

The Need to Belong

The need to belong *colors our thoughts and emotions*. As humans, we have a desire to be connected to others and to develop close, long-lasting relationships, and this need to belong affects the way we think and feel (*colors our thoughts and emotions*).

To be *shunned—given the cold shoulder or the silent treatment, with others' eyes avoiding yours*—is to have one's *need to belong threatened*. . . . For both adults and children, to be ignored (*shunned*), treated with disdain (*given the cold shoulder*), or deprived of verbal interactions with others (*given the silent treatment*) is very distressing and hurtful; this type of social ostracism makes us feel isolated and abandoned (*threatens our need to belong*) and can lead to depression and withdrawal.

Motivation at Work

28 MODULE

MODULE OVERVIEW

Research on worker motivation reveals that workers who view their careers as a meaningful calling, those working in jobs that optimize their skills, and those who become absorbed in activities that result in "flow" find work satisfying and enriching. Effective leaders recognize this and develop management styles that focus on workers' strengths and adapt their leadership style to the situation.

NOTE: Answer guidelines for all Module 28 questions begin on page 317.

MODULE REVIEW

First, skim each section, noting headings and boldface items. After you have read the section, review each objective by answering the fill-in and essay-type questions that follow it. As you proceed, evaluate your performance by consulting the answers beginning on page 317. Do not continue with the next section until you understand each answer. If you need to, review or reread the section in the textbook before continuing.

> David Myers at times uses idioms that are unfamiliar to some readers. If you do not know the meaning of any of the following words, phrases, or expressions in the context in which they appear in the text, refer to page 319 for an explanation: *beeped; what our gut tells us; ringtoss game . . . stake; holy grail; exude a self-confident charisma.*

Introduction (pp. 392–393)

Objective 1: Explain the concept of flow, and identify three subfields of industrial-organizational psychology.

1. According to Freud, the healthy life is filled with _____ and _____ .

2. Most people _____ (have/do not have) a predictable career path, which is one reason that many colleges focus less on _____ and more on _____ .

3. People who are unemployed _____ (report/do not report) lower well-being. People who view their work as a _____ report the greatest satisfaction.

4. Psychologist Mihaly Csikszentmihalyi formulated the concept of _____ , which is defined as a focused state of _____ and diminished awareness of _____ . People who experience this state also experience increased feelings of _____ , _____ , and _____ .

5. The nature of work has changed, from _____ to _____ to _____ .

6. The field of _____-_____ psychology applies psychology's principles to the workplace. The subfield of _____ _____ focuses on employee recruitment, training, appraisal, and development. Another subfield, _____ _____ , examines

313

how work environments and _____ styles influence worker motivation, satisfaction, and productivity. A third subfield,

_____ _____

psychology, focuses on the design of appliances, machines, and work environments.

Personnel Psychology (pp. 393–397)

Objective 2: Describe how personnel psychologists help organizations with employee selection, work placement, and performance appraisal.

1. Personnel psychologists have found that the corporate world is generally quite _____ (good/bad) at capitalizing on the strengths of workers. One remedy to this is instituting a _____ selection system which matches strengths to work.

2. (Close-Up) Satisfied and successful people devote less time to _____ _____ than to

   _____ _____ .

3. Interviewers tend to _____ (feel confident/lack confidence) in their ability to predict job performance from unstructured interviews. These impressions tend to be highly _____ (accurate/error-prone).

4. The best predictor of long-term job performance for most jobs is _____

   _____ _____ .

   Interviewers tend to _____ (over/under)estimate their interviewing skills and intuition—a phenomenon labeled the

   _____ _____ .

State four effects that fuel this phenomenon.

5. A more disciplined method of collecting information from job applicants is the

   _____ _____ , which asks the same questions of all applicants. This method enhances the _____ accuracy and _____ of the interview process.

6. Performance appraisal has several purposes, including helping organizations decide

   _____ ,

   how to appropriately _____

   _____ ,

   and how to better harness employees' _____ . Performance appraisal methods include _____ ,

   _____ _____ scales,

   and _____ _____ scales.

7. Some organizations practice _____- _____ feedback, in which employees not only rate themselves but are also rated by their supervisors and other colleagues.

Organizational Psychology: Motivating Achievement (pp. 398–402)

Objective 3: Discuss the nature and sources of achievement motivation.

1. Psychologists refer to the desire for significant accomplishments, mastering skills or ideas, and attaining a high standard as _____ _____ . People with high levels of this form of motivation prefer _____ (easy/moderately difficult/difficult) tasks, where success is _____ yet attributable to their _____ and _____ .

2. High-achieving children learn to associate achievement with _____ _____ . In addition to these _____ roots, achievement may also have _____ roots, as children learn to attribute their accomplishments to their own _____ and _____ .

Objective 4: Discuss how managers can create a motivated, productive, and satisfied workforce.

3. Positive moods at work contribute to worker

    _____ , _____ , and

    _____ . Researchers have also
    found a positive correlation between measures of
    organizational success and employee

    _____ , or the extent of workers'
    involvement, satisfaction, and enthusiasm.

4. The best managers help people to

    _____ ,

    match tasks to _____ , care how
    their people feel about their work, and

    _____ positive behaviors.

5. Higher worker achievement is motivated by a
    leader who sets _____ ,

    _____ goals.

6. Managers who are directive, set clear standards,
    organize work, and focus attention on specific
    goals are said to employ _____

    _____ . More democratic
    managers who aim to build teamwork and medi-
    ate conflicts in the work force employ

    _____ _____ .

7. Effective leaders tend to exude a self-confident

    _____ that is a mix of a

    _____ of some goal, an ability
    to _____ the goal clearly, and
    enough optimism to _____ oth-
    ers to follow. Leadership that inspires others to
    transcend their own self-interests for the sake of
    the group is called _____
    leadership.

8. The most effective style of leadership

    _____ (varies/does not vary)
    with the situation and/or the person.

9. Effective managers _____
    (rarely/often) exhibit a high degree of both task
    and social leadership. The _____
    effect occurs when people respond more positive-
    ly to managerial decisions on which they have
    voiced an opinion.

PROGRESS TEST

Multiple-Choice Questions

Circle your answers to the following questions and
check them with the answers on page 318. If your
answer is incorrect, read the explanation for why it is
incorrect and then consult the appropriate pages of
the text.

1. Which of the following is *not* an aspect of
    Murray's definition of achievement motivation?
    a. the desire to master skills
    b. the desire for control
    c. the desire to gain approval
    d. the desire to attain a high standard

2. The best predictor of on-the-job performance for
    all but less-skilled jobs is:
    a. age.
    b. general mental ability.
    c. motivation.
    d. stated intentions.

3. Psychologist Henry Murray asked research par-
    ticipants to invent stories about ambiguous pic-
    tures. The stories were then scored for content
    related to acts of heroism, pride, and other signs
    of:
    a. achievement motivation.
    b. leadership.
    c. optimum arousal.
    d. esteem needs.

4. In almost every industrialized nation, unem-
    ployed people report:
    a. better health.
    b. lower well-being.
    c. being bored.
    d. enjoying time to travel.

5. To increase employee productivity, industrial-
    organizational psychologists advise managers to:
    a. adopt a directive leadership style.
    b. adopt a democratic leadership style.
    c. instill competitiveness in each employee.
    d. deal with employees according to their indi-
    vidual motives.

6. Why do people with a high need for achievement prefer moderately difficult tasks?
   a. They are afraid of failing at more difficult tasks.
   b. They want to avoid the embarrassment of failing at easy tasks.
   c. Moderately difficult tasks present an attainable goal in which success is attributable to their own skill.
   d. They have high extrinsic motivation.

7. Which of the following was *not* identified as a contributing factor in the interviewer illusion?
   a. The fact that interviews reveal applicants' intentions but not necessarily their habitual behaviors.
   b. The tendency of interviewers to think that interview behavior only reflects applicants' enduring traits.
   c. The tendency of interviewers to more often follow the successful careers of applicants they hired rather than those who were not hired.
   d. The tendency of most interviewers to rely on unstructured rather than structured interviews.

8. Munson is conducting his annual appraisal of employees' performance. Which of the following is *not* a type of appraisal method?
   a. graphic rating
   b. behavior rating
   c. checklist
   d. unstructured interview

9. Because Brent believes that his employees are intrinsically motivated to work for reasons beyond money, Brent would be described as a(n) _____ manager.
   a. directive
   b. social-oriented
   c. task-oriented
   d. charismatic

10. Jack works for a company that requires employees to periodically rate their own performance and to be rated by their managers, other colleagues, and customers. This type of assessment is called:
    a. 360-degree feedback.
    b. multifactorial evaluation.
    c. analytical performance review.
    d. human resource management.

11. Which of the following individuals would be characterized as experiencing *flow*?
    a. Sheila, who, despite viewing her work as merely a job, performs her work conscientiously
    b. Larry, who sees his work as an artist as a calling
    c. Arnie, who views his present job as merely a stepping stone in his career
    d. Montel, who often becomes so immersed in his writing that he loses all sense of self and time

12. Darren, a sales clerk at a tire store, enjoys his job, not so much for the money as for its challenge and the opportunity to interact with a variety of people. The store manager asks you to recommend a strategy for increasing Darren's motivation. Which of the following is most likely to be effective?
    a. Create a competition among the salespeople so that whoever has the highest sales each week receives a bonus.
    b. Put Darren on a week-by-week employment contract, promising him continued employment only if his sales increase each week.
    c. Leave Darren alone unless his sales drop and then threaten to fire him if his performance doesn't improve.
    d. Involve Darren as much as possible in company decision making and use rewards to inform him of his successful performance.

13. For as long as she has been the plant manager, Juanita has welcomed input from employees and has delegated authority. Bill, in managing his department, takes a more authoritarian, iron-fisted approach. Juanita's style is one of _____ leadership, whereas Bill's is one of _____ leadership.
    a. task; social
    b. social; task
    c. directive; democratic
    d. democratic; participative

14. Dr. Iverson conducts research focusing on how management styles influence worker motivation. Dr. Iverson would most accurately be described as a(n):
    a. motivation psychologist.
    b. personnel psychologist.
    c. organizational psychologist.
    d. human factors psychologist.

Matching Items

Match each term with its definition or description.

Terms

_____ 1. transformational leadership
_____ 2. 360-degree feedback
_____ 3. personnel psychology
_____ 4. organizational psychology
_____ 5. task leadership
_____ 6. social leadership
_____ 7. flow
_____ 8. industrial-organizational (I/O) psychology

Definitions or Descriptions

a. state of focused consciousness
b. studies issues related to optimizing behavior in the workplace
c. applies psychological methods and principles to the selection and evaluation of workers
d. goal-oriented leadership that sets standards, organizes work, and focuses attention on goals
e. group-oriented leadership that builds teamwork, mediates conflict, and offers support
f. examines organizational influences on worker satisfaction and productivity
g. process that involves self-evaluation, along with evaluation from supervisors, colleagues, and customers
h. motivates others to commit themselves to the group's mission

KEY TERMS

Using your own words, write on a separate piece of paper a brief definition or explanation of each of the following terms.

1. flow

2. industrial-organizational psychology

3. personnel psychology

4. organizational psychology

5. structured interview

6. achievement motivation

7. task leadership

8. social leadership

ANSWERS
Module Review

Introduction

1. work; love

2. do not have; training job skills; enlarging capacities for understanding, thinking, and communicating in any work setting

3. report; calling

4. flow; consciousness; self; self-esteem, competence, well-being

5. farming; manufacturing; knowledge work

6. industrial-organizational; personnel psychology; organizational psychology; management; human factors

Personnel Psychology

1. bad; strengths-based

2. correcting deficiencies; accentuating strengths

3. feel confident; error-prone

4. general mental ability; over; interviewer illusion
   a. Interviews disclose the interviewee's good intentions, which are less revealing than their typical behaviors.
   b. Interviewers tend to follow the successful careers of people they hired and lose track of those they did not hire.
   c. Interviewers mistakenly presume that *how* interviewees present themselves reflects only their enduring traits.
   d. Interviewers' preconceptions and moods influence their perceptions of job applicants.

5. structured interview; predictive; reliability

6. whom to retain; reward and pay workers; strengths; checklists; graphic rating; behavior rating

7. 360-degree

Organizational Psychology: Motivating Achievement

1. achievement motivation; moderately difficult; attainable; skill; effort

2. positive emotions; emotional; cognitive; competence; effort

3. creativity; persistence; helpfulness; engagement

4. identify and measure their talents; talent; reinforce

5. specific; challenging

6. task leadership; social leadership

7. charisma; vision; communicate; inspire; transformational

8. varies

9. often; voice

Progress Test

Multiple-Choice Questions

1. **c.** is the answer.

2. **b.** is the answer.

3. **a.** is the answer.

4. **b.** is the answer.

5. **d.** is the answer. As different people are motivated by different things, in order to increase motivation and thus productivity, managers are advised to learn what motivates individual employees and to challenge and reward them accordingly.
a. & b. The most effective management style will depend on the situation.
c. This might be an effective strategy with some, but not all, employees.

6. **c.** is the answer.

7. **d.** is the answer. Although unstructured interviews *are* more prone to bias than structured interviews, the text does not suggest that they are used more often.

8. **d.** is the answer.
a., b., & c. These are all performance appraisal methods used by supervisors.

9. **b.** is the answer.
a. & c. Directive, or task-oriented, managers are likely to assume that worker motivation is low.
d. The most effective leaders are generally charismatic, which has nothing to do with whether they are directive or democratic leaders.

10. **a.** is the answer.

11. **d.** is the answer.

12. **d.** is the answer. Because Darren appears to resonate with the principle that people are intrinsically motivated to work for reasons beyond money, giving him feedback about his work and involving him in decision making are probably all he needs to be very satisfied with his situation.
a., b., & c. Creating competitions and using controlling, rather than informing, rewards may have the opposite effect and actually undermine Darren's motivation.

13. **b.** is the answer.
a. Bill's style is one of task leadership, whereas Juanita's is one of social leadership.
c. Juanita's style is democratic, whereas Bill's is directive.
d. Participative is another term used to refer to the social or group-oriented style of leadership.

14. **c.** is the answer.

Matching Items

1. h		5. d	
2. g		6. e	
3. c		7. a	
4. f		8. b	

Key Terms

1. **Flow** is a completely involved, focused state of consciousness on a task that optimally engages a person's skills, often accompanied by a diminished awareness of self and time.

2. **Industrial-organizational (I/O) psychology** is a subfield of psychology that studies and advises on issues related to optimizing behavior in workplaces.

3. **Personnel psychology** is a subfield of I/O psychology that applies psychological methods and principles to the selection and evaluation of workers.

4. **Organizational psychology** is a subfield of I/O psychology that explores how work environments and management styles affect worker motivation, satisfaction, and productivity.

5. A **structured interview** is one in which an interviewer asks the same job-relevant questions of all interviewees, who are then rated on established evaluation scales.

6. **Achievement motivation** is a desire for significant accomplishment; for mastery of things, people, or ideas; and for attaining a high standard.

7. **Task leadership** is goal-oriented leadership that sets standards, organizes work, and focuses attention on goals.

8. **Social leadership** is group-oriented leadership that builds teamwork, mediates conflict, and offers support.

FOCUS ON VOCABULARY AND LANGUAGE

When the researchers *beeped* people at random intervals . . . When researchers used pagers to randomly signal subjects (*they were beeped*) and report what they were doing and how they were feeling, those engaged in purposeful activities reported more positive emotions and flow than those who were idle and doing nothing much (*vegetating*).

Personnel Psychology

If there's a contest between *what our gut tells us* about someone and what test scores, work samples, and past performance tell us, we should distrust *our gut*. Subjective judgments (*gut feelings*) based on informal get-acquainted face-to-face meetings (*unstructured seat-of-the-pants interviews*) are very weak predictors of later behavior compared to what test scores, work samples, and previous performance reveal. Thus, we should not rely too much on subjective evaluations obtained (*gleaned*) from unstructured interviews (*we should distrust our gut*).

Organizational Psychology

In a *ring-toss game* they often stand at an *intermediate distance* from the *stake*, enabling some successes while providing a suitable *challenge*. When faced with the task of throwing a small rubber ring onto a vertical post (*stake*) some distance away (*ring-toss game*), those with a high need for achievement tend to stand neither too near nor too far away (*intermedi-*

ate distance). This makes the game somewhat difficult (*challenging*), yet ensures some correct responses which can then be attributed to skill and concentration. Those with low achievement motivation pick either a very close or a very far position from the stake.

Conclusive evidence of satisfaction's benefits is, some have said, the *holy grail* of I/O psychology. The reference here is to the medieval legend that the cup (*grail*) Jesus Christ drank from at the Last Supper, and which was later used to catch his blood when he was crucified, survived and may have been brought to England. The quest, or search, for this sacred cup (*Holy Grail*) symbolized spiritual regeneration and enlightenment. Finding definitive data that there are real benefits for the organization if employees are satisfied, engaged, and happy workers is one of *the major goals* (*the holy grail*) of I/O psychology.

Effective leaders of laboratory groups, work teams, and large corporations also tend to *exude a self-confident charisma*. Competent managers who lead groups of people in an effective and productive manner typically exhibit an ability to rely on their own capacities (*exude self-confidence*), project their vision of what needs to be done, and inspire others to follow them (*they have "charisma"*). This type of transformational leadership motivates others to want to belong to the group and to feel a strong commitment to its goal.

Emotions, Stress, and Health

Theories and Physiology of Emotion

29 MODULE

MODULE OVERVIEW

Emotions are responses of the whole individual, involving physiological arousal, expressive behaviors, and conscious experience. Module 29 first discusses several theoretical controversies concerning the relationship and sequence of the components of emotion. The focus is on whether the body's response to a stimulus causes the emotion that is felt and whether thinking is necessary to and must precede the experience of emotion. The module then describes the physiology of emotion.

NOTE: Answer guidelines for all Module 29 questions begin on page 329.

MODULE REVIEW

First, skim each section, noting headings and boldface items. After you have read the section, review each objective by answering the fill-in and essay-type questions that follow it. As you proceed, evaluate your performance by consulting the answers beginning on page 329. Do not continue with the next section until you understand each answer. If you need to, review or reread the section in the textbook before continuing.

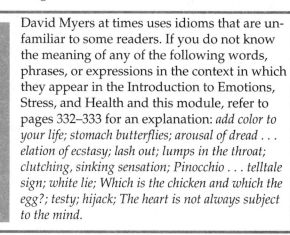

David Myers at times uses idioms that are unfamiliar to some readers. If you do not know the meaning of any of the following words, phrases, or expressions in the context in which they appear in the Introduction to Emotions, Stress, and Health and this module, refer to pages 332–333 for an explanation: *add color to your life; stomach butterflies; arousal of dread . . . elation of ecstasy; lash out; lumps in the throat; clutching, sinking sensation; Pinocchio . . . telltale sign; white lie; Which is the chicken and which the egg?; testy; hijack; The heart is not always subject to the mind.*

Theories of Emotion (pp. 407–409)

Objective 1: Identify the three components of emotion, and contrast the James-Lange, Cannon-Bard, and two-factor theories of emotion.

1. Emotions have three components: _____ _____ , _____ _____ , and _____ _____ .

2. According to the James-Lange theory, emotional states _____ (precede/follow) body arousal.

Describe two problems that Walter Cannon identified with the James-Lange theory.

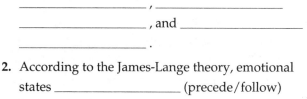

3. Cannon proposed that emotional stimuli in the environment are routed simultaneously to the _____ , which results in awareness of the emotion, and to the _____ nervous system, which causes the body's reaction. Because another scientist concurrently proposed similar ideas, this theory has come to be known as the _____-_____ theory.

4. The two-factor theory of emotion proposes that emotion has two components: _____ arousal and a _____ label. This theory was proposed by _____ and _____ .

Embodied Emotion (pp. 409–414)

Objective 2: Describe the physiological changes that occur during emotional arousal, and discuss the relationship between arousal and performance.

1. Describe the major physiological changes that each of the following undergoes during emotional arousal:

   a. heart: _____

   b. muscles: _____

   c. liver: _____

   d. breathing: _____

   e. digestion: _____

   f. pupils: _____

   g. blood: _____

   h. skin: _____

2. The responses of arousal are activated by the _____ nervous system. In response to its signal, the _____ glands release the hormones _____ and _____ , which increase heart rate, blood pressure, and blood sugar.

3. When the need for arousal has passed, the body is calmed through activation of the _____ nervous system.

Objective 3: Describe the relationship between physiological states and specific emotions.

4. The various emotions are associated with _____ (similar/different) forms of physiological arousal. In particular, the emotions of _____ , _____ , and _____ _____ are difficult to distinguish physiologically.

5. The emotions _____ and _____ are accompanied by differing _____ temperatures and _____ secretions.

6. The emotions _____ and _____ stimulate different facial muscles.

7. The brain circuits underlying different emotions _____ (are/are not) different. For example, seeing a fearful face elicits greater activity in the _____ than seeing a(n) _____ face. People who have generally negative personalities, and those who are prone to _____ , show more _____ _____ lobe activity.

8. When people experience positive moods, brain scans reveal more activity in the _____ _____ _____ .

9. Individuals with more active _____ (right/left) _____ lobes tend to be more cheerful than those in whom this pattern of brain activity is reversed.

Objective 4: Discuss the effectiveness of the polygraph in detecting lies.

10. (Thinking Critically) The technical name for the "lie detector" is the _____ .

(Thinking Critically) Explain how lie detectors supposedly indicate whether a person is lying.

11. (Thinking Critically) How well the lie detector works depends on whether a person exhibits _____ while lying.

12. (Thinking Critically) Those who criticize lie detectors feel that the tests are particularly likely to err in the case of the _____ (innocent/guilty), because different _____ all register as _____ .

13. (Thinking Critically) By and large, experts _____ (agree/do not agree) that lie detector tests are highly accurate.

14. (Thinking Critically) A test that assesses a suspect's knowledge of details of a crime that only the guilty person should know is the

_____ _____

_____ .

Objective 5: Explain the role of cognition in emotion, and discuss how neurological processes may enable us to experience some emotions prior to conscious thought.

15. The *spillover effect* refers to occasions when our _____ response to one event carries over into our response to another event.

16. Schachter and Singer found that physically aroused college men told that an injection would cause arousal _____ (did/did not) become emotional in response to an accomplice's aroused behavior. Physically aroused volunteers not expecting arousal _____ (did/did not) become emotional in response to an accomplice's behavior.

17. Arousal _____ emotion; cognition _____ emotion.

18. Robert Zajonc believes that the feeling of emotion _____ (can/cannot) precede our cognitive labeling of that emotion.

Cite two pieces of evidence that support Zajonc's position.

19. A pathway from the _____ via the _____ to the _____ enables us to experience emotion before _____ . For more complex emotions, sensory input is routed through the _____ for interpretation.

20. The researcher who disagrees with Zajonc and argues that most emotions require cognitive pro-

cessing is _____ . According to this view, emotions arise when we _____ an event as beneficial or harmful to our well-being.

21. Complex emotions are affected by our

_____ , _____ ,

and _____ .

Express some general conclusions that can be drawn about cognition and emotion.

PROGRESS TEST

Multiple-Choice Questions

Circle your answers to the following questions and check them with the answers beginning on page 330. If your answer is incorrect, read the explanation for why it is incorrect and then consult the appropriate pages of the text.

1. Which division of the nervous system is especially involved in bringing about emotional arousal?
   a. somatic nervous system
   b. peripheral nervous system
   c. sympathetic nervous system
   d. parasympathetic nervous system

2. Concerning emotions and their accompanying body responses, which of the following appears to be true?
   a. Each emotion has its own body response and underlying brain circuit.
   b. All emotions involve the same body response as a result of the same underlying brain circuit.
   c. Many emotions involve similar body responses but have different underlying brain circuits.
   d. All emotions have the same underlying brain circuits but different body responses.

3. The Cannon-Bard theory of emotion states that:
   a. emotions have two ingredients: physical arousal and a cognitive label.
   b. the conscious experience of an emotion occurs at the same time as the body's physical reaction.
   c. emotional experiences are based on an awareness of the body's responses to an emotion-arousing stimulus.
   d. emotional ups and downs tend to balance in the long run.

4. Which of the following was *not* raised as a criticism of the James-Lange theory of emotion?
   a. The body's responses are too similar to trigger the various emotions.
   b. Emotional reactions occur before the body's responses can take place.
   c. The cognitive activity of the cortex plays a role in the emotions we experience.
   d. People with spinal cord injuries at the neck typically experience less emotion.

5. (Thinking Critically) Current estimates are that the polygraph is inaccurate approximately _____ of the time.
   a. three-fourths
   b. one-half
   c. one-third
   d. one-fourth

6. In the Schachter-Singer experiment, which college men reported feeling an emotional change in the presence of the experimenter's highly emotional confederate?
   a. those receiving epinephrine and expecting to feel physical arousal
   b. those receiving a placebo and expecting to feel physical arousal
   c. those receiving epinephrine but not expecting to feel physical arousal
   d. those receiving a placebo and not expecting to feel physical arousal

7. Emotions consist of which of the following components?
   a. physiological reactions
   b. behavioral expressions
   c. conscious feelings
   d. all of these components

8. Law enforcement officials sometimes use a lie detector to assess a suspect's responses to details of the crime believed to be known only to the perpetrator. This is known as the:
   a. inductive approach.
   b. deductive approach.
   c. guilty knowledge test.
   d. screening examination.

9. In laboratory experiments, fear and joy:
   a. result in an increase in heart rate.
   b. stimulate different facial muscles.
   c. increase heart rate and stimulate different facial muscles.
   d. result in a decrease in heart rate.

10. Evidence that we prefer stimuli without being consciously aware of having seen the stimuli before has convinced Robert Zajonc that:
    a. the heart is always subject to the mind.
    b. emotional reactions involve deliberate rational thinking.
    c. cognition is not necessary for emotion.
    d. subliminal perception is a learned skill.

11. Which of the following most accurately describes emotional arousal?
    a. Emotions prepare the body to fight or flee.
    b. Emotions are voluntary reactions to emotion-arousing stimuli.
    c. Because all emotions have the same physiological basis, emotions are primarily psychological events.
    d. Emotional arousal is always accompanied by cognition.

12. Schachter's and Singer's two-factor theory emphasizes that emotion involves both:
    a. the sympathetic and parasympathetic divisions of the nervous system.
    b. verbal and nonverbal expression.
    c. physical arousal and a cognitive label.
    d. universal and culture-specific aspects.

13. Which theory of emotion emphasizes the simultaneous experience of body response and emotional feeling?
    a. James-Lange theory
    b. Cannon-Bard theory
    c. two-factor theory
    d. arousal theory

14. (Thinking Critically) The polygraph measures:
    a. lying.
    b. brain rhythms.
    c. chemical changes in the body.
    d. physiological indexes of arousal.

15. People who are exuberant and persistently cheerful show increased activity in the brain's _____ , which is rich in receptors for the neurotransmitter _____ .
    a. right frontal lobe; dopamine
    b. left frontal lobe; dopamine
    c. amygdala; serotonin
    d. thalamus; serotonin

16. Which theory of emotion implies that every emotion is associated with a unique physiological reaction?
    a. James-Lange theory
    b. Cannon-Bard theory
    c. two-factor theory
    d. arousal theory

17. Which of the following was *not* presented in the text as evidence that some emotional reactions involve no deliberate, rational thinking?
    a. Some of the neural pathways involved in emotion are separate from those involved in thinking and memory.
    b. Emotional reactions are sometimes quicker than our interpretations of a situation.
    c. People can develop an emotional preference for visual stimuli to which they have been unknowingly exposed.
    d. Arousal of the sympathetic nervous system will trigger an emotional reaction even when artificially induced by an injection of epinephrine.

18. In an emergency situation, emotional arousal will result in:
    a. increased rate of respiration.
    b. increased blood sugar.
    c. a slowing of digestion.
    d. all of these conditions.

19. Several studies have shown that physical arousal can intensify just about any emotion. For example, when people who have been physically aroused by exercise are insulted, they often misattribute their arousal to the insult. This finding illustrates the importance of:
    a. cognitive labels of arousal in the conscious experience of emotions.
    b. a minimum level of arousal in triggering emotional experiences.
    c. the simultaneous occurrence of physical arousal and cognitive labeling in emotional experience.
    d. all of these answers.

20. (Thinking Critically) Many psychologists are opposed to the use of lie detectors because:
    a. they represent an invasion of a person's privacy and could easily be used for unethical purposes.
    b. there are often serious discrepancies among the various indicators such as perspiration and heart rate.
    c. polygraphs cannot distinguish the various possible causes of arousal.
    d. they are accurate only about 50 percent of the time.

21. You are on your way to school to take a big exam. Suddenly, on noticing that your pulse is racing and that you are sweating, you feel nervous. With which theory of emotion is this experience most consistent?
    a. Cannon-Bard theory
    b. James-Lange theory
    c. two-factor theory
    d. Lazarus cognition theory

22. After Brenda scolded her brother for forgetting to pick her up from school, the physical arousal that had accompanied her anger diminished. Which division of her nervous system mediated her physical *relaxation*?
    a. sympathetic division
    b. parasympathetic division
    c. somatic division
    d. peripheral nervous system

23. Two years ago Maria was in an automobile accident in which her spinal cord was severed, leaving her paralyzed from her neck down. Today, Maria finds that she experiences emotions less intensely than she did before her accident. This tends to support which theory of emotion?
    a. James-Lange theory
    b. Cannon-Bard theory
    c. Zajonc theory
    d. Lazarus theory

24. After hitting a grand-slam home run, Mike noticed that his heart was pounding. Later that evening, after nearly having a collision while driving on the freeway, Mike again noticed that his heart was pounding. That he interpreted this reaction as fear, rather than as ecstasy, can best be explained by the:
    a. James-Lange theory.
    b. Cannon-Bard theory.
    c. two-factor theory.
    d. guilty knowledge theory.

25. As part of her job interview, Jan is asked to take a lie-detector test. Jan politely refuses and points out that:
    a. a guilty person can be found innocent by the polygraph.
    b. an innocent person can be found guilty.
    c. these tests err one-third of the time.
    d. all of these statements are true.

26. A student participating in an experiment concerned with physical responses that accompany emotions reports that her mouth is dry, her heart is racing, and she feels flushed. Can the emotion she is experiencing be determined?
    a. Yes, it is anger.
    b. Yes, it is fear.
    c. Yes, it is ecstasy.
    d. No, it cannot be determined from the information given.

27. Who will probably be angrier after getting a parking ticket?
    a. Bob, who has just awakened from a nap
    b. Veronica, who has just finished eating a big lunch
    c. Dan, who has just completed a tennis match
    d. Alicia, who has been reading a romantic novel

28. Nine-month-old Nicole's left frontal lobe is more active than her right frontal lobe. We can expect that, all other things being equal, Nicole:
    a. may suffer from mild depression for most of her life.
    b. may have trouble "turning off" upsetting feelings later in her life.
    c. may be more cheerful than those with more active right frontal lobes.
    d. may have trouble expressing feelings later in her life.

29. Julio was extremely angry when he came in for a routine EEG of his brain activity. When he later told this to the doctor, she was no longer concerned about the:
    a. increased electrical activity in Julio's right hemisphere.
    b. increased electrical activity in Julio's left hemisphere.
    c. decreased electrical activity in Julio's amygdala.
    d. increased electrical activity in Julio's amygdala.

Matching Items

Match each definition or description with the appropriate term.

Definitions or Descriptions

_____ 1. emotions consist of physical arousal *and* a cognitive label
_____ 2. an emotion-arousing stimulus triggers cognitive and body responses simultaneously
_____ 3. the division of the nervous system that calms the body following arousal
_____ 4. the division of the nervous system that activates arousal
_____ 5. a device that measures the physiological correlates of emotion
_____ 6. we are sad because we cry

Terms
a. two-factor theory
b. sympathetic nervous system
c. James-Lange theory
d. polygraph
e. Cannon-Bard theory
f. parasympathetic nervous system

True–False Items

Indicate whether each statement is true or false by placing *T* or *F* in the blank next to the item.

_____ **1.** The sympathetic nervous system triggers physiological arousal during an emotion.

_____ **2.** Physical arousal can intensify emotion.

_____ **3.** All emotions involve conscious thought.

_____ **4.** The two-factor theory states that emotions are given a cognitive label before physical arousal occurs.

Essay Question

Discuss biological influences on emotions. (Use the space below to list the points you want to make, and organize them. Then write the essay on a separate sheet of paper.)

KEY TERMS

Using your own words, on a separate piece of paper write a brief definition or explanation of each of the following terms.

1. emotion

2. James-Lange theory

3. Cannon-Bard theory

4. two-factor theory

5. polygraph

ANSWERS

Module Review

Theories of Emotion

1. physiological arousal; expressive behaviors; conscious experience

2. follow

Cannon argued that the body's responses were not sufficiently distinct to trigger the different emotions and, furthermore, that physiological changes occur too slowly to trigger sudden emotion.

3. cortex; sympathetic; Cannon-Bard

4. physiological; cognitive; Stanley Schachter; Jerome Singer

Embodied Emotion

1. **a.** Heart rate increases.

   b. Muscles become tense.

   c. The liver pours extra sugar into the bloodstream.

   d. Breathing rate increases.

   e. Digestion slows.

   f. Pupils dilate.

   g. Blood tends to clot more rapidly.

   h. Skin perspires.

2. sympathetic; adrenal; epinephrine (adrenaline); norepinephrine (noradrenaline)

3. parasympathetic

4. similar; fear; anger; sexual arousal

5. fear; rage; finger; hormone

6. fear; joy

7. are; amygdala; angry; depression; right frontal

8. left frontal lobe

9. left; frontal

10. polygraph

The polygraph measures several of the physiological responses that accompany emotion, such as changes in breathing, pulse rate, blood pressure, and perspiration. The assumption is that lying is stressful, so a person who is lying will become physiologically aroused.

11. anxiety

12. innocent; emotions; arousal

13. do not agree

14. guilty knowledge test

15. arousal

16. did not; did

17. fuels; channels

18. can

First, experiments on subliminal perception indicate that although stimuli are not consciously perceived, people later prefer these stimuli to others they have never been exposed to. Second, there is some separation of the neural pathways involved in emotion and cognition.

19. eye or ear; thalamus; amygdala; cognition; cortex
20. Lazarus; appraise
21. interpretations; expectations; memories

It seems that some emotional responses—especially simple likes, dislikes, and fears—involve no conscious thinking. Other emotions are greatly affected by our interpretations and expectations.

Progress Test

Multiple-Choice Questions

1. **c.** is the answer.
   a. The somatic division of the peripheral nervous system carries sensory and motor signals to and from the central nervous system.
   b. The peripheral nervous system is too general an answer, since it includes the sympathetic and parasympathetic divisions, as well as the somatic division.
   d. The parasympathetic nervous system restores the body to its unaroused state.

2. **c.** is the answer. Although many emotions have the same general body arousal, resulting from activation of the sympathetic nervous system, they appear to be associated with different brain circuits.

3. **b.** is the answer.
   a. This expresses the two-factor theory.
   c. This expresses the James-Lange theory.
   d. This theory was not discussed.

4. **d.** is the answer. The finding that people whose brains can't sense the body's responses experience considerably less emotion in fact supports the James-Lange theory, which claims that experienced emotion follows from body responses.
   a., b., & c. All these statements go counter to the theory's claim that experienced emotion is essentially just an awareness of the body's response.

5. **c.** is the answer.

6. **c.** is the answer. The men who received epinephrine without an explanation felt arousal and experienced this arousal as whatever emotion the experimental confederate in the room with them was displaying.
   a. Epinephrine recipients who expected arousal attributed their arousal to the drug and reported no emotional change in reaction to the confederate's behavior.
   b. & d. In addition to the two groups discussed in the text, the experiment involved placebo recipi-

ents; these subjects were not physically aroused and did not experience an emotional change.

7. **d.** is the answer. These are the three components of emotions identified in the text.

8. **c.** is the answer. If the suspect becomes physically aroused while answering questions about details only the perpetrator of the crime could know, it is presumed that he or she committed the crime.

9. **c.** is the answer. Both fear and joy increase heart rate but stimulate different facial muscles.

10. **c.** is the answer.
    a. & b. These answers imply that cognition *always* precedes emotion.
    d. Subliminal perception is unconscious and innate, but perception does not mean influence.

11. **a.** is the answer. Emotional arousal activates the sympathetic nervous system, causing the release of sugar into the blood for energy, pupil dilation, and the diverting of blood from the internal organs to the muscles, all of which help prepare the body to meet an emergency.
    b. Being autonomic responses, most emotions are *involuntary* reactions.
    c. All emotions do *not* have the same physiological basis.
    d. Some emotions occur without cognitive awareness.

12. **c.** is the answer. According to Schachter and Singer, the two factors in emotion are (1) physical arousal and (2) conscious interpretation of the arousal.

13. **b.** is the answer.
    a. The James-Lange theory states that the experience of an emotion is an awareness of one's physical response to an emotion-arousing stimulus.
    c. The two-factor theory states that to experience emotion one must be physically aroused and attribute the arousal to an emotional cause.
    d. There is no such theory; arousal is a general term referring to an increase in emotion.

14. **d.** is the answer. No device can literally measure lying. The polygraph measures breathing, pulse rate, blood pressure, and perspiration for changes indicative of physiological arousal.

15. **b.** is the answer.

16. **a.** is the answer. If, as the theory claims, emotions are triggered by physiological reactions, then each emotion must be associated with a unique physiological reaction.
    b. According to the Cannon-Bard theory, the same general body response accompanies many emotions.

c. The two-factor theory states that the cognitive interpretation of a general state of physical arousal determines different emotions.

d. There is no such theory; arousal is a general term referring to an increase in emotion.

17. **d.** is the answer. As the Schachter-Singer study indicated, physical arousal is not always accompanied by an emotional reaction. Only when arousal was attributed to an emotion was it experienced as such. The results of this experiment, therefore, support the viewpoint that conscious interpretation of arousal must precede emotion.

a., b., & c. Each of these was presented as a supporting argument in the text.

18. **d.** is the answer.

19. **a.** is the answer. That physical arousal can be misattributed demonstrates that it is the cognitive interpretation of arousal, rather than the intensity or specific nature of the body's arousal, that determines the conscious experience of emotions.

b. & c. The findings of these studies do not indicate that a minimum level of arousal is necessary for an emotional experience nor that applying a cognitive label must be simultaneous with the arousal.

20. **c.** is the answer. As heightened arousal may reflect feelings of anxiety or irritation rather than of guilt, the polygraph, which simply measures arousal, may easily err.

a. Misuse and invasion of privacy are valid issues, but Lykken primarily objects to the use of lie detectors because of their inaccuracy.

b. Although there are discrepancies among the various measures of arousal, this was not what Lykken objected to.

d. The lie detector errs about one-third of the time.

21. **b.** is the answer. The James-Lange theory proposes that the experienced emotion is an awareness of a prior body response: Your pulse races, and so you feel nervous.

a. According to the Cannon-Bard theory, your body's reaction would occur simultaneously with, rather than before, your experience of the emotion.

c. The two-factor theory states that emotion involves arousal plus the cognitive labeling of that arousal.

d. Lazarus suggested that even the most instantaneous emotions involve some cognitive appraisal.

22. **b.** is the answer. The parasympathetic division is involved in calming arousal.

a. The sympathetic division is active during states of arousal and hence would not be active in the situation described.

c. The somatic division is involved in transmitting sensory information and controlling skeletal muscles; it is not involved in arousing and calming the body.

d. This answer is too general, because the peripheral nervous system includes not only the parasympathetic division but also the sympathetic division and the somatic division.

23. **a.** is the answer. According to the James-Lange theory, Maria's emotions should be greatly diminished since her brain is unable to sense physical arousal.

b. Cannon and Bard would have expected Maria to experience emotions normally because they believed that the experiencing of emotions occurs separately from the body's responses.

c. & d. Zajonc and Lazarus were concerned with whether emotion was possible without cognition, not the intensity of emotion.

24. **c.** is the answer. According to the two-factor theory, it is cognitive interpretation of the same general physiological arousal that distinguishes the two emotions.

a. According to the James-Lange theory, if the same physical arousal occurred in the two instances, the same emotions should result.

b. The Cannon-Bard theory argues that conscious awareness of an emotion and body reaction occur at the same time.

d. Guilty knowledge is a test to determine a person's involvement in a crime.

25. **d.** is the answer.

26. **d.** is the answer.

27. **c.** is the answer. Because physical arousal tends to intensify emotions, Dan (who is likely to be physically aroused after playing tennis) will probably be angrier than Bob or Veronica, who are in more relaxed states.

28. **c.** is the answer.

a. Individuals with more active right frontal lobes tend to be less cheerful and are more likely to be depressed.

b. In fact, just the opposite is true: People with greater left frontal activity tend to be better able to turn off upsetting feelings.

d. The text does not suggest that greater left or right frontal activity influences a person's ability to express his or her feelings.

29. a. is the answer. As people experience negative emotions, such as anger, the right hemisphere becomes more electrically active.

c. & d. The EEG measures electrical activity on the surface of the cortex, not at the level of structures deep within the brain, such as the amygdala.

Matching Items

1.	a	4.	b
2.	e	5.	d
3.	f	6.	c

True–False Items

1.	T	3.	F
2.	T	4.	F

Essay Question

All emotions involve some degree of physiological arousal of the sympathetic nervous system. Although the arousal that occurs with different emotions is in most ways undifferentiated, there may be subtle differences in the brain pathways and hormones associated with different emotions. Other examples of the influence of biological factors on emotion are the universality of facial expressions of emotion (see Module 30).

Key Terms

1. **Emotion** is a response of the whole organism involving three components: (1) physical arousal, (2) expressive behaviors, and (3) conscious experience.

2. The **James-Lange theory** states that emotional experiences are based on an awareness of the body's responses to emotion-arousing stimuli: a stimulus triggers the body's responses that in turn trigger the experienced emotion.

3. The **Cannon-Bard theory** states that the subjective experience of an emotion occurs at the same time as the body's physical reaction.

4. The **two-factor theory** of emotion proposes that emotions have two ingredients: physical arousal and a cognitive label. Thus, physical arousal is a necessary, but not a sufficient, component of emotional change. For an emotion to be experienced, arousal must be attributed to an emotional cause.

5. The **polygraph**, or lie detector, is a device that measures several of the physiological responses accompanying emotion.

FOCUS ON VOCABULARY AND LANGUAGE

Theories of Emotion

No one needs to tell you that feelings add *color* to your life. . . . Without emotions we would experience a very dull and uninteresting existence; we would have no feelings of intense happiness or excitement nor would we experience depression and sadness. Thus, emotions add a variety of interesting qualities (*color*) to our lives.

Nervous about an important encounter, we feel *stomach butterflies*. Anxious over *speaking in public,* we *frequent the bathroom. Smoldering* over a conflict with a family member, we get a *splitting* headache. When you are apprehensive and fearful, you have visceral (*internal*) sensations that may feel as though small flying insects (*butterflies*) are fluttering around in your stomach (we feel *stomach butterflies*). Likewise, the prospect of talking to a group of people (*speaking in public*) may create an urgent need to use the toilet (*frequent the bathroom*), and being quietly angry (*smoldering*) can give rise to a painful (*splitting*) headache.

In an instant, the *arousal of dread* spilled into the *elation of ecstasy.* When Dr. Myers finally located his lost child (*toddler*) in the store, his apprehension and fear (*the arousal of dread*) transformed into a heightened and intense feeling of happiness (*the elation of ecstasy*) and he was overcome with positive emotions (*awash with joy*). This story illustrates the various components of emotion—physiological arousal, expressive behavior, and conscious experience.

Common sense tells most of us that we cry because we are sad, *lash out* because we are angry, *tremble* because we are afraid. The James-Lange theory states that physiological arousal precedes the experience of emotion. Thus, we cry first, then feel sad; we strike someone (*lash out*), then experience the anger; we shiver and shake (*tremble*), then feel fear. The Cannon-Bard theory proposes that physiological arousal and the experience of emotion occur at the same time but separately. One does not cause the other.

Virtually all the men Hohmann interviewed reported increases in *weeping, lumps in the throat,* and getting *choked up* when saying *good-bye, worshipping, or watching a touching movie.* For emotions expressed mostly in body areas above the neck, people with high spinal cord injuries reported more intense reactions, such as crying (*weeping*), becoming inarticulate (*lumps in the throat*), and being overcome emotionally (*choked up*) when parting company (*saying goodbye*), participating in religious ceremonies (*worshipping*), or viewing a sentimental film (*watching a touching movie*). On the other hand, emotional intensity for most other feelings decreased substantially, especially if they involved body areas below the neck. This provides partial support for the James-Lange theory (*breathed new life into it*), which proposes that physical reactions are important in the experience of emotions.

Embodied Emotion

If afraid, you may feel a *clutching, sinking sensation* in your chest and a *knot in your stomach.* Different emotions (anger, fear, sadness) feel and look different. Someone who is extremely afraid may have certain visceral (internal) reactions such as tightness in the upper abdomen (*a clutching, sinking sensation*) and a feeling of a lump (*knot*) in the stomach. An angry person may experience an increase in temperature and sweating (may feel *"hot under the collar"*). There is some evidence of different physiological or brain patterns corresponding to each emotion.

Given the physical indicators of emotion, might we, like *Pinocchio*, give some *telltale sign* whenever we lie? Pinocchio is a fictional character in a children's story whose nose grows longer every time he tells a lie. The polygraph, or lie detector, does not detect lies; rather, it measures a number of physiological reactions (heart rate, blood pressure, and perspiration) (*telltale signs*) which indicate a change in emotional state. Unlike Pinocchio, people display no reliable or valid indicators of whether they are lying or telling the truth.

(Box): . . . a white lie . . . When we tell a rather harmless or benign falsehood (*a white lie*), we are failing to reveal the truth about something relatively trivial. The polygraph can detect the physiological arousal that results from falsely answering control questions; this level of arousal is compared to reactions to the critical questions. Myers makes it clear that inferring guilt or innocence on the basis of these comparisons is fraught with problems. The innocent are more often labeled guilty than the guilty innocent; as Myers suggests, you should "never take a lie detector test if you are innocent."

Which is the chicken and which the egg? The old riddle asks, "Which came first, the chicken or the egg?" Myers asks which comes first, our cognitions or our emotions? The two-factor theory suggests that physiological arousal has to be cognitively interpreted in order for one to experience different emotions. Stanley Schachter's research showed that the same arousal (*stirred-up state*) can be experienced as two very different emotional states (e.g., euphoria or irritation) depending on how we interpret and label it. Thus, thinking comes before feeling.

. . . testy . . . This means to be ill-tempered or irritable. Those subjects who were physiologically aroused but did not know why were affected by (*"caught"*) the apparent emotional state of the person they were with. They made different attributions about their aroused (*stirred-up*) state ("I'm happy" or "I'm feeling testy") on the basis of whether the accomplice acted in a euphoric or irritated way.

This makes it easier for our feelings to *hijack* our thinking than for our thinking to *rule* our feelings . . . Some neural pathways go from the ear or eye via the thalamus to the amygdala, an emotional control center, and detour around (*bypass*) the cortical areas involved in thinking. This makes it possible to have extremely rapid (*greased-lightning*) emotional responses before cognitive factors become involved. Thus, our feelings can take over (*hijack*) our thinking, instead of our thinking controlling (*ruling*) our emotions.

The *heart* is not always subject to the *mind.* Robert Zajonc proposed that some emotional states are not preceded by cognitions. The emotions (*heart*) are not determined by our thoughts (*mind*). We can have *some* feelings, at least, without thinking first.

Expressing and Experiencing Emotion

30 MODULE

MODULE OVERVIEW

Module 30 discusses the various ways in which emotions are expressed, noting that nonverbal expressions are often important signs of emotion. The module concludes with a discussion of the experience of emotion, particularly as it relates to the emotions of anger and happiness.

NOTE: Answer guidelines for all Module 30 questions begin on page 341.

MODULE REVIEW

First, skim each section, noting headings and boldface items. After you have read the section, review each objective by answering the fill-in and essay-type questions that follow it. As you proceed, evaluate your performance by consulting the answers on page 341. Do not continue with the next section until you understand each answer. If you need to, review or reread the section in the textbook before continuing.

> David Myers at times uses idioms that are unfamiliar to some readers. If you do not know the meaning of any of the following expressions in the context in which they appear in the text, refer to pages 343–344 for an explanation: *good enough at reading; Fidgeting; sneer; Fake a big grin; hostile outbursts; drain off some of their tension; rush of euphoria; lob a bombshell; Off your duffs, couch potatoes.*

Expressed Emotion (pp. 417–422)

Objective 1: Describe our ability to perceive and communicate emotions nonverbally, and discuss gender differences in this capacity.

1. Most people are especially good at interpreting nonverbal _____ . We read fear and _____ mostly from the _____ , and happiness from the _____ .

2. Introverts are _____ (better/worse) at reading others' emotions, whereas extraverts are themselves _____ (easier/harder) to read.

3. Experience can _____ people to particular emotions, as revealed by the fact that physically abused children are quicker than others at perceiving _____ .

4. The absence of nonverbal cues to emotion is one reason that communications sent as _____ are easy to misread.

5. Women are generally _____ (better/worse) than men at detecting nonverbal signs of emotion and in spotting _____ . Women possess greater emotional _____ than men, as revealed by the tendency of men to describe their emotions in _____ terms. This gender difference may contribute to women's greater emotional _____ .

6. Although women are _____ (more/less) likely than men to describe themselves as empathic, physiological measures reveal a much _____ (smaller/larger) gender difference. Women are _____ (more/less) likely than men to express empathy.

335

Objective 2: Discuss the culture-specific and culturally universal aspects of emotional expression.

7. Gestures have _____ (the same/different) meanings in different cultures.

8. Studies of adults indicate that in different cultures facial expressions have _____ (the same/different) meanings. Studies of children indicate that the meaning of their facial expressions _____ (varies/does not vary) across cultures. The emotional facial expressions of blind children _____ (are/are not) the same as those of sighted children.

9. According to _____ , human emotional expressions evolved because they helped our ancestors communicate before language developed. It has also been adaptive for us to _____ faces in particular _____ .

10. In cultures that encourage _____ , emotional expressions are often intense and prolonged. Cultures such as that of Japan _____ (also show intense emotion/hide their emotions). This points to the importance of realizing that emotions are not only biological and psychological but also _____-_____ .

Objective 3: Describe the effects of facial expressions on emotional experience.

11. Darwin believed that when an emotion is accompanied by an outward facial expression, the emotion is _____ (intensified/diminished).

12. In one study, students who were induced to smile _____ (found/did not find) cartoons more humorous.

13. The _____ _____ effect occurs when expressions amplify our emotions by activating muscles associated with specific states.

14. Studies have found that imitating another person's facial expressions _____ (leads/does not lead) to greater empathy with that person's feelings.

15. Similarly, moving our body as we would when experiencing a particular emotion causes us to feel that emotion. This is the _____ _____ effect.

Experienced Emotion (pp. 423–432)

Objective 4: Name several basic emotions.

1. Izard believes that there are _____ basic emotions, most of which _____ (are/are not) present in infancy. Although others claim that emotions such as pride and love should be added to the list, Izard contends that they are _____ of the basic emotions.

Objective 5: Discuss anger in terms of causes, consequences, and ways of handling it.

2. In studying why we become angry, Averill has found that most people become angry several times per week and especially when another person's act seemed _____ , _____ , and _____ .

3. The belief that expressing pent-up emotion is adaptive is most commonly found in cultures that emphasize _____ . This is the _____ hypothesis. In cultures that emphasize _____ , such as those of _____ or _____ , expressions of anger are less common.

4. Psychologists have found that when anger has been provoked, retaliation may have a calming effect under certain circumstances. List the circumstances.

   a. _____
   b. _____
   c. _____

Identify some potential problems with expressing anger.

5. List two suggestions offered by experts for handling anger.

   a. _____

   b. _____

6. Researchers have found that students who mentally rehearsed the times they _____ someone who had hurt them had lower bodily arousal than when they thought of times when they did not.

Objective 6: Identify some potential causes and consequences of happiness, and describe two psychological phenomena that help explain the relatively short duration of emotions.

7. Happy people tend to perceive the world as _____ and live _____ and more energized and satisfied lives.

8. Happy people are also _____ (more/less) willing to help others. This is called the _____-_____ , _____-_____ phenomenon.

9. An individual's self-perceived happiness or satisfaction with life is called his or her _____ _____ .

10. Positive emotions _____ (rise/fall) early in the day and _____ (rise/fall) during the later hours. The gloom of stressful events usually _____ (is gone by/continues into) the next day.

11. After experiencing tragedy or dramatically positive events, people generally _____ (regain/do not regain) their previous degree of happiness.

12. Most people tend to _____ (underestimate/overestimate) the duration of emotions and _____ (underestimate/overestimate) their capacity to adapt.

13. Researchers have found that levels of happiness _____ (do/do not) mirror differences in standards of living.

14. During the last four decades, spendable income in the United States has more than doubled; personal happiness has _____ (increased/decreased/remained almost unchanged).

15. Research has demonstrated that people generally experience a higher quality of life and greater well-being when they strive for _____ _____ _____ than when they strive for _____ .

16. The idea that happiness is relative to one's recent experience is stated by the _____-_____ phenomenon.

Explain how this principle accounts for the fact that, for some people, material desires can never be satisfied.

17. The principle that one feels worse off than others is known as _____ _____ . This helps to explain why the middle- and upper-income people who compare themselves with the relatively poor are _____ (slightly more/slightly less/equally) satisfied with life.

18. List six factors that have been shown to be positively correlated with feelings of happiness.

   _____
   _____
   _____
   _____
   _____
   _____

19. List five factors that are evidently unrelated to happiness.

_____

_____

_____

_____

20. Research studies of identical and fraternal twins have led to the estimate that _____ percent of the variation in people's happiness ratings is heritable.

21. (Close-Up) State several research-based suggestions for increasing your satisfaction with life.

PROGRESS TEST

Multiple-Choice Questions

Circle your answers to the following questions and check them with the answers beginning on page 341. If your answer is incorrect, read the explanation for why it is incorrect and then consult the appropriate pages of the text.

1. Which of the following is true regarding happiness?
   a. People with more education tend to be happier.
   b. Beautiful people tend to be happier than plain people.
   c. Women tend to be happier than men.
   d. People who are socially outgoing or who exercise regularly tend to be happier.

2. Catharsis will be most effective in reducing anger toward another person if:
   a. you wait until you are no longer angry before confronting the person.
   b. the target of your anger is someone you feel has power over you.
   c. your anger is directed specifically toward the person who angered you.
   d. the other person is able to retaliate by also expressing anger.

3. Research on nonverbal communication has revealed that:
   a. it is easy to hide your emotions by controlling your facial expressions.
   b. facial expressions tend to be the same the world over, while gestures vary from culture to culture.
   c. most authentic expressions last between 7 and 10 seconds.
   d. most gestures have universal meanings; facial expressions vary from culture to culture.

4. Research suggests that people generally experience the greatest well-being when they strive for:
   a. wealth.
   b. modest income increases from year to year.
   c. slightly higher status than their friends, neighbors, and co-workers.
   d. intimacy and personal growth.

5. Research indicates that a person is most likely to be helpful to others if he or she:
   a. is feeling guilty about something.
   b. is happy.
   c. recently received help from another person.
   d. recently offered help to another person.

6. With regard to emotions, Darwin believed that:
   a. the expression of emotions helped our ancestors to survive.
   b. all humans express basic emotions using similar facial expressions.
   c. human facial expressions of emotion retain elements of animals' emotional displays.
   d. all of these statements are true.

7. A graph depicting the course of positive emotions over the hours of the day since waking would:
   a. start low and rise steadily until bedtime.
   b. start high and decrease steadily until bedtime.
   c. remain at a stable, moderate level throughout the day.
   d. rise over the early hours and dissipate during the day's last several hours.

8. When students studied others who were worse off than themselves, they felt greater satisfaction with their own lives. This is an example of the principle of:
   a. relative deprivation.
   b. adaptation level.
   c. behavioral contrast.
   d. opponent processes.

9. Izard believes that there are _____ basic emotions.
   a. 3   c. 7
   b. 5   d. 10

10. Which of the following is true regarding gestures and facial expressions?
    a. Gestures are universal; facial expressions, culture-specific.
    b. Facial expressions are universal; gestures, culture-specific.
    c. Both gestures and facial expressions are universal.
    d. Both gestures and facial expressions are culture-specific.

11. Concerning the catharsis hypothesis, which of the following is true?
    a. Expressing anger can be temporarily calming if it does not leave one feeling guilty or anxious.
    b. The arousal that accompanies unexpressed anger never dissipates.
    c. Expressing one's anger always calms one down.
    d. Psychologists agree that under no circumstances is catharsis beneficial.

12. In studying what makes people angry, James Averill found that most people become angry:
    a. once a day.
    b. once a week.
    c. several times a week.
    d. several times a month.

13. Which of these factors have researchers *not* found to correlate with happiness?
    a. a satisfying marriage or close friendship
    b. high self-esteem
    c. religious faith
    d. education

14. In cultures that emphasize social interdependence:
    a. emotional displays are typically intense.
    b. emotional displays are typically prolonged.
    c. negative emotions are rarely displayed.
    d. all of these answers are true.

15. When Professor Simon acquired a spacious new office, he was overjoyed. Six months later, however, he was taking the office for granted. His behavior illustrates the:
    a. relative deprivation principle.
    b. adaptation-level phenomenon.

c. two-factor theory.
    d. optimum arousal principle.

16. The candidate stepped before the hostile audience, panic written all over his face. It is likely that the candidate's facial expression caused him to experience:
    a. a lessening of his fear.
    b. an intensification of his fear.
    c. a surge of digestive enzymes in his body.
    d. increased body temperature.

17. Jane was so mad at her brother that she exploded at him when he entered her room. That she felt less angry afterward is best explained by the principle of:
    a. adaptation level.
    b. physiological arousal.
    c. relative deprivation.
    d. catharsis.

18. Children in New York, Nigeria, and New Zealand smile when they are happy and frown when they are sad. This suggests that:
    a. not until adulthood do emotional expressions vary by culture.
    b. some emotional expressions are learned at a very early age.
    c. all cultures also express emotions in the same intensity.
    d. facial expressions of emotion are universal and biologically determined.

19. Who is the *least* likely to display negative emotions openly?
    a. Paul, a game warden in Australia
    b. Niles, a stockbroker in Belgium
    c. Deborah, a physicist in Toronto
    d. Yoko, a dentist in Japan

20. As elderly Mr. Hooper crosses the busy intersection, he stumbles and drops the packages he is carrying. Which passerby is most likely to help Mr. Hooper?
    a. Drew, who has been laid off from work for three months
    b. Leon, who is on his way to work
    c. Bonnie, who graduated from college the day before
    d. Nancy, whose father recently passed away

21. Expressing anger can be adaptive when you:
   a. retaliate immediately.
   b. have mentally rehearsed all the reasons for your anger.
   c. count to 10, then blow off steam.
   d. first wait until the anger subsides, then deal with the situation in a civil manner.

22. Cindy was happy with her promotion until she found out that Janice, who has the same amount of experience, receives a higher salary. Cindy's feelings are *best* explained according to the:
   a. adaptation-level phenomenon.
   b. two-factor theory.
   c. catharsis hypothesis.
   d. principle of relative deprivation.

23. I am an emotionally literate person who is very accurate at reading others' nonverbal behavior, detecting lies, and describing my feelings. Who am I?
   a. an introvert
   b. an extravert
   c. a woman
   d. a man

Matching Items

Match each definition or description with the appropriate term.

Definitions or Descriptions

_____ **1.** the tendency to react to changes on the basis of recent experience

_____ **2.** an individual's self-perceived happiness

_____ **3.** emotional release

_____ **4.** the tendency to evaluate our situation negatively against that of other people

_____ **5.** the tendency of people to be helpful when they are in a good mood

Terms
   a. adaptation-level phenomenon
   b. catharsis
   c. relative deprivation principle
   d. feel-good, do-good phenomenon
   e. subjective well-being

True–False Items

Indicate whether each statement is true or false by placing *T* or *F* in the blank next to the item.

_____ **1.** Men are generally better than women at detecting nonverbal emotional expression.

_____ **2.** When one imitates an emotional facial expression, the body may experience physiological changes characteristic of that emotion.

_____ **3.** Wealthy people tend to be much happier than middle-income people.

Essay Question

Discuss cultural influences on emotions. (Use the space below to list the points you want to make, and organize them. Then write the essay on a separate sheet of paper.)

KEY TERMS

Using your own words, on a separate piece of paper write a brief definition or explanation of each of the following terms.

1. catharsis
2. feel-good, do-good phenomenon
3. subjective well-being
4. adaptation-level phenomenon
5. relative deprivation

ANSWERS

Module Review

Expressed Emotion

1. threats; anger; eyes; mouth
2. better; easier
3. sensitize; anger
4. e-mail
5. better; lies; literacy; simpler; responsiveness
6. more; smaller; more
7. different
8. the same; does not vary; are
9. Darwin; interpret; contexts
10. individuality; hide their emotions; social-cultural
11. intensified
12. found
13. facial feedback
14. leads
15. behavior feedback

Experienced Emotion

1. 10; are; combinations
2. willful; unjustified; avoidable
3. individuality; catharsis; interdependence; Tahiti; Japan
4. **a.** Retaliation must be directed against the person who provoked the anger.
   b. Retaliation must be justifiable.
   c. The target of the retaliation must not be someone who is intimidating.

One problem with expressing anger is that it breeds more anger, in part because it may trigger retaliation. Expressing anger can also magnify anger and reinforce its occurrence.

5. **a.** Wait to calm down.

b. Deal with anger in a way that involves neither chronic anger nor passive sulking.

6. forgave
7. safer; healthier
8. more; feel-good, do-good
9. subjective well-being
10. rise; fall; is gone by
11. regain
12. overestimate; underestimate
13. do not
14. remained almost unchanged
15. intimacy, personal growth, and contribution to the community; wealth
16. adaptation-level

If we acquire new possessions, we feel an initial surge of pleasure. But we then adapt to having these new possessions, come to see them as normal, and require other things to give us another surge of happiness.

17. relative deprivation; slightly more
18. high self-esteem; satisfying marriage or close friendships; meaningful religious faith; optimistic outgoing personality; good sleeping habits and regular exercise; having work and leisure that engage our skills
19. age; gender; education; parenthood; physical attractiveness
20. 50
21. Realize that happiness doesn't come from financial success. Take control of your time. Act happy. Seek work and leisure that engage your skills. Engage in regular aerobic exercise. Get plenty of sleep. Give priority to close relationships. Focus beyond self. Be grateful. Nurture your spiritual self.

Progress Test

Multiple-Choice Questions

1. **d.** is the answer. Education level, parenthood, gender, and physical attractiveness seem unrelated to happiness.

2. **c.** is the answer.
   a. This would not be an example of catharsis, since catharsis involves releasing, rather than suppressing, aggressive energy.
   b. Expressions of anger in such a situation tend to cause the person anxiety and thus tend not to be effective.
   d. One danger of expressing anger is that it will lead to retaliation and an escalation of anger.

3. **b.** is the answer.
   a. The opposite is true; relevant facial muscles are hard to control voluntarily.
   c. Authentic facial expressions tend to fade within 4 or 5 seconds.
   d. Facial expressions are generally universal; many gestures vary from culture to culture.

4. **d.** is the answer.

5. **b.** is the answer.
   a., c., & d. Research studies have not found these factors to be related to altruistic behavior.

6. **d.** is the answer.

7. **d.** is the answer.

8. **a.** is the answer. The principle of relative deprivation states that happiness is relative to others' attainments. This helps explain why those who are relatively well off tend to be slightly more satisfied than the relatively poor, with whom the better-off can compare themselves.
   b. Adaptation level is the tendency for our judgments to be relative to our prior experience.
   c. This phenomenon has nothing to do with the interpretation of emotion.
   d. Opponent processes are not discussed in the text in relation to emotion.

9. **d.** is the answer.

10. **b.** is the answer. Whereas the meanings of gestures vary from culture to culture, facial expressions seem to have the same meanings around the world.

11. **a.** is the answer.
    b. The opposite is true. Any emotional arousal will simmer down if you wait long enough.
    c. Catharsis often magnifies anger, escalates arguments, and leads to retaliation.
    d. When counterattack is justified and can be directed at the offender, catharsis may be helpful.

12. **c.** is the answer.

13. **d.** is the answer.

14. **c.** is the answer.
    a. & b. These are true of cultures that emphasize individuality rather than interdependence.

15. **b.** is the answer. Professor Simon's judgment of his office is affected by his recent experience: When that experience was of a smaller office, his new office seemed terrific; now, however, it is commonplace.
    a. Relative deprivation is the sense that one is worse off than those with whom one compares oneself.
    c. The two-factor theory has to do with the cognitive labeling of physical arousal.

d. This is the principle that there is an inverse relationship between the difficulty of a task and the optimum level of arousal.

16. **b.** is the answer. Expressions may amplify the associated emotions.
    a. Laboratory studies have shown that facial expressions *intensify* emotions.
    c. Arousal of the sympathetic nervous system, such as occurs when one is afraid, slows digestive function.
    d. Increased body temperature accompanies anger but not fear.

17. **d.** is the answer. In keeping with the catharsis hypothesis, Jane feels less angry after releasing her aggression.
    a. Adaptation level is our tendency to judge things relative to our experiences.
    b. This is not a specific theory.
    c. Relative deprivation is the sense that one is worse off relative to those with whom one compares oneself.

18. **d.** is the answer.
    a. Emotional expressions are universal throughout life.
    b. Even if it is true that emotional expressions are acquired at an early age, this would not necessarily account for the common facial expressions of children from around the world. If anything, the different cultural experiences of the children might lead them to express their feelings in very *different* ways.
    c. Different cultures display different amounts of emotion.

19. **d.** is the answer. In Japan and other Asian cultures that emphasize human connections and interdependence, negative emotional displays are rare and typically brief.
    a., b., & c. In cultures that encourage individuality, as in Western Europe, Australia, and North America, emotional displays often are intense and prolonged.

20. **c.** is the answer. People who are in a good mood are more likely to help others. Bonnie, who is probably pleased with herself following her graduation from college, is likely to be in a better mood than Drew, Leon, or Nancy.

21. **d.** is the answer.
    a. Venting anger immediately may lead you to say things you later regret and/or may lead to retaliation by the other person.
    b. Going over the reasons for your anger merely prolongs the emotion.

c. Counting to 10 may give you a chance to calm down, but "blowing off steam" may rekindle your anger.

22. **d.** is the answer. Cindy is unhappy with her promotion because she feels deprived relative to Janice.

   a. The adaptation-level phenomenon would predict that Cindy's raise would cause an increase in her happiness, since her most recent experience was to earn a lower salary.

   b. The two-factor theory has to do with the cognitive labeling of physical arousal.

   c. The catharsis hypothesis maintains that venting one's anger may relieve aggressive urges.

23. **c.** is the answer.

Matching Items

1. a   4. c
2. e   5. d
3. b

True–False Items

1. F
2. T
3. F

Essay Question

Unlike facial expressions of emotion, the meaning of many gestures is culturally determined. Culture also influences how people express their feelings. In cultures that encourage individuality, for example, emotional displays often are intense and prolonged. In cultures that emphasize human interdependence, negative emotions that might disrupt group harmony are rarely expressed, while displays of "other-sensitive" emotions such as sympathy, respect, and shame are more common than in the West.

Key Terms

1. **Catharsis** is emotional release; according to the catharsis hypothesis, by expressing our anger, we can reduce it.

2. The **feel-good, do-good phenomenon** is the tendency of people to be helpful when they are in a good mood.

3. **Subjective well-being** refers to a person's sense of satisfaction with his or her life.

4. The **adaptation-level phenomenon** refers to our tendency to judge things relative to a neutral level defined by our prior experience.

5. The principle of **relative deprivation** is the perception that we are worse off relative to those with whom we compare ourselves.

FOCUS ON VOCABULARY AND LANGUAGE

Expressed Emotion

Most of us are good enough at *reading* nonverbal cues to decipher the emotions in an old *silent film*. We communicate our feelings with words (verbally) and through body language (nonverbally). Without hearing a single word, as in a movie with no soundtrack (*silent film*), we can discern much about someone's emotional state by observing (*reading*) his or her bodily actions and facial expressions. As Myers notes, when we look at a large group of faces, a single angry one will be extremely noticeable (*it will "pop out"*) and will be detected more quickly than a single happy one.

Fidgeting, for example, may reveal *anxiety* or *boredom*. Many popular books and articles suggest what to look for in body language during interviews, business meetings, and so on. However, specific interpretations of gestures or posture cannot be made accurately or reliably. For example, restlessness, accompanied by frequent small movements (*fidgeting*), may be indicative of either disinterest (*boredom*) or extreme nervousness (*anxiety*).

A *sneer*, for example, retains elements of an animal's baring its teeth in *a snarl*. Darwin believed that all humans have inherited the ability to express emotions through very similar facial expressions. Thus, a person's scornful or contemptuous grimace (*sneer*) has many aspects of the fierce growl with teeth showing (*a snarl*) typical of dogs and other animals. Emotional expressions are one form of social communication.

Fake a big grin. Now scowl. Can you feel the smile therapy difference? Clearly, our moods affect how we look, but Myers is inviting you to test the idea that your facial expression can affect your mood. Make a large, false smile (*fake a grin*). Next, wrinkle or furrow your brow, frown and look sullen (*scowl*). Subjects in numerous experiments felt different emotions under these conditions. Smile and inside you feel happy, scowl and you may see the world as more miserable than it is.

Experienced Emotion

Popular books and articles on aggression at times advise that even releasing angry feelings as *hostile outbursts* can be better than internalizing them. The idea is that expressing your anger openly (*hostile outbursts or "venting your anger"*) provides some form of emotional release (*catharsis*) and that this is better than not expressing your feelings and holding your anger inside (*internalizing it*). Under certain circumstances, this may provide temporary relief, but the evidence also suggests that expressing anger can increase or magnify (*breed more*) anger.

If stressed managers find they can *drain off* some of their tension by *berating* an employee . . . Myers notes that if a supervisor severely and angrily scolds (*berates*) a worker this can increase or amplify the supervisor's hostile emotions, but, in addition, it may also be reinforcing because it releases some of the frustration (*it drains off some of the tension*). Consequently, the next time these feelings arise, the more likely it is that the hostile behavior will be repeated (*he or she will be more likely to explode*).

Once their *rush of euphoria* wears off, state lottery winners typically find their overall happiness unchanged. . . . We probably all dream of winning large amounts of money through gambling (*state lottery winners*) and then living happily ever after. However, once the initial feelings of excitement

(*rush of euphoria*) diminish, most winners discover that they are no happier. Myers puts it succinctly: "Wealth is like health. Its utter absence breeds misery, yet having it is no guarantee of happiness."

Such findings *lob a bombshell* at modern materialism. . . . The contemporary tendency to accumulate wealth and possessions (*modern materialism*) in industrialized and affluent countries has not resulted in greater happiness. This finding challenges and destroys (*lobs a bombshell at*) the myth that riches (*affluence*) bring happiness and social well-being.

(*Close-Up*): *Off your duffs, couch potatoes.* This Close-Up, How to Be Happier, lists a number of research-based suggestions for elevating our moods and for creating more contentment and fulfillment with life. One recommendation is to become more physically active (*join the "movement" movement*). A vast amount (*an avalanche*) of research shows very clearly the benefits of regular aerobic exercise in terms of better overall health, higher levels of energy, and lower levels of anxiety and depression. Myers advises sedentary people (*couch potatoes*) to get out of the sitting position (*get off your duffs*) and start exercising regularly.

Stress and Illness

31

M O D U L E

MODULE OVERVIEW

Behavioral factors play a major role in maintaining health and causing illness. Module 31 explores the effort to understand this role more fully through such questions as: How do our perceptions of a situation determine the stress we feel? How do our emotions and personality influence our risk of disease? Module 31 describes how stress affects our body, psychological factors that determine how it affects us, and how stress contributes to heart disease, infectious diseases, and cancer.

NOTE: Answer guidelines for all Module 31 questions begin on page 350.

MODULE REVIEW

First, skim each section, noting headings and boldface items. After you have read the section, review each objective by answering the fill-in and essay-type questions that follow it. As you proceed, evaluate your performance by consulting the answers on page 350. Do not continue with the next section until you understand each answer. If you need to, review or reread the section in the textbook before continuing.

> David Myers at times uses idioms that are unfamiliar to some readers. If you do not know the meaning of any of the following expressions in the context in which they appear in the text, refer to pages 352–353 for an explanation: *tense muscles, clenched teeth, . . . churning stomach; slippery concept; heart rate zooms; uprooting; a cluster of crises; Daily Hassles; mellow and laid-back; after the honeymoon period; headless horseman; hyping.*

Stress and Stressors (pp. 435–438)

Objective 1: Discuss the role of appraisal in the way we respond to stressful events, and describe the biology of the "fight-or-flight" response.

1. Out of every 10 people, _____ (how many?) report experiencing frequent stress.

2. Stress is not merely a _____ or a _____ . Rather, it is the _____ by which we perceive and respond to environmental threats and challenges.

3. This definition highlights the fact that stressors can have _____ (only negative/ both positive and negative) effects, depending on how they are perceived.

4. In the 1920s, physiologist Walter _____ began studying the effect of stress on the body. He discovered that the hormones _____ and _____ are released into the bloodstream in response to stress. This and other bodily changes due to stress are mediated by the _____ nervous system, thus preparing the body for _____ _____ _____ .

5. Another common response to stress among women has been called "_____ _____ _____ ," which refers to the increased tendency to _____ .

Objective 2: Describe the physical characteristics and phases of the general adaptation syndrome.

6. In studying animals' reactions to stressors, Hans Selye referred to the bodily response to stress as the _____ _____

   _____ .

7. During the first phase of the GAS—the _____ reaction—the person is in a state of shock due to the sudden arousal of the _____ nervous system.

8. This is followed by the stage of _____ , in which the body's resources are mobilized to cope with the stressor.

9. If stress continues, the person enters the stage of _____ . During this stage, a person is _____ (more/less) vulnerable to disease.

Objective 3: Discuss the health consequences of catastrophes, significant life changes, and daily hassles.

10. In the wake of catastrophic events, such as floods, hurricanes, and fires, there often is an increase in the rates of _____

    _____ .

11. Research studies have found that people who have recently been widowed, fired, or divorced are _____ (more/no more) vulnerable to illness than other people.

12. For most people, the most significant sources of stress are _____

    _____ . The stresses that accompany poverty and unemployment, for example, often compounded by _____ ,
    may account for the higher rates of _____ among residents of urban ghettos.

Stress and the Heart (pp. 438–439)

Objective 4: Discuss the role of stress in causing coronary heart disease, and contrast Type A and Type B personalities.

1. The leading cause of death in North America is

   _____ _____

   _____ . List several risk factors for

developing this condition: _____

_____

_____ .

2. Friedman and Rosenman discovered that tax accountants experience an increase in blood _____ level and blood- _____ speed during tax season. This showed there was a link between coronary warning indicators and _____ .

Friedman and Rosenman, in a subsequent study, grouped people into Type A and Type B personalities. Characterize these types, and indicate the difference that emerged between them over the course of this nine-year study.

3. The Type A characteristic that is most strongly linked with coronary heart disease is

   _____ _____ ,

   especially _____

   _____ .

4. When a _____ (Type A/Type B) person is angered, blood flow is diverted away from the internal organs, including the liver, which is responsible for removing _____ and fat from the blood. Thus, such people have elevated levels of these substances in the blood.

5. Another toxic emotion is _____ ; researchers have found that _____ are more than twice as likely to develop heart disease as _____ .

6. Depression _____ (increases/has no effect on) one's risk of having a heart attack or developing other heart problems.

Stress and Susceptibility to Disease
(pp. 440–443)

Objective 5: Define *psychophysiological illness*, and describe the effect of stress on immune system functioning.

1. In _____ illnesses, physical symptoms are produced by psychological causes.

2. Examples of such illnesses are certain types of _____ and _____ . Such illnesses appear to be linked to _____ .

3. The term _____ was once used to describe such illness. However, this term implied that symptoms were _____ .

4. The new field of _____ investigates how psychological, neural, and endocrine systems together affect the immune system and health.

5. The body's system of fighting disease is the _____ system. This system includes two types of white blood cells, called _____ : the _____ _____ , which fight bacterial infections, and the _____ _____ , which form in the _____ and attack viruses, cancer cells, and foreign substances.

6. Two other immune agents are the _____ , which pursues and ingests foreign substances, and _____ _____ , which pursue diseased cells.

7. Responding too strongly, the immune system may attack the body's tissues and cause _____ or an _____ reaction. Or it may _____ , allowing a dormant herpes virus to erupt or _____ cells to multiply.

8. _____ (Women/Men) are the immunologically stronger gender. This makes them less susceptible to _____ , but more susceptible to _____ diseases such as _____ and _____ _____ .

9. Stress can suppress the lymphocyte cells, resulting in a(n) _____ (increase/decrease) in disease resistance. Stress diverts energy from the _____ _____ to the _____ and _____ , mobilizing the body for action.

10. Worldwide, the fourth leading cause of death is _____ , caused by the _____ _____ _____ , which is spread primarily through the exchange of _____ and _____ .

11. Stressful life circumstances _____ (have/have not) been shown to accelerate the progression of this chronic disease.

12. Educational initiatives, support groups, and other efforts to control stress _____ (have/have not) been shown to have positive consequences on HIV-positive individuals.

13. Stress and _____ emotions _____ (have/have not) been linked to cancer's rate of progression.

14. When rodents were inoculated with _____ cells or given _____ , tumors developed sooner in those that were also exposed to _____ stress.

15. Stress _____ (does/does not) create cancer cells.

PROGRESS TEST

Multiple-Choice Questions

Circle your answers to the following questions and check them with the answers beginning on page 350. If your answer is incorrect, read the explanation for why it is incorrect and then consult the appropriate pages of the text.

1. Researchers Friedman and Rosenman refer to individuals who are very time-conscious, super-motivated, verbally aggressive, and easily angered as:
   a. ulcer-prone personalities.
   b. cancer-prone personalities.
   c. Type A.
   d. Type B.

2. During which stage of the general adaptation syndrome is a person especially vulnerable to disease?
   a. alarm reaction
   b. stage of resistance
   c. stage of exhaustion
   d. stage of adaptation

3. The leading cause of death in North America is:
   a. lung cancer.
   b. AIDS.
   c. coronary heart disease.
   d. alcohol-related accidents.

4. Genuine illnesses that are caused by stress are called _____ illnesses.
   a. psychophysiological
   b. psychological
   c. psychogenic
   d. psychotropic

5. Stress has been demonstrated to place a person at increased risk of:
   a. cancer.
   b. progressing from HIV infection to AIDS.
   c. bacterial infections.
   d. all of these conditions.

6. *Stress* is defined as:
   a. unpleasant or aversive events that cannot be controlled.
   b. situations that threaten health.
   c. the process by which we perceive and respond to challenging or threatening events.
   d. anything that decreases immune responses.

7. Research studies demonstrate that after a catastrophe rates of _____ often increase.
   a. depression
   b. anxiety
   c. sleeplessness
   d. all of these problems

8. In order, the sequence of stages in the general adaptation syndrome is:
   a. alarm reaction, stage of resistance, stage of exhaustion.
   b. stage of resistance, alarm reaction, stage of exhaustion.
   c. stage of exhaustion, stage of resistance, alarm reaction.
   d. alarm reaction, stage of exhaustion, stage of resistance.

9. AIDS is a disorder that causes a breakdown in the body's:
   a. endocrine system.
   b. circulatory system.
   c. immune system.
   d. respiratory system.

10. "Tend and befriend" refers to:
    a. the final stage of the general adaptation syndrome.
    b. the health-promoting impact of having a strong system of social support.
    c. an alternative to the "fight-or-flight" response that may be more common in women.
    d. the fact that spiritual people typically are not socially isolated.

11. Which of the following statements concerning Type A and B persons is true?
    a. Even when relaxed, Type A persons have higher blood pressure than Type B persons.
    b. When stressed, Type A persons redistribute blood flow to the muscles and away from internal organs.
    c. Type B persons tend to suppress anger more than Type A persons.
    d. Type A persons tend to be more outgoing than Type B persons.

12. The disease- and infection-fighting cells of the immune system are:
    a. B lymphocytes.
    b. T lymphocytes.
    c. types of lymphocytes.
    d. antigens.

13. One effect of stress on the body is to:
    a. suppress the immune system.
    b. facilitate the immune system response.
    c. increase disease resistance.
    d. increase the growth of B and T lymphocytes.

14. Compared to men, women:
    a. have stronger immune systems.
    b. are less susceptible to infections.
    c. are more susceptible to self-attacking diseases such as multiple sclerosis.
    d. have all of these characteristics.

15. Allergic reactions and arthritis are caused by:
    a. an overreactive immune system.
    b. an underreactive immune system.
    c. the presence of B lymphocytes.
    d. the presence of T lymphocytes.

16. Research on cancer patients reveals that:
    a. stress affects the growth of cancer cells by weakening the body's natural resources.
    b. patients' attitudes can influence their rate of recovery.
    c. cancer occurs slightly more often than usual among those widowed, divorced, or separated.
    d. all of these statements are true.

17. The component of Type A behavior that is the most predictive of coronary disease is:
    a. time urgency.   c. high motivation.
    b. competitiveness.   d. anger.

18. Each semester, Bob does not start studying until just before midterms. Then he is forced to work around the clock until after final exams, which makes him sick, probably because he is in the _____ phase of the _____ .
    a. alarm; post-traumatic stress syndrome
    b. resistance; general adaptation syndrome
    c. exhaustion; general adaptation syndrome
    d. depletion; post-traumatic stress syndrome

19. Connie complains to the campus psychologist that she has too much stress in her life. The psychologist tells her that the level of stress people experience depends primarily on:
    a. how many activities they are trying to do at the same time.
    b. how they appraise the events of life.
    c. their physical hardiness.
    d. how predictable stressful events are.

20. Karen and Kyumi attend different colleges, but both have rooms in on-campus dorms. Karen's dorm is large, roomy, with only two students to a suite. Kyumi attends a city college, where the dorms are small, overcrowded, and noisy, with five students to a room, which makes study very difficult. Which student is probably under more stress?
    a. Karen
    b. Kyumi
    c. There should be no difference in their levels of stress.
    d. It is impossible to predict stress levels in this situation.

21. Jill is an easygoing, noncompetitive person who is happy in her job and enjoys her leisure time. She would *probably* be classified as:
    a. Type A.
    b. Type B.
    c. Type C.
    d. There is too little information to tell.

22. A white blood cell that is formed in the thymus and that attacks cancer cells is:
    a. a macrophage.   c. a T lymphocyte.
    b. a B lymphocyte.   d. any of the above.

23. When would you expect that your immune responses would be *weakest*?
    a. during summer vacation
    b. during exam weeks
    c. just after receiving good news
    d. Immune activity would probably remain constant during these times.

True–False Items

Indicate whether each statement is true or false by placing *T* (*True*) or *F* (*False*) in the blank next to the item.

_____ 1. Stress arises more from the events themselves than from how we appraise them.
_____ 2. Type A persons are more physiologically reactive to stress than are Type B persons.
_____ 3. The symptoms of psychophysiological illnesses are not real.
_____ 4. Stressors tend to increase activity in the immune system and in this way make people more vulnerable to illness.
_____ 5. Stress causes the growth of cancer cells.

KEY TERMS

Using your own words, on a separate piece of paper write a brief definition or explanation of each of the following terms.

1. stress
2. general adaptation syndrome (GAS)
3. coronary heart disease
4. Type A
5. Type B
6. psychophysiological illness
7. psychoneuroimmunology (PNI)
8. lymphocytes

ANSWERS

Module Review

Stress and Stressors

1. 4
2. stimulus; response; process
3. both positive and negative
4. Cannon; epinephrine (adrenaline); norepinephrine (noradrenaline); sympathetic; fight or flight
5. tend and befriend; seek and give support
6. general adaptation syndrome
7. alarm; sympathetic
8. resistance
9. exhaustion; more
10. depression and other psychological disorders
11. more
12. daily hassles; racism; hypertension

Stress and the Heart

1. coronary heart disease; smoking, obesity, high-fat diet, physical inactivity, elevated cholesterol level
2. cholesterol; clotting; stress

Type A people were competitive, hard-driving, supermotivated, impatient, time-conscious, verbally aggressive, and easily angered. Type B people were more relaxed and easygoing. Heart attack victims over the course of the study came overwhelmingly from the Type A group.

3. negative emotions; the anger associated with an aggressively reactive temperament
4. Type A; cholesterol
5. pessimism; pessimists; optimists
6. increases

Stress and Susceptibility to Disease

1. psychophysiological
2. headaches; hypertension; stress
3. psychosomatic; unreal
4. psychoneuroimmunology
5. immune; lymphocytes; B lymphocytes; T lymphocytes; thymus
6. macrophage; natural killer (NK) cells
7. arthritis; allergic; underreact; cancer
8. Women; infections; self-attacking; lupus; multiple sclerosis
9. decrease; immune system; brain; muscles
10. AIDS; human immunodeficiency virus (HIV); blood; semen
11. have
12. have
13. negative; have
14. tumor; carcinogens; uncontrollable
15. does not

Progress Test

Multiple-Choice Questions

1. **c.** is the answer.
   a. & b. Researchers have not identified such personality types.
   d. Individuals who are more easygoing are labeled Type B.
2. **c.** is the answer.
   a. & b. During these stages, the body's defensive mechanisms are at peak function.
   d. This is not a stage of the GAS.
3. **c.** is the answer. Coronary heart disease is followed by cancer, stroke, and chronic lung disease. AIDS has not yet become one of the four leading causes of death in North America among the general population.
4. **a.** is the answer.
   b. Psychological is too broad a term.
   c. *Psychogenic* means "originating in the mind." One's reaction to stress is partially psychological, but this term is not used to refer to stress-related illness.
   d. There is no such term in psychology.
5. **d.** is the answer. Because stress depresses the immune system, stressed individuals are prone to all of these conditions.
6. **c.** is the answer.
   a., b., & d. Whether an event is stressful or not depends on how it is appraised.
7. **d.** is the answer.

8. **a.** is the answer.

9. **c.** is the answer.

10. **c.** is the answer.
    a. The final stage of the general adaptation syndrome is exhaustion.
    b. & d. Although both of these are true, neither has anything to do with "tend and befriend."

11. **b.** is the answer. The result is that their blood may contain excess cholesterol and fat.
    a. Under relaxed situations, there is no difference in blood pressure.
    c. Anger, both expressed and suppressed, is more characteristic of Type A people.
    d. The text doesn't indicate that Type A persons are more outgoing than Type B persons.

12. **c.** is the answer. B lymphocytes fight bacterial infections; T lymphocytes attack cancer cells, viruses, and foreign substances.
    d. Antigens cause the production of antibodies when they are introduced into the body.

13. **a.** is the answer. A variety of studies have shown that stress depresses the immune system, increasing the risk and potential severity of many diseases.

14. **d.** is the answer.

15. **a.** is the answer.
    b. An *under*reactive immune system would make an individual more susceptible to infectious diseases or the proliferation of cancer cells.
    c. & d. Lymphocytes are disease- and infection-fighting white blood cells in the immune system.

16. **d.** is the answer.

17. **d.** is the answer. The crucial characteristic of Type A behavior seems to be a tendency to react with negative emotions, especially anger; other aspects of Type A behavior appear not to predict heart disease, and some appear to be helpful to the individual.

18. **c.** is the answer. According to Selye's general adaptation syndrome, diseases are most likely to occur in this final stage.
    a. & b. Resistance to disease is greater during the alarm and resistance phases because the body's mobilized resources are not yet depleted.
    d. There is no such thing as the "depletion phase." Moreover, the post-traumatic stress syndrome refers to the haunting nightmares and anxiety of those who have suffered extreme stress, such as that associated with combat.

19. **b.** is the answer.

a., c., & d. Each of these is a factor in coping with stress, but it is how an event is *perceived* that determines whether it is stressful or not.

20. **b.** is the answer. Living under crowded conditions contributes to feeling a lack of control, which is the situation in Kyumi's case.

21. **b.** is the answer.
    a. Type A persons are hard-driving and competitive.
    c. There is no such thing as a "Type C" person.

22. **c.** is the answer.
    a. Macrophages are immune agents that search for and ingest harmful invaders.
    b. B lymphocytes form in the bone marrow and release antibodies that fight bacterial infections.

23. **b.** is the answer. Stressful situations, such as exam weeks, decrease immune responses.

True–False Items

1.	F	4.	F
2.	T	5.	F
3.	F		

Key Terms

1. **Stress** refers to the process by which people perceive and react to events, called stressors, that they perceive as threatening or challenging.

2. The **general adaptation syndrome (GAS)** is the three-stage sequence of bodily reaction to stress outlined by Hans Selye.

3. The leading cause of death in North America today, **coronary heart disease** results from the clogging of the vessels that nourish the heart muscle.

4. **Type A** personality is Friedman and Rosenman's term for the coronary-prone behavior pattern of competitive, hard-driving, impatient, verbally aggressive, and anger-prone people.

5. **Type B** personality is Friedman and Rosenman's term for the coronary-resistant behavior pattern of easygoing, relaxed people.

6. A **psychophysiological illness** is any genuine illness such as hypertension and some headaches that is apparently linked to stress rather than caused by a physical disorder.

   Memory aid: Psycho- refers to mind; *physio-* refers to body; a **psychophysiological illness** is a mind-body disorder.

7. **Psychoneuroimmunology (PNI)** is the study of how psychological, neural, and endocrine processes affect the immune system and resulting health.

8. **Lymphocytes** are the two types of white blood cells of the immune system that fight bacterial infections (B lymphocytes) and viruses, cancer cells, and foreign substances in the body (T lymphocytes).

FOCUS ON VOCABULARY AND LANGUAGE

Stress and Stressors

Afterward, she notices her *tense* muscles, *clenched teeth*, and *churning stomach*. Our response to stress can be beneficial (e.g., Karl's escape from the snake) or destructive (e.g., Karen's reaction to relatively minor routine problems or *daily hassles*). Following a number of stressful events (missing her train, rush-hour pedestrian traffic, late for an appointment, etc.), she becomes aware of her physiological reaction. Her muscles feel strained and taut (*tense*), her jaws are clamped shut (*clenched teeth*), and her stomach feels upset (*churning stomach*).

Stress is a *slippery concept*. The term *stress* is often used to describe a stimulus (a threatening or challenging event) or a response (fear or anxiety). Most psychologists refer to the former as a *stressor*, the latter as a *stress reaction*, and use the word *stress* to refer to the entire process of evaluating and dealing with threatening events. Thus, stress is not a simple or easily grasped (understood) construct (*it is a slippery concept*).

Your heart rate *zooms*. According to Selye's general adaptation syndrome (GAS), there are three phases in our response to stress: *alarm reaction, resistance,* and *exhaustion*. During the first phase, the sympathetic nervous system responds rapidly; your heart rate quickly increases (*zooms*), blood is directed to the muscles, and you experience the weakness associated with being startled. You are now ready to fight or cope with the stressor (*resistance phase*); if the situation is not resolved soon, you will experience *exhaustion* (the third phase).

. . . *uprooting* . . . Refugees and others who are forcibly made to leave their homes (*they are uprooted*) have increased rates of depression, anxiety, psychological disorders, and other stress symptoms. In most instances, the health impairments come from long-term exposure to stress.

Experiencing *a cluster of crises* puts one even more at risk. Important and significant changes in our lives are other types of life-event stressors that increase the probability of health problems. If a number of these events occur close together (*a cluster of crises*), people become more vulnerable to disease.

Daily Hassles Small, routine, annoying events and the little things that go wrong day by day (*daily hassles*) can have an accumulative effect on health and well-being. Some people can handle these daily hassles (*they shrug them off*) while others are severely distressed (*"driven up the wall"*) by these inconveniences. Continual work-related hassles can lead to mental, physical, and emotional exhaustion.

Stress and the Heart

Moreover, not one of the *"pure"* Type Bs —the most *mellow* and *laid-back* of their group—had suffered a *heart attack*. Researchers have identified two personality types: Type As are reactive (*easily angered*), competitive, verbally aggressive, highly motivated, always rushed, and lacking in patience; Type Bs are less easily angered (*mellow*), easy-going (*laid-back*), patient, understanding, and noncompetitive. The most prototypical (*"pure"*) Type Bs were the least likely to be afflicted by coronary heart disease (*heart attacks*).

But *after the honeymoon period,* in which the finding seemed definitive and revolutionary, other researchers began asking: Is the finding reliable? The discovery of the relationship between personality type (A or B) and health and well-being aroused much interest. However, once the initial excitement abated (*after the honeymoon period*), other investigators started more detailed research and asked questions about the specific mechanisms involved in personality type and risk of disease.

Stress and Susceptibility to Disease

Your immune system is not *a headless horseman*. The immune system does not operate as an autonomous system independent of other systems (*a headless horseman*). Instead, it works in close harmony with various brain systems and with the endocrine system, which secretes hormones. All these interact and affect each other in a very complex way.

One danger in *hyping* reports on attitudes and cancer is that some patients may be led to blame themselves for their illness. . . . One problem with overstating (*hyping*) the relationship between attitudes and cancer is that some cancer victims may feel that they have somehow caused their sickness. The biological factors involved in the disease cannot easily be mitigated (*derailed*) by believing good health is due to a healthy character (the *wellness macho*). Nor is it appropriate to blame (*lay a guilt trip on*) those who develop the illness. As Myers notes, we should be aware of the fine distinction (*thin line*) that separates science from desperately hopeful beliefs (*wishful thinking*).

Promoting Health

32 **MODULE**

MODULE OVERVIEW

Module 32 discusses the physical and psychological factors that promote good health. For example, research has shown that social support can improve one's chances of surviving a major illness such as cancer. A Thinking Critically box explores the growing market for complementary and alternative medicine.

NOTE: Answer guidelines for all Module 32 questions begin on page 359.

MODULE REVIEW

First, skim each section, noting headings and boldface items. After you have read the section, review each objective by answering the fill-in and essay-type questions that follow it. As you proceed, evaluate your performance by consulting the answers on page 359. Do not continue with the next section until you understand each answer. If you need to, review or reread the section in the textbook before continuing.

> David Myers at times uses idioms that are unfamiliar to some readers. If you do not know the meaning of any of the following expressions in the context in which they appear in the text, refer to page 361 for an explanation: *Laughter among friends is good medicine; heartaches; cold fact . . . nothing to sneeze at; "open heart therapy"; run away from their troubles; boosts our moods; overblown and oversold.*

Coping With Stress (pp. 445–449)

Objective 1: Identify two ways people cope with stress, and describe how a perceived lack of control can affect health.

1. People learn to _____ with stress by finding _____ , _____ , or _____ ways to alleviate it.

2. When we cope directly with a stressor, we are using _____-_____ coping.

3. When we attempt to alleviate stress by avoiding it and attending to emotional needs, we are using _____-_____ coping.

4. People tend to use _____-_____ coping when they feel a sense of _____ over a situation. They turn to _____-_____ coping when they cannot or believe they cannot _____ a situation.

5. Negative situations are especially stressful when they are appraised as _____ .

6. With higher economic status comes lower risks of infant _____ , a low _____ _____ , smoking, and _____ .

355

7. In animals and humans, sudden lack of control is followed by a drop in immune responses, a(n) _____ (increase/decrease) in blood pressure, and a rise in the levels of _____ _____ .

Objective 2: Discuss the links among explanatory style, social support, stress, and health.

8. People who have an _____ explanatory style are less likely than others to suffer ill health.

9. Another buffer against the effects of stress is _____ support.

10. Longitudinal research reveals that a _____ _____ at age 50 predicts healthy aging better than _____ _____ at the same age.

State some possible reasons for the link between health and social support.

11. James Pennebaker has found that emotional _____ can adversely affect our physical health.

12. Health can also be improved by _____ about personal traumas in a diary.

13. Another way to reduce stress is to talk about it. In another study by Pennebaker, Holocaust survivors who were the most _____ had the most improved health.

Managing Stress Effects (pp. 449–456)

Objective 3: Discuss the advantages of aerobic exercise as a technique for managing stress and fostering well-being.

1. Sustained exercise that increases heart and lung fitness is known as _____ exercise.

2. Experiments _____ (have/have not) been able to demonstrate conclusively that such exercise reduces anxiety, depression, and stress.

3. Exercise increases the body's production of mood-boosting neurotransmitters such as _____ , _____ , and the _____ . It also modestly enhances cognitive abilities, such as _____ .

4. By one estimate, moderate exercise adds _____ (how many?) years to one's life expectancy.

Objective 4: Compare the benefits of biofeedback and relaxation training as stress-management techniques, and discuss meditation as a relaxation technique.

5. A system for recording a physiological response and providing information concerning it is called _____ . The instruments used in this system _____ (provide/do not provide) the individual with a means of monitoring physiological responses.

6. Lowered blood pressure, heart rate, and oxygen consumption have been found to be characteristic of people who regularly practice _____ . The _____ response accompanies sitting quietly, with closed eyes, while breathing deeply.

7. Brain scans of experienced meditators reveal decreased activity in the _____ lobe and increased activity in the _____ lobe.

8. (Thinking Critically) Acupuncture, massage therapy, homeopathy, and similar treatments comprise the growing health care market called

_____ _____

_____ _____ . In

China, _____ therapies have flourished for centuries, as have acupuncture and acupressure therapies that claim to correct imbalances in the flow of the energy called

_____ .

9. (Thinking Critically) Critics of alternative medicine point out that such treatments seem especially effective with _____ diseases such as arthritis and _____ , as well as with diseases that disappear naturally—a phenomenon called _____

_____ . Critics also argue that the seeming effectiveness of alternative medicine is due to a _____ effect.

Objective 5: Discuss the correlation between religiosity and longevity, and offer some possible explanations for this link.

10. Until fairly recently in history, the healing traditions of _____ and

_____ have worked

_____ (together/separately).

11. Several recent studies demonstrate that religious involvement _____ (predicts/ does not predict) health and longevity.

State two possible intervening variables that might account for the "faith factor" in health.

PROGRESS TEST

Multiple-Choice Questions

Circle your answers to the following questions and check them with the answers beginning on page 359. If your answer is incorrect, read the explanation for why it is incorrect and then consult the appropriate pages of the text.

1. Attempting to alleviate stress directly by changing a stressor or how we interact with it is an example of:
   a. problem-focused coping.
   b. emotion-focused coping.
   c. managing rather than coping with stress.
   d. biofeedback.

2. A study in which people were asked to confide troubling feelings to an experimenter found that participants typically:
   a. did not truthfully report feelings and events.
   b. experienced a sustained increase in blood pressure until the experiment was finished.
   c. became physiologically more relaxed after confiding their problem.
   d. denied having any problems.

3. Which of the following was *not* mentioned in the text as a potential health benefit of exercise?
   a. Exercise can increase ability to cope with stress.
   b. Exercise can lower blood pressure.
   c. Exercise can reduce stress, depression, and anxiety.
   d. Exercise improves functioning of the immune system.

4. Social support _____ our ability to cope with stressful events.
   a. has no effect on
   b. usually increases
   c. usually decreases
   d. has an unpredictable effect on

5. Research has demonstrated that as a predictor of health and longevity, religious involvement:
   a. has a small, insignificant effect.
   b. is more accurate for women than men.
   c. is more accurate for men than women.
   d. rivals nonsmoking and exercise.

6. During biofeedback training:
   a. a person is given sensory feedback for a subtle body response.
   b. biological functions controlled by the autonomic nervous system may come under conscious control.
   c. the accompanying relaxation is much the same as that produced by other, simpler methods of relaxation.
   d. all of the above occur.

7. Which of the following was *not* suggested as a possible explanation of the "faith factor" in health?
   a. Having a coherent worldview is a buffer against stress.
   b. Religious people tend to have healthier lifestyles.
   c. Those who are religious have stronger networks of social support.
   d. Because they are more affluent, religiously active people receive better health care.

8. (Thinking Critically) Acupuncture, aromatherapy, and homeopathy are forms of:
   a. psychophysiological medicine.
   b. complementary and alternative medicine.
   c. Chi therapy.
   d. psychosomatic medicine.

9. Concluding her presentation on spirituality and health, Maja notes that:
   a. historically, religion and medicine joined hands in caring for the sick.
   b. religious involvement predicts health and longevity.
   c. people who attend religious services weekly have healthier life-styles.
   d. all of these statements are true.

10. Ricardo has been unable to resolve a stressful relationship with a family member. To cope, he turns to a close friend for social support. Ricardo's coping strategy is an example of:
    a. problem-focused coping.
    b. emotion-focused coping.
    c. managing rather than coping.
    d. general adaptation.

11. To help him deal with a stressful schedule of classes, work, and studying, Randy turns to a regular program of exercise and relaxation training. Randy's strategy is an example of:
    a. problem-focused coping.
    b. emotion-focused coping.

c. managing rather than coping.
d. general adaptation.

12. Which of the following would be the *best* piece of advice to offer a person who is trying to minimize the adverse effects of stress on his or her health?
    a. "Avoid challenging situations that may prove stressful."
    b. "Learn to play as hard as you work."
    c. "Maintain a sense of control and a positive approach to life."
    d. "Keep your emotional responses in check by keeping your feelings to yourself."

13. You have just transferred to a new campus and find yourself in a potentially stressful environment. According to the text, which of the following would help you cope with the stress?
    a. believing that you have some control over your environment
    b. having a friend to confide in
    c. feeling optimistic that you will eventually adjust to your new surroundings
    d. All of these things would help.

14. (Thinking Critically) Andrew, who is convinced that an expensive herbal remedy "cured" his arthritis, has decided to turn to homeopathy and herbal medicine for all of his health care. You caution him by pointing out that:
    a. arthritis is a cyclical disease that often improves on its own.
    b. botanical herbs have never been proven effective in controlled experiments.
    c. alternative medicine is a recent fad in this country that has few proponents in other parts of the world.
    d. all of these statements are true.

True–False Items

Indicate whether each statement is true or false by placing *T* or *F* in the blank next to the item.

_____ 1. Optimists cope more successfully with stressful events than do pessimists.
_____ 2. People with few social and community ties are more likely to die prematurely than are those who have many social ties.
_____ 3. Exercise not only reduces depression and anxiety but also strengthens the heart and lowers blood pressure.
_____ 4. Relaxation techniques are not as effective as biofeedback in reducing tension headaches.

Essay Question

Discuss several factors that enhance a person's ability to cope with stress. (Use the space below to list the points you want to make, and organize them. Then write the essay on a separate sheet of paper.)

KEY TERMS

Using your own words, on a separate piece of paper write a brief definition or explanation of each of the following terms.

1. aerobic exercise

2. biofeedback

3. complementary and alternative medicine

ANSWERS

Module Review

Coping With Stress

1. cope; emotional; cognitive; behavioral
2. problem-focused
3. emotion-focused
4. problem-focused; control; emotion-focused; change
5. uncontrollable
6. mortality; birth weight; violence
7. increase; stress hormones
8. optimistic
9. social
10. good marriage; low cholesterol

Close relationships provide the opportunity to confide painful feelings, which may mitigate physical reactions to stressful events. Environments that foster our need to belong also foster stronger immune functioning.

11. suppression

12. writing
13. self-disclosing

Managing Stress Effects

1. aerobic
2. have
3. norepinephrine; serotonin; endorphins; memory
4. two
5. biofeedback; do not provide
6. meditation (relaxation); relaxation
7. parietal; frontal
8. complementary and alternative medicine; herbal; Qi or Chi
9. cyclical; allergies; spontaneous remission; placebo
10. religion; medicine; together
11. predicts

Religiously active people have healthier life-styles. They also tend to have stronger networks of social support and are more likely to be married.

Progress Test

Multiple-Choice Questions

1. **a.** is the answer.
   b. In emotion-focused coping, we attempt to alleviate stress by avoiding or ignoring it.
   c. This is an example of coping rather than managing stress because it involves an attempt to actually alleviate a stressor.
   d. Biofeedback is a technique for controlling a subtle physiological state.

2. **c.** is the answer. The finding that talking about grief leads to better health makes a lot of sense in light of this physiological finding.
   a., b., & d. The study by Pennebaker did not find these to be true.

3. **d.** is the answer. Regular aerobic exercise has been shown to increase ability to cope with stress, lower blood pressure, and reduce depression and anxiety. The text does not cite evidence that exercise enhances immune function.

4. **b.** is the answer.

5. **d.** is the answer.
   b. & c. The text does not indicate that a gender difference exists in the "faith factor" in health.

6. **d.** is the answer. In biofeedback training, people are given sensory feedback about autonomic responses. Although biofeedback may promote relaxation, its benefits may be no greater than those produced by simpler, and less expensive, methods.

7. **d.** is the answer. As a group, religiously active people are no more affluent than other people.

8. **b.** is the answer.
   a. There is no such subfield of medicine.
   c. Chi is an alleged form of energy, imbalances of which Chinese herbal therapies and acupuncture are intended to treat.
   d. The term psychosomatic was once used to describe psychologically caused symptoms. Many forms of alternative medicine, including acupuncture, are intended to treat a full range of symptoms and diseases.

9. **d.** is the answer.

10. **b.** is the answer. Ricardo is attempting to address his emotional needs, since he has been unable to alleviate stress directly.

11. **c.** is the answer.

12. **c.** is the answer.
    a. This is not realistic.
    b. & d. These might actually *increase* the health consequences of potential stressors.

13. **d.** is the answer.

14. **a.** is the answer.
    b. In fact, botanical herbs have given us many widely used drugs, including morphine and penicillin, each of which was proven to be useful in controlled research studies.
    c. Herbal remedies and acupuncture—to name two forms of complementary and alternative medicine—have a long tradition in other parts of the world and remain enormously popular today.

True–False Items

1.	T	**3.**	T
2.	T	**4.**	F

Essay Question

When potentially stressful events occur, a person's appraisal is a major determinant of their impact.

Catastrophes, significant life events, and daily hassles are especially stressful when appraised as negative and uncontrollable and when the person has a pessimistic outlook on life. Under these circumstances, stressful events may suppress immune responses and make the person more vulnerable to disease. If stressors cannot be eliminated, aerobic exercise, biofeedback, relaxation, and spirituality can help the person cope. Aerobic exercise can reduce stress, depression, and anxiety, perhaps by increasing production of mood-boosting neurotransmitters. During biofeedback training, people enjoy a calm, relaxing experience that can be helpful in reducing stress. Research demonstrates that people who regularly practice relaxation techniques enjoy a greater sense of tranquility and have lower blood pressure and stronger immune responses. People with strong social ties eat better, exercise more, and smoke and drink less. Social support may also help people evaluate and overcome stressful events. In addition, confiding painful feelings to others has been demonstrated to reduce the physiological responses linked to stress.

Key Terms

1. **Aerobic exercise** is any sustained activity such as running, swimming, or cycling that promotes heart and lung fitness and may help alleviate depression and anxiety.

2. **Biofeedback** refers to a system for electronically recording, amplifying, and feeding back information regarding a subtle physiological state.

   Memory aid: A **biofeedback** device, such as a brain-wave trainer, provides auditory or visual feedback about biological responses.

3. **Complementary and alternative medicine** is a collection of health care remedies and treatments that have not been accepted by medical science or verified by controlled research trials.

FOCUS ON VOCABULARY AND LANGUAGE

Coping With Stress

(caption): . . . *Laughter among friends is good medicine.* This old saying proposes that mirthful humor may be good for our health. Some research has shown the beneficial effects of laughter, which appears to act as a block or buffer against stress-induced problems.

. . . *heartaches* . . . *Heartaches* is a term that refers to persistent mental anguish or suffering, usually re-

sulting from the loss of a loved one or from disappointment in love. Myers points out that while close relationships and family tend to contribute to our well-being and contentment, they also can be the cause of much misery, strain, and strife (*heartaches*).

The *cold fact* is that the effect of social ties is *nothing to sneeze at.* Myers is being humorous here. The expression "that is nothing to sneeze at" indicates that something (the object, event, accomplishment, etc.) is not minor or insignificant, and, of course, people with colds tend to sneeze a lot. In research on resistance to cold viruses, the finding that healthy volunteers who had the most social ties were less likely to catch a cold and produced less mucus (the *cold fact*) is not an insignificant result (*nothing to sneeze at*). In addition, research shows that social support calms the cardiovascular system, lowering blood pressure and stress hormones.

Talking about our troubles can be *"open heart therapy."* Research has shown that those with close, supportive friends and family tend to have fewer health problems and live longer. One reason for this may be that trusting relationships provide the opportunity to talk about our problems and feelings and, just as *"open-heart surgery"* can save lives, having someone to talk to can be a form of *"open-heart therapy."*

Managing Stress Effects

Many of them had, quite literally, *run away from their troubles.* Many research studies have shown the beneficial effect of aerobic exercise on depression and anxiety. In one study, women who took up jogging (*running*) showed a substantial reduction in depression. As Myers humorously puts it, they had, in reality, *run away from their problems.*

(caption): The mood boost. Regular exercise increases longevity and cardiovascular fitness, reduces anxiety and depression, and enhances positive emotional states (*boosts our moods*). So the popular trend toward being more physically active has many benefits.

After a decade of study, however, researchers decided the initial claims for biofeedback were *overblown and oversold* (Miller, 1985). Biofeedback became very popular in the 1970s, and the reports of its effectiveness for all kinds of problems led to much excitement. By the mid-1980s, however, when researchers took the time to evaluate the research findings objectively, it became clear that these assertions were exaggerated (*overblown*) and falsely promoted (*oversold*). Simple relaxation without the use of costly equipment is just as beneficial.

Personality

The Psychoanalytic Perspective

MODULE OVERVIEW

Personality refers to each individual's characteristic pattern of thinking, feeling, and acting. Module 33 describes and then evaluates the contributions, short-comings, and historical significance of the psychoanalytic perspective. Psychoanalytic theory emphasizes the unconscious and irrational aspects of personality. In addition, the module includes a brief description of some of the techniques used by the psychoanalytic perspective in analyzing personality. It concludes with an evaluation of the psychoanalytic perspective. This final section explores the status of the concept of the unconscious mind in psychology today.

NOTE: Answer guidelines for all Module 33 questions begin on page 372.

MODULE REVIEW

First, skim each section, noting headings and boldface items. After you have read the section, review each objective by answering the fill-in and essay-type questions that follow it. As you proceed, evaluate your performance by consulting the answers beginning on page 372. Do not continue with the next section until you understand each answer. If you need to, review or reread the section in the textbook before continuing.

> David Myers at times uses idioms that are unfamiliar to some readers. If you do not know the meaning of any of the following words, phrases, or expressions in the context in which they appear in the text, refer to pages 375–376 for an explanation: *ran up a bookstore debt; mind running; glimpse; virtuous . . . wantonly; utter biting sarcasm; twig of personality is bent; icebreaker; linguistic flip-flops; seared; scientific shortcomings.*

Introducing Personality and Exploring the Unconscious (pp. 459–463)

Objective 1: Define *personality*, and explain how Freud's treatment of psychological disorders led to his study of the unconscious mind.

1. Personality is defined as an individual's characteristic pattern of _____ , _____ , and _____ .

2. The psychoanalytic perspective on personality was proposed by _____ _____ . A second, historically significant perspective was the _____ approach, which focused on people's capacities for _____ and _____ .

3. Today's theories are more _____ and down-to-earth than these grand theories.

4. Sigmund Freud was a medical doctor who specialized in _____ disorders.

5. Freud developed his theory in response to his observation that many patients had disorders that did not make _____ sense.

Objective 2: Describe Freud's view of personality structure in terms of the id, ego, and superego.

6. At first, Freud thought _____ would unlock the door to the unconscious.

7. The technique later used by Freud, in which the patient relaxes and says whatever comes to mind, is called _____ _____ .

8. Freud called his theory and associated techniques, whereby painful unconscious memories are exposed, _____ .

9. According to this theory, many of a person's thoughts, wishes, and feelings are hidden in a large _____ region. Some of the thoughts in this region can be retrieved at will into consciousness; these thoughts are said to be _____ . Many of the memories of this region, however, are blocked, or _____ , from consciousness.

10. Freud believed that a person's _____ wishes are often reflected in his or her beliefs, habits, symptoms, and _____ of the tongue or pen. Freud called the remembered content of dreams the _____ _____ , which he believed to be a censored version of the dream's true _____ _____ .

11. Freud believed that all facets of personality arise from conflict between our _____ impulses and the _____ restraints against them.

12. According to Freud, personality consists of three interacting structures: the _____ , the _____ , and the _____ .

13. The id is a reservoir of psychic energy that is primarily _____ (conscious/unconscious) and operates according to the _____ principle.

14. The ego develops _____ (before/after) the id and consists of perceptions, thoughts, and memories that are mostly _____ (conscious/unconscious). The ego operates according to the _____ principle.

Explain why the ego is considered the "executive" of personality.

15. The personality structure that reflects moral values is the _____ , which Freud believed began emerging at about age _____ .

16. A person with a _____ (strong/weak) superego may be self-indulgent; one with an unusually _____ (strong/weak) superego may be continually guilt-ridden.

Objective 3: Identify Freud's psychosexual stages of development, and describe the effects of fixation on behavior.

17. According to Freud, personality is formed as the child passes through a series of _____ stages, each of which is focused on a distinct body area called an _____ _____ .

18. The first stage is the _____ stage, which takes place during the first 18 months of life. During this stage, the id's energies are focused on behaviors such as _____ .

19. The second stage is the _____ stage, which lasts from about age _____ months to _____ months.

20. The third stage is the _____ stage, which lasts roughly from ages _____ to _____ years. During this stage the id's energies are focused on the _____ . Freud also believed that during this stage children develop sexual desires for the _____ (same/opposite)-sex parent. Freud referred to these feelings as the _____ in boys. Some psychoanalysts in Freud's era believed that girls experience a parallel _____ .

21. Freud believed that _____ with the same-sex parent is the basis for what psychologists now call _____ .

Explain how this complex of feelings is resolved through the process of identification.

22. During the next stage, sexual feelings are repressed. This phase is called the _____ stage and lasts until puberty.

23. The final stage of development is called the _____ stage.

24. According to Freud, it is possible for a person's development to become blocked in any of the stages; in such an instance, the person is said to be _____ .

Objective 4: Discuss how defense mechanisms serve to protect the individual from anxiety.

25. The ego attempts to protect itself against anxiety through the use of _____

_____ . The process underlying each of these mechanisms is

_____ .

26. Dealing with anxiety by returning to an earlier stage of development is called

_____ .

27. When a person reacts in a manner opposite that of his or her true feelings, _____ _____ is said to have occurred.

28. When a person attributes his or her own feelings to another person, _____ has occurred.

29. When a person offers a false, self-justifying explanation for his or her actions, _____ has occurred.

30. When impulses are directed toward an object other than the one that caused arousal, _____ has occurred.

Matching Items

Match each defense mechanism in the following list with the proper example of its manifestation.

Defense Mechanisms

_____ 1. displacement
_____ 2. projection
_____ 3. reaction formation
_____ 4. rationalization
_____ 5. regression

Manifestations

a. nail biting or thumb sucking in an anxiety-producing situation
b. overzealous crusaders against "immoral behaviors" who don't want to acknowledge their own sexual desires
c. saying you drink "just to be sociable" when in reality you have a drinking problem
d. thinking someone hates you when in reality you hate that person
e. a child who is angry at his parents and vents this anger on the family pet, a less threatening target

31. Defense mechanisms are _____ (conscious/unconscious) processes.

The Neo-Freudian and Psychodynamic Theorists (pp. 463–464)

Objective 5: Contrast the views of the neo-Freudians and psychodynamic theorists with Freud's original theory.

1. The theorists who established their own, modified versions of psychoanalytic theory are called _____-_____ .

   These theorists typically place _____ (more/less) emphasis on the conscious mind than Freud did and _____ (more/less) emphasis on sex and aggression.

2. Briefly summarize how each of the following theorists departed from Freud.

   a. Adler _____

   b. Horney _____
   _____
   _____

   c. Jung _____
   _____

3. Today's psychologists _____ (accept/reject) the idea of inherited experiences, which _____ (which theorist?) called a _____
   _____ .

4. More recently, some of Freud's ideas have been incorporated into _____ theory. Unlike Freud, the theorists advocating this perspective do not believe that _____ is the basis of personality. They do agree, however, that much of mental life is _____ , that _____ shapes personality, and that we often struggle with _____ _____ .

Assessing Unconscious Processes (pp. 464–465)

Objective 6: Describe two projective tests used to assess personality, and discuss some criticisms of them.

1. Tests that provide subjects with ambiguous stimuli for interpretation are called _____ tests.

2. Henry Murray introduced the personality assessment technique called the _____ _____ Test.

3. The most widely used projective test is the _____ , in which subjects are shown a series of _____ . Generally, these tests appear to have _____ (little/significant) validity and reliability. This is because there _____ (is/is not) a universal system for scoring these tests, and they _____ (are/are not) successful at predicting behaviors.

Evaluating the Psychoanalytic Perspective (pp. 466–468)

Objective 7: Summarize psychology's current assessment of Freud's theory of psychoanalysis.

1. Contrary to Freud's theory, research indicates that human development is _____ (fixed in childhood/lifelong), children gain their gender identity at a(n) _____ (earlier/later) age, and the presence of a same-sex parent _____ (is/is not) necessary for the child to become strongly masculine or feminine.

2. Research also disputes Freud's belief that dreams disguise _____ and that defense mechanisms disguise _____ and _____ impulses. Another Freudian idea that is no longer widely accepted is that psychological disorders are caused by _____ _____ .

3. Psychoanalytic theory rests on the assumption that the human mind often _____ painful experiences. Many of today's researchers think that this process is much _____ (more common/rarer) than Freud believed. They also believe that when it does occur, it is a reaction to terrible _____ .

4. Today's psychologists agree with Freud that we have limited access to all that goes on in our minds. Research confirms the reality of

_____ _____

learning.

5. An example of the defense mechanism that Freud called _____ is what researchers today call the _____

_____ effect. This refers to our tendency to _____ the extent to which others share our beliefs and behaviors.

6. Criticism of psychoanalysis as a scientific theory centers on the fact that it provides

_____-_____-

_____ explanations and does not offer _____ _____ .

State several of Freud's ideas that have endured.

PROGRESS TEST

Multiple-Choice Questions

Circle your answers to the following questions and check them with the answers beginning on page 373. If your answer is incorrect, read the explanation for why it is incorrect and then consult the appropriate pages of the text.

1. The text defines *personality* as:
   a. the set of personal attitudes that characterizes a person.
   b. an individual's characteristic pattern of thinking, feeling, and acting.
   c. a predictable set of responses to environmental stimuli.
   d. an unpredictable set of responses to environmental stimuli.

2. Which of the following places the greatest emphasis on the unconscious mind?
   a. the humanistic perspective
   b. the social-cognitive perspective
   c. the trait perspective
   d. the psychoanalytic perspective

3. Which of the following is the correct order of psychosexual stages proposed by Freud?
   a. oral; anal; phallic; latency; genital
   b. anal; oral; phallic; latency; genital
   c. oral; anal; genital; latency; phallic
   d. anal; oral; genital; latency; phallic

4. According to Freud, defense mechanisms are methods of reducing:
   a. anger.   c. anxiety.
   b. fear.   d. lust.

5. Neo-Freudians such as Adler and Horney believed that:
   a. Freud placed too great an emphasis on the conscious mind.
   b. Freud placed too great an emphasis on sexual and aggressive instincts.
   c. the years of childhood were more important in the formation of personality than Freud had indicated.
   d. Freud's ideas about the id, ego, and superego as personality structures were incorrect.

6. Which of Freud's ideas would *not* be accepted by most contemporary psychologists?
   a. Development is essentially fixed in childhood.
   b. Sexuality is a potent drive in humans.
   c. The mind is an iceberg with consciousness being only the tip.
   d. Repression can be the cause of forgetting.

7. Projective tests such as the Rorschach inkblot test have been criticized because:
   a. their scoring system is too rigid and leads to unfair labeling.
   b. they were standardized with unrepresentative samples.
   c. they have low reliability and low validity.
   d. it is easy for people to fake answers in order to appear healthy.

8. Id is to ego as _____ is to _____ .
   a. reality principle; pleasure principle
   b. pleasure principle; reality principle
   c. conscious forces; unconscious forces
   d. conscience; "personality executive"

9. Recent research has provided more support for defense mechanisms such as _____ than for defense mechanisms such as _____ .

   a. displacement; reaction formation
   b. reaction formation; displacement
   c. displacement; regression
   d. displacement; projection

10. According to Freud's theory, personality arises in response to conflicts between:

    a. our unacceptable urges and our Oedipus complex.
    b. the process of identification and the ego's defense mechanisms.
    c. the collective unconscious and our individual desires.
    d. our biological impulses and the social restraints against them.

11. The _____ classifies people according to Carl Jung's personality types.

    a. Myers-Briggs Type Indicator
    b. MMPI
    c. Locus of Control Scale
    d. Kagan Temperament Scale

12. The Oedipus and Electra complexes have their roots in the:

    a. anal stage.   c. latency stage.
    b. oral stage.   d. phallic stage.

13. Which of the following was not mentioned in the text as a criticism of Freud's theory?

    a. The theory is sexist.
    b. It offers few testable hypotheses.
    c. There is no evidence of anything like an "unconscious."
    d. The theory ignores the fact that human development is lifelong.

14. According to Freud, _____ is the process by which children incorporate their parents' values into their _____ .

    a. reaction formation; superegos
    b. reaction formation; egos
    c. identification; superegos
    d. identification; egos

15. A psychoanalyst would characterize a person who is impulsive and self-indulgent as possessing a strong _____ and a weak _____ .

    a. id and ego; superego   c. ego; superego
    b. id; ego and superego   d. id; superego

16. Jill has a biting, sarcastic manner. According to Freud, she is:

    a. projecting her anxiety onto others.
    b. fixated in the oral stage of development.
    c. fixated in the anal stage of development.
    d. displacing her anxiety onto others.

17. The personality test Teresa is taking involves her describing random patterns of dots. What type of test is she taking?

    a. an empirically derived test
    b. the TAT
    c. a psychodynamic test
    d. a projective test

18. According to the psychoanalytic perspective, a child who frequently "slips" and calls her teacher "mom" probably:

    a. has some unresolved conflicts concerning her mother.
    b. is fixated in the oral stage of development.
    c. did not receive unconditional positive regard from her mother.
    d. can be classified as having a weak sense of personal control.

19. Suzy bought a used, high-mileage automobile because it was all she could afford. Attempting to justify her purchase, she raves to her friends about the car's attractiveness, good acceleration, and stereo. According to Freud, Suzy is using the defense mechanism of:

    a. displacement.   c. rationalization.
    b. reaction formation.   d. projection.

Matching Items 1

Match each definition or description with the appropriate term.

Definitions or Descriptions

_____ 1. redirecting impulses to a less threatening object

_____ 2. test consisting of a series of inkblots

_____ 3. the conscious executive of personality

_____ 4. disguising an impulse by imputing it to another person

_____ 5. switching an unacceptable impulse into its opposite

_____ 6. the unconscious repository of instinctual drives

_____ 7. personality structure that corresponds to a person's conscience

_____ 8. providing self-justifying explanations for an action

_____ 9. a projective test consisting of a set of ambiguous pictures

Terms

a. id
b. ego
c. superego
d. reaction formation
e. rationalization
f. displacement
g. projection
h. TAT
i. Rorschach

Matching Items 2

Match each term with the appropriate definition or description.

Terms

_____ 1. projective test
_____ 2. identification
_____ 3. collective unconscious
_____ 4. reality principle
_____ 5. psychosexual stages
_____ 6. pleasure principle
_____ 7. Oedipus complex
_____ 8. preconscious

Definitions or Descriptions

a. the id's demand for immediate gratification
b. a boy's sexual desires toward the opposite-sex parent
c. information that is retrievable but currently not in conscious awareness
d. stages of development proposed by Freud
e. personality test that provides ambiguous stimuli
f. the repository of universal memories proposed by Jung
g. the process by which children incorporate their parents' values into their developing superegos
h. the process by which the ego seeks to gratify impulses of the id in nondestructive ways

KEY TERMS

Using your own words, on a separate piece of paper write a brief definition or explanation of each of the following terms.

1. personality

2. free association

3. psychoanalysis

4. unconscious

5. id

6. ego

7. superego

8. psychosexual stages

9. Oedipus complex

10. identification

11. fixation

12. defense mechanisms

13. repression

14. regression

15. reaction formation

16. projection

17. rationalization

18. displacement

19. collective unconscious

20. projective tests

21. Thematic Apperception Test (TAT)

22. Rorschach inkblot test

ANSWERS

Module Review

Introducing Personality and Exploring the Unconscious

1. thinking; feeling; acting

2. Sigmund Freud; humanistic; growth; self-fulfillment

3. focused

4. nervous

5. neurological

6. hypnosis

7. free association

8. psychoanalysis

9. unconscious; preconscious; repressed

10. unconscious; slips; manifest content; latent content

11. biological; social

12. id; ego; superego

13. unconscious; pleasure

14. after; conscious; reality

The ego is considered the executive of personality because it directs our actions as it intervenes among the impulsive demands of the id, the reality of the external world, and the ideals of the superego.

15. superego; 4 or 5

16. weak; strong

17. psychosexual; erogenous zone

18. oral; sucking (also biting, chewing)

19. anal; 18; 36

20. phallic; 3; 6; genitals; opposite; Oedipus complex; Electra complex

21. identification; gender identity

Children eventually cope with their feelings for the opposite-sex parent by repressing them and by identifying with the rival (same-sex) parent. Through this process children incorporate many of their parents' values, thereby strengthening the superego.

22. latency

23. genital

24. fixated

25. defense mechanisms; repression

26. regression

27. reaction formation

28. projection

29. rationalization

30. displacement

Matching Items

1. e

2. d

3. b

4. c

5. a

31. unconscious

The Neo-Freudian and Psychodynamic Theorists

1. neo-Freudians; more; less

2. a. Adler emphasized the social, rather than the sexual, tensions of childhood and said that much of behavior is driven by the need to overcome feelings of inferiority.

   b. Horney questioned the male bias in Freud's theory, such as the assumptions that women have weak egos and suffer "penis envy." Like Adler, she emphasized social tensions.

   c. Jung emphasized an inherited collective unconscious.

3. reject; Jung; collective unconscious

4. psychodynamic; sex; unconscious; childhood; inner conflicts

Assessing Unconscious Processes

1. projective

2. Thematic Apperception

3. Rorschach; inkblots; little; is not; are not

Evaluating the Psychoanalytic Perspective

1. lifelong; earlier; is not

2. wishes; sexual; aggressive; sexual suppression

3. represses; rarer; trauma

4. unconscious implicit

5. projection; false consensus; overestimate

6. after-the-fact; testable predictions

Freud drew attention to the unconscious and the irrational, to human defenses against anxiety, to the importance of human sexuality, to the tension between our biological impulses and our social well-being, and to our potential for evil.

Progress Test

Multiple-Choice Questions

1. **b.** is the answer. Personality is defined as patterns of response—of thinking, feeling, and acting—that are relatively consistent across a variety of situations.

2. **d.** is the answer.
   a. & b. Conscious processes are the focus of these perspectives.
   c. The trait perspective focuses on the description of behaviors.

3. **a.** is the answer.

4. **c.** is the answer. According to Freud, defense mechanisms reduce anxiety unconsciously, by disguising one's threatening impulses.
   a., b., & d. Unlike these specific emotions, anxiety need not be focused. Defense mechanisms help us cope when we are unsettled but are not sure why.

5. **b.** is the answer.
   a. According to most neo-Freudians, Freud placed too much emphasis on the *unconscious* mind.
   c. Freud emphasized early childhood, and the neo-Freudians basically agreed with him.
   d. The neo-Freudians accepted Freud's ideas about the basic personality structures.

6. **a.** is the answer. Developmental research indicates that development is lifelong.
   b., c., & d. To varying degrees, research has partially supported these Freudian ideas.

7. **c.** is the answer. As scoring is largely subjective and the tests have not been very successful in predicting behavior, their reliability and validity have been called into question.
   a. This is untrue.
   b. Unlike empirically derived personality tests, projective tests are not standardized.
   d. Although this may be true, it was not mentioned as a criticism of projective tests.

8. **b.** is the answer. In Freud's theory, the id operates according to the pleasure principle; the ego operates according to the reality principle.
   c. The id is presumed to be unconscious.

d. The superego is, according to Freud, the equivalent of a conscience; the ego is the "personality executive."

9. **b.** is the answer.
   a., c., & d. The evidence supports defenses that defend self-esteem, rather than those that are tied to instinctual energy.

10. **d.** is the answer.
    a. The Oedipus complex refers to a boy's sexual desires for his mother and hatred for and jealousy of his father.
    b. Through identification, children *reduce* conflicting feelings as they incorporate their parents' values.
    c. Jung, rather than Freud, proposed the concept of the collective unconscious.

11. **a.** is the answer.

12. **d.** is the answer.

13. **c.** is the answer. Although many researchers think of the unconscious as information processing without awareness rather than as a reservoir of repressed information, they agree with Freud that we do indeed have limited access to all that goes on in our minds.

14. **c.** is the answer.
    a. & b. Reaction formation is the defense mechanism by which people transform unacceptable impulses into their opposites.
    d. It is the superego, rather than the ego, that represents parental values.

15. **d.** is the answer. Impulsiveness is the mark of a strong id; self-indulgence is the mark of a weak superego. Because the ego serves to mediate the demands of the id, the superego, and the outside world, its strength or weakness is judged by its decision-making ability, not by the character of the decision—so the ego is not relevant to the question asked.

16. **b.** is the answer. Sarcasm is said to be an attempt to deny the passive dependence characteristic of the oral stage.
    a. A person who is projecting attributes his or her own feelings to others.
    c. Such a person might be either messy and disorganized or highly controlled and compulsively neat.
    d. Displacement involves diverting aggressive or sexual impulses onto a more acceptable object than that which aroused them.

17. **d.** is the answer. Projective tests provide ambiguous stimuli, such as random dot patterns, in an attempt to trigger in the test-taker projection of his or her personality.

b. The TAT is a projective test, but it uses ambiguous pictures, not random patterns of dots.
c. Psychodynamic is not a category of tests.

18. **a.** is the answer. Freud believed that dreams and such slips of the tongue reveal unconscious conflicts.
    b. A person fixated in the oral stage might have a sarcastic personality; this child's slip of the tongue reveals nothing about her psychosexual development.
    c. & d. Unconditional positive regard and personal control are not psychoanalytic concepts.

19. **c.** is the answer. Suzy is trying to justify her purchase by generating (inaccurate) explanations for her behavior.
    a. Displacement is the redirecting of impulses toward an object other than the one responsible for them.
    b. Reaction formation is the transformation of unacceptable impulses into their opposites.
    d. Projection is the attribution of one's own unacceptable thoughts and feelings to others.

Matching Items

1. f	**4.** g	**7.** c
2. i	**5.** d	**8.** e
3. b	**6.** a	**9.** h

Matching Items

1. e	**5.** d
2. g	**6.** a
3. f	**7.** b
4. h	**8.** c

Key Terms

1. **Personality** is an individual's characteristic pattern of thinking, feeling, and acting.

2. **Free association** is the Freudian technique in which the person is encouraged to say whatever comes to mind as a means of exploring the unconscious.

3. **Psychoanalysis** is Freud's theory of personality that attributes thoughts and actions to unconscious motives and conflicts; also, the techniques used in treating psychological disorders by seeking to expose and interpret the tensions within a patient's unconscious.

4. In Freud's theory, the **unconscious** is the repository of mostly unacceptable thoughts, wishes, feelings, and memories. According to contemporary psychologists, it is a level of information processing of which we are unaware.

5. In Freud's theory, the **id** is the unconscious system of personality, consisting of basic sexual and aggressive drives, that supplies psychic energy to personality. It operates on the *pleasure principle.*

6. In psychoanalytic theory, the **ego** is the conscious division of personality that attempts to mediate between the demands of the id, the superego, and reality. It operates on the *reality principle.*

7. In Freud's theory, the **superego** is the division of personality that contains the conscience and develops by incorporating the perceived moral standards of society.

8. Freud's **psychosexual stages** are developmental periods children pass through during which the id's pleasure-seeking energies are focused on different erogenous zones.

9. According to Freud, boys in the phallic stage develop a collection of feelings, known as the **Oedipus complex**, that center on sexual attraction to the mother and resentment of the father. Some psychologists believe girls have a parallel *Electra complex.*

10. In Freud's theory, **identification** is the process by which the child's superego develops and incorporates the parents' values. Freud saw identification as crucial, not only to resolution of the Oedipus complex, but also to the development of *gender identity.*

11. In Freud's theory, **fixation** occurs when development becomes arrested, due to unresolved conflicts, in an immature psychosexual stage.

12. In Freud's theory, **defense mechanisms** are the ego's methods of unconsciously protecting itself against anxiety by distorting reality.

13. The basis of all defense mechanisms, **repression** is the unconscious exclusion of anxiety-arousing thoughts, feelings, and memories from the conscious mind. Repression is an example of motivated forgetting: One "forgets" what one really does not wish to remember.

14. **Regression** is the defense mechanism in which a person faced with anxiety reverts to a less mature pattern of behavior.

15. **Reaction formation** is the defense mechanism in which the ego converts unacceptable impulses into their opposites.

16. In psychoanalytic theory, **projection** is the unconscious attribution of one's own unacceptable feelings, attitudes, or desires to others.
    Memory aid: To project is to thrust outward. **Projection** is an example of thrusting one's own feelings outward to another person.

17. **Rationalization** is the defense mechanism in which one devises self-justifying but incorrect reasons for one's behavior.

18. **Displacement** is the defense mechanism in which a sexual or aggressive impulse is shifted to a more acceptable object other than the one that originally aroused the impulse.

19. The **collective unconscious** is Jung's concept of an inherited unconscious shared by all people and deriving from our species' history.

20. **Projective tests**, such as the TAT and Rorschach, present ambiguous stimuli onto which people supposedly *project* their own inner feelings.

21. The **Thematic Apperception Test (TAT)** is a projective test that consists of ambiguous pictures about which people are asked to make up stories, which are thought to reflect their inner feelings and interests.

22. The **Rorschach inkblot test**, the most widely used projective test, consists of 10 inkblots that people are asked to interpret; it seeks to identify people's inner feelings by analyzing their interpretations of the blots.

FOCUS ON VOCABULARY AND LANGUAGE

Exploring the Unconscious

He [Freud] had a prodigious memory and so loved reading plays, poetry, and philosophy that he once *ran up a bookstore debt* beyond his means. When he was young, Freud was a very serious student with an exceptionally good (*prodigious*) memory and an intense interest in a variety of topics. He obtained many books which he could not afford to pay for (*ran up a bookstore debt beyond his means*) in order to satisfy his curiosity about literature and the natural sciences.

Freud's search for a cause for such disorders set his *mind running* in a direction destined to change human self-understanding. Patients came to Freud with strange neurological (*nervous*) disorders which had no obvious physiological explanation. Freud suspected that the problems were psychological in nature, and the questions raised by this theorizing caused him to think (*set his mind running*) in a way that changed the way we view human nature.

He [Freud] believed he could *glimpse* the unconscious seeping not only into people's free associations, beliefs, habits, and symptoms but also into *slips of the tongue and pen*. Freud used the technique of free association to gain access to the unconscious. He also thought he got a fleeting look at (*glimpse of*) the unconscious in the content of people's dreams and in the inadvertent verbal mistakes we make in speech and writing (*slips of the tongue and pen*).

Someone with an exceptionally strong superego may be *virtuous* yet, ironically, guilt-ridden; another with a weak superego may be *wantonly* self-indulgent and remorseless. In Freud's theory, the superego (our conscience) develops when the 4-to-5-year-old child incorporates society's values through identification with the parent of the opposite sex. A person with a well-developed superego may behave in an appropriately moral way (*virtuous*) yet still feel ashamed and anxious (*guilt-ridden*); someone with a poorly developed superego may be excessively and willfully (*wantonly*) selfish and aggressive.

. . . uttering biting sarcasm. If there are unresolved conflicts at any of the psychosexual stages, the person may become stuck (**fixated**) at that stage, which will directly affect the development of a psychologically healthy personality. People fixated at the oral stage may become very dependent or may pretend to be the opposite by acting strong and independent and by using cruel and destructive humor (*biting sarcasm*) to attack the self-respect of others. In addition, this personality type may have an excessive need for oral gratification (smoking, nail biting, eating, chewing on pens, etc.).

In such ways, Freud suggested, the *twig of personality* is *bent* at an early age. Freud believed that adult personality was formed during the first 4 or 5 years of life and was a function of the way the conflicts of the first three psychosexual stages (oral, anal, and phallic) were handled. Just as the shape of the grown tree is the result of how the young tree (*twig*) was twisted (*bent*), adult personality is a function of early childhood experiences.

Assessing Unconscious Processes

Other clinicians view it [the Rorschach inkblot test] . . . as an *icebreaker* and a revealing interview technique. Because of problems in scoring and interpreting the Rorschach inkblot test, most researchers question its validity and reliability. Some clinicians use the test to help generate hypotheses about the client's problems, and others use it as a point of departure to help get the interview under way (*as an icebreaker*).

Evaluating the Psychoanalytic Perspective

(*margin note*): . . . *linguistic flip-flops ("spoonerisms")*. Professor Spooner became well known because of his habit of inadvertently twisting and distorting his sentences (*linguistic flip-flops*). For example, instead of saying "lighting a fire in the quadrangle," he said "fighting a liar in the quadrangle"; "you missed my history lecture" came out as "you hissed my mystery lecture," and "you have wasted two hours" appeared as "you have tasted two worms." Psychoanalysts call these "slips of the tongue" (Freudian slips) and believe that they represent unconscious motives and desires seeping through.

They are *seared into the soul*. Traumatic events are likely to be remembered very well; they can occur as unwanted, persistent, and intrusive memories (*flashbacks*) that appear often (*they haunt the survivors*). In a sense, they are indelibly impressed in memory (*seared into the soul*).

Psychologists also criticize Freud's theory for its *scientific shortcomings*. In order for a theory to be considered scientifically acceptable, it must be able to explain observations and provide testable hypotheses. Freud's theory fails on this account. In addition, his theory offers explanations only after the events or behaviors have occurred (*after-the-fact explanations*). Freud's theory does not meet acceptable or desired scientific standards (*it has scientific shortcomings*).

The Humanistic Perspective

34

M
O
D
U
L
E

MODULE OVERVIEW

Module 34 describes and then evaluates the contributions, shortcomings, and historical significance of the humanistic perspective. Humanistic theory draws attention to the concept of self and to human potential for healthy growth. In addition, the module includes a brief description of the techniques used by the humanistic perspectives in analyzing personality. It concludes with a discussion of the contributions of humanistic theory and some drawbacks of this point of view.

NOTE: Answer guidelines for all Module 34 questions begin on page 379.

MODULE REVIEW

First, skim each section, noting headings and boldface items. After you have read the section, review each objective by answering the fill-in and essay-type questions that follow it. As you proceed, evaluate your performance by consulting the answers on page 379. Do not continue with the next section until you understand each answer. If you need to, review or reread the section in the textbook before continuing.

> David Myers at times uses idioms that are unfamiliar to some readers. If you do not know the meaning of any of the following words, phrases, or expressions in the context in which they appear in the text, refer to page 380 for an explanation: *crippled spirits; thwarted . . . acorn, primed for growth; rugged individual.*

Abraham Maslow's Self-Actualizing Person
(p. 471)

Objective 1: Discuss Abraham Maslow's concept of self-actualization, and explain how his ideas illustrate the humanistic perspective.

1. Two influential theories of humanistic psychology were proposed by _____ and _____ . These theorists offered a _____-_____ perspective that emphasized human _____ .

2. According to Maslow, humans are motivated by needs that are organized into a _____ . Maslow refers to the process of fulfilling one's potential as _____ . Many people who fulfill their potential have been moved by _____ _____ that surpass ordinary consciousness.

List some of the characteristics Maslow associated with those who fulfilled their potential.

Carl Rogers' Person-Centered Perspective
(pp. 471–472)

Objective 2 : Discuss Carl Rogers' person-centered perspective, and explain the importance of unconditional positive regard.

1. According to Rogers, a person nurtures growth in a relationship by being _____ , _____ , and _____ .

2. People who are accepting of others offer them _____ _____ _____ . By so doing, they enable others to be _____ without fearing the loss of their esteem.

3. For both Maslow and Rogers, an important feature of personality is how an individual perceives himself or herself; this is the person's _____ .

Assessing the Self (p. 472)

Objective 3: Explain how humanistic psychologists assessed personality.

1. Humanistic psychologists sometimes use _____ to assess personality, that is, to evaluate the _____ .

2. Carl Rogers developed a questionnaire that asked people to describe themselves both as they would _____ like to be and as they _____ are. When these two selves are alike, the self-concept is _____ .

3. Some humanistic psychologists feel that questionnaires are _____ and prefer to use _____ to assess personality.

Evaluating the Humanistic Perspective
(pp. 472–473)

Objective 4: Discuss the major criticisms of the humanistic perspective on personality.

1. Humanistic psychologists have influenced such diverse areas as _____ , _____ , _____ , and _____ . They have also had a major impact on today's _____

psychology, perhaps because the emphasis on the individual self strongly reflects _____ cultural values.

State three criticisms of humanistic psychology.

PROGRESS TEST

Multiple-Choice Questions

Circle your answers to the following questions and check them with the answers beginning on page 379. If your answer is incorrect, read the explanation for why it is incorrect and then consult the appropriate pages of the text.

1. The humanistic perspective on personality:
   a. emphasizes the driving force of unconscious motivations in personality.
   b. emphasizes the growth potential of "healthy" individuals.
   c. emphasizes the importance of interaction with the environment in shaping personality.
   d. describes personality in terms of scores on various personality scales.

2. According to Rogers, three conditions are necessary to promote growth in personality. These are:
   a. honesty, sincerity, and empathy.
   b. high self-esteem, honesty, and empathy.
   c. high self-esteem, genuineness, and acceptance.
   d. genuineness, acceptance, and empathy.

3. For humanistic psychologists, many of our behaviors and perceptions are ultimately shaped by whether our _____ is _____ or _____ .
   a. empathy; strong; weak
   b. genuineness; real; fake
   c. personality; self-actualized; personalized
   d. self-concept; positive; negative

4. Which of the following is a common criticism of the humanistic perspective?
   a. Its concepts are vague and subjective.
   b. The emphasis on the self encourages selfishness in individuals.
   c. Humanism fails to appreciate the reality of evil in human behavior.
   d. All of these are common criticisms.

5. In promoting personality growth, the person-centered perspective emphasizes all but:
   a. empathy.   c. genuineness.
   b. acceptance.   d. altruism.

6. Andrew's grandfather, who has lived a rich and productive life, is a spontaneous, loving, and self-accepting person. Maslow might say that he:
   a. is empathic.
   b. is genuine and understanding.
   c. has resolved all of his lifelong internal conflicts.
   d. is a self-actualizing person.

7. Wanda wishes to instill in her children an accepting attitude toward other people. Maslow and Rogers would probably recommend that she:
   a. teach her children first to accept themselves.
   b. use discipline sparingly.
   c. be affectionate with her children only when they behave as she wishes.
   d. do all of these things.

KEY TERMS

Using your own words, on a separate piece of paper write a brief definition or explanation of each of the following terms.

1. self-actualization

2. unconditional positive regard

3. self-concept

ANSWERS

Module Review

Abraham Maslow's Self-Actualizing Person

1. Maslow; Rogers; third-force; potential

2. hierarchy; self-actualization; peak experiences

For Maslow, such people were self-aware, open, self-accepting, spontaneous, loving, caring, not paralyzed by others' opinions, secure, and problem-centered rather than self-centered.

Carl Rogers' Person-Centered Perspective

1. genuine; accepting; empathic

2. unconditional positive regard; spontaneous

3. self-concept

Assessing the Self

1. questionnaires; self-concept

2. ideally; actually; positive

3. depersonalizing; interviews

Evaluating the Humanistic Perspective

1. counseling; education; child-rearing; management; popular; Western

Three criticisms of humanistic psychology are that its concepts are vague and subjective; the individualism it encourages can lead to self-indulgence, selfishness, and an erosion of moral restraints; and it fails to appreciate the human capacity for evil.

Progress Test

Multiple-Choice Questions

1. **b.** is the answer.
   a. This is true of the psychoanalytic perspective.
   c. This is true of the social-cognitive perspective.
   d. This is true of the trait perspective.

2. **d.** is the answer.

3. **d.** is the answer.
   a. & b. Although empathy and genuineness are part of Rogers' growth-promoting climate, they do not actually shape personality.
   c. Self-actualization is the highest level in Maslow's hierarchy.

4. **d.** is the answer.

5. **d.** is the answer.

6. **d.** is the answer.
   a. & b. These are concepts used by Rogers, not Maslow.
   c. Humanistic psychologists are not concerned with internal conflicts.

7. **a.** is the answer.
   b. The text does not discuss the impact of discipline on personality.
   c. This would constitute *conditional*, rather than unconditional, positive regard and would likely cause the children to be *less* accepting of themselves and others.

Key Terms

1. In Maslow's theory, **self-actualization** describes the process of fulfilling one's potential and becoming spontaneous, loving, creative, and self-accepting. Self-actualization is at the very top of Maslow's need hierarchy and therefore becomes active only after the more basic physical and psychological needs have been met.

2. **Unconditional positive regard** is, according to Rogers, an attitude of total acceptance toward another person.

3. **Self-concept** refers to one's personal awareness of "who I am." In the humanistic perspective, the self-concept is a central feature of personality; life happiness is significantly affected by whether the self-concept is positive or negative.

FOCUS ON VOCABULARY AND LANGUAGE

Abraham Maslow's Self-Actualizing Person

(caption): . . . crippled spirits. Abraham Maslow, a humanistic psychologist, studied healthy, motivated, creative people and came to the conclusion that once our basic needs are met, we all seek **self-actualization.** He believed that any theory of personality and motivation must be based on more than the study of psychologically impaired individuals (crippled spirits); rather, it should also include those who have achieved or fulfilled their innate potential (self-actualized people).

Carl Rogers' Person-Centered Perspective

Unless thwarted by an environment that inhibits growth, each of us is like an acorn, primed for growth and fulfillment. Carl Rogers was another pioneer in humanistic psychology. We are born with an innate striving (we are primed) for achieving our potential and like the seed (acorn) of the oak tree we will grow and develop unless we are blocked (thwarted) by an uncaring and unaccepting environment. As Rogers puts it, genuineness, acceptance, and empathy are the water, sun, and nutrients that enable people to grow like vigorous oak trees.

Evaluating the Humanistic Perspective

Movie plots feature rugged individualists who, true to themselves, buck social conventions or take the law into their own hands. Humanistic psychology has been popular because it is consistent with Western cultural values, which emphasize strong, capable (rugged) individuals who follow their own beliefs and ambitions (are true to themselves) and oppose social norms and restrictions (they buck social conventions). This popular reception of the humanistic movement has elicited a strongly adverse and disapproving reaction from its critics (set off a backlash of criticism).

Contemporary Research on Personality

35 MODULE

MODULE OVERVIEW

Module 35 examines the trait and social-cognitive perspectives on personality as well as current research on the concept of self. Trait theory led to advances in techniques for evaluating and describing personality. The text first describes and then evaluates the contributions and shortcomings of the trait and social-cognitive perspectives. In addition, it includes a brief description of some of the techniques used by these perspectives in analyzing personality.

NOTE: Answer guidelines for all Module 35 questions begin on page 388.

MODULE REVIEW

First, skim each section, noting headings and boldface items. After you have read the section, review each objective by answering the fill-in and essay-type questions that follow it. As you proceed, evaluate your performance by consulting the answers on page 388. Do not continue with the next section until you understand each answer. If you need to, review or reread the section in the textbook before continuing.

> David Myers at times uses idioms that are unfamiliar to some readers. If you do not know the meaning of any of the following words, phrases, or expressions in the context in which they appear in the text, refer to pages 391–392 for an explanation: *blind date; spoofing; dubbed the Big Five; scoff; suckering methods; "stock spiel"; labeling and pigeonholing; cold shoulder; leaping a hurdle; dumbfounded; even after a blunder; negative about themselves; prowess; Lake Wobegon; flies in the face of pop psychology; pride does often go before a fall; swelled head; from fantasy to hogwash; put-downs.*

The Trait Perspective (pp. 475–483)

Objective 1: Discuss psychologists' interest in personality types, and describe research efforts to identify fundamental personality traits.

1. Gordon Allport developed trait theory, which defines personality in terms of people's characteristic _____ and conscious _____ . Unlike Freud, he was generally less interested in _____ individual traits than in _____ them.

2. The _____-_____ _____ _____ classifies people according to Carl Jung's personality types. Although recently criticized for its lack of predictive value, this test has been widely used in _____ and _____ counseling.

3. To reduce the number of traits to a few basic ones, psychologists use the statistical procedure of _____ _____ . The Eysencks think that two or three genetically influenced personality dimensions are sufficient; these include _____- _____ and emotional _____-_____ .

4. Some researchers believe that extraverts seek stimulation because their level of _____ _____ is relatively low. PET scans reveal an area of the brain's _____ lobe that is less active in _____ (extraverts/introverts) than in _____ (extraverts/introverts).

5. Research increasingly reveals that our _____ play an important role in defining our _____ and _____ style.

6. Jerome Kagan attributes differences in children's _____ and _____ to autonomic nervous system reactivity.

7. Personality differences among dogs, birds, and other animals _____ (are/are not) stable.

Objective 2: Discuss the value of using personality inventories to assess traits, and identify the Big Five trait dimensions.

8. Questionnaires that categorize personality traits are called _____ _____ .

9. The most widely used of all such personality tests is the _____ _____ _____ _____ ; its questions are grouped into _____ (how many?) clinical scales.

10. This test was developed by testing a large pool of items and selecting those that differentiated particular individuals; in other words, the test was _____ derived.

11. Researchers have arrived at a cluster of five factors that seem to describe the major features of personality. List and briefly describe the Big Five.
    a. _____
    b. _____
    c. _____
    d. _____
    e. _____

12. While some traits wane a bit after college, others increase. For example, as young adults mature and learn to manage their commitments, _____ increases. From the thirties through the sixties, _____ increases.

13. In adulthood, the Big Five are quite _____ (stable/variable), with heritability estimated at _____ percent or more for each dimension. Moreover, these traits _____ (describe/do not describe) personality in other cultures.

Objective 3: Summarize the person-situation controversy, and explain its importance as a commentary on the trait perspective.

14. Human behavior is influenced both by our inner _____ and by the external _____ . The issue of which of these is the more important influence on personality is called the _____-_____ controversy.

15. To be considered a personality trait, a characteristic must persist over _____ and across _____ . Research studies reveal that personality trait scores _____ (correlate/do not correlate) with scores obtained seven years later. The consistency of specific behaviors from one situation to the next is _____ (predictably consistent/not predictably consistent).

16. An individual's score on a personality test _____ (is/is not) very predictive of his or her behavior in any given situation.

Explain the apparent contradiction between behavior in specific situations and average behavior patterns.

17. People's expressive styles, which include their
_____ , manner of _____ ,
and _____ , are quite
_____ (consistent/inconsistent),
which _____ (does/does not)
reveal distinct personality traits.

(Thinking Critically) Explain several techniques used by astrologers to persuade people to accept their advice.

The Social-Cognitive Perspective (pp. 483–490)

Objective 4: Describe the social-cognitive perspective, and discuss the important consequences of personal control, learned helplessness, and optimism.

1. Social-cognitive theory, which focuses on how the individual and the _____ interact, was proposed by _____ .

2. Social-cognitive theorists propose that personality is shaped by the mutual influence of our internal _____ ,
_____ factors, and
_____ factors. This is the principle of _____ _____ .

Describe three different ways in which the environment and personality interact.

3. In studying how we interact with our environment, social-cognitive theorists point to the importance of our sense of _____
_____ . Individuals who believe

that they control their own destinies are said to perceive an _____
_____ _____
_____ . Individuals who believe that their fate is determined by outside forces are said to perceive an _____
_____ _____
_____ . Self-control, which is the ability to control _____ and
_____ gratification, predicts
good _____ , better _____ ,
and _____ success.

4. Seligman found that exposure to inescapable punishment produced a passive resignation in behavior, which he called _____
_____ .

5. People become happier when they are given _____ (more/less) control over what happens to them.

6. One measure of a person's feelings of effectiveness is his or her degree of _____ .
Our characteristic manner of explaining negative and positive events is called our
_____ _____ .

7. Our natural positive-thinking bias can sometimes promote an _____
_____ about future life events that can be unhealthy.

8. (Close-Up) During its first century, psychology focused primarily on understanding and alleviating _____ _____ .
Today, however, thriving Western cultures have an opportunity to create a more _____ psychology, focused on three pillars:

  a. _____

  b. _____

  c. _____

Objective 5: Explain why social-cognitive researchers assess behavior in realistic situations, and state the major criticism of the social-cognitive perspective.

9. People tend to be most overconfident of their abilities in areas where they are, in fact, most _____ (competent/incompetent).

10. It follows from the social-cognitive perspective that the best means of predicting people's future behavior is their _____

_____ .

11. The major criticism of the social-cognitive perspective is that it fails to appreciate a person's

_____ _____ .

Exploring the Self (pp. 490–494)

Objective 6: Explain why psychology has generated so much research on the self, and discuss the importance of self-esteem to human well-being.

1. One of Western psychology's most vigorously researched topics today is the _____ .

2. Hazel Markus and colleagues introduced the concept of an individual's _____

____ . _____ to emphasize how our aspirations motivate us through specific goals.

3. Our tendency to overestimate the extent to which others are noticing and evaluating us is called the

_____ _____ .

4. According to self theorists, personality development hinges on our feelings of self-worth, or _____ . People who feel good about themselves are relatively _____ (dependent on/independent of) outside pressures.

5. In a series of experiments, researchers found that people who were made to feel insecure were _____ (more/less) critical of other persons or tended to express heightened

_____ _____ .

6. Research studies demonstrate that ethnic minorities, people with disabilities, and women generally _____ (have/do not have) lower self-esteem.

7. Members of stigmatized groups maintain self-esteem in three ways:

a. _____

b. _____

c. _____

Objective 7: Discuss some evidence for self-serving bias, and contrast defensive and secure self-esteem.

8. Research has shown that most people tend to have _____ (low/high) self-esteem.

9. The tendency of people to judge themselves favorably is called the _____ bias.

10. Responsibility for success is generally accepted _____ (more/less) readily than responsibility for failure.

11. Most people perceive their own behavior and traits as being _____ (above/below) average.

12. Bushman and Baumeister found that students with unrealistically _____ (low/high) self-esteem were most likely to become exceptionally aggressive after criticism.

13. Some researchers distinguish _____ self-esteem, which is fragile and sensitive to _____ , from _____ self-esteem, which is less focused on _____ evaluations.

14. A number of psychologists have suggested that humans function best with modest self-enhancing _____ .

PROGRESS TEST

Multiple-Choice Questions

Circle your answers to the following questions and check them with the answers beginning on page 389. If your answer is incorrect, read the explanation for why it is incorrect and then consult the appropriate pages of the text.

1. Research on locus of control indicates that internals are _____ than externals.
  a. more dependent
  b. more intelligent
  c. better able to cope with stress
  d. more sociable

2. Which two dimensions of personality have the Eysencks emphasized?
   a. extraversion–introversion and emotional stability–instability
   b. internal–external locus of control and extraversion–introversion
   c. internal–external locus of control and emotional stability–instability
   d. melancholic–phlegmatic and choleric–sanguine

3. With regard to personality, it appears that:
   a. there is little consistency of behavior from one situation to the next and little consistency of traits over the life span.
   b. there is little consistency of behavior from one situation to the next but significant consistency of traits over the life span.
   c. there is significant consistency of behavior from one situation to the next but little consistency of traits over the life span.
   d. there is significant consistency of behavior from one situation to the next and significant consistency of traits over the life span.

4. Regarding the self-serving bias, psychologists who study the self have found that self-affirming thinking:
   a. is generally maladaptive to the individual because it distorts reality by overinflating self-esteem.
   b. is generally adaptive to the individual because it maintains self-confidence and minimizes depression.
   c. tends to prevent the individual from viewing others with compassion and understanding.
   d. tends *not* to characterize people who have experienced unconditional positive regard.

5. A major criticism of trait theory is that it:
   a. places too great an emphasis on early childhood experiences.
   b. overestimates the consistency of behavior in different situations.
   c. underestimates the importance of heredity in personality development.
   d. places too great an emphasis on positive traits.

6. In studying personality, a trait theorist would *most likely*:
   a. test for locus of control.
   b. observe a person in a variety of situations.
   c. use a personality inventory.
   d. check for self-serving bias.

7. Which of the following is the major criticism of the social-cognitive perspective?
   a. It focuses too much on early childhood experiences.
   b. It focuses too little on the inner traits of a person.
   c. It provides descriptions but not explanations.
   d. It lacks appropriate assessment techniques.

8. Seligman has found that humans and animals who are exposed to aversive events they cannot escape may develop:
   a. an internal locus of control.
   b. a reaction formation.
   c. learned helplessness.
   d. reciprocal determinism.

9. Research has shown that individuals who are made to feel insecure are subsequently:
   a. more critical of others.
   b. less critical of others.
   c. more likely to display a self-serving bias.
   d. less likely to display a self-serving bias.

10. An example of the self-serving bias described in the text is the tendency of people to:
    a. see themselves as better than average on nearly any desirable dimension.
    b. accept more responsibility for failures than for successes.
    c. be overly critical of other people.
    d. exhibit different selves in different situations.

11. The Minnesota Multiphasic Personality Inventory (MMPI) is a(n):
    a. projective personality test.
    b. empirically derived and objective personality test.
    c. personality test developed mainly to assess job applicants.
    d. personality test used primarily to assess locus of control.

12. Trait theory attempts to:
    a. show how development of personality is a lifelong process.
    b. describe and classify people in terms of their predispositions to behave in certain ways.
    c. determine which traits are most conducive to individual self-actualization.
    d. explain how behavior is shaped by the interaction between traits, behavior, and the environment.

13. With which of the following statements would a social-cognitive psychologist agree?

    a. People with an internal locus of control achieve more in school.

    b. "Externals" are better able to cope with stress than "internals."

    c. "Internals" are less independent than "externals."

    d. All of these statements are true.

14. Which of the following statements about self-esteem is *not* correct?

    a. People with low self-esteem tend to be negative about others.

    b. People with high self-esteem are less prone to drug addiction.

    c. People with low self-esteem tend to be non-conformists.

    d. People with high self-esteem suffer less from insomnia.

15. In studying personality, a social-cognitive theorist would *most likely* make use of:

    a. personality inventories.

    b. projective tests.

    c. observing behavior in different situations.

    d. factor analyses.

16. The Big Five personality factors are:

    a. emotional stability, openness, introversion, sociability, locus of control.

    b. neuroticism, extraversion, openness, emotional stability, sensitivity.

    c. neuroticism, gregariousness, extraversion, impulsiveness, conscientiousness.

    d. emotional stability, extraversion, openness, agreeableness, conscientiousness.

17. Which of the following groups tend to suffer from relatively low self-esteem?

    a. women

    b. ethnic minorities

    c. disabled persons

    d. none of these groups

18. Recent research on the Big Five personality factors provides evidence that:

    a. some tendencies decrease during adulthood, while others increase.

    b. these traits only describe personality in Western, individualist cultures.

    c. the heritability of individual differences in these traits generally runs about 25 percent or less.

    d. all of these statements are true.

19. James attributes his failing grade in chemistry to an unfair final exam. His attitude exemplifies:

    a. internal locus of control.

    b. learned helplessness.

    c. the self-serving bias.

    d. reciprocal determinism.

20. The behavior of many people has been described in terms of a *spotlight effect*. This means that they

    a. tend to see themselves as being above average in ability.

    b. perceive that their fate is determined by forces not under their personal control.

    c. overestimate the extent to which other people are noticing them.

    d. behave in all of these ways.

21. Because you have a relatively low level of brain arousal, a trait theorist would suggest that you are a(n) _____ who would naturally seek _____ .

    a. introvert; stimulation

    b. introvert; isolation

    c. extravert; stimulation

    d. extravert; isolation

22. A psychologist at the campus mental health center administered an empirically derived personality test to diagnose an emotionally troubled student. Which test did the psychologist *most likely* administer?

    a. the MMPI

    b. the TAT

    c. the Rorschach

    d. the Locus of Control Scale

23. Isaiah is sober and reserved; Rashid is fun-loving and affectionate. The Eysencks would say that Isaiah _____ and Rashid _____ .

    a. has an internal locus of control; has an external locus of control

    b. has an external locus of control; has an internal locus of control

    c. is an extravert; is an introvert

    d. is an introvert; is an extravert

24. In high school, Britta and Debbie were best friends. They thought they were a lot alike, as did everyone else who knew them. After high school, they went on to very different colleges, careers, and life courses. Now, at their twenty-fifth reunion, they are shocked at how little they have in common. Bandura would suggest that their differences reflect the interactive effects of environment, personality, and behavior, which he refers to as:

a. reciprocal determinism.
b. personal control.
c. the spotlight effect.
d. the self-serving bias.

25. For his class presentation, Bruce plans to discuss the Big Five personality factors used by people throughout the world to describe others or themselves. Which of the following is *not* a factor that Bruce will discuss?

a. extraversion   c. independence
b. openness   d. conscientiousness

26. Dayna is not very consistent in showing up for class and turning in assignments when they are due. Research studies would suggest that Dayna's inconsistent behavior:

a. indicates that she is emotionally troubled and may need professional counseling.

b. is a sign of learned helplessness.
c. is not necessarily unusual.
d. probably reflects a temporary problem in another area of her life.

27. Nadine has a relatively high level of brain arousal. Trait theorists would probably predict that she is:

a. an extravert.   c. an unstable person.
b. an introvert.   d. narcissistic.

28. (Close-Up) During a class discussion, Trevor argues that "positive psychology" is sure to wane in popularity, since it suffers from the same criticisms as humanistic psychology. You counter his argument by pointing out that, unlike humanistic psychology, positive psychology:

a. focuses on advancing human fulfillment.
b. is rooted in science.
c. is not based on the study of individual characteristics.
d. has all of these characteristics.

Matching Items

Match each definition or description with the appropriate term.

Definitions or Descriptions

_____ **1.** personality inventory
_____ **2.** a statistical technique that identifies clusters of personality traits
_____ **3.** the two-way interactions of behavior with personal and environmental factors
_____ **4.** developed by testing a pool of items and then selecting those that discriminate the group of interest

Terms

a. factor analysis
b. MMPI
c. empirically derived test
d. reciprocal determinism

KEY TERMS

Using your own words, on a separate piece of paper write a brief definition or explanation of each of the following terms.

1. traits

2. personality inventory

3. Minnesota Multiphasic Personality Inventory (MMPI)

4. empirically derived test

5. social-cognitive perspective

6. reciprocal determinism

7. personal control

8. external locus of control

9. internal locus of control

10. learned helplessness

11. positive psychology

12. spotlight effect

13. self-esteem

14. self-serving bias

ANSWERS

Module Review

The Trait Perspective

1. behaviors; motives; explaining; describing

2. Myers-Briggs Type Indicator; business; career

3. factor analysis; extraversion–introversion; stability–instability

4. brain arousal; frontal; extraverts; introverts

5. genes; temperament; behavioral

6. shyness; inhibition

7. are

8. personality inventories

9. Minnesota Multiphasic Personality Inventory; 10

10. empirically

11. a. Emotional stability: on a continuum from calm to anxious; secure to insecure
    b. Extraversion: from sociable to retiring
    c. Openness: from preference for variety to routine
    d. Agreeableness: from soft-hearted to ruthless
    e. Conscientiousness: from disciplined to impulsive

12. conscientiousness; agreeableness

13. stable; 50; describe

14. traits (or dispositions); situation (or environment); person-situation

15. time; situations; correlate; not predictably consistent

16. is not

At any given moment a person's behavior is powerfully influenced by the immediate situation, so that it may appear that the person does not have a consistent personality. But averaged over many situations a person's outgoingness, happiness, and carelessness, for instance, are more predictable.

17. animation; speaking; gestures; consistent; does

Astrologers use a "stock spiel" that includes information that is generally true of almost everyone. The willingness of people to accept this type of phony information is called the "Barnum effect." A second technique used by astrologers is to "read" a person's clothing, features, reactions, etc. and build their advice from these observations.

The Social-Cognitive Perspective

1. environment; Bandura

2. behaviors; personal; environmental; reciprocal determinism

Different people choose different environments partly on the basis of their dispositions. Our personality shapes how we interpret and react to events. It also helps create the situations to which we react.

3. personal control; internal locus of control; external locus of control; impulses; delay; adjustment; grades; social

4. learned helplessness

5. more

6. optimism; attributional style

7. unrealistic (illusory) optimism

8. negative states; positive
   a. positive emotions
   b. positive character
   c. positive groups, communities, and cultures

9. incompetent

10. past behavior in similar situations

11. inner traits

Exploring the Self

1. self

2. possible selves

3. spotlight effect

4. self-esteem; independent of

5. more; racial prejudice

6. do not have

7. a. They value the things at which they excel.
   b. They attribute problems to prejudice.
   c. They compare themselves to those in their own group.

8. high

9. self-serving

10. more

11. above

12. high

13. defensive; criticism; secure; external

14. illusions

Progress Test

Multiple-Choice Questions

1. **c.** is the answer.
   a. & d. In fact, just the opposite is true.
   b. Locus of control is not related to intelligence.

2. **a.** is the answer.
   b. & c. Locus of control is emphasized by the social-cognitive perspective.
   d. This is how the ancient Greeks described personality.

3. **b.** is the answer. Studies have shown that people do not act with predictable consistency from one situation to the next. But, over a number of situations, consistent patterns emerge, and this basic consistency of traits persists over the life span.

4. **b.** is the answer. Psychologists who study the self emphasize that for the individual, self-affirming thinking is generally adaptive (therefore, not a.); such thinking maintains self-confidence, minimizes depression, and enables us to view others with compassion and understanding (therefore, not c.); unconditional positive regard tends to promote self-esteem and thus self-affirming thinking (therefore, not d.).

5. **b.** is the answer. In doing so, it underestimates the influence of the environment.
   a. The trait perspective does not emphasize early childhood experiences.
   c. This criticism is unlikely since trait theory does not seek to explain personality development.
   d. Trait theory does not look on traits as being "positive" or "negative."

6. **c.** is the answer.
   a. & b. Locus of control is a concept of the social-cognitive perspective. Also, this type of theorist, not a trait theorist, would test a person in a variety of situations.
   d. The self-serving bias refers to the tendency to perceive oneself favorably.

7. **b.** is the answer. The social-cognitive theory has been accused of putting so much emphasis on the situation that inner traits are neglected.
   a. Such a criticism has been made of the psychoanalytic perspective but is not relevant to the social-cognitive perspective.
   c. Such a criticism might be more relevant to the trait perspective; the social-cognitive perspective offers an explanation in the form of reciprocal determinism.
   d. There are assessment techniques appropriate to the theory, namely, questionnaires and observations of behavior in situations.

8. **c.** is the answer. In such situations, passive resignation, called learned helplessness, develops.
   a. This refers to the belief that one controls one's fate; the circumstances described lead to precisely the opposite belief.
   b. Reaction formation is a defense mechanism in which unacceptable impulses are channeled into their opposites.
   d. Reciprocal determinism refers to the interaction of the person and the environment.

9. **a.** is the answer. Feelings of insecurity reduce self-esteem, and those who feel negative about themselves tend to feel negative about others as well.

10. **a.** is the answer.

11. **b.** is the answer. The MMPI was developed by selecting from many items those that differentiated between the groups of interest; hence, it was empirically derived. That it is an objective test is shown by the fact that it can be scored by computer.
    a. Projective tests present ambiguous stimuli for people to interpret; the MMPI is a questionnaire.
    c. Although sometimes used to assess job applicants, the MMPI was developed to assess emotionally troubled people.
    d. The MMPI does not focus on control but, rather, measures various aspects of personality.

12. **b.** is the answer. Trait theory attempts to describe behavior and not to develop explanations or applications. The emphasis is more on consistency than on change.

13. **a.** is the answer. "Internals," or those who have a sense of personal control, have been shown to achieve more in school. Relative to externals, they also cope better with stress and are more independent.

14. **c.** is the answer. In actuality, people with *high* self-esteem are generally more independent of pressures to conform.

15. **c.** is the answer. In keeping with their emphasis on interactions between people and situations, social-cognitive theorists would most likely make use of observations of behavior in relevant situations.
    a. & d. Personality inventories and factor analyses would more likely be used by a trait theorist.
    b. Projective tests would more likely be used by a psychologist working within the psychoanalytic perspective.

16. **d.** is the answer.

17. **d.** is the answer.

18. **a.** is the answer. Neuroticism, extraversion, and openness tend to decrease, while agreeableness and conscientiousness tend to increase.

    b. The Big Five dimensions describe personality in various cultures reasonably well.

    c. Heritability generally runs 50 percent or more for each dimension.

19. **c.** is the answer.

    a. A person with an internal locus of control would be likely to *accept* responsibility for a failing grade.

    b. Learned helplessness is the perceive lack of control a person develops from repeated exposure to inescapable aversive events. James obviously had control over his grade.

    d. Reciprocal determinism refers to the mutual influences among personality, environment, and behavior.

20. **c.** is the answer.

    a. This describes the self-serving bias.

    b. This describes external locus of control.

21. **c.** is the answer.

    a. & b. According to this theory, introverts have relatively *high* levels of arousal, causing them to crave solitude.

    d. Isolation might lower arousal level even further.

22. **a.** is the answer.

    b. & c. The TAT and Rorschach are projective tests that were not empirically derived.

    d. A personality test that measures locus of control would not be helpful in identifying troubled behaviors.

23. **d.** is the answer.

    a. & b. The traits of Isaiah and Rashid reveal nothing about their sense of personal control.

24. **a.** is the answer. Reciprocal determinism refers to the mutual influences among personal factors, environmental factors, and behavior.

    b. Personal control is one's sense of controlling, or being controlled by, the environment.

    c. The spotlight effect is the tendency of people to overestimate the extent to which other people are observing them.

    d. The self-serving bias describes our readiness to perceive ourselves favorably.

25. **c.** is the answer.

26. **c.** is the answer.

27. **b.** is the answer. Introverts do not need to seek stimulation because their normal level of brain arousal is already high.

    c. Nadine's high level of brain arousal might imply instability but not necessarily so.

    d. Nadine may be narcissistic, but that would not show up as brain arousal.

28. **b.** is the answer.

    a. Both positive psychology and humanistic psychology focus on advancing human fulfillment.

    c. Both perspectives focus, at least partly, on individual characteristics.

Matching Items
1. b   3. d
2. a   4. c

Key Terms

1. **Traits** are people's characteristic patterns of behavior.

2. **Personality inventories**, associated with the trait perspective, are questionnaires used to assess personality traits.

3. Consisting of 10 clinical scales, the **Minnesota Multiphasic Personality Inventory (MMPI)** is the most widely researched and clinically used personality inventory.

4. An **empirically derived test** is one developed by testing many items to see which best distinguish between groups of interest.

5. According to the **social-cognitive perspective,** behavior is the result of interactions between people (and their thinking) and their social context.

6. According to the social-cognitive perspective, personality is shaped through **reciprocal determinism,** or the interaction between personality and environmental factors.

7. **Personal control** refers to a person's sense of controlling the environment.

8. **External locus of control** is the perception that one's fate is determined by forces not under personal control.

9. **Internal locus of control** is the perception that, to a great extent, one controls one's own destiny.

10. **Learned helplessness** is the passive resignation and perceived lack of control that a person or animal develops from repeated exposure to inescapable aversive events.

11. Focusing on positive emotions, character virtues such as creativity and compassion, and healthy families and neighborhoods, **positive psychology** is the scientific study of optimal human functioning.

12. The **spotlight effect** is the tendency of people to overestimate the extent to which other people are noticing and evaluating them.

13. **Self-esteem** refers to an individual's sense of self-worth.

14. The **self-serving bias** is the tendency to perceive oneself favorably.

FOCUS ON VOCABULARY AND LANGUAGE

The Trait Perspective

. . . blind date . . . When a social outing (a *date*) is arranged with a person you have never met or seen before, the outing is called a *blind date*. Having the person (*your blind date*) ranked on the Big Five dimensions, for example, would tell you a lot about the person's character and personality.

Nevertheless, people have had fun *spoofing* the MMPI with their own *mock* items . . . Some items on the MMPI may appear nonsensical (*sound silly*), but they differentiated, say, depressed from nondepressed people, and so were retained in the form. Some people have created humorous but false (*mock*) items for a personality test that is a parody (*spoof*) of the MMPI.

A slightly expanded set of factors—*dubbed* the Big Five—does a better job. . . . The Eysencks use two prime personality dimensions, or factors—extraversion–introversion and emotional stability– instability. Other researchers offer another three dimensions (openness, agreeableness, and conscientiousness), bringing the total to five factors, which they named (*dubbed*) the Big Five.

(Thinking Critically): . . . *scoff* . . . This means to have a contemptuously mocking attitude toward something. Astronomers who study the universe scientifically *scoff* at astrologers who believe that the planets and stars determine human affairs.

(Thinking Critically): . . . *suckering methods* . . . To get suckered means to be easily fooled and exploited. Psychologists, such as Ray Hyman, show us how astrologers, palm (hand) readers, graphologists (who allegedly analyze handwriting to reveal personality), and others fool and exploit people by use of a few simple techniques (*suckering methods*).

(Thinking Critically): . . . *"stock spiel"* . . . A "stock spiel" is a well-rehearsed and glib story. Astrologers, horoscope writers, and such often use statements that are generally true of almost everybody (*their "stock spiel"*), and most people find it hard to resist believing the flattering descriptions of themselves; consequently, many view astrology as an authentic art.

If we remember such results, says Mischel, we will be more cautious about *labeling* and *pigeonholing* individuals. Research has shown that some behavior can be context specific (i.e., determined by the situation and not by the personality) and that personality test scores are poorly correlated with people's actual behavior on any particular occasion. Mischel warns that we should be careful about classifying individuals (*labeling*) and concluding that they belong in one particular slot (*pigeonholing*).

The Social-Cognitive Perspective

If we expect someone to be angry with us, we may give the person a *cold shoulder, touching off* the very anger we expect. The way we are (our personalities) may influence how we are treated by others. If we believe that someone has hostile intentions toward us, we may ignore and treat the person with indifference (*give the person a cold shoulder*), and this in turn may cause (*touch off*) the angry behavior we predicted or expected from that person. As Myers notes, we are both the results (*products*) and the creators (*architects*) of our environments.

Later placed in another situation where they *could* escape the punishment by simply *leaping a hurdle,* the dogs cowered as if without hope. In Seligman's experiments, dogs learned that nothing they did had any effect on what happened to them (**learned helplessness**), so they would not make even a minimal effort, such as jumping over a small barrier (*leaping a hurdle*), to escape being shocked. People, too, who feel they have no control over what happens to them may become depressed and feel hopeless and helpless.

. . . so many low-scoring students are *dumbfounded* after doing badly on an exam. People often are most overconfident when most incompetent, mainly because it is difficult for them to recognize incompetence without having competence in the first place. Consequently, many students who do not recognize that they are having problems are often astounded (*dumbfounded*) when they find they are not in the top half of the class. (As Myers notes, like pride, illusory or blind optimism may precede a negative outcome or fall.)

Exploring the Self

Even after a blunder . . . we stick out like a sore thumb less than we imagine. A person who sticks out like a sore thumb is someone who is very noticeable to everyone as odd or different. If we make a clumsy mistake (*a blunder*), we think that everyone is paying attention to us (*we stick out like a sore thumb*), but this is often not the case. For example, students who had to wear a very unfashionable T-shirt with the picture of a lounge singer on it (*they had to don a Barry Manilow T-shirt*) thought that many people would notice their odd attire (*dorky clothes*), but very few did. This is a good illustration of the **spotlight effect.**

Those who are *negative about themselves* also tend to be *thin-skinned* and *judgmental. . . .* People who have low self-esteem (*are negative about themselves*) are more likely to be anxious, depressed, insecure, and very sensitive to criticism (*thin-skinned*). In addition, they are also more likely to disparage and be critical (*judgmental*) of others.

Athletes often privately credit their victories to their own *prowess* and their losses to *bad breaks, lousy officiating,* or the other team's exceptional performance. Athletes, like the rest of us, want to feel that desirable outcomes are due to their own abilities (*prowess*) and that failures are due to factors beyond their control such as poor luck (*bad breaks*), unfair refereeing (*lousy officiating*), or their opponents' unexpectedly outstanding efforts. This is called the **self-serving bias.**

The world, it seems, is Garrison Keillor's *Lake Wobegon* writ large—a place where "all the women are strong, all the men are good-looking, and all the children are above average." Lake Wobegon is a fictional but ideal community satirized by comedian Garrison Keillor. Most abilities follow a bell-shaped distribution (the normal curve), so approximately half the population will be below average and half above on any given trait, such as strength, looks, or intelligence. The self-serving bias, which prompts most of us to rate ourselves as above average, appears to be almost universal, and the world is a magnified reflection of the Lake Wobegon community.

Self-serving bias *flies in the face of pop psychology.* A claim of pop psychology is that we all have inferiority complexes. As is often the case, scientific psychology has clearly demonstrated that the opposite is actually true and that empirically based research findings contradict or refute the popular beliefs (*they fly in the face of pop psychology claims*).

Moreover, *pride does often go before a fall.* Our conceit and self-important attitudes (*pride*) often precede a harsh lesson from reality (*a fall*). As Myers notes, it was nationalistic pride (the conceited belief that the Aryan race was superior) that facilitated and fostered (*fueled*) the growth of the Nazi movement and legitimized their inhumane and cruel deeds (*atrocities*).

An adolescent or adult with a *swelled head* that gets deflated by insult is potentially dangerous. Overly self-confident people with high self-esteem (*swelled heads or large egos*) do more than retaliate in kind (*put down others*) when criticized, insulted, or rejected. Instead, they are more likely to react violently and aggressively (they are potentially dangerous). Researchers suggest that this negative aspect (*dark side*) of self-esteem is the result of threatened egotism and not low self-esteem.

(margin): The enthusiastic claims of the self-esteem movement mostly range *from fantasy to hogwash.* The popular belief that having high self-esteem is essential to being a happy, well-adjusted, caring person is not supported by the research. Baumeister (1996) suggests that the claims of the self-esteem movement vary from being imaginative, wishful thinking (*fantasy*) to sheer nonsense (*hogwash*)—the effects of self-esteem are not very large or important.

Sometimes self-directed *put-downs* are subtly strategic: They *elicit* reassuring *strokes.* When people disparage themselves with criticisms aimed at themselves (*self-directed put-downs*), they sometimes have an insidious or hidden purpose (*are subtly strategic*). They may want to have people reassure them that the opposite is true (*they want strokes*), or they may want to prepare for the worst possible outcome and have a rationalization for failure ready, just in case.

Psychological Disorders

Introduction to Psychological Disorders

36

MODULE OVERVIEW

Although there is no clear-cut line between normal and abnormal behavior, we can characterize as abnormal those behaviors that are deviant, distressful, and dysfunctional. Module 36 introduces the *Diagnostic and Statistical Manual of Mental Disorders* (DSM-IV). Although this classification system follows a medical model, most psychologists today advocate a biopsychosocial approach. Thus, psychoanalytic theory, learning theory, social-cognitive theory, and other psychological perspectives are drawn on when relevant. The module concludes with a discussion of the incidence of serious psychological disorders in society today.

NOTE: Answer guidelines for all Module 36 questions begin on page 398.

MODULE REVIEW

First, skim each section, noting headings and boldface items. After you have read the section, review each objective by answering the fill-in and essay-type questions that follow it. As you proceed, evaluate your performance by consulting the answers beginning on page 398. Do not continue with the next section until you understand each answer. If you need to, review or reread the section in the textbook before continuing.

> David Myers at times uses idioms that are unfamiliar to some readers. If you do not know the meaning of any of the following words, phrases, or expressions from the context in which they appear in the text, refer to pages 400–401 for an explanation: *eerie sense of self-recognition; draw the line; "The devil made him do it"; chatters away and darts from one activity to the next; handy shorthand; have faulted the manual; "Hinckley Insane, Public Mad"; self-fulfilling prophecies.*

Defining Psychological Disorders
(pp. 499–500, 501)

Objective 1: Identify the criteria for judging whether behavior is psychologically disordered.

1. Psychological disorders are persistently harmful

   _____ , _____ ,

   and _____ .

2. Psychiatrists and psychologists label behavior disordered when it is _____ ,

   _____ , and _____ .

3. This definition emphasizes that standards of acceptability for behavior are

   _____ (constant/variable).

4. (Thinking Critically) ADHD, or _____-

   _____ _____

   _____ , plagues children who display one or more of three key symptoms:

   _____ , _____ ,

   and _____ .

5. (Thinking Critically) ADHD is diagnosed more often in _____ (boys/girls). In the past two decades, the proportion of American children being treated for this disorder _____ (increased/decreased) dramatically. Experts _____ (agree/do not agree) that ADHD is a real neurobiological disorder.

6. (Thinking Critically) ADHD _____ (is/is not) thought by some heritable, and it _____ (is/is not) caused by eating too much sugar or poor schools. ADHD is often accompanied by a _____ disorder or with behavior that is _____ or temper-prone.

Understanding Psychological Disorders
(pp. 500, 502)

Objective 2: Contrast the medical model of psychological disorders with the biopsychosocial approach to disordered behavior.

1. The view that psychological disorders are sicknesses is the basis of the _____ model. According to this view, psychological disorders are viewed as mental _____ , or _____ , diagnosed on the basis of _____ and cured through _____ .

2. Today's psychologists recognize that all behavior arises from the interaction of _____ and _____ . To presume that a person is "mentally ill" attributes the condition solely to an _____ problem.

3. Major psychological disorders such as _____ and _____ are universal; others, such as _____ _____ and _____ _____ , are culture-bound. These culture-bound disorders may share an underlying _____ , such as _____ , yet differ in their _____ .

4. Most mental health workers today take a _____ approach, whereby they assume that disorders are influenced by _____ _____ and _____ _____ , inner _____ _____ , and _____ and _____ circumstances.

Classifying Psychological Disorders
(pp. 502–503)

Objective 3: Describe the goals and content of the DSM-IV.

1. The most widely used system for classifying psychological disorders is the American Psychiatric Association manual, commonly known by its abbreviation, _____ . It was developed in coordination with the World Health Organization's _____

_____ of _____ . This manual _____ (does/does not) explain the cause of a disorder; rather, it _____ the disorder and lists its prevalence.

2. Independent diagnoses made with the current manual generally _____ (show/do not show) agreement.

3. One criticism of DSM-IV is that as the number of disorder categories has _____ (increased/decreased), the number of adults who meet the criteria for at least one psychiatric ailment has _____ (increased/decreased).

(Close-Up) Briefly describe the "unDSM."

Labeling Psychological Disorders (pp. 503–505)

Objective 4: Discuss the potential dangers and benefits of using diagnostic labels.

1. Studies have shown that labeling has _____ (little/a significant) effect on our interpretation of individuals and their behavior.

2. (Thinking Critically) Most people with psychological disorders _____ (are/are not) violent. A 1999 study found that 16 percent of U.S. prison inmates had severe _____ _____ .

Outline the pros and cons of labeling psychological disorders.

Rates of Psychological Disorders (pp. 506–507)

Objective 5: Discuss the prevalence of psychological disorders, and summarize the findings on the link between poverty and serious psychological disorders.

1. Research reveals that approximately 1 in every _____ (how many?) Americans suffered a clinically significant mental disorder during the prior year.

2. The incidence of serious psychological disorders is _____ (higher/lower) among those below the poverty line.

3. In terms of age of onset, most psychological disorders appear by _____ (early/middle/late) adulthood. Some, such as the

   _____ _____

   and _____ , appear during childhood.

PROGRESS TEST

Multiple-Choice Questions

Circle your answers to the following questions and check them with the answers on page 399. If your answer is incorrect, read the explanation for why it is incorrect and then consult the appropriate pages of the text.

1. The criteria for classifying behavior as psychologically disordered:
   a. are the same in all cultures.
   b. vary from culture to culture and from time to time.
   c. are based on legal definitions.
   d. have remained largely unchanged over the course of history.

2. Most mental health workers today take the view that disordered behaviors:
   a. are usually genetically triggered.
   b. are organic diseases.
   c. arise from the interaction of nature and nurture.
   d. are the product of learning.

3. The view that all behavior arises from the interaction of heredity and environment is referred to as the _____ approach.
   a. biopsychosocial
   b. psychoanalytic
   c. medical
   d. conditioning

4. Evidence of environmental effects on psychological disorders is seen in the fact that certain disorders, such as _____ , are universal, whereas others, such as _____ , are culture-bound.
   a. schizophrenia; depression
   b. depression; schizophrenia
   c. antisocial personality; neurosis
   d. depression; anorexia nervosa

5. The diagnostic reliability of DSM-IV:
   a. is unknown.
   b. depends on the age of the patient.
   c. is very low.
   d. is relatively high.

6. (Thinking Critically) The term *insanity* refers to:
   a. legal definitions.
   b. psychotic disorders only.
   c. personality disorders only.
   d. both psychotic disorders and personality disorders.

7. Which of the following is true concerning abnormal behavior?
   a. Definitions of abnormal behavior are culture-dependent.
   b. A behavior cannot be defined as abnormal unless it is considered harmful to society.
   c. Abnormal behavior can be defined as any behavior that is distressful.
   d. Definitions of abnormal behavior are based on physiological factors.

8. The fact that disorders such as schizophrenia are universal and influenced by heredity, whereas other disorders such as anorexia nervosa are culture-bound provides evidence for the _____ model of psychological disorders.
   a. medical   c. social-cultural
   b. biopsychosocial   d. psychoanalytic

9. Our early ancestors commonly attributed disordered behavior to:
   a. "bad blood."   c. brain injury.
   b. evil spirits.   d. laziness.

10. Which of the following statements concerning the labeling of disordered behaviors is *not* true?
    a. Labels interfere with effective treatment of psychological disorders.
    b. Labels promote research studies of psychological disorders.
    c. Labels may create preconceptions that bias people's perceptions.
    d. Labels may influence behavior by creating self-fulfilling prophecies.

11. Which of the following is true of the medical model?
    a. In recent years, it has been in large part discredited.
    b. It views psychological disorders as sicknesses that are diagnosable and treatable.
    c. It emphasizes the role of psychological factors in disorders over that of physiological factors.
    d. It focuses on cognitive factors.

12. Behavior is classified as disordered when it:
    a. is deviant.
    b. is distressful.
    c. is dysfunctional.
    d. has all of these characteristics.

13. Many psychologists dislike using DSM-IV because of its:
    a. failure to emphasize observable behaviors in the diagnostic process.
    b. learning theory bias.
    c. medical model bias.
    d. psychoanalytic bias.

14. (Thinking Critically) Thirteen-year-old Ronald constantly fidgets in his seat at school, frequently blurts out answers without being called, and is extremely distractible. A psychiatrist might diagnose Ronald with:
    a. bipolar disorder.
    b. panic disorder.
    c. attention-deficit hyperactivity disorder.
    d. obsessive-compulsive disorder.

Essay Question

Clinical psychologists label people disordered if their behavior is (1) deviant, (2) distressful, and (3) dysfunctional. Demonstrate your understanding of the classification process by giving examples of behaviors that might be considered deviant, distressful, or dysfunctional but, because they do not fit all three criteria, would not necessarily be labeled disordered. (Use the space below to list the points you want to make, and organize them. Then write the essay on a separate piece of paper.)

KEY TERMS

Using your own words, on a separate piece of paper write a brief definition or explanation of each of the following terms.

1. psychological disorder

2. attention-deficit hyperactivity disorder (ADHD)

3. medical model

4. DSM-IV

ANSWERS

Module Review

Defining Psychological Disorders

1. thoughts; feelings; actions
2. deviant; distressful; dysfunctional
3. variable
4. attention-deficit hyperactivity disorder; inattention; hyperactivity; impulsivity
5. boys; increased; agree
6. is; is not; learning; defiant

Understanding Psychological Disorders

1. medical; illness; psychopathology; symptoms; therapy
2. nature; nurture; internal
3. depression; schizophrenia; anorexia nervosa; bulimia nervosa; dynamic; anxiety; symptoms
4. biopsychosocial; genetic predispositions; physiological states; psychological dynamics; social; cultural

Classifying Psychological Disorders

1. DSM-IV; Internal Classification; Diseases; does not; describes
2. show
3. increased; increased

The "unDSM" is a new classification system that identifies 24 human strengths and virtues grouped into six clusters: wisdom and knowledge, courage, love, justice, temperance, and transcendence.

Labeling Psychological Disorders

1. a significant
2. are not; mental disorders

Psychological labels may be arbitrary. They can create preconceptions that bias our perceptions and interpretations and they can affect people's self-images. Moreover, labels can change reality, by serving as self-fulfilling prophecies. Despite these drawbacks, labels are useful in describing, treating, and researching the causes of psychological disorders.

Rates of Psychological Disorders

1. 7
2. higher
3. early; antisocial personality; phobias

Progress Test

Multiple-Choice Questions

1. **b.** is the answer.
2. **c.** is the answer. Most clinicians agree that psychological disorders may be caused by both psychological (d.) and physical (a. and b.) factors.
3. **a.** is the answer.
4. **d.** is the answer. Although depression is universal, anorexia nervosa and bulimia are rare outside of Western culture.
   a. & b. Schizophrenia and depression are both universal.

c. The text mentions only schizophrenia and depression as universal disorders. Furthermore, neurosis is no longer utilized as a category of diagnosis.

5. **d.** is the answer.
   b. The text does not mention DSM-IV's reliability in terms of a person's age.
6. **a.** is the answer.
7. **a.** is the answer. Different cultures have different standards for behaviors that are considered acceptable and normal.
   b. Some abnormal behaviors are simply maladaptive for the individual.
   c. Many individuals who are deviant, such as Olympic gold medalists, are not considered abnormal. There are other criteria that must be met in order for behavior to be considered abnormal.
   d. Although physiological factors play a role in the various disorders, they do not define abnormal behavior. Rather, behavior is said to be abnormal if it is deviant, distressful, and dysfunctional.
8. **b.** is the answer. The fact that some disorders are universal and at least partly genetic in origin implicates biological factors in their origin. The fact that other disorders appear only in certain parts of the world implicates sociocultural and psychological factors in their origin.
9. **b.** is the answer.
10. **a.** is the answer. In fact, just the opposite is true. Labels are useful in promoting effective treatment of psychological disorders.
11. **b.** is the answer.
    a. This isn't the case; in fact, the medical model has gained credibility from recent discoveries of genetic and biochemical links to some disorders.
    c. & d. The medical perspective tends to place more emphasis on physiological factors.
12. **d.** is the answer.
13. **c.** is the answer. DSM-IV was shaped by the medical model.
    a. In fact, just the opposite is true. DSM-IV was revised in order to improve reliability by basing diagnoses on observable behaviors.
    b. & d. DSM-IV does not reflect a learning or a psychoanalytic bias.
14. **c.** is the answer.

Essay Question

There is more to a psychological disorder than being different from other people. Gifted artists, athletes, and scientists have deviant capabilities, yet are not considered psychologically disordered. Also, what is deviant in one culture may not be in another, or at another time. Homosexuality, for example, was once classified as a psychological disorder, but it is no longer. Similarly, nudity is common in some cultures and disturbing in others. Deviant behaviors are more likely to be considered disordered when judged as distressful and dysfunctional to the individual. Prolonged feelings of depression or the use of drugs to avoid dealing with problems are examples of deviant behaviors that may signal a psychological disorder if the person is unable to function, to perform routine behaviors (become dysfunctional).

Key Terms

1. In order to be classified as a **psychological disorder**, behavior must be deviant, distressful, and dysfunctional.

2. **Attention-deficit hyperactivity disorder (ADHD)** is a psychological disorder characterized by one or more of three symptoms: extreme inattention, hyperactivity, and impulsivity.

3. The **medical model** holds that psychological disorders are illnesses that can be diagnosed, treated, and, in most cases, cured, often through treatment in a psychiatric hospital.

4. **DSM-IV** is a short name for the American Psychiatric Association's *Diagnostic and Statistical Manual of Mental Disorders (Fourth Edition, Text Revision)*, which provides a widely used system of classifying psychological disorders.

FOCUS ON VOCABULARY AND LANGUAGE

It's no wonder, then, that studying psychological disorders may at times evoke an *eerie sense* of self-recognition, one that *illuminates* the dynamics of our own personality. When reading this chapter, you may sometimes experience the strange, uncanny feeling (*eerie sense*) that Myers is writing about you. On occasion, we all feel, think, and behave in ways similar to disturbed people, and becoming aware of how alike we sometimes are may help shed some light on (*illuminate*) the processes underlying personality.

Defining Psychological Disorders

Where should we *draw the line* between sadness and depression? Between zany creativity and bizarre irrationality? Between normality and abnormality? Myers is addressing the problem of how exactly to define psychological disorders. How do we distinguish (*draw the line*) between someone who displays unusual or absurd innovative ability (*zany creativity*) and someone who has strange and unusual reasoning (*bizarre irrationality*)? Between someone who is "abnormal" and someone who is not? For psychologists and other mental-health workers, psychological disorders involve persistently harmful thoughts, feelings, and actions that are deviant, distressful, and dysfunctional.

Understanding Psychological Disorders

"The devil made him do it." Our ancestors explained strange and puzzling behavior by appealing to what they knew and believed about the nature of the world (e.g., gods, stars, demons, spirits, etc.). A person who today would be classified as psychologically disturbed because of his or her bizarre behavior in the past would have been considered to be possessed by evil spirits or demons (*the devil made him do it*). These types of nonscientific explanations persisted up until the nineteenth century.

(Thinking Critically): At home, he *chatters away* and *darts* from one activity to the next, rarely settling down to read a book or focus on a game. If a young boy talks constantly (*chatters away*), moves quickly (*darts*) from doing one thing to doing something else, is nervous and restless (*fidgety*), and seldom sits quietly (*settles down*) to read a book or focus on a game, he may be diagnosed with attention-deficit hyperactivity disorder (ADHD). There is some debate about whether this behavioral pattern is a real disorder or simply reflects the normal range of behavior of an overenergetic young person. Skeptics claim that it is being overdiagnosed, while others argue that the more frequent diagnosis of ADHD today reflects increased awareness of the disorder.

Classifying Psychological Disorders

"Schizophrenia" provides *a handy shorthand* for describing a complex disorder. Psychology uses a classification system (DSM-IV) to describe and impose order on complicated psychological problems. When a descriptive label (diagnostic classification) is used to identify a disorder, it does not explain the problem, but it does provide a quick and useful means of communicating a great deal of information in abbreviated form (*it is a handy shorthand*).

Some critics have *faulted* the manual for *casting too wide a net* and bringing "almost any kind of behavior within the *compass* of psychiatry." . . . The DSM-IV classification system has been received with a less-than-enthusiastic response by some practitioners (*they were not enthralled*). Many criticize (*fault*) the inclusion of a large number of behaviors as psychologically disordered (*it casts too wide a net*) and suggest that just about any behavior is now within the purview (*compass*) of psychiatry. Nevertheless, many other clinicians find DSM-IV a useful and practical tool or device.

Labeling Psychological Disorders

(*Thinking Critically*): "Hinckley *Insane*, Public *Mad.*" The word *mad* has a number of meanings: (a) angry, (b) insane, (c) foolish and irrational, (d) rash, (e) enthusiastic about something, (f) frantic. John Hinckley, who shot President Reagan, was not sent to prison; instead, he was confined to a mental hospital. The public was angry and upset (*mad*) because Hinckley was judged to be mad (*insane*).

Labels can serve as *self-fulfilling prophecies*. A prophecy is a prediction about the future. When we characterize or classify (*label*) someone as a certain type of person, the very act of labeling may help bring about or create the actions described by the label (*self-fulfilling prophesy*).

Anxiety, Dissociative, and Personality Disorders

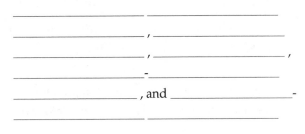

37 **MODULE**

MODULE OVERVIEW

Module 37 first discusses types of anxiety disorders, as classified by the *Diagnostic and Statistical Manual of Mental Disorders* (DSM-IV). After briefly describing generalized anxiety disorder, phobias, obsessive-compulsive disorder, and post-traumatic stress disorder, the module presents psychoanalytic, learning, and biological explanations for these disorders.

The module also discusses dissociative disorders, focusing on the controversial and unique dissociative identity disorder, and personality disorders. Although the dissociative identity disorder has received much attention, some critics are skeptical; they note that it may be a construct of therapists looking to explain certain behaviors. Personality disorders, on the other hand, are widely accepted; the antisocial personality in particular is thought to be a product of genetic and environmental factors.

Your major task in this module is to learn about several different types of psychological disorders, their characteristics, and their possible causes. Since the material to be learned is extensive, it may be helpful to rehearse it by mentally completing the fill-in questions several times.

NOTE: Answer guidelines for all Module 37 questions begin on page 408.

MODULE REVIEW

First, skim each section, noting headings and boldface items. After you have read the section, review each objective by answering the fill-in and essay-type questions that follow it. As you proceed, evaluate your performance by consulting the answers beginning on page 408. Do not continue with the next section until you understand each answer. If you need to, review or reread the section in the textbook before continuing.

David Myers at times uses idioms that are unfamiliar to some readers. If you do not know the meaning of any of the following words, phrases, or expressions from the context in which they appear in the text, refer to pages 411–412 for an explanation: *heart palpitations . . . fidgeting; lighting up doesn't lighten up; flashbacks and nightmares; Grooming gone wild; ruse; go fishing for multiple personalities; con artist; woven of biological and psychological strands.*

Anxiety Disorders (pp. 509–515)

Objective 1: Contrast the symptoms of generalized anxiety disorder and panic disorder.

1. Anxiety disorders are psychological disorders characterized by _____
   _____ . The key to differentiating anxiety disorders from normal anxiety is in the _____ and _____ of the anxiety.

2. Five anxiety disorders discussed in the text are
   _____ _____
   _____ , _____
   _____ , _____ ,
   _____ - _____
   _____ , and _____ -
   _____ _____
   _____ .

3. When a person is continually tense, apprehensive, and physiologically aroused for no apparent reason, he or she is diagnosed as suffering from a _____ _____ disorder. In Freud's term, the anxiety is _____-_____ .

4. Generalized anxiety disorder can lead to physical problems, such as _____ and _____ _____ _____ . In some instances, anxiety may intensify dramatically and unpredictably and be accompanied by chest pain or choking, for example; people with these symptoms are said to have _____ _____ . This anxiety may escalate into a minutes-long episode of intense fear, or a _____ _____ .

5. People who _____ have an increased risk of a first-time _____ _____ , because _____ is a stimulant.

Objective 2: Describe the symptoms of phobias, obsessive-compulsive disorder, and post-traumatic stress disorder.

6. When a person has an irrational fear of a specific object, activity, or situation, the diagnosis is a _____ . Although in many situations, the person can live with the problem, some _____ _____ , such as a fear of thunderstorms, are incapacitating.

7. When a person has an intense fear of being scrutinized by others, the diagnosis is a _____ _____ . People who fear situations in which escape or help might not be possible when panic strikes suffer from _____ .

8. When a person cannot control repetitive thoughts and actions, an _____-_____ disorder is diagnosed.

9. Older people are _____ (more/less) likely than teens and young adults to suffer from this disorder.

10. Traumatic stress, such as that associated with witnessing atrocities or combat, can produce _____-_____ _____ disorder. The symptoms of this disorder include _____ _____ , _____ , _____ _____ , _____ _____ , and _____ . People who have a sensitive _____ _____ are more vulnerable to this disorder.

11. Researchers who believe this disorder may be overdiagnosed point to the _____ _____ of most people who suffer trauma. Also, suffering can lead to _____-_____ _____ , in which people experience an increased appreciation for life.

Objective 3: Discuss the contributions of the learning and biological perspectives to understanding the development of anxiety disorders.

12. Freud assumed that anxiety disorders are symptoms of submerged mental energy that derives from intolerable impulses that were _____ during childhood.

13. Learning theorists, drawing on research in which rats are given unpredictable shocks, link general anxiety with _____ conditioning of _____ .

14. Some fears arise from _____ _____ , such as when a person who fears heights after a fall also comes to fear airplanes.

15. Phobias and compulsive behaviors reduce anxiety and thereby are _____ . Through _____ learning,

someone might also learn fear by seeing others display their own fears.

16. Humans probably _____ (are/are not) biologically prepared to develop certain fears. Compulsive acts typically are exaggerations of behaviors that contributed to our species' _____ .

17. The anxiety response probably _____ (is/is not) genetically influenced.

18. PET scans of persons with obsessive-compulsive disorder reveal excessive activity in a brain region called the _____ _____ cortex. Some antidepressant drugs dampen fear-circuit activity in the _____ , thus reducing this behavior.

Dissociative Disorders (pp. 515–517)

Objective 4: Describe the symptoms of dissociative disorders and the controversy regarding the diagnosis of dissociative identity disorder.

1. In _____ disorders, a person experiences a sudden loss of _____ or change in _____ .

2. A person who develops two or more distinct personalities is suffering from _____ _____ disorder.

3. Nicholas Spanos has argued that such people may merely be playing different _____ .

4. Those who accept this as a genuine disorder point to evidence that differing personalities may be associated with distinct _____ and _____ states.

Identify two pieces of evidence brought forth by those who do not accept dissociative identity disorder as a genuine disorder.

5. The psychoanalytic and learning perspectives view dissociative disorders as ways of dealing with _____ . Others view them as a protective response to histories of _____ _____ .

Skeptics claim these disorders are sometimes contrived by _____-_____ people and sometimes constructed out of the _____-_____ interaction.

Personality Disorders (pp. 517–518)

Objective 5: Contrast the three clusters of personality disorders, and describe the behaviors and brain activity associated with the antisocial personality disorder.

1. Personality disorders exist when an individual has character traits that are enduring and impair _____ _____ .

2. A fearful sensitivity to rejection may predispose the _____ personality disorder. Eccentric behaviors, such as emotionless disengagement, are characteristic of the _____ personality disorder. The third cluster exhibits dramatic or _____ behaviors.

3. An individual who seems to have no conscience, lies, steals, is generally irresponsible, and may be criminal is said to have an _____ personality. Previously, this person was labeled a _____ .

4. Studies of biological relatives of those with antisocial and unemotional tendencies suggest that there _____ (is/is not) a biological predisposition to such traits.

5. Some studies have detected early signs of antisocial behavior in children as young as _____ . Antisocial adolescents tended to have been _____ , _____ , unconcerned with _____ , and low in _____ .

6. PET scans of murderers' brains reveal reduced activity in the _____

   _____ , an area of the cortex that

   helps control _____ .

7. As in other disorders, in antisocial personality, genetics _____ (is/is not) the whole story.

PROGRESS TEST

Multiple-Choice Questions

Circle your answers to the following questions and check them with the answers beginning on page 409. If your answer is incorrect, read the explanation for why it is incorrect and then consult the appropriate pages of the text.

1. Because of some troubling thoughts, Carl recently had a PET scan of his brain that revealed excessive activity in the anterior cingulate area. Carl's psychiatrist believes that Carl suffers from:
   a. schizophrenia.
   b. a mood disorder.
   c. a personality disorder.
   d. obsessive-compulsive disorder.

2. Phobias and obsessive-compulsive behaviors are classified as:
   a. anxiety disorders.
   b. mood disorders.
   c. dissociative disorders.
   d. personality disorders.

3. Which of the following was presented in the text as evidence of biological influences on anxiety disorders?
   a. Identical twins often develop similar phobias.
   b. Brain scans of persons with obsessive-compulsive disorder reveal unusually high activity in the anterior cingulate cortex.
   c. Drugs that dampen fear-circuit activity in the amygdala also alleviate OCD.
   d. All of these statements were presented.

4. When expecting to be electrically shocked, people with an antisocial personality disorder, as compared to normal people, show:
   a. less fear and greater arousal of the autonomic nervous system.
   b. less fear and less autonomic arousal.
   c. greater fear and greater autonomic arousal.
   d. greater fear and less autonomic arousal.

5. The psychoanalytic perspective would most likely view phobias as:
   a. conditioned fears.
   b. displaced responses to incompletely repressed impulses.
   c. biological predispositions.
   d. manifestations of self-defeating thoughts.

6. Nicholas Spanos considers dissociative identity disorder to be:
   a. a genuine disorder.
   b. merely role-playing.
   c. a disorder that cannot be explained according to the learning perspective.
   d. a reflection of unconscious conflicts.

7. After falling from a ladder, Joseph is afraid of airplanes, although he has never flown. This demonstrates that some fears arise from:
   a. observational learning.
   b. reinforcement.
   c. stimulus generalization.
   d. stimulus discrimination.

8. Which of the following provides evidence that human fears have been subjected to the evolutionary process?
   a. Compulsive acts typically exaggerate behaviors that contributed to our species' survival.
   b. Most phobias focus on objects that our ancestors also feared.
   c. It is easier to condition some fears than others.
   d. All of these statements provide evidence.

9. Psychoanalytic and learning theorists both agree that dissociative and anxiety disorders are symptoms that represent the person's attempt to deal with:
   a. unconscious conflicts.
   b. anxiety.
   c. unfulfilled wishes.
   d. unpleasant responsibilities.

10. Joe has an intense, irrational fear of snakes. He is suffering from a(n):
    a. generalized anxiety disorder.
    b. obsessive-compulsive disorder.
    c. phobia.
    d. mood disorder.

11. As a child, Monica was criticized severely by her mother for not living up to her expectations. This criticism was always followed by a beating with a whip. As an adult, Monica is generally introverted and extremely shy. Sometimes, however, she acts more like a young child, throwing tantrums if she doesn't get her way. At other times, she is a flirting, happy-go-lucky young lady. Most likely, Monica is suffering from:
    a. a phobia.
    b. dissociative schizophrenia.
    c. dissociative identity disorder.
    d. bipolar disorder.

12. Bob has never been able to keep a job. He's been in and out of jail for charges such as theft, sexual assault, and spousal abuse. Bob would most likely be diagnosed as having:
    a. a dissociative identity disorder.
    b. social phobia.
    c. post-traumatic stress disorder.
    d. an antisocial personality.

13. Julia's psychologist believes that Julia's fear of heights can be traced to a conditioned fear she developed after falling from a ladder. This explanation reflects a _____ perspective.
    a. medical
    c. social-cognitive
    b. psychoanalytic
    d. learning

14. Before he can study, Rashid must arrange his books, pencils, paper, and other items on his desk so that they are "just so." The campus counselor suggests that Rashid's compulsive behavior may help alleviate his anxiety about failing in school, which reinforces the compulsive actions. This explanation of obsessive-compulsive behavior is most consistent with which perspective?
    a. learning
    c. humanistic
    b. psychoanalytic
    d. social-cognitive

15. Sharon is continually tense, jittery, and apprehensive for no specific reason. She would probably be diagnosed as suffering a(n):
    a. phobia.
    b. major depressive disorder.
    c. obsessive-compulsive disorder.
    d. generalized anxiety disorder.

16. Jason is so preoccupied with staying clean that he showers as many as 10 times each day. Jason would be diagnosed as suffering from a(n):
    a. dissociative disorder.
    b. generalized anxiety disorder.
    c. personality disorder.
    d. obsessive-compulsive disorder.

17. Although she escaped from war-torn Bosnia two years ago, Zheina still has haunting memories and nightmares. Because she is also severely depressed, her therapist diagnoses her condition as:
    a. dissociative identity disorder.
    b. generalized anxiety disorder.
    c. social phobia.
    d. post-traumatic stress disorder.

18. Irene occasionally experiences unpredictable episodes of intense dread accompanied by chest pains and a sensation of smothering. Since her symptoms have no apparent cause, they would probably be classified as indicative of:
    a. schizophrenia.
    b. bipolar disorder.
    c. post-traumatic stress disorder.
    d. panic attack.

19. To which of the following is a person *most* likely to acquire a phobia?
    a. heights
    b. being in public
    c. being dirty
    d. All of these are equally likely.

20. Dr. Jekyll, whose second personality was Mr. Hyde, had a(n) _____ disorder.
    a. anxiety
    c. mood
    b. dissociative
    d. personality

Matching Items

Match each term with the appropriate definition or description.

Terms

_____ 1. dissociative disorder
_____ 2. social phobia
_____ 3. obsessive-compulsive disorder
_____ 4. panic attack
_____ 5. dissociative identity disorder
_____ 6. phobia
_____ 7. panic disorder
_____ 8. antisocial personality
_____ 9. serotonin
_____ 10. agoraphobia

Definitions or Descriptions

a. a sudden escalation of anxiety often accompanied by a sensation of choking or other physical symptoms
b. a disorder in which conscious awareness becomes separated from previous memories, feelings, and thoughts
c. intense fear of being scrutinized by others
d. a disorder characterized by repetitive thoughts and actions
e. an individual who seems to have no conscience
f. an anxiety disorder marked by a persistent, irrational fear of a specific object or situation
g. a disorder formerly called multiple personality disorder
h. a neurotransmitter possibly linked to obsessive-compulsive behavior
i. an anxiety disorder marked by episodes of intense dread
j. a fear of situations in which help might not be available during a panic attack

KEY TERMS

Using your own words, on a separate piece of paper write a brief definition or explanation of each of the following terms.

1. anxiety disorders

2. generalized anxiety disorder

3. panic disorder

4. phobia

5. obsessive-compulsive disorder (OCD)

6. post-traumatic stress disorder (PTSD)

7. dissociative disorders

8. dissociative identity disorder

9. personality disorders

10. antisocial personality disorder

ANSWERS

Module Review

Anxiety Disorders

1. distressing, persistent anxiety or maladaptive behaviors that reduce anxiety; intensity; persistence

2. generalized anxiety disorder; panic disorder; phobias; obsessive-compulsive disorder; post-traumatic stress disorder

3. generalized anxiety; free-floating

4. ulcers; high blood pressure; panic disorder; panic attack

5. smoke; panic attack; nicotine

6. phobia; specific phobias

7. social phobia; agoraphobia

8. obsessive-compulsive

9. less

10. post-traumatic stress; haunting memories; nightmares; social withdrawal; jumpy anxiety; insomnia; limbic system

11. survivor resiliency; post-traumatic growth

12. repressed

13. classical; fears

14. stimulus generalization

15. reinforced; observational

16. are; survival

17. is

18. anterior cingulate; amygdala

Dissociative Disorders

1. dissociative; memory; identity

2. dissociative identity

3. roles

4. brain; body

Skeptics point out that the recent increase in the number of reported cases of dissociative identity disorder indicates that it has become a fad. The fact that the disorder is almost nonexistent outside North America also causes skeptics to doubt the disorder's genuineness.

5. anxiety; childhood trauma; fantasy-prone; therapist-patient

Personality Disorders

1. social functioning

2. avoidant; schizoid; impulsive

3. antisocial; psychopath or sociopath

4. is

5. 3 to 6; impulsive; uninhibited; social rewards; anxiety

6. frontal lobe; impulses

7. is not

Progress Test

Multiple-Choice Questions

1. **d.** is the answer. These areas show increased activity during compulsive behaviors.

2. **a.** is the answer.
   b. The mood disorders include major depressive disorder and bipolar disorder.
   c. Dissociative identity disorder is the only dissociative disorder discussed in the text.
   d. The personality disorders include the antisocial and schizoid personalities.

3. **d.** is the answer.

4. **b.** is the answer. Those with antisocial personality disorders show less autonomic arousal in such situations, and emotions, such as fear, are tied to arousal.

5. **b.** is the answer.
   a. This answer reflects the learning perspective.
   c. Although certain phobias are biologically predisposed, this could not fully explain phobias, nor is it the explanation offered by psychoanalytic theory.
   d. Social-cognitive theorists propose self-defeating thoughts as a cause of depression.

6. **b.** is the answer.
   c. Playing a role is most definitely a learned skill.
   d. This would be the view of a psychoanalyst.

7. **c.** is the answer. Joseph's fear has generalized from ladders to airplanes.
   a. Had Joseph acquired his fear after seeing someone *else* fall, observational learning would be implicated. This process would not, however, explain how his fear was transferred to airplanes.
   b. There is no indication that Joseph's phobia was acquired through reinforcement.
   d. Through stimulus discrimination, Joseph's fear would *not* have generalized from ladders to airplanes.

8. **d.** is the answer.

9. **b.** is the answer. The psychoanalytic explanation is that these disorders are a manifestation of incompletely repressed impulses over which the person is anxious. According to the learning perspective, the troubled behaviors that result from these disorders have been reinforced by anxiety reduction.
   a. & c. These are true of the psychoanalytic, but not the learning, perspective.

10. **c.** is the answer. An intense fear of a specific object is a phobia.
    a. His fear is focused on a specific object, not generalized.
    b. In this disorder a person is troubled by repetitive thoughts and actions.
    d. Conditioned fears form the basis for anxiety rather than mood disorders.

11. **c.** is the answer.
    a. Phobias focus anxiety on a specific object, activity, or situation.
    b. There is no such disorder.
    d. In this mood disorder, a person alternates between feelings of hopeless depression and overexcited mania.

12. **d.** is the answer. Repeated wrongdoing and aggressive behavior are part of the pattern associated with the antisocial personality disorder, which may also include marital problems and an inability to keep a job.

a. Although dissociative identity disorder may involve an aggressive personality, there is nothing in the example to indicate a dissociation.

b. Nothing in the question indicates that Bob is afraid of being in social situations, as he would be with a social phobia.

c. Nothing in the question indicates that Bob has suffered a trauma, nor does he have any of the symptoms of PTSD.

13. **d.** is the answer. In the learning perspective, a phobia, such as Julia's, is seen as a conditioned fear.

a. Because the fear is focused on a specific stimulus, the medical model does not easily account for the phobia. In any event, it would presumably offer an internal, biological explanation.

b. The psychoanalytic view of phobias would be that they represent incompletely repressed anxieties that are displaced onto the feared object.

c. The social-cognitive perspective would emphasize a person's conscious, cognitive processes, not reflexive conditioned responses.

14. **a.** is the answer. According to the learning view, compulsive behaviors are reinforced because they reduce the anxiety created by obsessive thoughts. Rashid's obsession concerns failing, and his desk-arranging compulsive behaviors apparently help him control these thoughts.

b. The psychoanalytic perspective would view obsessive thoughts as a symbolic representation of forbidden impulses. These thoughts may prompt the person to perform compulsive acts that counter these impulses.

c. & d. The text does not offer explanations of obsessive-compulsive behavior based on the humanistic or social-cognitive perspectives. Presumably, however, these explanations would emphasize growth-blocking difficulties in the person's environment (humanistic perspective) and the reciprocal influences of personality and environment (social-cognitive perspective), rather than symbolic expressions of forbidden impulses.

15. **d.** is the answer.

a. In phobias, anxiety is focused on a specific object.

b. Major depressive disorder does not manifest these symptoms.

c. The obsessive-compulsive disorder is characterized by repetitive and unwanted thoughts and/or actions.

16. **d.** is the answer. Jason is obsessed with cleanliness; as a result, he has developed a compulsion to shower.

a. Dissociative disorders involve a separation of conscious awareness from previous memories and thoughts.

b. Generalized anxiety disorder does not have a specific focus.

c. This disorder is characterized by maladaptive character traits.

17. **d.** is the answer.

a. There is no evidence that Zheina has *lost* either her memory or her identity, as would occur in dissociative disorders.

b. With generalized anxiety disorder, the anxiety is free-floating, not tied to specific events.

c. A social phobia is a fear of social situations, not depression resulting from traumatic events.

18. **d.** is the answer.

a. Baseless physical symptoms rarely play a role in schizophrenia.

b. There is no indication that she is exhibiting euphoric behavior.

c. There is no indication that she has suffered a trauma.

19. **a.** is the answer. Humans seem biologically prepared to develop a fear of heights and other dangers that our ancestors faced.

20. **b.** is the answer.

Matching Items

1.	b	**6.**	f
2.	c	**7.**	i
3.	d	**8.**	e
4.	a	**9.**	h
5.	g	**10.**	j

Key Terms

1. **Anxiety disorders** involve distressing, persistent anxiety or maladaptive behaviors that reduce anxiety.

2. In the **generalized anxiety disorder**, the person is continually tense, apprehensive, and in a state of autonomic nervous system arousal for no apparent reason.

3. A **panic disorder** is an episode of intense dread accompanied by chest pain, dizziness, or choking. It is essentially an escalation of the anxiety associated with generalized anxiety disorder.

4. A **phobia** is an anxiety disorder in which a person has a persistent, irrational fear and avoidance of a specific object or situation.

5. **Obsessive-compulsive disorder (OCD)** is an anxiety disorder in which the person experiences uncontrollable and repetitive thoughts (obsessions) and actions (compulsions).

6. **Post-traumatic stress disorder (PTSD)** is an anxiety disorder characterized by haunting memories, nightmares, social withdrawal, jumpy anxiety, and/or insomnia lasting four weeks or more following a traumatic experience.

7. **Dissociative disorders** involve a separation of conscious awareness from one's previous memories, thoughts, and feelings.

   Memory aid: To *dissociate* is to separate or pull apart. In the **dissociative disorders** a person becomes dissociated from his or her memories and identity.

8. The **dissociative identity disorder** is a dissociative disorder in which a person exhibits two or more distinct and alternating personalities; also called *multiple personality disorder*.

9. **Personality disorders** are characterized by inflexible and enduring maladaptive character traits that impair social functioning.

10. The **antisocial personality disorder** is a personality disorder in which the person is aggressive, ruthless, and shows no sign of a conscience that would inhibit wrongdoing.

FOCUS ON VOCABULARY AND LANGUAGE

Anxiety Disorders

heart palpitations . . . ringing in the ears . . . edgy . . . jittery . . . sleep-deprived . . . furrowed brows . . . twitching eyelids . . . fidgeting. These are all descriptions of the symptoms of generalized anxiety disorder. The person may may have increased heart rate (*heart palpitations*), may hear high-pitched sounds (*ringing in the ears*), may be nervous and jumpy (*edgy*), and may start trembling (*jittery*). The sufferer may worry all the time, be unable to sleep (*sleeplessness or insomnia*), and feel apprehensive, which may show in frowning (*furrowed brows*), rapidly blinking eyes (*twitching eyelids*), and restless movements (*fidgeting*).

Because nicotine is a stimulant, *lighting up doesn't lighten up.* People who smoke cigarettes have an increased risk (*two- to fourfold*) of a first time panic attack. So, igniting and smoking a cigarette (*lighting up*) doesn't necessarily lead to an elevated mood (*it doesn't lighten up our mood*).

Years later, images of these events intrude on him as *flashbacks* and *nightmares.* Many war veterans (*vets*) and others who experienced traumatic stressful events develop post-traumatic stress disorder. Symptoms include terrifying images of the event (*flashbacks*); very frightening dreams (*nightmares*); extreme nervousness, anxiety, or depression; and a tendency to become socially isolated.

Grooming gone wild becomes hair pulling. The biological perspective explains our tendency to be anxious (*anxiety-prone*) in evolutionary or genetic terms. A normal behavior that once had survival value in our evolutionary past may now be distorted into compulsive action. Thus, compulsive hair pulling may be an exaggerated version of normal grooming behavior (*grooming gone wild*).

Dissociative Disorders

. . . a ruse . . . Kenneth Bianchi is a convicted psychopathic murderer who pretended to be a multiple personality in order to avoid jail or the death penalty, and his cunning ploy (*ruse*) fooled many psychologists and psychiatrists. It also raised the question of the reality of dissociative identity as a genuine disorder.

Rather, note skeptics, some therapists *go fishing for multiple personalities.* Those who doubt the existence of dissociative identity disorder (*skeptics*) find it strange that the number of diagnosed cases in North America has increased dramatically (*exploded*) in the last decade. (In the rest of the world it is rare or nonexistent; in Britain, where it is rarely diagnosed, some consider it an eccentric [*wacky*] American fad [*fashionably popular*].) In addition, the average number of personalities has multiplied (*mushroomed*) from 3 to 12 per patient. One explanation for the disorder's popularity is that many therapists expect it to be there, so they actively solicit (*go fishing for*) symptoms of dissociative identity disorder from their patients.

Personality Disorders

. . . con artist . . . A person who has an antisocial personality is usually a male who has no conscience, who lies, steals, cheats, and is unable to keep a job or take on the normal responsibilities of family and society. When combined with high intelligence and no moral sense, the result may be a clever, smooth

412   Module 37 Anxiety, Dissociative, and Personality Disorders

talking, and deceitful trickster or confidence man (*con artist*).

Antisocial personality disorder is *woven* of biological and psychological *strands*. The analogy here is between the antisocial personality and how cloth is made (*woven*). Both psychological and biological factors (*strands*) combine to produce the disorder. If the biological predispositions are fostered (*channeled*) in more positive ways, the result may be a fearless hero; alternatively, the same disposition may produce a killer or a manipulative, calculating, self-centered, but charming and intelligent individual (a *clever con artist*). Research confirms that with antisocial behavior, as with many other things, nature and nurture interact.

Mood Disorders

38 M O D U L E

MODULE OVERVIEW

Module 38 discusses the mood disorders, which include major depressive disorder, the "common cold" of psychological disorders, and bipolar disorder, which is characterized by extreme mood swings. Suicide, sometimes a product of severe depression—is featured in a Close-Up box. This module focuses on the various explanations for mood disorders, particularly those provided by the biological and social-cognitive perspectives.

NOTE: Answer guidelines for all Module 38 questions begin on page 417.

MODULE REVIEW

First, skim each section, noting headings and boldface items. After you have read the section, review each objective by answering the fill-in and essay-type questions that follow it. As you proceed, evaluate your performance by consulting the answers on page 417. Do not continue with the next section until you understand each answer. If you need to, review or reread the section in the textbook before continuing.

> David Myers at times uses idioms that are unfamiliar to some readers. If you do not know the meaning of any of the following words, phrases, or expressions from the context in which they appear in the text, refer to page 419 for an explanation: *To grind temporarily to a halt; blue mood; slow motion . . . fast forward; view life through dark glasses; company does not love another's misery.*

Major Depressive Disorder and Bipolar Disorder (pp. 521–522)

Objective 1: Define *mood disorders,* and contrast major depressive disorder and bipolar disorder.

1. Mood disorders are psychological disorders characterized by _____ _____ . They come in two forms: The experience of prolonged depression with no discernible cause is called _____ _____ disorder. When a person's mood alternates between depression and the hyperactive state of _____ , a _____ disorder is diagnosed.

2. Although _____ are more common, _____ is the number one reason that people seek mental health services. It is also the leading cause of disability worldwide.

3. The possible signs of depression include

_____

_____ .

4. Major depression occurs when its signs last

_____ _____ or more with no apparent cause.

5. Depressed persons usually _____ (can/cannot) recover without therapy.

6. Symptoms of mania include _____

_____ .

7. Bipolar disorder is less common among creative professionals who rely on _____ and _____ than among those who rely on _____ expression and vivid _____ .

Explaining Mood Disorders (pp. 522–529)

Objective 2: Explain the development of mood disorders, and summarize the contributions of the biological perspective to the study of depression.

1. The commonality of depression suggests that its _____ must also be common.

2. Compared with men, women are _____ (more/less) vulnerable to major depression. In general, women are most vulnerable to disorders involving _____ states, such as _____ _____ .

3. Men's disorders tend to be more _____ and include _____ _____ .

4. It usually _____ (is/is not) the case that a depressive episode has been triggered by a stressful event. An individual's vulnerability to depression also increases following, for example, _____ .

5. With each new generation, the rate of depression is _____ (increasing/decreasing) and the disorder is striking _____ (earlier/later). In North America today, young adults are _____ times (how many?) more likely than their grandparents to suffer depression.

State the psychoanalytic explanation of depression.

6. Mood disorders _____ (tend/do not tend) to run in families. Studies of _____ also reveal that genetic influences on mood disorders are _____ (weak/strong).

7. To determine which genes are involved in depression, researchers use _____ _____ , in

which they examine the _____ of both affected and unaffected family members.

(Close-Up) Identify several group differences in suicide rates.

8. Depression may also be caused by _____ (high/low) levels of two neurotransmitters, _____ and _____ .

9. Drugs that alleviate mania reduce _____ ; drugs that relieve depression increase _____ or _____ supplies by blocking either their _____ or their chemical _____ .

10. Most people with a history of depression also were habitual _____ . The brains of depressed people tend to be _____ (more/less) active, especially in an area of the _____ _____ lobe. In severely depressed patients, this brain area may also be _____ (smaller/larger) in size. The brain's _____ , which is important in processing _____ , is vulnerable to stress-related damage. Antidepressant drugs that boost _____ may promote recovery by stimulating neurons in this area of the brain.

Objective 3: Summarize the contributions of the social-cognitive perspective to the study of depression.

11. According to the social-cognitive perspective, depression may be linked with _____ beliefs and a _____ _____ style.

12. Such beliefs may arise from _____
_____ , the feeling that can arise
when the individual repeatedly experiences
uncontrollable, painful events.

13. Gender differences in responding to
_____ help explain why women
have been twice as vulnerable to depression.

14. According to Susan Nolen-Hoeksema, when trouble strikes, men tend to _____
and women tend to _____ .

Describe how depressed people differ from others in
their explanations of failure and how such explanations tend to feed depression.

15. According to Martin Seligman, depression is
more common in Western cultures that emphasize _____ and that have shown
a decline in commitment to _____
and family.

16. Depression-prone people respond to bad events
in an especially _____ way.

17. Being withdrawn, self-focused, and complaining
tends to elicit social _____
(empathy/rejection).

Outline the vicious cycle of depression.

PROGRESS TEST

Multiple-Choice Questions

Circle your answers to the following questions and
check them with the answers beginning on page 417.
If your answer is incorrect, read the explanation for
why it is incorrect and then consult the appropriate
pages of the text.

1. Gender differences in the prevalence of depression may be partly due to the fact that when
stressful experiences occur:
   a. women tend to act, while men tend to think.
   b. women tend to think, while men tend to act.
   c. women tend to distract themselves by drinking, while men tend to delve into their work.
   d. women tend to delve into their work, while men tend to distract themselves by drinking.

2. Which of the following is *not* true concerning
depression?
   a. Depression is more common in females than in males.
   b. Most depressive episodes appear not to be preceded by any particular factor or event.
   c. Most depressive episodes last less than 3 months.
   d. Most people recover from depression without professional therapy.

3. According to the social-cognitive perspective, a
person who experiences unexpected aversive
events may develop helplessness and manifest
a(n):
   a. obsessive-compulsive disorder.
   b. dissociative disorder.
   c. personality disorder.
   d. mood disorder.

4. In treating depression, a psychiatrist would probably prescribe a drug that would:
   a. increase levels of acetylcholine.
   b. decrease levels of dopamine.
   c. increase levels of norepinephrine.
   d. decrease levels of serotonin.

5. In general, women are more vulnerable than men
to:
   a. external disorders such as anxiety.
   b. internal disorders such as depression.
   c. external disorders such as antisocial conduct.
   d. internal disorders such as alcohol abuse.

6. Which neurotransmitter is present in overabundant amounts during the manic phase of bipolar disorder?
   a. dopamine
   b. serotonin
   c. epinephrine
   d. norepinephrine

7. Social-cognitive theorists contend that depression is linked with:
   a. negative moods.
   b. maladaptive explanations of failure.
   c. self-defeating beliefs.
   d. all of these characteristics.

8. According to psychoanalytic theory, memory of losses, especially in combination with internalized anger, is likely to result in:
   a. learned helplessness.
   b. the self-serving bias.
   c. weak ego defense mechanisms.
   d. depression.

9. For the past 6 months, a woman has complained of feeling isolated from others, dissatisfied with life, and discouraged about the future. This woman could be diagnosed as suffering from:
   a. bipolar disorder.
   b. major depressive disorder.
   c. generalized anxiety disorder.
   d. a dissociative disorder.

10. On Monday, Matt felt optimistic, energetic, and on top of the world. On Tuesday, he felt hopeless and lethargic, and thought that the future looked very grim. Matt would *most* likely be diagnosed as having:
   a. bipolar disorder.
   b. major depressive disorder.
   c. schizophrenia.
   d. panic disorder.

11. Connie's therapist has suggested that her depression stems from unresolved anger toward her parents. Evidently, Connie's therapist is working within the _____ perspective.
   a. learning
   b. social-cognitive
   c. biological
   d. psychoanalytic

12. Ken's therapist suggested that his depression is a result of his self-defeating thoughts and negative assumptions about himself, his situation, and his future. Evidently, Ken's therapist is working within the _____ perspective.
   a. learning
   b. social-cognitive
   c. biological
   d. psychoanalytic

13. Alicia's doctor, who thinks that Alicia's depression has a biochemical cause, prescribes a drug that:
   a. reduces norepinephrine.
   b. increases norepinephrine.
   c. reduces serotonin.
   d. increases acetylcholine.

Matching Items

Match each term with the appropriate definition or description.

Terms

_____ 1. mood disorders
_____ 2. mania
_____ 3. norepinephrine
_____ 4. bipolar disorder

Definitions or Descriptions

a. a neurotransmitter that is overabundant during mania and scarce during depression
b. an extremely elevated mood
c. a disorder in which the person alternates between depression and euphoria
d. psychological disorders marked by emotional extremes

KEY TERMS

Using your own words, on a separate piece of paper write a brief definition or explanation of each of the following terms.

1. mood disorders

2. major depressive disorder

3. mania

4. bipolar disorder

ANSWERS

Module Review

Major Depressive Disorder and *Bipolar Disorder*

1. emotional extremes; major depressive; mania; bipolar

2. phobias; depression

3. lethargy, feelings of worthlessness, and loss of interest in family, friends, and activities

4. two weeks

5. can

6. euphoria, hyperactivity, and a wildly optimistic state

7. precision; logic; emotional; imagery

Explaining Mood Disorders

1. causes

2. more; internal; depression, anxiety, and inhibited sexual desire

3. external; alcohol abuse, antisocial conduct, and lack of impulse control

4. is; a family member's death, loss of a job, a marital crisis, or a physical assault

5. increasing; earlier; three

The psychoanalytic perspective suggests that adulthood depression can be triggered by losses that evoke feelings associated with earlier childhood losses. Alternatively, unresolved anger toward one's parents is turned inward and takes the form of depression.

6. tend; twins; strong

7. linkage analysis; DNA

Suicide rates are higher among white Americans, the rich, older men, the nonreligious, and those who are single, widowed, or divorced. Although women more often attempt suicide, men are more likely to succeed. Suicide rates also vary widely around the world.

8. low; norepinephrine; serotonin

9. norepinephrine; norepinephrine; serotonin; reuptake; breakdown

10. smokers; less; left frontal; smaller; hippocampus; memories; serotonin

11. self-defeating; negative explanatory

12. learned helplessness

13. stress

14. act; think (or overthink)

Depressed people are more likely than others to explain failures or bad events in terms that are stable (it's going to last forever), global (it will affect everything), and internal (it's my fault). Such explanations lead to feelings of hopelessness, which in turn feed depression.

15. individualism; religion

16. self-blaming

17. rejection

Depression is often brought on by stressful experiences. Depressed people brood over such experiences with maladaptive explanations that produce self-blame and amplify their depression, which in turn triggers other symptoms of depression. In addition, being withdrawn and complaining tends to elicit social rejection and other negative experiences.

Progress Test

Multiple-Choice Questions

1. **b.** is the answer.
   c. & d. Men are more likely than women to cope with stress in these ways.

2. **b.** is the answer. Depression is often preceded by a stressful event related to work, marriage, or a close relationship.

3. **d.** is the answer. Learned helplessness may lead to self-defeating beliefs, which in turn are linked with depression, a mood disorder.

4. **c.** is the answer. Drugs that relieve depression tend to increase levels of norepinephrine.
   a. Acetylcholine is a neurotransmitter involved in muscle contractions.
   b. It is in certain types of schizophrenia that decreasing dopamine levels is known to be helpful.
   d. On the contrary, it appears that a particular type of depression may be related to *low* levels of serotonin.

5. **b.** is the answer.
   a. Anxiety is an internal disorder.
   c. & d. Alcohol abuse and antisocial conduct are external disorders, most often exhibited by men.

6. **d.** is the answer. In bipolar disorder, norepinephrine appears to be overabundant during mania and in short supply during depression.

   a. There is an overabundance of dopamine receptors in some schizophrenia patients.

   b. Serotonin sometimes appears to be scarce during depression.

   c. Epinephrine has not been implicated in psychological disorders.

7. **d.** is the answer.

8. **d.** is the answer. A loss may evoke feelings of anger associated with an earlier loss. Such anger is turned against the self. This internalized anger results in depression.

   a. Learned helplessness would be an explanation offered by the social-cognitive perspective.

   b. The self-serving bias is not discussed in terms of its relationship to depression.

   c. This is the psychoanalytic explanation of anxiety.

9. **b.** is the answer. The fact that this woman has had these symptoms for more than two weeks indicates that she is suffering from major depressive disorder.

10. **a.** is the answer. Matt's alternating states of the hopelessness and lethargy of depression and the energetic, optimistic state of mania are characteristic of bipolar disorder.

    b. Although he was depressed on Tuesday, Matt's manic state on Monday indicates that he is not suffering from major depressive disorder.

    c. Matt was depressed, not detached from reality.

    d. That Matt is not exhibiting episodes of intense dread indicates that he is not suffering from panic disorder.

11. **d.** is the answer. Freud believed that the anger once felt toward parents was internalized and would produce depression.

    a. & b. The learning and social-cognitive perspectives focus on environmental experiences, conditioning, and self-defeating attitudes in explaining depression.

c. The biological perspective focuses on genetic predispositions and biochemical imbalances in explaining depression.

12. **b.** is the answer.

13. **b.** is the answer. Norepinephrine, which increases arousal and boosts mood, is scarce during depression. Drugs that relieve depression tend to increase norepinephrine.

    c. Increasing serotonin, which is sometimes scarce during depression, might relieve depression.

    d. This neurotransmitter is involved in motor responses but has not been linked to psychological disorders.

Matching Items

1. d
2. b
3. a
4. c

Key Terms

1. **Mood disorders** are characterized by emotional extremes.

2. **Major depressive disorder** is the mood disorder that occurs when a person exhibits the lethargy, feelings of worthlessness, or loss of interest in family, friends, and activities characteristic of depression for more than a two-week period and for no discernible reason. Because of its relative frequency, depression has been called the "common cold" of psychological disorders.

3. **Mania** is the wildly optimistic, euphoric, hyperactive state that alternates with depression in the bipolar disorder.

4. **Bipolar disorder** is the mood disorder in which a person alternates between depression and the euphoria of a manic state.

   Memory aid: *Bipolar* means having two poles, that is, two opposite qualities. In **bipolar disorder,** the opposing states are mania and depression.

FOCUS ON VOCABULARY AND LANGUAGE

Major Depressive Disorder

To grind temporarily to a halt and *ruminate,* as depressed people do, is to reassess one's life when feeling threatened and to *redirect energy in more promising ways.* From a biological point of view, depression is a natural reaction to stress and painful events. It is like a warning signal that brings us to a complete stop (*we grind to a halt*) and allows us time to reflect on life and contemplate (*ruminate on*) the meaning of our existence and to focus more optimistically on the future.

But the difference between a *blue mood* after bad news and a mood disorder is like the difference between gasping for breath for a few minutes after a hard run and being chronically short of breath. We all feel depressed and sad (*we have blue moods*) in response to painful events and sometimes just to life in general. These feelings are points on a continuum; at the extreme end, and very distinct from ordinary depression, are the serious mood disorders (e.g., major depressive disorder) in which the signs of chronic depression (loss of appetite, sleeplessness, tiredness, low self-esteem, and a disinterest in family, friends and social activities) last two weeks or more.

Bipolar Disorder

If depression is living in slow motion, mania is *fast forward.* Bipolar disorder is characterized by mood swings. While depression slows the person down (*like living in slow motion*), the hyperactivity and heightened exuberant state (*mania*) at the other emotional extreme seems to speed the person up, similar to the images you get when you press the fast forward button on the DVD player or see a "speeded-up" film.

Explaining Mood Disorders

Depressed people *view life through dark glasses.* Social-cognitive theorists point out that biological factors do not operate independently of environmental influences. People who are depressed often have negative beliefs about themselves and about their present and future situations (*they view life through dark glasses*). These self-defeating beliefs can accentuate or amplify a nasty (*vicious*) cycle of interactions between chemistry, cognition, and mood.

Misery may love another's company, *but company does not love another's misery.* The old saying *"misery loves company"* means that depressed, sad people like to be with other people. The possible social consequence of being withdrawn, self-focused, self-blaming, and complaining (*depressed*), however, is rejection by others (*company does not love another's misery*).

Schizophrenia

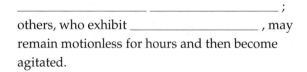

39 MODULE

MODULE OVERVIEW

Module 39 discusses schizophrenia, including the general symptoms and how this disorder develops. The major portion of this module is devoted to exploring the possible causes of schizophrenia, both psychological and physiological.

NOTE: Answer guidelines for all Module 39 questions begin on page 424.

MODULE REVIEW

First, skim each section, noting headings and boldface items. After you have read the section, review each objective by answering the fill-in and essay-type questions that follow it. As you proceed, evaluate your performance by consulting the answers on page 424. Do not continue with the next section until you understand each answer. If you need to, review or reread the section in the textbook before continuing.

> David Myers at times uses idioms that are unfamiliar to some readers. If you do not know the meaning of the following phrase and expression from the context in which they appear in the text, refer to page 425 for an explanation: *hodge-podge; flat affect*.

Symptoms of Schizophrenia (pp. 531–532)

Objective 1: Describe the symptoms of schizophrenia.

1. Schizophrenia, or "split mind," refers not to a split personality but rather to a split from
   _____ .

2. Three manifestations of schizophrenia are disorganized _____ , disturbed _____ , and inappropriate _____ and _____ . People with schizophrenia who display inappropriate behavior are said to have _____ _____ , while those with toneless voices and expressionless faces are said to have
   _____ _____ .

3. The distorted, false beliefs of schizophrenia patients are called _____ .

4. Many psychologists attribute the disorganized thinking of schizophrenia to a breakdown in the capacity for _____
   _____ .

5. The disturbed perceptions of people suffering from schizophrenia may take the form of _____ , which usually are _____ (visual/auditory).

6. Some victims of schizophrenia lapse into a zombielike state of apparent apathy, or
   _____ _____ ;
   others, who exhibit _____ , may remain motionless for hours and then become agitated.

Onset and Development of Schizophrenia
(pp. 532–533)

Objective 2: Contrast chronic and acute schizophrenia.

1. When schizophrenia develops slowly (called _____ schizophrenia), recovery is _____ (more/less) likely than when it develops rapidly in reaction to particular life stresses (called _____ schizophrenia).

Understanding Schizophrenia (pp. 533–537)

Objective 3: Outline some abnormal brain chemistry, functions, and structures associated with schizophrenia, and discuss the possible link between prenatal viral infections and schizophrenia.

1. The brain tissue of schizophrenia patients has been found to have an excess of receptors for the neurotransmitter _____ . Drugs that block these receptors have been found to _____ (increase/decrease) schizophrenia symptoms.

2. Brain scans have shown that many people suffering from schizophrenia have abnormally _____ (high/low) brain activity in the _____ lobes.

3. Enlarged, _____-filled areas and a corresponding _____ of cerebral tissue is also characteristic of schizophrenia. Schizophrenia patients also have a smaller-than-normal _____ , which may account for their difficulty in filtering _____ _____ and focusing _____ .

4. Some scientists contend that the brain abnormalities of schizophrenia may be caused by a prenatal problem, such as _____ _____ _____ ; birth complications, such as _____ _____ ; or a _____ _____ contracted by the mother.

List several pieces of evidence for this theory.

Objective 4: Discuss the evidence for a genetic contribution to the development of schizophrenia.

5. Twin studies _____ (support/do not support) the contention that heredity plays a role in schizophrenia.

6. The role of the prenatal environment in schizophrenia is demonstrated by the fact that identical twins who share the same _____ , and are therefore more likely to experience the same prenatal _____ , are more likely to share the disorder.

7. Adoption studies _____ (confirm/do not confirm) a genetic link in the development of schizophrenia.

8. It appears that for schizophrenia to develop there must be both a _____ predisposition and other factors such as those listed earlier that "_____" the _____ that predispose this disease.

PROGRESS TEST

Multiple-Choice Questions

Circle your answers to the following questions and check them with the answers beginning on page 424. If your answer is incorrect, read the explanation for why it is incorrect and then consult the appropriate pages of the text.

1. Which of the following is *not* true regarding schizophrenia?
   a. It occurs more frequently in people born in winter and spring months.
   b. It occurs less frequently as infectious disease rates have declined.
   c. It occurs more frequently in lightly populated areas.
   d. It usually appears during adolescence or early adulthood.

2. The effect of drugs that block receptors for dopamine is to:

   a. alleviate schizophrenia symptoms.
   b. alleviate depression.
   c. increase schizophrenia symptoms.
   d. increase depression.

3. Most of the hallucinations of schizophrenia patients involve the sense of:

   a. smell.   c. hearing.
   b. vision.   d. touch.

4. Hearing voices would be a(n) _____ ; believing that you are Napoleon would be a(n) _____ .

   a. obsession; compulsion
   b. compulsion; obsession
   c. delusion; hallucination
   d. hallucination; delusion

5. When schizophrenia is slow to develop, called _____ schizophrenia, recovery is _____ .

   a. reactive; unlikely   c. process; unlikely
   b. process; likely   d. reactive; likely

6. Many psychologists believe the disorganized thoughts of people with schizophrenia result from a breakdown in:

   a. selective attention.   c. motivation.
   b. memory storage.   d. memory retrieval.

7. Research evidence links the brain abnormalities of schizophrenia to _____ during prenatal development.

   a. maternal stress
   b. a viral infection contracted
   c. abnormal levels of certain hormones
   d. the weight of the unborn child

8. Which of the following is *not* a symptom of schizophrenia?

   a. inappropriate emotions
   b. disturbed perceptions
   c. panic attacks
   d. disorganized thinking

9. Among the following, which is generally accepted as a possible cause of schizophrenia?

   a. an excess of endorphins in the brain
   b. being a twin
   c. extensive learned helplessness
   d. a genetic predisposition

10. Claiming that she heard a voice commanding her to warn other people that eating is harmful, Sandy attempts to convince others in a restaurant not to eat. The psychiatrist to whom she is referred finds that Sandy's thinking and speech are often fragmented and incoherent. In addition, Sandy has an unreasonable fear that someone is "out to get her" and consequently trusts no one. Her condition is most indicative of:

    a. schizophrenia.
    b. generalized anxiety disorder.
    c. a phobia.
    d. obsessive-compulsive disorder.

11. Wayne's doctor attempts to help Wayne by prescribing a drug that blocks receptors for dopamine. Wayne has apparently been diagnosed with:

    a. a mood disorder.
    b. an anxiety disorder.
    c. a personality disorder.
    d. schizophrenia.

12. Janet, whose class presentation is titled "Current Views on the Causes of Schizophrenia," concludes her talk with the statement:

    a. "Schizophrenia is caused by intolerable stress."
    b. "Schizophrenia is inherited."
    c. "Genes may predispose some people to react to particular experiences by developing schizophrenia."
    d. "As of this date, schizophrenia is completely unpredictable and its causes are unknown."

Matching Items

Match each term with the appropriate definition or description.

Terms

_____ **1.** schizophrenia
_____ **2.** hallucination
_____ **3.** dopamine
_____ **4.** delusions
_____ **5.** process schizophrenia
_____ **6.** reactive schizophrenia

Definitions or Descriptions

a. a false sensory experience
b. a group of disorders marked by disorganized thinking, disturbed perceptions, and inappropriate emotions and actions
c. slow-developing schizophrenia in which recovery is doubtful
d. a neurotransmitter for which there are excess receptors in some schizophrenia patients
e. rapidly developing schizophrenia, usually as a reaction to life's stresses
f. false beliefs that may accompany psychological disorders

KEY TERMS

Using your own words, on a separate piece of paper write a brief definition or explanation of each of the following terms.

1. schizophrenia

2. delusions

ANSWERS
Module Review

Symptoms of Schizophrenia

1. reality

2. thinking; perceptions; emotions; actions; positive symptoms; negative symptoms

3. delusions

4. selective attention

5. hallucinations; auditory

6. flat affect; catatonia

Onset and Development of Schizophrenia

1. chronic (or process); less; acute (or reactive)

Understanding Schizophrenia

1. dopamine; decrease

2. low; frontal

3. fluid; shrinkage; thalamus; sensory input; attention

4. low birth weight; oxygen deprivation; viral infection

Risk of schizophrenia increases for those who undergo fetal development during a flu epidemic, or simply during the flu season. People born in densely populated areas and those born during winter and spring months are at increased risk. The months of excess schizophrenia births are reversed in the Southern Hemisphere, where the seasons are the reverse of the Northern Hemisphere's. Mothers who were sick with influenza during their pregnancy may be more likely to have children who develop schizophrenia. Blood drawn from pregnant women whose children develop schizophrenia have higher-than-normal levels of viral infection antibodies.

5. support

6. placenta; viruses

7. confirm

8. genetic; turn on; genes

Progress Test

Multiple-Choice Questions

1. **c.** is the answer.

2. **a.** is the answer.
   b. & d. Thus far, only norepinephrine and serotonin have been implicated in depression and bipolar disorder.
   c. Schizophrenia has been associated with an excess of dopamine receptors. Blocking them alleviates, rather than increases, schizophrenia symptoms.

3. **c.** is the answer.

4. d. is the answer. Hallucinations are false sensory experiences; delusions are false beliefs.

a. & b. Obsessions are repetitive and unwanted thoughts. Compulsions are repetitive behaviors.

5. c. is the answer.

6. a. is the answer. Schizophrenia sufferers are easily distracted by irrelevant stimuli, evidently because of a breakdown in the capacity for selective attention.

7. b. is the answer.

8. c. is the answer. Panic attacks are characteristic of certain anxiety disorders, not of schizophrenia.

9. d. is the answer. Risk for schizophrenia increases for individuals who are related to a schizophrenia victim, and the greater the genetic relatedness, the greater the risk.

a. Schizophrenia victims have an overabundance of the neurotransmitter dopamine, not endorphins.

b. Being a twin is, in itself, irrelevant to developing schizophrenia.

c. Although learned helplessness has been suggested by social-cognitive theorists as a cause of self-defeating depressive behaviors, it has not been suggested as a cause of schizophrenia.

10. a. is the answer. Because Sandy experiences hallucinations (hearing voices), delusions (fearing someone is "out to get her"), and incoherence, she would most likely be diagnosed as suffering from schizophrenia.

b., c., & d. These disorders are not characterized by disorganized thoughts and perceptions.

11. d. is the answer. Schizophrenia patients sometimes have an excess of receptors for dopamine. Drugs that block these receptors can therefore reduce symptoms of schizophrenia.

a., b., & c. Dopamine receptors have not been implicated in these psychological disorders.

12. c. is the answer.

Matching Items

1. b **4.** f
2. a **5.** c
3. d **6.** e

Key Terms

1. Schizophrenia refers to the group of severe disorders whose symptoms may include disorganized and delusional thinking, inappropriate emotions and actions, and disturbed perceptions.

2. Delusions are false beliefs that often are symptoms of psychotic disorders.

FOCUS ON VOCABULARY AND LANGUAGE

Symptoms of Schizophrenia

. . . *hodge-podge* . . . The symptoms of schizophrenia include fragmented and distorted thinking, disturbed perception, and inappropriate feelings and behaviors. Schizophrenia victims, when talking, may move rapidly from topic to topic and idea to idea so that their speech is incomprehensible (*a word salad*). This may be the result of a breakdown in selective attention, whereby an assorted mixture (*hodge-podge*) of stimuli continually distracts the person.

A person with schizophrenia may also lapse into an emotionless *flat affect*, a zombielike state of apparent apathy. The emotions of schizophrenia are frequently not appropriate for the situation. There may be laughter at a funeral, anger and tears for no apparent reason, or no expression of emotion whatsoever (*flat affect*), which resembles a half-dead, trancelike (*zombielike*) state of indifference (*apathy*).

Therapy

The Psychological Therapies

40

MODULE OVERVIEW

Module 40 discusses the major psychotherapies for maladaptive behaviors. The various psychotherapies all derive from the personality theories discussed earlier, namely, the psychoanalytic, humanistic, behavioral, and cognitive theories. The module groups the therapies by perspective.

NOTE: Answer guidelines for all Module 40 questions begin on page 436.

MODULE REVIEW

First, skim each section, noting headings and boldface items. After you have read the section, review each objective by answering the fill-in and essay-type questions that follow it. As you proceed, evaluate your performance by consulting the answers beginning on page 436. Do not continue with the next section until you understand each answer. If you need to, review or reread the section in the textbook before continuing.

> David Myers at times uses idioms that are unfamiliar to some readers. If you do not know the meaning of any of the following words or expressions in the context in which they appear in the Therapy introduction and this module, refer to pages 440–441 for an explanation: *bewildering array of harsh and gentle methods; gawk; fueled . . . residue; aim to boost; "knocks the props out from under you"; lore; drinks laced with a drug; aggressive and self-abusive behaviors; colors our feelings; catastrophizing.*

Introducing the Psychological Therapies
(p. 541)

Objective 1: Define *psychotherapy*, and explain what we mean by an *eclectic approach* to therapy.

1. Psychological therapy is more commonly called _____ . This type of therapy is appropriate for disorders that are

   _____ .

2. Some therapists, particularly those who adopt a biopsychosocial view, blend several psychotherapy techniques and so are said to take an

   _____ approach. Closely related to this approach is _____

   _____ , which attempts to combine methods into a single, coherent system.

Psychoanalysis (pp. 541–543)

Objective 2: Define *psychoanalysis*, and discuss the aims, methods, and criticisms of this form of therapy.

1. The goal of Freud's psychoanalysis, which is based on his personality theory, is to help the patient gain _____ .

2. Freud assumed that many psychological problems originate in childhood impulses and conflicts that have been _____ .

3. Psychoanalysts attempt to bring

   _____ feelings into

   _____ awareness where they can be dealt with.

4. Freud's technique in which a patient says whatever comes to mind is called

   _____ _____ .

5. When, in the course of therapy, a person omits shameful or embarrassing material, _____ is occurring. Insight is facilitated by the analyst's _____ of the meaning of such omissions, of dreams, and of other information revealed during therapy sessions.

6. Freud referred to the hidden meaning of a dream as its _____

   _____ .

7. When strong feelings, similar to those experienced in other important relationships, are developed toward the therapist, _____ has occurred.

8. Critics point out that psychoanalysts' interpretations are hard to _____ and that therapy takes a long time and is very

   _____ .

Objective 3: Contrast psychodynamic therapy and interpersonal therapy with traditional psychoanalysis.

9. Therapists who are influenced by Freud's psychoanalysis but who talk to the patient face to face are _____ therapists. In addition, they work with patients only _____ (how long?) and for only a few weeks or months.

10. A brief alternative to psychodynamic therapy that has proven effective with _____ patients is _____

    _____ .

11. While this approach aims to help people gain _____ into their difficulties, it focuses on _____

    _____ rather than on past hurts.

Humanistic Therapies (pp. 543–545)

Objective 4: Identify the basic characteristics of the humanistic therapies, and describe the specific goals and techniques of Carl Rogers' client-centered therapy.

1. Humanistic therapies attempt to help people meet their potential for _____ .

List several ways that humanistic therapy differs from psychoanalysis.

2. The humanistic therapy based on Rogers' theory is called _____-_____ therapy, which is described as _____ therapy because the therapist _____ (interprets/does not interpret) the person's problems.

3. In order to promote growth in clients, Rogerian therapists exhibit _____ , _____ , and _____ .

4. Rogers' technique of restating and clarifying what a person is saying is called

   _____ _____ .

   Given a nonjudgmental environment that provides _____ _____ _____ , patients are better able to accept themselves as they are and to feel valued and whole.

5. Three tips for listening more actively in your own relationships are to _____ ,

   _____ _____ , and _____ _____ .

Behavior Therapies (pp. 545–548)

Objective 5: Explain how the basic assumption of behavior therapy differs from those of traditional psychoanalytic and humanistic therapies, and describe the techniques used in exposure therapies and aversive conditioning.

1. Behavior therapy applies principles of _____ to eliminate troubling behaviors.

Contrast the assumptions of the behavior therapies with those of psychoanalysis and humanistic therapy.

2. One cluster of behavior therapies is based on the principles of _____ _____ , as developed in Pavlov's experiments. This technique, in which a new, incompatible response is substituted for a mal-adaptive one, is called _____ . Two examples of this technique are

_____ _____

and _____ _____ .

3. The most widely used techniques of behavior therapy are the _____ _____ . The technique of system-atic desensitization has been most fully devel-oped by the therapist _____ . The assumption behind this technique is that one cannot simultaneously be _____ and relaxed.

4. The first step in systematic desensitization is the construction of a _____ of anxiety-arousing stimuli. The second step involves training in _____ _____ . In the final step, the per-son is trained to associate the _____ state with the _____-arousing stimuli.

5. For those who are unable to visually imagine an anxiety-arousing situation, or too afraid or embarrassed to do so, _____

_____ _____

therapy offers a promising alternative.

6. In aversive conditioning, the therapist attempts to substitute a _____ (positive/ negative) response for one that is currently _____ (positive/negative) to a harmful stimulus. In this technique, a person's unwanted behaviors become associated with _____ feelings.

Objective 6: State the main premise of therapy based on operant conditioning principles, and describe the views of proponents and critics of behavior modifica-tion.

7. Reinforcing desired behaviors and withholding reinforcement for undesired behaviors are key aspects of _____

_____ .

8. Therapies that influence behavior by controlling its consequences are based on principles of _____ conditioning. One appli-cation of this form of therapy to institutional settings is the _____ _____ , in which desired behaviors are rewarded.

State two criticisms of behavior modification.

State some responses of proponents of behavior mod-ification.

Cognitive Therapies (pp. 548–551)

Objective 7: Contrast cognitive therapy and cognitive-behavior therapy, and give some examples of cognitive therapy for depression.

1. Therapists who teach people new, more constructive ways of thinking are using _____ therapy.

2. One variety of cognitive therapy attempts to reverse the _____ beliefs often associated with _____ by helping clients see their irrationalities. This therapy was developed by _____ .

3. Training people to restructure their thinking in stressful situations is the goal of _____ _____ training. Students trained to _____ their negative thoughts are less likely to experience future depression.

4. Treatment that combines an attack on negative thinking with efforts to modify behavior is known as _____- _____ therapy.

Group and Family Therapies (p. 551)

Objective 8: Discuss the rationale and benefits of group therapy, including family therapy.

List several advantages of group therapy.

1. The type of group interaction that focuses on the fact that we live and grow in relation to others is _____ _____ .

2. In this type of group, therapists focus on improving _____ within the family.

PROGRESS TEST

Multiple-Choice Questions

Circle your answers to the following questions and check them with the answers beginning on page 437. If your answer is incorrect, read the explanation for why it is incorrect and then consult the appropriate pages of the text.

1. The technique in which a person is asked to report everything that comes to his or her mind is called _____ ; it is favored by_____ therapists.
   a. active listening; cognitive
   b. spontaneous remission; humanistic
   c. free association; psychoanalytic
   d. systematic desensitization; behavior

2. Of the following categories of psychotherapy, which is known for its nondirective nature?
   a. psychoanalysis
   b. humanistic therapy
   c. behavior therapy
   d. cognitive therapy

3. Which of the following is *not* a common criticism of psychoanalysis?
   a. It emphasizes the existence of repressed memories.
   b. It provides interpretations that are hard to disprove.
   c. It is generally a very expensive process.
   d. It gives therapists too much control over patients.

4. Which of the following types of therapy does *not* belong with the others?
   a. cognitive therapy
   b. family therapy
   c. behavior therapy
   d. psychosurgery

5. Which of the following is *not* necessarily an advantage of group therapies over individual therapies?
   a. They tend to take less time for the therapist.
   b. They tend to cost less money for the client.
   c. They are more effective.
   d. They allow the client to test new behaviors in a social context.

6. Cognitive-behavior therapy aims to:
   a. alter the way people act.
   b. make people more aware of their irrational negative thinking.
   c. alter the way people think and act.
   d. countercondition anxiety-provoking stimuli.

7. An eclectic psychotherapist is one who:
   a. takes a nondirective approach in helping clients solve their problems.
   b. views psychological disorders as usually stemming from one cause, such as a biological abnormality.
   c. uses one particular technique, such as psychoanalysis or counterconditioning, in treating disorders.
   d. uses a variety of techniques, depending on the client and the problem.

8. The technique in which a therapist echoes and restates what a person says in a nondirective manner is called:
   a. active listening.
   b. free association.
   c. systematic desensitization.
   d. transference.

9. Unlike traditional psychoanalytic therapy, interpersonal psychotherapy:
   a. helps people gain insight into the roots of their problems.
   b. offers interpretations of patients' feelings.
   c. focuses on current relationships.
   d. does all of these things.

10. The technique of systematic desensitization is based on the premise that maladaptive symptoms:
    a. are a reflection of irrational thinking.
    b. are conditioned responses.
    c. are expressions of unfulfilled wishes.
    d. have all of these characteristics.

11. The operant conditioning technique in which desired behaviors are rewarded with points or poker chips that can later be exchanged for various rewards is called:
    a. counterconditioning.
    b. systematic desensitization.
    c. a token economy.
    d. exposure therapy.

12. One variety of _____ therapy is based on the finding that depressed people often attribute their failures to _____ .
    a. humanistic; themselves
    b. behavior; external circumstances
    c. cognitive; external circumstances
    d. cognitive; themselves

13. Carl Rogers was a _____ therapist who was the creator of _____ .
    a. behavior; systematic desensitization
    b. psychoanalytic; insight therapy
    c. humanistic; client-centered therapy
    d. cognitive; cognitive therapy for depression

14. Using techniques of classical conditioning to develop an association between unwanted behavior and an unpleasant experience is known as:
    a. aversive conditioning.
    b. systematic desensitization.
    c. transference.
    d. electroconvulsive therapy.

15. Which type of psychotherapy emphasizes the individual's inherent potential for self-fulfillment?
    a. behavior therapy   c. humanistic therapy
    b. psychoanalysis   d. cognitive therapy

16. Which type of psychotherapy focuses on changing unwanted behaviors rather than on discovering their underlying causes?
    a. behavior therapy
    b. cognitive therapy
    c. humanistic therapy
    d. psychoanalysis

17. The techniques of counterconditioning are based on principles of:
    a. observational learning.
    b. classical conditioning.
    c. operant conditioning.
    d. behavior modification.

18. In which of the following does the client learn to associate a relaxed state with a hierarchy of anxiety-arousing situations?
    a. cognitive therapy
    b. aversive conditioning
    c. counterconditioning
    d. systematic desensitization

19. Principles of operant conditioning underlie which of the following techniques?
    a. counterconditioning
    b. systematic desensitization
    c. stress inoculation training
    d. the token economy

20. Which of the following is *not* a common criticism of behavior therapy?
    a. Clients may rely too much on extrinsic rewards for their new behaviors.
    b. Behavior control is unethical.
    c. Outside the therapeutic setting, the new behavior may disappear.
    d. All of these are criticisms of behavior therapy.

21. Which type of therapy focuses on eliminating irrational thinking?
    a. psychoanalysis
    b. client-centered therapy
    c. cognitive therapy
    d. behavior therapy

22. Family therapy differs from other forms of psychotherapy because it focuses on:
    a. using a variety of treatment techniques.
    b. conscious rather than unconscious processes.
    c. the present instead of the past.
    d. how family tensions may cause individual problems.

23. One reason that aversive conditioning may only be temporarily effective is that:
    a. for ethical reasons, therapists cannot use sufficiently intense unconditioned stimuli to sustain classical conditioning.
    b. patients are often unable to become sufficiently relaxed for conditioning to take place.
    c. patients know that outside the therapist's office they can engage in the undesirable behavior without fear of aversive consequences.
    d. most conditioned responses are elicited by many nonspecific stimuli and it is impossible to countercondition them all.

24. During a session with his psychoanalyst, Jamal hesitates while describing a highly embarrassing thought. In the psychoanalytic framework, this is an example of:
    a. transference.   c. mental repression.
    b. insight.   d. resistance.

25. During psychoanalysis, Jane has developed strong feelings of hatred for her therapist. The analyst interprets Jane's behavior in terms of a _____ of her feelings toward her father.
    a. projection   c. regression
    b. resistance   d. transference

26. Given that Jim's therapist attempts to help him by offering genuineness, acceptance, and empathy, she is probably practicing:
    a. psychoanalysis.
    b. behavior therapy.
    c. cognitive therapy.
    d. client-centered therapy.

27. To help Sam quit smoking, his therapist blew a blast of smoke into Sam's face each time Sam inhaled. Which technique is the therapist using?
    a. exposure therapy
    b. behavior modification
    c. systematic desensitization
    d. aversive conditioning

28. After Darnel dropped a pass in an important football game, he became depressed and vowed to quit the team because of his athletic incompetence. The campus psychologist used gentle questioning to reveal to Darnel that his thinking was irrational: his "incompetence" had earned him an athletic scholarship. The psychologist's response was most typical of a _____ therapist.
    a. behavior   c. client-centered
    b. psychoanalytic   d. cognitive

29. Leota is startled when her therapist says that she needs to focus on eliminating her problem behavior rather than gaining insight into its underlying cause. Most likely, Leota has consulted a _____ therapist.
    a. behavior   c. cognitive
    b. humanistic   d. psychoanalytic

30. In order to help him overcome his fear of flying, Duane's therapist has him construct a hierarchy of anxiety-triggering stimuli and then learn to associate each with a state of deep relaxation. Duane's therapist is using the technique called:
    a. systematic desensitization.
    b. aversive conditioning.
    c. shaping.
    d. free association.

31. A patient in a hospital receives poker chips for making her bed, being punctual at meal times, and maintaining her physical appearance. The poker chips can be exchanged for privileges, such as television viewing, snacks, and magazines. This is an example of the:
    a. psychodynamic therapy technique called systematic desensitization.
    b. behavior therapy technique called token economy.

c. cognitive therapy technique called token economy.

d. humanistic therapy technique called systematic desensitization.

32. Ben is a cognitive-behavior therapist. Compared to Rachel, who is a behavior therapist, Ben is more likely to:

a. base his therapy on principles of operant conditioning.

b. base his therapy on principles of classical conditioning.

c. address clients' attitudes as well as behaviors.

d. focus on clients' unconscious urges.

33. Which type(s) of psychotherapy would be most likely to use the interpretation of dreams as a technique for bringing unconscious feelings into awareness?

a. humanistic therapy

b. psychodynamic therapy

c. cognitive therapy

d. self-help groups

34. Of the following therapists, who would be most likely to interpret a person's psychological problems in terms of repressed impulses?

a. a behavior therapist

b. a cognitive therapist

c. a humanistic therapist

d. a psychoanalyst

Matching Items

Match each term with the appropriate definition or description.

Terms

_____ 1. cognitive therapy
_____ 2. behavior therapy
_____ 3. systematic desensitization
_____ 4. cognitive-behavior therapy
_____ 5. client-centered therapy
_____ 6. exposure therapy
_____ 7. aversive conditioning
_____ 8. psychoanalysis
_____ 9. counterconditioning
_____ 10. active listening
_____ 11. token economy
_____ 12. free association
_____ 13. stress inoculation training

Definitions or Descriptions

a. associates unwanted behavior with unpleasant experiences

b. associates a relaxed state with anxiety-arousing stimuli

c. integrated therapy that focuses on changing self-defeating thinking and unwanted behavior

d. category of therapies that teach people more adaptive ways of thinking and acting

e. the most widely used method of behavior therapy

f. therapy developed by Carl Rogers

g. therapy based on Freud's theory of personality

h. classical conditioning procedure in which new responses are conditioned to stimuli that trigger unwanted behaviors

i. category of therapies based on learning principles derived from classical and operant conditioning

j. empathic technique used in person-centered therapy

k. technique of psychoanalytic therapy

l. an operant conditioning procedure

m. cognitive-behavior therapy in which people are trained to restructure their thinking in stressful situations

Essay Question

Willie has been diagnosed as suffering from major depressive disorder. Describe the treatment he might receive from a psychoanalyst and a cognitive therapist. (Use the space below to list points you want to make, and organize them. Then write the essay on a separate sheet of paper.)

KEY TERMS

Using your own words, on a separate piece of paper write a brief definition or explanation of each of the following terms.

1. psychotherapy

2. eclectic approach

3. psychoanalysis

4. resistance

5. interpretation

6. transference

7. client-centered therapy

8. active listening

9. behavior therapy

10. counterconditioning

11. exposure therapies

12. systematic desensitization

13. virtual reality exposure therapy

14. aversive conditioning

15. token economy

16. cognitive therapy

17. cognitive-behavior therapy

18. family therapy

ANSWERS

Module Review

Introducing the Psychological Therapies

1. psychotherapy; learned

2. eclectic; psychotherapy integration

Psychoanalysis

1. insight

2. repressed

3. repressed; conscious

4. free association

5. resistance; interpretation

6. latent content

7. transference

8. disprove; expensive

9. psychodynamic; once a week

10. depressed; interpersonal psychotherapy

11. insight; current relationships

Humanistic Therapies

1. self-fulfillment

Unlike psychoanalysis, humanistic therapy is focused on the present and future instead of the past, on conscious rather than unconscious processes, on promoting growth and fulfillment instead of curing illness, and on helping clients take immediate responsibility for their feelings and actions rather than on uncovering the obstacles to doing so.

2. client-centered; nondirective; does not interpret

3. genuineness; acceptance; empathy

4. active listening; unconditional positive regard

5. paraphrase; invite clarification; reflect feelings

Behavior Therapies

1. learning

Whereas psychoanalysis and humanistic therapies assume that problems diminish as self-awareness grows, behavior therapists doubt that self-awareness is the key. Instead of looking for the inner cause of unwanted behavior, behavior therapy applies learning principles to directly attack the unwanted behavior itself.

2. classical conditioning; counterconditioning; systematic desensitization; aversive conditioning
3. exposure therapies; Joseph Wolpe; anxious
4. hierarchy; progressive relaxation; relaxed; anxiety
5. virtual reality exposure
6. negative; positive; unpleasant
7. behavior modification
8. operant; token economy

Behavior modification is criticized because the desired behavior may stop when the rewards are stopped. Also, critics contend that one person should not be allowed to control another.

Proponents of behavior modification contend that some clients request this therapy. Also, control already exists.

Cognitive Therapies

1. cognitive
2. catastrophizing; depression; Aaron Beck
3. stress inoculation; dispute
4. cognitive-behavior

Group and Family Therapies

Group therapy saves therapists time and clients money. The social context of group therapy allows people to discover that others have similar problems and to try out new ways of behaving.

1. family therapy
2. communication

Progress Test

Multiple-Choice Questions

1. **c.** is the answer.
   a. Active listening is a Rogerian technique in which the therapist echoes, restates, and seeks clarification of the client's statements.
   b. Spontaneous recovery refers to improvement without treatment.
   d. Systematic desensitization is a process in which a person is conditioned to associate a relaxed state with anxiety-triggering stimuli.
2. **b.** is the answer.
3. **d.** is the answer. This is not among the criticisms commonly made of psychoanalysis. (It would more likely be made of behavior therapies.)

4. **d.** is the answer.
   a., b., & c. Each of these is a type of psychological therapy.
5. **c.** is the answer. Outcome research on the relative effectiveness of different therapies reveals no clear winner; the other factors mentioned are advantages of group therapies.
6. **c.** is the answer.
7. **d.** is the answer. Today, half of all psychotherapists describe themselves as eclectic—as using a blend of therapies.
   a. An eclectic therapist may use a nondirective approach with certain behaviors; however, a more directive approach might be chosen for other clients and problems.
   b. In fact, just the opposite is true. Eclectic therapists generally view disorders as stemming from many influences.
   c. Eclectic therapists, in contrast to this example, use a combination of treatments.
8. **a.** is the answer.
9. **c.** is the answer.
10. **b.** is the answer.
    a. This reflects a cognitive perspective.
    c. This reflects a psychoanalytic perspective.
11. **c.** is the answer.
    a. & b. Counterconditioning is the replacement of an undesired response with a desired one by means of aversive conditioning or systematic desensitization.
    d. Exposure therapy exposes a person, in imagination or in actuality, to a feared situation.
12. **d.** is the answer.
13. **c.** is the answer.
    a. This answer would be a correct description of Joseph Wolpe.
    b. There is no such thing as insight therapy.
    d. This answer would be a correct description of Aaron Beck.
14. **a.** is the answer.
    b. In systematic desensitization, a hierarchy of anxiety-provoking stimuli is gradually associated with a relaxed state.
    c. Transference refers to a patient's transferring of feelings from other relationships onto his or her psychoanalyst.
    d. Electroconvulsive therapy is a biomedical shock treatment.
15. **c.** is the answer.
    a. Behavior therapy focuses on behavior, not self-awareness.

b. Psychoanalysis focuses on bringing repressed feelings into awareness.

d. Cognitive therapy teaches people to think and act in more adaptive ways.

16. **a.** is the answer. For behavior therapy, the problem behaviors *are* the problems.

b. Cognitive therapy teaches people to think and act in more adaptive ways.

c. Humanistic therapy promotes growth and self-fulfillment by providing an empathic, genuine, and accepting environment.

d. Psychoanalytic therapy focuses on uncovering and interpreting repressed feelings.

17. **b.** is the answer. Counterconditioning techniques involve taking an established stimulus, which triggers an undesirable response, and pairing it with a new stimulus in order to condition a new, and more adaptive, response.

a. As indicated by the name, counterconditioning techniques are a form of conditioning; they do not involve learning by observation.

c. & d. The principles of operant conditioning are the basis of behavior modification, which, in contrast to counterconditioning techniques, involves use of reinforcement.

18. **d.** is the answer.

a. This is a confrontational therapy, which is aimed at teaching people to think and act in more adaptive ways.

b. Aversive conditioning is a form of counterconditioning in which unwanted behavior is associated with unpleasant feelings.

c. Counterconditioning is a general term, including not only systematic desensitization, in which a hierarchy of fears is desensitized, but also other techniques, such as aversive conditioning.

19. **d.** is the answer.

a. & b. These techniques are based on classical conditioning.

c. This is a type of cognitive therapy.

20. **d.** is the answer.

21. **c.** is the answer.

a. Psychoanalysis focuses on uncovering unconscious thoughts.

b. In this humanistic therapy, the therapist facilitates the client's growth by offering a genuine, accepting, and empathic environment.

d. Behavior therapy concentrates on modifying the actual symptoms of psychological problems.

22. **d.** is the answer.

a. This is true of most forms of psychotherapy.

b. & c. This is true of humanistic, cognitive, and behavior therapies.

23. **c.** is the answer. Although aversive conditioning may work in the short run, the person's ability to discriminate between the situation in which the aversive conditioning occurs and other situations can limit the treatment's effectiveness.

a., b., & d. These were not offered in the text as limitations of the effectiveness of aversive conditioning.

24. **d.** is the answer. Resistances are blocks in the flow of free association that hint at underlying anxiety.

a. In transference, a patient redirects feelings from other relationships to his or her analyst.

b. The goal of psychoanalysis is for patients to gain insight into their feelings.

c. Although such hesitation may well involve material that has been repressed, the hesitation itself is a resistance.

25. **d.** is the answer. In transference, the patient develops feelings toward the therapist that were experienced in important early relationships but were repressed.

a. Projection is a defense mechanism in which a person imputes his or her own feelings to someone else.

b. Resistances are blocks in the flow of free association that indicate repressed material.

c. Regression is a defense mechanism in which a person retreats to an earlier form of behavior.

26. **d.** is the answer. According to Rogers' client-centered therapy, the therapist must exhibit genuineness, acceptance, and empathy if the client is to move toward self-fulfillment.

a. Psychoanalysts are much more directive in providing interpretations of clients' problems than are humanistic therapists.

b. Behavior therapists focus on modifying the behavioral symptoms of psychological problems.

c. Cognitive therapists teach people to think and act in new, more adaptive ways.

27. **d.** is the answer. Aversive conditioning is the classical conditioning technique in which a positive response is replaced by a negative response. (In this example, the US is the blast of smoke, the CS is the taste of the cigarette as it is inhaled, and the intended CR is aversion to cigarettes.) (p. 504)

a. Exposure therapy exposes someone, in imagination (virtual reality exposure therapy) or actuality, to a feared situation.

b. Behavior modification applies the principles of operant conditioning and thus, in contrast to the example, uses reinforcement.

c. Systematic desensitization is used to help people overcome specific anxieties.

28. d. is the answer. Because the psychologist is focusing on Darnel's irrational thinking, this response is most typical of Beck's cognitive therapy for depression.

a. Behavior therapists treat behaviors rather than thoughts.

b. Psychoanalysts focus on helping patients gain insight into previously repressed feelings.

c. Client-centered therapists attempt to facilitate clients' growth by offering a genuine, accepting, empathic environment.

29. a. is the answer.

b. & c. These types of therapists are more concerned with promoting self-fulfillment (humanistic) and healthy patterns of thinking (cognitive) than with correcting specific problem behaviors.

d. Psychoanalysts see the behavior merely as a symptom and focus their treatment on its presumed underlying cause.

30. a. is the answer.

b. Aversive conditioning associates unpleasant states with unwanted behaviors.

c. Shaping is an operant conditioning technique in which successive approximations of a desired behavior are reinforced.

d. Free association is a psychoanalytic technique in which a patient says whatever comes to mind.

31. b. is the answer.

32. c. is the answer.

a. & b. Behavior therapists make extensive use of techniques based on both operant and classical conditioning.

d. Neither behavior therapists nor cognitive behavior therapists focus on clients' unconscious urges.

33. b. is the answer. Psychodynamic therapy seeks insight into a patient's unconscious feelings. The analysis of dreams, slips of the tongue, and resistances are considered a window into these feelings.

a. Humanistic therapy aims to help people grow in self-awareness and self-acceptance.

c. Cognitive therapists avoid reference to unconscious feelings and would therefore be uninterested in interpreting dreams.

d. Psychodynamic therapies cannot be practiced in groups.

34. d. is the answer. A key aim of psychoanalysis is to unearth and understand repressed impulses.

a., b., & c. Behavior and cognitive therapists avoid concepts such as "repression" and "unconscious"; behavior and humanistic therapists focus on the present rather than the past.

Matching Items

1. d	6. e	11. l
2. i	7. a	12. k
3. b	8. g	13. m
4. c	9. h	
5. f	10. j	

Essay Question

Psychoanalysts assume that psychological problems such as depression are caused by unresolved, repressed, and unconscious impulses and conflicts from childhood. A psychoanalyst would probably attempt to bring these repressed feelings into Willie's conscious awareness and help him gain insight into them. He or she would likely try to interpret Willie's resistance during free association, the latent content of his dreams, and any emotional feelings he might transfer to the analyst.

Cognitive therapists assume that a person's emotional reactions are influenced by the person's thoughts in response to the event in question. A cognitive therapist would probably try to teach Willie new and more constructive ways of thinking in order to reverse his catastrophizing beliefs about himself, his situation, and his future.

Key Terms

1. **Psychotherapy** is an interaction between a trained therapist and someone who suffers from psychological difficulties or wants to achieve personal growth.

2. With an **eclectic approach**, therapists are not locked into one form of psychotherapy, but draw on whatever combination seems best suited to a client's needs.

3. **Psychoanalysis**, the therapy developed by Sigmund Freud, attempts to give clients self-insight by bringing into awareness and interpreting previously repressed feelings.

   Example: The tools of the **psychoanalyst** include free association, the analysis of dreams and transferences, and the interpretation of repressed impulses.

4. **Resistance** is the psychoanalytic term for the blocking from consciousness of anxiety-laden memories. Hesitation during free association may reflect resistance.

5. **Interpretation** is the psychoanalytic term for the analyst's helping the client to understand resistances and other aspects of behavior, so that the client may gain deeper insights.

6. **Transference** is the psychoanalytic term for a patient's redirecting to the analyst emotions from other relationships.

7. **Client-centered therapy** is a humanistic nondirective therapy developed by Carl Rogers, in which growth and self-awareness are facilitated in an environment that offers genuineness, acceptance, and empathy.

8. **Active listening** is a nondirective technique of Rogers' client-centered therapy, in which the listener echoes, restates, and seeks clarification of, but does not interpret, clients' remarks.

9. **Behavior therapy** is therapy that applies learning principles to the elimination of problem behaviors.

10. **Counterconditioning** is a category of behavior therapy in which new responses are classically conditioned to stimuli that trigger unwanted behaviors.

11. **Exposure therapies** treat anxiety by exposing people to things they normally fear and avoid. Among these therapies are systematic desensitization and virtual reality exposure therapy.

12. **Systematic desensitization** is a type of exposure therapy in which a state of relaxation is classically conditioned to a hierarchy of gradually increasing anxiety-provoking stimuli.

    Memory aid: This is a form of **counterconditioning** in which sensitive, anxiety-triggering stimuli are *desensitized* in a progressive, or **systematic**, fashion.

13. **Virtual reality exposure therapy** progressively exposes people to simulations of feared situations to treat their anxiety.

14. **Aversive conditioning** is a form of counterconditioning in which an unpleasant state becomes associated with an unwanted behavior.

15. A **token economy** is an operant conditioning procedure in which desirable behaviors are promoted in people by rewarding them with tokens, or positive reinforcers, which can be exchanged for privileges or treats. For the most part, token economies are used in hospitals, schools, and other institutional settings.

16. **Cognitive therapy** focuses on teaching people new and more adaptive ways of thinking and acting. The therapy is based on the idea that our feelings and responses to events are strongly influenced by our thinking, or cognition.

17. **Cognitive-behavior therapy** is an integrated therapy that focuses on changing self-defeating thinking (cognitive therapy) and unwanted behaviors (behavior therapy).

18. **Family therapy** views problem behavior as partially engendered by the client's family system and environment. Therapy therefore focuses on relationships and problems among the various members of the family.

FOCUS ON VOCABULARY AND LANGUAGE

Introducing the Psychological Therapies

. . . bewildering array of harsh and gentle methods . . . Myers is referring to the many odd and strange techniques (*bewildering variety of harsh and gentle methods*) used to deal with people suffering from psychological disorders, such as cutting holes in the skull, piercing veins or attaching leeches to remove blood from the body (*bleeding*), and whipping or striking people in order to force demons out of the body (*"beating the devil" out of people*). Today's less harsh (*gentle*) therapies are classified into two main categories, psychological and biomedical.

(caption): . . . visitors paid to *gawk* at the *patients* as though they were viewing zoo animals. In the past, mentally disordered people (*patients*) were confined to hospitals (*insane asylums*) and were often treated badly. For instance, some hospitals raised money by selling tickets to the public who could come and stare (*gawk*) at the inmates (*patients*), much as we do today when we visit the zoo and look at the captive animals.

Psychoanalysis

. . . Freud assumed that many psychological problems are *fueled* by childhood's *residue* of *repressed impulses and conflicts.* Freud's psychoanalytic techniques are used by many therapists; their fundamental tenet (*assumption*) is that mental disorders are created and kept in existence (*fueled*) by hidden (*repressed*) childhood urges and opposing psychic forces (*conflicts*). Psychoanalysis attempts to restore the patient to mental health by bringing these submerged (*buried*) feelings into conscious awareness where they can be examined and dealt with (*worked through*). As Myers puts it, psychoanalysis digs up (*unearths*) the past in the hopes of uncovering (*unmasking*) the present.

Humanistic Therapies

Not surprisingly, humanistic therapists *aim to boost* self-fulfillment by helping people grow in self-awareness and self-acceptance. The most popular humanistic technique is Carl Rogers' nondirective person-centered therapy. The goal is to increase (*the aim is to boost*) the client's feelings of accomplishment and achievement (self-actualization) by providing nonthreatening opportunities for living in the present, for becoming less critical of one's self, and for becoming more self-aware.

"And that just really knocks the props out from under you." In Carl Rogers' therapy sessions, he attempts to be genuine, accepting, and empathic; he also mirrors (*reflects*) back to the client in different words the feelings that were expressed. The client said he had been told that he was no good, and Rogers reflects the feelings he detects by saying that it must seem that the client's self-worth had been undermined (*knocked the props out from under you*).

Behavior Therapies

. . . Jones' story of Peter and the rabbit did not immediately become part of psychology's *lore*. Mary Cover Jones was the first to demonstrate **counterconditioning** (replacing a fear response with an incompatible response, such as relaxation through classical conditioning). This technique, however, did not become part of psychology's tradition and store of knowledge (*lore*) until Wolpe developed systematic desensitization more than 30 years later.

To treat alcoholism, an aversion therapist offers the client appealing drinks *laced* with a drug that produces *severe nausea*. Behavior therapists, focusing on observable behaviors, use a number of techniques based on well-established learning principles. Two counterconditioning techniques based on classical conditioning are **systematic desensitization** and **aversive conditioning.** In aversive therapy, people who regularly drink too much are given enticing

alcoholic beverages which are infused (*laced*) with a substance that induces sickness (*severe nausea*). Alcohol should now be a potent conditioned stimulus that elicits unpleasant feelings; as a result, the person with alcoholism should want to avoid these drinks. Research shows some limited success with this approach.

The combination of positively reinforcing desired behaviors and ignoring or punishing *aggressive and self-abusive* behaviors *worked wonders* for some. Another type of behavior therapy is based on operant conditioning principles and involves voluntary behavior followed by pleasant or unpleasant consequences. Socially withdrawn autistic children, treated to an intensive two-year program of positive reinforcement for desired behaviors and punishment for violent and self-injurious (*aggressive and self-abusive*) behaviors, responded extremely well (*it worked wonders for them*).

Cognitive Therapies

The **cognitive therapies** assume that our thinking *colors* our feelings. . . . The underlying assumption of the cognitive approach to therapy is that thoughts precede and influence (*color*) our feelings. If certain destructive patterns of thinking are learned, then it must be possible to unlearn them and replace them with more constructive ways of viewing what happens to us.

. . . *catastrophizing* . . . Aaron Beck, a cognitive therapist, believes that the way to help depressed people feel better is to turn around (*reverse*) their negative, distorted thinking, which tends to transform ordinary events into disasters (*catastrophizing*). The goal is to get them to think about their lives in more positive terms (*convince them to take off the dark glasses*).

Evaluating Psychotherapy

41 M O D U L E

MODULE OVERVIEW

In evaluating the therapies, the module points out that, although people who are untreated often improve, those receiving psychotherapy tend to improve somewhat more, regardless of the type of therapy they receive. The module also includes a discussion of several popular alternative therapies.

Because the origins of problems often lie beyond the individual, the module includes a Close-Up on approaches that aim at preventing psychological disorders by focusing on the family or on the larger social environment as possible contributors to psychological disorders.

NOTE: Answer guidelines for all Module 41 questions begin on page 447.

MODULE REVIEW

First, skim each section, noting headings and boldface items. After you have read the section, review each objective by answering the fill-in and essay-type questions that follow it. As you proceed, evaluate your performance by consulting the answers on page 447. Do not continue with the next section until you understand each answer. If you need to, review or reread the section in the textbook before continuing.

> David Myers at times uses idioms that are unfamiliar to some readers. If you do not know the meaning of any of the following words or expressions in the context in which they appear in the text, refer to pages 448–449 for an explanation: *"Hang in there"; testimonials; ebb and flow of events; clear-cut; fertile soil for pseudotherapies; harness; Warmth and empathy are hallmarks; upstream work.*

Is Psychotherapy Effective? (pp. 554–556)

Objective 1: Explain why clients and clinicians tend to overestimate the effectiveness of psychotherapy.

1. An interaction between a trained therapist and someone suffering from a psychological disorder is called _____ .

2. In contrast to earlier times, most therapy today _____ (is/is not) provided by psychiatrists.

3. A majority of psychotherapy clients express _____ (satisfaction/dissatisfaction) with their therapy.

Give three reasons why client testimonials are not persuasive evidence for psychotherapy's effectiveness.

4. Clinicians tend to _____ (overestimate/underestimate) the effectiveness of psychotherapy.

5. One reason clinicians' perceptions of the effectiveness of psychotherapy are inaccurate is that clients justify entering therapy by emphasizing their _____ and justify leaving therapy by emphasizing their _____ .

Objective 2: Discuss some of the findings of outcome studies in judging the effectiveness of psychotherapies.

6. In hopes of better assessing psychotherapy's effectiveness, psychologists have turned to _____ research studies.

7. The debate over the effectiveness of psychotherapy began with a study by _____ ; it showed that the rate of improvement for those who received therapy _____ (was/was not) higher than the rate for those who did not.

8. Overall, the results of Smith's statistical digest of outcome studies indicate that psychotherapy is _____ (somewhat effective/ineffective).

9. Psychotherapy is cost-effective when compared with the greater costs of _____ care for psychological problems.

The Relative Effectiveness of Different Therapies (p. 557)

Objective 3: Describe which psychotherapies are most effective for specific disorders.

1. Comparisons of the effectiveness of different forms of therapy reveal _____ (clear/no clear) differences, that the type of therapy provider _____ (matters greatly/does not matter), and that whether therapy is provided by an individual therapist or within a group _____ (makes a difference/does not make a difference).

2. With phobias, compulsions, and other specific behavior problems, _____ _____ therapies have been the most effective. Other studies have demonstrated that depression may be effectively treated with _____ therapy.

3. As a rule, psychotherapy is most effective with problems that are _____ (specific/nonspecific).

Evaluating Alternative Therapies (pp. 557–559)

Objective 4: Evaluate the effectiveness of eye movement desensitization and reprocessing (EMDR) and light exposure therapies.

1. Today, many forms of _____ _____ are touted as effective treatments for a variety of complaints.

2. Aside from testimonials, there is very little evidence based on _____ research for such therapies.

3. In one popular alternative therapy, a therapist triggers eye movements in patients while they imagine _____ _____ . This therapy, called _____ _____ _____ _____ _____ , has proven _____ (completely ineffective/somewhat effective) as a treatment for nonmilitary _____- _____ _____ . However, skeptics point to evidence that _____ _____ is just as effective as triggered eye movements in producing beneficial results. The key seems to be in the person's _____ traumatic memories and in a _____ effect.

4. For people who suffer from the wintertime form of depression called _____ _____ _____ , timed _____- _____ therapy may be beneficial.

Commonalities Among Psychotherapies (pp. 559–561)

Objective 5: Describe the three benefits attributed to all psychotherapies.

1. All forms of psychotherapy offer three benefits: _____ for demoralized people; a new _____ on oneself; and a relationship that is _____ , _____ , and _____ .

2. Therapy outcomes vary with the _____ of the person seeking help.

3. The emotional bond between therapist and client—the _____ _____—is a key aspect of effective therapy. In one study of depression treatment, the most effective therapists were those who were perceived as most _____ and _____ .

4. Several studies found that treatment for mild problems offered by paraprofessionals _____ (is/is not) as effective as that offered by professional therapists.

Culture and Values in Psychotherapy
(pp. 561–563)

Objective 6: Discuss the role of values and cultural differences in the therapeutic process.

1. Generally speaking, psychotherapists' personal values _____ (do/do not) influence their therapy. This is particularly significant when the therapist and client are from _____ (the same/different) cultures.

2. In North America, Europe, and Australia, most therapists reflect their culture's _____ .

3. Differences in values may help explain the reluctance of some _____ populations to use mental health services.

(Close-Up) Preventing Psychological Disorders by Treating the Social Contexts that Breed Them (p. 562)

Objective 7: Explain the rationale of preventive mental health programs.

1. Psychotherapies and biomedical therapies locate the cause of psychological disorders within the _____ .

2. An alternative viewpoint is that many psychological disorders are responses to _____ _____ .

3. According to this viewpoint, it is not just the _____ who needs treatment but

also the person's _____ _____ .

4. One advocate of _____ mental health, George Albee, believes that many social stresses undermine people's sense of _____ , _____ _____ , and _____ . These stresses include _____ , work that is _____ , constant _____ , _____ , _____ , and _____ .

5. Albee's views remind us that disorders are not just biological and not just environmental or psychological, because we are all an _____ _____ system.

PROGRESS TEST

Multiple-Choice Questions

Circle your answers to the following questions and check them with the answers beginning on page 447. If your answer is incorrect, read the explanation for why it is incorrect and then consult the appropriate pages of the text.

1. The effectiveness of psychotherapy has been assessed both through clients' perspectives and through controlled research studies. What have such assessments found?
   a. Clients' perceptions and controlled studies alike strongly affirm the effectiveness of psychotherapy.
   b. Whereas clients' perceptions strongly affirm the effectiveness of psychotherapy, studies point to more modest results.
   c. Whereas studies strongly affirm the effectiveness of psychotherapy, many clients feel dissatisfied with their progress.
   d. Clients' perceptions and controlled studies alike paint a very mixed picture of the effectiveness of psychotherapy.

2. The results of outcome research on the effectiveness of different psychotherapies reveal that:
   a. no single type of therapy is consistently superior.
   b. behavior therapies are most effective in treating specific problems, such as phobias.
   c. cognitive therapies are most effective in treating depressed emotions.
   d. all of these statements are true.

3. Psychologists who advocate a _____ approach to mental health contend that many psychological disorders could be prevented by changing the disturbed individual's _____ .
   a. biomedical; diet
   b. family; behavior
   c. humanistic; feelings
   d. preventive; environment

4. A person can derive benefits from psychotherapy simply by believing in it. This illustrates the importance of:
   a. spontaneous recovery.
   b. the placebo effect.
   c. the transference effect.
   d. interpretation.

5. Before 1950, the main mental health providers were:
   a. psychologists.   c. psychiatrists.
   b. paraprofessionals.   d. the clergy.

6. Light-exposure therapy has proven useful as a form of treatment for people suffering from:
   a. bulimia.
   b. seasonal affective disorder.
   c. schizophrenia.
   d. dissociative identity disorder.

7. Which form of therapy is *most* likely to be successful in treating depression?
   a. behavior modification c. cognitive therapy
   b. psychoanalysis   d. humanistic therapy

8. An analysis of 39 research studies comparing the effectiveness of professional therapists with paraprofessionals found that:
   a. the professionals were much more effective than the paraprofessionals.
   b. the paraprofessionals were much more effective than the professionals.
   c. except in treating depression, the paraprofessionals were about as effective as the professionals.
   d. the paraprofessionals were about as effective as the professionals.

9. Among the common ingredients of the psychotherapies is:
   a. the offer of a therapeutic relationship.
   b. the expectation among clients that the therapy will prove helpful.
   c. the chance to develop a fresh perspective on oneself and the world.
   d. all of these characteristics.

10. Seth enters therapy to talk about some issues that have been upsetting him. The therapist prescribes some medication to help him. The therapist is most likely a:
    a. clinical psychologist.
    b. psychiatrist.
    c. psychiatric social worker.
    d. clinical social worker.

11. A close friend who for years has suffered from wintertime depression is seeking your advice regarding the effectiveness of light-exposure therapy. What should you tell your friend?
    a. "Don't waste your time and money. It doesn't work."
    b. "A more effective treatment for seasonal affective disorder is eye movement desensitization and reprocessing."
    c. "You'd be better off with a prescription for lithium."
    d. "It might be worth a try. There is some evidence that morning light exposure produces relief."

12. A relative wants to know which type of therapy works best. You should tell your relative that:
    a. psychotherapy does not work.
    b. behavior therapy is the most effective.
    c. cognitive therapy is the most effective.
    d. no one type of therapy is consistently the most successful.

13. A psychotherapist who believes that the best way to treat psychological disorders is to prevent them from developing would be *most* likely to view disordered behavior as:
    a. maladaptive thoughts and actions.
    b. expressions of unconscious conflicts.
    c. conditioned responses.
    d. an understandable response to stressful social conditions.

KEY TERM

Using your own words, on a separate piece of paper write a brief definition or explanation of the following term.

1. psychotherapy

ANSWERS

Module Review

Is Psychotherapy Effective?

1. psychotherapy
2. is not
3. satisfaction

   People often enter therapy in crisis. When the crisis passes, they may attribute their improvement to the therapy. Clients, who may need to believe the therapy was worth the effort, may overestimate its effectiveness. Clients generally find positive things to say about their therapists, even if their problems remain.
4. overestimate
5. unhappiness; well-being
6. controlled
7. Hans Eysenck; was not
8. somewhat effective
9. medical

The Relative Effectiveness of Different Therapies

1. no clear; does not matter; does not make a difference
2. behavioral conditioning; cognitive
3. specific

Evaluating Alternative Therapies

1. alternative therapy
2. controlled
3. traumatic events; eye movement desensitization and reprocessing (EMDR); somewhat effective; post-traumatic stress disorder; finger tapping; reliving; placebo
4. seasonal affective disorder; light-exposure

Commonalities Among Psychotherapies

1. hope; perspective; caring; trusting; empathic
2. attitude
3. therapeutic alliance; empathic; caring
4. is

Culture and Values in Psychotherapy

1. do; different
2. individualism
3. minority

(Close-Up) Preventing Psychological Disorders by Treating the Social Contexts That Breed Them

1. person
2. a disturbing and stressful society
3. person; social context
4. preventive; competence; personal control; self-esteem; poverty; meaningless; criticism; unemployment; racism; sexism
5. integrated biopsychosocial

Progress Test

Multiple-Choice Questions

1. **b.** is the answer. Clients' testimonials regarding psychotherapy are generally very positive. The research, in contrast, seems to show that therapy is only *somewhat* effective.
2. **d.** is the answer.
3. **d.** is the answer.
4. **b.** is the answer.
   a. Spontaneous recovery refers to improvement without any treatment.
   c. Transference is the psychoanalytic phenomenon in which a client transfers feelings from other relationships onto his or her analyst.
   d. Interpretation is the psychoanalytic procedure through which the analyst helps the client become aware of resistances and understand their meaning.
5. **c.** is the answer.
6. **b.** is the answer.
7. **c.** is the answer.
   a. Behavior modification is most likely to be successful in treating specific behavior problems, such as bed wetting.
   b. & d. The text does not single out particular disorders for which these therapies tend to be most effective.
8. **d.** is the answer. Even when dealing with seriously depressed adults, the paraprofessionals were as effective as the professionals.
9. **d.** is the answer.
10. **b.** is the answer. Psychiatrists are physicians who specialize in treating psychological disorders. As doctors they can prescribe medications.
    a., c., & d. These professionals cannot prescribe drugs.
11. **d.** is the answer.

a. In fact, there is evidence that light-exposure therapy can be effective in treating SAD.

b. There is no evidence that EMDR is effective as a treatment for SAD.

c. Lithium is a mood-stabilizing drug that is often used to treat bipolar disorder.

12. **d.** is the answer.

a. Psychotherapy has proven "somewhat effective" and more cost-effective than physician care for psychological disorders.

b. & c. Behavior and cognitive therapies are both effective in treating depression, and behavior therapy is effective in treating specific problems such as phobias.

13. **d.** is the answer.

a. This would be the perspective of a cognitive behavior therapist.

b. This would be the perspective of a psychoanalyst.

c. This would be the perspective of a behavior therapist.

Key Term

1. **Psychotherapy** is an interaction between a trained therapist and someone who suffers from psychological difficulties or wants to achieve personal growth.

FOCUS ON VOCABULARY AND LANGUAGE

Introduction

"*Hang in there* until you find [a psychotherapist] *who fills the bill.*" Each year in the United States about 15 percent of the population seek help for psychological and addictive disorders. Many people, including the late advice columnist Ann Landers, recommend that troubled people get professional help and that they persevere (*hang in there*) in finding the right therapist to meet their needs (*who fills the bill*).

Is Psychotherapy Effective?

If clients' *testimonials* were the only measuring stick, we could strongly affirm the effectiveness of psychotherapy. The question of whether or not psychotherapy is effective is a very complex issue. If the only gauge (*measuring stick or yardstick*) we have was what clients said about their therapy (*testimonials*), then the conclusion would have to be that psychotherapy works. (Three-quarters, or more, of those surveyed were satisfied.) Myers points out that such testimonials can be misleading and invalid.

When, with the normal *ebb and flow* of events, the crisis passes, people may attribute their improvement to the therapy. Because of some serious traumatic events (*crises*) in their lives, people may end up seeing a therapist; after many sessions they may feel much better. During the ordinary course (*ebb and flow*) of events, however, the crisis is likely to have passed; thus, their present feelings of well-being may have little to do with the psychotherapy.

The Relative Effectiveness of Different Therapies

Moreover, we can say that therapy is most effective when the problem is *clear-cut* (Singer, 1981; Westen & Morrison, 2001). Psychotherapy tends to work best when the disturbances are well-defined (*clear-cut*) and explicitly stated or understood. For example, those who suffer from irrational fears (*phobias*), are timid or shy (*unassertive*), or have a psychologically caused sexual disorder respond better to therapy than those who suffer from schizophrenia or who want a total personality change. As Myers notes, the more specific the problem, the greater the hope.

Evaluating Alternative Therapies

The tendency of many abnormal states of mind to return to normal, combined with the placebo effect, creates *fertile soil* for *pseudotherapies*. So-called alternative therapies may appear to be effective for a couple of reasons: worse-than-normal mental states tend to diminish and move back to more normal mental states over time, and if people expect that a particular therapy will help them, they may get better as a result of their belief alone (*the placebo effect*). These factors provide a basis (*fertile soil*) for the growth and popularity of therapies that have not been empirically validated (*pseudotherapies*). Indeed, supported (*bolstered*) by anecdotes, exuberantly reported (*heralded*) by the media, given accolades (*praised*) on the Internet, alternative therapies can thrive and flourish (*can spread like wildfire*).

Commonalities Among Psychotherapies

Thus, each therapy, in its individual way, may *harness* the person's own healing powers. Research has shown that actual therapy is better than no treatment, but that placebo-treated people improve significantly. This suggests that therapies work in part because they offer hope; each different type of therapy may be effective to the extent that it capitalizes on and uses (*harnesses*) the clients' ability for self-healing.

Warmth and *empathy* are *hallmarks* of healers everywhere, whether psychiatrists, witch doctors, or shamans (Torrey, 1986). In general, therapies are approximately the same in effectiveness, but that does not mean that all therapists are equal in this respect. Fundamental qualities (*hallmarks*) of effective therapists are an ability to understand other people's experiences (*empathy*) and a capacity to show genuine concern and care (*warmth*). In addition, good listening skills, a reassuring manner, and concern for gaining (*earning*) the client's respect and trust help in the therapeutic process.

(Close-Up) Preventing Psychological Disorders by Treating the Social Contexts That Breed Them

Preventive mental health is *upstream work*. Some psychologists believe that prevention is better than cure and they support programs that help relieve and stop poverty, racism, discrimination, and other disempowering or demoralizing situations. The attempt to prevent psychological disorders by getting rid of conditions that may cause them is extremely difficult (*upstream work*).

The Biomedical Therapies

42

MODULE OVERVIEW

The biomedical therapies discussed are drug therapies, electroconvulsive therapy, and psychosurgery, which is seldom used. By far the most important of these, drug therapies are being used in the treatment of psychotic, anxiety, and mood disorders.

NOTE: Answer guidelines for all Module 42 questions begin on page 454.

MODULE REVIEW

First, skim each section, noting headings and boldface items. After you have read the section, review each objective by answering the fill-in and essay-type questions that follow it. As you proceed, evaluate your performance by consulting the answers beginning on page 454. Do not continue with the next section until you understand each answer. If you need to, review or reread the section in the textbook before continuing.

> David Myers at times uses idioms that are unfamiliar to some readers. If you do not know the meaning of any of the following words or expressions in the context in which they appear in the text, refer to page 456 for an explanation: *sluggishness, tremors, and twitches; "Popping a Xanax"; lift people up; barbaric image; jump-starting the depressed brain.*

Introduction and Drug Therapies (pp. 565–568)

Objective 1: Identify the biomedical therapies, and explain how double-blind studies help researchers evaluate a drug's effectiveness.

1. Biomedical therapies include the use of

_____ _____

and medical procedures that act directly on the patient's _____ _____ .

2. The most widely used biomedical treatments are the _____ therapies. Thanks to these therapies, the number of residents in mental hospitals has _____ (increased/decreased) sharply. Other biomedical therapies include _____ therapy and

_____ .

3. The field that studies the effects of drugs on the mind and behavior is _____ .

4. To guard against the _____ effect and normal _____ , neither the patients nor the staff involved in a study may be aware of which condition a given individual is in; this is called a _____-

_____ study.

Objective 2: Describe the characteristics of antipsychotic, antianxiety, antidepressant, and mood-stabilizing drugs, and discuss their use in treating psychological disorders.

5. One effect of _____ drugs such as _____ is to help those experiencing _____ (positive/negative) symptoms of schizophrenia by decreasing their responsiveness to irrelevant stimuli; schizophrenia patients who are apathetic and withdrawn may be more effectively treated with the drug _____ .

6. These drugs work by blocking the receptor sites for the neurotransmitter _____ .

7. Long-term use of antipsychotic drugs can produce _____ _____ ,
   which involves involuntary movements of the
   muscles of the _____ ,
   _____ , and _____ .

8. Xanax and Ativan are classified as
   _____ drugs.

9. These drugs depress activity in the _____
   _____ _____ .

10. When used in combination with
    _____ _____ ,
    these drugs can help people cope with frighten-
    ing situations.

11. Antianxiety drugs have been criticized for merely
    reducing _____ , rather than
    resolving underlying _____ .
    These drugs can also cause _____
    _____ .

12. Drugs that are prescribed to alleviate depression
    are called _____ drugs. These
    drugs also work by increasing levels of the neuro-
    transmitters _____ or
    _____ .

13. One example of this type of drug is
    _____ , which works by blocking
    the reabsorption and removal of
    _____ from synapses and is
    therefore called a _____-
    _____-_____-
    _____ drug.

14. Equally effective in calming anxious people and
    energizing depressed people is
    _____ _____ ,
    which has positive side effects. Even better is to
    use drugs, which work _____
    (bottom-up/top-down), in conjunction with
    _____-_____
    therapy, which works _____
    (bottom-up/top-down).

15. Although people with depression often improve
    after one month on antidepressants, studies

demonstrate that a large percentage of the
effectiveness is due to _____
_____ or a _____
_____ .

16. In order to stabilize the mood swings of a bipolar
    disorder, the simple salt _____ is
    often prescribed.

17. Another effective drug in the control of mania
    was originally used to treat epilepsy; it is
    _____ .

Brain Stimulation (pp. 568–570)

Objective 3: Describe the use of brain stimulation
techniques in treating specific disorders, and discuss
possible alternatives to ECT.

1. The therapeutic technique in which the patient
   receives an electric shock to the brain is referred
   to as _____ therapy, abbreviated
   as _____ .

2. ECT is most often used with patients suffering
   from severe _____ . Research evidence _____ (confirms/does not
   confirm) ECT's effectiveness with such patients.

3. The mechanism by which ECT works is
   _____ .

4. A gentler alternative is a chest _____
   that intermittently stimulates the
   _____ nerve.

5. Another gentler procedure called _____
   _____ _____
   _____ aims to treat depression
   by presenting pulses through a magnetic coil held
   close to a person's skull above the right eyebrow.
   Unlike ECT, this procedure produces no
   _____ , _____
   loss, or other side effects. This procedure may
   work by energizing the brain's left
   _____ _____ ,
   which is relatively inactive in depressed patients.

Psychosurgery (pp. 570–571)

Objective 4: Summarize the history of the psychosurgical procedure known as the lobotomy, and discuss the use of psychosurgery today.

1. The biomedical therapy in which a portion of brain tissue is removed or destroyed is called

   _____ .

2. In the 1930s, Moniz developed an operation called the _____ . In this procedure, the _____ lobe of the brain is disconnected from the rest of the brain.

3. Today, most psychosurgery has been replaced by the use of _____ or some other form of treatment.

PROGRESS TEST

Multiple-Choice Questions

Circle your answers to the following questions and check them with the answers on page 455. If your answer is incorrect, read the explanation for why it is incorrect and then consult the appropriate pages of the text.

1. Electroconvulsive therapy is most useful in the treatment of:
   a. schizophrenia.
   b. depression.
   c. personality disorders.
   d. anxiety disorders.

2. Which biomedical therapy is *most* likely to be practiced today?
   a. psychosurgery
   b. electroconvulsive therapy
   c. drug therapy
   d. counterconditioning

3. The antipsychotic drugs appear to produce their effects by blocking the receptor sites for:
   a. dopamine.   c. norepinephrine.
   b. epinephrine.   d. serotonin.

4. Antidepressant drugs are believed to work by affecting serotonin or:
   a. dopamine.   c. norepinephrine.
   b. lithium.   d. acetylcholine.

5. After many years of taking antipsychotic drugs, Greg's facial muscles sometimes twitch involuntarily. This behavior is called:
   a. tardive dyskinesia.
   b. spontaneous recovery.
   c. repetitive transcranial magnetic stimulation.
   d. EMDR.

6. Which of the following is the mood-stabilizing drug most commonly used to treat bipolar disorder?
   a. Ativan   c. Xanax
   b. chlorpromazine   d. lithium

7. The type of drugs criticized for reducing symptoms without resolving underlying problems are the:
   a. antianxiety drugs.
   b. antipsychotic drugs.
   c. antidepressant drugs.
   d. amphetamines.

8. Although Moniz won the Nobel prize for developing the lobotomy procedure, the technique is not widely used today because:
   a. it produces a lethargic, immature personality.
   b. it is irreversible.
   c. calming drugs became available in the 1950s.
   d. of all of these reasons.

9. In an experiment testing the effects of a new antipsychotic drug, neither Dr. Cunningham nor her patients know whether the patients are in the experimental or the control group. This is an example of:
   a. outcome research.
   b. within-subjects research.
   c. the double-blind technique.
   d. the single-blind technique.

10. Linda's doctor prescribes medication that blocks the activity of dopamine in her nervous system. Evidently, Linda is being treated with an _____ drug.
    a. antipsychotic   c. antidepressant
    b. antianxiety   d. anticonvulsive

11. Abraham's doctor prescribes medication that increases the availability of norepinephrine or serotonin in his nervous system. Evidently, Abraham is being treated with an _____ drug.
    a. antipsychotic
    b. antianxiety
    c. antidepressant
    d. anticonvulsive

12. In concluding her talk entitled "Psychosurgery Today," Ashley states that:

   a. "Psychosurgery is still widely used throughout the world."

   b. "Electroconvulsive therapy is the only remaining psychosurgical technique that is widely practiced."

   c. "With advances in psychopharmacology, psychosurgery has largely been abandoned."

   d. "Although lobotomies remain popular, other psychosurgical techniques have been abandoned."

13. A psychiatrist has diagnosed a patient as having bipolar disorder. It is likely that she will prescribe:

   a. an antipsychotic drug.

   b. lithium.

   c. an antianxiety drug.

   d. a drug that blocks receptor sites for serotonin.

Matching Items

Match each term with the appropriate definition or description.

Terms

_____ **1.** biomedical therapy
_____ **2.** placebo effect
_____ **3.** lobotomy
_____ **4.** lithium
_____ **5.** psychopharmacology
_____ **6.** double-blind technique
_____ **7.** Xanax

Definitions or Descriptions

a. type of psychosurgery
b. mood-stabilizing drug
c. the beneficial effect of a person's expecting that treatment will be effective
d. treatment with psychosurgery, electroconvulsive therapy, or drugs
e. antianxiety drug
f. the study of the effects of drugs on the mind and behavior
g. experimental procedure in which both the patient and staff are unaware of a patient's treatment condition

KEY TERMS

Using your own words, on a separate piece of paper write a brief definition or explanation of each of the following terms.

1. biomedical therapy

2. psychopharmacology

3. electroconvulsive therapy (ECT)

4. repetitive transcranial magnetic stimulation (rTMS)

5. psychosurgery

6. lobotomy

ANSWERS

Module Review

Introduction and *Drug Therapies*

1. prescribed medications; nervous system

2. drug; decreased; electroconvulsive; psychosurgery

3. psychopharmacology

4. placebo; recovery; double-blind

5. antipsychotic; chlorpromazine (Thorazine); positive; clozapine (Clozaril)

6. dopamine

7. tardive dyskinesia; face; tongue; limbs

8. antianxiety

9. central nervous system

10. psychological therapy
11. symptoms; problems; physiological dependence
12. antidepressant; norepinephrine; serotonin
13. fluoxetine (Prozac); serotonin; selective-serotonin-reuptake-inhibitor
14. aerobic exercise; bottom-up; cognitive-behavior; top-down
15. spontaneous recovery; placebo effect
16. lithium
17. Depakote

Brain Stimulation

1. electroconvulsive; ECT
2. depression; confirms
3. unknown
4. implant; vagus
5. repetitive transcranial magnetic stimulation (rTMS); seizures; memory; frontal lobe

Psychosurgery

1. psychosurgery
2. lobotomy; frontal
3. drugs

Progress Test

Multiple-Choice Questions

1. **b.** is the answer. Although no one is sure how ECT works, one possible explanation is that it increases release of norepinephrine, the neurotransmitter that elevates mood.

2. **c.** is the answer.
   a. The fact that its effects are irreversible makes psychosurgery a drastic procedure, and with advances in psychopharmacology, psychosurgery was largely abandoned.
   b. ECT is still widely used as a treatment of severe depression, but in general it is not used as frequently as drug therapy.
   d. Counterconditioning is not a biomedical therapy.

3. **a.** is the answer. By occupying receptor sites for dopamine, these drugs block its activity and reduce its production.

4. **c.** is the answer.

5. **a.** is the answer.

6. **d.** is the answer. Lithium works as a mood stabilizer.
   a. & c. Ativan and Xanax are antianxiety drugs.
   b. Chlorpromazine is an antipsychotic drug.

7. **a.** is the answer.

8. **d.** is the answer.

9. **c.** is the answer.
   a. This is a statistical technique used to combine the results of many different research studies.
   b. In this design, which is not mentioned in the text, there is only a single research group.
   d. This answer would be correct if the experimenter, but not the research participants, knew which condition was in effect.

10. **a.** is the answer.

11. **c.** is the answer.

12. **c.** is the answer.
   b. Although still practiced, electroconvulsive therapy is not a form of psychosurgery.

13. **b.** is the answer.

Matching Items

1.	d	5.	f
2.	c	6.	g
3.	a	7.	e
4.	b		

Key Terms

1. **Biomedical therapy** is the use of prescribed medications or medical procedures that act on a patient's nervous system to treat psychological disorders.

2. **Psychopharmacology** is the study of the effects of drugs on mind and behavior.

   Memory aid: Pharmacology is the science of the uses and effects of drugs. *Psycho*pharmacology is the science that studies the psychological effects of drugs.

3. In **electroconvulsive therapy (ECT)**, a biomedical therapy often used to treat severe depression, electric shock is passed through the brain.

4. **Repetitive transcranial magnetic stimulation (rTMS)** is the delivery of repeated pulses of magnetic energy to stimulate or suppress brain activity.

5. **Psychosurgery** is a biomedical therapy that attempts to change behavior by removing or destroying brain tissue. Since drug therapy became widely available in the 1950s, psychosurgery has been infrequently used.

6. Once used to control violent patients, the **lobotomy** is a form of psychosurgery in which the nerves linking the emotion centers of the brain to the frontal lobes are severed.

FOCUS ON VOCABULARY AND LANGUAGE

Drug Therapies

Antipsychotics are powerful drugs. Some can produce *sluggishness, tremors, and twitches* similar to those of Parkinson's disease, which is marked by too little dopamine (Kaplan & Saddock, 1989). Because of the serious side effects of some antipsychotic drugs—tiredness and apathy (*sluggishness*), shaking limbs (*tremors*), and sudden involuntary spasms (*twitches*)—therapists have to be very careful (*they have to tread a fine line*) in selecting the dose of both first- and new-generation drugs that will relieve the symptoms but will not produce the side effects.

"Popping a Xanax" at the first sign of tension can produce psychological dependence; . . . The most popular antianxiety drugs (Xanax and Valium) are central nervous system depressants, and they reduce tension without causing too much drowsiness. As a consequence, they are prescribed for a variety of problems, including minor emotional stresses. If a person regularly takes an antianxiety drug (*routinely "pops a Xanax"*) whenever there is the slightest feeling of anxiety, the result can be psychological dependence on the drug. Withdrawal symptoms for heavy users include increased anxiety and an inability to sleep (insomnia).

The antidepressants derive their name from their ability to *lift people up from* a state of depression, . . . Antidepressants work by either increasing the availability of the neurotransmitters norepinephrine or serotonin, blocking their reabsorption, or by inhibit-ing an enzyme that breaks them down. Thus, they tend to make depressed people feel more alive and aroused (*they lift them up*). As Myers notes, these drugs are also used to treat anxiety disorders such as obsessive-compulsive disorder.

Brain Stimulation

ECT therefore gained a *barbaric* image, one that lingers still. **Electroconvulsive therapy (ECT)** has proven quite effective and is used mainly for chronically depressed people who have not responded to drug therapy. In 1938, when ECT was first introduced, wide-awake patients were strapped to a table to prevent them from hurting themselves during the convulsions and were shocked (*jolted*) with 100 volts of electricity to the brain. Although the procedure is different today, these inhumane (*barbaric*) images tend to remain in people's minds. As Myers points out, ECT is credited with saving many from suicide, but its Frankensteinlike image lingers on. (Note: Dr. Frankenstein is a fictional character who created a living monster from the body parts of dead people.)

Hopes are now rising for gentler alternative for *jump-starting* the depressed brain. (Using power from another car's battery to start a car with a flat or dead battery is called *jump-starting*.) Depressed moods appear to improve when a painless procedure called repetitive transcranial magnetic stimulation (rTMS) is used on wide-awake patients. Thus, optimism is increasing (*hopes are rising*) for a better way to activate (*jump-start*) the depressed brain.

Social Psychology

Social Thinking

MODULE OVERVIEW

Module 43 examines the process by which we decide whether to attribute behavior to the person or the situation. It focuses on the fundamental attribution error, which is our tendency to attribute other people's behavior to their personalities while attributing our own behavior to the situation. The module concludes with a discussion of the reciprocal relationship between attitudes and actions.

NOTE: Answer guidelines for all Module 43 questions begin on page 461.

MODULE REVIEW

First, skim each section, noting headings and boldface items. After you have read the section, review each objective by answering the fill-in and essay-type questions that follow it. As you proceed, evaluate your performance by consulting the answers beginning on page 461. Do not continue with the next section until you understand each answer. If you need to, review or reread the section in the textbook before continuing.

> David Myers at times uses idioms that are unfamiliar to some readers. If you do not know the meaning of any of the following words, phrases, or expressions in the context in which they appear in the text, refer to page 463 for an explanation: *tart-tongued remark; freeloaders; stand up for; "brainwashed"; chicken-and-egg spiral; heartening implication.*

Introduction and Attributing Behavior to Persons or to Situations (pp. 575–577)

Objective 1: Describe the three main focuses of social psychology.

1. Psychologists who study how we think about, influence, and relate to one another are called

   _____ _____ .

Objective 2: Contrast dispositional and situational attributions, and explain how the fundamental attribution error can affect our analyses of behavior.

2. Heider's theory of how we explain others' behavior is the _____ theory. According to this theory, we attribute behavior either to an internal cause, which is called a

   _____ _____ ,

   or to an external cause, which is called a

   _____ _____ .

3. Most people tend to_____ (overestimate/underestimate) the extent to which people's actions are influenced by social situations because their _____ is focused on the person. This tendency is called the

   _____
   _____ . When explaining our own behavior, or that of someone we know well, this tendency is _____ (stronger/weaker). When observers view the world from others' perspectives, attributions are _____ (the same/reversed).

Give an example of the practical consequences of attributions.

Attitudes and Actions (pp. 577–580)

Objective 3: Define *attitude*, and explain how attitudes and actions affect each other.

1. Feelings, often based on our beliefs, that predispose our responses are called

_____ .

List three conditions under which our attitudes do predict our actions. Give examples.

2. Many research studies demonstrate that our attitudes are strongly influenced by our
_____ . One example of this is the tendency for people who agree to a small request to comply later with a larger one. This is the _____-_____-
_____-_____
phenomenon.

3. When you follow the social prescriptions for how you should act as, say, a college student, you are adopting a _____ .

4. Taking on a set of behaviors, or acting in a certain way, generally _____
(changes/does not change) people's attitudes.

5. According to _____
_____ theory, thoughts and feelings change because people are motivated to justify actions that would otherwise seem hypocritical. This theory was proposed by

_____ .

6. Dissonance theory predicts that people induced (without coercion) to behave contrary to their true attitudes will be motivated to reduce the resulting _____ by changing their _____ .

PROGRESS TEST

Multiple-Choice Questions

Circle your answers to the following questions and check them with the answers on page 462. If your answer is incorrect, read the explanation for why it is incorrect and then consult the appropriate pages of the text.

1. According to cognitive dissonance theory, dissonance is most likely to occur when:
   a. a person's behavior is not based on strongly held attitudes.
   b. two people have conflicting attitudes and find themselves in disagreement.
   c. an individual does something that is personally disagreeable.
   d. an individual is coerced into doing something that he or she does not want to do.

2. Which of the following phenomena is best explained by cognitive dissonance theory?
   a. the fundamental attribution error
   b. the foot-in-the-door phenomenon
   c. dispositional attributions
   d. situational attributions

3. When male students in an experiment were told that a woman to whom they would be speaking had been instructed to act in a friendly or unfriendly way, most of them subsequently attributed her behavior to:
   a. the situation.
   b. the situation *and* her personal disposition.
   c. her personal disposition.
   d. their own skill or lack of skill in a social situation.

4. Which of the following is true?
   a. Attitudes and actions rarely correspond.
   b. Attitudes predict behavior about half the time.
   c. Attitudes are excellent predictors of behavior.
   d. Attitudes predict behavior under certain conditions.

5. Which theory describes how we explain others' behavior as being due to internal dispositions or external situations?
   a. cognitive dissonance theory
   b. reward theory
   c. two-factor theory
   d. attribution theory

6. Before she gave a class presentation favoring gun control legislation, Wanda opposed it. Her present attitude favoring such legislation can best be explained by:
   a. attribution theory.
   b. cognitive dissonance theory.
   c. reward theory.
   d. evolutionary psychology.

7. Which of the following situations should produce the *greatest* cognitive dissonance?
   a. A soldier is forced to carry out orders he finds disagreeable.
   b. A student who loves animals has to dissect a cat in order to pass biology.
   c. As part of an experiment, a subject is directed to deliver electric shocks to another person.
   d. A student volunteers to debate an issue, taking the side he personally disagrees with.

8. Professor Washington's students did very poorly on the last exam. The tendency to make the fundamental attribution error might lead her to conclude that the class did poorly because:
   a. the test was unfair.
   b. not enough time was given for students to complete the test.
   c. students were distracted by some social function on campus.
   d. students were unmotivated.

9. Which of the following is an example of the foot-in-the-door phenomenon?
   a. To persuade a customer to buy a product a store owner offers a small gift.
   b. After agreeing to wear a small "Enforce Recycling" lapel pin, a woman agrees to collect signatures on a petition to make recycling required by law.
   c. After offering to sell a car at a ridiculously low price, a car salesperson is forced to tell the customer the car will cost $1000 more.
   d. All of these are examples.

True–False Items

Indicate whether each statement is true or false by placing *T* or *F* in the blank next to the item.

_____ 1. When explaining another's behavior, we tend to underestimate situational influences.

_____ 2. When explaining our own behavior, we tend to underestimate situational influences.

_____ 3. Counterattitudinal behavior (acting contrary to our beliefs) often leads to attitude change.

KEY TERMS

Using your own words, on a separate piece of paper write a brief definition or explanation of each of the following terms.

1. social psychology
2. attribution theory
3. fundamental attribution error
4. attitudes
5. foot-in-the-door phenomenon
6. role
7. cognitive dissonance theory

ANSWERS

Module Review

Introduction and *Attributing Behavior to Persons or to Situations*

1. social psychologists
2. attribution; dispositional attribution; situational attribution
3. underestimate; attention; fundamental attribution error; weaker; reversed

Our attributions—to individuals' dispositions or to situations—have important practical consequences. A hurtful remark from an acquaintance, for example, is more likely to be forgiven if it is attributed to a temporary situation than to a mean disposition.

Attitudes and Actions

1. attitudes

Attitudes predict actions when other influences on the attitudes and actions are minimized, when the attitude is specifically relevant to the behavior, and when we are especially aware of our attitudes. Thus, our attitudes are more likely to predict behavior when we are not attempting to adjust our behavior to please others, when we are in familiar situations in which we don't have to stop and think about our attitudes, and when the attitude pertains to a specific behavior, such as purchasing a product or casting a vote.

2. actions or behavior; foot-in-the-door

3. role

4. changes

5. cognitive dissonance; Leon Festinger

6. dissonance; attitudes

Progress Test

Multiple-Choice Questions

1. c. is the answer. Cognitive dissonance is the tension we feel when we are aware of a discrepancy between our thoughts and actions, as would occur when we do something we find distasteful.
   a. Dissonance requires strongly held attitudes, which must be perceived as not fitting behavior.
   b. Dissonance is a personal cognitive process.
   d. In such a situation the person is less likely to experience dissonance, since the action can be attributed to "having no choice."

2. b. is the answer.
   a. The fundamental attribution error is the tendency to overestimate the impact of personal dispositions on behavior.
   c. & d. Situational and dispositional attributions have to do with how we interpret other people's behavior, not how our attitudes affect our actions, or vice versa.

3. c. is the answer. In this example of the fundamental attribution error, even when given the situational explanation for the woman's behavior, students ignored it and attributed her behavior to her personal disposition.

4. d. is the answer. Our attitudes are more likely to guide our actions when other influences are minimal, when there's a specific connection between the two, and when we're keenly aware of our beliefs. The presence of other people would more likely be an outside factor that would lessen the likelihood of actions being guided by attitude.

5. d. is the answer.

6. b. is the answer. Dissonance theory focuses on what happens when our actions contradict our attitudes.
   a. Attribution theory holds that we give causal explanations for others' behavior, often by crediting either the situation or people's dispositions.
   c. Reward theory maintains that we continue relationships that maximize benefits and minimize costs. This has nothing to do with relationships.
   d. This is not a theory of social psychology.

7. d. is the answer. In this situation, the counterattitudinal behavior is performed voluntarily and cannot be attributed to the demands of the situation.
   a., b., & c. In all of these situations, the counterattitudinal behaviors should not arouse much dissonance because they can be attributed to the demands of the situation.

8. d. is the answer. The fundamental attribution error refers to the tendency to underestimate situational influences in favor of this type of dispositional attribution when explaining the behavior of other people.

9. b. is the answer. In the foot-in-the-door phenomenon, compliance with a small initial request, such as wearing a lapel pin, later is followed by compliance with a much larger request, such as collecting petition signatures.

True–False Items

1. T   **3.** T
2. F

Key Terms

1. Social psychology is the scientific study of how we think about, influence, and relate to one another.

2. Attribution theory deals with our causal explanations of behavior. We attribute behavior to the individual's disposition or to the situation.

3. The **fundamental attribution error** is our tendency to underestimate the impact of situations and to overestimate the impact of personal dispositions upon the behavior of others.

4. Attitudes are feelings, often based on beliefs, that may predispose a person to respond in particular ways to objects, people, and events.

5. The **foot-in-the-door phenomenon** is the tendency for people who agree to a small request to comply later with a larger request.

6. A **role** is a set of explanations (norms) about how people in a specific social position ought to behave.

7. **Cognitive dissonance theory** refers to the theory that we act to reduce the psychological discomfort we experience when our behavior conflicts with what we think and feel, or more generally, when two of our thoughts are inconsistent. This is frequently accomplished by changing our attitude rather than our behavior.

Memory aid: *Dissonance* means "lack of harmony." **Cognitive dissonance** occurs when two thoughts, or cognitions, are at variance with one another.

FOCUS ON VOCABULARY AND LANGUAGE

Introduction and *Attributing Behavior to Persons or to Situations*

Happily married couples attribute *a spouse's tart-tongued remark* to a temporary situation ("She must have had a bad day at work"). How we make attributions can have serious consequences. Couples who think that their partner's sarcastic or unkind comment (*tart-tongued remark*) was due to a cruel personality (*mean disposition*) are more likely to be dissatisfied with their marriages than couples who believe that the same remark was simply a result of some situational influence, such as a stressful day at work.

. . . freeloaders. This refers to people who voluntarily live off other people. Those who believe that people are poor and/or unemployed because of personal dispositions tend to underestimate the influence of situational variables. Thus, they might call someone on welfare a *freeloader* rather than simply a victim of circumstances.

Attitudes and Actions

Not only will people sometimes *stand up for* what they believe, they will also come to believe in what *they have stood up for*. Not only do people support (*stand up for*) their strong convictions by taking appropriate action, but people will also develop convictions about things that they have taken action in support of (*that they have stood up for*). Many lines (*streams*) of evidence confirm the principle that beliefs can be changed to correspond with people's actions (*attitudes follow behavior*).

. . . "brainwashed" . . . This refers to a person's beliefs, values, and attitudes being changed by relentless indoctrination and mental torture. One component of this mind-changing process ("*thought-control*") involves use of the **foot-in-the-door phenomenon**, whereby a person is first coerced into agreeing to a small request, then to complying with much greater requests. Frequently, people will change their attitudes to be consistent with their new behavior.

This *chicken-and-egg spiral*, of actions-feeding-attitudes-feeding-actions, enables behavior to escalate. Whether used for good or for bad, the foot-in-the-door strategy involves starting with small requests, then slowly increasing the level of demand. The new behavior will be followed by a change in attitude which, in turn, will make the behavior more likely and that will then lead to more change in belief, etc. (*the chicken-and-egg spiral*).

The attitudes-follow-behavior principle has a *heartening implication*: When our attitudes and behaviors are inconsistent, we feel a certain amount of tension (**cognitive dissonance**), which makes us want to do something to reduce this uncomfortable state. Thus, if we are feeling depressed (*down in the dumps*) and we behave in a more outgoing manner, talk in a more positive way, and *act* as though we are happy, we may, in fact, start feeling much better. As Myers notes, the feelings-follow-actions notion has positive ramifications (*heartening implications*).

Social Influence

MODULE OVERVIEW

Module 44 demonstrates the powerful influences of social situations on the behavior of individuals. Central to this topic are research studies on conformity, compliance, and group and cultural influences. The social principles that emerge help us to understand how individuals are influenced by advertising, political candidates, and the various groups to which they belong. Although social influences are powerful, it is important to remember the significant role of individuals in choosing and creating the social situations that influence them.

Although there is some terminology for you to learn in this module, your primary task is to absorb the findings of the many research studies discussed. The module headings, which organize the findings, should prove especially useful to you here. In addition, you might, for each main topic (conformity, group influence, etc.), ask yourself the question, "What situational factors promote this phenomenon?" The research findings can then form the basis for your answers.

NOTE: Answer guidelines for all Module 44 questions begin on page 469.

MODULE REVIEW

First, skim each section, noting headings and boldface items. After you have read the section, review each objective by answering the fill-in and essay-type questions that follow it. As you proceed, evaluate your performance by consulting the answers beginning on page 469. Do not continue with the next section until you understand each answer. If you need to, review or reread the section in the textbook before continuing.

David Myers at times uses idioms that are unfamiliar to some readers. If you do not know the meaning of any of the following words, phrases, or expressions in the context in which they appear in the text, refer to pages 472–473 for an explanation: *"open-minded"; draw slips from a hat; draw back; kindness and obedience on a collision course; zap; devilish villains; tug-of-war; waffles.*

Conformity and Obedience (pp. 582–587)

Objective 1: Describe the chameleon effect, and discuss Asch's experiments on conformity.

1. The *chameleon effect* refers to our natural tendency to unconsciously _____ others' expressions, postures, and voice tones. This helps us to feel what they are feeling, referred to as _____ _____ .

2. Copycat violence is a serious example of the effects of _____ on behavior.

3. Sociologists have found that suicides sometimes increase following a _____ _____ suicide.

4. The term that refers to the tendency to adjust one's behavior to coincide with an assumed group standard is _____ .

5. The psychologist who first studied the effects of group pressure on conformity is _____ .

6. In this study, when the opinion of other group members was contradicted by objective evidence, research participants _____ (were/were not) willing to conform to the group opinion.

7. One reason that people comply with social pressure is to gain approval or avoid rejection; this is called _____

   _____ _____ .

   Understood rules for accepted and expected behavior are called social _____ .

8. Another reason people comply is that they have genuinely been influenced by what they have learned from others; this type of influence is called _____

   _____ _____ .

Objective 2: Describe Milgram's experiments on obedience, and explain how the conformity and obedience studies can help us understand our susceptibility to social influence.

9. The classic social psychology studies of obedience were conducted by _____ . When ordered by the experimenter to electrically shock the "learner," the majority of participants (the "teachers") in these studies _____ (complied/refused). More recent studies have found that women's compliance rates in similar situations were _____ (higher than/lower than/similar to) men's.

List the conditions under which obedience was highest in Milgram's studies.

10. In getting people to administer increasingly larger shocks, Milgram was in effect applying the

    _____-_____-

    _____-_____

    technique.

11. The Asch and Milgram studies demonstrate that strong _____ influences can make _____ people _____ to falsehoods and _____ orders to commit cruel acts.

Group Influence (pp. 588–592)

Objective 3: Describe conditions in which the presence of others is likely to result in social facilitation, social loafing, or deindividuation.

1. The tendency to perform a task better when other people are present is called _____

   _____ . In general, people become aroused in the presence of others, and arousal enhances the correct response on a(n) _____ (easy/difficult) task. Later research revealed that arousal strengthens the response that is most _____ in a given situation.

2. Researchers have found that the reactions of people in crowded situations are often _____ (lessened/amplified).

3. Ingham found that people worked _____ (harder/less hard) in a team tug-of-war than they had in an individual contest. This phenomenon has been called

   _____ _____ .

4. The feeling of anonymity and loss of self-restraint that an individual may develop when in a group is called _____ .

Objective 4: Discuss how group interaction can facilitate group polarization and groupthink, and identify the characteristic common to minority positions that successfully sway majorities.

5. Over time, the initial differences between groups usually _____ (increase/decrease).

6. The enhancement of each group's prevailing tendency over time is called _____

   _____ . Future research studies will reveal whether electronic discussions on the _____ also demonstrate this tendency.

7. When the desire for group harmony overrides realistic thinking in individuals, the phenomenon known as _____ has occurred.

8. In considering the power of social influence, we cannot overlook the interaction of

_____ _____

(the power of the situation) and

_____ _____

(the power of the individual).

9. The power of one or two individuals to sway the opinion of the majority is called

_____ _____ .

10. A minority opinion will have the most success in swaying the majority if it takes a stance that is _____ (unswerving/flexible).

PROGRESS TEST

Multiple-Choice Questions

Circle your answers to the following questions and check them with the answers beginning on page 470. If your answer is incorrect, read the explanation for why it is incorrect and then consult the appropriate pages of the text.

1. In his study of obedience, Stanley Milgram found that the majority of subjects:
   a. refused to shock the learner even once.
   b. complied with the experiment until the "learner" first indicated pain.
   c. complied with the experiment until the "learner" began screaming in agony.
   d. complied with all the demands of the experiment.

2. Which of the following statements is true?
   a. Groups are almost never swayed by minority opinions.
   b. Group polarization is most likely to occur when group members frequently disagree with one another.
   c. Groupthink provides the consensus needed for effective decision making.
   d. A group that is like-minded will probably not change its opinions through discussion.

3. Conformity increased under which of the following conditions in Asch's studies of conformity?
   a. The group had three or more people.
   b. The group had high status.
   c. Individuals were made to feel insecure.
   d. All of these situations increased conformity.

4. The phenomenon in which individuals lose their identity and relinquish normal restraints when they are part of a group is called:
   a. groupthink.   c. empathy.
   b. social facilitation. d. deindividuation.

5. Subjects in Asch's line-judgment experiment conformed to the group standard when their judgments were observed by others but not when they were made in private. This tendency to conform in public demonstrates:
   a. social facilitation.
   b. overjustification.
   c. informational social influence.
   d. normative social influence.

6. Based on findings from Milgram's obedience studies, participants would be *less* likely to follow the experimenter's orders when:
   a. they hear the "learner" cry out in pain.
   b. they merely administer the test while someone else delivers the shocks.
   c. the "learner" is an older person or mentions having some physical problem.
   d. they see another subject disobey instructions.

7. Which of the following most accurately states the effects of crowding on behavior?
   a. Crowding makes people irritable.
   b. Crowding sometimes intensifies people's reactions.
   c. Crowding promotes altruistic behavior.
   d. Crowding usually weakens the intensity of people's reactions.

8. Research has found that for a minority to succeed in swaying a majority, the minority must:
   a. make up a sizable portion of the group.
   b. express its position as consistently as possible.
   c. express its position in the most extreme terms possible.
   d. be able to convince a key majority leader.

9. Which of the following conclusions did Milgram derive from his studies of obedience?

   a. Even ordinary people, without any particular hostility, can become agents in a destructive process.

   b. Most people are able, under the proper circumstances, to suppress their natural aggressiveness.

   c. The need to be accepted by others is a powerful motivating force.

   d. All of these conclusions were reached.

10. Which of the following best summarizes the relative importance of personal control and social control of our behavior?

    a. Situational influences on behavior generally are much greater than personal influences.

    b. Situational influences on behavior generally are slightly greater than personal influences.

    c. Personal influences on behavior generally are much greater than situational influences.

    d. Situational and personal influences interact in determining our behavior.

11. Which of the following is important in promoting conformity in individuals?

    a. whether an individual's behavior will be observed by others in the group

    b. whether the individual is male or female

    c. the size of the room in which a group is meeting

    d. whether the individual is of a higher status than other group members

12. Which of the following is most likely to promote groupthink?

    a. The group's leader fails to take a firm stance on an issue.

    b. A minority faction holds to its position.

    c. The group consults with various experts.

    d. Group polarization is evident.

13. Which of the following would most likely be subject to social facilitation?

    a. proofreading a page for spelling errors

    b. typing a letter with accuracy

    c. playing a difficult piece on a musical instrument

    d. running quickly around a track

14. Jane and Sandy were best friends as freshmen. Jane joined a sorority; Sandy didn't. By the end of their senior year, they found that they had less in common with each other than with the other members of their respective circles of friends. Which of the following phenomena most likely explains their feelings?

    a. group polarization   c. deindividuation

    b. groupthink   d. social facilitation

15. José is the one student member on the college board of trustees. At the board's first meeting, José wants to disagree with the others on several issues but in each case decides to say nothing. Studies on conformity suggest all except one of the following are factors in José's not speaking up. Which one is *not* a factor?

    a. The board is a large group.

    b. The board is prestigious and most of its members are well known.

    c. The board members are already aware that José and the student body disagree with them on these issues.

    d. Because this is the first meeting José has attended, he feels insecure and not fully competent.

16. Maria recently heard a speech calling for a ban on aerosol sprays that endanger the earth's ozone layer. Maria's subsequent decision to stop using aerosol sprays is an example of:

    a. informational social influence.

    b. normative social influence.

    c. deindividuation.

    d. social facilitation.

17. Concluding her presentation on deindividuation, Renée notes that deindividuation is less likely in situations that promote:

    a. anonymity.

    b. decreased self-awareness.

    c. increased self-awareness.

    d. arousal.

Matching Items

Match each term with the appropriate definition or description.

Terms

_____ 1. social facilitation
_____ 2. social loafing
_____ 3. conformity
_____ 4. normative social influence
_____ 5. informational social influence
_____ 6. group polarization

True–False Items

Indicate whether each statement is true or false by placing *T* or *F* in the blank next to the item.

_____ 1. An individual is more likely to conform when the rest of the group is unanimous.

_____ 2. The tendency of people to conform is influenced by the culture in which they were socialized.

_____ 3. Group polarization tends to prevent groupthink from occurring.

_____ 4. Crowded conditions usually subdue people's reactions.

_____ 5. When individuals lose their sense of identity in a group, they often become more uninhibited.

Essay Question

The Panhellenic Council on your campus has asked you to make a presentation on the topic "Social Psychology" to all freshmen who have signed up to "rush" a fraternity or sorority. In a fit of cynicism following your rejection last year by a prestigious fraternity or sorority, you decide to speak on the negative influences of groups on the behavior of individuals. What will you discuss? (Use the space below to list the points you want to make, and organize them. Then write the essay on a separate sheet of paper.)

Definitions or Descriptions

a. people work less hard in a group
b. performance is improved by an audience
c. the effect of social approval or disapproval
d. adjusting one's behavior to coincide with a group standard
e. group discussion enhances prevailing tendencies
f. the effect of accepting others' opinions about something

KEY TERMS

Using your own words, on a separate piece of paper write a brief definition or explanation of each of the following terms.

1. social psychology
2. conformity
3. normative social influence
4. informational social influence
5. social facilitation
6. social loafing
7. deindividuation
8. group polarization
9. groupthink

ANSWERS

Module Review

Conformity and Obedience

1. mimic; mood linkage
2. suggestibility
3. highly publicized
4. conformity
5. Solomon Asch
6. were
7. normative social influence; norms
8. informational social influence
9. Stanley Milgram; complied; similar to

Obedience was highest when the person giving the orders was close at hand and perceived to be a legitimate authority figure, the authority figure was supported by a prestigious institution, the victim was depersonalized, and when there were no role models for defiance.

10. foot-in-the-door

11. social; ordinary; conform; obey

Group Influence

1. social facilitation; easy; likely
2. amplified
3. less hard; social loafing
4. deindividuation
5. increase
6. group polarization; Internet
7. groupthink
8. social control; personal control
9. minority influence
10. unswerving

Progress Test

Multiple-Choice Questions

1. **d.** is the answer. In Milgram's initial experiments, 63 percent of the subjects fully complied with the experiment.

2. **d.** is the answer. In such groups, discussion usually strengthens prevailing opinion; this phenomenon is known as group polarization.
   a. Minority opinions, especially if consistently and firmly stated, can sway the majority in a group.
   b. Group polarization, or the strengthening of a group's prevailing tendencies, is most likely in groups where members agree.
   c. When groupthink occurs, there is so much consensus that decision making becomes less effective.

3. **d.** is the answer.

4. **d.** is the answer.
   a. Groupthink refers to the mode of thinking that occurs when the desire for group harmony overrides realistic and critical thinking.
   b. Social facilitation is the improved performance before a group that occurs with well-learned tasks.
   c. Empathy is feeling what another person feels.

5. **d.** is the answer. Normative social influence refers to influence on behavior that comes from a desire to look good to others. Subjects who were observed conformed because they didn't want to look like oddballs.

a. Social facilitation involves performing tasks better or faster in the presence of others.
b. Overjustification occurs when a person is rewarded for doing something that is already enjoyable.
c. Informational social influence is the tendency of individuals to accept the opinions of others, especially in situations where they themselves are unsure.

6. **d.** is the answer. Role models for defiance reduce levels of obedience.
   a. & c. These did not result in diminished obedience.
   b. This "depersonalization" of the victim resulted in increased obedience.

7. **b.** is the answer.
   a. & c. Crowding may amplify irritability or altruistic tendencies that are already present. Crowding does not, however, produce these reactions as a general effect.
   d. In fact, just the opposite is true. Crowding often intensifies people's reactions.

8. **b.** is the answer.
   a. Even if they made up a sizable portion of the group, although still a minority, their numbers would not be as important as their consistency.
   c. & d. These aspects of minority influence were not discussed in the text; however, they are not likely to help a minority sway a majority.

9. **a.** is the answer.

10. **d.** is the answer. The text emphasizes the ways in which personal and social controls interact in influencing behavior. It does not suggest that one factor is more influential than the other.

11. **a.** is the answer. As Solomon Asch's experiments demonstrated, individuals are more likely to conform when they are being observed by others in the group. The other factors were not discussed in the text and probably would not promote conformity.

12. **d.** is the answer. Group polarization, or the enhancement of a group's prevailing attitudes, promotes groupthink, which leads to the disintegration of critical thinking.
   a. Groupthink is more likely when a leader highly favors an idea, which may make members reluctant to disagree.
   b. A strong minority faction would probably have the opposite effect: It would diminish group harmony while promoting critical thinking.
   c. Consulting experts would discourage groupthink by exposing the group to other opinions.

13. **d.** is the answer. Social facilitation, or better performance in the presence of others, occurs for easy tasks but not for more difficult ones. For tasks such as proofreading, typing, playing an instrument, or giving a speech, the arousal resulting from the presence of others can lead to mistakes.

14. **a.** is the answer. Group polarization means that the tendencies within a group—and therefore the differences among groups—grow stronger over time. Thus, because the differences between the sorority and nonsorority students have increased, Jane and Sandy are likely to have little in common.

   b. Groupthink is the tendency for realistic decision making to disintegrate when the desire for group harmony is strong.

   c. Deindividuation is the loss of self-restraint and self-awareness that sometimes occurs when one is part of a group.

   d. Social facilitation refers to improved performance of a task in the presence of others.

15. **c.** is the answer. Prior commitment to an opposing view generally tends to work against conformity. In contrast, large group size, prestigiousness of a group, and an individual's feelings of incompetence and insecurity all strengthen the tendency to conform.

16. **a.** is the answer. As illustrated by Maria's decision to stop buying aerosol products, informational social influence occurs when people have genuinely been influenced by what they have learned from others.

   b. Had Maria's behavior been motivated by the desire to avoid rejection or to gain social approval (which we have no reason to suspect is the case), it would have been an example of normative social influence.

   c. Deindividuation refers to the sense of anonymity a person may feel as part of a group.

   d. Social facilitation is the improvement in performance of well-learned tasks that may result when one is observed by others.

17. **c.** is the answer. Deindividuation involves the loss of self-awareness and self-restraint in group situations that involve arousal and anonymity, so a., b., and d. cannot be right.

Matching Items

1. b
2. a
3. d
4. c
5. f
6. e

True–False Items

1. T
2. T
3. F
4. F
5. T

Essay Question

Your discussion might focus on some of the following topics: normative social influence; conformity, which includes suggestibility; obedience; group polarization; and groupthink.

   As a member of any group with established social norms, individuals will often act in ways that enable them to avoid rejection or gain social approval. Thus, a fraternity or sorority pledge would probably be very suggestible and likely to eventually conform to the attitudes and norms projected by the group—or be rejected socially. In extreme cases of pledge hazing, acute social pressures may lead to atypical and antisocial individual behaviors—for example, on the part of pledges complying with the demands of senior members of the fraternity or sorority. Over time, meetings and discussions will probably enhance the group's prevailing attitudes (group polarization). This may lead to the unrealistic and irrational decision making that is groupthink. The potentially negative consequences of groupthink depend on the issues being discussed, but may include a variety of socially destructive behaviors.

Key Terms

1. **Social psychology** is the scientific study of how we think about, influence, and relate to one another.

2. **Conformity** is the tendency to change one's thinking or behavior to coincide with a group standard.

3. **Normative social influence** refers to the pressure on individuals to conform in order to avoid rejection or gain social approval.

   Memory aid: *Normative* means "based on a norm, or pattern, regarded as typical for a specific group." **Normative social influence** is the pressure groups exert on the individual to behave in ways acceptable to the group standard.

4. **Informational social influence** results when one goes along with a group when one is willing to accept others' opinions about reality.

5. **Social facilitation** is stronger performance of simple or well-learned tasks that occurs when other people are present.

6. **Social loafing** is the tendency for individual effort to be diminished when one is part of a group working toward a common goal.

7. **Deindividuation** refers to the loss of self-restraint and self-awareness that sometimes occurs in group situations that foster arousal and anonymity.

   Memory aid: As a prefix, *de-* indicates reversal or undoing. To **de**individuate is to undo one's individuality.

8. **Group polarization** refers to the enhancement of a group's prevailing tendencies through discussion, which often has the effect of accentuating the group's differences from other groups.

Memory aid: To *polarize* is to "cause thinking to concentrate about two poles, or contrasting positions."

9. **Groupthink** refers to the unrealistic thought processes and decision making that occur within groups when the desire for group harmony overrides a realistic appraisal of alternatives.

   Example: The psychological tendencies of self-justification, conformity, and group polarization foster the development of the "team spirit" mentality known as **groupthink**.

FOCUS ON VOCABULARY AND LANGUAGE

Conformity and Obedience

When influence supports what we approve, we applaud those who are *"open-minded"* and *"sensitive"* enough to be *"responsive."* We can be influenced by others because they provide useful knowledge (**informational influence**) or because we want them to view us favorably and not ignore us (**normative influence**). Conformity that is consistent with what we believe is true will be seen in a positive light (the conformists are *"open-minded,"* etc.), and conformity that is not will be viewed negatively (*"submissive conformity"*).

You and another person *draw slips from a hat* to see who will be the "teacher" (which your slip says) and who will be the "learner." In Milgram's famous obedience experiments participants were deceived into believing they were randomly assigned to one of two conditions ("teacher" or "learner") by picking a piece of paper out of a container (*drawing slips from a hat*). All the subjects were actually "teachers" and were asked to "shock" the "learners" whenever they made mistakes on a memory task. A majority of the participants complied with the experimenter's request.

When you hear these pleas, you *draw back*. But the experimenter *prods* you: "Please continue—the experiment requires that you continue." If you were a participant ("teacher") in Milgram's experiment, you would be pressured (*prodded*) by the research assistant to carry on with the experiment even though you may show great reluctance (*you draw back*) after hearing the "learner's" cries of distress at being "shocked."

With *kindness and obedience on a collision course*, obedience usually won. Milgram's research on obedience showed that social factors that foster conformity are powerful enough to make almost any one of us behave in ways inconsistent with our beliefs. When subjects were in a conflict over (*torn between*) whether to refuse to harm an individual or to follow orders (*kindness and obedience were on a collision course*), they usually did what they were asked to do.

Milgram did not entrap his "teachers" by asking them first to *zap* "learners" with enough electricity to make their hair stand on end. Milgram used the foot-in-the-door tactic to get his subjects to comply with his requests to shock (*zap*) the "learners" with larger and larger voltages of electricity (*enough to make their hair stand on end*). He started with a small amount (*a little tickle*) of electricity; after obtaining compliance (*obedience*), he asked them to increase the level, and so on. Subjects tended to rationalize their behavior; for some, their attitudes became consistent with their behavior over the course of the experiment.

Contrary to images of *devilish villains*, cruelty does not require *monstrous characters*; all it takes is ordinary people corrupted by an evil situation. . . . We tend to think that pain and suffering (*cruelty*) are always caused by inhumane and cruel people (*devilish villains* or *monstrous characters*), but the research in social psychology shows that almost anyone can be led to behave badly given the right (or wrong) circumstances.

Group Influence

In a team *tug-of-war*, for example, do you suppose the effort that a person puts forth would be more than, less than, or the same as the effort he or she would exert in a *one-on-one tug-of-war*? In a game in which opponents pull on each end of a rope (*tug-of-war*), when two individuals compete (*one-on-one*), they work much harder (*exert more effort*) than if they were members of a group competing on the same task. This lowering of individual effort when part of a team is called **social loafing**. (Note: The term *to loaf* means *to work less hard, to slack off, to take it easy,* or *to free ride*.)

They repeatedly found that a minority that unswervingly holds to its position is far more successful in swaying the majority than is a minority that *waffles*. Committed individuals and small groups of individuals can convince (*sway*) the majority to their point of view if they adhere strictly to their agenda and do not appear to be uncertain or unsure (*to waffle*).

Social Relations

45 M O D U L E

MODULE OVERVIEW

Module 45 discusses how people relate to one another in a negative fashion—developing prejudice, behaving aggressively, and provoking conflict—and in a positive fashion—being attracted to people who are nearby and/or similar and behaving altruistically. The module concludes with a discussion of techniques that have been shown to promote conflict resolution.

Although there is some terminology for you to learn in this module, your primary task is to absorb the findings of the many research studies discussed. The module headings, which organize the findings, should prove especially useful to you here. In addition, you might, for each main topic (prejudice, aggression, attraction, altruism, and conflict and peacemaking), ask yourself the question, "What situational factors promote this phenomenon?" The research findings can then form the basis for your answers.

NOTE: Answer guidelines for all Module 45 questions begin on page 483.

MODULE REVIEW

First, skim each section, noting headings and boldface items. After you have read the section, review each objective by answering the fill-in and essay-type questions that follow it. As you proceed, evaluate your performance by consulting the answers beginning on page 483. Do not continue with the next section until you understand each answer. If you need to, review or reread the section in the textbook before continuing.

David Myers at times uses idioms that are unfamiliar to some readers. If you do not know the meaning of any of the following words, phrases, or expressions in the context in which they appear in the text, refer to pages 487–488 for an explanation: *"horsing around"; with the toss of a coin; Ferdinand; she melts; an outlet for bottled-up impulses; familiarity breeds fondness; "beauty is only skin deep"; opposites retract; revved up; bystanders turns people away from the path that leads to helping; blasé; diabolical images; "sneaky," "smart-alecky stinkers"; down the tension ladder to a safer rung.*

Prejudice (pp. 594–599)

Objective 1: Identify the three components and various forms of prejudice.

1. Prejudice is an _____ (and usually _____) attitude toward a group that involves overgeneralized beliefs known as _____ .

2. Like all attitudes, prejudice is a mixture of

   _____ , _____ , and predispositions to _____ .

3. Prejudice is a negative _____ , and _____ is a negative

   _____ .

4. Americans today express _____ (less/the same/more) racial and gender prejudice than they did 50 years ago.

5. (text and Close-Up) Blatant forms of prejudice _____ (have/have not) diminished. However, even people who deny holding prejudiced attitudes may carry negative _____ about race or gender.

6. (Close-Up) Studies of prejudice indicate that it is often an unconscious, or _____, action. In one study, people who displayed the most _____ _____ were the quickest to perceive apparent threat in black faces.

7. (Close-Up) Today's biopsychosocial approach has stimulated neuroscience studies that have detected implicit prejudice in people's _____-muscle responses and in the activation of their brain's _____ .

8. Worldwide, _____ (women/men) are more likely to live in poverty. People tend to perceive women as being more _____ and _____ and less _____ than men.

Objective 2: Discuss the social factors that contribute to prejudice, and explain how scapegoating illustrates the emotional component of prejudice.

9. For those with money, power, and prestige, prejudice often serves as a means of _____ social inequalities.

10. Discrimination increases prejudice through the tendency of people to _____ victims for their plight.

11. Through our _____ _____ , we associate ourselves with certain groups.

12. Prejudice is also fostered by the _____ _____ , a tendency to favor groups to which one belongs— called the _____—while excluding others, or the _____ .

13. Research studies also reveal that the terror of facing _____ tends to heighten aggression toward people who threaten one's _____ .

14. That prejudice derives from attempts to blame others for one's frustration is proposed by the _____ theory.

15. People who feel loved and supported become more _____ to and _____ of those who differ from them.

Objective 3: Cite four ways that cognitive processes help create and maintain prejudice.

16. Research suggests that prejudice may also derive from _____ , the process by which we attempt to simplify our world by classifying people into groups. One by-product of this process is that people tend to _____ the similarity of those within a group.

17. Another factor that fosters the formation of group stereotypes and prejudice is the tendency to _____ from vivid or memorable cases.

18. The belief that people get what they deserve— that the good are rewarded and the bad punished—is expressed in the _____-_____ phenomenon. This phenomenon is based in part on _____ _____ , the tendency to believe that one would have foreseen how something turned out.

Aggression (pp. 599–606)

Objective 4: Explain how psychology's definition of *aggression* differs from everyday usage, and describe various biological influences on aggression.

1. Aggressive behavior is defined by psychologists as _____ _____ . Thus, psychologists _____ (do/ do not) consider assertive salespeople to be aggressive.

2. Like other behaviors, aggression emerges from the interaction of _____ and _____ .

3. Today, most psychologists _____ (do/do not) consider human aggression to be instinctive.

4. In humans, aggressiveness _____ (varies/does not vary) greatly from culture to culture, era to era, and person to person.

5. That there are genetic influences on aggression can be shown by the fact that many species of animals have been _____ for aggressiveness.

6. Twin studies suggest that genes _____ (do/do not) influence human aggression. One genetic marker of those who commit the most violence is the _____ chromosome. Studies of violent criminals reveal diminished activity in the brain's _____ _____ , which play an important role in controlling _____ .

7. In humans and animals, aggression is facilitated by _____ systems, which are in turn influenced by _____ and other substances in the blood.

8. The aggressive behavior of animals can be manipulated by altering the levels of the hormone _____ . When this level is _____ (increased/decreased), aggressive tendencies are reduced.

9. High levels of testosterone correlate with _____ , low tolerance for _____ , _____ , and _____ . Among teenage boys and adult men, high testosterone also correlates with _____ , hard _____ _____ , and aggressive responses to _____ . With age, testosterone levels—and aggressiveness— _____ (increase/decrease). Although testosterone heightens aggressiveness, aggression _____ (increases/ decreases) testosterone level.

10. One drug that unleashes aggressive responses to provocation is _____ .

Objective 5: Outline psychological triggers of aggression, noting the relationship between violent video games and aggressive behavior.

11. According to the _____- _____ principle, inability to achieve a goal leads to anger, which may generate aggression.

12. Other aversive stimuli can provoke hostility, including _____ .

13. Aggressive behavior can be learned through _____ , as shown by the fact that people use aggression where they've found it pays, and through _____ of others.

14. Crime rates are higher in countries in which there is a large disparity between those who are _____ and those who are _____ . High violence rates also are typical of cultures and families in which there is minimal _____ _____ .

15. Once established, aggressive behavior patterns are _____ (difficult/not difficult) to change. However, _____- _____ programs have been successful in bringing down re-arrest rates of juvenile offenders.

16. Violence on television tends to _____ people to cruelty and _____ them to respond aggressively when they are provoked.

17. The "rape myth" is the mistaken idea that _____ . Most rapists _____ (accept/do not accept) this myth.

Comment on the impression of women that pornography frequently conveys and the effects this impression has on attitudes and behavior.

Summarize the findings of the Zillmann and Bryant study on the effects of pornography on attitudes toward rape.

18. Experiments have shown that it is not eroticism but depictions by the media of _____ _____ that most directly affect men's acceptance and performance of aggression against women. Such depictions may create

_____ _____

to which people respond when they are in new situations or are uncertain how to act.

19. (Thinking Critically) Kids who play a lot of violent video games see the world as more _____ , get into more _____ and _____ , and get worse _____ .

20. (Thinking Critically) Research studies of the impact of violent video games _____ (confirm/disconfirm) the idea that we feel better if we "blow off steam" by venting our emotions. This idea is the _____ _____ . Expressing anger breeds _____ _____ .

21. Many factors contribute to aggression, including _____ factors, such as an increase in testosterone; _____ factors, such as frustration; and _____-_____ factors, such as deindividuation.

Attraction (pp. 607–612)

Objective 6: Describe the influence of proximity, physical attractiveness, and similarity on interpersonal attraction.

1. A prerequisite for, and perhaps the most powerful predictor of, attraction is _____ .

2. When people are repeatedly exposed to unfamiliar stimuli, their liking of the stimuli

_____ (increases/decreases). This phenomenon is the _____ _____ effect. Robert Zajonc contends that this phenomenon was _____ for our ancestors, for whom the unfamiliar was often dangerous. One implication of this is that _____ against those who are culturally different may be a primitive, _____ , emotional response.

3. Our first impression of another person is most influenced by the person's _____ .

4. In a sentence, list several of the characteristics that physically attractive people are judged to possess: _____ _____ .

5. A person's attractiveness _____ (is/is not) strongly related to his or her self-esteem or happiness.

6. Cross-cultural research reveals that men judge women as more attractive if they have a _____ appearance, whereas women judge men who appear _____ , _____ , and _____ as more attractive.

7. Compared with strangers, friends and couples are more likely to be similar in terms of _____ _____ .

Explain what a reward theory of attraction is and how it can account for the three predictors of liking—proximity, attractiveness, and similarity.

Objective 7: Describe the effect of physical arousal on passionate love, and identify two predictors of enduring companionate love.

8. Hatfield has distinguished two types of love: _____ love and _____ love.

9. According to the two-factor theory, emotions have two components: physical _____ and a _____ label.

10. When college men were placed in an aroused state, their feelings toward an attractive woman _____ (were/were not) more positive than those of men who had not been aroused.

11. Companionate love is promoted by _____—mutual sharing and giving by both partners. Another key ingredient of loving relationships is the revealing of intimate aspects of ourselves through _____ .

Altruism (pp. 613–615)

Objective 8: Define *altruism,* and describe the steps in the decision-making process involved in bystander intervention.

1. An unselfish regard for the welfare of others is called _____ .

Give an example of altruism.

2. According to Darley and Latané, people will help only if a three-stage decision-making process is completed: Bystanders must first _____ the incident, then _____ it as an emergency, and finally _____ _____ for helping.

3. When people who overheard a seizure victim calling for help thought others were hearing the same plea, they were _____ (more/less) likely to go to his aid than when they thought no one else was aware of the emergency.

4. In a series of staged accidents, Latané and Darley found that a bystander was _____ (more/less) likely to help if other bystanders were present. This phenomenon has been called the _____ _____ .

Identify the circumstances in which a person is most likely to offer help during an emergency.

Conflict and Peacemaking (pp. 615–618))

Objective 9: Discuss effective ways of encouraging peaceful cooperation and reducing social conflict.

1. A perceived incompatibility of actions, goals, or ideas is called _____ . This perception can take place between individuals, _____ , or _____ .

2. The distorted images people in conflict form of each other are called _____ - _____ perceptions.

3. In most situations, establishing contact between two conflicting groups _____ (is/is not) sufficient to resolve conflict.

4. In Sherif's study, two conflicting groups of campers were able to resolve their conflicts by working together on projects in which they shared _____ goals. Shared _____ breed solidarity, as demonstrated by a surge in use of the word _____ in the weeks after 9/11.

5. When conflicts arise, a third-party _____ may facilitate communication and promote understanding.

6. Osgood has advanced a strategy of conciliation called GRIT, which stands for

_____ and _____

_____ in _____ -

_____ . The key to this method is each side's offering of a small

_____ gesture in order to increase mutual trust and cooperation.

PROGRESS TEST

Multiple-Choice Questions

Circle your answers to the following questions and check them with the answers beginning on page 484. If your answer is incorrect, read the explanation for why it is incorrect and then consult the appropriate pages of the text.

1. Violent criminals often have diminished activity in the _____ of the brain, which play(s) an important role in _____ .
   a. occipital lobes; aggression
   b. hypothalamus; hostility
   c. frontal lobes; controlling impulses
   d. temporal lobes; patience

2. *Aggression* is defined as behavior that:
   a. hurts another person.
   b. is intended to hurt another person.
   c. is hostile, passionate, and produces physical injury.
   d. has all of these characteristics.

3. Which of the following is true about aggression?
   a. It varies too much to be instinctive in humans.
   b. It is just one instinct among many.
   c. It is instinctive but shaped by learning.
   d. It is the most important human instinct.

4. Research studies have found a positive correlation between aggressive tendencies in animals and levels of the hormone:
   a. estrogen.   c. noradrenaline.
   b. adrenaline.   d. testosterone.

5. Research studies have indicated that the tendency of viewers to misperceive normal sexuality, devalue their partners, and trivialize rape is:
   a. increased by exposure to pornography.
   b. not changed after exposure to pornography.
   c. decreased in men by exposure to pornography.
   d. decreased in both men and women by exposure to pornography.

6. Increasing the number of people that are present during an emergency tends to:
   a. increase the likelihood that people will cooperate in rendering assistance.
   b. decrease the empathy that people feel for the victim.
   c. increase the role that social norms governing helping will play.
   d. decrease the likelihood that anyone will help.

7. Which of the following was *not* mentioned in the text discussion of the roots of prejudice?
   a. people's tendency to overestimate the similarity of people within groups
   b. people's tendency to assume that exceptional, or especially memorable, individuals are unlike the majority of members of a group
   c. people's tendency to assume that the world is just and that people get what they deserve
   d. people's tendency to discriminate against those they view as "outsiders"

8. The mere exposure effect demonstrates that:
   a. familiarity breeds contempt.
   b. opposites attract.
   c. birds of a feather flock together.
   d. familiarity breeds fondness.

9. In one experiment, college men were physically aroused and then introduced to an attractive woman. Compared to men who had not been aroused, these men:
   a. reported more positive feelings toward the woman.
   b. reported more negative feelings toward the woman.
   c. were ambiguous about their feelings toward the woman.
   d. were more likely to feel that the woman was "out of their league" in terms of attractiveness.

10. The deep affection that is felt in long-lasting relationships is called _____ love; this feeling is fostered in relationships in which _____ .
   a. passionate; there is equity between the partners
   b. passionate; traditional roles are maintained
   c. companionate; there is equity between the partners
   d. companionate; traditional roles are maintained

11. Which of the following is associated with an increased tendency on the part of a bystander to offer help in an emergency situation?
    a. being in a good mood
    b. having recently needed help and not received it
    c. observing someone as he or she refuses to offer help
    d. being a female

12. The belief that those who suffer deserve their fate is expressed in the:
    a. just-world phenomenon.
    b. phenomenon of ingroup bias.
    c. fundamental attribution error.
    d. mirror-image perception principle.

13. (Close-Up) Which of the following is an example of implicit prejudice?
    a. Jake, who is White, gives higher evaluations to essays he believes to be written by Blacks than to white-authored essays.
    b. Carol believes that white people are arrogant.
    c. Brad earns more than Jane, despite having the same job skills, performance level, and seniority.
    d. In certain countries, women are not allowed to drive.

14. We tend to perceive the members of an ingroup as _____ and the members of an outgroup as _____ .
    a. similar to one another; different from one another
    b. different from one another; similar to one another
    c. above average in ability; below average in ability
    d. below average in ability; above average in ability

15. Regarding the influence of alcohol and testosterone on aggressive behavior, which of the following is true?
    a. Consumption of alcohol increases aggressive behavior; injections of testosterone reduce aggressive behavior.
    b. Consumption of alcohol reduces aggressive behavior; injections of testosterone increase aggressive behavior.
    c. Consumption of alcohol and injections of testosterone both promote aggressive behavior.
    d. Consumption of alcohol and injections of testosterone both reduce aggressive behavior.

16. Most people prefer mirror-image photographs of their faces. This is best explained by:
    a. the principle of equity.
    b. the principle of self-disclosure.
    c. the mere exposure effect.
    d. mirror-image perceptions.

17. Research studies have shown that frequent exposure to sexually explicit films:
    a. makes a woman's friendliness seem more sexual.
    b. diminishes the attitude that rape is a serious crime.
    c. may lead individuals to devalue their partners.
    d. may produce all of these effects.

18. Research studies indicate that in an emergency situation, the presence of others often prevents:
    a. people from even noticing the situation.
    b. people from interpreting an unusual event as an emergency.
    c. people from assuming responsibility for assisting.
    d. all of these behaviors.

19. Which of the following factors is the *most* powerful predictor of friendship?
    a. similarity in age
    b. common racial and religious background
    c. similarity in physical attractiveness
    d. physical proximity

20. Most researchers agree that:
    a. media violence is a factor in aggression.
    b. there is a negative correlation between media violence and aggressiveness.
    c. paradoxically, watching excessive pornography ultimately diminishes an individual's aggressive tendencies.
    d. media violence is too unreal to promote aggression in viewers.

21. People with power and status may become prejudiced because:
    a. they tend to justify the social inequalities between themselves and others.
    b. those with less status and power tend to resent them.
    c. those with less status and power appear less capable.
    d. they feel proud and are boastful of their achievements.

22. Which of the following best describes how GRIT works?
    a. The fact that two sides in a conflict have great respect for the other's strengths prevents further escalation of the problem.
    b. The two sides engage in a series of reciprocated conciliatory acts.
    c. The two sides agree to have their differences settled by a neutral, third-party mediator.
    d. The two sides engage in cooperation in those areas in which shared goals are possible.

23. After waiting in line for an hour to buy concert tickets, Teresa is told that the concert is sold out. In her anger she pounds her fist on the ticket counter, frightening the clerk. Teresa's behavior is best explained by:
    a. evolutionary psychology.
    b. deindividuation.
    c. reward theory.
    d. the frustration-aggression principle.

24. Which of the following strategies would be *most* likely to foster positive feelings between two conflicting groups?
    a. Take steps to reduce the likelihood of mirror-image perceptions.
    b. Separate the groups so that tensions diminish.
    c. Increase the amount of contact between the two conflicting groups.
    d. Have the groups work on a superordinate goal.

25. Given the tendency of people to categorize information according to preformed schemas, which of the following stereotypes would Juan, a 65-year-old political liberal and fitness enthusiast, be most likely to have?
    a. "People who exercise regularly are very extraverted."
    b. "All political liberals are advocates of a reduced defense budget."
    c. "Young people today have no sense of responsibility."
    d. "Older people are lazy."

26. Ever since their cabin lost the camp softball competition, the campers have become increasingly hostile toward one camper in their cabin, blaming her for every problem in the cabin. This behavior is best explained in terms of:
    a. the ingroup bias.
    b. prejudice.
    c. the scapegoat theory.
    d. catharsis.

27. Mr. and Mrs. Samuels are constantly fighting, and each perceives the other as hard-headed and insensitive. Their conflict is being fueled by:
    a. self-disclosure.
    b. stereotypes.
    c. a social norm.
    d. mirror-image perceptions.

28. Students at State University are convinced that their school is better than any other; this most directly illustrates:
    a. an ingroup bias.
    b. prejudice and discrimination.
    c. the scapegoat effect.
    d. the just-world phenomenon.

29. Ahmed and Monique are on a blind date. Which of the following will probably be *most* influential in determining whether they like each other?
    a. their personalities
    b. their beliefs
    c. their social skills
    d. their physical attractiveness

30. Opening her mail, Joan discovers a romantic greeting card from her boyfriend. According to the two-factor theory, she is likely to feel the most intense romantic feelings if, prior to reading the card, she has just:
    a. completed her daily run.
    b. finished reading a chapter in her psychology textbook.
    c. awakened from a nap.
    d. finished eating lunch.

31. Summarizing his report on the biology of aggression, Sam notes that:
    a. biology does not significantly influence aggression.
    b. when one identical twin has a violent temperament, the other member of the twin pair rarely does.
    c. hormones and alcohol influence the neural systems that control aggression.
    d. testosterone reduces dominance behaviors in animals.

32. Having read the module, which of the following is best borne out by research on attraction?
    a. Birds of a feather flock together.
    b. Opposites attract.
    c. Familiarity breeds contempt.
    d. Absence makes the heart grow fonder.

Matching Items

Match each term with the appropriate definition or description.

Terms

_____ 1. bystander effect
_____ 2. ingroup bias
_____ 3. stereotype
_____ 4. altruism
_____ 5. mere exposure effect

Definitions or Descriptions

a. a generalized belief about a group of people
b. the tendency to favor one's own group
c. unselfish regard for others
d. the tendency that a person is less likely to help someone in need when others are present
e. the increased liking of a stimulus that results from repeated exposure to it

KEY TERMS

Using your own words, on a separate piece of paper write a brief definition or explanation of each of the following terms.

1. social psychology
2. prejudice
3. stereotype
4. discrimination
5. ingroup
6. outgroup
7. ingroup bias
8. scapegoat theory
9. just-world phenomenon
10. aggression
11. frustration-aggression principle
12. mere exposure effect
13. passionate love
14. companionate love
15. equity
16. self-disclosure
17. altruism
18. bystander effect
19. conflict
20. superordinate goals
21. GRIT

ANSWERS

Module Review

Prejudice

1. unjustifiable; negative; stereotypes
2. beliefs; emotions; action
3. attitude; discrimination; behavior
4. less
5. have; associations
6. implicit; implicit prejudice
7. facial; amygdala
8. women; nurturant; sensitive; aggressive
9. justifying
10. blame
11. social identities
12. ingroup bias; ingroup; outgroup
13. death; world
14. scapegoat
15. open; accepting
16. categorization; overestimate
17. overgeneralize
18. just-world; hindsight bias

Aggression

1. any physical or verbal behavior intended to hurt or destroy; do not
2. biology; experience
3. do not
4. varies
5. bred
6. do; Y; frontal lobes; impulses

7. neural; hormones

8. testosterone; decreased

9. irritability; frustration; assertiveness; impulsiveness; delinquency; drug use; frustration; decrease; increases

10. alcohol

11. frustration-aggression

12. physical pain, personal insults, foul odors, hot temperatures, cigarette smoke

13. rewards; observation (or imitation)

14. rich; poor; father care

15. difficult; aggression-replacement

16. desensitize; prime

17. some women invite or enjoy rape; accept

Pornography tends to portray women as enjoying being the victims of sexual aggression, and this perception increases the acceptance of coercion in sexual relationships. Repeatedly watching X-rated films also makes one's partner seem less attractive, makes a woman's friendliness seem more sexual, and makes sexual aggression seem less serious.

The Zillmann and Bryant study found that after viewing sexually explicit films for several weeks, undergraduates were more likely to recommend a lighter prison sentence for a convicted rapist than were subjects who viewed nonerotic films.

18. sexual violence; social scripts

19. hostile; arguments; fights; grades

20. disconfirm; catharsis hypothesis; more anger

21. biological; psychological; social-cultural

Attraction

1. proximity

2. increases; mere exposure; adaptive; prejudice; automatic

3. appearance

4. Attractive people are perceived as happier, more sensitive, more successful, and more socially skilled.

5. is not

6. youthful; mature; dominant; affluent

7. attitudes, beliefs, interests, religion, race, education, intelligence, smoking behavior, economic status, age

Reward theories of attraction say that we are attracted to, and continue relationships with, those people whose behavior provides us with more benefits than costs. Proximity makes it easy to enjoy the benefits of friendship at little cost, attractiveness is pleasing, and similarity is reinforcing to us.

8. passionate; companionate

9. arousal; cognitive

10. were

11. equity; self-disclosure

Altruism

1. altruism

An example of altruism is giving food and shelter to people displaced by a hurricane or other major disaster without expectation of reward.

2. notice; interpret; assume responsibility

3. less

4. less; bystander effect

People are most likely to help someone when they have just observed someone else being helpful; when they are not in a hurry; when the victim appears to need and deserve help; when they are in some way similar to the victim; when in a small town or rural area; when feeling guilty; when not preoccupied; and when in a good mood.

Conflict and Peacemaking

1. conflict; groups; nations

2. mirror-image

3. is not

4. superordinate; predicaments; "we"

5. mediator

6. Graduated; Reciprocated Initiatives; Tension-Reduction; conciliatory

Progress Test

Multiple-Choice Questions

1. **c.** is the answer.

2. **b.** is the answer. Aggression is any behavior, physical or verbal, that is intended to hurt or destroy.
   a. A person may accidentally be hurt in a nonaggressive incident; aggression does not necessarily prove hurtful.
   c. Verbal behavior, which does not result in physical injury, may also be aggressive. Moreover, acts of aggression may be cool and calculated, rather than hostile and passionate.

3. **a.** is the answer. The very wide variations in aggressiveness from culture to culture indicate that aggression cannot be considered an unlearned instinct.

4. **d.** is the answer.

5. a. is the answer.

6. d. is the answer. This phenomenon is known as the bystander effect.
a. This answer is incorrect because individuals are less likely to render assistance at all if others are present.
b. Although people are less likely to assume responsibility for helping, this does not mean that they are less empathic.
c. This answer is incorrect because norms such as the social responsibility norm encourage helping others, yet people are less likely to help with others around.

7. b. is the answer. In fact, people tend to overgeneralize from vivid cases, rather than assume that they are unusual.
a., c., & d. Each of these is an example of a cognitive (a. & c.) or a social (d.) root of prejudice.

8. d. is the answer. Being repeatedly exposed to novel stimuli increases our liking for them.
a. For the most part, the opposite is true.
b. & c. The mere exposure effect concerns our tendency to develop likings on the basis, not of similarities or differences, but simply of familiarity, or repeated exposure.

9. a. is the answer. This result supports the two-factor theory of emotion and passionate attraction, according to which arousal from any source can facilitate an emotion, depending on how we label the arousal.

10. c. is the answer. Deep affection is typical of companionate love, rather than passionate love, and is promoted by equity, whereas traditional roles may be characterized by the dominance of one sex.

11. a. is the answer.
b. & c. These factors would most likely decrease a person's altruistic tendencies.
d. There is no evidence that one sex is more altruistic than the other.

12. a. is the answer.
b. Ingroup bias is the tendency of people to favor their own group.
c. The fundamental attribution error is the tendency of people to underestimate situational influences when observing the behavior of other people.
d. The mirror-image perception principle is the tendency of conflicting parties to form similar, diabolical images of each other.

13. a. is the answer.
b. This is an example of overt prejudice.
c. & d. These are examples of discrimination.

14. b. is the answer.
a. We are keenly sensitive to differences within our group, less so to differences within other groups.
c. & d. Although we tend to look more favorably on members of the ingroup, the text does not suggest that ingroup bias extends to evaluations of abilities.

15. c. is the answer.

16. c. is the answer. The mere exposure effect refers to our tendency to like what we're used to, and we're used to seeing mirror images of ourselves.
a. Equity refers to equality in giving and taking between the partners in a relationship.
b. Self-disclosure is the sharing of intimate feelings with a partner in a loving relationship.
d. Although people prefer mirror images of their faces, mirror-image perceptions are often held by parties in conflict. Each party views itself favorably and the other negatively.

17. d. is the answer.

18. d. is the answer.

19. d. is the answer. Because it provides people with an opportunity to meet, proximity is the most powerful predictor of friendship, even though, once a friendship is established, the other factors mentioned become more important.

20. a. is the answer.

21. a. is the answer. Such justifications arise as a way to preserve inequalities. The just-world phenomenon presumes that people get what they deserve. According to this view, someone who has less must deserve less.

22. b. is the answer.
a. GRIT is a technique for reducing conflict through a series of conciliatory gestures, not for maintaining the status quo.
c. & d. These measures may help reduce conflict but they are not aspects of GRIT.

23. d. is the answer. According to the frustration-aggression principle, the blocking of an attempt to achieve some goal—in Teresa's case, buying concert tickets—creates anger and can generate aggression.
a. Evolutionary psychology maintains that aggressive behavior is a genetically based drive. Teresa's behavior clearly was a reaction to a specific situation.

b. Deindividuation refers to loss of self-restraint in group situations that foster arousal. Teresa's action has only to do with her frustration.

c. Reward theory views behavior as an exchange process in which people try to maximize the benefits of their behavior by minimizing the costs. Teresa's behavior likely brought her few benefits while exacting some costs, including potential injury, embarrassment, and retaliation by the clerk.

24. **d.** is the answer. Sherif found that hostility between two groups could be dispelled by giving the groups superordinate, or shared, goals.
    a. Although reducing the likelihood of mirror-image perceptions might reduce mutually destructive behavior, it would not lead to positive feelings between the groups.
    b. Such segregation would likely increase in-group bias and group polarization, resulting in further group conflict.
    c. Contact by itself is not likely to reduce conflict.

25. **c.** is the answer. People tend to overestimate the similarity of people within groups other than their own. Thus, Juan is not likely to form stereotypes of fitness enthusiasts (a.), political liberals (b.), or older adults (d.), because these are groups to which he belongs.

26. **c.** is the answer. According to the scapegoat theory, when things go wrong, people look for someone on whom to take out their anger and frustration.
    a. These campers are venting their frustration on a member of their *own* cabin group (although this is not always the case with scapegoats).
    b. Prejudice refers to an unjustifiable and usually negative attitude toward another group.
    d. Catharsis is the idea that releasing aggressive energy relieves aggressive urges.

27. **d.** is the answer. The couple's similar, and presumably distorted, feelings toward each other fuel their conflict. (p. 566)
    a. Self-disclosure, or the sharing of intimate feelings, fosters love.
    b. Stereotypes are overgeneralized ideas about groups.
    c. A social norm is an understood rule for expected and accepted behavior.

28. **a.** is the answer.
    b. Prejudices are unjustifiable and usually negative attitudes toward other groups. They may result from an ingroup bias, but they are probably not why students favor their own university.

c. Scapegoats are individuals or groups toward which prejudice is directed as an outlet for the anger of frustrated individuals or groups.
    d. The just-world phenomenon is the tendency for people to believe others "get what they deserve."

29. **d.** is the answer. Hundreds of experiments indicate that first impressions are most influenced by physical appearance.

30. **a.** is the answer. According to the two-factor theory, physical arousal can intensify whatever emotion is currently felt. Only in the situation described in a. is Joan likely to be physically aroused.

31. **c.** is the answer.
    a. & b. Biology is an important factor in aggressive behavior. This includes genetics, which means identical twins would have similar temperaments.
    d. Just the opposite is true.

32. **a.** is the answer. Friends and couples are much more likely than randomly paired people to be similar in views, interests, and a range of other factors.
    b. The opposite is true.
    c. The mere exposure effect demonstrates that familiarity tends to breed fondness.
    d. This is unlikely, given the positive effects of proximity and intimacy.

Matching Items

1. d	**4.** c
2. b	**5.** e
3. a	

Key Terms

1. **Social psychology** is the scientific study of how we think about, influence, and relate to one another.

2. **Prejudice** is an unjustifiable (and usually negative) attitude toward a group and its members.

3. A **stereotype** is a generalized (sometimes accurate but often overgeneralized) belief about a group of people.

4. **Discrimination** is unjustifiable negative behavior toward a group or its members.

5. The **ingroup** refers to the people and groups with whom we share a common identity.

6. The **outgroup** refers to the people and groups that are excluded from our ingroup.

7. The **ingroup bias** is the tendency to favor one's own group.

8. The **scapegoat theory** proposes that prejudice provides an outlet for anger by finding someone to blame.

9. The **just-world phenomenon** is a manifestation of the commonly held belief that good is rewarded and evil is punished. The logic is indisputable: "If I am rewarded, I must be good."

10. **Aggression** is any physical or verbal behavior intended to hurt or destroy.

11. The **frustration-aggression principle** states that aggression is triggered when people become angry because their efforts to achieve a goal have been blocked.

12. The **mere exposure effect** refers to the fact that repeated exposure to an unfamiliar stimulus increases our liking of it.

13. **Passionate love** refers to an aroused state of intense positive absorption in another person, especially at the beginning of a relationship.

14. **Companionate love** refers to a deep, enduring, affectionate attachment.

15. **Equity** refers to the condition in which there is mutual giving and receiving between the partners in a relationship.

16. **Self-disclosure** refers to a person's sharing intimate feelings with another.

17. **Altruism** is unselfish regard for the welfare of others.

18. The **bystander effect** is the tendency of a person to be less likely to offer help to someone if there are other people present.

19. **Conflict** is a perceived incompatibility of actions, goals, or ideas between individuals or groups.

20. **Superordinate goals** are mutual goals that require the cooperation of individuals or groups otherwise in conflict.

21. **GRIT** (Graduated and Reciprocated Initiatives in Tension-Reduction) is a strategy of conflict resolution based on the defusing effect that conciliatory gestures can have on parties in conflict.

FOCUS ON VOCABULARY AND LANGUAGE

Prejudice

In one 1970s study, most white participants perceived a white man shoving a black man as *"horsing around."* Prejudices involve beliefs, emotions, and tendencies to behave in certain ways. They are a form of prejudgment that influences (*colors*) how we interpret what we see. Thus, in an experiment in which white people saw a white man pushing a black person, most interpreted the behavior as playful activity (*horsing around*); when the roles were reversed, the behavior was more likely to be described as aggressive or hostile (*violent*).

Even arbitrarily creating an us-them distinction—by grouping people *with the toss of a coin*—leads people to show favoritism to their own group when dividing any rewards (Tajfel, 1982; Wilder, 1981). One of the factors affecting prejudice is our propensity to define ourselves through identification with a particular group (**ingroup bias**); this in turn creates an outgroup consisting of those who do not belong to our group. Even if the groups are artificially created by random assignment (*with the toss of a coin*), we will tend to see our own group as more deserving, superior, and so on.

Aggression

A raging bull will become a gentle *Ferdinand* when castration reduces its testosterone level. Biological explanations of aggression examine the influences of genes, clusters of neurons in the brain, and biochemical agents in the blood, such as hormones and alcohol. Levels of the male sex hormone can be reduced by castration; thus, an aggressive, ferocious bull can be reduced to a playful, friendly animal similar to the fictional character (*Ferdinand*) of children's stories.

In less graphic form, the same unrealistic script—she resists, he persists, *she melts*—is commonplace on TV and in romance novels. A common theme in certain types of films and books is the idea that if the main male character overcomes (*he persists*) the lovely female's reluctance (*she resists*) to be romantically or sexually involved, then she will be totally devoted to him (*she melts*). This depiction of male-female relationships, in both pornographic and non-pornographic media, has little to do with reality and may, in fact, promote sexual aggression.

Contrary to much popular opinion, viewing such *depictions* does not provide *an outlet* for *bottled-up impulses.* Laboratory studies have demonstrated that watching media that show sexual violence against women does not decrease the acceptance and performance of aggression against females. In contrast to what many believe, such portrayals (*depictions*) do not allow vicarious expression (*an outlet*) for pent-up hostile urges (*bottled-up impulses*) and may have the opposite effect.

Attraction

Within certain limits . . . *familiarity breeds fondness.* Under some circumstances, the more often we see (*become familiar with*) someone, the more likely it is that we will grow to like (*become fond of*) that person. This is called the **mere exposure effect.** This effect suggests that the popular saying "familiarity breeds contempt" may not be completely accurate.

. . . *"beauty is only skin deep"* . . . This saying suggests that physical attractiveness (*beauty*) is only a superficial quality (*skin deep*). Research, however, has shown that how we look influences social interactions, how frequently we date, our popularity, how we are perceived by others, etc.

In real life, *opposites retract.* The old saying *"opposites attract"* has not been supported by research in social psychology. In fact, we tend to dislike those we do not perceive as similar to ourselves (*opposites retract*). Rather than fostering *contempt*, Myers humorously suggests that similarity breeds *content.*

To be *revved up* and to associate some of that arousal with a desirable person is to feel the pull of passion. Research has shown that one component of romantic or passionate love is physiological arousal; a second aspect is some cognitive interpretation and labeling of that feeling. So, if a person is in an aroused state (*revved up*) and this is easily linked to the presence of an attractive person, then attributions of romantic love may be made. As Myers cheerfully notes, rather than *absence, adrenaline makes the heart grow fonder* (intensifies love).

Altruism

At each step, the presence of other *bystanders turns people away from the path that leads to helping.* Darley and Latané displayed their findings in a flow diagram (See Figure 45.7, p. 613). At each decision point (i.e., noticing the event, interpreting it as an emer-

gency, and assuming responsibility), the presence of others who appear to have observed the event (*bystanders*) causes people to be less likely to give assistance to someone in need (*they are turned away from the path that leads to helping*).

. . . *blasé* . . . This means to be indifferent or uncaring. We arrive at the decision (especially in ambiguous situations) to help or not to help by watching the reactions of others. If they appear to be unconcerned (*blasé*), we may conclude that there is no emergency and thus may not intervene or help. This **bystander effect** means that the presence of others decreases the probability that any particular observer will provide help.

Conflict and Peacemaking

Psychologists have noted that those in conflict have a curious tendency to form *diabolical images* of one another. We have a propensity to perceive our enemies in a very distorted manner, often categorizing them as evil, cruel, untrustworthy, and devilish (*diabolical*). They, of course, view us in the same way; the biased pictures we form of each other are called *mirror-image perceptions.*

Before long, each group became intensely proud of itself and hostile to the other group's *"sneaky," "smart-alecky stinkers."* In Sherif's experiment, competitive conditions were created in order to foster the formation of two antagonistic groups. Each group soon saw itself as superior to the other group's "dishonest and sly" (*sneaky*) "rotten know-it-alls" (*smart-alecky stinkers*). Sherif then used shared objectives and common problems (**superordinate goals**) to create reconciliation and cooperation.

Conciliations allow both parties to begin edging *down the tension ladder to a safer rung* where communication and mutual understanding can begin. Social psychologist Charles Osgood has developed a tactic called **GRIT** (Graduated and Reciprocated Initiatives in Tension-Reduction) for increasing cooperation and trust between parties in conflict. When one side makes a small gesture or offer of goodwill (*a conciliatory act*), the other side has an opportunity to reciprocate and thus move the conflict toward some resolution (*down the tension ladder to a safer rung*) and start the process of mutual respect and understanding.

Statistical Reasoning in Everyday Life

APPENDIX OVERVIEW

A basic understanding of statistical reasoning has become a necessity in everyday life. Statistics are tools that help the psychologist and layperson to interpret the vast quantities of information they are confronted with on a daily basis. Appendix A discusses how statistics are used to describe data and to generalize from instances.

In studying this appendix, you must concentrate on learning a number of procedures and understanding some underlying principles in the science of statistics. The graphic and computational procedures in the section called "Describing Data" include how data are distributed in a sample; measures of central tendency such as the mean, median, and mode; variation measures such as the range and standard deviation; and correlation, or the degree to which two variables are related. Most of the conceptual material is then covered in the section entitled "Making Inferences." You should be able to discuss three important principles concerning populations and samples, as well as the concept of significance in testing differences. The ultimate goal is to make yourself a better consumer of statistical research by improving your critical thinking skills.

NOTE: Answer guidelines for all questions in Appendix A begin on page 497.

APPENDIX REVIEW

First, skim each section, noting headings and boldface items. After you have read the section, review each objective by answering the fill-in and essay-type questions that follow it. As you proceed, evaluate your performance by consulting the answers on page 497. Do not continue with the next section until you understand each answer. If you need to, review or reread the section in the textbook before continuing.

Introduction and Describing Data
(pp. A-1–A-7)

> David Myers at times uses idioms that are unfamiliar to some readers. If you do not know the meaning of any of the following words, phrases, or expressions in the context in which they appear in the introduction and this section, refer to pages 501–502 for an explanation: *top-of-the-head estimates often misread reality and mislead the public; national income cake; gauges; naked eye; Data are "noisy."*

Objective 1: Describe one way of organizing data, and differentiate the three measures of central tendency.

1. We should be skeptical when presented with numbers that are _____ , _____ , and _____ .

2. The first step in describing data is to _____ it, such as by displaying it as a _____ _____ .

3. The three measures of central tendency are the _____ , the _____ , and the _____ .

4. The most frequently occurring score in a distribution is called the _____ .

5. The mean is computed as the _____ of all the scores divided by the _____ of scores.

6. The median is the score at the _____ percentile.

7. When a distribution is lopsided, or
_____ , the _____
(mean/median/mode) can be biased by a few
extreme scores.

Objective 2: Identify two measures of variation, and discuss the normal curve as a means of describing large amounts of data.

8. Averages derived from scores with
_____ (high/low) variability are
more reliable than those with
_____ (high/low) variability.

9. The measures of variation include the
_____ and the
_____ _____ .

10. The range is computed as the _____
_____ .

11. The range provides a(n) _____
(crude/accurate) estimate of variation because it
_____ (is/is not) influenced by
extreme scores.

12. The standard deviation is a _____
(more accurate/less accurate) measure of variation than the range. Unlike the range, the standard deviation _____ (uses/does
not use) information from each score in the distribution.

13. The bell-shaped distribution that often describes
large amounts of data is called the
_____ _____ .

14. In this distribution, approximately
_____ percent of the individual
scores fall within 1 standard deviation on either
side of the mean. Within 2 standard deviations on
either side of the mean fall _____
percent of the individual scores.

Calculate what a score of 116 on the normally distributed Wechsler IQ test would mean with regard to
percentile rank. (Recall that the mean is 100; the standard deviation is ±15 points. Hint: You might find it
helpful to draw the normal curve first.)

Objective 3: Describe the correlation coefficient, and explain its importance in assessing relationships between variables.

15. A measure of the direction and extent of relationship between two sets of scores is called the
_____ _____ .
Numerically, this measure can range from
_____ to _____ .

16. When there is no relationship at all between two
sets of scores, the correlation coefficient is
_____ . The strongest possible correlation between two sets of scores is either
_____ or _____ .
When the correlation between two sets of scores
is negative, as one increases, the other
_____ .

Cite an example of a positive correlation and a negative correlation. Your examples can be drawn from
previous chapters of the text or can be based on observations from daily life.

An example of a positive correlation is

An example of a negative correlation is

17. The correlation coefficient _____
(gives/does not give) information about cause-
and-effect relationships. It does, however, tell
how well one factor _____ the
other related factor.

18. To depict a correlation, researchers create a graph
called a _____ , which uses dots to
represent the values of the two variables.

Objective 4: Explain how people can be misled by failing to recognize a normal statistical regression toward the mean.

19. A correlation that is perceived but doesn't really
exist is called an _____
_____ .

20. When we believe that a relationship exists
between two things, we are most likely to recall
instances that _____ (confirm/dis-
confirm) our belief.

21. This type of correlation feeds the illusion of
_____—that we can control events
that actually are due to _____ .
It is also fed by a statistical phenomenon called

_____ _____

_____ _____ , the
idea that average results are more typical than
extreme results.

Making Inferences (pp. A-7–A-8)

Objective 5: Identify three important principles in
generalizing from samples to populations, and
explain what we mean when we say an observed difference is statistically significant.

1. The best basis for generalizing is not from
_____ cases but from a
_____ sample of cases.

2. (Close-Up) Researchers use _____-
_____ studies to investigate a randomly sampled group of people of
_____ (the same/different) age(s).
This type of study generally extends over a very
_____ (long/short) period of time.

3. (Close-Up) Researchers use _____
studies to study, test, and re-test
_____ (the same/different)
group(s) over a _____ (long/short)
period of time.

4. (Close-Up) The first kind of study found evidence
of intellectual _____ (stability/
decline) during adulthood; the second found evidence of intellectual _____ (stabili-
ty/decline).

(Close-Up) Explain why the conflicting results of
these two types of studies point to the importance of
knowing how researchers reached their conclusions.

5. Averages are more reliable when they are based
on scores with _____ (high/low)
variability.

6. Averages based on a large number of cases are
_____ (more/less) reliable than
those based on a few cases.

7. Tests of statistical _____ are used
to estimate whether observed differences are real,
that is, to make sure they are not simply the
result of _____ variation. The differences are probably real if the sample averages
are _____ and the difference
between them is _____ .

PROGRESS TEST

Multiple-Choice Questions

Circle your answers to the following questions and
check them with the answers beginning on page 497.
If your answer is incorrect, read the explanation for
why it is incorrect and then consult the appropriate
pages of the text. Use the page margins if you need
extra space for your computations.

1. What is the mean of the following distribution of
scores: 2, 3, 7, 6, 1, 4, 9, 5, 8, 2?
a. 5   **c.** 4.7
b. 4   **d.** 3.7

2. What is the median of the following distribution
of scores: 1, 3, 7, 7, 2, 8, 4?
a. 1   **c.** 3
b. 2   **d.** 4

3. What is the mode of the following distribution: 8,
2, 1, 1, 3, 7, 6, 2, 0, 2?
a. 1   **c.** 3
b. 2   **d.** 7

4. Compute the range of the following distribution:
9, 14, 2, 8, 1, 6, 8, 9, 1, 3.
a. 10   **c.** 8
b. 9   **d.** 13

5. Which of the following is true of the longitudinal
method?
a. It compares people of different ages.
b. It studies the same people at different times.
c. It usually involves a larger sample than do
cross-sectional tests.
d. It usually involves a smaller sample than do
cross-sectional tests.

6. If two sets of scores are negatively correlated, it means that:
   a. as one set of scores increases, the other decreases.
   b. as one set of scores increases, the other increases.
   c. there is only a weak relationship between the sets of scores.
   d. there is no relationship at all between the sets of scores.

7. Regression toward the mean is the:
   a. tendency for unusual scores to fall back toward a distribution's average.
   b. basis for all tests of statistical significance.
   c. reason the range is a more accurate measure of variation than the standard deviation.
   d. reason the standard deviation is a more accurate measure of variation than the range.

8. In a normal distribution, what percentage of scores fall between +2 and –2 standard deviations of the mean?
   a. 50 percent   c. 95 percent
   b. 68 percent   d. 99.7 percent

9. Which of the following statistics must fall on or between –1.00 and +1.00?
   a. the mean
   b. the standard deviation
   c. the correlation coefficient
   d. none of these statistics

10. In generalizing from a sample to the population, it is important that:
    a. the sample is representative of the population.
    b. the sample is large.
    c. the scores in the sample have low variability.
    d. all of these situations are observed.

11. When a difference between two groups is "statistically significant," this means that:
    a. the difference is statistically real but of little practical significance.
    b. the difference is probably the result of sampling variation.
    c. the difference is not likely to be due to chance variation.
    d. all of these statements are true.

12. A lopsided set of scores that includes a number of extreme or unusual values is said to be:
    a. symmetrical.   c. skewed.
    b. normal.   d. dispersed.

13. Which of the following is *not* a measure of central tendency?
    a. mean   c. median
    b. range   d. mode

14. Which of the following is the measure of central tendency that would be most affected by a few extreme scores?
    a. mean   c. median
    b. range   d. mode

15. The symmetrical, bell-shaped distribution in which most scores are near the mean and fewer near the extremes forms a:
    a. skewed curve.   c. normal curve.
    b. bimodal curve.   d. bar graph.

16. A homogeneous sample with little variation in scores will have a(n) _____ standard deviation.
    a. small
    b. moderate
    c. large
    d. unknown (It is impossible to determine.)

17. If there is no relationship between two sets of scores, the correlation coefficient equals:
    a. 0.00   c. +1.00
    b. –1.00   d. 0.50

18. Illusory correlation refers to:
    a. the perception that two negatively correlated variables are positively correlated.
    b. the perception of a relationship between two unrelated variables.
    c. an insignificant correlation coefficient.
    d. a correlation coefficient that equals –1.00.

19. Gamblers who blow on their dice "for luck" are victims of:
    a. regression toward the mean.
    b. the illusion of control.
    c. hindsight bias.
    d. the fundamental attribution error.

20. What is the mode of the following distribution of scores: 2, 2, 4, 4, 4, 14?
    a. 2   c. 5
    b. 4   d. 6

21. What is the mean of the following distribution of scores: 2, 5, 8, 10, 11, 4, 6, 9, 1, 4?
    a. 2
    b. 10
    c. 6
    d. 15

22. What is the median of the following distribution: 10, 7, 5, 11, 8, 6, 9?
    a. 6
    b. 7
    c. 8
    d. 9

23. Which statistic is the average amount by which the scores in a distribution vary from the average?
    a. standard deviation
    b. range
    c. median
    d. mode

24. The most frequently occurring score in a distribution is the:
    a. mean.
    b. median.
    c. mode.
    d. range.

25. In the following distribution, the mean is _____ the mode and _____ the median: 4, 6, 1, 4, 5.
    a. less than; less than
    b. less than; greater than
    c. equal to; equal to
    d. greater than; equal to

26. Which of the following is the measure of variation that is most affected by extreme scores?
    a. mean
    b. standard deviation
    c. mode
    d. range

27. Which of the following is true of the cross-sectional method?
    a. It compares people of different ages with one another.
    b. It studies the same group of people at different times.
    c. It tends to paint too favorable a picture of the effects of aging on intelligence.
    d. It is more appropriate than the longitudinal method for studying intellectual change over the life span.

28. Which of the following sets of scores would likely be most representative of the population from which it was drawn?
    a. a sample with a relatively large standard deviation
    b. a sample with a relatively small standard deviation
    c. a sample with a relatively large range
    d. a sample with a relatively small range

29. The *value* of the correlation coefficient indicates the _____ of relationship between two variables, and the *sign* (positive or negative) indicates the _____ of the relationship.
    a. direction; strength
    b. strength; direction
    c. direction; reliability
    d. reliability; strength

30. If a difference between two samples is *not* statistically significant, which of the following can be concluded?
    a. The difference is probably not a true one.
    b. The difference is probably not reliable.
    c. The difference could be due to sampling variation.
    d. All of these statements are true.

31. The first step in constructing a bar graph is to:
    a. measure the standard deviation.
    b. organize the data.
    c. calculate a correlation coefficient.
    d. determine the range.

32. Standard deviation is to mode as _____ is to _____ .
    a. mean; median
    b. variation; central tendency
    c. median; mean
    d. central tendency; variation

33. In a normal distribution, what percentage of scores fall between −1 and +1 standard deviation units of the mean?
    a. 50 percent
    b. 68 percent
    c. 95 percent
    d. 99.7 percent

34. The precision with which sample statistics reflect population parameters is greater when the sample is:
    a. large.
    b. characterized by high variability.
    c. small in number but consists of vivid cases.
    d. statistically significant.

35. The following scatterplot depicts a correlation coefficient that would be close to:

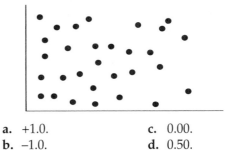

    a. +1.0.
    b. −1.0.
    c. 0.00.
    d. 0.50.

36. Which of the following correlation coefficients indicates the strongest relationship between two variables?
    a. −.73   c. 0.00
    b. +.66   d. −.50

37. A correlation coefficient:
    a. indicates the direction of relationship between two variables.
    b. indicates the strength of relationship between two variables.
    c. does *not* indicate whether there is a cause-and-effect relationship between two variables.
    d. does all of these things.

38. Cross-sectional studies of intelligence are potentially misleading because:
    a. they are typically based on a very small and unrepresentative sample of people.
    b. retesting the same people over a period of years allows test performance to be influenced by practice.
    c. they compare people who are not only different in age, but of different eras, education levels, and affluence.
    d. of all of these reasons.

39. Jane usually averages 175 in bowling. One night her three-game average is 215. What will probably happen to her bowling average over the next several weeks of bowling?
    a. It will return to about the level of her average.
    b. It will continue to increase.
    c. It will dip down to about 155.
    d. There is no way to predict her average scores.

40. If height and body weight are positively correlated, which of the following is true?
    a. There is a cause-effect relationship between height and weight.
    b. As height increases, weight decreases.
    c. Knowing a person's height, one can predict his or her weight.
    d. All of these statements are true.

41. The football team's punter wants to determine how consistent his punting distances have been during the past season. He should compute the:
    a. mean.   c. mode.
    b. median.   d. standard deviation.

42. If about two-thirds of the cases in a research study fall within 1 standard deviation from the mean, and 95 percent within 2 standard deviations, researchers know that their data form a:
    a. skewed distribution.   c. normal curve.
    b. plot.   d. bar graph.

43. Which of the following exemplifies regression toward the mean?
    a. In his second season of varsity basketball, Edward averaged 5 points more per game than in his first season.
    b. A gambler rolls 5 consecutive "sevens" using her favorite dice.
    c. After earning an unusually low score on the first exam in a class, a "B student" scores much higher on the second exam.
    d. A student who usually gets Bs earns grades of A, C, C, and A on four exams, thus maintaining a B average overall for the class.

44. Which score falls at the 50th percentile of a distribution?
    a. mean   c. mode
    b. median   d. standard deviation

45. If scores on an exam have a mean of 50, a standard deviation of 10, and are normally distributed, approximately 95 percent of those taking the exam would be expected to score between:
    a. 45 and 55.   c. 35 and 65.
    b. 40 and 60.   d. 30 and 70.

46. Joe believes that his basketball game is always best when he wears his old gray athletic socks. Joe is a victim of the phenomenon called:
    a. regression toward the mean.
    b. the availability heuristic.
    c. illusory correlation.
    d. skewed scoring.

47. Five members of Terry's sorority reported the following individual earnings from their sale of raffle tickets: $3, $6, $8, $6, and $12. In this distribution, the mean is _____ the mode and _____ the median.
    a. equal to; equal to
    b. greater than; equal to
    c. greater than; greater than
    d. equal to; less than

48. If a distribution has a standard deviation of 0:
  a. it must be very small in size.
  b. it cannot be representative of the population from which it is drawn.
  c. all of the scores in the distribution are equal.
  d. nothing can be determined from the information given.

49. Esteban refuses to be persuaded by an advertiser's claim that people using their brand of gasoline average 50 miles per gallon. His decision probably is based on:
  a. the possibility that the average is the mean, which could be artificially inflated by a few extreme scores.
  b. the absence of information about the size of the sample studied.
  c. the absence of information about the variation in sample scores.
  d. all of these facts.

50. Which of the following sets of scores best fits the description of a bell-shaped distribution that forms a normal curve?
  a. 1, 2, 4, 8, 16, 32
  b. 2, 2, 2, 2, 2, 2
  c. 1, 2, 3, 4, 4, 4, 5, 6, 7
  d. 2, 8, 10, 18, 35

51. Which of the following distributions has the largest standard deviation?
  a. 1, 2, 3   **c.** 6, 10, 14
  b. 4, 4, 4   **d.** 30, 31, 32

52. Bob scored 43 out of 70 on his psychology exam. He was worried until he discovered that most of the class earned the same score. Bob's score was equal to the:
  a. mean.   **c.** mode.
  b. median.   **d.** range.

53. The four families on your block all have annual household incomes of $25,000. If a new family with an annual income of $75,000 moved in, which measure of central tendency would be most affected?
  a. mean   **c.** mode
  b. median   **d.** standard deviation

54. How would you describe a scatterplot depicting a perfect correlation between two sets of scores?
  a. All the points fall on a straight line.
  b. The points are spread randomly about the plot.
  c. All the points fall on a curved line.
  d. It is impossible to determine from the information given.

55. Dr. Numbers passed back an exam and announced to the class that the mean, the median, and the mode of the scores were equal. This means that:
  a. the scores formed a normal curve.
  b. the distribution had a large standard deviation.
  c. the students did very well on the exam.
  d. all of these statements are true.

56. Dr. Salazar recently completed an experiment in which she compared reasoning ability in a sample of females and a sample of males. The means of the female and male samples equaled 21 and 19, respectively, on a 25-point scale. A statistical test revealed that her results were not statistically significant. What can Dr. Salazar conclude?
  a. Females have superior reasoning ability.
  b. The difference in the means of the two samples is probably due to chance variation.
  c. The difference in the means of the two samples is reliable.
  d. None of these conclusions is true.

Matching Items

Match each term with the appropriate definition or description.

Terms

_____ **1.** bar graph
_____ **2.** median
_____ **3.** normal curve
_____ **4.** regression toward the mean
_____ **5.** mode
_____ **6.** range
_____ **7.** standard deviation
_____ **8.** skewed
_____ **9.** mean
_____ **10.** measures of central tendency
_____ **11.** measures of variation

Definitions or Descriptions

a. the mean, median, and mode
b. the difference between the highest and lowest scores
c. the arithmetic average of a distribution
d. the range and standard deviation
e. a symmetrical, bell-shaped distribution
f. the most frequently occurring score
g. the tendency for extremes of unusual scores to fall back toward the average
h. a graph depicting a table of data
i. the middle score in a distribution
j. an asymmetrical distribution
k. the square root of the average squared deviation of scores from the mean

True–False Items

Indicate whether each statement is true or false by placing a *T* or *F* in the blank next to the item.

_____ **1.** The first step in describing raw data is to organize it.
_____ **2.** In almost all distributions, the mean, the median, and the mode will be the same.
_____ **3.** When a distribution has a few extreme scores, the range is more misleading than the standard deviation.
_____ **4.** If increases in the value of variable *x* are accompanied by decreases in the value of variable *y*, the two variables are negatively correlated.
_____ **5.** Over time, extreme results tend to fall back toward the average.
_____ **6.** If a sample has low variability, it cannot be representative of the population from which it was drawn.
_____ **7.** The mean is always the most precise measure of central tendency.
_____ **8.** Averages that have been derived from scores with low variability are more reliable than those derived from scores that are more variable.
_____ **9.** A relationship between two variables is depicted on a scatterplot.
_____ **10.** Small samples are less reliable than large samples for generalizing to the population.

Essay Question

Discuss several ways in which statistical reasoning can improve your own everyday thinking. (Use the space below to list the points you want to make, and organize them. Then write the essay on a separate sheet of paper.)

KEY TERMS

Using your own words, on a separate piece of paper write a brief definition or explanation of each of the following terms.

1. mode

2. mean

3. median

4. range

5. standard deviation

6. normal curve

7. correlation coefficient

8. scatterplot

9. regression toward the mean

10. cross-sectional study

11. longitudinal study

12. statistical significance

ANSWERS

Appendix Review

Introduction and *Describing Data*

1. big; round; undocumented

2. organize; bar graph

3. mean; median; mode

4. mode

5. sum; number

6. 50th

7. skewed; mean

8. low; high

9. range; standard deviation

10. difference between the lowest and highest scores in a distribution

11. crude; is

12. more accurate; uses

13. normal curve

14. 68; 95

Since the mean equals 100 and the standard deviation is 15 points, a score of 116 is just over one standard deviation unit above the mean. Since 68 percent of the population's scores fall within one standard deviation on either side of the mean, 34 percent fall between 0 and +1 standard deviation unit. By definition, 50 percent of the scores fall below the mean. Therefore, a score at or above 115 is higher than that obtained by 84 percent of the population (50 percent + 34 percent = 84 percent).

15. correlation coefficient; +1.00; –1.00

16. 0.00; +1.00; –1.00; decreases

An example of a positive correlation is the relationship between air temperature and ice cream sales: As one increases so does the other.

An example of a negative correlation is the relationship between good health and the amount of stress a person is under: As stress increases, the odds of good health decrease.

17. does not give; predicts

18. scatterplot

19. illusory correlation

20. confirm

21. control; chance; regression toward the mean

Making Inferences

1. fewer; larger

2. cross-sectional; different; short

3. longitudinal; the same; long

4. decline; stability

Because cross-sectional studies compare people not only of different ages but also of different eras, education levels, family size, and affluence, it is not surprising that such studies reveal cognitive decline with age. In contrast, longitudinal studies test one group over a span of years. However, because those who survive to the end of longitudinal studies may be the brightest and healthiest, these studies may underestimate the average decline in intelligence. It is therefore important to know what type of methodology was used and whether the sample was truly representative of the population being studied.

5. low

6. more

7. significance; chance; reliable; large

Progress Test

Multiple-Choice Questions

1. **c.** is the answer. The mean is the sum of scores divided by the number of scores. [$(2 + 3 + 7 + 6 + 1 + 4 + 9 + 5 + 8 + 2)/10 = 4.7$.]

2. **d.** is the answer. When the scores are put in order (1, 2, 3, 4, 7, 7, 8), 4 is at the 50th percentile, splitting the distribution in half.

3. **b.** is the answer. The mode is the most frequently occurring score. Since there are more "twos" than any other number in the distribution, 2 is the mode.

4. **d.** is the answer. The range is the gap between the highest and lowest scores in a distribution. (14 – 1 = 13.)

5. **b.** is the answer.
   a. This answer describes cross-sectional research.
   c. & d. Sample size does not distinguish cross-sectional from longitudinal research.

6. **a.** is the answer.
   b. This situation indicates that the two sets of scores are positively correlated.
   c. Whether a correlation is positive or negative does not indicate the strength of the relationship, only its direction.
   d. In negative correlations, there *is* a relationship; the correlation is negative because the relationship is an inverse one.

7. **a.** is the answer.
   b. Regression toward the mean has nothing to do with tests of statistical significance.
   c. In fact, just the opposite is true.
   d. This is true, but not because of regression toward the mean.

8. **c.** is the answer.
   a. 50 percent of the normal curve falls on either side of its mean.
   b. 68 percent of the scores fall between –1 and +1 standard deviation units.
   d. 99.7 percent fall between –3 and +3 standard deviations.

9. **c.** is the answer.

10. **d.** is the answer.

11. **c.** is the answer.
    a. A statistically significant difference may or may not be of practical importance.
    b. This is often the case when a difference is *not* statistically significant.

12. **c.** is the answer.

13. **b.** is the answer.

14. **a.** is the answer. As an average, calculated by adding all scores and dividing by the number of scores, the mean could easily be affected by the inclusion of a few extreme scores.
    b. The range is not a measure of central tendency.
    c. & d. The median and mode give equal weight to all scores; each counts only once and its numerical value is unimportant.

15. **c.** is the answer.
    a. A skewed curve is formed from an asymmetrical distribution.
    b. A bimodal curve has two modes; a normal curve has only one.
    d. A bar graph depicts a distribution of scores.

16. **a.** is the answer. The standard deviation is the average deviation in a distribution; therefore, if variation (deviation) is small, the standard deviation will also be small.

17. **a.** is the answer.
    b. & c. These are "perfect" correlations of equal strength.
    d. This indicates a much stronger relationship between two sets of scores than does a coefficient of 0.00.

18. **b.** is the answer.

19. **b.** is the answer.

20. **b.** is the answer.

21. **c.** is the answer. The mean is the sum of the scores divided by the number of scores. (60/10 = 6.)

22. **c.** is the answer. When the scores are put in order (5, 6, 7, 8, 9, 10, 11), 8 is at the 50th percentile, splitting the distribution in half.

23. **a.** is the answer.
    b. The range is the difference between the highest and lowest scores in a distribution.
    c. The median is the score that falls at the 50th percentile.
    d. The mode is the most frequently occurring score.

24. **c.** is the answer.
    a. The mean is the arithmetic average.
    b. The median is the score that splits the distribution in half.
    d. The range is the difference between the highest and lowest scores.

25. **c.** is the answer. The mean, median, and mode are equal to 4.

26. **d.** is the answer. Since the range is the difference between the highest and lowest scores, it is by definition affected by extreme scores.
    a. & c. The mean and mode are measures of central tendency, not of variation.
    b. The standard deviation is less affected than the range because, when it is calculated, the deviation of *every* score from the mean is computed.

27. **a.** is the answer.
    b. This answer describes the longitudinal research method.
    c. & d. Cross-sectional studies have tended to exaggerate the negative effects of aging on intellectual functioning; for this reason they may not be the most appropriate method for studying lifespan development.

28. **b.** is the answer. Averages derived from scores with low variability tend to be more reliable estimates of the populations from which they are drawn. Thus, a. and c. are incorrect. Because the standard deviation is a more accurate estimate of variability than the range, d. is incorrect.

29. **b.** is the answer.

30. **d.** is the answer. A difference that is statistically significant is a true difference, rather than an apparent difference due to factors such as sampling variation, and it is reliable.

31. **b.** is the answer. A bar graph is based on a data distribution.

32. **b.** is the answer. Just as the standard deviation is a measure of variation, so the mode is a measure of central tendency.

33. **b.** is the answer.
    a. 50 percent of the scores in a normal distribution fall on one side of the mean.
    c. 95 percent fall between –2 and +2 standard deviations.
    d. 99.7 percent fall between –3 and +3 standard deviations.

34. **a.** is the answer. Figures based on larger samples are more reliable.
    b. & c. These sample characteristics would tend to lower precision.
    d. A test of significance is a determination of the likelihood that an obtained result is real.

35. **c.** is the answer.

36. **a.** is the answer. The closer the correlation coefficient is to either +1 or –1, the stronger the relationship between the variables.

37. **d.** is the answer.

38. **c.** is the answer. Because several variables (education, affluence, etc.) generally distinguish the various groups in a cross-sectional study, it is impossible to rule out that one or more of these, rather than aging, is the cause of the measured intellectual decrease.
    a. Small sample size and unrepresentativeness generally are not limitations of cross-sectional research.
    b. This refers to longitudinal research.

39. **a.** is the answer. Although Jane's individual scores cannot be predicted, over time her scores will fall close to average. This is the phenomenon of regression toward the mean.

40. **c.** is the answer. If height and weight are positively correlated, increased height is associated with increased weight. Thus, one can predict a person's weight from his or her height.
    a. Correlation does not imply causality.
    b. This situation depicts a negative correlation between height and weight.

41. **d.** is the answer. A small or large standard deviation indicates whether a distribution is homogeneous or variable.
    a., b., & c. These statistics would not give any information regarding the consistency of performance.

42. **c.** is the answer.
    a. In a skewed distribution, the scores are not evenly distributed.
    b. A scatterplot is a graph that depicts the nature and degree of relationship between two variables.
    d. A bar graph depicts a data distribution.

43. **c.** is the answer. Regression toward the mean is the phenomenon that average results are more typical than extreme results. Thus, after an unusual event (the low exam score in this example) things tend to return toward their average level (in this case, the higher score on the second exam).
    a. Edward's improved average indicates only that, perhaps as a result of an additional season's experience, he is a better player.
    b. Because the probability of rolling 5 consecutive "sevens" is very low, the gambler's "luck" will probably prove on subsequent rolls to be atypical and things will return toward their average level. This answer is incorrect, however, because it states only that 5 consecutive "sevens" were rolled.
    d. In this example, although the average of the student's exam grades is her usual grade of B, they are all extreme grades and do not regress toward the mean.

44. **b.** is the answer.
    a. The mean is the arithmetic average of the scores in a distribution.
    c. The mode is the most frequently occurring score in a distribution.
    d. The standard deviation is the average deviation of scores from the mean.

45. **d.** is the answer. 95 percent of the scores in a normal distribution fall between 2 standard deviation units below the mean and 2 standard deviation units above the mean. In this example, the test score that corresponds to –2 standard deviation units is 50 – (2 x 10) = 30; the score that corresponds to +2 standard deviation units is 50 + (2 x 10) = 70.

46. **c.** is the answer. A correlation that is perceived but doesn't actually exist, as in the example, is known as an illusory correlation.
   a. Regression toward the mean is the tendency for extreme scores to fall back toward the average.
   b. The availability heuristic is the tendency of people to estimate the likelihood of something in terms of how readily it comes to mind (see Module 23).
   d. There is no such thing as skewed scoring.

47. **c.** is the answer. In this case, the mean, or average (7), is greater than both the mode, or most frequently occurring score (6), and the median, or middle score (6).

48. **c.** is the answer.

49. **d.** is the answer.

50. **c.** is the answer. This best approximates a normal distribution because most of the scores are near the mean, fewer scores are at the extremes, and the distribution is symmetrical.

51. **c.** is the answer. Even without actually computing its value, it is evident that the standard deviation of these three scores will be greater than that in a., b., or d., because the scores in this distribution are much more variable.

52. **c.** is the answer.
   a. The mean is computed as the sum of the scores divided by the number of scores.
   b. The median is the midmost score in a distribution.
   d. The range is the difference between the highest and lowest scores in a distribution.

53. **a.** is the answer. The mean is strongly influenced by extreme scores. In this example, the mean would change from $25,000 to (75,000 + 25,000 + 25,000 + 25,000 + 25,000)/5 = $35,000.
   b. & c. Both the median and the mode would remain $25,000, even with the addition of the fifth family's income.
   d. The standard deviation is a measure of variation, not central tendency.

54. **a.** is the answer.
   b. This will occur when the correlation coefficient is near 0.00.
   c. Correlations are linear, rather than curvilinear, relationships.

55. **a.** is the answer.
   b. & c. Neither of these can be determined from the information given.

56. **b.** is the answer.
   a. If the difference between the sample means is not significant, then the groups probably do not differ in the measured ability.

c. When a result is not significant it means that the observed difference is unreliable.

Matching Items

1. h	5. f	9. c
2. i	6. b	10. a
3. e	7. k	11. d
4. g	8. j	

True–False Items

1. T	6. F
2. F	7. F
3. T	8. T
4. T	9. T
5. T	10. T

Essay Question

The use of tables and bar graphs is helpful in accurately organizing, describing, and interpreting events, especially when there is too much information to remember and one wishes to avoid conclusions based on general impressions. Computing an appropriate measure of central tendency provides an index of the overall average of a set of scores. Knowing that the mean is the most common measure of central tendency, but that it is very sensitive to unusually high or low scores, can help one avoid being misled by claims based on misleading averages. Being able to compute the range or standard deviation of a set of scores allows one to determine how homogeneous the scores in a distribution are and provides a basis for realistically generalizing from samples to populations. Understanding the correlation coefficient can help us to see the world more clearly by revealing the extent to which two things relate. Being aware that unusual results tend to return to more typical results (regression toward the mean) helps us to avoid the practical pitfalls associated with illusory correlation. Finally, understanding the basis for tests of statistical significance can make us more discerning consumers of research reported in the media.

Key Terms

1. The **mode** is the most frequently occurring score in a distribution; it is the simplest measure of central tendency to determine.

2. The **mean** is the arithmetic average, the measure of central tendency computed by adding together the scores in a distribution and dividing by the number of scores.

3. The **median**, another measure of central tendency, is the score that falls at the 50th percentile, cutting a distribution in half.

   Example: When the *mean* of a distribution is affected by a few extreme scores, the **median** is the more appropriate measure of central tendency.

4. The **range** is a measure of variation computed as the difference between the highest and lowest scores in a distribution.

5. The **standard deviation** is the average amount by which the scores in a distribution deviate from the mean. Because it is based on every score in the distribution, it is a more precise measure of variation than the range.

6. The **normal curve** is the symmetrical, bell-shaped curve that describes many types of data, with most scores centering around the mean and progressively fewer scores occurring toward the extremes.

7. The **correlation coefficient** is a statistical measure of how much two factors vary together, and thus how well either predicts the other.

Example: When the **correlation coefficient** is positive, the two sets of scores increase together. When it is negative, increases in one set are accompanied by decreases in the other.

8. A **scatterplot** is a graph consisting of dots, each of which represents the value of two variables.

9. **Regression toward the mean** is the tendency for extreme scores to return back, or regress, toward the average.

10. In a **cross-sectional study,** people of different ages are compared with one another.

11. In a **longitudinal study,** the same people are tested and retested over a period of years.

12. **Statistical significance** means that an obtained result, such as the difference between the averages for two samples, very likely reflects a real difference rather than sampling variation or chance factors. Tests of statistical significance help researchers decide when they can justifiably generalize from an observed instance.

FOCUS ON VOCABULARY AND LANGUAGE

Top-of-the-head estimates often misread reality and mislead the public. Without knowing actual data and numbers (statistics), people may guess at the figures (*top-of-the-head estimates*), which do not reflect the facts (*misreads reality*) and can deceive (*mislead*) the public. The figures generated in this manner are often easy to articulate, such as 10 percent or 50 percent (*a big round number*) and, when repeated (*echoed*) by others, may eventually be believed to be true by most people (*they become public myths*).

Describing Data

Because the bottom *half* of British income earners receive only a *quarter* of the *national income cake*, most British people, like most people everywhere, make less than the mean. Incomes are not normally distributed (they do not follow a bell-shaped curve when plotted as a data distribution), so a better measure of central tendency than the mean (arithmetic average) is either the median (the score in the middle) or the mode (the most frequently occurring score). In Myers' example, half the people account for 25 percent of all the money earned in the country (*national income cake*); in this uneven (*skewed*) distribution, therefore, most people earn below-average wages.

It [**standard deviation**] better *gauges* whether scores are packed together or dispersed, because it uses information from each score (Table A.1). The most commonly used statistic for measuring (*gauging*) how much scores differ from one another (their variation) is the standard deviation (SD). Using this formula, each score is compared to the mean; the result is an index of how spread out (*dispersed*) the scores are. A relatively small SD indicates that most of the scores are close to the average; a relatively large SD indicates that they are much more variable.

Statistics can help us see what the *naked eye* sometimes misses. When looking at an array of data consisting of different measures (e.g., height and temperament) for many subjects, it is very difficult to discern what, if any, relationships exist. Statistical tools, such as the correlation coefficient and the scatterplot, can help us see clearly what the unaided (*naked*) eye might not see. As Myers notes, we sometimes need statistical illumination to see what is in front of us.

Making Inferences

Data are *"noisy."* Differences between groups may simply be due to random (*chance*) variations (*fluctuations*) in those particular samples. When data have a great deal of variability, they are said to be *"noisy,"* which may limit our ability to generalize them to the larger population. In order to determine if differences are reliable, we should be sure that (a) samples are random and representative, (b) scores in the sample are similar to each other (have low variability), and (c) a large number of subjects or observations are included. If these principles are followed, we can confidently make inferences about the differences between groups.